THE OFFICIAL
1999
BLACKBOOK PRICE GUIDE TO UNITED STATES POSTAGE STAMPS

TWENTY-FIRST EDITION

BY MARC HUDGEONS, N.L.G., AND TOM HUDGEONS

HOUSE OF COLLECTIBLES

The Ballantine Publishing Group • New York

Important Notice. All of the information, including valuations, in this book has been compiled from the most reliable sources, and every effort has been made to eliminate errors and questionable data. Nevertheless, the possibility of error, in a work of such immense scope, always exists. The publisher will not be held responsible for losses which may occur in the purchase, sale, or other transaction of items because of information contained herein. Readers who feel they have discovered errors are invited to *write* and inform us, so they may be corrected in subsequent editions. Those seeking further information on the topics covered in this book are advised to refer to the complete line of *Official Price Guides* published by the House of Collectibles.

Copyright © 1998 by Random House, Inc.

H This is a registered trademark of Random House, Inc.
C

All rights reserved under International and Pan-American Copyright Conventions.

Published by: House of Collectibles
The Ballantine Publishing Group
201 East 50th Street
New York, New York 10022

Distributed by The Ballantine Publishing Group, a division of Random House, Inc., New York, and simultaneously in Canada by Random House of Canada Limited, Toronto.

Stamp designs © United States Postal Service

Manufactured in the United States of America

ISSN: 0195-3559

ISBN: 0-676-60065-4

Cover design by Dreu Pennington-McNeil
Cover photo by George Kerrigan

Twenty-first Edition: July 1998

10 9 8 7 6 5 4 3 2 1

TABLE OF CONTENTS

OFFICIAL BOARD OF CONTRIBUTORS

The author would like to express a special thank you to:

Mr. Armin R. Crowe at the COLLECTORS INSTITUTE, LTD., Omaha, NE, 68144, for color photographs,

Robert Lamb, Executive Director, Kathleen Wunderly, Education Director, and Frank Sente, Membership Director at THE AMERICAN PHILATELIC SOCIETY, State College, PA, 16803, for directory listings,

Michael Laurence and Leenie Folsom, Circulation Director at LINN'S STAMP NEWS, Sidney, OH 45365, for their article,

Donald Sundman and Karen Ostrander at Mystic Stamp Company, Camden, NJ, 13316 for their article and pricing information,

Daisy Ridgway, Public Affairs Manager at THE NATIONAL POSTAL MUSEUM, Smithsonian Institution, Washington, D.C, 20560, for articles,

Alex Bereson at UNITED NATIONS PHILATELIST, San Francisco, CA, 94131, for his pricing information,

Barry Newton of THE AMERICAN FIRST DAY COVER SOCIETY, Cleveland, OH, 44120, for his pricing information,

Robert Dumaine of DUCK STAMP COLLECTORS SOCIETY, Houston, TX 77282,

Kelly L. Spinks at THE UNITED STATES POSTAL SERVICE, Washington, D.C., 20260, for permission to reproduce the photography of U.S. stamps. *The designs for the stamps issued from 1978 to date are copyrighted by THE U.S. POSTAL SERVICE and are used with the permission of the U.S. Postal Service.*

NOTE TO READERS

HOW TO FIND YOUR STAMP

This new stamp catalog takes the confusion out of finding and identifying individual stamps. A complete, new FULL-COLOR FAST-FIND PHOTO INDEX is illustrated in the insert in this book. All of the stamp photographs are arranged in Scott numerical order and date of issue. Below each stamp picture is the Scott number.

Scott No.	Date	Page	Scott No.	Date	Page
1–138	1847–1871	A–1	1038–1065	1954–1955	A–22
139–236	1870–1893	A–2	1066–1076	1955–1956	A–23
237–287	1893–1898	A–3	1077–1093	1956–1957	A–24
288–323	1898–1904	A–4	1094–1113	1957–1958	A–25
324–551	1904–1922	A–5	1114–1132	1958–1959	A–26
552–620	1922–1925	A–6	1133–1149	1959–1960	A–27
621–689	1925–1930	A–7	1150–1167	1960	A–28
690–733	1931–1933	A–8	1168–1186	1960–1961	A–29
734–777	1933–1936	A–9	1187–1202	1961–1962	A–30
782–801	1936–1937	A–10	1203–1237	1962–1963	A–31
802–830	1937–1938	A–11	1238–1257	1963–1964	A–32
831–867	1938–1940	A–12	1258–1273	1964–1965	A–33
868–896	1940	A–13	1274–1306	1965–1966	A–34
897–927	1940–1945	A–14	1307–1321	1966	A–35
928–942	1945–1946	A–15	1322–1343	1966–1968	A–36
943–954	1946–1948	A–16	1344–1372	1968–1969	A–37
955–970	1948	A–17	1373–1396	1969–1970	A–38
971–986	1948–1950	A–18	1397–1425	1970–1971	A–39
987–1005	1950–1952	A–19	1426–1447	1971–1972	A–40
1006–1020	1952–1953	A–20	1448–1473	1972	A–41
1021–1037	1953–1954	A–21	1474–1497	1972–1973	A–42

THE OFFICIAL®

1999
BLACKBOOK
PRICE GUIDE TO
UNITED STATES
POSTAGE
STAMPS

LINN'S LOOK AT THE NEW STAMP ISSUES

by George Amick,
courtesy of Michael Laurence at
Linn's Stamp News

One hundred fifty years after the first two United States postage stamps appeared, bearing the portraits of Benjamin Franklin and George Washington, the U.S. Postal Service issued 130 new varieties of postal paper, including a stamp picturing Bugs Bunny.

Whether the latter total represents progress is debatable, but it surely signifies change.

Though high by earlier standards, the 1997 total of 130 is the lowest number of new face-different and perforation-different U.S. stamps and postal stationery items since the 116 varieties of 1993. The total is down from 166 new stamps last year and 214 in 1995.

The Postal Service may have merely been catching its breath this year. With 1998 expected to include a rate change and the launch of the already announced, lengthy Celebrate the Century commemorative series, this relative restraint won't last. Commemoratives are stamps with one printing that are usually issued to mark an anniversary.

Self-adhesive stamps, hugely popular with the public, continue to command an ever larger share of total stamp production. The Postal Service expected to sell 32 billion self-adhesives this year—80 percent of its stamp total—compared to 60 percent in 1996 and 20 percent in 1995.

For the first time, all the year's standard-rate definitive stamps and special stamps were self-adhesives.

As usual, the year brought some technical innovations. The long promised linerless self-adhesive coil stamps (stamps without backing paper that peel off like adhesive tape), made to come off a roll like transparent tape, were introduced on an experimental basis.

The most interesting new gimmick, however, accompanied the Department of the Air Force, Classic Movie Monsters and the Mars Pathfinder commemoratives. Their designs include hidden images called "scrambled indicia" that are visible only through a special plastic decoder lens sold by the Postal Service.

Scrambled indicia have a dual purpose: They provide a counterfeit-proof security element, and they are likely to appeal to the kids whom the Postal Service is trying hard to recruit as stamp collectors.

Kids also were the target audience for the Bugs Bunny stamp, the most controversial issue of 1997.

Many adult collectors protested that this self-adhesive—the first of a promised series featuring Warner Bros. animated Looney Tunes cartoon characters—cheapened the U.S. stamp program and was a shameless promotion for the commercial enterprise, in violation of Citizens' Stamp Advisory Committee guidelines.

But Postal Service officials replied that Bugs was more of an American icon than an item of commerce. Furthermore, they said, Bugs would also produce a windfall.

Their projections showed that the Postal Service would net $38 million from Bugs Bunny stamps purchased and retained rather than used on mail. This would beat the $36 million the Postal Service claims to have netted from its 1993 record-setter, the 29-cent Elvis Presley stamp.

As usual, the year's total number of commemoratives (93) was boosted by several se-tenant multiple issues.

The words "classic" and "legend" got a workout in 1997. Besides the 5 Classic Movie Monsters stamps, there were 15 Classic American Dolls stamps and 20 Classic American Aircraft stamps (the latter being the 1997 entry in what the Postal Service calls the Classic Collections series).

There were also eight Legendary Football Coaches stamps (four designs but eight total varieties), plus eight Composers and Conductors stamps and four Opera Singers stamps in the Legends of American Music series.

The 15 Dinosaurs stamps that were featured in a pane of their own were prehistoric rather than classic.

Several of the continuing commemorative series received new entries in 1996.

The series ranged in longevity from Black Heritage, which got its 20th annual stamp, to Legends of Hollywood, which got its 3rd (this year's featured movie star was Humphrey Bogart).

The Lunar New Year and Literary Arts series were also extended in 1997.

The Postal Service issued two pairs of stamps to celebrate Pacific 97, the international stamp show held in San Francisco, California, to commemorate the sesquicentennial of the first U.S. postage stamps.

Both issues were created specifically to appeal to tradition-minded collectors. They were intaglio engraved—the only solely line-engraved stamps of the year. (There was also the offset-intaglio 32-cent Marshall Plan stamp, but its engraved lettering was created by computer.)

The first Pacific 97 stamps were triangular, the first of that shape to be issued by the United States.

The second set comprised two souvenir sheets (small panes with commemorative inscriptions in the selvage), each including 12 modified reproductions of the original U.S. Franklin and Washington stamps of 1847.

The Postal Service deliberately limited the sale of these sheets as to place (Pacific 97 and through mail order) and time (80 days for mail order), and it destroyed most, but not all, of the unsold remainders, to impart to them the aura of scarcity.

Ironically, however, these sheets proved to be far less scarce and desirable to collectors than a variety the Postal Service created almost casually and with no apparent thought to its implications.

The variety was a Bugs Bunny stamp without its normal die-cut simulated perforations. It was created as part of a special printing of the Bugs panes that was made to fill orders from youthful participants in the Postal Service's Stampers program.

Although the imperforate stamps themselves weren't sent to the Stampers club members, the full panes that included them were offered briefly to collectors through the Philatelic Fulfillment Service Center. An estimated 83,000 of these panes were sold, making them scarcer than the 150,000 sets of Pacific 97 souvenir sheets distributed during their limited time on the market.

In October, a mint Bugs Bunny variety pane brought $220 in an Internet auction, and later a first-day cover bearing an imperforate stamp went for $500.

The year's special stamps included two new Love stamps and two Christmas stamps, the smallest number in the Christmas category since 1988. The Postal Service issued the second of its so-called Holiday Celebrations series with a stamp honoring Kwanzaa.

Most of the year's new definitives used previous stamp designs. The exceptions were a se-tenant pair, issued in two sizes and two formats, that reproduced botanical prints by the 17th-century German artist Maria Sibylla Merian, and the final item of the year, a $3 Priority Mail rate stamp that saluted the Mars Pathfinder mission and that was sold in small one-stamp panes, a kind of souvenir sheet.

There was no new entry in the Great American definitive series for the first time since that lengthy set was launched in 1980. And, for the first time since 1987, no new stamped envelope was issued.

There were 14 picture postal cards (cards with an imprinted stamp and a large picture on the back). Of these were eight 20-cent Swans Love cards depicting current and past Love stamp designs and their picture sides, five cards showing Classic Movie Monsters and one card for Bugs Bunny. Plus there were four conventional commemorative postal cards with plain backs.

Two of the conventional cards, issued for Pacific 97 and showing views of the Golden Gate Bridge, followed the growing Postal Service trend of using designs based on photographs rather than original artwork.

The Postal Service continued to intensify its efforts to harvest profits from the stamp program. Seven different issues were offered for sale in uncut press sheets, a larger number than ever before. And new kinds of ancillary products proliferated. This included Bugs Bunny neckties, stationery decorated with stamp designs, clothing, mugs, clocks and more.

A new so-called last-day-of-sale program, with appropriate cancellations, was created for selected older commemoratives when they were officially removed from sale at the Philatelic Fulfillment Service Center.

And all subtlety was abandoned in a print and television marketing campaign that specifically urged customers to buy the colorful new commemorative stamps, but not to use them on mail.

Ads for the Humphrey Bogart stamp, for instance, carried

this message: "Thugs, gangsters and cheap gunmen couldn't lick him. Perhaps you shouldn't either."

Dinosaur stamp ads proclaimed, "Licking a special edition Stegosaurus stamp is a futile primordial urge. It won't be around forever, so what will you gain by mailing it?. . . . Don't be a Neanderthal and slap them on an envelope."

A Postal Service internal memo, obtained by Linn's, instructed postal clerks to tell customers buying the Classic Movie Monsters Stamps that the stamps were special editions and should be saved.

Postal Service marketing officials seemed oblivious to collectors' complaints that this policy was harmful to stamp collecting.

The policy, if effective, would reduce the number of postally used commemoratives that might attract newcomers to the hobby when they found them on mail.

George Amick is the author of Linn's annual U.S. Stamp Yearbook.

MARKET REVIEW
by Donald Sundman

The U.S. stamp market shows continued strength with high-quality stamps very much in demand. Profits from the increase in stock and bond prices benefit stamps as investors feel free to add to their collections. All 19th-century U.S. stamps seem in short supply and prices are quite strong. Demand for 20th-century commemorative stamps continues from newer collectors working to fill in early spaces in their collection. Washington–Franklin definitive stamps issued between 1908 and 1920 are underpriced relative to their scarcity. Greater collector demand for commemoratives accounts for the difference in price. U.S. possessions, Hawaii, Puerto Rico, Cuba and Guam stamps are rising in price as dealers seek to build or replenish stocks.

The stamp market in Great Britain is strong, in part because the British economy is also strong. Continued weakness in the economies of continental Europe has resulted in a drop off in stamp activity, prices are flat or sagging. European stamp prices should strengthen when the overall domestic economic activity turns up. Likewise, the financial turmoil in Asia has thrown those overheated stamp markets into a confused state.

Pacific 97, the international stamp show held in San Francisco marked the 150th anniversary of America's first postage stamps. The 1847 stamp images were altered with a higher face value (50¢ instead of the 5¢ Franklin and 60¢ instead of the 10¢ Washington) and printed in different colors than the originals and issued in two souvenir sheets of twelve stamps each. The stamps were on sale only during the eleven-day show in an effort to create speculative demand. The USPS expected the retail value of the sheets to rise and increase the speculation in new U.S. stamps. Sales lagged USPS expectations, although in time they promise to become difficult to find.

Bugs Bunny stamps marked the first in a new annual series of Warner Brothers cartoon figures to appear on U.S. stamps. Bugs became the official spokesmen for the "Stampers Program": a club with the purpose of introducing stamps to kids. Stampers was created by USPS marketers borrowing concepts from baseball cards, kids mount new stamps on slick cards the size and shape of baseball cards. While Stampers is a huge success with more than one million members, the Bugs stamp generated controversy and national media attention. First, Bugs Bunny is a commercial product owned by a large media company (Time Warner) and U.S. stamps are prohibited from promoting profit-making organizations. Second, is Bugs alive? Living Americans are not allowed to be pictured on U.S. stamps. Michael Laurence, publisher/editor of *Linn's Stamp News* feels picturing Bugs on stamps trivializes the entire stamp program and empowers fringe special-interest groups to push their own stamp with the argument, "If they put Bugs Bunny on a stamp, why not XYZ?"

A special edition of only 117,000 Bugs Bunny panes of ten stamps (Scott #3138) with the righthand single-stamp imperforate was created for the Stampers program. Overlooked by collectors and dealers, the special pane rocketed upward in price when its relative rarity became public knowledge. With a face value of just $3.20, panes traded as high as $220 before settling in the $150 retail range. This scarce Bugs Bunny pane is rarer than the 1993 Legends of the West error stamp sheet showing the image of Bill Picketts's brother Ben instead of Bill. That sheet was recalled and reprinted with a corrected picture of Pickett. One hundred fifty thousand of the recalled sheets with the design error (Scott #2870) were distributed in a special never repeated lottery to collectors who ordered one. Current retail price for the recalled Pickett sheet is $300.

The United States is scheduled to issue its first semi-postal postage stamp in 1998. Semi-postals, postage stamps with an additional fee charged for a specific charity, have been issued by European countries for many years, and by Canada to pay for the 1976 Montreal Olympics. The theory behind semi-postals is that it is supposed to be an easy and voluntary way to raise money for a good cause and raising public interest in a specific charity at the same time. In practice, it is a tax on stamp collectors and a very inefficient way to collect funds. Most of the money raised is consumed by the overhead and accounting necessary to collect and distribute the funds.

Diana, Princess of Wales, tragically killed in a Paris auto accident, was commemorated when dozens of countries issued stamps bearing her likeness. Great Britain was set to issue a set of five stamps showing the Princess early in 1998. Demand for affordable stamps showing Princess Diana and other contemporary individuals is a new and fast-growing part of the stamp hobby.

Krause Publications added the Minkus catalog and album line to their *Stamp Collector* and *Stamp Wholesale* newspapers. Krause is investing heavily in their desire to compete with stamp publishing industry leader Amos Press's *Linn's Stamp News* and Scott's albums and catalogs. The competition will benefit collectors as the two companies provide more and better products.

The absence of "fresh material" on the wholesale market means people with stamps for sale are seeing strong prices bid for their collections. This trend is continuing.

Theodore J. Kaczynski, a hermit living in Montana, was arrested and accused as the infamous Uni-bomber. Bombs mailed by the Uni-bomber over a seventeen-year period killed or maimed many people while the U.S. Postal Inspection Service sought to catch the bomber. DNA was collected from the saliva used to stick postage stamps to the bomb packages. It is expected this evidence will be introduced during the trial. This case highlights a unique position occupied by stamps and those fortunate individuals who share the passion for philately.

Mystic's U.S. Stamp Catalog
The White House
1792
1992

- Latest Edition
- 3400 Color Photos
- Collecting Tips
- Fascinating Stories
- Collector's Supplies

Yours Free – Mystic's New U.S. Stamp Catalog

A free copy of America's best U.S. stamp catalog is waiting for you. Enjoy 112 pages of color photographs, valuable collecting tips, fascinating history, and more. Collectors agree, a catalog like this is worth its weight in gold, but we'll send yours Free!

Send today for Mystic's Free 112-page catalog and also receive other stamp offers on approval.

Mail your name and address to:
Mystic Stamp Co., Dept. SC579, Camden, New York 13316
Or call toll free 1-800-433-7811 and give Customer Service the department number.

Do you have all the "Flag Over Porch" Stamps?
Complete set of 12 – *only $8.95*

Are these new Flag Over Porch definitive stamps missing from your collection? It's easy to overlook them, so now's the time to get this complete mint set of 12 from Mystic – while they're still available at the special low price of only $8.95. All major Scott numbers are included!

The "Porch" stamps represent a historic change in producing U.S. definitives. Each stamp has a date in the bottom margin – small or large in size, red or blue in color. Four have traditional gum (water-activated), while eight are self-adhesives. And they were produced by four different printers. Now, Mystic makes it easy for you to tell these look-alike stamps apart, and get them all for your collection before they disappear. We've identified each one and even packaged them individually! **Please note that #2915C is very, very hard to get. We believe it will be the "key" to the set.**

Many of the stamps in this important set are no longer available at the Post Office. Order now to get your complete mint set of the Flag Over Porch stamps – limit one set please. You'll receive special collector's information plus Mystic's 112-page color U.S. Stamp Catalog (mailed separately) and other interesting offers on approval. Your satisfaction is guaranteed.

Mail your name, address, and $8.95 to:

Mystic Stamp Company, Dept. CA170, Camden, NY 13316 Or call toll-free 1-800-433-7811 and give Customer Service the department number.

THE NATIONAL POSTAL MUSEUM

On July 30, 1993 the National Postal Museum opened its doors to the public, marking the creation of a new Smithsonian Institution museum, and making way for the nation's first major museum devoted to postal history and philately.

In what is a sophisticated and highly interactive museum, the National Postal Museum features exhibitions that tell the history of the nation's mail service, from the Colonial era and the Pony Express to the art of letters and the beauty and lore of stamps.

"The theme of the museum is 'America's history is in the mail.' We are presenting American history from a new perspective," says James H. Bruns, director of the National Postal Museum. "The museum is intended to inspire appreciation for a system that affects our lives every day. The history of America's mail service is the history of our success as a nation. The museum tells an upbeat and endearing story of American ingenuity and remarkable progress."

The Postal Museum is located at First Street and Massachusetts Avenue N.E. on the lower level of the former Washington City Post Office Building, which is on Capitol Hill next to Union Station. The new museum houses and displays the nation's stamp and postal history collection, the largest and most comprehensive of its kind in the world.

"Not only is America's history in the mail, its future is in the mail, too," says Marvin Runyon, Chief Executive Officer and Postmaster General of the U.S. Postal Service. "We want people to understand the role the Postal Service has played for more than two centuries in helping our nation grow and prosper, and the important social and economic role the mail continues to play for the United States."

The museum occupies approximately 75,000 square feet, with more than 25,000 square feet devoted to exhibit space. It also features a Library Research Center, a Discovery Room for educational programs, a museum shop, and a philatelic sales center. The Library Research Center, available to the public by appointment, is among the largest postal history and philatelic research centers in the world, with more than 40,000 volumes and manuscripts. The museum also houses collections, conservation facilities, and curatorial and administrative offices. A full-service U.S. post office will be accessible from a corridor within the museum.

HISTORY

The National Postal Museum was made possible by an agreement between the Smithsonian and the United States Postal Service. The museum was established after lengthy negotiations about relocating the Smithsonian's vast postal history and philatelic collection of more than 16 million stamps, covers, and artifacts. Previously housed on the third and fourth floors of the National Museum of American History, the collection lacked adequate exhibit, storage, and research space in that location.

On Nov. 6, 1990, the Smithsonian Institution and the U.S. Postal Service signed an agreement in which the Postal Service would provide the site and approximately $15.4 million for start-up and construction costs and the Smithsonian would administer the museum and its staff.

The National Postal Museum is funded by both the Postal Service and the Smithsonian, as well as by money raised from endowments and on-going fund-raising campaigns. The museum's annual operating budget calls for $3 million ($2 million from the Postal Service and $1 million from the Smithsonian in direct and indirect costs). The Smithsonian contribution to the new museum has been the same as that spent on the collection when it was at the Museum of American History. The more than $3 million raised from private organizations through March 1993 went toward the installation of the new and expanding exhibits. Private funds continue to be used to develop and expand exhibits.

THE COLLECTION

The National Philatelic Collection was established at the Smithsonian in 1886 with the donation of a sheet of 10-cent Confederate postage stamps. Generous gifts from individuals and foreign governments, transfers from government agencies and purchases have increased the collection to today's total of more than 16 million items.

From 1908 until 1963, the collection was housed in the Smithsonian's Arts and Industries Building on the National Mall. In 1964, the collection was moved to the National Museum of American History where it was expanded to include postal history and stamp production. In addition to the stamp collection, the museum has postal stationery covers, postal history material that pre-dates stamps, vehicles used to transport the mail, mailboxes, meters, greeting cards, and letters.

INAUGURAL EXHIBITIONS

More than 50,000 stamps and objects, and 400 graphics are on display throughout the museum's five major exhibit galleries that explore different facets of mail communication and history. The galleries include:

MOVING THE MAIL

Faced with the challenge of moving the mail quickly, the postal service looked to trains, automobiles, airplanes, and buses to deliver the mail, all of which are the focus of the museum's 90-foot-high Atrium gallery. After the Civil War, postal officials began to take advantage of railway trains for moving and sorting the mail. Sorting the mail while it was being carried between towns was a revolutionary approach to mail delivery, involving generations of devoted postal employees who worked as railway mail clerks.

Airmail service was established between New York, Philadelphia and Washington, D.C. in 1918 with the remarkable pioneering flights of pilots Torrey Webb, James Edgerton, H. Paul Culver, and George Boyle. Airmail service was the base from which America's commercial aviation industry developed.

Some of the most ambitious movers of the mail were not aviators, railway mail clerks, or even postal employees. They are the star route contractors, who have delivered mail with everything from mules to motorcycles, including the 1850s Concord-style stagecoach on display in the museum.

THE ART OF CARDS AND LETTERS

While other galleries focus on systems of mail service, this gallery emphasizes letters. A cherished art form, letters are windows into history, used throughout museum displays to relate personal stories of survival, success, and tragedy. Through an array of wartime correspondence from World War I to Desert Storm, as well as objects and a video, one section highlights the struggle between soldiers and their loved ones to maintain ties during war. Changing exhibits in this gallery will concentrate on the important stories letters tell of families and friends bound by these missives over land and across time.

BINDING THE NATION

The museum's first gallery provides an overview of the events in America from colonial times through the 19th century, stressing the importance of written communication in the young nation. As early as 1673, regular mail was carried between New York and Boston following Indian trails. That route, once known as the King's Best Highway, is now U.S. Route 1.

Benjamin Franklin, a colonial postmaster for the British government, played a key role in establishing mail service in the colonies, as well as in forging a strong link between colonial publishers and the postal service. Many newspapers that relied heavily on information carried in the mail customarily adopted the word "Post" into their title. Newspapers were so important to the dissemination of information to the people that they were granted cheaper postage rates.

By 1800, mail was carried over more than 9,000 miles of postal roads. The challenge of developing mail service over long distances is the central theme of "The Expanding Nation," which features the famed Pony Express and the Southern Postal Administration of the Civil War. At an interactive video station, visitors can create their own postal route.

CUSTOMERS AND COMMUNITIES

By the turn of the 20th century, nearly 10,000 letter carriers worked in over 400 cities. The nation's population was expanding at top speed, and with it, the nation's mail volume and the need for personal mail delivery. This gallery focuses on the modern changes in mail service introduced at the turn of the century.

Crowded cities inspired postal officials to experiment with a variety of mail delivery systems, such as the impressive but ultimately impractical underground pneumatic tubes. Home delivery of mail began in the cities during the Civil War, when postal officials decided it was inhumane to require soldiers' families to receive death notices at post office windows.

As rural Americans watched city residents receive free home delivery, they began to demand equal treatment. This was the start of Rural Free Delivery. Facets of Rural Free Delivery and its important and often heart-warming role in the fabric of the nation is explored with photographs, mail vehicles, and a variety of rural mailboxes.

The history of the vast direct mail industry is the subject of a special interactive gallery. Through the use of sophisticated technology, the exhibition *What's in the Mail for You!* uses touch screen panels, three-dimensional projections, video work stations, holograms, and computer interactives to tell the story of the mailing industry and its function as a major means of commerce in America. This hands-on exhibit allows visitors to create a mailer and "target" customers; related exhibit topics look at different mail marketing techniques, the key to a successful mail campaign, and the success stories of well-known mail order entrepreneurs like L.L. Bean.

STAMPS AND STORIES

Among some 20 million stamp collectors in the United States, many are casual collectors, while others work at the hobby with a devotion to detail and scholarship unmatched by other pastimes. This gallery is for all collectors, as well as for those who know little about the renowned hobby of philately. The history of the stamp begins in 1840, when Great Britain issued the first gummed postage stamp. Since then stamps of every subject, shape, and design have been produced for consumer use or as collectibles.

Serving not only as proof of postage, stamps are also miniature works of art, keepsakes and rare treasures—as well as the workhorses of the automated postal system. Some stamps tell stories while others contain secrets and hidden meanings.

Some of the highlights of the gallery are priceless rarities from the museum's vast collection, including inverted stamps and scarce covers. Videos address questions of how and why stamps were invented, and how they are printed. A selection of more than 55,000 stamps is on display, and will be rotated every six months.

Within the exhibit galleries are more than 30 interactive areas, including, for example, video games that invite visitors to choose the best mail route between various cities in the 1800s, or deliver mail in a DeHavilland biplane. The museum features 17 video presentations, with topics ranging from America's railway mail clerks, the star route contractors, early letter carriers, and transportation technology, to stories about mail-train wrecks and robberies, and postal workers.

THE JEANETTE CANTRELL RUDY GALLERY

In this 800-square-foot gallery, a major exhibition devoted to federal duck stamps, entitled "Artistic License: The Duck Stamp Story," opened in Spring 1996. Made possible by a generous donation from Jeanette Cantrell Rudy of Nashville, Tn., the exhibition explores the history of duck stamps, their contribution to the conservation of America's waterways, and the extraordinary craftsmanship that goes into their creation. A selection of rare duck stamps is on display, drawn from the collections of Mrs. Rudy and from the National Postal Museum.

TOURS

One hour highlights tours are offered weekdays at 11 A.M., 1 P.M. and 2 P.M., and weekends at 11 A.M. and 1 P.M. The National Postal Museum's Education Office will arrange guided tours for school and camp groups throughout the year. Group leaders should call (202) 357-2991 (Voice) and (202) 633-9849 (TTY) for more information.

MUSEUM DESIGNED SPECIFICALLY TO HOUSE UNIQUE COLLECTION

The National Postal Museum was designed by the firm of Florance Eichbaum Esocoff King Architects. Chief among the objectives for designing the museum was the desire to create a maximum-security facility to protect the Smithsonian's priceless stamp collection, while at the same time creating an aesthetically rich setting that will attract visitors and encourage exploration of the museum's themes of postal history and philately.

The new museum's centerpiece is a 90-foot-high atrium that projects through the center of the quadrangle-shaped City Post Office Building. Three air mail planes hang from steel girders inside the atrium, which has a glass ceiling 1.5 inches thick. The entire atrium area houses mail transportation vehicles and related displays; however, enough space on the atrium's marble floor remains for visitors to observe the intricate envelope and stamp design within the floor's tiles.

The museum is equipped with an array of sophisticated surveillance and safety equipment. The museum's research facilities, including the 6,000-square-foot Library Research Center, are meant to enhance the work and study of visiting researchers and scholars. The library features a specimen study room, an audio-visual viewing room, and a separate library of rare books.

HISTORIC BUILDING ENHANCES MUSEUM'S MESSAGE

The Washington City Post Office Building was built between 1911 and 1914 to serve as the District's central post office facility. Designed by architect Daniel Burnham, architect of Union Station, the City Post Office Building was built next door to the elegant train station in order to expedite the distribution of incoming mail to the nation's capital.

Completely renovated and restored to its original appearance, the City Post Office Building houses the National Postal Museum as well as a full-service post office and several federal agencies. The museum is located in what was once the building's mail processing and distribution center. An impressively ornate historic marble lobby, formerly the main service area of the City Post Office Building, will now serve as the foyer to the National Postal Museum. The Beaux Arts–style building is eligible for listing in the National Register of Historic Places.

EDUCATION PROGRAMS AND CHANGING EXHIBITIONS

The National Postal Museum offers a series of educational outreach activities. Through scheduled events in the museum's Discovery Center, individuals from pre-school age to adult will be invited to participate in events that aim to enhance the information presented in exhibits. Activities range from learning more about the art of stamps, postal transportation, automation, and mail delivery to letter writing and the analysis of historic letters. The museum also engages in school and community collaborative projects.

LIBRARY RESEARCH CENTER

With its more than 40,000 volumes and manuscripts, the museum's new Library Research Center is among the world's largest philatelic and postal history research facilities. The 6,000-square-foot library features a rare book reading room, an audiovisual room, research cubbies, and a workroom for viewing items from the collection. The library also offers current philatelic and postal magazines and newsletters as well as U.S. Postal Service publications and annual reports. The center is operated by the Smithsonian Institution Libraries. It is open to the public by appointment from 10 A.M. to 4 P.M., Monday through Friday. For more information, call (202) 633-9370.

PUBLICATIONS

The official newsletter of the National Postal Museum is a quarterly, titled "EnRoute," and is available by becoming a member of the National Postal Museum for $25.00 annually. A six-month calendar of events and membership information is offered by request by calling (202) 633-9385.

STAFF

The museum staff includes a director (who also serves as a curator), one curator, two museum specialists, an exhibition director, an education director, a collections staff of four, and a conservation staff of one.

THE STORY OF U.S. STAMPS

The world's first postage stamps were issued by Great Britain in 1840 and pictured its new queen, Victoria, then 21 years old. It was not until 1847 that the United States released postage stamps, but prior to that time some city postmasters issued stamps of their own. These very valuable stamps, known as "postmaster provisionals," were used in St. Louis, New York, Annapolis, and a number of other cities.

The first federally released postage stamps comprised a 5¢ denomination picturing Benjamin Franklin and a 10¢ showing George Washington. Their size was very similar to that of modern non-commemoratives and they had gummed backs, just like our stamps. The chief difference was that they carried no little holes or perforations between each specimen on a sheet, to aid in separation. Instead they had to be cut apart with scissors or creased and torn by hand. These stamps are called "imperforates," or "without perforations." All stamps in those days, including Europe's, were made in this way. The United States did not start perforating its stamps until 1857, ten years later.

Imperforates rank today as the hobby's aristocrats, its elder statesmen and foremost classics. They have long been dear to the hearts of collectors, and not merely on grounds of their antiquity. Some specialists maintain that these issues, every one of them bearing a statesman's portrait, are more elegantly engraved than any of their descendants. In addition, they can be found (with luck and the necessary cash) in super specimens that put ordinary perforated stamps to shame. When a stamp is perforated, every one on the sheet is of identical size. Some sheets may be better centered than others, depending on how the paper is fed, but no specimens will be physically larger than any others. With imperforates, it's quite another matter. The cutting was never done very evenly. Some specimens were cropped or cut into by scissor wielders and left with margins so immense that portions of all the surrounding stamps are visible. These are called jumbo margin copies and the prices collectors will give for them are often astronomic, provided the condition is otherwise good. It is not at all unusual for one of these oversized beauties to command three or four times the normal sum. Collectors must take care though, because in philately, as in most other things, all that sparkles is not necessarily diamonds. Larcenous persons have been known to take very ordinary average stamps and add fake margins.

Not all imperforates are equally easy (or hard) to get with four full margins. This is all a matter of how closely together they were printed on the sheet. The cutter is less apt to make a mistake if the stamps are further apart on the sheet. Scott's #11, the 3¢ 1851, is by far the most difficult to find with full margins. It also happens to be the least expensive imperforate, thanks to the enormous quantities printed. While the usual specimen will fetch only $8–$10 used, a jumbo margin #11 has no trouble selling for $20, $30 or more.

The second series of imperforates, issued from 1851 to 1856, comprised values from 1¢ to 12¢. There were five stamps, with Washington appearing on three of them; the other two used portraits of Franklin and Jefferson. In 1857 the same group of stamps was released again, this time with perforations and three high values: a 24¢ and 90¢ pictured Washington, and a 30¢ portrayed Franklin. The 90¢ stamp was not exceeded in face value until the Columbian Exposition series in 1893. Because very little mail required the paying of so much postage, most specimens of the 90¢, 1857–1861 that went to private hands never got on letters. Consequently, this stamp is much more difficult to find used than unused, a rare circumstance for a U.S. issue. Needless to say, counterfeit cancels exist.

There was no question that by this time postage stamps had scored a big success. Any doubts or complaints that some users may have had about them at the beginning had long since vanished. Certain persons became so fond of stamps that they began saving them, used as well as unused, and thus the hobby of philately was born. For the government, stamps brought greater economy to the postal service than anticipated. They also allowed mail to travel faster. There was just one problem: some people were abusing the system. During the Civil War, and shortly thereafter, it became apparent that many stamps were going through the mails twice or more. People were cleaning off the cancels and using them again. This may have been done by individuals but, more likely, it was a large-scale operation in which used stamps were cleaned in wholesale quantities and sold to business houses and other volume mailers at a discount. The government was being bilked out of thousands of dollars, but there seemed no solution until a plan was devised to use "grills" on the faces of stamps in 1867. These were networks of tiny embossed dots which weakened the paper and would, presumably, cause it to break apart if any attempt was made at erasing the cancel. After just two years the grill was dropped, but it had appeared on enough stamps in that short time to provide philatelists with an intriguing subspecialty. Not all the grills were alike. They differed in size and style and collecting them is quite a sport.

The year 1869 marked the first year of U.S. pictorial stamps that portrayed things or events rather than portraits. They cannot really be termed commemoratives in the modern sense, but they were extremely pictorial. Subjects included a pony express rider, a rail locomotive, panoramas of the landing of Columbus, the signing of the Declaration of Independence, and others. This series also presented the first stamps to be printed in more than one color. Multicolor printing was no small operation in those days. It required two separate plates; one consisting of frames to be printed in one color, and the other central designs to be printed in a different color. The sheets were fed through one press, allowed to dry, then fed into the next to receive the final printing. As the feeding was done by hand, human error occasionally occurred. A few sheets were fed upside down the second time around, resulting in the first, but not the most famous, U.S. inverts, or stamps with upside down centers. These are very valuable and seldom offered on the market. The king of all U.S. inverts is a twentieth-century stamp, the 24¢ airmail of 1918. This small stamp has a central design of a Curtiss Jenny single engine plane. It was printed 100 to a sheet. On the day it was issued, a Washington, D.C.

collector, William T. Robey, took a few minutes from his lunch hour to go into the local post office and buy a sheet. He had no intention of using the stamps but merely wanted them for his collection. After putting down his $24 he received what appeared to be a normal sheet, but after looking closer, Mr. Robey found that on every stamp the airplane was upside down. This incident stirred a furor of considerable proportion. The government was embarrassed since it had claimed that the old 1869 inverts could not happen again with its new machinery and rigid controls. It tried, without success, to buy the sheet back from Robey. Meanwhile it notified postmasters around the country to check their stocks for further error sheets. No more were found, and when it became evident that Robey's sheet was the only one in existence he began receiving substantial offers from collectors and dealers. The offers seemed tempting and he finally sold his treasure for $15,000 to Eugene Klein of Philadelphia, a prominent dealer. Klein immediately resold the sheet to Col. Edward H. R. Green of New York, the legendary collector who also owned the only five known specimens of the 1913 Liberty nickel. It is believed Green paid at least $17,500 for this philatelic morsel, a huge sum in those days but only about one third as much as each of the 100 stamps are now individually worth. Green broke up the sheet into blocks, selling most of them and recovering his entire cost. Several single specimens were subsequently lost; one was supposed to have disappeared into a vacuum cleaner while Green's housekeeper was tidying up.

FACTORS THAT DETERMINE STAMP VALUES

The collector value (or "market value") of any stamp rests with a variety of factors. Philately becomes a bit less mysterious when one understands the forces at work in the stamp marketplace.

A beginner will normally presume that expensive stamps are expensive because of rarity. Certainly there is a great deal of talk about stamp rarities within the hobby, and so it is natural enough to ascribe high prices to the phenomenon of rarity. In fact, rarity is only one of several factors that influence stamp prices, and the influence it carries is not particularly clear-cut.

In this book you will note some stamps (mostly among the early regular issues) with values of $1,000, $2,000, and even higher. Obviously these stamps are rarer than those selling for $10 or $15. But having said that, we have virtually summed up our useful knowledge of rarity and its effect on prices. A comparison of prices, between stamps in roughly similar ranges of value, does not indicate which is the rarer. A stamp selling for $1,000 is not necessarily rarer than one selling for $500. A $10,000 stamp may actually be more abundant than one which commands $5,000. This hard-to-comprehend fact of philatelic life prevails because of the other factors involved in determining a stamp's price. If rarity were the only factor, one could, of course, easily see which stamps are the rarest by the prices they fetch.

The word "rare" is an elixir to many collectors, not only of stamps but other collectors' items. Sellers are well aware of this, and seldom fail to sprinkle the word liberally in their sales literature. There is no law against calling a stamp rare, as this represents a personal opinion more than anything else and opinions are allowable in advertising. Unfortunately, there is no standard definition for rarity. Does "rare" mean just a handful of specimens in existence, with one reaching the sales portals once in five years? Does it mean 100 in existence, or 1,000, or some other number? Since stamps are—today, at any rate— printed in the multimillions, a thousand surviving specimens might seem a very tiny total to some people. Further complicating this situation is the fact that the specific rarity of most stamps cannot be determined, or even estimated, with any hope of accuracy. The quantities printed are recorded for most of our stamps, going back even into the nineteenth century, but the quantity *surviving* of any particular stamp is anyone's guess. It is obvious that a stamp that goes through the auction rooms once a year is fairly rare, but this provides no sound basis for guessing the number of specimens in existence. That could only be accomplished if some sort of grand census could be taken, and all specimens tallied. This, of course, is nothing but a pipe dream. Some collectors would not participate in such a census; some might be unaware that it was being conducted. Then, too, there are many scarce or rare stamps in hands other than those of collectors, such as dealers and museums. Additionally, there could be (and probably are) existing specimens of rare stamps yet to be discovered, as fresh discoveries are made periodically in the hobby through attic cleaning and the like.

In terms of influence on price, rarity is outdistanced somewhat by *popularity*. Some stamps, for one reason or other, are simply more popular than others. They have a sort of innate appeal for hobbyists, either through reputation, exquisite designing, circumstances of issue, oddity, or various other potential reasons. These stamps sell out rapidly from the stocks of dealers, while some stamps that are supposedly scarcer will linger in stock albums for ages and ages waiting to tempt a customer. It is no wonder, then, that the prices of popular stamps rise more quickly than those that are scarce but not in brisk demand. The Columbian series typifies the effect of popularity on stamp values. If stamp prices were fixed by scarcity alone, none of the Columbians would be selling for nearly as much. Much of their value derives from their overwhelming popularity with collectors of U.S. stamps. It would be safe to say, in fact, that *all* of the Columbians from the lowest face value to the $5, are more plentiful than other U.S. stamps selling for precisely the same sums. Every dealer has Columbians in stock, and quite a few dealers have the high value of the set, too. They are not "hard to get." But they *are* very costly.

Popularity, of course, does not remain constant forever. There are shifts in philatelic popularity, usually slight but occasionally extreme. The popularity of commemoratives as a whole versus regular issues as a whole can change from time to time. Then, too, there are swings of popularity for airmails, first day covers, blocks, coil pairs, mint sheets, and all other philatelic material. A climb or decline in the price of any philatelic item is often an indication of the forces of popularity at work. Then there are activities of investors to consider, whose buying habits seldom reflect those of the pure collector. A great deal of buying by investors in any short period of time (such as occurred during 1979 and 1980, and to less extent in 1981) can make prices seem well out of balance.

Also on the subject of prices, it is important for the beginner to realize that arithmetic is usually futile when dealing with stamp values. You cannot determine the price of one philatelic item by knowing the value of a similar one. This can best be shown by the relative values of singles and blocks of four. A block of four is, as one would expect, worth *more* than four times as much as single specimens of that stamp. It is not just four specimens of the stamp, but four of them *attached*, which lends added scarcity and appeal. The difficulty lies in trying to use mathematics to determine a block's value. Some blocks are worth five times as much as the single stamp; some six times; some ten times as much or even more. Almost all blocks—except very common ones—will vary somewhat in value, in relation to the value of the individual stamp. There is no satisfactory explanation for this, other than the presumption that some blocks are scarcer than others or just in greater demand than others.

In the case of common philatelic items, the value hinges greatly on the method of sale. If you want to buy one specimen of a common cover, you may have to pay $1.50. But if you were willing to buy a hundred common first day covers *of the dealer's choice*, you could very likely get them for $75 or 75¢ each. Buying in quantity, and allowing the dealer to make the selections, can save a great deal of money. Of course one may then ask: What is the real value of those covers? Is it $1.50 or 75¢? The only answer is that it depends on how you buy!

If this article seems to raise a great many questions without supplying many answers, it will, hopefully, serve to show that stamp collecting is not bound to rigid formulas. What happens in the stamp market is largely beyond prediction, or precise explanation. This, indeed, is one of the exciting aspects of the hobby.

STAMP COLLECTORS' TERMINOLOGY

Adhesives—A term given to stamps that have gummed backs and are intended to be pasted on articles and items that are to be mailed.

Aerophilately—The collecting of airmail or any form of stamps related to mail carried by air.

Airmail—Any mail carried by air.

Albino—An uncolored embossed impression of a stamp generally found on envelopes.

Approvals—Stamps sent to collectors. They are examined by the collector, who selects stamps to purchase and returns balance with payment for the stamps he retained.

Arrow Block—An arrow-like mark found on blocks of stamps in the selvage. This mark is used as a guide for cutting or perforating stamps.

As-is—A term used when selling a stamp. It means no representation is given as to its condition or authenticity. Buyers should beware.

Backprint—Any printing that may appear on reverse of stamp.

Backstamp—The postmark on the back of a letter indicating what time or date the letter arrived at the post office.

Bantams—A miniature stamp given to a war economy issue of stamps from South Africa.

Batonne—Watermarked paper used in printing stamps.

Bicolored—A two-color printed stamp.

Bisect—A stamp that could be used by cutting in half and at half the face value.

Block—A term used for a series of four or more stamps attached at least two high and two across.

Bourse—A meeting or convention of stamp collectors and dealers where stamps are bought, sold, and traded.

Cachet—A design printed on the face of an envelope, generally celebrating the commemoration of a new postage stamp issue. Generally called a first day cover.

Cancellation—A marking placed on the face of a stamp to show that it has been used.

Cancelled to Order—A stamp cancelled by the government without being used. Generally remainder stamps or special issues. Common practice of Russian nations.

Centering—The manner in which the design of a stamp is printed and centered upon the stamp blank. A perfectly centered stamp would have equal margins on all sides.

Classic—A popular, unique, highly desired or very artistic stamp. Not necessarily a rare stamp, but one sought after by the collector. Generally used only for nineteenth-century issues.

Coils—Stamps sold in rolls for use in vending machines.

Commemorative—A stamp issued to commemorate or celebrate a special event.

Crease—A fold or wrinkle in a stamp.

Cut Square—An embossed staple removed from the envelope by cutting.

Dead Country—A country no longer issuing stamps.

Demonetized—A stamp no longer valid for use.

Error—A stamp printed or produced with a major design or color defect.

Essay—Preliminary design for a postage stamp.

Face Value—The value of a stamp indicated on the face or surface of the stamp.

Frank—A marking on the face of an envelope indicating the free and legal use of postage. Generally for government use.

Fugitive Inks—A special ink used to print stamps, which can be rubbed or washed off easily, to eliminate erasures and forgeries.

General Collector—One who collects all kinds of issues and all types of stamps from different countries.

Granite Paper—A type of paper containing colored fibers to prevent forgery.

Gum—The adhesive coating on the back of a stamp.

Handstamped—A stamp that has been handcancelled.

Hinge—A specially gummed piece of glassine paper used to attach a stamp to the album page.

Imperforate—A stamp without perforations.

Inverted—Where one portion of a stamp's design is inverted or upside down from the remainder of the design.

Local Stamps—Stamps that are only valid in a limited area.

Margin—The unprinted area around a stamp.

Miniature Sheet—A smaller than usual sheet of stamps.

Mint Condition—A stamp in original condition as it left the postal printing office.

Mirror Print—A stamp error printed in reverse as though looking at a regular stamp reflected in a mirror.

Multicolored—A stamp printed in three or more colors.

Never Hinged—A stamp in original mint condition never hinged in an album.

Off Paper—A used stamp that has been removed from the envelope to which it was attached.

On Paper—A used stamp still attached to the envelope.

Original Gum—A stamp with the same or original adhesive that was applied in the manufacturing process.

Pair—Two stamps unseparated.

Pen Cancellation—A stamp cancelled by pen or pencil.

Perforation Gauge—A printed chart containing various sizes of perforation holes used in determining the type or size of perforation of a stamp.

Perforations—Holes punched along stamp designs allowing stamps to be easily separated.

Philatelist—One who collects stamps.

Pictorial Stamps—Stamps that bear large pictures of animals, birds, flowers, etc.

Plate Block Number—The printing plate number used to identify a block of four or more stamps taken from a sheet of stamps.

Postally Used—A stamp that has been properly used and cancelled.

Precancels—A stamp that has been cancelled in advance. Generally used on bulk mail.

Reissue—A new printing of an old stamp that has been out of circulation.

Revenue Stamp—A label or stamp affixed to an item as evidence of tax payment.

Seals—An adhesive label that looks like a stamp, used for various fund raising campaigns.

Se-tenant—Two or more stamps joined together, each having a different design or value.

Sheet—A page of stamps as they are printed, usually separated before distribution to post offices.

Soaking—Removing used stamps from paper to which they are attached by soaking in water. *(NOTE: Colored cancels may cause staining to other stamps.)*

Souvenir Sheet—One or more specially designed stamps printed by the government in celebration of a special stamp.

Splice—The splice made between rolls of paper in the printing operation. Stamps printed on this splice are generally discarded.

Tete-Bechs—A pair of stamps printed together so that the images point in opposite vertical directions.

Transit Mark—A mark made by an intermediate post office between the originating and final destination post office.

Typeset Stamp—A stamp printed with regular printer's type, as opposed to engraved, lithographed, etc.

Ungummed—Stamps printed without an adhesive back.

Unhinged—A stamp that has never been mounted with the use of a hinge.

Unperforated—A stamp produced without perforations.

Vignette—The central design portion of a stamp.

Want List—A list of stamps a collector needs to fill gaps in his collection.

Watermark—A mark put into paper by the manufacturer, not readily seen by the naked eye.

Wrapper—A strip of paper with adhesive on one end, used for wrapping bundles of mail. Especially in Britain, it refers to any bit of paper to which a used stamp is still attached.

HOW TO GRADE STAMPS

A person need not be an expert to judge the quality or grade of a stamp. All he needs is a discerning eye, possibly a small linear measuring device, and the grading instructions listed below.

The major catalogs traditionally list stamps simply as "Unused" or "Used." Auction houses, however, will describe the stamps for sale in a more informative manner. The greater the value of the stamp, the more thoroughly it is described.

There is no officially accepted system of grading stamps. What we have done in this book is essentially to set up a system of grading stamps using the suggestions and practices of stamp dealers from all over the country. Total agreement was made to the following categories and grades of stamps that are most frequently traded.

CATEGORIES

Mint—The perfect stamp with superb centering, no faults and usually with original gum (if issued with gum).

Unused—Although unused this stamp may have a hinge mark or may have suffered some change in its gum since it was issued.

Used—Basically this will be the normal stamp that passed through the government postal system and will bear an appropriate cancellation.

Cancelled to Order—These are stamps that have not passed through the postal system but have been carefully cancelled by the government usually for a commemoration. These are generally considered undesirable by collectors.

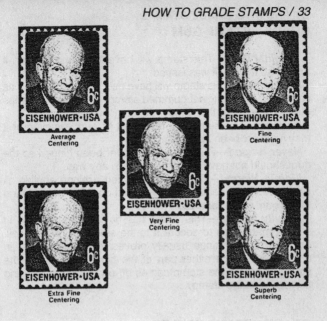

Average
Centering

Fine
Centering

Very Fine
Centering

Extra Fine
Centering

Superb
Centering

GRADE—STAMP CENTERING

Average—The perforations cut slightly into the design.

Fine—The perforations do not touch the design at all, but the design will be off center by 50 percent or more of a superb centered stamp.

Very Fine—The design will be off center by less than 50 percent of a superb stamp. The off centered design will be visibly noticeable.

Extra Fine—The design will be almost perfectly centered. The margin will be off by less than 25 percent of a superb stamp.

Superb—This design will be perfectly centered with all four margins exactly the same. On early imperforate issues, superb specimens will have four clear margins that do not touch the design at any point.

GRADE—STAMP GUM

Original Gum—This stamp will have the same gum on it that it had the day it was issued.

Regummed—This stamp will have new gum applied to it as compared to an original gummed stamp. Regummed stamps are worth no more than those with gum missing.

No Gum—This stamp will have had its gum removed or it may have not been issued with gum.

Never Hinged—This stamp has never been hinged so the gum should not have been disturbed in any way.

Lightly Hinged—This stamp has had a hinge applied. A lightly wetted or peelable hinge would do very little damage to the gum when removed.

Heavily Hinged—This stamp has had a hinge applied in such a manner as to secure it to the stamp extremely well. Removal of this hinge usually proves to be disastrous, in most cases, since either part of the hinge remains on the stamp or part of the stamp comes off on the hinge, causing thin spots on the stamp.

GRADE—STAMP FAULTS

Any fault in a stamp such as thin paper, bad perforations, creases, tears, stains, ink marks, pin holes, etc., and depending upon the seriousness of the fault, usually results in grading the stamp to a lower condition.

OTHER STAMP CONSIDERATIONS

CANCELLATIONS

Light Cancel—This stamp has been postally cancelled but the wording and lines are very light and almost unreadable.

Normal Cancel—This stamp has been postally cancelled with just the right amount of pressure. Usually the wording and lines are not distorted and can be made out.

Heavy Cancel—This stamp has been postally cancelled. In the process excessive pressure was used, and the wording and lines are extremely dark and sometimes smeared and in most cases unreadable.

PERFORATIONS

Not to be overlooked in the appearance of a stamp are its perforations. The philatelist might examine these "tear apart" holes with a magnifying glass or microscope to determine the cleanliness of the separations. One must also consider that the different types of paper, upon which the stamp was printed, will sometimes make a difference in the cleanliness of the separations. The term "pulled perf" is used to denote a badly separated stamp in which the perforations are torn or ragged.

COLOR

Other important factors such as color affect the appearance and value of stamps. An expert will have a chart of stamp colors. Chemical changes often occur in inks. Modern printing sometimes uses metallic inks. These "printings" will oxidize upon contact with the natural secretions from human skin.

The color of certain stamps has been deliberately altered by chemicals to produce a rare shade. Overprints can be eliminated. Postmarks may be eradicated. Replacing gum is a simple process. Some stamps have been found to bear forged watermarks. The back of the paper was cut away and then the stamps rebacked with appropriately watermarked paper.

There are stamp experts who earn a living in the business of stamp repairing. They are craftsmen of the first order. A thin spot on a stamp can be repaired by gluing it on a new layer of paper. Missing perforations can be added. Torn stamps can be put back together. Pieces of stamps may be joined.

In some countries it is accepted practice for an expert, upon examination of a stamp, to certify the authenticity by affixing his signature to the back of the stamp. If the stamp is not genuine, it is his right and duty to so designate on the stamp; but these signatures can also be faked.

WHAT IS AN ERROR, FREAK, OR ODDITY?

In an attempt to answer the questions above, an article, *Listing of Existing EFO Variations According to Group,* by Mr. John M. Hotchner, was published originally in the June 1982 issue of *The EFO Collector,* the quarterly journal of the Errors, Freaks, Oddities Collectors Club. Resulting correspondence and experience in the efo field, plus selected portions of Mr. Hotchner's article, are contained herein to attempt to provide some guidance as to what constitutes an error, freak or oddity.

Nothing makes a philatelist's head turn so fast as an obvious error in an issued stamp. Many of philately's true blue-chip errors are from the early days. The United States 1869 inverts on the fifteen cent, twenty-four cent and thirty cent values, Spain's 1851 two real value in a six real blue sheet, New South Wales stamps of the 1850's and 60's with the wrong watermark, etc.

Why? Most stamps of this era had relatively small printings compared to today's. In addition, they were used with little thought given to looking for or saving errors or misprints of lesser significance. Most of the varieties that have been found were used, and exist in very small quantities. Incidentally, this is a very good reason for one to keep one's eye open, for there remains a possibility that classic errors can still be found in old albums or accumulations.

In the early days of philately, collectors gathered efos (errors, freaks, oddities) to dress up their country or topical collections. Many modern collectors continue to collect efos in that fashion. There has, however, been a recent increase in collecting and studying efos as a specialty area.

Modern-day specialization has been fostered by the greatly

increased awareness of and search for efo material. This is a search which is often rewarded because of the increasing complexity of modern production equipment and the continuing pressure to reduce cost.

The lack of commonly accepted definitions of efo terms has been an impediment to the growth of efo philately. Absence of a clear sense of what efos include, philatelists, in large numbers, have found the area complex and difficult. It has been hard to understand how values developed, so collectors merely kept what they came across, but rarely sought out efo material unless it was listed in a catalog.

Catalog listing is, of course, reserved for errors. Catalog listed errors get space in albums. Thus, recognized errors tend to have an increased value because collectors search for them because they like to fill their empty album spaces. Without a catalog listing, the remainder of efo material tended to wallow in a valley of conflicting and confusing opinion and wildly varying prices. Also, if an item lacks catalog recognition, one might call the item a "freak," "oddity" or "variety."

The answer to an often-asked question regarding efos— "Aren't they expensive?"—is that while some efos are valued in the thousands of dollars, others cost no more than a regular used stamp. In fact, it is quite possible for one to find a spectacular efo item in one's own mailbox. You have probably heard of collectors who bought stamps or postal stationery at their local post office only to find something wrong with the purchase. Think of some of the people who used their find before they realized they had an efo item. *Knowledge* is the key to recognizing efo material when you find it.

The best possible source of information and education can be obtained by becoming a member of a philatelic organization such as the American Philatelic Society (APS), The American Topical Association (ATA), etc.; by joining specialty groups such as the Bureau Issues Association (BIA), The Errors, Freaks, Oddities Collectors Club (EFOCC), etc.; by subscribing to publications such as Linn's, Meekels, Stamp Collector, etc.; by joining libraries such as the Cardinal Spellman Museum, the Western Philatelic Library, etc. Through these organizations and publications, one will obtain knowledge so that one can differentiate between what a postal entity designs and what is the produced product.

The following is the best tool, to date, to attempt to type efo material that is at variance from the intended design.

ERRORS

To be classed as such, an item must be *completely missing* a production step, i.e. the item must be *completely missing* a color, *completely missing* required perforations, contain an inverted design step, etc. Other examples might be:

• Perforations *entirely missing* between stamps—one or more sides.
• Perforations *fully* doubled or tripled.
• Perforations of *wrong gauge* applied.
• Items unintentionally printed on paper watermarked for another issue, or not watermarked at all.

FREAKS

To be classed as such, an item might have a lesser degree of production problem, or problems that are partial and not repeatable. Examples might be:

• Perforations shifted into the design portion of an issue.
• Over inking, under inking, smeared inking.
• Foldovers, foldunders, creases creating crazy perforations.
• Printer's waste (by definition, "Unlawfully Salvaged"). This category would include rejection markings that indicate material that should have been destroyed.
• Gutter snipes (less than a full stamp on one side).

ODDITIES

"Oddities" or, as European collectors seem to favor, "Varieties" include unusual issuances. Examples might be:

• Stamps printed on backs of stamps.
• Usages (bisects).
• Essays, proofs, specimens.
• Cancel/meter varieties.

- Unusual local overprints.
- Double transfers, layout lines, position dots.
- Pre-first day of issue cancels.

The bottom line is any item, be it freak, error, oddity or variety, can be collected as a specialty, or a collector can try to obtain an example of each. Some collectors will restrict their collecting to one country, or even one major issue within a country. Others simply accumulate and enjoy anything they come across with no particular rhyme or reasoned order.

The Errors, Freaks, Oddities Collectors Club has an international membership, quarterly publication and mail auction, heir's assistance program, study groups, etc. Annual dues are $16 USD North America, Europe $30 USD. Sample copy of *The EFO Collector* is $3 USD, or mint postage. EFOCC, 138 Lakemont Drive East, Kingsland, GA 31548-7603, FAX: (912) 729-1585, Email—cwouscg@aol.com

REPAIRS, FAKES, AND
OTHER UNDESIRABLES

Philately, like most hobbies, is not without its pitfalls. The collector who buys from reputable dealers runs very little risk, as today's stamp pros have high principles and are hard to fool. Buying from auction sales and small dealers, who may not have expert knowledge, is another matter. Here the collector must call into play his own expertise and learn to distinguish the bad from the good.

In the early years of philately, stamps provided a playground for fakers and swindlers. They took advantage of the public's gullibility and the general lack of published information about stamps. Copies were printed of rare stamps, as well as of stamps that never existed in the first place. Cancels were bleached from used specimens to make them appear unused. Fake margins were added to imperforates, to allow ordinary copies to be sold as "superb with jumbo margins." Perforated stamps were reperforated to make them better centered. Thin spots in the paper were filled in, tears closed, missing portions of paper replaced. Stamps were doctored and manipulated in more ways than could be imagined, all in the hope of fooling collectors and making anywhere from a few extra cents to thousands of dollars on them. One of the favorite tricks of fakers was to apply bogus overprints or surcharges. By merely using a rubber handstamp and a pad of ink, they could stamp out a hundred or more "rarities" in a few minutes, turning ordinary British or other issues into varieties not found in any catalog. It was all a great game and proved very profitable, until collectors and the philatelic public at large became wary of such practices. Even though most of these fakes from the hobby's pioneer years have disappeared out of circulation, a few still turn up and must be guarded against.

U.S. stamps have not been faked nearly so extensively as those of many other nations, notably South America and Japan. Still, the collector should learn to watch for fakes and also repaired specimens.

Total Fake. The counterfeit stamp always varies somewhat from a genuine specimen, though the difference may be very slight. Detection can usually be made if the suspect stamp is examined alongside one known to be genuine. By using a magnifier, the lines of engraving and paper quality can be compared. The ink on a fake is likely to have a fresher appearance and will lie on the surface as a result of being printed at a later date and on less sophisticated equipment; however, this is not always the case. Experts say that when a stamp appears to be a fake, or a reprint, the odds are very good that it is. Some experience is necessary before anyone can get a first glance reaction to a stamp. The presence or absence of a cancel has no bearing on the likelihood of a stamp being a fake, as cancels can be faked too.

Faked Cancel. Faked cancels are very rare on U.S. stamps, as nearly all are worth more unused than used. One notable exception is the 90¢, 1857–1861. These are applied either with a fake handstamp or simply drawn with pen and ink. Skillfully drawn faked cancels can be very deceptive. Faked cancels are *much more numerous* on covers than loose stamps.

Removed Cancels. So-called cleaned copies of used stamps, sold as unused, were once very plentiful and are still encountered from time to time. The faker, of course, chooses lightly cancelled specimens from which the obliteration can be removed without leaving telltale evidence. In the case of imperforates he may trim down the margins to remove part of the cancel. Rarely will he attempt to clean a stamp whose cancel falls across the face or any important portion of the stamp. Holding the stamp to a strong light may reveal the cancel lines. X-ray examination provides positive proof.

Added Margin(s). When margins have been added to an imperforate stamp, the paper fibers are woven together (after moistening) along the back and at the front where the margin extends beyond the stamp's design. They can usually be detected by looking closely for a seam or joint at the point where the design ends and the margin begins. A magnifying glass will be necessary for this. When held against a light, the reverse side will probably show evidence of the weaving operation. Sometimes the added margins are of a slightly different grade of paper.

Reperforated. A stamp that has been reperforated to improve its centering will usually be slightly smaller than a normal specimen, and this can be revealed by placing it atop an untampered copy.

Filled in Thin Spots. If held to a light and examined with a good magnifier, filled in thin spots will normally appear darker than the remainder of the stamp. Such spots are often mistaken for discoloration by beginners. Thin spots are filled in by making a paste of paper pulp and glue and applying it gradually to the injured area. After drying, the stamp is placed in a vise so that no telltale hills or valleys are left. This is not really considered forgery but honest repair work; it becomes forgery only if done with the intent of selling the stamp as undamaged.

Closed Tears. These are almost always visible against a light with a magnifier, even if small. A routine examination of any rare stamp should include a check of its margins for possible closed or open tears.

HOW TO USE THIS BOOK

The main section of this book lists all U.S. stamps with the exception of special issues such as airmail, revenues, etc. Special issues are grouped separately in sections of their own. Please refer to the Table of Contents.

Before pricing your stamps, be sure they are correctly identified. Use the photo section as an aid. In some cases, two or more stamp issues are very similar in appearance and can be distinguished only by minor details. These are always noted in the text. Sometimes the evidence is obvious. If a stamp has perforations, it cannot be earlier than 1857.

Prices are given in columns for used and unused specimens, usually in two grades of condition. You need only refer to the column that applies to your stamp and its condition grade.

Prices shown in this book are actual selling prices, so one should not necessarily expect to receive a discount when buying from dealers.

When a dash (—) appears in place of a price, this indicates that the item is either unavailable in that condition grade or is so seldom available that its price is open to question. It should not be assumed, however, that such items are invariably more valuable than those for which prices are shown.

Prices are given for hinged stamps that have been in collections. In today's stamp market a premium value is placed on stamps that have never been hinged. To determine the premium on any stamp, refer to the premium percentages shown on every page.

The stated values are general guides only and cannot

reflect the price of occasional superb specimens, such as imperforates with four wide margins, which may sell considerably higher.

A small box has been provided to the left of each listing for keeping a record of the stamps in your collection.

IMPORTANT

Because of the space limitation on each page we have not been able to include very fine, extra fine, never hinged, or lightly hinged pricing on each stamp. To determine these prices please use the following procedure.

Very Fine Pricing—Prior to 1941: *Double the average price quoted.*

Very Fine Pricing—After 1941: *Add 25 percent to the fine price.*

Extra Fine Pricing—Prior to 1941: *Triple the average price quoted.*

Never Hinged Pricing—Prior to 1941: *Add the percentage indicated at the right of the issue to any price listed. Example: (N-H add 5 percent).*

Never Hinged Pricing—After 1941: *Add 15 percent to any price listed.*

Lightly Hinged Pricing—*Add one half of the N-H percentage indicated for each issue to any price listed.*

DEALER BUYING PRICES

Buying prices will vary greatly depending upon condition, rarity, and existing dealers' stock of a particular stamp. With these facts in mind, a dealer can be expected to buy stamps between 40 percent and 50 percent of their quoted prices; but this will depend upon supply and demand.

THREE TIPS FOR
STAMP COLLECTORS:
Soaking Stamps,
Choosing an Album,
and Using Tongs

Courtesy of the American Philatelic Society.

- ## TIP 1: SOAKING STAMPS

BEFORE SOAKING

Set aside any stamps on colored paper, or on paper with a colored backing. Pick out any stamps with colored cancellations, especially with red or purple ink.

Set aside any dark-colored stamps, stamps on poor-quality paper, or with strange-looking inks that might dissolve in the water and stain other stamps being soaked, etc. Any "problem" stamps must be handled carefully later, one at a time.

Trim the envelope paper close to the stamp, being careful not to cut the perforated edges or otherwise damage the stamp.

SOAKING THE STAMPS

Use a shallow bowl and fill it with several inches of cool-to-lukewarm water. (Never use hot water.) Float the stamps with the picture side up. Make sure the stamps have room to float and do not stick to one another. Don't soak too many at one time.

Let the stamps float until the glue dissolves and the stamps *slide easily* off the paper. Paper is very weak when it is wet and it's easy to tear a wet stamp if you handle it roughly. Be patient, and let the water do its work!

Rinse the back of the stamp gently in fresh water to make sure all the glue is off. Change the water in the soaking bowl often to make sure it is clean.

Place the stamps to dry on paper towels or old newspapers. (Don't use the Sunday comics! The colored inks might stick to the wet stamps.) It's a good idea to use your stamp tongs (see next page!) to lift the wet stamps, instead of using your fingers. Lay the stamps in a single layer, and so they are not touching one another.

Let the stamps dry on their own. They may curl a little or look wrinkled, but don't worry about that. When they are completely dry, lift them with your tongs and put them in a phone book or a dictionary or some other book. (Special "stamp drying books" also can be purchased.) It's important not to put the stamps in a book until they are completely dry. After a few days, they should be nice and flat, and you can put them in your collection.

STAMPS ON COLORED PAPER OR WITH COLORED INK CANCELS

Cut away all the excess envelope paper without harming the edges of the stamp.

Fill a shallow dish with cool water (cooler than you would usually use for soaking) and float the stamp *face up*. If the water becomes stained before the stamp is free from the paper, empty it out and use clean water, to prevent the stamp from being stained.

Dry as before.

DIRTY OR STAINED STAMPS

These can be soaked carefully in a small amount of undiluted liquid dishwashing detergent (*not dishwasher* detergent), then rinsed in clean cool water.

Very badly stained stamps can be washed gently in a weak solution of water and a bit of enzyme laundry detergent. Careful! This can work *too* well and remove the printing ink!

SELF-ADHESIVE STAMPS

Some self-adhesive stamps have a special, water-soluble backing, and they *can* be soaked off envelopes. You just need extra patience, as they may have to soak for an hour or more before they will separate from the backing paper. In general, **U.S. self-adhesive stamps from about 1990 and later can be soaked with water; earlier ones cannot.** If you don't want to try soaking, just trim the paper closely around a self-adhesive stamp on cover, and then mount it in your collection with a stamp mount.

• TIP 2: CHOOSING AN ALBUM

You've raided the mailbox, rummaged in the wastebasket in the post office lobby, and pestered your friends to save their envelopes. Now that you have all these philatelic goodies, where will you put them?

True, an ordinary shoebox gives storage space, but you should want a nicer home for your treasures—a place to *display* your material, not just store it. And, on the practical side, stamps and covers (envelopes with stamps on them, used in the mail) kept in a shoebox or paper folder risk damage from dirt or creases, losing value as well as beauty.

Since the first known commercial stamp album was published in 1862, the stamp hobby has grown tremendously, and many types of albums have become available.

When buying a home for your collection, here are some things to think about:

It may be your first album, but it probably will not be your last or only one. Your first album may be a kind of experiment, unless you already have seen someone else's album and think that kind would be right for you too. You also may have tried homemade pages and got some ideas of what you would want in a standard album.

If you are buying an album in person, rather than by mail, listen to the seller's advice, but don't be fully convinced by claims that one or another album is "the best." An album may be by a famous maker, and expensive, but that doesn't make it "the best" one for you. Be a careful shopper; **consider all the factors—appearance, price, format—** and make the best choice. Good beginners' albums are available that are not too expensive, are fully illustrated to show which stamp goes where, and may even contain extra information, such as maps and facts about the countries.

Certain styles of albums can present problems. For example, if an album is designed for stamps to be mounted on the front and back of each page, when the book is closed, the stamps can become tangled with one another on the facing pages. Opening the book may tear the mounted stamps apart. If you are looking at an album with this page format and don't like that aspect, but do like other things about the album, buy some good-quality plastic sheets to insert between the pages, and prevent the tangles.

You may choose not to buy a top-of-the-line album because of cost, but do **be willing to pay for some quality**. An album with pages of flimsy paper will not stand up to the stress of increasing numbers of stamps as you fill the album. An album with torn, falling-out pages is not much better than the old shoebox.

Homemade pages can be experimented with before album-shopping or may even become your permanent storage choice. Some options include a notebook or looseleaf binder of plain paper, though longtime, safest storage of your stamps should be on acid-free paper. If you have an unusual specialty, or enjoy unique arrangements, no standard album may ever suit your needs, and homemade will be best.

Blank, acid-free album pages punched for three-hole binders are widely available. It is easy to assemble a safe, stable home for your personalized collection, if you don't need or want the kind of structured format that standard albums provide. Makers of custom pages and albums advertise regularly in the philatelic press.

Buying an album is not so different from buying anything else: **Think before and during the purchase;** buy as wisely as you can and not over your budget; and don't be too discouraged if your first acquisition turns out to be less than perfect. You will always need places for temporary storage as you continue in the hobby. Old albums never go to waste!

• TIP 3: USING TONGS

Philatelic tongs (not to be confused with the tweezers in the medicine cabinet) are must-have items for every stamp collector. Get into the habit early of using your tongs every time you work with your stamps. They will act as clean extensions of your fingers and keep dirt, skin oil, and other harmful things from getting on your philatelic paper.

It's important to use tongs correctly and carefully. As with knives, scissors, and other helpful tools, tongs used carelessly are harmful rather than helpful. Cut some plain paper into stamp-sized pieces and practice using your tongs, watching what happens as you change the angle, pressure, and method of using them.

Grip a bit of paper strongly with the pointy-end style of tongs and watch what happens. If that were a favorite stamp, would you have wanted that hole poked in the middle of it? Keep experimenting, and you will find that it's not difficult to hold a stamp firmly but gently with tongs.

There are several common styles of tongs, to suit your preference and for special purposes.

Some have very pointed ends; they touch only a tiny part of the stamp, but there is the risk of poking holes through it. Working with extra-long tongs (five or six inches) with small pointed tips requires a lot of dexterity, and while experts may prefer them, they may not be comfortable or necessary for "everyday" stamp work.

The rounded, spatula-type style known as the "spade" are good, general-purpose tongs. **A squared-off version** of the spade also is commonly available, though the rather sharp corners present the same kind of risk as the thin, pointy tongs. **One handy style is angled,** with a bend near the tips that makes it easier to remove stamps from watermark or soaking trays, or to insert and remove stamps from stockbooks or mounts.

Tongs cost anywhere from a couple of dollars to quite a few for some of the imported, high-quality models. A special gift for a philatelist would be some gold-plated tongs, which are not hard to find, believe it or not! Tongs can be found anywhere stamp supplies are sold; check under "Accessories" in the philatelic press ads.

Tongs are among the least expensive and most essential stamp-hobby needs. You may even want to have several different kinds on hand—instead of your hands! Your stamps will appreciate it.

EQUIPMENT

To collect stamps properly a collector will need some "tools of the trade." These need not be expensive and need not all be bought at the very outset. That might, in fact, be the worst thing to do. Many a beginning collector has spent his budget on equipment, only to have little or nothing left for stamps and then loses interest in the hobby.

It may be economical in the long run to buy the finest quality accessories, but few collectors, just starting out, have a clear idea of what they will and will not be needing. It is just as easy to make impulse purchases of accessories as of stamps and just as unwise. Equipment must be purchased on the basis of what sort of collection is being built *now*, rather than on what the collection may be in the future. There is no shame in working up from an elementary album.

Starter Kits. Starter or beginner outfits are sold in just about every variety shop, drugstore, etc. These come in attractive boxes and contain a juvenile or beginner's album; some stamps, which may be on paper and in need of removal; a packet of gummed hinges; tongs; a pocket stockbook or file; and often other items such as a perforation gauge, booklet on stamp collecting, magnifier, and watermark detector. These kits are specially suited to young collectors and can provide a good philatelic education.

Albums. When the hobby began, more than a century ago, collectors mounted their stamps in whatever albums were at hand. Scrapbooks, school exercise tablets and diaries all were used, as well as homemade albums. Today a number of firms specialize in printing albums of all kinds for philatelists, ranging from softbounds for the cautious type to huge multi-volume sets that cost hundreds of dollars. There are general worldwide albums, country albums, U.N. albums, and albums for mint sheets, covers, and every other conceivable variety of philatelic material. Choose your album according to the specialty you intend to pursue. It is not necessary, however, to buy a printed album at all. Many collectors feel there is not enough room for creativity in a printed album and prefer to use a binder with unprinted sheets. This allows items to be arranged at will on the page, rather than following the publisher's format, and for a personal write-up to be added. Rod-type binders will prove more durable and satisfactory than ring binders for heavy collections. The pages of an album should not be too thin, unless only one side is used. The presence of tiny crisscrossing lines (quadrilled sheets) is intended as an aid to correct alignment. Once items have been mounted and written up, these lines are scarcely visible and do not interfere with the attractiveness of the page.

Hinges. These are small rectangular pieces of lightweight paper, usually clear or semiopaque, gummed and folded. One side is moistened and affixed to the back of the stamp and the other to the album page. Hinges are sold in packets of 1,000 and are very inexpensive. Though by far the most popular device for mounting stamps, the hobbyist has his choice of a number of other products if hinges are not satisfactory to him. These include cello mounts, which encase the stamp in clear sheeting and have a black background to provide a kind of frame. These are self-sticking. Their cost is much higher than hinges. The chief advantage of cello mounts is that they prevent injuries to the stamp and eliminate the moistening necessary in using hinges; however, they add considerably to the weight of each page, making flipping through an album less convenient, and become detached from the page more readily than hinges.

Glassine Interleaving. These are sheets made of thin semitransparent glassine paper, the same used to make envelopes in which stamps are stored. They come punched to fit albums of standard size and are designed to be placed between each set of sheets, to prevent stamps on one page from becoming entangled with those on the facing page. Glassine interleaving is not necessary if cello mounts are used, but any collection mounted with conventional hinges should be interleaved. The cost is small. Glassine interleaving is sold in packets of 100 sheets.

Magnifier. A magnifier is a necessary tool for *most* stamp collectors, excepting those who specialize in first day covers or other items that would not likely require study by magnification. There are numerous types and grades on the market, ranging in price from about $1 to more than $20. The quality of magnifier to buy should be governed by the extent to which it is likely to be used, and the collector's dependence upon it for identification and study. A collector of plate varieties ought to have the best magnifier he can afford and carry it whenever visiting dealers, shows, or anywhere that he may wish to examine specimens. A good magnifier is also necessary for a specialist in grilled stamps and for collectors of Civil War and other nineteenth-century covers. Those with built-in illumination are best in these circumstances.

Tongs. Beginners have a habit of picking up stamps with their fingers, which can cause injuries, smudges and grease stains. Efficient handling of tongs is not difficult to learn, and the sooner the better. Do not resort to ordinary tweezers, but get a pair of philatelic tongs which are specially shaped and of sufficiently large size to be easily manipulated.

Perforation Gauge. A very necessary inexpensive article, as the identification of many stamps depends upon a correct measuring of their perforations.

TEN LOW-COST WAYS TO START COLLECTING STAMPS
Courtesy of the American Philatelic Society.

If you have recently started collecting stamps, or are thinking about starting, you may be wondering if the hobby is expensive. Can you enjoy it with limited financial resources? What if you have no money at all for the hobby?

One of the biggest questions any stamp collector faces is where to find stamps inexpensively. If you intend to save stamps of the United States or the world and want to save used as well as unused stamps, the opportunities are really great. Not all collections consist mainly of unused stamps that you buy in the post office. Used stamps are worth saving, have value, and they may cost you nothing.

Many stamp collectors save only used stamps. Others save both used and unused ones. Others save stamps only from one country or one part of the world. Some collectors save stamps by "topic," for example, stamps that depict horses or trains or birds. There are any number of different types of collections.

1. All postally used stamps started out being received in someone's mailbox, at no cost to the person receiving them. The first place to search for stamps, then, is your own mailbox. Don't be discouraged when you notice that many senders use postage meters or the imprint "Bulk Rate Postage Paid" on their envelopes to enjoy a better postal rate or to keep from affixing stamps. Also, when people do use real stamps, they often use the same common small ones.

You can begin to change this by asking people who write to you to use *commemorative* stamps on their mail. These are normally the larger stamps issued to honor famous people, places, or events. These stamps are printed in lesser quantities than the common smaller *(definitive)* stamps and usually are of much more interest to collectors. Many people will remember to ask for commemorative stamps at the post office when mailing letters to you or your family if you let them know you are a stamp collector. Also, if you write away for offers that require postage or a self-addressed, stamped envelope, you can put commemoratives on your return envelope, knowing that they will come back to you later.

2. Neighbors, friends, and relatives are another good source of stamps. The majority of people just throw away stamps when they receive them on mail and are only too happy to save them for someone who appreciates them. You may even know someone who gets letters from other countries who can save these stamps, too. Always be on the lookout for potentially good stamp contacts, and don't be afraid to ask them to go through their mail for you before they throw away all the envelopes.

3. Office mail may be even better. You may know someone who works in an office that gets a lot of mail. Out of 100 letters a day, there may be ten or twenty good stamps that are being thrown away. Many businesses get a lot of foreign mail and regularly throw away stamps that have interest and/or value to a collector.

4. Ask your parents if they have any old letters, which may have stamps on the envelopes. When taking stamps off envelopes, always tear off the corner so that there is paper all around the stamp, and the stamp and all its perforations are undamaged. Anyone who is saving stamps for you should be told that this is the way to do it; otherwise, he/she may try to peel the stamp off the envelope. This will cause thin spots or tears, both of which ruin a stamp's appearance and lessen its value to collectors. If you run across envelopes that are very old or have postal markings that may be of particular interest, it is best to save the entire envelope until you can find out if the stamp is worth more attached to the cover.

Now that you have stamps on paper, what do you do with them? The most common way to get stamps off paper is to soak them in cool water, then dry them on paper. To understand more about soaking stamps, it is best to find a handbook on stamp collecting at the library.

There is a lot to learn about stamps as you get more and more of them. For example, different shades of color may exist on stamps with the same design, or they may have different perforation measurements (number of holes per side). Major varieties of stamps and "catalog values" are listed in stamp catalogs, which are available in most libraries. The most common one, the *Scott Standard Postage Stamp Catalogue*, has a very good section in front that explains how stamps are made and how to tell varieties apart, as well as how to use the catalog. Having access to a catalog in a nearby library is very useful until you decide if you want one of your own.

5. Longtime collectors may be another source of stamps. Usually a person who has been a collector for a number of years has developed many sources for stamps. The collector may have thousands of duplicates, some of which may be very inexpensive while others may have more value. Often older collectors are willing to help new philatelists get started by giving them stamps, or at least providing packets of stamps much more cheaply than can be purchased in stores or by mail.

6. Many stamp companies advertise free stamps. However, these ads must be read carefully before you send away for anything. Usually these ads offer "approvals," which means they will send you the free stamps advertised, *plus* an assortment of other stamps which you may either buy or return. By sending for the free stamps, you have already agreed that you will return the other stamps within a reasonable period of time if you do not buy anything. Usually you must pay the return postage. This is a convenient way to buy stamps from your own home.

7. Stamp clubs are another place to get stamps. A club may offer stamps as prizes, or have inexpensive stamps you can afford to buy.

Some stamp clubs sponsor junior clubs that meet at schools or the local YMCA or community center. If you are fortunate enough to have one of these in your area, it can be a great source of both stamps and advice.

8. One way to increase your sources for stamps and also have a lot of fun is to help *start* a local club, if one does not already exist. All it takes are four or five other stamp collectors who are interested in getting together to learn about and trade stamps and ideas.

9. Obtaining a pen pal in another country is a very good way to get stamps from that country. His or her extra stamps may seem really common in that country, but over here they are much scarcer. Your own stamps may look fairly common to you, but he or she is sure to appreciate them.

10. Trading off your duplicate stamps can be a lot of fun. Even if you don't know many collectors where you live, stamps are so lightweight that they can easily be traded by mail. Check out the stamp newspapers and magazines available at your local library for classified ads that list stamp trades. You may find, for example, that another collector will send you 100 large foreign stamps if you send 100 U.S. commemoratives. Usually schools do not subscribe to any of the periodical stamp publications, so you will have to go to your public library. (Many stamp publications also offer to send one free sample issue if you request it, because they are always looking for potential new subscribers.)

Collecting stamps need not be an expensive hobby. Thousands of stamps are issued every year, and while some of them cost many dollars, others cost just a few cents each. Nobody expects you to try to save every stamps that exists, and the key to enjoying philately is to save whatever you enjoy the most! With free stamps and a few inexpensive accessories, such as a small album and a package of stamp hinges, even collectors with little money can have a great time. Don't forget to mention stamps, stamp albums, and hinges before your birthday or Christmas! Also remember that a great many inexpensive stamps in the past have turned into more valuable stamps over the years.

TIPS ON STAMP BUYING

There are many ways to buy stamps: packets, poundage mixtures, approvals, new issue services, auctions and a number of others. To buy wisely, a collector must get to know the language of philately and the techniques used by dealers and auctioneers in selling stamps.

Packets of all different worldwide stamps are sold in graduated sizes from 1,000 up to 50,000. True to their word, they contain no duplicates. The stamps come from all parts of the world and date from the 1800s to the present. Both mint and used are included. When you buy larger quantities of most things, a discount is offered; with stamp packets, it works in reverse. The larger the packet, the higher its price per stamp. This is because the smaller packets are filled almost exclusively with low-grade material.

Packets are suitable only as a collection base. A collector should never count on them to build his entire collection. The contents of one worldwide packet are much like that of another. Country jackets are sold in smaller sizes, but there are certain drawbacks with packets.

1. Most packets contain some cancelled-to-order stamps, which are not very desirable for a collection. These are stamps released with postmarks already on them, and are classified as used but have never gone through the mail. Eastern Europe and Russia are responsible for many C.T.O.'s.

2. The advertised value of packets bears little relation to the actual value. Packet makers call attention to the catalog values of their stamps, based on prices listed in standard reference works. The lowest sum at which a stamp can be listed in these books is 2¢, therefore, a packet of 1,000 automatically has a minimum catalog value of $20. If the retail price is $3 this seems like a terrific buy when, in fact, most of those thousand stamps are so common they are almost worthless.

Poundage mixtures are very different than packets. Here the stamps are all postally used (no C.T.O.'s) and still attached to small fragments of envelopes or parcel wrappings. Rather than sold by count, poundage mixtures are priced by the pound or ounce and quite often by kilos. Price varies depending on the grade, and the grade depends on where the mixture was assembled. Bank mixtures are considered the best, as banks receive a steady flow of foreign registered mail. Mission mixtures are also highly rated. Of course, the mixture should be sealed and unpicked. Unless a mixture is advertised as unpicked, the high values have been removed. The best poundage mixtures are sold only by mail. Those available in shops are of medium or low quality. Whatever the grade, poundage mixtures can be counted on to contain duplicates.

If you want to collect the stamps of a certain country, you can leave a standing order for its new releases with a new issue service. Whenever that government puts out stamps, they will be sent to the collector along with a bill. Usually the service will supply only mint copies. The price charged is not the face value, but the face value with a surcharge added to meet the costs of importing, handling, and the like. New issue services are satisfactory only if the collector is positive he wants all the country's stamps, no matter what. Remember that its issues could include semipostals, long and maybe expensive sets, and extra high values.

By far the most popular way to buy stamps is via approvals. There is nothing new about approvals, as they go back to the Victorian era. Not all services are alike, though. Some offer sets, while others sell penny approvals. Then there are remainder approvals, advanced approvals, and seconds on approval. Penny approvals are really a thing of the past, though the term is still used. Before inflation, dealers would send a stockbook containing several thousand stamps, all priced at a penny each. If all the stamps were kept, the collector got a discount plus the book! Today the same sort of service can be found, but instead of 1¢ per stamp, the price is anywhere from 3¢ to

10¢. Remainder approvals are made up from collection remainders. Rather than dismount and sort stamps from incoming collections, the approval merchant saves himself time by sending them out right on the album pages. The collector receives leaves from someone else's collection with stamps mounted just as he arranged them. Seconds on approval are slightly defective specimens of scarce stamps, which would cost more if perfect. Advanced approvals are designed for specialized collectors who know exactly what they want and have a fairly substantial stamp budget.

In choosing an approval service you should know the ground rules of approval buying and not be unduly influenced by promotional offers. Most approval merchants allow the selections to be kept for ten days to two weeks. The unbought stamps are then returned along with payment for those kept. As soon as the selection is received back, another is mailed. This will go on, regardless of how much or how little is bought, until the company is notified to refrain from sending further selections. The reputable services will always stop when told.

Approval ads range from splashy full pagers in the stamp publications to small three-line classified announcements in magazines and newspapers. Most firms catering to beginners offer loss leaders, or stamps on which they take a loss for the sake of getting new customers. If an approval dealer offers 100 pictorials for a dime, it is obvious he is losing money on that transaction, as 10¢ will not even pay the postage. It is very tempting to order these premiums. Remember that when ordering approvals. What sort of service is it? Will it offer the kind of stamps desired? Will prices be high to pay for the loss leaders? Be careful of confusing advertisements. Sometimes the premium offers seem to promise more than they actually do. A rare, early stamp may be pictured. Of course you do not receive the stamp, but merely a modern commemorative picturing it.

Auction Sales. Stamp auctions are held all over the country and account for millions of dollars in sales annually. Buying at auction is exciting and can be economical. Many sleepers turn up—stamps that can be bought at less than their actual value. To be a good auction buyer, the philatelist must know stamps and their prices pretty well, and know the ropes of auctions. An obvious drawback of auctions is that purchases are not returnable. A dealer will take back a stamp that proves not to a collector's liking, but an auctioneer will not. Also, auctioneers require immediate payment while a dealer may extend credit.

Stamps sold at auction come from private collections and the stocks of dealers; not necessarily defunct dealers, but those who want to get shelf space. Because they were brought together from a variety of sources, the nature and condition will vary. In catalog descriptions the full book value will be given for each stamp, but of course defective stamps will sell for much less than these figures. A bidder must calculate how much less. Other lots which can be difficult for the bidder to evaluate are those containing more than one stamp. Sometimes a superb specimen will be lotted along with a defective one. Then there are bulk lots which contain odds and ends from collections and such. It is usual in auctioning a collection for the better stamps to be removed and sold separately. The remainder is then offered in a single lot, which may consist of thousands or even tens of thousands of stamps. By all means examine lots before bidding. A period of inspection is always allowed before each sale, usually for several days. There may or may not be an inspection on sale day. If the bidder is not able to make a personal examination but must bid on strength of the catalog description, he should scale his bids for bulk lots much lower than for single stamp lots. He might bid $50 on a single stamp lot with a catalog value of $100, if the condition is listed as top notch, but to bid one-half catalog value on a bulk lot would not be very wise. These lots are not scrutinized very carefully by the auctioneers and some stamps are bound to be disappointing. There may be some heavily canceled, creased, torn, etc. Also, there will very likely be duplication. A bid of one-fifth the catalog value on a bulk lot is considered high. Often a one-tenth bid is successful.

The mechanics of stamp auctions may strike the beginner as complicated. They are run no differently than other auctions. All material to be sold is lotted by the auctioneer; that is, broken down into lots or units and bidding is by lot. Everything in the lot must be bid on, even if just one of the stamps is desired. The motive of bulk lotting is to save time and give each lot a fair sales value.

Before the sale a catalog is published listing all the lots, describing the contents and sometimes picturing the better items. Catalogs are in the mail about 30 days before the sale date. If a bid is to be mailed, it must be sent early. Bids that arrive after the sale are disqualified, even if they would have been successful.

When the bid is received it is entered into a bidbook, along with the bidder's name and address. On sale day each lot opens on the floor at one level above the second highest mail bid. Say the two highest mail bids are $30 and $20. The floor bidding would begin at $25. If the two highest bids are $100 and $500, the opening bid would probably be $150. The larger the amounts involved, the bigger will be the advances. The auctioneer will not accept an advance of $5 on a $500 lot; but on low value lots even dollar advances are sometimes made. Then it becomes a contest of floor versus book. The auctioneer acts as an agent, bidding for the absentee until his limit is reached. If the floor tops him, he has lost. If the floor does not get as high as his bid, he wins the lot at one advance over the highest floor bid.

When a collector buys stamps by mail from a dealer, he should choose one who belongs to the American Stamp Dealers' Association or A.S.D.A. The emblem is carried in their ads.

HOW TO ORDER STAMPS "TOLL-FREE" FROM THE USPS

You can now order stamps, toll-free, from the USPS by calling the Philatelic Fulfillment Service Center located in Kansas City, Missouri, 1-800-782-6724. Listening to a computerized voice, you can choose from six options using a touchtone phone: 1) ordering stamps, 2) catalog requests, subscription programs information, 3) customer assistance, 4) personalized envelopes, post offices and official mail agencies. This is a very useful service. It is recommended that you first order one of the catalogs, "Stamps, Etc." or "Not Just Stamps" in order to correctly place your order for stamps.

SELLING YOUR STAMPS

Almost every collector becomes a stamp seller sooner or later. Duplicates are inevitably accumulated, no matter how careful one may be in avoiding them. Then there are the G and VG stamps that have been replaced with F and VF specimens, and have become duplicates by intent. In addition to duplicates, a more advanced collector is likely to have stamps that are not duplicates but for which he has no further use. These will be odds and ends, sometimes quite valuable ones, that once suited the nature of his collection but are now out of place. Collectors' tastes change. The result is a stockpile of stamps that can be converted back to cash.

The alternative to selling the stamps you no longer need or want is trading them with a collector who does want them, and taking his unwanted stamps in return. All stamp clubs hold trading sessions. Larger national stamp societies operate trade-by-mail services for their members. The APS (American Philatelic Society) keeps $8,000,000 worth of stamps constantly circulating in its trading books or "circuit" books. Trading can be an excellent way of disposing of surplus stamps. In most cases it takes a bit longer than selling. Another potential drawback, especially if you are not a club member, is finding the right person with the right stamps.

The nature and value of the material involved may help in deciding whether to sell outright or trade. Also, there are your own personal considerations. If you're not going to continue in the stamp hobby, or need cash for some purpose other than stamp buying, trading is hardly suitable. Likewise, if you have developed an interest in some very exotic group of stamps or other philatelic items it may be impossible to find someone to trade with.

Once you have decided to sell, if indeed you do make that decision, the matter revolves upon how. To a stamp shop? To another collector? Through an auction house? Possibly by running your own advertisements and issuing price lists, if you have enough stamps and spare time to make this worthwhile?

While some individuals have an absolute horror at the prospect of selling anything, stamp collectors tend to enjoy selling. It is difficult to say why. Some enjoy it so much they keep right on selling stamps, as a business, long after their original objective is achieved. Nearly all professional stamp dealers were collectors before entering the trade.

Selling your stamps outright to a dealer, especially a local dealer whom you can personally visit, is not necessarily the most financially rewarding but it is quick and very problem-free. Of course it helps if the dealer knows you and it's even better if he knows some of your stamps. Dealers have no objection to repurchasing stamps they've sold to you. You will find that the dealers encourage their customers to sell to them just as much as they encourage them to buy. The dealers are really anxious to get your stamps if you have good salable material from popular countries. In fact most dealers would prefer buying from the public rather than any other source.

The collector selling stamps to a dealer has to be reasonable in his expectations. A dealer may not be able to use all the stamps you have. It is simply not smart business for a dealer to invest money in something he may not be able to sell. So, if you have esoteric or highly specialized items for sale, it might be necessary to find a specialist who deals in those particular areas rather than selling to a neighborhood stamp shop.

The local stamp shop will almost certainly want to buy anything you can offer in the way of medium to better grade United States stamps of all kinds, including the so-called "back of the book" items. He may not want plate blocks or full sheets of commemoratives issued within the past 20 years. Most dealers are well supplied with material of this nature and have opportunities to buy more of it every day. The same is true of first day covers, with a few exceptions, issued from the 1960s to the present. The dealers either have these items abundantly or can get them from a whole-saler at rock-bottom prices. They would rather buy stamps that are a bit harder to get from the wholesalers, or for which the wholesalers charge higher prices. On the whole you will meet with a favorable reception when offering U.S. stamps to a local dealer. With foreign stamps it becomes another matter: what do you have and how flexible are you in price? Nearly all the stamp shops in this country do stock foreign stamps to one extent or another. They do not, as a rule, attempt to carry comprehensive or specialized stocks of them. In the average shop you will discover that the selection of general foreign consists of a combination of modern mint sets, topicals, souvenir sheets, packets which come from the wholesaler, and a small sprinkling of older material, usually pre-1900. The price range of this older material will be $5 to $50. Non-specialist collectors of foreign stamps buy this type of item and that is essentially who the local shop caters to. When a local dealer buys rare foreign stamps or a large foreign collection, it is not for himself. He buys with the intent of passing them along to another dealer who has the right customers lined up. He acts only as a middleman or go-between. Therefore the price you receive for better grade foreign stamps tends to be lower than for better grade U.S., which the dealer buys for his own use.

What is a fair price to get for your stamps? This is always difficult to say, as many variable factors are involved. Consider their condition. Think in terms of what the dealer could reasonably hope to charge for them at retail and stand a good chance of selling them. Some of your stamps may have to be discounted because of no gum, poor centering, bent perfs, hinge remnants, repairs, or other problems. But even if your stamps are primarily F or VF, a dealer cannot pay book values for them. If you check his selling prices on his specimens of those same stamps, you can usually count on receiving from 40 to 50 percent of those prices. Considering the discount made from book values by the dealer in pricing his stock, your payment may work out to about 25 percent of book values. For rare U.S. stamps in top condition you can do better than 25 percent, but on most stamps sold to a dealer this is considered a fair offer. Keep in mind that the difference between a dealer's buying and selling prices is not just "profit margin." Most of the markup goes toward operating costs, for without this markup, there would be no stamp dealers.

PUBLICATIONS—
LINN'S STAMP NEWS

Linn's Stamp News is a tabloid-size newspaper for stamp collectors. It has been published continuously as a weekly since 1928. Both in terms of page count and circulation, *Linn's* is the largest publication in the stamp hobby. Each issue of *Linn's* contains a vast quantity of words and pictures designed to appeal to stamp collectors at every level of interest.

As the dominant publication in the stamp hobby, each weekly issue of *Linn's* is crammed with news and other information stamp collectors need to know, including details on how to order first-day covers directly from the U.S. Postal Service and information on how to order new-issue stamps at face value directly from overseas post offices. Lavishly illustrated features discuss virtually every aspect of the world's most popular collecting hobby, in terms that beginners and newcomers can easily understand. "Trends of Stamp Values" monitors prices (and price changes) for more than 100,000 stamps from every nation of the world. "Linn's Stamp Market Index" is the stamp equivalent of the Dow Jones Industrial Average. "U.S. Stamp Facts" provides weekly information about classic U.S. stamps in a compact and highly visual format. "Stamp Collecting Made Easy" explains complexities of stamp collecting in an illustrated how-to feature. "Focus on Forgeries" provides visual clues to identify common fake stamps.

One of the most interesting features of *Linn's* is its advertising. Each issue contains 50 or more pages of ads from dealers seeking to buy or sell stamps. *Linn's* classified advertising section consists of 15 or more pages of small ads from dealers and collectors, all arranged by classification, to help busy collectors locate just what they need.

The publication isn't cheap (current subscription price is $39 a year), but stamp collectors say they can't do without it. You can see for yourself, because the publishers of *Linn's* will send a free sample copy to *Blackbook* readers. Write to Linn's Blackbook Offer, P.O. Box 29, Sidney, OH 45365.

THE JUNIOR PHILATELISTS
OF AMERICA

The Junior Philatelists of America, founded in 1963, is an organization primarily for stamp collectors under age 18. The JPA brings together young collectors from every part of the United States and many foreign counties. One benefit of membership is receiving the bi-monthly newsletter, *The Philatelic Observer.* As a member, you also can write articles for the newsletter, or buy and sell stamps through free or low-cost advertising.

Other JPA services include auctions where members may buy or sell their stamps, a service to help find penpals throughout the world, awards for junior stamp exhibitors, study groups, local chapter clubs, and contests.

To learn more about the Junior Philatelists of America, send a **business size, self-addressed, stamped envelope** to JPA, P.O. Box 850, Boalsburg, PA 16827.

The JPA also offers an Adult Supporting Membership for adult collectors who want to support and assist the collectors of the future.

THE AMERICAN PHILATELIC SOCIETY

The American Philatelic Society is an internationally recognized association of both stamp experts and enthusiasts that offers a number of services and educational opportunities for stamp collectors. The APS is the national representative to the Federation Internationale de Philatelie and is affiliated with more than 700 local stamp clubs (APS Chapters) and almost 200 "specialty groups" (APS Affiliates).

The services that are available with an APS membership include a monthly subscription to *The American Philatelist*, one of the premier stamp magazines in the world, as well as numerous other brochures and publications that are available at a discount to members. The APS Sales Division provides an opportunity for collectors to buy or sell stamps through the mail. Members may request "circuits" of stamps or covers in more than 150 categories of countries and topics. Selections of circuit books are mailed at intervals, and members can choose any items they wish to purchase, and then mail the books on to the next APS member on the circuit. The items are priced by the submitting members, and most range from under $1 to $5.

The APS also provides an insurance program for members living in the United States, Canada, the United Kingdom, and other countries in western Europe and Scandinavia. The insurance policy does not require a detailed inventory, only a general description of a collection and a value estimate, and may be applied for along with APS membership.

The Society also runs the American Philatelic Research Library, with a wide range of resource material including thousands of books, journals, auction catalogs, and other material that are loaned or photocopied and available to members by mail for a nominal fee. The APRL also publishes the *Philatelic Literature Review*, a quarterly journal covering literature of interest to collectors. The magazine is available by separate subscription.

The APS offers a week-long Summer Seminar on Philately that features hands-on instruction by prominent experts. In addition, the APS Education Department produces many brochures and other materials and answers inquiries from beginner and intermediate collectors on various "how-to" aspects of the hobby.

Other APS services include authentication of members' stamps by the APS Expert Committee, estate advice, a translation service for international trading, and an annual convention-exhibition stamp show.

THE AMERICAN PHILATELIST

The Society's monthly magazine, which is included in the membership fee, features regular columns on U.S. stamps, stamp clubs, exhibitions, topical collecting, and more; articles by experienced philatelists; how-to columns on using the Society's Sales Division; and detailed listings of all new stamps and postal stationery issued by the U.S. Postal Service.

MEMBERSHIP INFORMATION

The APS offers a variety of memberships including special rates for other family members, foreign members, and lifetime memberships. The Society operates on a calendar year, and membership fees are pro-rated on a quarterly basis and include a $3 admission fee. The current schedule of membership fees is listed below.

Application received by APS National Headquarters	Admission Fee	Membership Fee	U.S.	Total Canada	Foreign
October, November, December	$3.00	$22.00	$25.00	$28.00	$31.00
January, February, March	3.00	16.50	19.50	21.75	24.00
April, May, June	3.00	11.00	14.00	15.50	17.00
July, August, September	3.00	5.50	8.50	9.25	10.00

For more information, call or write the American Philatelic Society at:

APS
P.O. Box 8000, Dept. HC
State College, PA 16803
(814) 237-3803, Fax (814) 237-6128
e-mail FLSENTE@STAMPS.ORG

For those with access to the Internet, the APS maintains a home page at http://www.west.net/~stamps1/aps.html. The site contains current APS news, such as minutes of recent official meetings and upcoming events; access to the American Philatelic Research Library; descriptions of member services; listings of books and other items for sale by the APS; and an online membership application form. The page also has links to many other philatelic sites on the Net.

NATIONAL STAMP ORGANIZATIONS LISTED ALPHABETICALLY BY COLLECTING SPECIALTY

All of the listed organizations are affiliated with the APS, but each is a separate organization and offers its own services to its members, including, in most cases, a specialized journal. Affiliates that also are affiliated with the American Topical Association are identified by an asterisk (*).

HOW TO BECOME AN APS AFFILIATE

Any organization that is at least national in scope, that was formed for the study of a special phase of philately, and that has objectives and activities compatible with those of the APS may affiliate with the Society upon approval of the APS Board of Directors. Further information may be obtained by contacting APS Headquarters, P.O. Box 8000, State College, PA 16803.

Aerophilatelic Society, Canadian — #189

APS REP: MAJ R. K. Malott, 16 Harwick Cres., Nepean, ON K2H 6R1, Canada.

The Canadian Aerophilatelist: 4 per year. **Dues:** U.S. $15; outside U.S. $20. **Services:** directory, expertizing (Canadian material only), exhibition awards, library, annual convention.

Air Mail Society, American — #77

APS REP: Cheryl Ganz, P.O. Box A3843, Chicago, IL 60690-3843. Home page.

The Airpost Journal: monthly. **Dues:** U.S. $20; outside U.S. $25. **Services:** local chapters, study groups, sales book circuits, auctions, slide programs, handbooks, exhibition awards, special awards, annual convention.

Air Mail Society, Jack Knight — #181

APS REP: Wayne Fitzgibbons, P.O. Box 1239, Elgin, IL 60121-1239.

Jack Knight Air Log: quarterly. **Dues:** U.S. $15; outside U.S. $20. **Services:** auction, handbooks, exhibition awards, special awards, library, annual convention.

Air Post Society, Metropolitan — #192

APS REP: Edward Lettick, 31 Orangewood West, Derby, CT 06418.

MAPS Bulletin: quarterly. **Dues:** $8. **Services:** study groups, auctions, expertizing, speakers bureau, exhibition awards, special awards.

Alaska Collectors Club — #218

APS REP: Seely Hall, Jr., P.O. Box 20574, Juneau, AK 99802,

The Alaskan Philatelist: bimonthly. **Dues:** U.S. $10; outside U.S. $15. **Services:** auctions, library.

American First Day Cover Society — #33

APS REP: Douglas A. Kelsey, P.O. Box 65960, Tuscon, AZ 85728-5960. E-mail to afdcs@aol.com

First Days: 8 per year. **Dues:** U.S. $20; outside U.S. $28 **Services:** local chapters, study groups, directory, auctions, expertizing, slide programs, cover service, handbooks, exhibition awards, special awards, annual convention.

American Indian Philatelic Society* — #220

APS REP: Bud Keeton, P.O. Box 523, Warrenton, MO 6338.

The Council Fire: bimonthly. **Dues:** U.S. $10; Can/Mex $15; others $20. **Services:** mail sales, cover service, library.

American Philatelic Congress — #139

APS REP: Janet Klug, P.O. Box 250, Pleasant Plain, OH 45162.

American Congress Book: annually. **Dues:** U.S. $25; outside U.S. $30. **Services:** exhibition awards, special awards, annual convention.

American Topical Association — #177

APS REP: Douglas A. Kelsey, P.O. Box 65749, Tucson, AZ 85728. E-mail ataoffice@aol.com.

Topical Time: bimonthly. **Dues:** U.S. $20; outside U.S. $25. **Services:** local chapters, study groups, directory, slide programs, handbooks, exhibition awards, special awards, annual convention.

Americana Unit* — #40

APS REP: David A. Kent, P.O. Box 127, New Britain, CT 06050.

Americana Philatelic News: bimonthly. **Dues:** U.S. $5. **Services:** exhibition awards, annual convention.

Arizona – New Mexico Postal History Society — #188

APS REP: Owen H. Kriege, 370 Deer Pass Dr., Sedona, AZ 86351.

The Roadrunner: quarterly.

Dues: $10. Services: directory, auctions, expertizing, cover service, annual convention.

Ascension. See St. Helena

Asociacion Mexicana de Filatelia — #194
APS REP: Alejandro Grossmann, Apartado Postal 18-933, Mexico City, D.F. 11800, Mexico.
Boletin AMEXFIL: bimonthly. **Dues:** U.S. $37. **Services:** auctions.

Australasian Specialists/ Oceania, Society of — #22
APS REP: Margaret H. Sayre, 2 Providence Ave., Falmouth, ME 04105-2133.
The Informer: quarterly. **Dues:** U.S. $15; outside U.S. $20. **Services:** directory, sales book circuits, auctions, slide programs, handbooks, exhibition awards, special awards, library, annual convention.

Authors. See JAPOS

Belgian Philatelic Society, American — #138
APS REP: Harry G. Dober, 25190 Canyon Dr., Carmel, CA 93923.
The Belgiophile: quarterly. **Dues:** U.S. $7.50; Can $8.50; others $12.50. **Services:** directory, auctions, expertizing, library.

Bermuda Collectors Society — #186
APS REP: Thomas J. McMahon, 364 Nash Road, Purdys, NY 10578.
Bermuda Post: quarterly. **Dues:** U.S. $22; outside U.S. $27; Far East $30. **Services:** auctions, handbooks, annual convention.

Biblical Topics Study Unit* — #203
APS REP: Frank Pieper, P.O. Box 169, Emden, IL 62635.
Biblical Philately: quarterly. **Dues:** U.S./Can $7; outside U.S. $10. **Services:** directory, annual convention.

Biology Unit* — #172
APS REP: Carl H. Spitzer, Jr., 610 N. Bedford Dr., Tucson, AZ 85710-2620.
Biophilately: quarterly. **Dues:** U.S. $15. **Services:** special awards, library, annual convention.

Brazil Philatelic Association — #32
APS REP: Kurt Ottenheimer, 462 W. Walnut St., Long Beach, NY 11561-3133.
Bull's Eyes: quarterly. **Dues:** U.S. $15; Can $17.50; others $20. **Services:** auctions, library, annual convention.

British Caribbean Philatelic Study Group — #27
APS REP: Gale J. Raymond, Bali-Hai, P.O. Box 228, Sugarlane, TX 77478-0228. Home Page—http://ourworld.compuserve.com/homepages/BCPSG/
British Caribbean Philatelic Journal: quarterly. **Dues:** U.S./Can $18; outside U.S. $21. **Services:** local chapters, study groups, directory, auctions, slide programs, speakers bureau, handbooks, exhibition awards, special awards, library, annual convention.

British North American Philatelic Society — #144

APS REP: Jerome C. Jarnick, 108 Duncan Dr., Troy, MI 48098-4613. Home Page—http://www.compusmart.ab.ca/Stalbert/bnaps.htm

BNA TOPICS: quarterly. **Dues:** U.S. $18; outside U.S. $24. **Services:** local chapters, study groups, sales book circuits, speakers bureau, handbooks, exhibition awards, special awards, annual convention.

Bureau Issues Association — #150

APS REP: David Lee, P.O. Box 2641, Reston, VA 22090.

The United States Specialist: monthly. **Dues:** U.S. $25; Canada $28, others $32. **Services:** study groups, speakers bureau, handbooks, exhibition award, special awards, annual convention.

Canada, Postal History Society of — #67

APS REP: R.F. Narbonne, 216 Mailey Dr., Carleton Place, ON K7C 3X9, Canada.
PHSC Journal: quarterly. **Dues:** $15. **Services:** speakers bureau, exhibition awards.

Canadiana Study Unit* — #213

APS REP: Robert A. Haslewood, 4416 Harvard Ave., Montreal, PQ H4A 2X1, Canada.

The Canadian Connection: quarterly. **Dues:** U.S./Can $10; others $15. **Services:** auctions.

Canal Zone Study Group — #42

APS REP: Richard H. Salz, 60 27th Ave., San Francisco, CA 94121.

Canal Zone Philatelist: quarterly. **Dues:** $8. **Services:** local chapters, mail sales, handbooks, exhibition awards, convention.

Carriers and Locals Society — #211

APS REP: Helen M. Galaton-Stone, P.O. Box 770334, Woodside, NY 11377.

The Penny Post: quarterly. **Dues:** $25. **Services:** directory, slide programs, annual convention.

Cats on Stamps Study Unit* — #179

APS REP: Mary Ann Brown, 3006 Wade Rd., Durham, NC 27705.

Cat Mews: quarterly. **Dues:** $5. **Services:** directory.

Censorship, Civil, Study Group—No. 86

Civil Censorship Study Group Bulletin, Quarterly. **Dues:** U.S. $15.00; outside U.S. £10. **Services:** auctions, library. APS REP: Charles J. LaBlonde, 2940 Underwood Springs #5, Colorado Springs, CO 80920.

Ceremony Program Society, The American — #217

APS REP: Frederick G. Bean, 1500 E. 79th St., Bloomington, MN 55425,

The Ceremonial: bimonthly. **Dues:** $12. **Services:** directory, auctions, new issue service, annual convention.

Chemistry and Physics on Stamps Study Unit* — #123

APS REP: John Sharkey,

1559 Grouse Lane, Mountain-side, NJ 07092-1340.

Philatelia Chimica et Physica: quarterly. **Dues:** U.S. $11; outside U.S. $12. **Services:** slide programs, handbooks, special awards, library.

Chess on Stamps Study Unit* — #180

APS REP: Russell E. Ott, P.O. Box 9789, Midland, TX 79708-2789.

Chesstamp Review: quarterly. **Dues:** U.S./Can/Mex $12; others $18. **Services:** directory, auctions, annual convention.

China Stamp Society — #10

APS REP: Donald R. Alexander, 5 Valley View, Norman, OK 73069.

The China Clipper: bimonthly. **Dues:** $15. **Services:** local chapters, study group, directory, sales book circuits, auctions, handbooks, exhibition awards, special awards, library, annual convention.

Home page: http//:www.azstarnet.com/~gersten/China.Stamp.Society.html

Christmas Philatelic Club* — #74

APS REP: Richard F. Norris, 5386 Roscommon Rd., Dublin, OH 43017.

Yule Log: bimonthly. **Dues:** U.S./Can $15; outside U.S. $22. **Services:** directory, auctions, handbooks, exhibition awards, special awards, library.

Christmas Seal & Charity Stamp Society — #101

APS REP: Joseph S. Wheeler, Jr., P.O. Box 41096, Sacramento, CA 95841.

Seal News: bimonthly. **Dues:** $8. **Services:** local chapters, auctions, handbooks, library.

Churchill Society, International* — #49

APS REP: Sue M. Hefner, 1837 Latham Ave., Lima, OH 45805-1635.

Finest Hour: quarterly. **Dues:** U.S. $25. **Services:** local chapters, cover service, annual convention.

Cinderella Stamp Club — #91

APS REP: L.N. Williams, 44 The Ridgeway, Golders Green, London NW11 8QS, England.

The Cinderella Philatelist: quarterly. **Dues:** £12. **Services:** study groups, sales book circuits (UK only), handbooks, library.

Colombia. See COPAPHIL

Colorado Postal History Society — #200

APS REP: William H. Bauer, P.O. Box 519, Unadilla, NY 13849-0519.

Colorado Postal Historian: quarterly. **Dues:** $10 **Services:** annual convention.

Columbus, Christopher, Philatelic Society* — #124

APS REP: John F. O'Brien, 136 Wentworth Dr., Berkeley Heights, NJ 07922.

Discovery: quarterly. **Dues:** U.S. $15. **Services:** directory, auctions, expertizing, slide programs, exhibition awards, special awards.

Commemorative Panels. See Philatelic Pages

Computers. See Philatelic Computing

Confederate Stamp Alliance — #73

APS REP: Richard H. Byne, 7518 Buckskin Lane, San Antonio, TX 78227-2716.

Confederate Philatelist: bimonthly. **Dues:** U.S./Can/Mex $20; outside U.S. $25. **Services:** directory, expertiams, handbooks, exhibition awards, special awards, library, annual convention.

Connecticut, Postal History Society of — #195

APS REP: Stephen W. Ekstrom, P.O. Box 207, Cromwell, CT 06416-0207.

The Journal: CPHS: quarterly. **Dues:** $12. **Services:** directory, auctions, handbooks, library.

Home page: http://ymug.cs.yale,edu/YMUG/CPHS/info.html.

COPAPHIL (Colombia-Panama Philatelic Study Group) — #142

APS REP: Larry Crain, 2919 Aldersgate, Medford, OR 97504.

COPACARTA: quarterly. **Dues:** U.S./Can $8.50; outside U.S. $12 **Services:** study groups, directory, auctions, slide programs, special awards, library, biennial convention.

COROS. See Religion on Stamps, Collectors of

Costa Rica Collectors, Society of — #96

APS REP: Paul Hernandez, 4204 Haring Rd., Metaire, LA 70006 .

Oxcart: quarterly. **Dues:** U.S. $12; outside U.S. $15. **Services:** directory, auctions, slide programs, handbooks, library, annual convention.

Cover Collectors Circuit Club — #215

APS REP: Tom Fortunato, 42 Maynard St., Rochester, NY 14615-2022.

CCCC News: 10 per year. **Dues:** U.S. $7.50; outside U.S. $5.

Croatian Philatelic Society — #53

APS REP: Eck Spahich, P.O. Box 696 Fritch, TX 79036-0696.

The Trumpeter: quarterly. **Dues:** U.S. $22. **Services:** local chapters, study groups, directory, auctions, expertizing, slide programs, speakers bureau, special awards, library, annual convention.

Home Page: http://www.dalmatia.net/cps/index.htm

Cuban Philatelic Society of America — #173

APS REP: Silvia Garcia-Frutos, P.O. Box 141656, Coral Gables, FL 33114-1656.

The Cuban Philatelist: quarterly. **Dues:** U.S. $15: outside U.S. $30. **Services:** local chapters, study groups, auctions, handbook, special awards, annual convention.

Czechoslovak Philately, Society for — #18

APS REP: Henry Hahn, 2936 Rosemoor Lane, Fairfax, VA 22031.

The Czechoslovak Specialist: 6 yearly. **Dues:** U.S. $18; outside U.S. $23, air mail $28. **Services:** local chapters, directory, sales book circuits, auctions, expertizing, slide programs, handbooks, exhibition awards, special awards, library, annual convention.

Dakota Postal History Society — #216

APS REP: Gordon Twedt, P.O. Box 280, Maddock, ND 58348.

Dakota Collector: quarterly. **Dues:** $10. **Services:** directory, exhibition awards, annual convention.

Disabled Collector's Correspondence Club — #214

APS REP: John Luong, P.O. Box 4960-177, Irving, CA 92716-4960.

Stampabilities: quarterly. **Dues:** $5. **Services:** directory.

Home page: http://members. aol.com/DisabledCC.

Disinfected Mail Study Circle, The — #219

APS REP: William A. Sandrik, P.O. Box 3277, Arlington, VA 22203,

Pratique: quarterly. **Dues:** U.S. $32; UK £12; others £15. **Services:** study groups, auctions, expertizing, speakers bureau, handbooks.

Duck Stamp Collectors Society, National — #210

APS REP: Robert Dumaine, P.O. Box 820087, Houston, TX 77282.

Duck Tracks: quarterly. **Dues:** $20.

Eire Philatelic Association — #21

APS REP: Joseph E. Foley, P.O. Box 183, Riva, MD 21140-0183.

Revealer: quarterly. **Dues:** U.S. $12; Can/Mex $15; other $20. **Services:** local chapters, study group, directory, auctions, expertizing, slide programs, speakers bureau, handbooks, exhibition awards, special awards, library, annual convention.

El Salvador, Associated Collectors of — #89

APS REP: Jeff Brasor, 7365 N. W. 68th Way, Parkland, FL 33067.

El Faro: quarterly. **Dues:** $20. **Services:** auctions.

Empire State Postal History Society — #28

APS REP: William J. Hart, P.O. Box 167, Shrub Oak, NY 10588.

ESPHS Bulletin: quarterly. **Dues:** $10. **Services:** directory, auctions, slide programs, handbooks, exhibition awards, annual convention.

Errors, Freaks & Oddities Collectors Club — #103

APS REP: CWO J. E. McDevitt, 138 Lakemont Dr., E., Kingsland, GA 31548-8921.

EFO Collector: bimonthly. **Dues:** U.S. $16; outside U.S. $30. **Services:** study groups, directory, sales book circuits, auctions, expertizing, slide programs, speakers bureau, exhibition awards, special awards, annual convention.

Ethiopian Philatelic Society — #145

APS REP: Huguette Gagnon, P.O. Box 8110-45, Blaine, WA 98231-8110.

MENELIK'S Journal: quarterly. **Dues:** U.S./Can $7.50; outside U.S. $12. **Services:** directory, auctions, expertizing, new issue service, FDC service, library.

Europa Study Unit* — #17

APS REP: Hank Klos, 4N 512 S. Church Rd, Bensenville, IL 60106-2929.

Europa News: bimonthly. **Dues:** U.S. $10; Can $11; others $16. **Services:** auctions, handbooks, library.

Exhibitors, Philatelic, American Association of — #157

APS REP: Russell V. Skavaril, 222 E. Torrence Rd., Columbus, OH 43214-3834.

The Philatelic Exhibitor: quarterly. **Dues:** U.S. $18; outside U.S. $20. **Services:** exhibition awards, annual convention.

Falkland Islands Philatelic Study Group — #83

APS REP: Carl J. Faulkner, Williams Inn, On The Green, Williamstown, MA 01267.

The Upland Goose: quarterly. **Dues:** U.S./Can $20; Europe £10; others £15. **Services:** sales book circuits (Great Britain only) auctions, handbooks, special awards, library, annual convention.

Federation Quebecquoise de Philatelie — #169

APS REP: Pierre Dorval, C.P. 40, St. Lambert, PQ G0S 2W0, Canada.

Philatelie Quebec: 10 per year. **Dues:** U.S. $30; outside U.S. $42. **Services:** local chapters, study groups, expertizing, speakers bureau, exhibition awards, special awards, library, annual convention.

Fine Arts Philatelists* — #160

APS REP: Beatrice M. Killough, 7234 River Rd., Conestoga, PA 17516-9761,

Journal of Fine and Peforming Arts Philately: quarterly. **Dues:** U.S. $20; outside U.S. $25. **Services:** directory, slide programs, new issue service, handbooks.

First Day Cover Society. See American First Day Cover Society

First Issues Collector Club — #232

APS REP: Floyd A. Walker, P.O. Box 82, Grandview, MO 64030. First Issues, bimonthly **Dues:** U.S. $6.

Flag Cancels. See Machine Cancel Society

Florida Postal History Society — #227

APS REP: Deane R. Briggs, 160 E. Lake Howard Dr., Winter Haven, FL 33881-3100.

Florida Postal History Journal: semi-annual. **Dues:** U.S. $10.

France & Colonies Philatelic Society — #45

APS REP: Edward J. J. Grabowski, P.O. Box 364., Garwood, NJ 07027.

France & Colonies Philatelist: quarterly. **Dues:** U.S. $11; outside U.S. $15. **Services:** expertizing, slide programs, speakers bureau, handbooks, exhibition awards, special awards.

Georgia Postal History Society — #224

APS REP: Douglas N. Clark, P.O. Box 51, Lexington, GA 30648. E-mail dnc@alpha. math.uga.edu

Georgia Post Roads: bimonthly. **Dues:** $10.

Germany Philatelic Society — #48

APS REP: Christopher Deterding, P.O. Box 29, Arnold, MD 21012.

The German Postal Specialist: monthly. **Dues:** U.S. $18; Can/Mex $25; others $28. **Services:** local chapters, study groups, slide programs, handbooks, exhibition awards, special awards, library, annual convention.

Germany. See also Plebiscite

Golf Society, International Philatelic* — #183

APS REP: Kevin J. Hadlock, 447 Skyline Dr., Orange, CT 06477.

Tee Time: quarterly. **Dues:** U.S. $12; outside U.S. £7. **Services:** directory, auctions, cover service.

Graphics Philately Association* — #133

APS REP: Dulcie Apgar, P.O. Box 1513, Thousand Oaks, CA 91358.

Philateli-Graphics: quarterly. **Dues:** U.S. $5; outside U.S. $8. **Services:** handbooks.

Great Britain Collectors Club — #191

APS REP: F. J. Koch, 4769 Silverwood Dr., P.O. Box 309, Batavia, OH 45103-0309.

GBCC Chronicle: quarterly. **Dues:** U.S. $15; outside U.S. $22. **Services:** study group, directory, sales book circuits, auctions, handbook.

Greece. See Hellenic

Guatemala Collectors, International Society of — #36

APS REP: Wesley S. Waite, 2818 W. Telegraph Ave., Stockton, CA 95204-2610.

El Quetzal: quarterly. **Dues:** U.S. $15. **Services:** study group, directory, auctions, handbooks, exhibition awards, library.

G.B. Overprints Society — #72

APS REP: F. E. Kiddle, Punch Tree House, Reading Rd. North, Fleet, Hants GU13 8HS, England.

The Overprinter: quarterly. **Dues:** U.S. $18; outside U.S. £10. **Services:** study groups, sales book circuits, auctions, expertizing, speakers bureau, handbooks, library, annual convention.

Haiti Philatelic Society — #81

APS REP: Carroll L. Lloyd, 2117 Oak Lodge Rd. Baltimore, MD 21228.

Haiti Philately: quarterly. **Dues:** U.S. $12; outside U.S. $20. **Services:** directory, auctions, expertizing.

Hawaiian Philatelic Society — #136

APS REP: Louis A. Howard, 84-770 Kili Dr., #839, Waianae, HI 96792.

Po'Oleka O Hawaii: quarterly. **Dues:** $12. **Services:** auctions, expertizing, handbooks, library.

Home page: http://www.stamp-shows.com/hps.html

Hellenic Philatelic Society of America — #120

APS REP: Nicholas Asimakopulos, 541 Cedar Hill Ave., Wyckoff, NJ 07481.

HPSA News Bulletin: quarterly. **Dues:** U.S. $15; Can $20; others $25. **Services:** local chapter, handbooks, exhibition awards, special awards, library, annual convention.

Helvetia Philatelic Society, American — #52

APS REP: Charles J. LaBlonde, 2940 Underwood Point #5, Colorado Springs, CO 80920.

Tell: bimonthly. **Dues:** U.S./Can/Mex $20; others $30. **Services:** sales book circuits, auctions, expertizing, slide programs, exhibition awards, biennial convention.

Honduras Collectors Club— #229

APS REP: Jeff Brasor, P.O. Box 173, Coconut Creek, FL 33097. *El Hondureno:* Quarterly. **Dues:** U.S. $11. **Services:** new issue service.

Hong Kong Stamp Society — #209

APS REP: Ming W. Tsang, P.O. Box 206, Glenside, PA 19038.

HKSS Bulletin: quarterly. **Dues:** U.S. $10; Can/Mex $15; others $20. **Services:** auctions, expertizing, library, annual convention.

Hungarian Philately, Society for — #34

APS REP: Thomas Phillips, P.O. Box 1162, Fairfield, CT 06432.

News of Hungarian Philately: quarterly. **Dues:** U.S./Canada $15; outside U.S. $20. **Services:** study group, directory, sales book circuits, auctions, expertizing, handbooks, exhibition awards, special awards, library, annual convention.

Illinois Postal History Society — #112

APS REP: Harvey M. Karlen, 1008 N. Marion St., Oak Park, IL 60302.

Illinois Postal Historian: bimonthly. **Dues:** $12. **Services:** local chapters, directory, slide programs, speakers bureau, handbooks, annual convention.

India Study Circle — #111

APS REP: John Warren, P.O. Box 70775, Washington, DC 20024.

India Post: quarterly. **Dues:** U.S. $22; outside U.S. £12. **Services:** chapters, directory, auctions, slide programs, handbooks, exhibition awards, library, annual convention.

Indo-China Philatelists, Society of — #38

APS REP: Mark Isaacs, P.O. Box 531, Chicago, IL 60690.

Indo-China Philatelist: bimonthly. **Dues:** U.S./Can/Mex $15; others $18. **Services:** directory, auctions, exhibition awards, annual convention.

Iowa Postal History Society — #168

APS REP: Steven J. Bahnsen, 2901 South King Dr., #608, Chicago, IL 60616-3310.

IPHS Bulletin: quarterly. **Dues:** $13. **Services:** directory, auctions, exhibition awards, annual convention.

Iran Philatelic Study Circle — No. American Chapter — #208

APS REP: Arthur J. Palmer, Jr., 6081 Carriage House Way, Reno, NV 89509.

I.P.S.C. Bulletin: 5 per year. **Dues:** U.S. $15; outside U.S. £8.

Ireland. See Eire

Israel Philatelists, Society of — #105

APS REP: Howard D. Chapman, 28650 Settlers Lane, Pepper Pike, OH 44124.

The Israel Philatelist: bimonthly. **Dues:** U.S. $17; outside U.S. $22. **Services:** local chapters, study groups, slide programs, handbooks, exhibition awards, special awards, library, annual convention.

Italian American Stamp Club — #175

APS REP: Ralph West, 1135 S. 75th St., West Allis, WI 53214.

Italian American Stamp Club Newsletter: monthly. **Dues:** U.S. $6; outside U.S. $10.

Italy and Colonies Study Circle (GB) — #132

APS REP: Richard Harlow, 6 Marston Rd., Teddington, Middx. TW11 9JU, England.

Fil-Italia: quarterly. **Dues:** U.S. $25 others £15. **Services:** local chapter, directory, sales book circuits, auctions, speakers bureau, handbooks, exhibition awards, library, annual convention.

Italy and Colonies Study Circle (USA) — #140

APS REP: David F. Emery, P.O. Box 86, Phillipsburg, NJ 08865.

Mare Nostrum: quarterly. **Dues:** $12. **Services:** local chapter, annual convention.

Japanese Philately, International Society for — #58

APS REP: Kenneth Kamholz, P.O. Box 1283, Haddonfield, NJ 08033-0760.

Japanese Philately: bimonthly. **Dues:** $12. **Services:** local chapters, directory, sales book circuits, expertizing, new issue service handbooks, library. ISJP Library: WIlliam L. Chang, 12105 Fort Craig Dr., Woodbridge, VA 22192-1007.

JAPOS [Journalists, Authors and Poets on Stamps] Study Group* — #68

APS REP: Louis Forster, 7561 E. 24th St., Pawtucket, RI 02860-1217.

JAPOS Bulletin: bimonthly. **Dues:** $10. **Services:** handbook.

Journalists. See JAPOS

Junior Philatelists of America — #26

APS REP: Mary Ann Owens, P.O. Box 021164, Brooklyn, NY 11202-0026.

Philatelic Observer: bimonthly. **Dues:** U.S. $9; outside U.S. $14. **Services:** local chapters, study groups, auctions, exhibition awards, library.

Kirbati. See Tuvalu

Korea Stamp Society — #113

APS REP: William M. Collyer,

P.O. Box 4158, Saticoy, CA 93007-0158.

Korean Philately: quarterly. **Dues:** $25. **Services:** directory, handbooks, library. Visit their Home Page.

Latin America. See also Spanish Main

Latin American Philatelic Society — #104

APS REP: Piet Steen, P.O. Box 6420, Hinton, AB T7V 1X7, Canada.

Latin American Post: quarterly. **Dues:** U.S./Can $15; others $17.50. **Services:** directory, expertizing, biannual convention.

Liberian Philatelic Society — #176

APS REP: Wm. Thomas Lockard, 1 S. Ohio Ave., P.O. Box 267, Wellston, OH 45692.

Liberian Philatelic Society Newsletter: quarterly. **Dues:** U.S. $15; outside U.S. $20. **Services:** expertizing, slide programs, annual convention. Visit their Home Page.

Lighthouse Stamp Society — #221

APS REP: Dalene Thomas, 8612 W. Warren Lane, Lakewood, CO 80227-2352.

The Philatelic Beacon: quarterly. **Dues:** U.S. $10, outside U.S. $15. **Services:** directory, handbooks, exhibition awards, annual convention.

Lions International Stamp Club* — #153

APS REP: Stanley E. Kenison, 13412 Grenoble Dr., Rockville, MD 20853.

Lions International Philatelist: quarterly. **Dues:** U.S. $10; outside U.S. $12. **Services:** local chapters, study groups, directory, auctions, slide programs, speakers bureau, new issue service, cover service, handbooks, exhibition awards, library, annual convention.

Lithuania Philatelic Society — #223

APS REP: Fred Baumgartner, 446 S. 6th Ave., LaGrange, IL 60525.

Lithuania Philatelic Society Bulletin: biannual. **Dues:** $10.

Local Post Collectors Society — #126

APS REP: Joseph J. Frasketi Jr., 2019 Maravilla Circle, Fort Myers, FL 33901.

The Poster: bimonthly. **Dues:** U.S./Can $9; others $15. **Services:** directory, auctions, handbooks.

Locals. See Carriers and Locals

Long Island Postal History Society — #154

APS REP: Brian R. Levy, 1983 Guildford Park Dr., Seaford, NY 11783.

Long Island Postal Historian: quarterly. **Dues:** $15. **Services:** exhibition awards, annual convention.

Lundy Collectors Club — #121

APS REP: Roger S. Cichorz, 3925 Longwood Ave., Boulder, CO 80303.

L.C.C. Philatelic Quarterly: quarterly. **Dues;** U.S. $12.50; outside U.S. $18.75. **Services:** sales book circuits (UK only), auctions, expertizing, library, annual convention.

Machine Cancel Society — #24

APS REP: Arthur R. Hadley,

3407 North 925 East, Hope, IN 47246.

Machine Cancel Forum: quarterly. **Dues:** U.S. $15; Can/Mex $22; others $24. **Services:** study groups, directory, sales book circuits, auctions, slide programs, handbooks, library, annual convention.

Mailer's Postmark Permit Club — #100

APS REP: Herbert H. Harrington, P.O. Box 0585, Vienna, OH 44473-0585.

Permit Patter: bimonthly. **Dues:** U.S. $6; outside U.S. $9. **Services:** directory, auctions, handbooks.

Maritime Postmark Society — #37

APS REP: Tom Hirschinger, 141 Gordon Ave., Wadsworth, OH 44281

Seaposter: bimonthly. **Dues:** $10. **Services:** directory, auctions, handbooks, library.

Maryland Postal History Society — #199

APS REP: Carroll L. Lloyd, 2117 Oak Lodge Rd., Baltimore, MD 21228.

Newsletter of the MPHS: quarterly. **Dues:** $10. **Services:** directory, exhibition awards, annual convention.

Masonic Study Unit* — #94

APS REP: Stanley R. Longenecker, 930 Wood St., Mount Joy, PA 17552-1926.

The Philatelic Freemason: bimonthly. **Dues:** U.S./Can $8; outside U.S. $14.

Massachusetts Postal Research Society—#93

APS REP: H.J. W. Daugherty,

P.O. Box 1146, Eastham, MA 02642. *The Massachusetts Spy:* quarterly. **Dues:** $8.

Mathematical Study Unit* — #130

APS REP: Monty Strauss, 4209 88th St., Lubbock, TX 79423.

PHILAMATH: quarterly. **Dues:** U.S. $10; outside U.S. $13.

Maximum Card Study Unit — #106

APS REP: Gary Denis, 3284 Winterberry Lane, Virginia Beach, VA 23456-5910.

Maximaphily: quarterly. **Dues:** U.S. $10; outside U.S. $15. **Services:** directory, auctions.

Memel. See Plebiscite

Mesoamerican Archeology Study Unit* — #82

APS REP: Phillips B. Freer, Apartado 646, Oaxaca, Oax. 68000, Mexico.

Codex Filatelica: bimonthly. **Dues:** U.S. $8; Can/Mex $9; others $22. **Services:** handbooks.

Meter Stamp Society — #193

APS REP: Alexander J. Savakis, P.O. Box 609, Warren, OH 44482-0609.

Meter Stamp Society Bulletin: quarterly. **Dues:** U.S. $12; Can/Mex $14; others $16. **Services:** study groups, directory, auctions, handbooks, library, annual convention.

Home Page: http://icgroup.net/-Skaplan/mss

Mexico-Elmurst Philatelic Society International — #43

APS REP: Frank E. Preisler,

500 E. Queen St., #3, Annville, PA 17003-1916.

Mexicana: quarterly. **Dues:** $20. **Services:** local chapters, directory, sales book circuits, auctions, expertizing, slide programs, speakers bureau, new issue service, exhibition awards, special awards, library, annual convention.

Military Postal History Society — #19

APS REP: Robert T. Kinsley, 1701 Goldfinch Ct., West Richland, WA 99353.

M.P.H.S. Bulletin: quarterly. **Dues:** U.S. $15; Can $18; others $22.50. **Services:** study groups, auctions, handbooks, exhibition awards, special awards, annual convention.

Minnesota, Postal History Society of — #84

APS REP: John Grabowski, P.O. Box 536, Willernie, MN 55090-0536.

Dues: $4. **Services:** auctions, speakers bureau, exhibition awards.

Mobile Post Office Society — #64

APS REP: Douglas N. Clark, P.O. Box 51, Lexington, GA 30648-0051.

Transit Postmark Collector: bimonthly. **Dues:** $15. **Services:** directory, auctions, slide programs, speakers bureau, handbooks, exhibition awards, special awards, library, annual convention. E-mail: dnc@alpha.math.uga.edu

Music Circle, Philatelic* — #141

APS REP: Cathleen F. Osborne, P.O. Box 1781, Sequim, WA 98382.

The Baton: 3 per year. **Dues:** U.S. $15; outside U.S. £8. **Services:** sales book circuits, slide programs, handbooks, special awards, library, annual convention.

Nepal and Tibet Philatelic Study Circle — #122

APS REP: Roger D. Skinner, 1020 Covington Road, Los Altos, CA 94024.

Postal Himal: quarterly. **Dues:** U.S. $18.75; outside U.S. £12. **Services:** study group, auctions, slide programs, exhibition awards, library, annual convention.

Netherlands Philately, American Society for — #60

APS REP: Jan Enthoven, W6428 Riverview Dr., Onalaska, WI 54650.

Netherlands Philately: quarterly. **Dues:** U.S. $16; Can $21; outside U.S. and Can $21 (surface), $26 (airmail). **Services:** auctions, library.

New Jersey Postal History Society — #95

APS REP: Brad Arch, 144 Hamilton Ave., Clifton, NJ 07011.

NJPH: bimonthly. **Dues:** U.S. $15; outside U.S. $20. **Services:** study groups, directory, auctions, slide programs, speakers bureau, handbooks, exhibition awards, special awards, annual convention.

New Mexico. See Arizona

New York. See Empire State

North Carolina Postal History Society — #155

APS REP: Tony Crumbley, P.O. Box 219, Newell, NC 28126.

NCPHS Newsletter: quarterly. **Dues:** $15. **Services:** directory, auctions, speakers bureau, handbooks, exhibition awards, special awards, annual convention.

North Dakota. See Dakota

Ohio Postal History Society — #66

APS REP: James L. Baumann, 5248 Sheila Dr., Toledo, OH 43613-2442.

Ohio Postal History Journal: quarterly. **Dues:** U.S. $15; outside U.S. by arrangement. **Services:** auctions, handbooks, exhibition awards, annual meeting.

Home Page://http://members.aol.com/OPHS3/ophs.html

Old World Archaeological Study Unit* — #92

APS REP: Eileen Meier, P.O. Box 369, Palmyra, VA 22963.

Old World Archaeologist: quarterly. **Dues:** $10. **Services:** auctions, exhibition awards, library, annual convention.

Orange Free State Study Circle — #196

APS REP: Alan MacGregor, 7 Little Woodfalls Dr., Woodfalls, Salisburg, Wilts. SP5 2NN, England.

Orange Free State Bulletin: quarterly. **Dues:** U.S. $11; outside U.S. £7. **Services:** auctions, expertizing, handbooks.

Pacific Islands Study Circle — #226

APS REP: John D. Ray, 24 Woodvale Ave., London SE25 4AE, England.

Pacifica: quarterly. **Dues:** U.S./others £12.50; UK/Europe £7.50. **Services:** auctions, speakers bureau, handbooks, special awards.

E-mail: jray@dial.pipex.com

Pacific Northwest Postal History Society — #147

APS REP: Len Lukens, 2710 N.E. 131 St, Portland, OR 97230.

The Oregon Country: quarterly. **Dues:** U.S. $10; outside U.S. $15. **Services:** study groups, sales book circuits, auctions, expertizing, slide programs, speakers bureau, annual convention.

Panama. See COPAPHIL

Papuan Philatelic Society — #228

APS REP: Steven G. Zirinsky, P.O. Box 49, Ansonia Sta., New York, NY 10023.

Pennsylvania Postal History Society — #50

APS REP: Norman Shachat, 382 Tall Meadow Lane, Yardley, PA 19067.

Pennsylvania Postal Historian: quarterly. **Dues:** $15. **Services:** directory, auction, handbooks, exhibition awards, annual convention.

Perfins Club, The — #57

APS REP: Kurt Ottenheimer, 462 W. Walnut, Long Beach, NY 11561. E-mail the editor: John Lyding at Bo618@yfn.ysu.edu

The Perfins Bulletin: 10 per year. **Dues:** U.S. $15; Can $17; others $20. **Services**: directory, auctions, slide programs, speakers bureau, handbooks, special awards, library, annual convention.

Performing Arts. See Fine Arts

Petroleum Philatelic Society International* — #170

APS REP: Thomas C. Hughes, 1740 S.W. 84th Ave., Hollywood, FL 33025-2127.

The Petro-Philatelist: quarterly. **Dues:** U.S. $9; outside U.S. $11. **Services:** auctions, handbooks, library.

Philatelic Computing Study Group — #212

APS REP: Bill F. Sharpe, 455 Lincoln Blvd., Santa Monica, CA 90402.

The Compulatelist: quarterly. **Dues:** U.S. $10; Can/Mex $12; others $15. **Services:** annual meeting.

Home Page: http://www.west.net/~stamps1/pcsg.html

Philatelic History Society — #161

APS REP: V. T. Short, Hunters Lodge, Cottesmore Rd., Ashwell, Oakham, Leics. LE15 7LJ, England.

Philatelic Paraphernalia: quarterly. **Dues:** $20. **Services:** speakers bureau.

Philatelic Museum, Cardinal Spellman — #166

APS REP: Guy R. Dillaway, 235 Wellesley St., Weston, MA 02193.

Museum Post Rider: monthly. **Dues:** $15. **Services:** library.

Philatelic Pages and Panels, American Society for — #165

APS REP: Gerald Blankenship, P.O. Box 475, Crosby, TX 77532.

Page & Panel Journal: quarterly. **Dues:** U.S. $15; outside U.S. $21. **Services:** directory, auctions, annual convention, free member buy/sell/ trade ads.

Philatelists and Numismatists, Society of — #116

APS REP: Eunice Alter, 19472 Catfish Circle, Huntington Beach, CA, 92646-2806.

ExSPANsion: quarterly. **Dues:** $10 **Services:** special award, annual convention.

Philippine Philatelic Society, International — #54

APS REP: David S. Durbin, 1608 S.W. 22nd St., Blue Springs, MO 64015-5231.

Philippine Philatelic News: quarterly. **Dues:** U.S. $15; outside U.S. $20. **Services:** local chapters, study groups, directory, auctions, expertizing, slide programs, new issue service, exhibition awards, special awards, library, annual convention.

Physics. See Chemistry and Physics

Pitcairn Islands Study Group — #46

APS REP: Nelson A.L. Weller, 2940 Wesleyan Lane, Winston-Salem, NC 27106.

Pitcairn Log: bimonthly. **Dues:** $10. **Services:** local chapters, study groups, auctions, handbooks.

Home Page: http://wavefront.wavefront.com/~pjlareau/pisg.html

Plate Number Coil Collectors Club — #185

APS REP: Gene C. Trinks, 3603 Bellows Ct., Troy, MI 48083.

Coil Line: monthly. **Dues:** U.S. $10; Can/Mex $14; others $20. **Services:** directory, auctions, slide programs, exhibition awards, special awards, annual convention.

Plate Number Single Society, American — #178

APS REP: James E. Ragsdale, P.O. Box 409, Pittsboro, IN 46167-0409.

Plate Numbers: bimonthly. **Dues:** U.S. $7.50, outside U.S. $10. **Services:** directory, sales book circuits, auctions, library, annual convention.

Plebiscite-Memel-Saar Study Group, GPS — #197

APS REP: Clay Wallace, 158 Arapahoe Circle, San Ramon, CA 94583.

PMS Study Group Bulletin: 3 per year. **Dues:** U.S. $15; outside U.S. $20. **Services:** study groups, sales book circuits, expertizing, library, annual convention.

Poets. See JAPOS

Polar Philatelists, American Society of — #31

APS REP: Robert de Violini, P.O. Box 5025, Oxnard, CA 93031.

Ice Cap News: quarterly. **Dues:** $19. **Services:** local chapters, directory, auctions, new issue service, cover service, exhibition awards, library, annual convention.

E-mail: dviolini@west.net

Polonus Philatelic Society — #119

APS REP: Roman H. Strze-lecki, 7006 W. 29th St., Berwyn, IL 60402.

Polonus Bulletin: bimonthly. **Dues:** U.S. $16. **Services:** study groups, directory, auctions, expertizing, handbooks, exhibition awards, library, annual convention.

Portuguese Philately, International Society for — #35

APS REP: Clyde J. Homen, 1491 Bonnie View Rd., Hollister, CA 95023-5117.

Portu-Info: quarterly. **Dues:** U.S. $15; outside U.S. $20. **Services:** local chapters, directory, auctions, expertizing, handbooks, exhibition awards, library, annual convention.

E-mail: cJh@hollinet.com

Post Mark Collectors Club — #62

APS REP: Paul T. Schroeder, 1750 W. 5th Ave., Apt. F, Oshkosh, WI 54901-5586.

PMCC Bulletin: 11 per year. **Dues:** U.S. $16.50; outside U.S. $25. **Services:** local chapters, study group, directory, auctions, special awards, library, annual convention.

Postal History Foundation — #148

APS REP: Donald N. Vivian, P.O. Box 40725, Tucson, AZ 85717.

The Heliograph: quarterly. **Dues:** U.S. $18; outside U.S. $30. **Services:** exhibition awards, library.

Postal History Society — #44

APS REP: Diane D. Boehret,

P.O. Box 61774, Virginia Beach, VA 23466-1774.

Postal History Journal: 3 per year. **Dues:** U.S. $30; outside U.S. $40. **Services:** exhibition awards, special awards, annual convention.

Postal Label Study Group — #207

APS REP: Raymond R. Erickson, 5427 Delia Way, Livermore, CA 94550.

The Postal Label Bulletin: quarterly. **Dues:** U.S./Can $7; others $10. **Services:** auctions, handbooks, library, annual convention.

Postal Order Society, The — #167

APS REP: Jack Harwood, P.O. Box 32015, Sarasota, FL 34239.

Postal Order News: quarterly. **Dues:** U.S. $10; outside U.S. £5. **Services:** directory, sales book circuits, auctions, new issue service, library, annual convention.

Postal Stationery Society, United — #20

APS REP: LeRoy Ferber, P.O. Box 210, West Berlin, NJ 08091-0210.

Postal Stationery: quarterly. **Dues:** U.S. $18; outside U.S. $25. New members have an additional $1.00 admission fee. **Services:** local chapters, directory, sales book circuits, auctions, expertizing, slide programs, speakers bureau, handbooks, exhibition awards, special awards, library, annual convention.

Postcard Dealers, International Federation of — #174

APS REP: Roy Cox, P.O. Box 3610, Baltimore, MD 21214.

IFPD Newsletter: quarterly. **Dues:** $35. **Services:** directory, expertizing, annual convention.

Postcard History Society — #187

APS REP: Roy Cox, P.O. Box 3610, Baltimore, MD 21214.

Postcard History Society: quarterly. **Dues:** U.S. $6 outside U.S. $8. **Services:** auctions, expertizing (post cards only), library, annual convention.

Precancel Stamp Society — #65

APS REP: Arthur A. Damm, 1750 Skippack Pk., #1603, Center Square, PA 19422.

The Precancel Forum: monthly. **Dues:** U.S. $15; others $20. **Services:** local chapters, directory, handbooks, annual convention.

Ration Token Collectors, Society of—No. 230

APS REP: Dennis Dillman, 15907 Erin Creek Ct., Houston, Tx 77062. *The Ration Board:* quarterly. **Dues:** U.S. $8. **Services:** auctions, exhibit awards, library.

Religion on Stamps, Collectors of — #206

APS REP: Verna Shackleton, 425 N. Linwood Ave., Apt. 110, Appleton, WI 54914-3433.

The COROS Chronicle: bimonthly. **Dues:** U.S. $15; outside U.S. $18. **Services:** study group, directory, slide programs, handbooks, exhibition awards.

Revenue Association, American — #51

APS REP: Ronald E. Lesher, P.O. Box 1663, Easton, MD 21601.

The American Revenuer: 10 per year. **Dues:** $21. **Services:** local chapters, directory, sales book circuits, auctions, handbooks, exhibition award, library, annual convention.

Rhodesian Study Circle — #107

APS REP: William R. Wallace, P.O. Box 16381, San Francisco, CA 94116.

The Journal of the RSC: quarterly. **Dues:** £8. **Services:** local chapters, study groups, sales book circuits (UK only), auctions, handbooks, exhibition awards, special awards, library, annual convention.

Rotary-on-Stamps* — #117

APS REP: Donald Fiery, P.O. Box 333, Hanover, PA 17331.

Rotary on Stamps Bulletin: 6 per year. **Dues:** U.S. $20. **Services:** slide programs, new issue service, handbooks, exhibition awards, library, annual convention.

Russian Philately, Rossica Society of — #171

APS REP: G. Adolph Ackerman, 629 Sanbridge Circle, E., Worthington, OH 43085. E-mail: gcombs@erols.com.

Rossica Journal: 2 per year. **Dues:** $20. **Services:** local chapters, directory, expertizing, slide programs, handbooks, exhibition awards, library, annual convention.

Ryukyu Philatelic Specialist Society — #47

APS REP: LTC Robert C. Effinger, P.O. Box 279, Jacksonville, AL 36265-0279.

From the Dragon's Den: quarterly. **Dues:** U.S. $12.50; outside U.S. $15. **Services:** local chapters, directory, auctions, expertizing, slide programs, handbooks, exhibition awards, special awards.

Saar. See Plebiscite

Sarawak Specialists' Society — #110

APS REP: Art Bunce, P.O. Box 2516, Escondido, CA 92033.

The Sarawak Journal: quarterly. **Dues:** £7. **Services:** sales book circuits, auctions, handbooks, exhibition awards, library, annual convention.

Scandinavian Collectors Club — #79

APS REP: Jared H. Richter, 1353 Plum St., San Diego, CA 92106.

The Posthorn: quarterly. **Dues:** $15. **Services:** local chapters, study groups, directory, sales book circuits, slide programs, speakers bureau, handbooks, exhibition awards, special awards, library, annual convention.

Home Page: http://www.nb.net/~downs/scc/scc.htm

Scandinavian Philatelic Foundation — #137

APS REP: Alan Warren, P.O. Box 17124, Philadelphia, PA 19105-7124.

Semiannual (informal newsletters). **Dues:** $10 or greater donation. **Services:** handbooks.

Scouts on Stamps Society International* — #202

APS REP: Walter M. Creitz,

830 Berkshire Dr., Reading, PA 19601.

SOSSI Journal: monthly. **Dues:** U.S. $15.00; outside U.S. $18. **Services:** local chapters, directory, slide programs, exhibition awards, special awards, library, annual convention.

Ship Cancellation Society, Universal — #98

APS REP: David A. Kent, P.O. Box 127, New Britain, CT 06050.

USCS Log: monthly. **Dues:** U.S. $16; outside U.S. $21. **Services:** local chapters, study groups, directory, sales book circuits, slide programs, auctions, handbooks, annual convention.

Home Page: http://www.esva.net/~fairwinds/

Ships on Stamps Unit* — #152

APS REP: Robert P. Stuckert, 2750 Hwy. 21 East, Paint Lick, KY 40461.

Watercraft Philately: bimonthly. **Dues:** U.S. $7; Can $9.50, outside U.S. $16. **Services:** directory, handbooks, exhibition awards, special awards, annual convention.

South Dakota. See Dakota

Southern Africa, Philatelic Society for Greater — #190

APS REP: Robert F. Taylor, 674 Chelsea Dr., Sanford, NC 27330-8587.

Forerunners: 3 per year. **Dues:** $20. **Services:** auctions, expertizing, exhibition awards, special awards, library, annual convention.

Souvenir Card Collectors Society — #149

APS REP: Douglas B. Holl,

P.O. Box 234, Annandale, VA 22003.

The Souvenir Card Journal: quarterly. **Dues:** U.S. $20; outside U.S. $25. **Services:** local chapters, auctions, handbooks, annual convention.

Space Topics Study Group* — #29

APS REP: Bernice Scholl, P.O. Box 522579, Marathon Shores, FL, 33052-2579.

Astrophile: bimonthly. **Dues:** $15. **Services:** directory, auctions, expertizing, slide programs, handbooks exhibition awards, library, annual convention.

Spanish Main, The — #162

APS REP: Brian Moorhouse, P.O. Box 105, Peterborough PE3 8TQ, England.

The Mainsheet: quarterly. **Dues:** U.S. $20; outside U.S. £8. **Services:** study groups, sales books circuits, auctions, handbooks, special awards, convention.

Spanish Philatelic Society —#201

APS REP: Jerry A. Wells, 1400 Preston Rd., Ste. 200, Plano, TX 75093

Spanish Philatelic Society: quarterly. **Dues:** U.S. $15; outside U.S. $22.50. **Services:** auction, library, annual convention.

Sports Philatelists International* — #39

APS REP: Glenn A. Estus, P.O. Box 451, Westport, NY 12993.

Journal of Sports Philately: bimonthly. **Dues:** U.S. $12; outside U.S. $18. **Services:** directory, auctions, cover service, handbooks, exhibition awards, annual convention.

Stamp Dealers Association, National — #225

APS REP: Edward G. Rosen, P.O. Box 7176, Redwood City, CA 94063-7176.

NSDA "Update." **Dues:** $50. **Services:** directory.

Stamps on Stamps Centenary Unit* — #127

APS REP: Boris Politziner, P.O. Box 25, Grand Island, NY 14072.

SOS Signal: quarterly. **Dues:** U.S. $8, others $11. **Services:** directory, auctions, exhibition awards.

State Revenue Society — #164

APS REP: Terrence Hines, P.O., Box 629, Chappaqua, NY 10514-0629.

State Revenue News: bimonthly. **Dues:** U.S. $10; outside U.S. $15. **Services:** study groups, directory, auctions, slide programs, speakers bureau, handbooks, exhibition awards, special awards, library, annual convention.

St. Helena, Ascension and Tristan Da Cunha Philatelic Society — #85

APS REP: Russell V. Skavaril, 222 E. Torrence Road, Columbus, OH 43214-3834.

South Atlantic Chronicle: quarterly. **Dues:** U.S. $20; outside U.S. $23–$25. **Services:** local chapters, directory, auctions, handbooks, special awards, library.

Switzerland. See Helvetia

Texas Postal History Society — #76

APS REP: Karl Gebert, 700 N. St. Mary's, Ste. 900, San Antonio, TX 78205.

Texas Postal History Journal: quarterly. **Dues:** U.S. $10; outside U.S. $15. **Services:** directory, auctions, annual convention.

Thai Philately, Society for — #78

APS REP: H. R. Blakeney, P.O. Box 25644, Oklahoma City, OK 73125-0644.

Thai Philately: 3 per year. **Dues:** $20. **Services:** study groups, directory, auctions, exhibition awards, special awards, library.

Tibet. See Nepal

Tonga/Tin Can Mail Study Circle — #128

APS REP: Janet Klug, 6854 Newtonsville Road, Pleasant Plain, OH 45162.

Tin Canner: bimonthly. **Dues:** U.S. $12; outside U.S. $15. **Services:** directory, auctions, slide programs, handbooks, special awards, library, annual convention.

Topical. See American Topical Association

Tristan Da Cunha. See St. Helena

Turkish and Ottoman Philatelic Society, The — #109

APS REP: Gary F. Paiste, 4249 Berritt St., Fairfax, VA 22030.

The Tughra Times: quarterly. **Dues:** U.S. $15; outside U.S.

$20. **Services:** auctions, expertizing, exhibition awards, annual convention.

Ukrainian Philatelic and Numismatic Society — #134

APS REP: Peter Bylen, P.O. Box 11184, Chicago, IL 60611-0184. *Ukrainian Philatelist:* quarterly. **Dues:** U.S. $18; outside U.S. $25. **Services:** local chapters, study groups, directory, auctions, expertising, handbooks, exhibition awards, library, annual convention.

United Nations Philatelists* — #71

APS REP: Alex Bereson, 18 Portola Dr., San Francisco, CA 94131.

The Journal of the UNP: bimonthly. **Dues:** U.S. $15; outside U.S. $25. **Services:** local chapters, auctions, handbooks, exhibition awards, special awards, annual convention.

Universal Postal Union Collectors* — #70

APS REP: Robert Malch, P.O. Box 607117, Orlando, FL 32860-7117.

Global Union: quarterly. **Dues:** U.S./Can $12; outside U.S. $19. **Services:** directory, auctions.

U. S. Cancellation Club — #75

APS REP: Roger D. Curran, 20 University Ave., Lewisburg, PA 17837.

U.S. Cancellation Club News: quarterly. **Dues:** U.S. $8; outside U.S. $15. **Services:** directory, sales book circuits, exhibition awards, library.

U.S. Philatelic Classics Society — #11

APS REP: Patricia S. Walker, Briarwood, P.O. Box 99, Lisbon, MD 21765-0099.

U.S. Chronicle: quarterly. **Dues:** U.S. $22.50; outside U.S. $30.50. **Services:** local chapters, directory, handbooks, exhibition awards, special awards, annual convention.

U.S. Possessions Philatelic Society — #99

APS REP: Geoffrey Brewster, 141 Lyford Dr., Tiburon, CA 94920.

Possessions: quarterly. **Dues:** $12. **Services:** directory, auctions, handbooks, exhibition awards, library.

Vatican Philatelic Society — #129

APS REP: Frederick J. Levitsky, 13 Lesley Ave., Auburn, MA 01501.

Vatican Notes: bimonthly. **Dues:** U.S. $9; outside U.S. $16. **Services:** local chapters, directory, auctions, expertizing, slide programs, exhibition awards, special awards, library.

Vermont Philatelic Society — #156

APS REP: William Lizotte, R 1, Box 384-8, Morrisville, VT 05661.

Vermont Philatelist: quarterly. **Dues:** U.S. $10; outside U.S. $15. **Services:** local chapters, directory, auctions, cover service, exhibition awards, library, annual convention.

Virginia Postal History Society — #41

APS REP: Renate W. Thayer,

P. O. Box 29771, Richmond, VA 23242-0771.

Way Markings: quarterly. **Dues:** U.S. $14; outside U.S. $25. **Services:** auctions, slide programs, handbooks, exhibition awards, special awards, annual convention.

War Covers. See Military

West Africa Study Circle— #231

APS REP: Jack Ince, P.O. Box 858, Stirling, ON K0K 3E0, Canada. *Cameo:* biannually. **Dues:** U.S. $24; Canada $30, UK £12; others £14. **Services:** biannual auctions, handbooks, library.

Home Page: http://ourworld. compuserve.com/homepages/ FrankWAlton/homepage.htm

Western Cover Society — #14

APS REP: Edward A. Weinberg, 887 Litchfield Ave., Sebastopol, CA 95472.

Western Express: quarterly. **Dues:** $15. **Services:** handbooks, special awards, annual convention.

Wine on Stamps Study Unit — #233

APS REP: Dr. James D. Vrum, 5132 Sepulveda, San Bernadino, CA 92304-1134

Wisconsin Postal History Society — #61

APS REP: James Maher, 150 Terrace Lane, Hartland, WI 53029.

Badger Postal History: quarterly. **Dues:** U.S. $10; outside U.S. $15. **Services:** auctions, handbooks, special awards, library, annual convention.

Women on Stamps Study Unit* — #118

APS REP: Davida Kristy, 515 Ocean Ave., #608S, Santa Monica, CA 90402.

The Topical Woman: quarterly. **Dues:** U.S. $6; outside U.S. $8. **Services:** directory, handbooks, exhibition awards.

Worldwide Stamp Collectors, International Society of — #151

APS REP: Thomas Fortunato, c/o Carol Cervenka, R 1, Box 69A, Caddo Mills, TX 75135.

The Circuit: quarterly. **Dues:** $10. **Services:** local chapters, directory, sales book circuits, auctions, exhibition awards, annual convention.

Writers Unit, APS — #30

APS REP: George Griffenhagen, 2501 Drexel St., Vienna, VA 22180.

The Philatelic Communicator: quarterly. **Dues:** U.S. $10; Can/Mex $12.50; others $17. **Services:** annual convention, publication critique service.

Zeppelin Collectors Club — #135

APS REP: Cheryl Ganz, P.O. Box A3843, Chicago, IL 60690-3843.

The Zeppelin Collector: quarterly. **Dues:** U.S. $15; outside U.S. $20. **Services:** annual convention.

NATIONAL STAMP CLUBS LISTED BY GEOGRAPHICAL LOCATION

All of the listed stamp clubs are chapter members of the APS, but each is a separate organization offering its own services to its members. APS Chapters located in the United States are listed alphabetically by state and city. Those outside the United States are listed alphabetically by country and city. The name and APS number of each chapter are given, the time and location of meetings, and, finally, the name and address of a local contact from whom additional information may be obtained.

When communicating with chapters by mail, be sure to use the contact address and *not* the meeting location address. The latter generally is not a valid mailing address.

Clubs that have maintained APS Chapter status for 25, 50, and 75 years are identified as follows:

* = 25 years
** = 50 years
*** = 75 years

SUPPORT FOR CHAPTERS

The APS Chapter Activities Committee serves as the focal point for most services available to APS Chapters. The committee publishes a quarterly newsletter, sponsors a publications contest, and conducts other programs for local clubs. APS Chapters may schedule APS Sales Division circuits and philatelic slide programs produced by the Society exclusively for use by chapters for their meetings through the APS Headquarters.

Local stamp clubs interested in the benefits of APS Chapter membership may obtain detailed information from the APS, P.O. Box 8000, State College, PA 16803; 814-237-3803.

ALABAMA

BIRMINGHAM: * Birmingham Philatelic Society, (0485-041050), 7:30 p.m., 2nd & 4th Tues., except Dec., Jewish Community Center, 3960 Montclair Road. CONTACT: Charles Hancock, P.O. Box 531330, Birmingham, AL 35253.

FAIRHOPE: Eastern Shore Stamp Collectors, (1328-142530), 7:15 p.m., 2nd & 4th Thurs., 2nd Thurs. July, Nov. & Dec., Trinity Presbyterian Church. CONTACT: Ian L. Robertson, 117 Kiefer Ave., Fairhope, AL 36532.

HUNTSVILLE: * Huntsville Philatelic Club, (0597-047322), 7:30 p.m., 1st and 3rd Tues., Trinity Methodist Church, Rm. 268, 607 Airport Road. CONTACT: Michael C. O'Reilly, P.O. Box 1131, Huntsville, AL 35807-0131.

JACKSONVILLE: * Calhoun County Stamp Club, (0629-049489), 7 p.m., 2nd & 4th Tues., Compass Bank N.A., Kitchen/Dining Area. CONTACT: LTC Robert C. Effinger, P.O. Box 279, Jacksonville, AL 36265.

MONTGOMERY: Montgomery Area Stamp Club, (0893-076748), 7 p.m., 2nd & 4th Thurs., Nov. & Dec. 2nd Thurs. only, Crump Community Center, 1735 Highland Ave. CONTACT: George Wall, 5741 Ainsworth Dr., Montgomery, AL 36117.

TUSCALOOSA: Tuscaloosa Stamp Club, (1432-166150), 7 p.m., 2nd Mon. & 4th Tues., Tuscaloosa Public Library, River Rd. CONTACT: Wallace H. Lancaster, P.O. Box 020744, Tuscaloosa, AL 35402.

ALASKA

ANCHORAGE: * Anchorage Philatelic Society, (0326-029280), 7:30 p.m., 2nd & 4th Wed., Senior Center, 1300 E. 19th St. CONTACT: Robert E. Spaugy, P.O. Box 102214, Anchorage, AK 99510-2214.

FAIRBANKS: Northern Lights Stamp Club, (1326-142053), 1 p.m., 1st and 3rd Sun. (Sept.–May), Mary Saih Rec. Center. CONTACT: Donval R. Simpson, 2130 Nottingham Dr., Fairbanks, AK 99709-6518.

JUNEAU: Gastineau Philatelic Society, (0863-072342), 7 p.m., 3rd Tues., KTOO Studio, 4th & Franklin Sts. CONTACT: Virginia B. Post, P.O. Box 240363, Douglas, AK 99824-0363.

ARIZONA

CASA GRANDE: * Arizona Federation of Stamp Clubs, (0792-064416), 7 p.m., 3rd Thurs. of Jan./Mar./May/Sept./Nov., Golden Corral Steak House, 1295 E. Florence. CONTACT: Carl L. John, 5063 E. North Regency Circle, Tucson, AZ 85711-3000.

FLAGSTAFF: Flagstaff Stamp Club, (1132-110956), 7 p.m., 2nd Mon., Citizen's Utilities, 420 N. San Francisco Ave. CONTACT: Robert J. Lackner, P.O. Box 43, Flagstaff, AZ 86002.

MESA: Mesa Stamp Club, (0938-083978), 7 p.m., 2nd & 4th Tues., Members' Homes. CONTACT: Fred A. Scheuer, P.O. Box 2356, Mesa, AZ 85214.

PHOENIX: * Phoenix Philatelic Association, (0307-028554), 6:30 p.m., 2nd Mon. & 4th Wed., 2nd Mon.-July/Aug./Nov./Dec.,

Los Olivos Senior Center, Rm. 1–3, 2802 E. Devonshire. CONTACT: Harold A. Egy, P.O. Box 7648, Phoenix, AZ 85011-7648.

PRESCOTT: Prescott Stamp Club, (1008-094275), 7 p.m., 1st & 3rd Tues., Prescott Community Church, 3151 Willow Creek Rd. CONTACT: Box Rosenbaum, 655 Talwatha Dr., Prescott, AZ 86301.

SEDONA: Verde Valley Stamp Club, (182657), 7 p.m., 2nd & 4th Wed., VOCA Community Bldg., 690 Bell Rock Blvd. CONTACT: Karen McClelland, P.O. Box 2997, Sedona, AZ 86339.

SIERRA VISTA: Roadrunner Stamp Club, (1447-170641), 4th Wed., Oscar Yrun Community Center, 3020 Tacoma. CONTACT: Robert G. Wendel, P.O. Box 3781, Sierra Vista, AZ 85635.

SUN CITY: Sun City Stamp Club, (0887-076248), 7:30 p.m. 1st Mon. & 3rd Tues., Marinette Rec. Center, 99th Ave. & Union Hills Dr. CONTACT: Sam Allen, 11125 Cameo Dr., Sun City, AZ 85351-2840.

SUN CITY WEST: Sun City West Coin & Stamp Club, (1204-122188), 7 p.m. 2nd Tues., 2 p.m. 4th Tues., 2nd-Kuentz Recreation Center, 4th-Johnson Recreation Center. CONTACT: Dick Scanlon, 15919 Heritage Dr., Sun City West, AZ 85375.

SUN LAKES: Sun Lakes Stamp Club, (1456-172828), 7 p.m., 1st Tues., Sun Lakes Ph. I Country Club, 25601 N. Sun Lakes Blvd. CONTACT:

John R. Storm, 1568 E. Winged Foot Dr., Chandler, AZ 85249.

TUCSON: ** Tucson Stamp Club, (0059-007566), 7 p.m., 1st & 3rd Tues., Armory Park Senior Center, Dining Rm., 220 S. 5th Ave. CONTACT: Stephen Brainerd, P.O. Box 77923, Tucson, AZ 85703.

— * Arizona Philatelic Rangers, (0585-046188), 9 a.m.–2 p.m., Mon., Wed., & Fri., 920 N. First Ave. CONTACT: Donald N. Vivian, 5670 N. Calle De La Reina, Tucson, AZ 85718.

ARKANSAS

FAYETTEVILLE: Fayetteville Stamp Club, (1322-140752), 7 p.m., 1st & 3rd Tues., various locations. CONTACT: Donald E. Cook, 1715 Horseshoe Dr., Springdale, AR 72762.

FORT SMITH: Westark Stamp Club, (0960-087767), 7 p.m., 1st Tues., St. Luke Lutheran Church, 5401 Free Ferry Road. CONTACT: John C. Schmitt, 522 N. 21st St., Fort Smith, AR 72901.

LITTLE ROCK: Pinnacle Stamp Club of Arkansas, (1300-136599), 7 p.m., 4th Thurs., University Mall, Community Rm., 300 S. University Ave. CONTACT: Lon Griffin, 3 Shepherds Cove 109, Little Rock, AR 72205-7068.

MOUNTAIN HOME: Mountain Home Area Stamp Club, (0844-070020), 1 p.m., 2nd Sat., Library, Guy Berry Intermediate School, 1001 S. Main St., CONTACT: Everett Wheeler, P.O. Box 203, Mountain Home, AR 72653.

ROGERS: Razorback Stamp

Club, (1111-105688), 7 p.m., 2nd & 4th Thurs., Peace Lutheran Church, 805 W. Olrich St. CONTACT: Herbert E. Kauffman, 100 N. Dixieland Rd., Rogers, AR 72756.

CALIFORNIA

NORTHERN CALIFORNIA: * Council of Northern California Philatelic Societies, (0456-039063), Quarterly, Various Affiliated Clubs. CONTACT: Charles R. Waller, 561 Bustos Pl., Bay Point, CA 94565-6711.

ANAHEIM: * Orange County Philatelic Society, (0726-057548), 7:30 p.m., 1st Fri., Brookhurst Community Center, Brookhurst & Crescent. CONTACT: Michael Cress, P.O. Box 847, Anaheim, CA 92815-0847.

ARCADIA: Arcadia Stamp Club, (1158-114972), 7 p.m., 2nd & 4th Tues., Our Saviour Lutheran Church, 512 W. Duarte Road. CONTACT: C. Allan Spencer, 4644 Vineta Ave., La Canada, CA 91011-2617.

AVERY: Stamp Club of Calaveras County, (1386-153404), 7:30 p.m., 4th Tues., St. Clair's Episcopal Church. CONTACT: Pat Lix, 5853 Pettinger Road, Valley Springs, CA 95252.

BAKERSFIELD: * Bakersfield Stamp Club, (0652-051445), 7:30 p.m., 3rd Thurs., except Dec., Jim Burkeford Conference Rm. A, 21st & Oak St., CONTACT: Robert A. Johnston, 2001 Canter Way, Bakersfield, CA 933309. E-mail contact: Sarah Perelli-Minetti (sarahpm@igalaxy.net)

BURBANK: * Burbank Stamp Club, (0257-025176), 6:30 p.m., 2nd Tues., 1358 N. Naomi St. CONTACT: Max Bunshaft, P.O. Box 9215, North Hollywood, CA 91609-1215.

BURLINGAME: * Peninsula Stamp Club, (0265-025999), 7:30 p.m., 2nd & 4th Thurs., Bank of America Bldg., El Camino & Chapin. CONTACT: Martin H. Feibusch, P.O. Box 331, Burlingame, CA 94010.

CAPITOLA: Santa Cruz County Stamp Club, (0894-076749), 7 p.m., 3rd Tues., City Hall council chambers, 420 Capitola Ave. CONTACT: Harold A. Short, P.O. Box 2864, Santa Cruz, CA 95063.

CARMEL: * Monterey Peninsula Stamp Club, (0413-035961), 7:30 p.m., 2nd Wed., 3029 Lorca Lane. CONTACT: Harold Seyferth, 50 Yankee Point, Carmel, CA 93923.

DOWNEY: Downey California Stamp Club, (1440-167738), 1st Wed., Maude Price School, 9500 Tweedy Lane. CONTACT: William Sherman, 7315 Bluff Rd., Downey, CA 90240.

EL CAJON: East County Stamp Club, (1154-113999), 11 a.m., 2nd & 4th Sat., 126 Rea St. CONTACT: Gerhard Lorenzen, 4262 Blackton Dr., La Mesa, CA 91941.

EL SEGUNDO: Hughes El Segundo Employees Association Stamp Club, (0942-084311), 7 p.m., 2nd & 4th Mon., 2nd-Westside Pavilion, LA, 4th-HESEA Clubhouse. CONTACT: Gerald C. Tobin, 366 S. Westgate Ave., Los Angeles, CA 90049.

EUREKA: Humboldt Collectors Club, (0978-089465),

7:30 p.m., 4th Tues., except June, Redwood Acres Fairgrounds, Turf Room, 3750 Harris Ave. CONTACT: John E. Burke, 2236 G St., Eureka, CA 95501.

FORT BRAGG: Mendocino Coast Stamp Club, (1410-159697), 7:30 p.m., 1st Thurs., F.B. Library Community Rm., 499 E. Laurel. CONTACT: Dennis M. Tuomala, P.O. Box 2910, Fort Bragg, CA 95437.

FREMONT: Fremont Stamp Club, (1120-107688), 7 p.m., 2nd Thurs., Fremont Cultural Arts Center, 3375 Country Dr. CONTACT: Leonard Holmsten, 396 Smalley Ave., Hayward, CA 94541.

FRESNO: * Fresno Philatelic Society, (0767-061202), 1 p.m. 1st Sun., 7 p.m. 3rd Thurs., American Legion Post #509, 3509 N. 1st Ave. CONTACT: Gilbert P. Parent, 5050 E. White, Fresno, CA 93727. Home Page for FRE-SPEX '96: www.cybergate.com/~rsoppe/frespex.html

FULLERTON: * Beckman Philatelic Society, (0555-044422), 8 p.m., 3rd Mon., various locations. CONTACT: Louise Van Ingen, P.O. Box 369, Placentia, CA 92670.

HEMET: Hemet-San Jacinto Stamp Club, (0848-070418), 7:30 p.m., 2nd Wed., Provident Savings, 1690 E. Florida. CONTACT: Delmar J. Albright, 41665 Johnston Ave., Hemet, CA 92544-7501.

HUNTINGTON BEACH: * McDonnell Douglas Philatelic Club, (0673-052804), 7:30 p.m., 1st & 3rd Tues., MDC Huntington Beach. CONTACT: Robert J. Gunkel, 1227 Devon Lane, Newport Beach, CA 92660.

LAGUNA HILLS: Saddleback Stamp Club, (0872-073155), 7 p.m., 2nd & 4th Mon., Iglesia Comm. Park, Senior Center Bldg., off Moulton Pkwy. CONTACT: Mark R. Winters, 24721 Paseo Vendaval, El Toro, CA 92630.

LANCASTER: A. V. Stamp Club, (1468-174561), 2 p.m., 2nd Sun., Lancaster Estates Clubhouse, 45465 25th St., E. CONTACT: Mary E. Escarcega, 41844 Shain Lane, Quartz Hill, CA 93536-3147.

LONG BEACH: * Long Beach Stamp Club, (0744-059314), 7:30 p.m., 1st & 3rd Tues., Millikan High School, Cafeteria, 2800 Snowden Ave. CONTACT: H. David Cooper, 15072 Capetown Lane, Huntington Beach, CA 92647.

LOS ALTOS: Foothill Stamp Club, (1463-174383), 7:30 p.m., 1st & 3rd Mon., Great Western Bank Bldg., 199 Main St. CONTACT: Lucy Berardi, 160 S. Springer Road, Los Altos, CA 94022.

LOS ANGELES: ** Philatelic Society of Los Angeles, (0090-010294), 7:30 p.m., 2nd & 4th Tues., 2nd-US Reserve Center, 4th-Westside Pavilion. CONTACT: Richard Willing, P.O. Box 2217, Culver City, CA 90230.

— * Collectors Club of Hollywood, (0383-033713), 8 p.m., 2nd Tues., except Dec., St. Kliment Church, Virginia & Bronson Aves. CONTACT: George J. Tacheff, 723 N. Edgemont St., Los Angeles, CA 90029.

— Scandinavian Philatelic

Library of Southern California, (0860-071935), 7:30 p.m., 1st Wed., Except Aug., Union Fed. Bank, 13300 Ventura, Sherman Oaks. CONTACT: Paul A. Nelson, P.O. Box 310, Claremont, CA 91711.

— Society of Israel Philatelist-L.A. Chapter (185528), 2:00 p.m., 4th Sun., California Federal Bank, 8485 Wilshire Blvd., Los Angeles, CA. CONTACT: N.L. Senensieb, 15032 Acre St., Sepulveda, CA 91343.

MONTROSE: * Glendale Stamp Club, (0589-046674), 8 p.m., 4th Mon. except Dec., Glendale Federal Savings. CONTACT: Joseph H. Mirsky, 4359 Ramsdell Ave., La Crescenta, CA 91214.

NEWBURY PARK: Conejo Valley Philatelic Society, (1337-145089), 7:30 p.m., 2nd Wed., King of Glory Lutheran Church, 2500 Borchard Road. CONTACT: Harlan M. Walker, 637 Paseo Esmeralda, Newbury Park, CA 91320.

OCEANSIDE: * Tri City Stamp Club, (0592-046968), 7 p.m., 1st & 3rd Thurs., Boys/Girls Club of Oceanside, 450 Country Club Lane. CONTACT: Ronald Couchot, P.O. Box 1413, Oceanside, CA 92051.

PACIFIC PALISADES: Pacific Palisades Stamp Club, (0929-082327), 7:30 p.m., 1st & 3rd Tues., Pacific Palisades Library, 861 Alma Real Dr. CONTACT: Hazel Marshall, 600 Lachman Lane, Pacific Palisades, CA 90272.

PASADENA: J.P.L. Stamp Club, (0948-086293), 12 Noon,

2nd Tues., Visitor Control Conference Rm., 4800 Oak Grove Dr. CONTACT: James R. Rose, P.O. Box 771, La Canada, CA 91012-0771.

PETALUMA: Petaluma Philatelic Society, (0968-088227), 7:30 p.m., 1st & 3rd Sat., Westamerican Bank, Comm. Rm., Washington Sq. Shopping Center. CONTACT: Ronald W. Thurner, 1161 Adrienne Way, Santa Rosa, CA 95401-4476.

— Redwood Empire Collectors Club, (1465-174385), 6 p.m., 3rd Wed., Fino Restaurant, 208 Petaluma Blvd. CONTACT: Kurt Schau, P.O. Box 659, Petaluma, CA 94953.

POWAY: Poway Stamp Club, (1137-112097), 7:30 p.m., 2nd & 4th Wed., Meadowbrook School Auditorium, 12320 Meadowbrook Lane. CONTACT: Erik Nilsen, 4524 Castleton Way, San Diego, CA 92117.

— Virtual Stamp Club on Delphi, (1461-174150), 9:30 p.m., 2nd & 4th Wed., Genie Online Service. CONTACT: Ed Ozmun, 13619 Powers Road, Poway, CA 92064-3615.

REDDING: Redding Stamp Club, (1411-160290), 2 p.m. 1st Sun., 7 p.m. 3rd Tues., River Oaks Retirement Resid., 301 Hartnell Ave. CONTACT: Harold H. Hammen, 3435 Santa Rosa Way, Apt. 8, Redding, CA 96003-1755.

REDLANDS: * Redlands Stamp Club, (0484-040866), 7:30 p.m., 4th Tues., except July, Church of Christ, 1000 Roosevelt Road. CONTACT:

Arthur Thomas, P.O. Box 48, Redlands, CA 92373.

REDONDO BEACH: TRW Stamp Club, (0979-089466), 12 p.m., 2nd & 4th Tues., TRW Complex, E2/1200. CONTACT: A.F. Conrad, 7755 Quimby Ave., Canoga Park, CA 91304.

REDWOOD CITY: * Sequoia Stamp Club, (0687-054588), 8:15 p.m., 2nd & 4th Tues., Community Activities Center, 1400 Roosevelt Ave. CONTACT: William Dutcher, 1842 Los Altos Dr., San Mateo, CA 94402-3642.

RIVERSIDE: * Riverside Stamp Club, (0507-042328), 7:30 p.m., 2nd Mon., Recreation Rm., 9391 California Ave. CONTACT: J.L. Meyer, 20112 Westpoint Dr., Riverside, CA 92507.

SACRAMENTO: * Sacramento Philatelic Society, (0390-034230), 7 p.m., Wed., Easter Seal Society, 3205 Hurley Way. CONTACT: Bob V. Short, 1831 Discovery Dr., Roseville, CA 95747-6203.

SALINAS: * Monterey County Stamp Club, (0598-047341), 7:30 p.m., 4th Tues., Seventh Day Adventist Church, Social Hall, 46 Villa St. CONTACT: Ruth Pantry, 37 Young Dr., Salinas, CA 93901.

SAN BERNARDINO: * Arrowhead Stamp Club, (0340-030432), 7 p.m., 2nd Wed., Riley School, All Purpose Rm., 13th & G Sts. CONTACT: William C. Brooks VI, P.O. Box 2698, San Bernardino, CA 92406-2698.

SAN DIEGO: * San Diego Stamp Club, (0313-028844), 7:30 p.m., 2nd & 4th Tues., North Park Recreation Center, 4044 Idaho St. CONTACT: Janice Madsen, 5225 Trojan Ave., #2, San Diego, CA 92115.

— Philatelic "25," (0822-067620), 7:30 p.m., 3rd Wed., Members' Homes. CONTACT: Les Lanphear, P.O. Box 80843, San Diego, CA 92138.

— San Diego County Philatelic Council, (0930-082328), 7:30 p.m., Last Mon. of Jan., Apr., July & Oct., San Diego County Philatelic Library, 4133 Popular St. CONTACT: Manuel Marti, 1832 Craigmore Ave., Escondido, CA 92127.

SAN FRANCISCO: *** San Francisco-Pacific Philatelic Society, (0003-003387), 7 p.m., 2nd Tues., SFPD-Richmond Station, 461 6th Ave. CONTACT: Carl Prodinger, 1939 30th Ave., San Francisco, CA 94116-1147.

— * California Collectors Club, (0244-024516), 7 p.m., Fri., 1st United Lutheran Church, 6555 Geary at 30th Ave. CONTACT: Ed Jarvis, P.O. Box 210453, San Francisco, CA 94121-0453.

— * Collectors Club of San Francisco, (0516-042997), 7:30 p.m., 2nd Wed., except July & Dec., Iron Horse Restaurant, 19 Maiden Lane. CONTACT: Ross Towle, 400 Clayton St., San Francisco, CA 94117.

— * Golden Gate Stamp Club, (186030) 8 p.m. 2nd & 4th Mon., Police Station, 2345 24th Ave. Contact: Hans Hansson, 2334 35th Ave., San Francisco, CA 94116.

SAN JOSE: * San Jose Stamp Club, (0264-025791), 7 p.m., 1st

& 3rd Wed., San Jose Scottish Rite Temple, 2455 Masonic Dr. CONTACT: M.R. Renfro, P.O. Box 21429, San Jose, CA 95151.

—West Valley Philatelic Society, (1419-161485) 10:30 a.m., every Thursday, Cypress Senior Center, 403 S. Cypress Ave. CONTACT: Dr. Alvin C. Beckett, c/o Cypress Senior Center, 403 S. Cypress Ave., San Jose, CA 95117-1530.

SAN LEANDRO: ** Philatelic Society of San Leandro, (0170-015388), 8 p.m., 3rd Tues., San Leandro City Library, Harrison St. & Estudillo. CONTACT: A. "Sandy" McNichols, 16193 Via Del Robles, San Lorenzo, CA 94580.

SAN LUIS OBISPO: San Luis Obispo Philatelic Society, (179443). CONTACT: Joe Funderburg, P.O. Box 391, San Luis Obispo, CA 93406.

SAN PABLO: * San Pablo Pines Stamp Club, (0638-050333), 8 p.m., Mon., except 5th Mon., Kidd Manor, 100 Austin Ct. CONTACT: John Stansfield, 1952 Vine St., Berkeley, CA 94709-2032.

SAN RAFAEL: Tamalpais Stamp Club, (1170-116381), 7:30 p.m., 2nd & 4th Fri., 930 Tamalpais Ave. CONTACT: Jay R. Losselyong, 26 Jefferson Ave., San Rafael, CA 94903.

SANTA BARBARA: * Santa Barbara Stamp Club, (0236-024016), 7 p.m., 1st & 3rd Tues., City Recreation Center, 100 E. Carrillo St. CONTACT: David A. Johannsen, 5290 Overpass Road, Suite 208, Santa Barbara, CA 93111.

SEBASTOPOL: * Sonoma

County Philatelic Society, (0404-034768), 8 p.m., 1st & 3rd Tues., Glendale Federal Community Rm., Main St. & McKinley. CONTACT: Giles A. Gibson, P.O. Drawer B, Rio Nido, CA 95471.

SIMI VALLEY: Simi Valley Stamp Club, (1344-145935), 7 p.m., 1st Mon. & 3rd Thurs. CONTACT: Marian Bowman, P.O. Box 3631, Simi Valley, CA 93063.

SONORA: Tuolumne County Stamp Club, (1086-103923), 7:30 p.m., 2nd Wed., Tuolumne County Library, Greenly Rd. CONTACT: Robert Adam, 17300 Blackbird Lane, Sonora, CA 95370.

STOCKTON: ** Stockton Stamp Club, (0145-014118), 7:30 p.m., 2nd Wed., 2818 W. Telegraph Ave. CONTACT: Wesley S. Waite, 2818 W. Telegraph Ave., Stockton, CA 95204.

SUNNYVALE: Sunnyvale Stamp Club, (0460-039214), 7 p.m., Tues., Sunnyvale Community Center, Remington Ave. CONTACT: Bernard A. Ross, P.O. Box 2909, Sunnyvale, CA 94084.

— Friends Western Philatelic Library, (0836-069388), 7 p.m., 1st Wed., location varies. CONTACT: Roger D. Skinner, P.O. Box 2219, Sunnyvale, CA 94087.

TORRANCE: Torrance Stamp Club, (0934-082768), 7:30 p.m., 1st & 3rd Mon., Torrance Airport, 3301 Airport Dr. CONTACT: Raymond D. Rodgers, 3023 Lomina Ave., Long Beach, CA 90808.

VACAVILLE: Solano Stamp Club, (1332-143811), 7 p.m.,

1st & 3rd Thurs., McBride Senior Center, 411 Kendal St. CONTACT: Edgar Pica, P.O. Box 133, Elmira, CA 95625.

VALLEJO: Vallejo Stamp Club, (1289-133895), 7 p.m., 1st & 3rd Tues., Vallejo Community Center, Club Rm., 225 Amador. CONTACT: Michael S. Turrini, P.O. Box 121, Vallejo, CA 94590.

VAN NUYS: * Greater Valley Philatelic Society, (0403-034767), 7 p.m., 1st Fri. & 3rd Thurs., Sherman Oaks Senior Citizen Center, 5166 Van Nuys Blvd. CONTACT: Lynne Gershenow, P.O. Box 8191, Van Nuys, CA 91409.

VENTURA: * Ventura County Philatelic Society, (0535-043840), 7:30 p.m., 1st & 3rd Mon., Church of the Foothills, 6279 Foothill Rd. CONTACT: John Weigle, P.O. Box 6536, Ventura, CA 93006.

VISALIA: Visalia Philatelic Society, (0849-070419), 7:30 p.m., 2nd & 4th Tues., YMCA Bldg. CONTACT: Thomas Z. Stillman, 2529 Dartmouth, Visalia, CA 93277.

WALNUT CREEK: * Diablo Valley Stamp Club, (0454-038809), 7:30 p.m., 2nd & 4th Thurs., except Nov. & Dec., 1st Thurs., Leisure Serv. Bldg., Multi-Purpose Rm., 1650 N. Broadway. CONTACT: T.H. Kammerer, 260 Stevenson Dr., Pleasant Hill, CA 94523.

YUCCA VALLEY: Yucca Valley Stamp Club, (1428-164956), 3 p.m., 2nd & 4th Wed., American Savings, 56711 29 Palms Hwy. CONTACT: Bret Chlup, 57175 Hillcrest Dr., Yucca Valley, CA 92284-2131.

COLORADO

AURORA: * Aurora Stamp Club, (0803-066112), 7:30 p.m., 1st Wed. & 3rd Mon., Aurora Public Library. CONTACT: Roger Rydberg, 354 S. Nile St., Aurora, CO 80012

BOULDER: * Boulder Stamp Club, (0361-031904), 7:30 p.m., 4th Wed., except July & Dec., Crossroads Mall Meeting Place, 28th St. & Canyon Blvd. CONTACT: James L. Williams, 395 Erie Dr., Boulder, CO 80303.

COLORADO SPRINGS: Colorado Springs Stamp Club, (0837-069389), 7:30 p.m., 1st & 3rd Tues., Aug. 1st Tues. only, Colorado Springs Police Operations Center, 705 S. Nevada. CONTACT: Phil Zook, P.O. Box 7921, Colorado Springs, CO 80933.

DENVER: *** Denver Stamp Club, (0022-002554), 7:30 p.m., 3rd Tues., Church of the Ascension, 6th Ave. & Gilpin. CONTACT: COL David C. Snyder, Sr., P.O. Box 94, Evergreen, CO 80439-0094.

— ** Collectors' Club of Denver, (0176-015797), 7:30 p.m., 2nd Tues., BPOE Elk's Lodge #17, 2475 W. 26th Ave. CONTACT: George E. Wright, 5405 Iris St., Arvada, CO 80002.

— Rocky Mountain Philatelic Exhibition, ROMPEX, (1014,-094728), 7:30 p.m., 4th Tues., except May, June & Dec., Holiday Inn, 13500 E. 40th Ave. CONTACT: Steven Schweighofer, 8725 E. Eastman Ave., Denver, CO 80231-4504.

— Denver Germany Stamp Club, (1264-129844), 7:30 p.m., 2nd Wed., VFW South Denver

Post 2461, 1350 S. Broadway. CONTACT: Gary Lee Shum, 4768 S. Bannock, Englewood, CO 80110-6533.

ENGLEWOOD: * Cherrelyn Stamp Club, (0279-026937), 7 p.m., 2nd. Mon., except Aug., Grace Lutheran Church, 4750 S. Clarkson. CONTACT: Robert Gross, 4920 S. Huron St., Englewood, CO 80110.

FORT COLLINS: Northern Colorado Philatelic Society, (1223-123774), 7:30 p.m., 3rd Wed., St. Luke's Episcopal Church, 2000 Stover, CONTACT: Ted Beers, 719 Locust St., Fort Collins, CO 80524.

GRAND JUNCTION: * Stamp Club of Grand Junction, (0346-030810), 7 p.m., 2nd Wed., Federal Bldg., Conference Rm. 217, 4th & Rood. CONTACT: Don Garner, P.O. Box 1394, Grand Junction, CO 81502.

—Delta-Montrose Stamp Club, (179441). CONTACT: Charles Teed, 510 W. Mesa Ave., Grand Junction, CO 81501.

LA JUNTA: Centennial Stamp Club, (1376-151682), 7 p.m., 1st Thurs., members' homes. CONTACT: Malcolm Buller, 1210 Reed Lane, La Junta, CO 81050.

LAKEWOOD: * West Side Stamp Club, (0761-060087), 7:30 p.m., 1st Tues. & 3rd Thurs., First Presbyterian Church, 8210 W. 10th Ave. CONTACT: Dalene Thomas, c/o 1st Presbyterian Church, 8210 W. 10th Ave., Lakewood, CO 80215.

LITTLETON: * Arapahoe Stamp Club, (0596-047269), 7 p.m., 1st Wed., Bemis Public Library, 6014 S. Datura St. CONTACT: M. L. Jacobs, 7022 S. Dexter St., Littleton, CO 80122-2159.

PUEBLO: * Pueblo Stamp Club, (0338-030220), 7:30 p.m., 1st & 3rd Wed., 1111 Bonforte, Apt. 1111. CONTACT: Linton Zang, 1111 Bonforte Ave., Apt. 1111, Pueblo, CO 81004.

CONNECTICUT

BRANFORD: Branford Philatelic Society, (1080-102907), 7:30 p.m., 1st & 3rd Mon., Branford Community House, Church St. CONTACT: Kenneth H. Warner, 11 Bassett Road, Branford, CT 06405.

BROOKFIELD: Brookfield Philatelic Society, (1093-104280), 7:30 p.m., 2nd Fri., Community Center, Town Hall, Pocono Road. CONTACT: Alan Vale, 6 Beechwood Cir., Brookfield, CT 06804.

CHESHIRE: * Cheshire Philatelic Society, (0475-040052), 7:30 p.m., 1st & 3rd Fri., except July & Aug., Cheshire Convalescent Center in the Day Room, 745 Highland Ave. CONTACT: Robert A. Cawood, P.O. Box 206, Cheshire, CT 06410.

CLINTON: Clinton Stamp Club, (0855-071064), 8 p.m., 4th Thurs., except July & Aug., Andrews Memorial Town Hall, Boston Post Road. CONTACT: David E. Hill, 146 Wildcat Road, Madison, CT 06443.

DARIEN: * Ye Olde King's Highway Stamp Club, (0411-035831), 8 p.m., 2nd & 4th Thurs., Noroton Presbyterian Church, Corner Post Rd. & Noroton Ave. CONTACT: Nanette Smith,

21 Ledge Road, Rowayton, CT 06853-1037.

MANCHESTER: * Manchester Philatelic Society, (0626-049353), 6 p.m., 2nd & 4th Tues., Hartford Courant Comm. Conf. Rm., 200 Adams St. CONTACT: Richard W. Steele, P.O. Box 448, Manchester, CT 06040.

MIDDLETOWN: * Middletown Stamp Club, (0733-057917), 7:30 p.m., 1st & 3rd Tues., except July & Aug., The Hartford Courant Office, E. Main St. CONTACT: Stephen W. Ekstrom, P.O. Box 207, Cromwell, CT 06416.

NEW BRITAIN: Hardware City Stamp Club, (1009-094276), 7:30 p.m., 1st & 3rd Tues., except July & Aug., St. Andrew's Church Hall, 396 Church St. CONTACT: David A. Kent, P.O. Box 127, New Britain, CT 06050.

NEW HAVEN: * New Haven Philatelic Society, (0054-025889), 7:30 p.m., Tues., except July & Aug., New Haven Colony Hist. Society, 114 Whitney Ave. CONTACT: Gerhard G. Korn, 30 Perry Road, Hamden, CT 06514.

NORWALK: * Norwalk Stamp Club, (0599-047348), 8 p.m., 1st & 3rd Mon., except July & Aug., Nathan Hale Middle School, Strawberry Hill Ave. CONTACT: John A. Fahey, P.O. Box 267, Norwalk, CT 06856.

SIMSBURY: Simsbury Stamp Club, (180442), 7:30 p.m., 2nd Mon. (Sept.–June), Eno Memorial Hall, 754 Hopmeadow St. CONTACT: George Boissard, 15 Simscroft Road, Simsbury, CT 60670.

STRATFORD: * Nutmeg Stamp Club, (0794-064418),

6 p.m., 2nd & 4th Wed., except July & Aug., Baldwin Senior Center, 1000 W. Broad St. CONTACT: Elliott Myers, 43 Surry Lane, Monroe, CT 06468.

WATERBURY: Waterbury Stamp Club, (1087-103924), 7 p.m., 1st, 3rd & 4th Mon., Mill Plain Union Church, 242 Southmayd Road. CONTACT: Pat J. Rinaldi, P.O. Box 581, Waterbury, CT 06720.

— United Stamp Societies, (1293-135604), Jan., even years, various cities. CONTACT: Lawrence LeBel, 40-2A Woodsedge Dr., Newington, CT 06111.

WATERFORD: * Thames Stamp Club, (0784-063332), 7:30 p.m., 2nd & 4th Wed., except July & Aug., Clark Lane Middle School Library, Clark Lane. CONTACT: Anthony B. Bruno, P.O. Box 1447, New London, CT 06320.

DELAWARE

DOVER: Dover Stamp Club, (1002-093318), 7 p.m., 4th Tues., W. Reily Brown Elem. School, 360 Webb's Lane. CONTACT: Edwin F. Englehart, 1170 E. Lebanon Road, Dover, DE 19901.

GEORGETOWN: Sussex County Stamp Club, (1413-161195), 7:30 p.m., 2nd Tues., Delaware Tech. Comm. College, Adult Plus Center, Ennis Road, CONTACT: Frank J. Morris, R 2, Box 387A, Milton, DE 19968.

ODESSA: Corbit-Calloway Philatelists, (1387-153677), 7 p.m., 3rd Tues., Corbit-Calloway Library. CONTACT: Carole H. Kadie, 215 Main St., Box 636, Odessa, DE 19730.

VARIOUS: * DuPont Stamp Club, (0276-026893), 7:30 p.m., 1st Wed., except July & Aug., Various. CONTACT: John A. Harris, 5 Tunison Ct., Devonshire, Wilmington, DE 19810-2120.

WILMINGTON: * Wilmington Stamp Club, (0268-026339), 8 p.m., 2nd Wed., except July & Aug., Hanby Jr. High School, 2525 Berwyn Road. CONTACT: C. Allison Floyd, 206 Glennside Ave., Wilmington, DE 19803.

— Scandinavian Collectors Club. #13, (1271-131172), 8 p.m., last Tues., members' homes. CONTACT: Dewey H. Smith, P.O. Box 325, Rockland, DE 19732.

DISTRICT OF COLUMBIA

WASHINGTON: ** Washington Philatelic Society, (0169-015412), 8 p.m., 2nd & 4th Wed., except July & Aug., St. John's Parish House, 1525 H St., N.W. CONTACT: Brock R. Covington, P.O. Box 160, Glen Echo, MD 20812.

— * Philatelic Club, Library of Congress, (0747-059427), 11:30 a.m., 1st & 3rd Tues., LOC, James Madison Bldg., Copyright Cataloging Conference. CONTACT: Harry H. Price, 13223 Greenmount Ave., Beltsville, MD 20705-1056.

— Collectors Club of Washington, (1292-135603), 7:30 p.m., 1st & 3rd Wed., Christ Methodist Church, 300 Block, I St., S.W. CONTACT: Donald J. Peterson,

7408 Alaska Ave., N.W., Washington, DC 20012.

— Palisades Stamp Club, (1297-136036), 7:30 p.m., 3rd Tues., Palisades Branch Library, 49th & V Sts., N.W. CONTACT: Daniel W. Lozier, Jr., 5230 Sherier Pl., N.W., Washington, DC 20016.

FLORIDA

FLORIDA: * Florida Federation of Stamp Clubs, (0406-035107), semi-annually, various cities. CONTACT: Edward W. Parker, P.O. Box 523, Crystal Beach, FL 34681.

AVON PARK: Highlands Stamp Club, (1452-172490), 7 p.m., 1st Mon., Union Congregational Church, 105 N. Forest Ave. CONTACT: Paul Hoffman, 99 Rally Road, Avon Park, FL 33825.

BOYNTON BEACH: Delray Beach Stamp Club, (1185-118816), 7 p.m., 1st & 3rd Wed., Congress Middle School Library, 101 S. Congress Ave. CONTACT: Edward Greenfield, 1120 Mahogany Way, Apt. 102, Delray Beach, FL 33445.

CAPE CORAL: * Cape Coral Stamp Club, (0741-059033), 6:30 p.m., 4th Tues., Epiphany Episcopal Church, Del Prado Blvd. at Everest Pkwy. CONTACT: Bayard T. Cowper, 6937 Wittman Dr., S.W., Fort Myers, FL 33919.

CLEARWATER: * Clearwater Stamp Club, (0684-054339), 7 p.m., 2nd & 4th Mon., Morningside Recreation Center, 2400 Harn Blvd. CONTACT: Ron Yankowski, P.O. Box 5442, Clearwater, FL 34618.

DEERFIELD BEACH: Century Village East Stamp & Coin Club, (1201-121747), 11 a.m. to 12:30 p.m., Every Thurs., Clubhouse, General Purpose Rm. "D." CONTACT: Ben Wagner, Prescott C 61, Deerfield Beach, FL 33442.

DELAND: West Volusia Stamp Club, (1272-131173), 2 p.m., 1st & 4th Tues., Faith Lutheran Church, 509 E. Penn. Ave. CONTACT: William Dure, 243 S. Hull Ave., DeLand, FL 32720.

ELFERS: New Port Richey Area Stamp Club, (1069-100984), 1 p.m., 1st & 3rd Sun., Elfers Senior Center, 3146 Barker St., CONTACT: Don Roberts, P.O. Box 684, New Port Richey, FL, 34656-0684.

FORT LAUDERDALE: * Germany Philatelic Society Chapter 7, (0588-046673), 10 a.m., 1st & 3rd Sat., South Medical Bldg., 2nd Fl., 4800 N. Federal Hwy. CONTACT: Werner Vogel, 2710 S.W. 15th St., #CB58, Delray Beach, FL 33445.

GAINESVILLE: * University City Stamp Club, (0795-064419), 8 p.m., 1st & 3rd Tues., Doyle Connor Bldg., 1911 S.W. 34th St. CONTACT: LTC Stanley M. Lucas, 21 N.W. 79th Dr., Gainesville, FL 32607-1543.

HOLLY HILL: * Halifax Area Philatelic Society, (0344-030719), 7 p.m., 2nd Wed., Holly Hill Club House. CONTACT: Ron Edwards, 1625 Ridge Ave., Holly Hill, FL 32117.

HOLLYWOOD: * Hollywood Stamp Club, (0665-052140), 6:30 p.m., Tues., Senior Citizens Center, 2030 Polk St. CONTACT: Robert L. Welky, P.O. Box 24474, Fort Lauderdale, FL, 33307-4474.

JACKSONVILLE: Jacksonville Stamp Collectors Club, (1052-098565), 7:30 p.m., 1st & 3rd Tues., Arlington Jr. High Library, 8141 Lone Star Road. CONTACT: Charles F. Winney, 857 S. Edgewood Ave., Jacksonville, FL 32205.

KEYSTONE HEIGHTS: Keystone Heights Stamp Club (APS#185527), 2nd Tues., except July, Keystone Heights High School, Bldg. #24, Keystone Heights, FL. CONTACT: Robert E. Havens, 4564 S.E. 3rd Ave., Keystone Heights, FL 32656.

LAKELAND: Ridge Stamp Club of Lakeland, (1230-124824), 7:30 p.m., 1st & 3rd Tues., Magnolia Bldg., Lake Mirror. CONTACT: Paul Pritchett, 3160 Tanager E., Mulberry, FL 33860.

— Germany Philatelic Society, Chapter 23, (1377-151683), 2 p.m., 2nd Sun., except June, July, & Aug., St. Paul Lutheran Church, 3020 S. Florida Ave. CONTACT: George E. Kuhn, P.O. Box 711, Fruitland Park, FL 34731.

MAITLAND: * Central Florida Stamp Club, (0699-055178), 8 p.m., 1st & 3rd Thurs., 1st Presbyterian Church, 341 N. Orlando Ave. CONTACT: Wade H. Beery, Jr., P.O. Box 3781, Orlando, FL 32802.

MELBOURNE: Missile Stamp Club, (1213-122933), 7 p.m., 1st Wed. & 3rd Tues., Carrier Annex Postal Bldg., Seminole & Elizabeth Sts. CONTACT: Terry I. Cooper, P.O. Box 362321, Melbourne, FL 32936-2321.

MIAMI: * Club Cubano De

Coleccionistas, (0951-086296), 7 p.m., 2nd & 4th Tues., 901 S.W. 62nd Ave. CONTACT: Aldo Marti, 3251 S.W. 21st St., Miami, FL 33145.

— South Miami Stamp Club, (1149-113285), 7 p.m., Thurs., Sunset Congregational Church, 9025 Sunset Dr. CONTACT: Carol Barrus, c/o Sunset Congregational Church, 9025 Sunset Dr., Miami, FL 33173.

MOUNT DORA: Golden Triangle Stamp Club, (1471-174903), 1 p.m., 3rd Fri., Community Center, Baker & 6th Ave., CONTACT: Joseph J. Kopczak, P.O. Box 931, Mount Dora, FL 32757-0931.

NAPLES: Collier County Stamp Club., (1015-094729), 7 p.m., 4th Thurs., except Nov & Dec., 1st Natl. Bank of Naples, 800 Goodlette Road. CONTACT: Ruth Fenton, 777 Walker-bilt Road, Lot 12, Naples, FL 33963.

OAKLAND PARK: Ft. Lauderdale/Oakland Park Stamp Club, (1298-136370), 2nd & 4th Thurs., Collins Community Center, 3900 N.W. 3rd Ave. CONTACT: Bill Ogden, 248 Utah Ave., Fort Lauderdale, FL 33312.

OCALA: General Francis Marion Stamp Club, (1422-162111), 1:30 p.m., 1st & 3rd Wed., Friendship Community Bank, 8375 S.W. State Road 200. CONTACT: Lester A. Sanders, 8831C S.W. 94th Lane, Ocala, FL 34481.

PANAMA CITY: * Bay County Stamp Club, (0740-059032), 7:30 p.m., 1st & 3rd Thurs., General Mail Facility. CONTACT:

Maureen Knipper, 303 Alexander Dr., Lynn Haven, FL 32444.

PENSACOLA: * Pensacola Philatelic Society, (0591-046901), 7 p.m., 1st & 3rd Mon., Pensacola Jr. College Campus. CONTACT: Dewey J. Baker, 341 Kelson Road, Pensacola, FL 32514-3841.

PORT CHARLOTTE: Port Charlotte Stamp Club, (1088-103925), 2 p.m 2nd Thurs., 7 p.m. 4th Thurs., 2nd-Nations Bank, 4th-1st of America Bank. CONTACT: Katherine C. Foltuz, P.O. Box 3645, Port Charlotte, FL 33949.

PORT ST. LUCIE: Port St. Lucie Stamp Club, (0866-072805), 7:30 p.m., 2nd Thurs., Port St. Lucie Community Center, 200 S.W. Prima Vista Blvd. CONTACT: Ed Kozak, 6009 Lantana Dr., Fort Pierce, FL 34951.

SARASOTA: * Sarasota Philatelic Club, (0353-031238), 7:30 p.m., 2nd Tues, except Dec., Nations Bank, 5th Floor, 1605 Main St. CONTACT: Jack Harwood, P.O. Box 3553, Sarasota, FL 34239.

ST. AUGUSTINE: St. Augustine Stamp Club, (1152-113730), 7:30 p.m., 1st Tues, except July & Aug., Trinity Episcopal Church, Meeting Rm., 215 St. George. CONTACT: Philip D. Beall, 24 D'Allyon Ave., St. Augustine, FL 32084.

ST. PETERSBURG: ** St. Petersburg Stamp Club, (0157-014836), 7:30 p.m., Wed., Trinity Lutheran Church, 401 5th St., N. CONTACT: Arnold Selengut, P.O. Box 16681, Temple Terrace, FL 33687.

SUNRISE: Sunrise Stamp Club, (1160-115325), 1 p.m., 2nd Sun., Knob-Hill Center, 10400 Sunset Strip. CONTACT: S.J. Cohan, 1101 N.W. 58th Terr., Sunrise, FL 33313.

TALLAHASSEE: Tallahassee Stamp/Cover Club, (1414-161196), 7:30 p.m., 2nd Tues., Art Annex-Senior Citizens Center, N. Monroe & 7th St., CONTACT: Larry Benson, 1832 Jean Ave., Tallahassee, FL 32308-5227.

TAMPA: ** Tampa Collectors Club, (0123-013182), 7 p.m., 2nd & 4th Mon., Dec. 2nd Mon. only, Morrison's Cafet., Comm. Rm., 11810 N. Dale Mabry Hwy. CONTACT: Edward K. Lyons, P.O. Box 24831, Tampa, FL 33623-4831.

TITUSVILLE: Titusville Moonport Stamp Club, (0879-074119), 6:30 p.m., 1st Mon., Miracle City Mall, Rm. 51, 2500 S. Washington Ave. CONTACT: Roy L. Whitson, 2875 Armadillo Tr., Titusville, FL 32780.

VENICE: * Venice Stamp Club, (0653-051446), 7 p.m., 3rd Tues., Venice Area Public Library. CONTACT: Robert H. Agan, P.O. Box 1501, Venice, FL 34285.

WEST MIAMI: Cuban Philatelic Society of America, (0797-064880), 7 p.m., 2nd & 4th Tues., West Miami City Hall Bldg., 901 S.W. 62nd Ave. CONTACT: Gerardo Alvarez, P.O. Box 141656, Coral Gables, FL 33114-1656.

WINTER HAVEN: Winter Haven Stamp Club, (1343-145426), 7:30 p.m., 2nd & 4th Thurs., Nov. & Dec. 2nd Thurs. only, 1st Presbyterian Church, 637 6th St., N.W. CONTACT: L.R. Newkirk, 1435 Drexel Ave., N.E., Winter Haven, FL 33881.

— CompuServe Stamp Section, (1466-174386), 24 hours a day. CompuServe Go Collect Section, 2. CONTACT: Dudley L. Bauerlein, 2117 Greenway Dr., Winter Haven, FL 33881.

GEORGIA

GEORGIA: Georgia Federation of Stamp Club, (1462-164386), varies, Oct. show, Gwinnett Civic Center. CONTACT: John Camp, 1766 Austin Dr., Decatur, GA 30032.

AMERICUS: Americus Philatelic Society, (1438-167283), 7 p.m., 1st Thurs., Main Post Office, 128 E. Forsyth St. CONTACT: Horton Davis, 211 W. Furlow St., Americus, GA 22310.

ATHENS: * Athens Philatelic Society, (0482-040782), 7:30 p.m, 2nd Tues., 1st Presbyterian Fellowship Hall, Dougherty St. & College Ave. CONTACT: Edwin L. Jackson, 255 Greystone Terr., Athens, GA 30606.

ATLANTA: * Atlanta Stamp Collectors Club, (0357-031583), 7:30 p.m., 2nd & 4th Wed., Dec. 2nd Wed. only, 1st United Methodist Church Bldg., 360 Peachtree St. CONTACT: Robert J. Lewallyn, 2442 Kings Point Dr., Dunwoody, GA 30338-5927.

— Stone Mountain Philatelic Society, (1178-117707), 7:30 p.m., 2nd & 4th Thurs., Central Congregational Church, 2676 Clairmont Road, N.E. CONTACT: Frank Kana, 723 Windy Dr., S.W., Stone Mountain, GA 30087.

AUGUSTA: Greater Augusta Stamp Club, (0884-075673), 7 p.m., 2nd & 4th Thurs., Warren Road Community Center, 300 Warren Road. CONTACT: Pete Gray, 527 San Salvador Dr., North Augusta, SC 29841.

COLUMBUS: Columbus Area Stamp Club, (1470-174902), 7:30 p.m, 2nd Tues., Post Office Conference Rm., Milgen Road. CONTACT: Ted Whealton, 3702 Willis Road, Columbus, GA 31904.

DECATUR: DeKalb Stamp Club, (0924-081339), 1:30 p.m., 2nd Sun., Decatur Library, 215 Sycamore St. CONTACT: Dick Beauchesne, 27 Glenn Ct., Ellenwood, GA 30049.

LILBURN: Button Gwinnett Stamp Club, (1392-155240), 7:30 p.m., 3rd Wed., Lilburn City Hall, 2nd Fl., Main St. CONTACT: David C. Will, P.O. Box 2066, Lilburn, GA 30226-2066.

LITHIA SPRINGS: Sweetwater Stamp Society, (1436-166735), 2 p.m., Last Sun., 1st Baptist Church, 3566 Bankhead Hwy. CONTACT: Russell Turner, Jr., 4063 Bearden Lane, Douglasville, GA 30135-3603.

MARIETTA: Cobb County Stamp Club, (1184-118815), 1:30 p.m., 4th Sun., except Dec., Fuller Park Rec. Center, 3499 Robinson Road, CONTACT: Susan Schweitzer-Solida, 274 Shaded Oaks Lane, Marietta, GA 30067.

ROME: Coosa Valley Stamp Club, (1393-155609), 7:30 p.m., 4th Thurs., Berry College, Hoge Hall. CONTACT: Horace G. Edmondson, 203 Venetian Way, Rome, GA 30165.

VALDOSTA: Valdosta Stamp Club, (0940-083980), 7:30 p.m., 2nd Mon., South Ga. Regional Library, 300 Woodrow Wilson Dr. CONTACT: Clarence M. Paine, 406 Mack Dr., Valdosta, GA 31602.

WARNER ROBINS: Heart of Georgia Philatelic Society, (1398-156218), 7 p.m., Warner Robins Rec. Dept., 800 Watson Blvd. CONTACT: Russell M. Williamson, Jr., 102 Island Blvd., Warner Robins, GA 31088-7600.

HAWAII

HONOLULU: * Hawaiian Philatelic Society, (0296-027905), 7 p.m., 2nd & 4th Mon., Nuuanu YMCA, 1441 Pali Hwy. CONTACT: Louis A. Howard, 84-770 Kili Dr., #839, Waianae, HI 96792.

IDAHO

IDAHO FALLS: Snake River Stamp Club, (1070-100985), 7:30 p.m., 3rd Tues., Idaho Falls Public Library, Rm. B, 457 Broadway. CONTACT: Lee Reeves, P.O. Box 2622, Idaho Falls, ID 83403.

POCATELLO: Pocatello Stamp Club, (1372-150544), 7 p.m., 4th Wed., K & S, 781 Yellowstone. CONTACT: Richard E. Baker, P.O. Box 4485, Pocatello, ID 83205.

TWIN FALLS: South Central Idaho Stamp Club, (1395-155611), 7:30 p.m., 3rd Mon., Sodbuster Restaurant, 598 Blue Lakes Blvd. CONTACT: Philip D. Furman, 428 6th Ave., W., Jerome, ID 83338.

ILLINOIS

BELLEVILLE: * Belleville/Scott AFB Stamp Club, (0587-

046632), 7 p.m., 2nd & 4th Wed., Governor French Academy, 219 W. Main St. CONTACT: William A. Jenner, 307 Alma St., O'Fallon, IL 62269.

BRADLEY: Kankakee Coin, Stamp, & Sports Card Club, (1108-105685), 7:30 p.m., 2nd Thurs., Super K-mart Community Rm. CONTACT: Howard Sharkey, P.O. Box 150, Bradley, IL 60915-0150.

BROOKFIELD: * Suburban Collectors' Club, (0772-061737), 8 p.m., 2nd & 4th Wed., July, Aug., Dec. 2nd Wed. only, Sokol Brookfield Hall, 3909 S. Prairie Ave. CONTACT: John Borgeaud, P.O. Box 1146, Oak Park, IL 60304.

CARBONDALE: * Southern Illinois Stamp Club, (0458-039106), 5:30–8:30 p.m., 2nd & 4th, Thurs., except Nov./Dec. 2nd Thurs., Hillside Nursery, 1900 W. Sycamore. CONTACT: Joseph A. Beatty, Dept. Zoology, Southern Illinois University, Carbondale, IL 62901.

CHAMPAIGN-URBANA:
* Champaign-Urbana Stamp Club, (0746-059426), 7 p.m., 1st & 3rd Mon., 1st-Urbana Free Library, 3rd-Champaign Public Library. CONTACT: Peter Michalove, 307 S. McKinley Ave., Champaign, IL 61821.

CHICAGO: *** Chicago Philatelic Society, (0001-001775), 7:30 p.m., 1st & 3rd Thurs., Bismarck Hotel, 3rd Floor, 171 W. Randolph St. CONTACT: Eliot Landau, 5329 Main St., Suite 105, Downers Grove, IL 60515-4845.

— ** Beverly Hills Philatelic Society, (0104-012009), 7:30 p.m.,

2nd & 4th Tues., except June, July & Aug., Ridge Park Fieldhouse, 9611 S. Longwood Dr. CONTACT: Clarence W. Reiels, 9538 S. Richmond Ave., Evergreen Park, IL 60642.

— ** The Philaterians, (0158-014851), when called, members' homes. CONTACT: Lester E. Winick, 1501 E. Central Road, Apt. 101, Arlington Heights, IL 60005.

— ** North Shore Philatelic Society, (0223-021536), 7:30 p.m., 4th Wed., Warren Park Fieldhouse, 6601 N. Western Ave. CONTACT: Ronald L. Schloss, P.O. Box 60223, Chicago, IL 60660.

— * Roosevelt Philatelic Society, (0231-022504), 7 p.m., 1st & 3rd Tues., Hayes Park Fieldhouse, 2936 W. 85th St. CONTACT: Stan Urban, P.O. Box 73, Oak Lawn, IL 60454-0073.

— * Germany Philatelic Society Chapter 5, (0690-054878), 7:30 p.m., 4th Fri., Congress Hotel, 520 S. Michigan. CONTACT: Austin Dulin, P.O. Box 980, Oak Park, IL 60303.

— Austin Philatelic Club, (1020-095307), 8 p.m., 1st & 3rd Wed., Sts. Cyril and Methodius Hall, 5800 W. Diversey Ave. CONTACT: Robert Outlaw, P.O. Box A3960, Chicago, IL 60690.

— Scandinavian Collectors Club, Chapter 4, (1119-107014), 7:30 p.m., 4th Thurs., except June, July & Aug., Golden Flame, Foster & Nagle Ave. CONTACT: Willy E. Melberg, P.O. Box 134, Allenton, WI 53002.

— Polonus Philatelic Society, (1134-111613), 8 p.m., 4th Fri., Sts. Cyril & Methodius Annex, 5800 W. Diversey. CONTACT: Roman Strzelecki, 7006 W. 29th St., Berwyn, IL 60402.

— Chicagoland Chapter, American Topical Association, (1234-125083), 8 p.m., 3rd Fri., various locations. CONTACT: Gary W. Hall, P.O. Box 218, Berwyn, IL 60402-0218.

— Chicago Air Mail Society, (1365-149352), 7:30 p.m., 4th Tues., except July & Dec., Oriole Park Field House, 5430 N. Olcott. CONTACT: Stephen Neulander, P.O. Box 25, Deerfield, IL 60015-0025.

— SOSSI Baden-Powell, Chapter 1, (1389-154754), meets 6 times per year. Various stamp shows & other locations in the Chicago area. CONTACT: Richard F. Thill, 305 Hillside Pl., North Aurora, IL 60542.

DECATUR: * Decatur Stamp Club, (0293-027772), 7 p.m., 1st Wed. & 3rd Thurs., except June, July, Aug., Decatur Stamp & Coin, 104 N. Main. CONTACT Ervin Runion, P.O. Box 114, Decatur, IL 62525.

EAST PEORIA: * Caterpillar Stamp Club, (0492-041377), 7 p.m., 1st & 3rd Tues., July 1st Tues. only, Fon Du Lac Park Adm. Center, 201 Veterans Dr. CONTACT: Lawrence J. Miller, Jr., 417 Redbud Dr., Washington, IL 61571-1638.

— * Tri-County Stamp Club, (0628-049453), 7 p.m., 1st Tues., Fon Du Lac Park Admin. Center, 201 Bloomington Road. CON-

TACT: Vernon Martin, 1006 Lincoln Ave., Pekin, IL 61554.

EVANSTON: Evanston-New Trier Philatelic Society, (0852-070422), 8 p.m., 1st & 3rd Wed., Bank One Bldg., Sherman Ave. & Davis St. CONTACT: Milton J. Schober, 4032 Lee St., Skokie, IL 60076.

GALESBURG: Galesburg Philatelic Society, (1384-153402), 7 p.m., 3rd Tues., 150 E. Simmons St. CONTACT: Shirley C. Daddona, 453 N. Pleasant Ave., Galesburg, IL 61401.

GRAYSLAKE * Lake County Philatelic Society, (0423-036864), 7 p.m., 4th Tues., except Dec., Grayslake Library, 100 Library Lane. CONTACT: Fred L. Schaefer, 27 Westshore Dr., Grayslake, IL 60030-1528.

MOLINE: * Quad City Stamp Club, (0249-024667), 7 p.m., 2nd Thurs., Moline Township Hall, 620 18th St. CONTACT: George Pettigrew, P.O. Box 10301, Moline, IL 61265-9301.

MOUNT PROSPECT: Northwest Stamp Club, (1054-098567), 7:30 p.m., 2nd & 4th Wed., Mount Prospect Library, 10 S. Emerson. CONTACT: Peter J. Zachar, 275 University Dr., Buffalo Grove, IL 60089.

NAPERVILLE: Naperville Stamp Club, (1404-158352), 7:30 p.m., John Greene Realty, 1111 S. Washington. CONTACT: William J. Thomas, 413 W. Gartner Road, Naperville, IL 60540.

NORMAL: * Corn Belt Philatelic Society, (0263-025751), 7 p.m., 3rd Tues. & Last Wed., First of America Bank, College

& Towanda Aves. CONTACT: Jack L. Jenkins, P.O. Box 625, Bloomington, IL 61702-0625.

PARK FOREST: * Park Forest Stamp Club, (0522-043135), 7:30 p.m., 1st, 3rd, & 5th Tues., Freedom Hall, Lakewood Blvd. & Orchard Dr. CONTACT: Paul A. Larsen, P.O. Box 606, Park Forest, IL 60466.

PEORIA: * Peoria Philatelic Society, (0243-024460), 7 p.m., 3rd Wed., Lakeview Public Library, 1137 W. Lake Ave. CONTACT: Paul R. King, 104 Montclair Ct., East Peoria, IL 61611.

ROCKFORD: * Rockford Stamp Club, (0735-057919), 6:30 p.m., 1st Wed., Ken Rock Community Center, 3218 11th St. CONTACT: Charles Teeman, 6291 Valley Knoll Dr., Rockford, IL 61109-1824.

ROSEMONT: Midwest Stamp Dealers Association, (1446-169967), 7 p.m., Holiday Inn O'Hare, 5440 N. River Road. CONTACT: James L. DeBruin, P.O. Box 5573, Buffalo Grove, IL 60089.

SKOKIE: Smith Center Stamp Club, (1443-168336), 1:30 p.m., 1st & 3rd Wed., Smith Center, 5120 Galitz. CONTACT: Harold M. Stral, 4438 Estes Ave., Lincolnwood, IL 60646-2228.

SPRINGFIELD: * Springfield Philatelic Society, (0339-030371), 7:30 p.m., 4th Tues, except June, Security Federal Bldg., 510 E. Monroe St. CONTACT: Geraldine Broadie, 2712 Bennington Dr., Springfield, IL 62704.

URBANA: See Champaign.

WEST DUNDEE: Spring Hill Stamp Club, (1373-150545), 7:30 p.m., 1st & 3rd Mon., First United Methodist Church, 318 W. Main. CONTACT: Robert C. Barkhurst, 319 N. River St., East Dundee, IL 60118-1300.

WHEATON: ** Glen Ellyn Philatelic Club, (0202-018782), 7 p.m., 1st & 3rd Mon., Mid-America Federal Savings, Roosevelt & Napersville Roads. CONTACT: Mark Isaacs, P.O. Box 217, Glen Ellyn, IL 60138.

INDIANA

ANDERSON: Madison County Bicentennial Stamp Club, (0991-091760), 7 p.m., 3rd Thurs., Anderson Public Library, Sagamore & Carnegie Room. CONTACT: Bonnie Lyons, 1732 Mockingbird Lane, Anderson, IN 46013.

BLOOMINGTON: Bloomington Stamp Club, (1416-161482), 7 p.m., 2nd Wed., Monroe County Public Library, 303 E. Kirkwood Ave. CONTACT: Mark W. Goodson, 202 W. Temperance St., Ellettsville, IN 47429.

EVANSVILLE: ** Evansville Stamp Club, (0175-015519), 7 p.m., 1st & 3rd Tues., C.K. Newsome Center, 100 E. Walnut St. CONTACT: Paul Adam, P.O. Box 161, Evansville, IN 47702-0161.

FORT WAYNE: ** Anthony Wayne Stamp Society, (0186-016444), 7 p.m., 2nd Mon., Allen County Public Library, 900 W. Webster & W. Washington. CONTACT: James Mowrer,

124 S. Barr St., Fort Wayne, IN 46802.

HAMMOND: Calumet Stamp Club, (0953-086239), 7 p.m., Thurs., Calumet Fed. Savings & Loan, 7007 Calumet Ave. CONTACT: Don Strom, 3207 Martha St., Highland, IN 46322.

INDIANAPOLIS: * Indiana Stamp Club, (0372-032548), 7:30 p.m., 1st Mon., Children's Museum, 30th & Meridian St. CONTACT: Jeanette Adams, P.O. Box 40792, Indianapolis, IN 46240.

LAPORTE: LaPorte County Stamp Club, (1242-126585), 7 p.m., 2nd & 4th Mon., Library, Indiana Ave. & Maple Ave. CONTACT: Sam Zerbe, 1008 E. Michigan Blvd., Michigan City, IN 46360.

RICHMOND: Centerville Stamp Club, (1094-104281), 7:30 p.m., 3rd Fri., The Cabin, Glenn Miller Park. CONTACT: Webster Hall, 10 Audree Lane, Richmond, IN 47374.

SOUTH BEND: Northern Indiana Philatelic Society, (1081-102908), 7:30 p.m., 2nd & 4th Thurs., except Nov., Northway Church of Christ, Auten Road. CONTACT: Betty Skopec, P.O. Box 393, Mishawaka, IN 46546.

TERRE HAUTE: * Wabash Valley Stamp Club, (0605-047983), 7 p.m., Last Thurs., except Nov. & Dec., Vigo County Public Library, 7th & Poplar Sts. CONTACT: S.R. Dawson, 10901 Ole Foxe Road, Terre Haute, IN 47803.

IOWA

ALLISON: Allison Stamp Club,

(0908-079744), 7:30 p.m., 2nd Sat., Allison Library Community Rm., 410 N. Main St. CONTACT: Kenneth Trettin, P.O. Box 56, Rockford, IA 50468-0056.

BURLINGTON: Hawkeye Stamp Club, (1339-145091), 7 p.m., Burlington Public Library, 501 N. 4th. CONTACT: William G. Comben, 2610 F Newbury Circle, Burlington, IA 52601.

CEDAR RAPIDS: ** Cedar Rapids Stamp Club, (0106-012487), 7:30 p.m., 1st Mon., except June–Sept., Mutual Fire Ins. Co. Bldg., 1111 1st Ave., S.E. CONTACT: Ida Mahan, P.O. Box 2554, Cedar Rapids, IA 52406-2554.

DECORAH: Oneota Stamp Club, (1350-146599), 7 p.m., 4th Mon., Interstate Meeting Room, 219 W. Water St. CONTACT: Verne Koenig, 110 Elm Ct., Decorah, IA 52101.

DES MOINES: * Des Moines Philatelic Society, (0294-027884), 7 p.m., 2nd Fri., Staves Memorial Methodist Church, E. 28th St. & Madison Ave. CONTACT: David Phelps, 3031 64th St., Urbandale, IA 50322.

— * Iowa Women's Philatelic Society, (0427-037027), 6:45 p.m., 1st Fri., except July & Aug., Bishops Cafeteria, 5030 N.E. 14th St. CONTACT: Barbara Good, 2804 E. 40th St., Des Moines, IA 50317.

DUBUQUE: Dubuque Stamp Club, (1434-166366), 4th Wed., except June–Aug., Cycare Building. CONTACT: Merwyn R. Ellis, 1652 Finley St., Dubuque, IA 52001.

WATERLOO: * Cedar Valley

Stamp Club, (0774-062335), 7:30 p.m., 2nd & 4th Wed., Waterloo Rec. & Arts Center, 225 Commercial. CONTACT: T. Wayne Black, 843 Olympic Dr., Waterloo, IA 50701.

KANSAS

LAWRENCE: Lawrence Stamp Club, (1186-118817), 7 p.m., 1st Thurs., Watkins Museum, South Door, 11th & Mass. CONTACT: Jon Dunham, 2712 Westdale Circle, Lawrence, KS 66049.

LINDSBORG: Lindsborg Stamp Club, (1045-097885), 7:30 p.m., 4th Mon., Villa Ro Center. CONTACT: Joyce Crowe, 706 Colonial Ct., Salina, KS 67401.

MANHATTAN: Flint Hills Stamp Club, (1190-119647), 7:30 p.m., 2nd Thurs., Post Office Civil Service Rm., 500 Leavenworth St. CONTACT: Gerry Ungerer, 8620 E. Hwy. 24, Manhattan, KS 66502.

TOPEKA: Topeka Stamp Club, (1352-147411), 7:30 p.m., 3rd Thurs., Crestview United Methodist Church, 2245 S.W. Eveningside Dr. CONTACT: Michael Keil, P.O. Box 14, Topeka, KS 66601.

WICHITA: ** Wichita Stamp Club, (0134-013615), 7 p.m., 1st & 3rd Thurs., 3rd July & Aug., 1st Dec., Downtown Wichita Public Library. Patio Room. CONTACT: Rex Cornelius, 1208 N. Crestway, Wichita, KS 67208. Home Page: http://www.southwind.net/~rexc/wsc/

— Cessna Stamp Club, (1161-115941), 7 p.m., 2nd Thurs., except June, July & Aug., Cessna Activity Center,

2744 Geo. Washington Blvd. CONTACT: Ralph E. Lott, 914 2nd Circle, Douglass, KS 67039.

KENTUCKY

LEXINGTON: Henry Clay Philatelic Society, (1317-140420), 7:00 p.m., 3rd Mon., Second Presbyterian Church, E. Main at Ransom Ave. CONTACT: Linda L. Lawrence, 312 Northwood Dr., Lexington, KY 40505.

LOUISVILLE: * Louisville Stamp Society, (0521-043117), 8 p.m., 1st & 3rd Fri., except Dec., Crescent Hill Presbyterian, Church, 142 Crescent Ave. CONTACT: Fred J. Lopp, 1406G Browns Lane, Louisville, KY 40207.

— * Philatelic Club of Louisville, (0580-045821), 7 p.m., 1st Thurs., River Road Country Club, 2930 Upper River Road. CONTACT: Prescott Van Horn Jr., 3017 Chimneywood Dr., Floyds Knobs, IN 47119.

OWENSBORO: Owensboro Area Stamp Club, (1425-163243), 7 p.m., 1st Fri., Trinity Episcopal Church, 720 Ford Ave. CONTACT: Wilfred L. Gorrell, 1025 Peninsula Ct., Maceo, KY 42355.

LOUISIANA

ALEXANDRIA: Cenla Stamp Club, (1439-167284), 6 p.m., 1st Tues., Alexandria Post Office, 1715 Odom St. CONTACT: J. Dean McAlister, 157 Spring Creek Dr., Pineville, LA 71360.

BATON ROUGE: * Baton Rouge Stamp Club, (0260-

025503), 7 p.m., 1st & 3rd Wed., Council on Aging Municipal, Bldg., 5790 Florida Blvd. CONTACT: Ron Snider, 743 Bourbon Ave., Baton Rouge, LA 70808.

BOSSIER CITY: * Red River Stamp Society, (0721-056951), 7 p.m., 1st Wed., Aulds Library, 3950 Wayne Ave. CONTACT: John P. Thomas, 1525 Concord Dr., Shreveport, LA 71105.

LAFAYETTE: Acadiana Stamp Club, (1138-112098), 7 p.m., 2nd Thurs., U.S. Regional Postal Facility, Conference Rm., 1105 Moss St. CONTACT: Janiece C. Young, P.O. Box 90214, Lafayette, LA 70509-0214.

MONROE: Twin City Stamp Club, (0981-090013), 7 p.m., 1st Mon., U.S. Post Office, 2nd Fl., 501 Sterlington Road. CONTACT: James G. Shows, 3612 Jefferson Davis, Monroe, LA 71201.

NEW ORLEANS: * Crescent City Stamp Club, (0517-042967), 7:30 p.m., 2nd Tues., Jefferson Parish (Lakeshore, Br) Library, 1000 W. Esplanade. CONTACT: H.J. Berthelot, 132 Livingston Pl. W., Metairie, LA 70005.

MAINE

FAIRFIELD: Waterville Stamp Club, (1323-141243), 6:30 p.m., 1st & 3rd Fri., June–Aug. 3rd Fri. only, Kennebec Valley Tech. College, Western Ave. CONTACT: Richard Williams Jr., 20 Ridge Road, Waterville, ME 04901-4121.

SANFORD: * York County Stamp Club, (0549-044268), 7:30 p.m., 2nd & 4th Thurs., Peoples Heritage Bank, R 109, Lower Main St. CONTACT: C. Rick Stambaugh, R 3, Box 491, North Berwick, ME 03906.

MARYLAND

ABERDEEN: * Harford County Stamp Club, (0700-055179), 7 p.m., 2nd & 4th Tues., Graie United Methodist Church. CONTACT: Rich Foichheimer, 2909 Shelley Ct., Abingdon, MD 21009.

ADELPHI: Beltway Stamp Club, (1245-127079), 7:30 p.m., 1st & 3rd Wed., except Dec., Adelphi Professional Bldg., 8508 Adelphi Road. CONTACT: D.H. Elliott, 8508 Adelphi Road, Adelphi, MD 20783.

ANNAPOLIS: * Annapolis Stamp Club, (0392-034247), 6 p.m., 1st, 3rd & 4th Tues., Annapolis Public Library, 1410 West St. CONTACT: Frank G. Soeder, Jr., 1183 Ramblewood Dr., Annapolis, MD 21401-4667.

BALTIMORE: ** Baltimore Philatelic Society, (0137-013722), 8 p.m., every Wed., 1224 N. Calvert St. CONTACT: Carroll L. Lloyd, 1224 N. Calvert St., Baltimore, MD 21202.

— Germany Philatelic Society, Herman L. Halle Chapter 16, (1333-144414), 1:30 p.m., 3rd Sun., except July & Aug., BPS Clubhouse, 1224 N. Calvert St. CONTACT: Christopher D. Deterding, R 10, 741 Holly Dr., N., Annapolis, MD 21401.

BOWIE: * Bowie Stamp Club, (0634-049876), 8 p.m., every

Mon., except legal holidays, Bowie City Hall, 2614 Kenhill Dr. CONTACT: Jared P. Jacobs, 5307 Russett Road, Rockville, MD 20853.

COLUMBIA: * Howard County Stamp Club, (0798-064881), 7:30 p.m., 1st & 3rd Wed., Harpers Choice Middle School. CONTACT: Gordon Trotter, 10626 Fable Row, Columbia, MD 21044.

CUMBERLAND: Tri-State Stamp Club, (1467-174387), 7 p.m., 2nd Wed., South Cumberland Library. CONTACT: Ted Rissell, 365 Back Bay Road, Swanton, MD 21561.

EASTON: Tidewater Stamp Club, (1382-153104), 7:30 p.m., 2nd & 4th Tues., City Hall, 14 S. Harrison St. CONTACT: Carol Armstrong, P.O. Box 2000, Easton, MD 21601.

FORT WASHINGTON: Silver Hill Lions Club, (1315-139412), time and location vary. CONTACT: Earl M. Whitehouse, Jr., 1008 Palmer Road, #6, Fort Washington, MD 20744.

GAITHERSBURG: Rockville-Gaithersburg Stamp Club, (0905-078421), 7:30 p.m., 2nd & 4th Thurs., Gaithersburg Sr. High School, 314 S. Frederick Ave. CONTACT: Catherine Russell, 18517 Kingshill Road, Germantown, MD 20874-2211.

GREENBELT: Goddard Space Flight Center Stamp Club, (1027-095720), 11:30 a.m., 2nd Tues, Bldg. 3, Room 200. CONTACT: Manfred Owe, P.O. Box 261, Greenbelt, MD 20768-0261.

HAGERSTOWN: Hagerstown Stamp Club, (0874-073392), 7:30 p.m., 2nd Tues., St. John's Lutheran Church, Ed. Bldg., 141 S. Potomac St. CONTACT: John Curlis, P.O. Box 2265, Hagerstown, MD 21741-2265.

NORTH EAST: Cecil County Stamp Club, (1420-161736), 7 p.m., 2nd & 4th Wed., VFW Post, 6027 Turkey Point Road. CONTACT: Robert J. Loller, 111 Quail Ct., Elkton, MD 21921.

POTOMAC: Potomac Philatelic Society, (1156-114548), 8 p.m., 2nd Tues., members' homes. CONTACT: Robert S. Dyer, 6102 Bayliss Pl., Alexandria, VA 22310.

SALISBURY: Eastern Shore Stamp Club, (1390-154755), 1st & 3rd Wed., except July & Aug., Wicomico County Youth/ Civic Center, Glen Ave. CONTACT: Gene Wharton, 26883 S. Tourmaline Dr., Hebron, MD 21830.

SILVER SPRING: * Silver Spring Philatelic Society, (0595-047100), 8 p.m., 2nd & 4th Tues., M. Schweinhaut Senior Center, 1000 Forest Glen Road. CONTACT: Raymond R. Goldberg, 11602 Milbern Dr., Potomac, MD 20854.

MASSACHUSETTS

MASSACHUSETTS: Northeastern Federation of Stamp Clubs, (1131-110585), time varies, Cardinal Spellman Philatelic Museum, Regis College. CONTACT: Guy R. Dillaway, P.O. Box 181, Weston, MA 02193.

BRIGHTON: * Boston Philatelic Society, (0300-028001), 7 p.m., 2nd & 4th Tues., except July & Aug., Brighton Police

Station, Community Rm., Washington St. CONTACT: John W. McGovern, 67 Perry St., Brookline, MA 02146.

CHELMSFORD: Chelmsford Stamp Club, (1021-095308), 8 p.m., 2nd & 4th Tues., Greater Lowell Council #238, 60 Carlisle St. CONTACT: Len Andexler, 192 Tahattawan Road, Littleton, MA 01460.

DUDLEY: * Webster-Dudley Stamp Club, (0620-048795), 7 p.m., 1st Tues., except July & Aug., Dudley Town Hall, Schofield Ave. (Rte. 12). CONTACT: Edith C. Ackerman, 156 W. Main St., Dudley, MA 01571.

EAST ORLENNA: Harwich Stamp Club, (179442). CONTACT: Caxton C. Foster, P.O. Box 488, East Orlenna, MA 02643.

EVERETT: * Malden Stamp Club, (0379-033586), 7:30 p.m., 2nd & 4th Wed., July & Aug. 4th Wed. only, Mystic Side Congregational, Church, 420 Main St. CONTACT: Phil Collins, 97 Central St., Saugus, MA 01906-1277.

FALL RIVER: Fall River Philatelic Society, (1325-142052), 7 p.m., 3rd Mon., Super Stop & Shop, Marianno Bishop Blvd. CONTACT: Donald F. Craig, P.O. Box 9002, Fall River, MA 02720-9002.

FRAMINGHAM: Lincoln Stamp Club, (0992-091761), Inactive. CONTACT: David Borghi, 9 McCarthy Cr., Framingham, MA 01701.

GREENFIELD: Franklin Stamp Club, (1354-148251), 3rd Wed., Senior Center, Weldon Bldg., 54 Light St. CONTACT: K. Russell Shillieto, P.O. Box 819, Greenfield, MA 01302.

LEOMINSTER: Wachusett Philatelic Society, (1082-102909), 7:30 p.m., 3rd Tues., except July & Aug., All Saints Chapel Annex, 1469 Main St. CONTACT: Emidio Martini, 153 Union St., Leominster, MA 01453-4125.

NEEDHAM: Needham Stamp Club, (1472-174904), 3rd Fri., Needham Memorial Park Bldg. CONTACT: Robert W. Muther, 37 Grosvenor Road, Needham, MA 02192.

NEW BEDFORD: Whaling City Stamp Club, (1004-093320), 7 p.m., 2nd & 4th Mon., except July & Aug., New Bedford Boys Club, 166 Jenny St. CONTACT: Gilbert Borges, 7 W. Bliss St., South Dartmouth, MA 02748.

NEWBURYPORT: Newburyport Stamp Club, (1478-176876), 7:15 p.m., 2nd & 4th Wed., Newburyport 5 Cent Savings, 63 State St., Conference Room. CONTACT: Neil Foley, P.O. Box 204, Newburyport, MA 01950-1935.

NORTH ADAMS: Mohawk Stamp Club, (1288-133894), 7:30 p.m., 3rd Wed., except July, Aug. & Dec., St. John's Episcopal Church, 59 Summer St. CONTACT: Roy Germaine, 757 Simonds Road, Williamstown, MA 01267.

NORTH ANDOVER: * Samuel Osgood Stamp Club, (0640-050725), 7 p.m., 1st & 3rd Wed., July & Aug. 3rd Wed. only, The Greenery, 75 Park St. CONTACT: Roger G. Brand, 30

Sharon Road, South Hamilton, MA 01982.

NORTH READING: Philatelic Group of Boston, (1400-156220), 7:30 p.m., 4th Wed., (except August), location varies. CONTACT: Stephen A. Hartwell, 137 Chestnut St., North Reading, MA 01864.

OXFORD: Clara Barton Stamp Club, (1424-163242), 7:30 p.m., 2nd Wed., Zion Lutheran Church, Main St. CONTACT: Peter Pierce, P.O. Box 560, Oxford, MA 01540-0760.

PITTSFIELD: * Berkshire Museum Stamp Club, (0593-046985), 7:30 p.m., 2nd & 4th Tues., Berkshire Museum. CONTACT: Robert M. Cancilla, 769 Williams St., Pittsfield, MA 01201.

PLYMPTON: Golden Bee Stamp Club, (1159-115324), 7 p.m., 2nd Wed., Upland Sportsman's Club. CONTACT: Robert J. Martin, P.O. Box 277, Bryantville, MA 02327.

QUINCY: Granite City Stamp Club, (180764). CONTACT: Edward L. Fitzpatrick, 89 St. Agatha Road, Milton MA 02186.

SPRINGFIELD: *** William C. Stone Chapter, (0028-003305), 7:30 p.m., Every other Thurs., except July & Aug., members' homes. CONTACT: Martin D. Turpie, 243 Prospect St., East Longmeadow, MA 01028.

STOUGHTON: Stoughton Stamp Club, (0856-071589), 7 p.m., 1st & 3rd Mon., First Congregational Church, 76 Pierce St. CONTACT: Irving Aronson, 702 West St., Stoughton, MA 02072.

SWAMPSCOTT: Lynn Philatelic Society, (0957-087134), 7 p.m., 1st & 3rd Tues., except July & Aug., Swampscott Public Library, 61 Burrill St. CONTACT: Michael J. Bourgault, 17 Lakeview Pl., East Lynn, MA 01904.

WESTFIELD: * Westfield Stamp Club, (0796-064420), 6:30 p.m., 1st & 3rd Tues., except July & Aug., Westfield Anthaneum, 6 Elm St. CONTACT: Ronald A. Skoog, 16 Chestnut St., Westfield, MA 01085-2717.

WESTON: * Waltham Stamp Club, (0683-054003), 8 p.m., 1st & 3rd Tues., July & Aug. 3rd Tues. only, Cardinal Spellman Philatelic Museum, Regis College, 235 Wellesley. CONTACT: Jeffrey Shapiro, 155-10 Broadmeadow St., Marlborough, MA 01752.

WORCESTER: Worchester County Philatelic Society, (1233-124827), 7:30 p.m., 2nd Fri., Greendale Peoples Church, 25 Francis St. CONTACT: John C. Root, 404 Pleasant St., Paxton, MA 01612-1375.

MICHIGAN

MICHIGAN: * Peninsular State Philatelic Society, (0226-022015), Annually, Chapter Club Host. CONTACT: Richard G. Ebach, 2265 Linda Ave., Saginaw, MI 48603.

ANN ARBOR: * Ann Arbor Stamp Club, (0806-066368), 7:30 p.m. 3rd Mon., except Nov. & Dec., Salvation Army Citadel, 100 Arbana. CONTACT:

Harry C. Winter, P.O. Box 2012, Ann Arbor, MI 48106.

BIRMINGHAM: Birmingham Stamp Club, (1172-116758), 7 p.m., 2nd & 4th Tues., BASCC Senior Center. CONTACT: Stefan Karadian, c/o BASCC Senior Center, 2121 Midvale Ave., Birmingham, MI 48009-4440.

DEARBORN: * Motor City Stamp & Cover Club, (0442-038192), last Sun., 3–6 p.m., Prince of Peace Lutheran Church, 19100 Ford Road. CONTACT: Robert Quintero, 22608 Poplar Ct., Hazel Park, MI 48030.

— * Dearborn Stamp Club, (0523-43209), 7 p.m., 2nd & 4th Wed., except July & Aug., Dearborn Civic Center, Michigan Ave. at Greenfield. CONTACT: Elmer Beck, 711 N. Waverly, Dearborn, MI 48128.

— Ford Stamp Club, (1310-138565), 1st Mon., P&A Bldg., Res. & Eng. Center, 2nd Fl., Conference Rm. CONTACT: R.L. Hyzy, P.O. Box 2388, Dearborn, MI 48123.

DETROIT: *** Detroit Philatelic Society, (0025-003219), 6 p.m., 1st & 3rd Wed., except July, Aug. & Sept., various locations. CONTACT: Jerome C. Jarnick, 108 Duncan Dr., Troy, MI 48098-4613.

— *** Michigan Stamp Club, (0047-004753), 7 p.m., 2nd & 4th Mon., Prince of Peace Lutheran Church, 19100 Ford Road. CONTACT: Robert F. Rinke, 31890 Hoover Road, Warren, MI 48093-1786.

— Collectors Club of Michigan, (0883-074901), 7:30 p.m., 1st Mon., Oak Park Community Center, 13500 Oak Park Dr. CONTACT: Gerald Berks, 138 Pointe West Dr., Amherstburg, ON N9V 3N9, Canada.

EAST LANSING: * Lansing Area Stamp Club, (0780-062751), 7 p.m., 2nd & 4th Thurs., East Lansing Rec. Center, 201 Hillside Ct. CONTACT: John N. Nelson, P.O. Box 20242, Lansing, MI 48901-8242.

FERDALE: Ferndale Stamp Club, (1175-117291), 7:30 p.m., 1st & 3rd Tues., Ferndale FOP Hall, 2905 Hilton Road. CONTACT: Robert K. Helbig, 21624 Jacksonville St. Farmington Hills, MI, 48336-5730.

FLINT: * Vehicle City Stamp Club—(Formerly Greater Flint Stamp Club,) (0660-051908), 6:30 p.m., 1st Wed., GMI-Campus Center, 5th Fl. CONTACT: Roger Larman, 132 First St., Mt. Morris, MI 48458.

GRAND RAPIDS: * Kent Philatelic Society, (0476-040322), 7 p.m., 2nd & 4th Wed., Forest Hills Senior Center, 660 Forest Hills, S.E. CONTACT: Reeves Simms, P.O. Box 1156, Grand Rapids, MI 49501-1156.

IRON MOUNTAIN: Northwoods Philatelic Society, (1477-176162), 7 p.m., 3rd Tues., First Lutheran Church, 1210 S. Stephenson Ave. CONTACT: James D. Stearns, W8071 Old Carney Lake Road, Iron Mountain, MI 49801.

KALAMAZOO: Kalamazoo Stamp Club, (1247-127323), 6:30 p.m., 4th Tues., Fidelity

Fed. Bank, Maple Hill Br., W. Main & Drake Rd. CONTACT: George E. McKay, Jr., 170 Frances Dr., Battle Creek, MI 49015.

MONROE: Floral City Stamp Club, (0899-077113), 7:30 p.m., 2nd Mon., Monroe Bank & Trust, Comm. Rm. CONTACT: Howard V. Thoma, 720 Jerome St., Monroe, MI 48161.

MOUNT PLEASANT: Mid Michigan Stamp Club, (1474-175687), 7–9 p.m., 4th Tues., Veteran Memorial Library, 301 S. University. CONTACT: Tom Culver, 2880 Fitch Dr., Mount Pleasant, MI 48858.

OAK PARK: Oak Park Stamp Club of Michigan, (1039-097002), 7:30 p.m., 2nd Tues., Oak Park Community Center, 14300 Oak Park Blvd. CONTACT: Irvin Girer, 27436 Aberdeen, Southfield, MI 48076.

PLYMOUTH: * West Suburban Stamp Club, (0783-062965), 7:30 p.m., 1st & 3rd Fri., Plymouth Cultural Center, 525 Farmer. CONTACT: Paul Stanton, P.O. Box 700049, Plymouth, MI 48170. E-MAIL CONTACT: Joe Picard (PICARDJ@aa.wl.com)

PONTIAC: * Pontiac Stamp Club, (0666-052141), 7 p.m., 2nd & 4th Tues., Don Tatro Instruction, Materials Center. CONTACT: John E. Kibble, 3817 Long Meadow Lane, Orion, MI 48359.

SAGINAW: ** Saginaw Valley Stamp Society, (0322-029149), 7:30 p.m., 1st & 3rd Wed., except July & Aug., Chemical Bank, Community Rm., Weiss & M-47. CONTACT: Richard G. Ebach, 2265 Linda Ave., Saginaw, MI 48603.

ST. JOSEPH: Southwestern Michigan Stamp Club, (1249-127800), 7 p.m., 3rd Wed., St. Luke's Lutheran Church, 5020 Cleveland Ave. CONTACT: William Kintup, 2612 Pixley Ave., St. Joseph, MI 49085.

TRAVERSE CITY: * Grand Traverse Stamp Club, (0441-038146), inactive. CONTACT: Richard E. Bond, P.O. Box 224, Traverse City, MI 49685.

MINNESOTA

DULUTH: * Arrowhead Stamp Club, (0502-042017), 7:30 p.m., 2nd & 4th Mon., Duluth Rainbow Senior Center, 211 N. 3rd Ave., E. CONTACT: Howard Pramann, 2137 Appalachian St., Duluth, MN 55811.

EXCELSIOR: Lake Minnetonka Stamp Club, (1222-123773), 7 p.m., 2nd Tues., Excelsior Elementary School, Highways 7 & 19. CONTACT: Rossmer V. Olson, P.O. Box 23377, Richfield, MN 55423.

FAIRMONT: Fairmont Area Stamp Club, (1476-176006), 7 p.m., 4th Mon., Martin County Library, 110 N. Park. CONTACT: Roger Welchlin, 415 Woodland, Fairmont, MN 56031.

MAPLEWOOD: * Maplewood Stamp Club, (0681-054001), 7 p.m., 1st Mon., except holidays-2nd Mon., American Bank-Community Rm., 2965 White Bear Ave. CONTACT: Bryan J. McGinnis, P.O. Box 9073, North St. Paul, MN 55109.

MARSHALL: Lyon County

Philatelic Society, (1210-122930), 7 p.m., 3rd Mon., except June, July & Aug., Marshall Middle School, Cafeteria, 207 N. 4th St. CONTACT: Steve Klein, 401 Charles Ave., Marshall, MN 56258.

MINNEAPOLIS: Minnehaha Stamp Club, (0861-071936), 7 p.m., 2nd Thurs., except July & Aug., Pearl Park Rec. Center, 414 E. Diamond Lake Road. CONTACT: Frederick E. Dickinson, 1701 James Pl., Burnsville, MN 55337.

— ** Twin City Philatelic Society, (0097-011353), 7:30 p.m., 1st & 3rd Thurs., except June, July & Aug., 1st-Bryant Ave. Park, Minneapolis, 3rd-Christ Lutheran Church, St Paul. CONTACT: Gladys M. Henslin, 26 E. Exchange St., Ste. 400, St. Paul, MN 55101.

MOORHEAD: Fargo Moorhead Philatelic Society, (0819-067286), 6:30 p.m., 2nd & 4th Thurs., June/July/Aug. & Dec. 2nd Thurs., Lake Agassiz Regional Library, KL Room. CONTACT: James Olsen, 7511 Ellis Lane, Horace, ND 58047-9535.

ROCHESTER: Rochester Stamp & Coin Club, (0889-076250), 7:30 p.m., Last Wed., except Dec., Denny's Restaurant, 1226 S. Broadway. CONTACT: Jerry Swanson, P.O. Box 565, Rochester, MN 55903.

ST. CLOUD: St. Cloud Area Stamp Club, (1336-144703), 7:30 p.m. 1st & 3rd Wed., St. Cloud/Great River. Reg., Library Bldg. CONTACT: Robert W.

Becker, 320 3rd Ave., S., St. Cloud, MN 56301.

ST. LOUIS PARK: Minnesota Israel Philatelic Society, American Topical Association, (1260-128886), 2:30 p.m., 3rd Sun., except June, July & Aug., St. Louis Park-Nov.-Dec.-Jan.-Apr.; St. Paul-Sept.-Oct.-Mar.-May. CONTACT: Wayne Hassell, 1765 Juno Ave., St. Paul, MN 55116.

ST. PAUL: ** Twin City Philatelic Society, (0097-011353), 7:30 p.m., 1st & 3rd Thurs., except June, July & Aug., 1st-Bryant Ave. Park, Minneapolis, 3rd-Christ Lutheran Church, St. Paul. CONTACT: Gladys M. Henslin, 26 E. Exchange St., Ste. 400, St. Paul, MN 55101.

VERGAS: Lake Area Stamp Society, (1445-169652), 7 p.m., 1st & 3rd Tues., Dec. 1st Tues. only, Vergas Bank, Main St. CONTACT: Ella R. Sauer, R 1, Box 501, Dent, MN 56528.

WILLMAR: West Central Minnesota Stamp Club, (1171-116382), 7:30 p.m., 2nd Thurs. & 4th Tues., except June, July & Aug., Willmar Jr. High. CONTACT: Elmond Ekblad, 501 13th Ave., S.W., Willmar, MN 56201.

MISSISSIPPI

BAY ST. LOUIS: Rotten Bayou Stamp Club, (1319-140422), 11:30 a.m., 1st & 3rd Wed., Conference Room, Bldg. 1003, Stennis Space Center. CONTACT: Van O. Light, 1321 Evangeline Dr., Picayune, MS 39466.

BILOXI: Gulf Coast Stamp Club, (0932-082330), 7:30 p.m.,

1st Sat., except Sept., Knights of Columbus Hall, 717 Water St. CONTACT: John Brauchle, 258 Porter Ave., Biloxi, MS 39530-2914.

HATTIESBURG: Hattiesburg Philatelic Society, (1084-103419), 7 p.m., 4th Fri., Unifirst Bank for Savings, University Mall. CONTACT: Alan E. Gould, 38 University Pl., Hattiesburg, MS 39402.

JACKSON: * Jackson Philatelic Society, (0631-049526), 7:30 p.m., 2nd Fri., MP & L Auditorium. CONTACT: Donald Garrett, P.O. Box 12369, Jackson, MS 39236.

MISSOURI

CHESTERFIELD: Greater St. Louis Stamp Club, (1011-094278), 8 p.m., 4th Mon., Parkway Central High School, 369 N. Woods Mill Road. CONTACT: Gary Hendren, 12737 Glenage Dr., Maryland Heights, MO 63043.

COLUMBIA: * Columbia Philatelic Society, (0763-060765), 7 p.m., 4th Tues., Columbia Public Library, 100 W. Broadway. CONTACT: Terry W. Edwards, 3611 Berrywood Dr., Columbia, MO 65201.

FULTON: * Kingdom Philatelic Association, (0702-055181), 7:30 p.m., 3rd Thurs., except July & Aug., Methodist Church, Educational Bldg., 719 Court St. CONTACT: Albert E. White, 8175 Country Road 403, Fulton, MO 65251.

GLADSTONE: Gladstone Philatelic Club, (1351-147410), 7 p.m., 2nd Thurs., Gladstone Community Bldg., 69th & N. Holmes. CONTACT: Howard Buhl III, 002 Frank St., Edgerton, MO 64444.

JOPLIN: Joplin Stamp Club, (1399-156219), 7 p.m., 1st & 3rd Tues., Southwest Missouri Bank, 32nd & Indiana. CONTACT: James P. Latimer, 305 Crestwood Dr., Webb City, MO 64870.

KANSAS CITY: **** Midwest Philatelic Society, (0010-000826), 1:30 p.m., 1st Sat., Plaza Library, 4801 Main St. CONTACT: Ted Hetzler, 1304 Morningside Dr., Blue Springs, MO 64015.

— Collectors Club of Kansas City, (0839-069391), 7 p.m., 2nd Wed., Interstate Savings Bldg., 8000 State Line. CONTACT: Randy L. Neil, P.O. Box 7088, Shawnee Mission, KS 66207.

SPRINGFIELD: Ozark Mountain Stamp Club, (1207-122462), 7 p.m., 3rd Thurs., except Dec., 39 Boonville. CONTACT: David H. Jones, 939 Boonville, Springfield, MO 65802.

ST. JOSEPH: * St. Joseph Stamp Collectors Club, (0627-049410), 1 p.m., 3rd Sat., Senior Citizens Bldg., 10th & Edmond. CONTACT: Opal O. Nussbaum, 1416 Pacific, St. Joseph, MO 64503.

ST. LOUIS: **** St. Louis Branch No. 4, (0004-000460), 1 p.m., 3rd Sat., except July & Aug., members' homes. CONTACT: David O. Semsrott, 2615 Briar Valley Ct., Des Peres, MO 63122.

— * Mound City Stamp Club, (0334-029614), 7:30 p.m., 1st &

3rd Mon., Olivette Community Center, 9723 Grandview Dr. CONTACT: Michael Rybalka, 708 Radcliffe, St. Louis, MO 63130.

WARRENSBURG: Warrensburg Stamp Club, (1415-161197), 7 p.m., Methodist Church, 141 E. Gay St. CONTACT: Peter L. Viscusi, 328 Jones Ave., Warrensburg, MO 64093.

WEBSTER GROVES: Webster Groves Stamp Club, (1475-175688), 8 p.m., 1st & 3rd Fri., Congregational Church, 10 W. Lockwood. CONTACT: Hans Stoltz, 34 N. Gore, St. Louis, MO 63119.

MONTANA

BILLINGS: Billings Stamp Club, (1346-146241), 7:30 p.m, 1st Tues., 360 N. 23rd St. CONTACT: David L. Servies, 3115 Zinnia Dr., Billings, MT 59102.

GREAT FALLS: Great Falls Stamp Club, (1287-133893), 7 p.m., Last Mon., 1021 Central Ave. CONTACT: Shirley Turner, 1625 3rd Ave., S., Great Falls, MT 59405.

KALISPELL: Glacier Stamp Club, (1265-129845), 7:30 p.m., 1st Mon., Flathead County Library. CONTACT: Richard B. Hunt, P.O. Box 126, West Glacier, MT 59936-0126.

MISSOULA: * Garden City Stamp Club, (0594-047026), 8 p.m., 1st Tues. & 3rd Thurs., except Aug., Montana Power Co., 1903 Russell. CONTACT: James Hirstein, 415 Crestline Dr., Missoula, MT 59803.

NEBRASKA

GRAND ISLAND: Central Nebraska Stamp Club, (1058-098569), 2 p.m., 2nd Sun., except May, June & July, Golden Towers, 910 N. Boggs Ave. CONTACT: Doris Sundermeier, P.O. Box 248, Cairo, NE 68824.

LINCOLN: * Lincoln Stamp Club, (0799-064882), 7:30 p.m., 2nd & 4th Thurs., Gere Library, 56th & Normal. CONTACT: Kenneth Pruess, 1441 Urbana Lane, Lincoln, NE 68505.

NORFOLK: Northeast Nebraska Philatelic Society, (1451-172097), 3rd Sun., except Dec., Norfolk Public Library, 4th & Prospect. CONTACT: Jane M. Juhlin, 103 Applewood Dr., Norfolk, NE 68701.

NORTH PLATTE: Buffalo Bill Stamp Club, (1195-120809), 2 p.m., 2nd Sun., Sun.-Blue Flame Rm. 215, E 5. CONTACT: Kirk Nichols, 721 Sioux Lane, North Platte, NE 69101.

OMAHA: Omaha Philatelic Society, (1122-108144), 7:30 p.m., 2nd & 4th Fri., Pacific Hills Lutheran Church, 90th & Pacific Sts. CONTACT: R.L. McConnell, Apt. 421, 2235 St. Mary's Ave., Omaha, NE 68102.

— West Omaha Stamp Club, (1278-132256), 7 p.m., 3rd Wed., 209 S. 72nd St. CONTACT: M.A. Eveland, 209 S. 72nd St., Omaha, NE 68114.

NEVADA

LAS VEGAS: Southern Nevada Stamp Club, (0816-067283), 8 p.m., 1st & 3rd Fri., except

Dec., University of Nevada Las Vegas, Beam Hall, Rm. 112. CONTACT: Betty Mauck, 3860 San Francisco Ave., Las Vegas, NV 89115.

RENO: Nevada Stamp Study Society, (0970-088229), 2 p.m., 2nd & 4th Sat., University of Nevada, Physics Building, Room 203. CONTACT: Ruthe Dreiling, P.O. Box 2907, Sparks, NV 89432-2907.

NEW HAMPSHIRE

BEDFORD: * Manchester Stamp Club, (0805-066114), 7:30 p.m., 4th Mon., Carlisle Place, Rte. 101. CONTACT: Robert A. Dion, P.O. Box 1, North Salem, NH 03073.

CONWAY: White Mountain Stamp Club, (1098-104708), 7:30 p.m., 3rd Mon., secretary's home. CONTACT: Barbara M. Savary, P.O. Box 393, Conway, NH 03818-0393.

DERRY: Greater Derry Philatelic Society, (1329-142958), 7:30 p.m., 3rd Mon., Derry Public Library. CONTACT: Jim Gorton, 150 W. River Road, Hooksett, NH 03106.

DOVER: Great Bay Stamp Club, (1228-124447), 7 p.m., 2nd Tues., Strafford Lodge Bldg., Upper 6th St. CONTACT: Lew Jennison, 28 High Road, Lee, NH 03824-6200.

NASHUA: Nashua Philatelic Society, (0825-067623), 7 p.m., 1st Mon., Chandler Memorial Library. CONTACT: Ralph L. Bauer, P.O. Box 364, Nashua, NH 03061.

NEW JERSEY

NORTHERN NEW JERSEY: * North Jersey Federated Stamp Clubs, (0508-042423), 7:30 p.m., 4th Wed., Bloomfield Civic Center, 84 Broad St. CONTACT: Nathan Zankel, P.O. Box 267, New Brunswick, NJ 08903.

BERGENFIELD: Bergen County Stamp Club, (1112-106164), 8:15 p.m., 3rd Thurs., except July & Aug., Corner Square, 49 W. Church St. CONTACT: Steve Marino, 124 Grove St., Bergenfield, NJ 07621.

CLIFTON: Clifton Stamp Society, (1294-135605), 7 p.m., 1st, 3rd, & 5th Mon., Community Recreation Center, 1232 Main Ave. CONTACT: Brad Arch, 144 Hamilton Ave., Clifton, NJ 07011.

CRANBURY: Clearbrook Stamp Club, (1290-134656), 8 p.m., 1st Thurs., Clearbrook Club House, Applegarth Road. CONTACT: George Corlin, 797B Sparta Road, Cranbury, NJ 08512.

DOVER: * Middle Forge Philatelic Society, (0611-048304), 7:30 p.m., 2nd & 4th Mon., First Memorial Presbyterian Church. CONTACT: Willard H. Hawley, 63 Quaker Church Road, Randolph, NJ 07869.

FAIR LAWN: * Fair Lawn Stamp Club, (0672-052632), 8 p.m., 2nd & 4th Tues., Fair Lawn Arts Center, 12-56 River Road. CONTACT: Michael Demski, 148 Cedar Ave., Hawthorne, NJ 07506.

— * American Helvetia Philatelic Society, New Jersey Chapter, (0739-058507), 8 p.m., 2nd

Tues., except Jan./Feb./ Mar./Jul./Aug./Dec., Fair Lawn Boro Hall, Room 25, Fair Lawn Ave. CONTACT: Frank J. Lawson, III, 35 Hudson Dr., Newburgh, NY 12553.

FREEHOLD: * Molly Pitcher Stamp Club, (0510-042467), 6:30 p.m., 1st & 3rd Wed., Grace Lutheran Church, Rte. 33 & 537. CONTACT: Raymond J. Rossi, 2811 Constitution Way, Wall, NJ 07719.

HAMILTON TOWNSHIP: Hamilton Township Philatelic Society, (1095-104282), 7:30 p.m., 3rd Tues., except July & Aug., Hamilton Township Library, Whitehouse Mercerville Road. CONTACT: Sherman R. Britton, Jr., 476 S. Olden Ave., Trenton, NJ 08629.

HAZLET: Hazlet Stamp Club, (0912-080082), 8 p.m., 2nd & 4th Tues., July & Aug. 4th Tues. only, James Cullen Rec. Center, 1776 Union Ave. CONTACT: Charles M. Rosario, Sr., 11 W. Susan St., Hazlet, NJ 07730.

LAMBERTVILLE: * Coryell's Ferry Stamp Club, (0807-066369), 8 p.m., 1st & 3rd Mon., July-Sept. 3rd Mon. only, 1st Mon-Lambertville, 3rd Mon-Washington Crossing. CONTACT: Bertha Davis, P.O. Box 52, Penns Park, PA 18943.

MONTCLAIR: * West Essex Philatelic Society, (0440-038021), 6 p.m., 2nd & 4th Mon., Montclair Public Library, 50 S. Fullerton Ave. CONTACT: Ronald Gollhardt, P.O. Box 110104, Nutley, NJ 07110.

MORGANTOWN: Foothills Stamp Club (184867), 2nd Thur.

Morgantown Recreation Center, Collett St. Morgantown, CONTACT: Phillip T. Howerton, 201 E. Parker Rd., Morgantown, NC 28655.

MORRISTOWN: Jockey Hollow Stamp Club, (0867-072806), 8 p.m., 1st & 3rd Mon., July-Sept. 3rd Mon. only, Morristown Memorial Hospital, 95 Mt. Kemble Ave. (Rt. 202 S). CONTACT: Julius F. Revesz, 7 Mendham Ave., Morristown, NJ 07960.

NEWTON: * Sussex County Stamp Club, (0778-062339), 7:30 p.m., 2nd Wed., except July & Aug., various locations. CONTACT: Joyce Storms, 25 Prospect St., Branchville, NJ 07826.

PENNSAUKEN: Merchantville Stamp Club, (0817-067284), 8:30 p.m., 1st Thurs. & 3rd Wed., Temple Lutheran Church, R 130 & Merchantville Ave. CONTACT: Paul Schumacher, P.O. Box 2913, Cherry Hill, NJ 08034.

PHILLIPSBURG: Bi-State Stamp Club, (1076-102413), 7 p.m., 4th Tues., Chemical Bank of New Jersey, 411 Roseberry St. CONTACT: Lloyd E. Foss, 474 Route 173, Stewartsville, NJ 08886.

RIDGEWOOD: * North Jersey Stamp Club, (0776-062337), 8 p.m., 2nd & 4th Wed., except July & Aug., Bethlehem Lutheran Church, 155 Linwood Ave. CONTACT: Ronald P. Morgan, 42 DeBaun Ave., Ramsey, NJ 07446.

TEANECK: Association of Bergen County Philatelists, (0903-077911), 8 p.m., 1st Wed., except July and Aug., Teaneck Community House, Teaneck Road & Forest Ave. CONTACT: Kathy Jucker, P.O. Box 37, River Edge, NJ 07661.

TOMS RIVER: Ocean County Stamp Club, (0918-080518), 7:30 p.m., 1st & 3rd Wed., Presbyterian Church, R 549, Hooper Ave. & Chestnut St. CONTACT: John Karch, 4 Ronda Road, Toms River, NJ 08755.

WARREN: Queen City-Warren Stamp & Cover Club, (1198-120812), 7:30 p.m., 1st & 3rd Mon., Natwest New Jersey Bank, 59 Mountain Blvd. CONTACT: Jean Balinky, P.O. Box 4503, Warren, NJ 07059.

WESTFIELD: * Westfield Stamp Club, (0540-043965), 8 p.m., 4th Thurs., Westfield Municipal Bldg., 425 E. Broad St. CONTACT: Henry Laessig, 117 Pearl St., Westfield, NJ 07090.

WESTWOOD: * Pascack Stamp Club, (0472-039650), 8 p.m., 2nd & 4th Mon., Westwood Public Library, 49 Park Ave. CONTACT: Donald Dietel, P.O. Box 52, Emerson, NJ 07630.

NEW MEXICO

NEW MEXICO: * New Mexico Philatelic Association, (0446-038436), semi-annually, various cities. CONTACT: Paul Tyler, 1023 Rocky Point Ct., N.E., Albuquerque, NM 87123.

ALAMOGORDO: Rocket City Stamp Club, (1449-171911), 6:30 p.m., 2nd Mon., Alamogordo Public Library, 10th & Oregon. CONTACT: Frank Kovacich, 402 Sunrise Ave., Alamogordo, NM 88310-4141.

ALBUQUERQUE: * Albuquerque Philatelic Society, (0250-024690), 7 p.m., 2nd & 4th Thurs., except Nov. & Dec. 4th Thurs., Redeemer Lutheran Church, 210 Alvarado, S.E. CONTACT: James J. Kaiser, 7102 Menaul Blvd., N.E., Albuquerque, NM 87110.

— Palo Duro Philatelic Society, (1318–140421), 12:30 p.m., Mon., except Holidays, Palo Duro Senior Center, 5221 Palo Duro Ave., N.E. CONTACT: Dora L. Sylvester, 2013 White Cloud, N.E., Albuquerque, NM 87112.

LAS CRUCES: Mesilla Valley Stamp Club, (1157-114549), 7:30 p.m., 1st & 3rd Thurs., except Aug., Branigan Library, 200 E. Picacho. CONTACT: Irwin Smith, 1604 Ralph Dr., Las Cruces, NM 88001.

LOS ALAMOS: * Los Alamos Stamp Collectors Association, (0298-027929), 7 p.m., 2nd & 4th Tues., Mesa Public Library, 2400 Central Ave. CONTACT: Eva Lee M. Wentworth, 2161-B 36th St., Los Alamos, NM 87544.

SANTA FE: * Santa Fe Stamp Club, (0481-040587), 7:15 p.m., 3rd Wed., except Dec., LaFarge Branch Library, 1730 Llano St., CONTACT: Harold Baxter, 1204 Seville Road, Santa Fe, NM 87501.

NEW YORK

CENTRAL NEW YORK: ** Federation of Central New York Philatelic Societies, (0191-016560), Bi-annually. CON-

TACT: William J. Apel, 22 Oriskany Blvd., Yorkville Plaza, Yorkville, NY 13495.

ALBANY: ** Fort Orange Stamp Club, (0138-013745), 7 p.m., 2nd & 4th Tues., except June, July & Aug., First Lutheran Church, 646 State St. CONTACT: Jack Haefeli, 57 S. Manning Blvd., Albany, NY 12203-1719.

BATAVIA: * Batavia-Genesee County Coin & Stamp Club, (0698-055177), 7:30 p.m., 3rd Thurs., Batavia YMCA, 209 E. Main St. CONTACT: Dennis A. Kane, 268 Ross St., Batavia, NY 14020-1642.

BINGHAMTON: * Johnson City Stamp Club, (0359-031785), 7:30 p.m., 1st & 3rd Mon., Grand Blvd. Methodist Church, Grand Blvd. & Floral Ave. CONTACT: John H. Fiske, 20 McNamara Ave., Binghamton, NY 13903.

BROOKLYN: St. Matthew Emanuel Stamp Club, (1385-153403), 7:30 p.m., 1st & 3rd Wed., 444 Neptune Ave. CONTACT: Rita J. Immerman, 160 Nevins St., Brooklyn, NY 11217.

BUFFALO: *** Buffalo Stamp Club, (0037-003691), 8 p.m., 2nd & 4th Fri., except June, July & Aug., Ramada Inn Buffalo Airport, 6643 Transit Road. CONTACT: William Kleinfelder, 18 Ebling Ave., Tonawanda, NY 14150.

CARMEL: Putnam Philatelic Society, (1061-099576), 7:30 p.m., 1st & 3rd Fri., Guideposts Assoc. Auditorium, Seminary Hill Road. CONTACT: Drew A. Nicholson, 18 Valley Dr., Pawling, NY 12564.

CHEEKTOWAGA: Cheektowaga Stamp & Coin Society, (1167-116378), 8 p.m., 2nd & 4th Mon., except July & Aug., Cheektowaga Rec. Center, Rm. A, across from St. Joe's Hospital. CONTACT: Thomas K. Butts, 97 Fairhaven Dr., Cheektowaga, NY 14225.

COOPERSTOWN: Leatherstocking Stamp Club, (1334-144415), 8 p.m., 2nd Tues., George Tillapaugh Home, 28 Pioneer St. CONTACT: Albert Keck, 3 Delaware St., Cooperstown, NY 13326-1209.

DANSVILLE: Dansville Area Coin & Stamp Club, (1196-120810), 2 p.m., 3rd Sun., Dansville Town Hall, 14 Clara Barton St. CONTACT: Robert Stickney, P.O. Box 574, Dansville, NY 14437.

DEPEW: * Plewacki Stamp Society, (0609-048166), 8 p.m., 2nd & 4th Wed., F.O.E. #2962, 4569 Broadway. CONTACT: Matt A. Gajewski, P.O. Box 2531, Buffalo, NY 14240-2531.

DUNKIRK: Northern Chautauqua Philatelic Society, (0857-071590), Inactive. CONTACT: Richard Long, 419 Robin St., Dunkirk, NY 14048.

ELMIRA: * Elmira Stamp Club, (0237-024110), 8 p.m., 3rd Tues., Binghamton Savings Bank, Comm. Room, 351 N. Main St. CONTACT: Alan Parsons, 809 Holley Road, Elmira, NY 14905.

FULTON: Fulton Stamp Club, (1193-120322), 6:30 p.m., 2nd Wed., except July & Aug., Fulton Public Library, 13069 S. First St.

CONTACT: John A. Cali, P.O. Box 401, Fulton, NY 13069.

FULTON: Federation of Central New York Philatelic Societies, (APS# 016560), Biannual meetings at various hotel meeting rooms in greater Utica area. CONTACT: John A. Cali, P.O. Box 401, Fulton, NY 13069.

GENEVA: * Finger Lakes Stamp Club, (0428-037260), 8 p.m., 2nd & 4th Wed., except July & Aug., Sawdust Cafe. CONTACT: Bob LaBelle, 3520 Lamoka Lake Road, Bradford NY 14815

GREAT NECK: Sperry Stamp Club, (1165-115945), 12 Noon, 1st Thurs.-Business, 3rd Thurs.-Trading, Sperry Corp., Marcus Ave., Lake Success. CONTACT: Michael L. Currie, Paramax Systems Corp., 365 Lakeville Road, Great Neck, NY 11020-1696.

HAMILTON: * Chenango Valley Stamp Club, (0781-062616), 7:45 p.m., 1st Mon., except July & Aug., Room 110, Huntington Gym, Colgate University. CONTACT: Braden Houston, R 2, Box 78C, Hamilton, NY 13346.

HORNELL: Steuben Stamp Club, (1357-148254), 7:30 p.m., 2nd Mon., DeSales Hall, 440 Monroe Ave. CONTACT: Arthur Gaisser, 39 Sayles St., Alfred, NY 14802.

HOUGTON: Allegany Stamp Club, (1130-110584), 8 p.m., 1st Thurs., Houghton Academy. CONTACT: William L. Howden, 7 Colonial Village, Allegany, NY 14706.

ITHACA: ** Ithaca Philatelic Society, (0210-019654), 7:30 p.m.,

Wed., Cornell University, 348 Morrison Hall. CONTACT: Yoram B. Szekely, 104 Kline Woods Road, Ithaca, NY 14850.

JAMESTOWN: * Reuben E. Fenton Philatelic Society, (0705-055184), 7:30 p.m., last Tues., Brooklyn Heights Methodist Church, 120 Delaware Ave. CONTACT: Leslie Davis, P.O. Box 266, Bemus Point, NY 14712.

KINGSTON: * Stamptrotters Society of Kingston, (0559-044549), 7:30 p.m., 2nd & 4th Thurs., except July & Aug., Chambers Elementary School, Albany Ave. CONTACT: Philip Bruno, 4 Willow Dr., Red Hook, NY 12571.

LOCKPORT: Lockport Coin and Stamp Club, (1163-115943), 7 p.m., 2nd & 4th Tues., Emanuel Methodist Church, 75 East Ave. CONTACT: Burwyn L. Schweigert, 6104 Corwin Ave., Newfane, NY 14108-1119.

MASSENA: St. Lawrence International Stamp Club, (0847-070417), 7 p.m., 1st Thurs. & 3rd Tues., except July & Aug., Warren Public Library, Second St., E. CONTACT: Robert Patten, 707 Ferris Road, Nicholville, NY 12965-9705.

MONTICELLO: Sullivan County Philatelic Society, (0920-080520), 7:30 p.m., 1st Sun., Temple Sholom, East Dillion Road. CONTACT: Arthur Rosenzweig, P.O. Box 230, Monticello, NY 12701.

NEW HARTFORD: ** Utica Stamp Club, (0066-008021), 7 p.m., 1st Tues., except July & Aug., Zion Lutheran Church, 630 French Road. CONTACT:

Janet E. Collmer, P.O. Box 85, Franklin Springs, NY 13341.

NEW YORK: International Stamp Club (1355-148252), 12 noon–4 p.m., varies (Sunday), Soldiers', Sailors' & Airmen's Club, Inc., 283 Lexington Ave. CONTACT: Ruth Gazes, 75 Henry St., Apt. 6D, Brooklyn, NY 11201.

— American Topical Association, New York Chapter, (1383-153401), 7:15 p.m., 2nd Thurs., Collectors Club, 22 E. 35th St. CONTACT: Harlan Hamilton, 170 E. 83rd St., Apt 3L, New York, NY 10028-1923.

NEWBURGH: * Newburgh Stamp Club, (0704-055183), 7:30 p.m., 4th Mon., except May & Dec. 3rd Mon., 1st Baptist Church, South & West Sts. CONTACT: William T. McCaw, 368 Grand St., Newburgh, NY 12550-3612.

OLEAN: Olean Stamp Club, (1442-168335), 7:30 p.m., 1st Mon., St. Stephens Episcopal Church, 109 S. Barry St. CONTACT: Leslie Crane, R 1, Box 832, Shinglehouse, PA 16748.

OSWEGO: * Oswego Stamp Club, (0728-057786), 7 p.m., 4th Mon., except June, July & Aug., Oswego Post Office, 391 W. First St. CONTACT: Charles Sweeting, 63 Ridgeway Sites Ave., Oswego, NY 13126-6506.

PLATTSBURGH: Plattsburgh Stamp Club, (1248-127324), 7:30 p.m., 4th Mon., except May & Dec., Clinton County Govt. Center, Margaret St. CONTACT: Glenn Estus, P.O. Box 451, Westport, NY 12993.

POUGHKEEPSIE: * Dutchess Philatelic Society, (0480-040579), 7:30 p.m., 2nd & 3rd Tues., except July & Aug., Friends Meeting Hall, Corner Hooker Ave. & Whittier Blvd. CONTACT: Rudy Schaelchli, P.O. Box 515, Millerton, NY 12546.

RIVERHEAD: Riverhead Stamp Club, (1341-145424), 2nd & Last Thurs., Riverhead Free Library, 330 Court St. CONTACT: Ted Fredericks, c/o Riverhead Free Library, 330 Court St., Riverhead, NY 11901.

ROCHESTER: ** Rochester Philatelic Association, (0207-019273), 8 p.m., 2nd & 4th Thurs., Nov. & Dec. 2nd Thurs. only, St. Paul's Episcopal Church Hall, East Ave. & Vick Park B. CONTACT: Norman E. Wright, Sr., 33 Northumberland Road, Rochester, NY 14618.

— * Kodak Stamp Club, (0655-051448), 7:30 p.m., 4th Tues., B-28, Room 151 A & B, Kodak Park, 1699 Lake Ave. CONTACT: Joseph K. Doles, 34 Carlisle St., Rochester, NY 14615.

ROME: Fort Stanwix Stamp Club, (1227-124446), 7:30 p.m., 2nd & 4th Thurs., except June, July & Aug., Rome City Hall, 2nd Floor, 100 Block of W. Liberty St. CONTACT: Phillip W. Brown, 400 Mayberry Rd., Rome, NY 13440-5510

ROSLYN: * North Shore Philatelic Society, (0607-048152), 8 p.m., 1st & 3rd Wed., Bryant Library. CONTACT: Adolph H. Stephani, 4 Ann St., Glen Cove, NY 11542.

SCHENECTADY: ** Schenectady Stamp Club, (0153-014474),

7:30 p.m., 1st & 3rd Mon., except July & Aug., Union Presbyterian Church, 1068 Park Ave. CONTACT: Stephen E. Gray, Apt. C-1, 10 Hillcrest Village W., Schenectady, NY 12309.

SHERRILL: Community Stamp Club, (1100-104710), 7:30 p.m., 3rd Thurs., except June, July & Aug., CAC Clubhouse, 139 E. Hamilton Ave. CONTACT: Don P. Connelly, R 1, Box 461, 68 Glenwood Ave., Oneida, NY 13421–2717.

SHRUB OAK: Shrub Oak Stamp Club, (1388-154423), 7:30 p.m., 1st & 3rd Mon., United Methodist Church. CONTACT: Alfred F. Schaum, P.O. Box 616, Shrub Oak, NY 10588.

SIDNEY: * Tri-County Stamp Club, (0292-027733), 7 p.m., 3rd Mon., except July & Aug., Sidney Civic Center. CONTACT: Robert Finnegan, 27 Pearl St. E., Sidney, NY 13838.

SODUS: Sodus Stamp Club, (1077-102414), 7:30, 3rd Wed., Methodist Church, Basement. CONTACT: Paul R. Spiers, 54 Orchard Terr., Sodus, NY 14551.

SPENCERPORT: * Western Monroe Philatelic Society, (0560-044599), 7:30 p.m., 3rd Mon., except July & Aug., Ogden Baptist Church, 721 Washington St. CONTACT: Mary W. Gerew, 3401 Brockport-Spencerport Road, Spencerport, NY 14559.

STATEN ISLAND: Staten Island Philatelic Society, (0814-066935), 8 p.m., 1st & 3rd Wed., except July & Aug., Rev. Paul Kroon Center, 199 Jefferson Blvd.

CONTACT: Charles R. Carlson, 30 Hopping Ave., Staten Island, NY 10307-1219.

SYRACUSE: *** Syracuse Stamp Club, (0050-005911), 8 p.m., 1st & 3rd Fri., Reformed Church of Syracuse, 1228 Teall Ave. CONTACT: Michael Ammann, 217 Inwood Dr., Syracuse, NY 13219.

TROY: * Uncle Sam Stamp Club of Troy, (0240-024176), 7:30 p.m., 2nd & 4th Wed., Holmes & Watson, Ltd., 450 Broadway, 2nd Fl. CONTACT: Arnold A. Leiter, 811 2nd Ave., Troy, NY 12182.

WATERTOWN: * Jefferson County Stamp Club, (0579-045718), 7:30 p.m., 1st & 3rd Tues., U.S. Postal Facility, Training Room, Commerce Dr. CONTACT: Gerald F. Wiley, 921 Mill St., Watertown, NY 13601.

NORTH CAROLINA

NORTH CAROLINA: Carolinas Chapter 37, Germany Philatelic Society, (1251-128124), Varies (Saturday), 12 Noon, various locations in North & South Carolina. CONTACT: Robert W. Soeder, P.O. Box 15, Todd, NC 28684.

ARDEN: Hendersonville Stamp Club, (0840-069392), 7 p.m., 4th Mon., Nativity Lutheran Church. CONTACT: Edward A. Gibson, 4 Breezy Dr., Fletcher, NC 28732.

ASHEVILLE: * Asheville Stamp Club, (0793-064417), 2 p.m., 3rd Sun., except Dec., Main Post Office Facility, 591 Brevard Road. CONTACT: Steven I.

Goldstein, P.O. Box 8317, Asheville, NC 28814.

CHAPEL HILL: Triangle Stamp Club, (0958-087135), 7:30 p.m., 2nd Mon., Parish House Library, Church of the Holy Family, 200 Hayes Rd. CONTACT: Edward G. Siebert, P.O. Box 16183, Chapel Hill, NC 27516-6183.

CHARLOTTE: ** Fortnightly Collectors Club, (0177-015882), 8 p.m., Every three weeks, members' homes. CONTACT: John Dohmlo, P.O. Box 242053, Charlotte, NC 28224-2053.

— * Charlotte Philatelic Society, (0738-058506), 2 p.m., 1st Sun., Metrolina Association for Blind, 704 Louise Ave. CONTACT: Robert R. Reeves, P.O. Box 30101, Charlotte, NC 28230.

COLUMBUS: Thermal Belt Stamp Club, (1179-117708), 7:30 p.m., 1st & 3rd Mon., Tryon Federal Savings & Loan, Conference Rm., Mills St. CONTACT: Clarke Taube, 108 Laurel Ave., Tryon, NC 28782.

EMERALD ISLE: Emerald Isle Stamp Club, (181643), 7 p.m., 2nd & 4th Thur., Emerald Isle Recreation Center, Leasure Dr. CONTACT: George A. Kuhhorn, P.O. Box 4486, Emerald Isle, NC 28594.

GREENSBORO: Greensboro Stamp Club, (1064-100357), 7:30 p.m., 2nd & 4th Thurs., except Nov. & Dec., Lindley Recreation Center, 2907 Springwood Dr. CONTACT: Danny Beane, 2816 Cyrus Rd., Greensboro, NC 27406.

NEW BERN: Eastern Carolina Stamp & Coin Club, (1374-150942), Inactive. CONTACT: Joe B. Knight, P.O. Box 1338, New Bern, NC 28563.

RALEIGH: * Raleigh Stamp Club, (0538-043937), 7:30 p.m., 1st Mon., Jaycee Center, 2405 Wade Ave. CONTACT: Jack C. Scott, P.O. Box 26863, Raleigh, NC 27611.

WILMINGTON: Wilmington Philatelic Society, (1283-132954), 7 p.m., 1st Tues., UNCW, Room 110. CONTACT: R. E. Vogelin, 2716 Shandy Lane, Wilmington, NC 28409-2041

WINSTON-SALEM: Winston-Salem Stamp Club, (1284-132955), 7:30 p.m., last Tues., Miller Park Recreation Center, 400 Miller Park Circle. CONTACT: Nelson A. L. Weller, 2940 Wesleyan Lane, Winston-Salem, NC 27106.

OHIO

AKRON: *** Rubber City Stamp Club, (0051-005912), 8 p.m., 1st & 3rd Fri., except July & Aug., Montrose-Zion U. M. Church, 565 N. Cleveland-Massillon Road. CONTACT: George C. Mayer, P.O. Box 13572, Akron, OH 44334.

— * Collectors Club of Akron, (0251-024886), 7 p.m., 3rd Tues., Papa Joe's Restaurant. CONTACT: Roger O. Gilruth, P.O. Box 1721, Akron, OH 44309-1721.

ATHENS: Athens Stamp Club, (0862-071937), 7:30 p.m., 2nd Wed., except July & Aug., Community Mental Health Bldg., 8000 Dairy Lane. CONTACT: Marvin Fletcher, 45 Avon Pl., Athens, OH 45701.

CANTON: ** McKinley Stamp Club, (0078-009294), 7:30 p.m., 4th Wed., Sippo Lake Club House, 5300 Tyner Ave., N.W. CONTACT: Dale E. Hart, 1730 Coventry Road, N.E., Massillon, OH 44646-4132.

— * Stark County Stamp Club, (0656-051449), 7:30 p.m., 2nd Wed., Sippo Lake Club House, 5300 Tyner Ave., N.W. CONTACT: Brian Mumford, 1210 31st St., N.W., Canton, OH 44709.

CINCINNATI: *** Greater Cincinnati Philatelic Society, (0046-004752), 7:30 p.m., 2nd Mon. & 4th Wed., except July & Dec., Star Bank, Mon-Clifton/Wed-Roselawn. CONTACT: Steven R. Unkrich, 5886 Cheviot Road, Cincinnati, OH 45247.

CLEVELAND: *** Garfield-Perry Stamp Club, (0030-003208), 8 p.m., Fri., Holiday Inn, 1111 Lakeside Ave. CONTACT: Richard H. Parker, 1526 Marview Dr., Westlake, OH 44145.

— * Cuy-Lor Stamp Club, (0601-047445), 8 p.m., 2nd & 4th Fri., July & Aug. 2nd Fri. only, West Park United Church, 3909 Rocky River Dr. CONTACT: Bernard Cross, Jr., P.O. Box 45042, Westlake, OH 44145.

— Shaker Heights Philatelic Society, (0900-077114), 8:30 p.m., 3rd Mon., except Summer, members' homes. CONTACT: Larry Cohn, 23351 Chagrin Blvd., #403, Beachwood, OH 44122.

COLUMBUS: ** Columbus Philatelic Club, (0195-017071), 7 p.m., 2nd & 4th Mon., Linden Lutheran Church, 1230 Oakland Park Ave. CONTACT: Russell V. Skavaril, 222 E. Torrence Road, Columbus, OH 43214-3834.

— * Nationwide Stamp Club, (0414-036094), Currently inactive, Nationwide Ins. Home Office. CONTACT: Ken Bonvallet, 3-26-08, 1 Nationwide Plaza, Columbus, OH 43216.

CUYAHOGA FALLS: * Cuyahoga Falls Stamp Club, (0562-044664), 7:30 p.m., 1st & 3rd Mon., Cuyahoga Falls Eagles Club, Front St. Mall at Stow St. CONTACT: Henry Lehr, P.O. Box 104, Cuyahoga Falls, OH 44222-0104.

DAYTON: Dayton Stamp Club, (0913-080083), 7:30 p.m. 1st & 3rd Mon. 4, Wegerzyn Garden Center, 1301 E. Siebenthaler Ave. CONTACT: John E. Pappas, 2922 Southfield Dr., Beavercreek, OH 45434.

ELYRIA: * Black River Stamp Club, (0615-048561), 8 p.m., 1st Fri., Elyria Savings Natl. Bank, West Side Office, 1000 Lowell St. CONTACT: James M. Forbes, 6443 Lake Ave., Elyria, OH 44035.

EUCLID: * Euclid Stamp Club, (0657-051450), 8 p.m., 2nd & 4th Mon., Euclid Lutheran Church, Forestview & E. 260th St. CONTACT: Frank Zoretich, P.O. Box 32211, Euclid, OH 44132. Visit their home page.

FINDLAY: * Fort Findlay Stamp Club, (0378-033563), 7:30 p.m., 2nd & 4th Wed., Society Bank, 1920 Tiffin Ave. CONTACT: Tom Foust, 5578 State Rte. 186, McComb, OH 45858.

HAMILTON: Fort Hamilton Philatelic Society, (1362-148908),

7:30 p.m., 2nd Thurs., Hamilton West YMCA. CONTACT: Richard F. Freuler, P.O. Box 224, Hamilton, OH 45012.

KINGSVILLE: Ashtabula County Stamp Club, (1429-165211), 7:30 p.m., 2nd Mon., Kingsville Public Library, Academy St. CONTACT: Douglas J. Gryczan, 1658 S. Denmark Road, Jefferson, OH 44047.

MEDINA: Medina County Stamp Club, (1145-112553), 7:30 p.m., 1st Thurs., Sylvester Library, 210 S. Broadway. CONTACT: Thomas Bieniosek, 8020 Spieth Rd., Litchfield, OH 44253.

MIDDLETOWN: * Miami Valley Stamp Club, (0614-048457), 7 p.m., 4th Thurs., Lebanon Citizens Natl. Bank, 4441 Marie Dr. CONTACT: James P. Bruner, 1813 Galway Circle, Middletown, OH 45042.

MILFORD: Clermont County Stamp Club, (1366-149353), 7 p.m., 3rd Thurs., Mulberry Church of Christ, 5857 Highview Dr. CONTACT: Janet Klug, 6854 Newtonsville Road, Pleasant Plain, OH 45162-9616.

NEW PHILADELPHIA: Tuscora Stamp Club, (1433-166151), 1st & 3rd Wed., Lutheran Church, 202 E. High Ave. CONTACT: Floyd Swinderman, 1113 Sherman Ave., New Philadelphia, OH 44663.

NORWALK: Firelands Stamp Club, (180986). CONTACT: Dr. Richard P. Germann, 6 Vinewood Dr., Norwalk, OH 44897-1919.

PARMA HEIGHTS: * Southwestern Stamp Club, (0706-055185), 7:30 p.m., 2nd & 4th Tues., Parma Heights Library, Pearl & Olde York Roads. CONTACT: Merlin J. Mason, 6392 Stratford Dr., Parma Heights, OH 44130.

POLAND: ** Mahoning Valley Stamp Club, (0072-008537), 6:45 p.m., 2nd & 4th Thurs., American Legion Hall, 35 Cortland St. CONTACT: George C. Riebe, Jr., 3139 Sunnybrook Dr., Youngstown, OH 44511-2823.

SIDNEY: Sidney Stamp Club, (1291-135207), 7 p.m., 3rd Mon., Dorothy Love Center, Conference Room. CONTACT: Susan Minniear, 610 E. Russell Road, Sidney, OH 45365.

STEUBENVILLE: Fort Steuben Stamp Club, (0864-072343), 7:30 p.m., 4th Mon., Jefferson Tech. College, Rm. 2000, 4000 Sunset Blvd. CONTACT: Verna Tarr, R 2, Box 296A, Colliers, WV 26035.

TIFFIN: * Tiffin Stamp Club, (0754-059698), 7:30 p.m., 3rd Thurs., Tiffin Public Library. CONTACT: Virgil Mathias, 30 Gibson Ct., Tiffin, OH 44883.

TOLEDO: ** Stamp Collectors Club of Toledo, (0181-016230), 7:30 p.m., 1st & 3rd Thurs., except June, July & Aug., Wernert's Corner Civic Assn. Hall, 5068 Douglas Road. CONTACT: Jerry Zachman, 7035 Edinburgh, Lambertville, MI 48144-9539.

WARREN: * Warren Area Stamp Club, (0755-059699), 7:30 p.m., 4th Fri., Cortland Bank, Warren Branch, 2935 Elm Road, N.E. CONTACT: Alexander J. Savakis, P.O. Box 609, Warren, OH 44482-0609.

WAVERLY: Pike County Stamp Collectors, (182213), 2nd Mon., Activity Center of Bristol Village, 625 Fifth St. CONTACT: Raymond Overmire, 430 Robin Road, Waverly, OH 45690.

WORTHINGTON: * Worthington Stamp Club, (0667-052142), 7:30 p.m., 1st & 3rd Mon., except July & Aug., Sharon Township Hall, Dublin-Granville Rd. & Morning St. CONTACT: Robert Baldridge, 8590 Dornoch Ct., Dublin, OH 43017.

OKLAHOMA

OKLAHOMA: Oklahoma Philatelic Society, (1308-138176), Varies, Annually. CONTACT: Lavoy Hatchett, P.O. Box 700334, Tulsa, OK 74170.

ENID: Enid Stamp Club, (1321-140751), 7 p.m., 2nd Thurs., Enid-Garfield County Public Library. CONTACT: Sammye Cupp, 118 N. Hoover, Enid, OK 73701.

LAWTON: Lawton-Fort Sill Stamp Club, (1066-100359), 7:30 p.m., 1st & 3rd Tues., Town Hall, 5th & B Sts. CONTACT: Glen Stebelton, 5210 Sherwood, Lawton, OK 73505.

MUSKOGEE: Muskogee Stamp Club, (1141-112101), 7:30 p.m., 1st & 3rd Tues., U.S. Post Office, 525 W. Okmulgee. CONTACT: Gilbert E. Weisser, 450 Palmer Dr., Muskogee, OK 74401.

NORMAN: Norman Stamp Club, (1266-130256), 7:30 p.m., 4th Thurs., Mid Town Plaza, Main St. & Blvd. CONTACT: Robert V. Owens, P.O. Box 1688, Norman, OK 73070.

OKLAHOMA CITY: Oklahoma City Stamp Club, (0841-069393), 7:30 p.m., 1st & 3rd Tues., except July & Aug.-3rd Tues., St. David's Church, Scout Hut, 3333 N. Meridian. CONTACT: Ray Janz, P.O. Box 26542, Oklahoma City, OK 73126.

TULSA: * Tulsa Stamp Club, (0678-053316), 7 p.m., 1st & 3rd Thurs., Southern Hills Baptist Church, 5600 S. Lewis. CONTACT: Lavoy Hatchett, P.O. Box 700334, Tulsa, OK 74170.

OREGON

BANDON: Surf N' Sand Stamp Society, (1381-152210), 8 p.m., 3rd Wed., Ocean Crest School, Teachers Lounge. CONTACT: Louis Prahar, R 1, Box 620, Bandon, OR 97411.

COOS BAY: Coos Stamp Club, (1012-094279), 8 p.m., 3rd Fri., North Bend Medical Center, 1900 Woodland Dr. CONTACT: Charles Lindsay, P.O. Box 341, North Bend, OR 97459-0029.

EUGENE: * Greater Eugene Stamp Society, (0437-037822), 7:30 p.m., 2nd & 4th Wed., 590 Good Pasture Island Road. CONTACT: Gary Schweiger, P.O. Box 734, Eugene, OR 97440.

GRANTS PASS: Rogue Valley Stamp Club, (178924). CONTACT: Richard K. Collins, 176 Teel Lane, Grants Pass, OR 97527.

MEDFORD: * Southern Oregon Philatelic Society, (0526-043418), 7 p.m., 1st Thurs., 1st Presbyterian Church, 8th & Holly. CONTACT: James D. Bryan, 855 Shafer Lane, Medford, OR 97501.

PORTLAND: ** Oregon Stamp Society, (0068-008234), 8 p.m., 2nd & 4th Tues., Clubhouse, 4828 N.E. 33rd Ave. CONTACT: Tom Current, P.O. Box 18165, Portland, OR 97218-0165.

SALEM: Salem Stamp Society, (0736-057920), 7:30 p.m., 2nd Wed., Fire Hall, Cordon Road at State St. CONTACT: Marc Dochez, 17001 Fairview Dr., Dundee, OR 97115.

PENNSYLVANIA

ALLENTOWN: ** Allentown Philatelic Society, (0060-007655), 7 p.m., 1st Tues., Sacred Heart Hospital Conference Center, 4th & Chew Sts. CONTACT: David E. Fisher, 909 N. Penn St., Allentown, PA 18102.

ALTOONA: Blair County Stamp Club, (1378-152207), 2 p.m., 3rd Sun., Subway Stamp Shop, 2121 Beale Ave. CONTACT: Elvin G. Liebegott, 530 W. 14th St., Duncansville, PA 16635.

BRADFORD: Bradford Stamp Club, (1348-146597), 7:30 p.m., 3rd Mon., Northwest Savings & Loan Bank, Main St. CONTACT: John Hallstrom, 209 Minard Run Road, Bradford, PA 16701.

BROOKHAVEN: Brookhaven Stamp Club, (1437-167085), 7:30 p.m., 1st Thurs., Brookhaven Municipal Bldg., Edgemont Ave. & Brookhaven Rd.

CONTACT: John Riper, 3617 Victor Ave., Brookhaven, PA 19015.

CAMP HILL: Susquehanna Valley Stamp/Postcard Club, (1146-112554), 7 p.m., 4th Mon., Camp Hill Shopping Mall, Community Rm., 32nd & Trindle. CONTACT: Edward J. Lukanuski, 3809 Conestoga Rd., Camp Hill, PA 17011.

CHURCHILL: Wilkinsburg Stamp Club, (1214-122934), 2 p.m., 2nd & 4th Sun., Borough Bldg., 2300 Wm. Penn Hwy. CONTACT: Andy Novotny, P.O. Box 8711, Pittsburgh, PA 15221-0711.

EASTON: See New Jersey, Phillipsburg.

ERIE: Erie Stamp Club, (1280-132951), 7 p.m., 2nd & 4th Thurs., except June, July & Aug., First Free Methodist Church, Fellowship Hall. CONTACT: John J. Pfister, 1808 Manchester Road, Erie, PA 16505-2632.

FAYETTEVILLE: Cumberland Valley Philatelic Society, (0829-067627), 6:30 p.m., 4th Wed., Farmer's Bank, 5035 Lincoln Way E. CONTACT: Richard W. Bower, 87 Quarry Road, Chambersburg, PA 17201-8475.

GETTYSBURG: Blue and Gray Stamp Club, (1312-139409), 7:30 p.m., 1st Wed., St. James Lutheran Church, 109 York St. CONTACT: Robert G. Zeigler, 175 Gordon Ave., Gettysburg, PA 17325.

GREENSBURG: * Westmoreland County Philatelic Society, (0649-051054), 2:15 p.m., 2nd

Sun., Greengate Mall, Community Hall, R 30, W. CONTACT: James Vaughn, R 5, Box 549, Mt. Pleasant, PA 15666.

HARRISBURG: * Capital City Philatelic Society, (0321-029127), 7:15 p.m., 1st & 3rd Tues., East Shore Area Library, 4501 Ethel St. CONTACT: Frank J. Schatt, 512 Ellencroft Road, Lewisberry, PA 17339.

HAVERTOWN: * Havertown Stamp Club, (0463-039274), 7:30 p.m., 1st & 3rd Wed., except July & Aug., Union Methodist Church, Brookline Blvd. & Allston Rd. CONTACT: Dr. Stanley R. Sandler, 221 Hemlock Lane, Springfield, PA 19064-1112.

HAZLETON: Hazelton Stamp Club, (1105-105295), 7 p.m., 2nd & 4th Mon., Former Nurses Dorm. across from Hazleton State Hospital. CONTACT: Genie Kutzor, P.O. Box 127, Ebervale, PA 18223-0127.

JOHNSTOWN: * Johnstown Stamp Club, (0318-029033), 8 p.m., 4th Mon., except Sept. & Dec., Seniors Activity Center, 550 Main St., 2nd Fl. Conf. Rm. CONTACT: Jay Hewitt, 443 Corning St., Johnstown, PA 15905-3109.

KING OF PRUSSIA: * Philadelphia National Stamp Exhibition, (0651-051056), 7 p.m., 1st Mon., except July & Aug., Valley Forge Convention Center, 1200 First Ave. CONTACT: Robert Lana, P.O. Box 358, Broomall, PA 19008-0358.

LAFAYETTE HILL: Collectors Club of Philadelphia, (1417-161483), 8 p.m., 1st Tues., Wm. Jeanes Library, 4051 Joshua Road. CONTACT: Chip Blumberg, P.O. Box 176, Lafayette Hill, PA 19444.

LANCASTER: ** Lancaster County Philatelic Society, (0173-015492), 7:30 p.m., 2nd Wed., except Aug., Stauffer Mansion, 1241 Lititz Pike. CONTACT: James G. Boyles, P.O. Box 982, Lancaster, PA 17603.

LEBANON: * Lebanon Stamp Collectors Club, (0703-055182), 7:30 p.m., 2nd Tues., Chamber of Commerce, 250 N. 8th St. CONTACT: Richard A. Colberg, 126 Crosswick Lane, Lancaster, PA 17601.

LOCK HAVEN: Bald Eagle Stamp Society, (1345-146240), 7:30 p.m., 1st Mon., except July & Aug., Yost Community Center, Linden Circle, CONTACT: Ralph L. Harnishfeger, Apt. 5, 73 Cider Press Road, Lock Haven, PA 17745.

LOWER BURRELL: Alle-Kiski Valley Numismatic & Philatelic Society, (1304-137366), 8 p.m., 2nd Thurs., except July & Aug., Grace Community Church, 2751 Grant St. CONTACT: Glen E. Nordmark, 331 Claremont Dr., Lower Burrell, PA 15068.

LYNDORA: Butler County Philatelic Society, (1135-111614), 7 p.m., 1st & 3rd Wed., except July & Aug., Dunbar Community Center, Hansen Ave. & Pillow St. CONTACT: Bro. James Merva, P.O. Box 990, Butler, PA 16003.

MIFFLINTOWN: Juniata River Stamp Club, (184237), 7 p.m., Thurs., St. Jude Catholic Church, Old Route 22. CONTACT: Richard

E. Kepler, R 2, Box 595, McAlisterville, PA 17049.

MONTOURSVILLE: * Williamsport Stamp Club, (0299-027974), 8 p.m., 4th Wed., except July & Aug., Montoursville American Legion, 1312 Broad St. CONTACT: Harold E. Gottshall, 1009 Weldon St., P.O. Box 402, Williamsport, PA 17754-0402.

MORRISVILLE: Summerseat Stamp Collectors, (1358-148255), 7:30 p.m., 4th Wed., Morrisville United Meth. Church, Ed. Bldg., Taft & Maples Ave. CONTACT: Doris G. Burkhardt, 216 Osborne Ave., Morrisville, PA 19067.

PHILADELPHIA: *** Philadelphia Chapter No. 18, (0018-001978), 8 p.m., 3rd Tues., except July & Aug., Phila. College of Textiles, Henry Ave. & School House Lane. CONTACT: Victor B. Krievins, P.O. Box 373, Bryn Mawr, PA 19010.

— * Frankford Arsenal Stamp Club, (0242-024403), members' homes. CONTACT: Michael A. Stefanowicz, 7610 Lexington Ave., Philadelphia, PA 19152-3912.

— * Germantown-Chestnut Hill Stamp Club, (0612-048409), 8 p.m., 1st Tues. & 3rd, Wed., Water Tower Recreation Center, Hartwell Lane & Ardleigh St. CONTACT: Harvey Fleegler, P.O. Box 128, Flourtown, PA 19031.

— Greater Northeast Stamp Club, (1368-149723), 8 p.m., 3rd Thurs., Rhawnhurt Recreation Center, Bustleton & Solly Ave. CONTACT: Samuel B. Rothkoff, 3177 Kensington Ave., Philadelphia, PA 19134.

PHOENIXVILLE: Phoenixville/King of Prussia Stamp Club, (180765). CONTACT: Gus Spector, 750 S. Main St., Suite 203, Phoenixville, PA 19460.

PITTSBURGH: **** Philatelic Society of Pittsburgh, (0005-000457), 7:30 p.m., 1st & 3rd Mon., First Lutheran Church, 615 Grant St. CONTACT: Ronald Carr, 60 Robinhood Dr., Pittsburgh, PA 15220.

POTTSTOWN: Pottstown Area Stamp Club, (1169-116380), 7 p.m., 1st Mon., Leader Nursing & Rehab. Center, Basement. CONTACT: Robert Brown, 192 W. Cedarville Road, Pottstown, PA 19464.

QUAKERTOWN: North Penn Stamp Club, (1206-122461), 7 p.m., 1st Tues., James A. Michener Library, California Road. CONTACT: Wolfgang S. Pohl, 916 W. Broad St., Quakertown, PA 18951.

READING: ** Reading Stamp Collectors Club, (0192-016695), 7:30 p.m., 2nd Tues., GPU Service Corp. Bldg., Bernville Road (Rte. 183). CONTACT: Walter M. Creitz, 830 Berkshire Dr., Reading, PA 19601.

ROYERSFORD: * Spring-Ford Philatelic Society, (0802-065722), 7 p.m., last Thurs., Patriot Savings Bank, 5th & Main St. CONTACT: Anna Wilson, P.O. Box 396, Kimberton, PA 19442.

SCRANTON: * Northeastern Pennsylvania Philatelic Society, (0360-031880), 7:30 p.m., 1st & 3rd Wed., except July & Aug., Covenant Presbyterian Church, Madison & Olive St. CONTACT:

Rev. J. Harry McElroy, P.O. Box 450, Moscow, PA 18444.

STATE COLLEGE: ** Mt. Nittany Philatelic Society, (0199-018536), 7:30 p.m., 1st Wed. & 3rd Thurs., American Philatelic Building, 100 Oakwood Ave. CONTACT: William F. Donovan, 111 Sowers St., Suite 600, State College, PA 16801.

WARMINSTER: * Bux-Mont Stamp Club, (0679-053999), 8 p.m., 2nd & 4th Tues., except Dec., Grace Lutheran Church, W. Street Road. CONTACT: Mike Matusko, P.O. Box 448, Abington, PA 19001.

WARREN: Warren County Stamp Club, (0959-087136), 7:30 p.m., 3rd Tues., Northwest Savings Hospitality Rm., Ludlow St. CONTACT: Karl H.G. Henninger, 430 Follett Run Road, Warren, PA 16365.

WILKES BARRE: * Wyoming Valley Stamp Club, (0641-050726), 7:30 p.m., 1st & 3rd Tues., except July & Aug., Wilkes Barre YMCA, 2nd Fl., 40 W. Northampton St. CONTACT: E.V. Chadwick, YMCA, 40 W. Northampton St., Wilkes-Barre, PA 18701.

YORK: * White Rose Philatelic Society of York, Pennsylvania, (0550-044283), 7:30 p.m., 1st & 3rd Wed., Aldersgate Methodist Church, 397 Tyler Run Road. CONTACT: Jerry Kotek, 424 Corbin Road, York, PA 17403.

RHODE ISLAND

CRANSTON: * Rhode Island Philatelic Society, (0370-032462), 8 p.m., 1st & 3rd Tues., Meshanticut Pk. Baptist Church, 180 Oak Lawn Ave. CONTACT: Stephan I. Frater, P.O. Box 40665, Providence, RI 02940.

MIDDLETOWN: Newport Philatelic Society, (0999-092951), 7:30 p.m., 2nd Thurs., Newport Electric Corp., Turner Road. CONTACT: Morrie P. Seiple, 35 Linden St., Middletown, RI 02842-4924.

SOUTH CAROLINA

SOUTH CAROLINA: Carolinas Chapter 37, Germany Philatelic Society, (1251-128124), varies (Saturday), 12 Noon, various locations in North & South Carolina. CONTACT: Robert W. Soeder, P.O. Box 15, Todd, NC 28684.

COLUMBIA: * Columbia Philatelic Society, (0519-043067), 7:30 p.m., 2nd Tues. & 4th Thurs., except Nov./Dec., State-Record Newspaper Bldg., Shop Road. CONTACT: Harry L. McDowell, P.O. Box 1675, Columbia, SC 29202.

GREENVILLE: Greenville Stamp Club, (0890-076251), 7 p.m., 3rd Thurs., Sears Shelter, corner N. Main & E. Park. CONTACT: Susan Reshni, P.O. Box 2212, Greenville, SC 29602-2212.

HILTON HEAD ISLAND: Hilton Head Island Philatelic Society, (1441-167739), 4:30 p.m., 1st Tues., Palmetto Electric, 111 Mathews Dr. CONTACT: Richard F. Bland, P.O. Box 23015, Hilton Head Island, SC 29925.

MYRTLE BEACH: Myrtle Beach Stamp Club, (1455-

172827), 7 p.m., 1st Tues., Grand Strand Senior Center, Hwy. 17 Bypass. CONTACT: Donn Ebert, 117 Cedar Ridge Lane, Conway, SC 29526.

NORTH CHARLESTON: * Charleston Stamp Club, (0544-044098), 7:30 p.m., 1st & 3rd Thurs., Park Circle Community Center, inside Park Circle. CONTACT: Kit Byrd, P.O. Box 5042, North Charleston, SC 29406.

SPARTANBURG: Spartanburg Stamp Club, (1183-118225), 6:30 p.m., 1st Thurs., Woodland Heights Rec. Center, 1214 Reidville Road. CONTACT: Larry Vincent, 335 Weblin St., Spartanburg, SC 29306.

SOUTH DAKOTA

ABERDEEN: Ringneck Stamp Club, (0843-069739), 7:30 p.m., 3rd Mon., Aberdeen Area Senior Center, 1307 7th Ave. S.E. CONTACT: Elaine Roth, 118 Elizabeth Dr., Aberdeen, SD 57401.

SIOUX FALLS: Sioux Falls Stamp Club, (1212-122932), 7 p.m., 1st & 3rd Thurs., McKennan Hospital. CONTACT: R.C. Schmidt, 1609 E. 32nd, Sioux Falls, SD 57105.

TENNESSEE

BRENTWOOD: Brentwood Philatelic Society, (1349-146598), 6:30 p.m., 3rd Tues., Brentwood Public Library, 5055 Maryland Way. CONTACT: Richard E. Rouse, 6545 Cloverbrook Dr., Brentwood, TN 37027.

CLARKSVILLE: Clarksville Stamp Club, (179440). CON-TACT: Wesley W. Petrouske, 1584 Freestone Dr., Clarksville, TN 37042.

CHATTANOOGA: * Chattanooga Stamp Club, (0731-057915), 7:30 p.m., 2nd Thurs., except Aug. & Dec., USPS General Mail Facility, Shallowford Road. CONTACT: Ernest Seagle, P.O. Box 22022, Chattanooga, TN 37422.

HENDERSONVILLE: Sumner County Stamp Club, (1473-175205), 6:30 p.m., 3rd Thurs., Hendersonville Public Library, 116 Dunn St. CONTACT: Forrest Wise, 104 Greenyards Pl., Hendersonville, TN 37075.

JACKSON: West Tennessee Stamp Club, (1188-118819), 7 p.m., 3rd Tues., Jackson-Madison County Library, 433 E. Lafayette. CONTACT: Frank E. Kos, P.O. Box 204, Medina, TN 38355-0204.

JOHNSON CITY: * Holston Stamp Club, (0662-051910), 3rd Thurs., Asbury Center, 400 N. Boone St. CONTACT: John L. Sanks, 3832 Skyland Dr., Kingsport, TN 37664.

MEMPHIS: * Memphis Stamp Collectors Society, (0542-044035), 7 p.m., 1st & 3rd Thurs., Raleigh Library, 3157 Powers Road. CONTACT: Carol Strobush, P.O. Box 11310, Memphis, TN 38112.

NASHVILLE: * Nashville Philatelic Society, (0431-037461), 6:45 p.m., 2nd & 4th Mon., Inglewood Branch Library, 4312 Gallatin Road. CONTACT: Terry M. Chaney, P.O. Box 60531, Nashville, TN 37206.

OAK RIDGE: * Atomic City

Stamp Club, (0531-043626), 7:30 p.m., 3rd Thurs., Oak Ridge Civic Center, 1401 Oak Ridge Tpke. CONTACT: John Lund, P.O. Box 5055, Oak Ridge, TN 37831-5055.

PARIS: Kentucky Lake Stamp Club, (1205-122460), 7:30 p.m., 2nd Thurs., WG Rhea Library. CONTACT: Carl Glasgow, P.O. Drawer D, New Johnsonville, TN 37134.

TEXAS

TEXAS: Texas Philatelic Association, (0632-049588), Annually 4, Dallas. CONTACT: Jane K. Fohn, 17209 Whippoorwill Trl., Leander, TX 78645-9734.

ARLINGTON: Mid-Cities Stamp Club, (0891-076252), 7:30 p.m., 1st & 3rd Wed., 1st-Arlington Community Center, 3rd-Irving Center for the Arts. CONTACT: Arthur P. Von Reyn, P.O. Box 201514, Arlington, TX 76006.

AUSTIN: * Austin Texas Stamp Club, (0462-039231), 7:30 p.m., 1st & 3rd Tues., Howson Branch library, 2500 Exposition Blvd. CONTACT: John G. Karabaic, 9409 Queenswood Dr., Austin, TX 78748.

BORGER: Borger Stamp Club, (1391-155239), 7:30 p.m., 1st & 3rd Tues., Hutchinson County Library, Club Room, 625 Weatherly. CONTACT: Ann Whitesides, P.O. Box 3244, Borger, TX 79008-3244.

COLLEGE STATION: Texas A&M University Stamp Club, (1096-104283), 7 p.m., 1st & 3rd Wed., Texas A & M University, Memorial Student Center. CONTACT: George Dresser,

501 Fairview Ave., College Station, TX 77840.

CORPUS CHRISTI: * Sea Gulf Stamp Club, (0371-032523), 7 p.m., 2nd & 4th Wed., Main Library, 805 Comanche. CONTACT: Steve Powell, P.O. Box 30574, Corpus Christi, TX 78463-0574.

DALLAS: Collectors Club of Dallas, (0909-079745), 6:30 p.m., Last Wed., members' homes. CONTACT: A.E. Gaddy, 9817 Kingsley Road, Dallas, TX 75238.

DENTON: Denton Stamp Club, (1444-168809), 2nd Mon., Senior Citizen Center, 509 N. Bell Ave. CONTACT: Dieter Gaupp, 2416 Nottingham Dr., Denton, TX 76201-2202.

EL PASO: * El Paso Philatelic Society, (0301-028021), 7:30 p.m., 1st Thurs., 1280 Hawkins Blvd. CONTACT: Bruce G. Bixler, 1280 Hawkins Blvd., El Paso, TX 79925.

FARMERS BRANCH: Dallas Philatelic Society, (0835-068806), 7:15 p.m., 1st & 3rd Fri., Farmers Branch Community Bldg. 2910 Amber Lane. CONTACT: Lois S. Petty, 3964 Goodfellow Dr., Dallas, TX 75229.

FORT WORTH: ** Panther City Philatelic Society, (0132-013590), 7:30 p.m., 2nd & 4th Tues., Dec. 2nd Tues. only, Texas College of Osteopathic Medicine, Room 218-Mez. CONTACT: Charles W. Brock, 4633 El Campo Ave., Fort Worth, TX 76107-4913.

HARKER HEIGHTS: Fort Hood Area Coin & Stamp Club, (1421-162110), 6:30 p.m., Last Tues., Harker Heights Public

Library, 100 E. Beeline. CONTACT: Robert B. Knowles, P.O. Box 5087, Temple, TX 76505.

HOUSTON: * Houston Philatelic Society, (0347-030827), 7:30 p.m., 1st & 3rd Mon., Central Presbyterian Church, 3788 Richmond Ave. CONTACT: Jonathan Topper, P.O. Box 610002, Houston, TX 77208-0002.

— * JSC Stamp Club, (0809-066371), 7 p.m., 2nd & 4th Mon., Gilruth Recreation Center, JSC, Nasa Road 1. CONTACT: Diane Kerkhove, 109 Royal Dr., League City, TX 77573.

IRVING: See Arlington.

KINGWOOD: Kingwood Stamp Club, (1397-155845), 7 p.m., 2nd & 4th Tues., First American Title Co., 1387 Kingwood Dr. CONTACT: Myra B. McCain, 2222 Rolling Meadows Dr., Kingwood, TX 77339.

LONGVIEW: Longview Stamp Club, (1237-125515), 7:30 p.m., 1st Tues. Longview Art Museum, 102 W. College. CONTACT: Max Statman, P.O. Box 56, Judson, TX 75660.

LUBBOCK: * South Plains Stamp Club, (0771-061736), 7:30 p.m., 1st & 3rd Mon., Lubbock Garden & Arts Center, 4215 University. CONTACT: Howard Medlock, 4123 W. 18th St., Lubbock, TX 79416-6008.

MARSHALL: Marshall Stamp Club, (0967-087774), 7:30 p.m., 2nd Tues., Pacific Southwest Bank, Alamo at Travis. CONTACT: Barney C. Wyatt, 2701 Cedarcrest Dr., Marshall, TX 75670.

MIDLAND: Permian Basin Stamp Club. (1330-143239), 7:30 p.m., 2nd Tues. & 4th Thurs., Midland Airport Reg. Mail Facility. CONTACT: Michael D. Cherrington, P.O. Box 60141, Midland, TX 79711-0141.

NEDERLAND: South East Texas Stamp Club (186356) 7 p.m. 4th Thurs., 2748 Viterbo Rd., CONTACT: William J. Windle, 6927 Olympic Dr.; Port Arthur, TX 77642.

PORT LAVACA: * Port Lavaca Philatelic Society, (0509-042421), 7 p.m., 2nd Thurs., International Bank of Commerce. CONTACT: Ruth Oliver, P.O. Box 834, Port Lavaca, TX 77979.

SAN ANGELO: Concho Valley Stamp Club, (1457-173093), 7 p.m. 2nd Tues. & 4th Thurs., Main Post Office, Norwest Bank. CONTACT: Gene Rowden, 106 Windham St., San Angelo, TX 76903-8650.

SAN ANTONIO: * San Antonio Philatelic Association, (0388-034143), 7:30 p.m., Fri., St. Luke's Lutheran Church, 514 Santa Monica. CONTACT: Manfred Groth, 531 Santa Helena, San Antonio, TX 78232. E-MAIL CONTACT: welfare@netxpress.com.

VICTORIA: Victoria Stamp Club, (181644), 7 p.m., 1st Mon., Victoria Mall, Meeting Room. CONTACT: Gerald FitzSimmons, 105 Calle Ricardo, Victoria, TX 77904.

WACO: Heart of Texas Stamp Club, (1062-099577), 7 p.m., 1st Thurs., Wiethorn Visitors Center, University Park Dr. CONTACT:

James Berryhill, 1700 Plum Circle, Waco, TX 76706.

WICHTA FALLS: Texoma Stamp Club, (1406-158932), 7:30 p.m., 2nd Thurs., U.S. Post Office, Rm. 312, 1000 Lamar St. CONTACT: Terrence L. Mish, P.O. Box 1253, Wichita Falls, TX 76307.

UTAH

SALT LAKE CITY: * Utah Philatelic Society, (0352-031236), 7 p.m., 1st & 3rd Thurs., Senior Citizen Rec. Center, 237 South 1000 East. CONTACT: Michael K. Sullivan, P.O. Box 27742, Salt Lake City, UT 84127-0742.

VERMONT

BENNINGTON: Green Mountain Stamp Society, (1375-150943), 7:30 p.m., 2nd & 4th Wed., Crescent Manor Nursing Home, Crescent Blvd. CONTACT: Norman Hendrickson, P.O. Box 571, Bennington, VT 05201.

BRATTLEBORO: Brattleboro Stamp Club, (1123-108145), 7 p.m., 3rd Mon., except Jan. & Feb. 4th Mon., Brooks Memorial Library, Meeting Room, Main St. CONTACT: Janet O'Keefe, 104 Williams St., Brattleboro, VT 05301.

MONTPELIER: * Washington County Stamp Club, (0722-056952), 7:30 p.m., 3rd Tues., except July & Aug., 1st Baptist Church, School & St. Paul St. CONTACT: William Lizotte, Brooklyn Heights, R 1, Box 384-8, Morrisville, VT 05661-9795.

RUTLAND: * Rutland County Stamp Club, (0314-028954), 7 p.m., Every Other Thurs., except June, July & Aug., Pleasant Manor, 46 Nichols St. CONTACT: James P. Monegeon, 31 Burnham Ave., Rutland, VT 05701.

SOUTH BURLINGTON: Chittenden County Stamp Club, (0915-080085), 7 p.m., 2nd Mon., New England Telephone, 800 Hinesburg Road. CONTACT: Everett Engles, P.O. Box 114, Burlington, VT 05402.

WOODSTOCK: Woodstock Stamp Club (APS# 183679), 7 p.m., 3rd Mon., St. James Episcopal Church "On the Green." CONTACT: W. Bruce Dudley, P.O. Box 355. Woodstock, VT 05091-0355.

VIRGINIA

VIRGINIA: Virginia Philatelic Federation, (1107-105297), Quarterly, various locations. CONTACT: Joan R. Bleakley, 15906 Crest Dr., Woodbridge, VA 22191-4211.

CHARLOTTESVILLE: * Charlottesville Stamp Club, (0416-036394), 8 p.m., 3rd Mon., Heritage Hall, 550 W. Rio Road. CONTACT: George T. Waaser, 3835 Graemont Dr., Earlysville, VA 22936.

DANVILLE: Dan River Philatelic Society, (0830-067628), 7:30 p.m., 3rd Tues., except Dec., American National Bank, S. Main St. office. CONTACT: W.H. Bogart, Jr., 318 Pendleton Road, Danville, VA 24541-3339.

HAMPTON: ** Peninsula Stamp Club, (0224-021542), 7:15 p.m., 2nd & 4th Wed., phone for information, (804-851-8712). CONTACT: Norman F. Bretschneider,

4 Riding Path, Hampton, VA 23669.

— * Tidewater Stamp Club, (0633-049590), 7:30 p.m., 1st & 3rd Wed., Central United Methodist Church, 225 Chapel St. CONTACT: J.M. Melson, P.O. Box 633, Hampton, VA 23669.

LYNCHBURG: Lynchburg Stamp Club, (1356-148253), 7 p.m., 2nd Tues., except July, First Colony Life Ins. Co., 700 Main St. CONTACT: Karl Wuttke, 1801 Clayton Ave., Lynchburg, VA 24503.

MCLEAN: Dolley Madison Stamp Club, (0831-067629), 7:30 p.m., 1st & 3rd Fri., McLean Governmental Center, 1437 Balls Hill Road. CONTACT: John M. Hotchner, P.O. Box 1125, Falls Church, VA 22041.

**NORFOLK: ** Norfolk Philatelic Society, (0345-030753), 8 p.m., 1st & 3rd Tues., Virginia Power Bldg., 2700 Cromwell Dr. CONTACT: Leroy P. Collins III, P.O. Box 2183, Norfolk, VA 23501.

RICHMOND: * Richmond Stamp Club, (0218-020653), 8 p.m., 1st & 3rd Tues., Virginia Science Museum, 2500 W. Broad St. CONTACT: Robert D. Thornhill Jr., P.O. Box 27012, Richmond VA 23261.

ROANOKE: Big Lick Stamp Club, (1025-095312), 2:30 p.m., 2nd Sun., St. Mark's Lutheran Church, 1008 Franklin Road. CONTACT: William K. Kellaris, 3355 Longhorn Road, S.W., Roanoke, VA 24018-3233.

SPRINGFIELD: Springfield Stamp Club, (0993-091762), 7:30 p.m., every Wed., Lynbrook Elementary School, 5801 Backlick Road. CONTACT: Joe Schoen, 8616 Greeley Blvd., Springfield, VA 22152

VIENNA: Ayrhill Stamp Club, (0973-088232), 7 p.m., 1st & 3rd Thurs., Patrick Henry Library, Maple Ave. & Center St. CONTACT: Miles B. Manchester, 9508 Rockport Road, Vienna, VA 22180.

VIRGINIA BEACH: Virginia Beach Stamp Club, (0984-090593), 7:30 p.m., 2nd & 4th Tues., St. Gregory's School Library, 5345 Virginia Beach Blvd. CONTACT: LCDR Rudolph J. Roy Jr., P.O. Box 5367, Virginia Beach, VA 23471-0367.

— Tidewater International Topics Society, (1258-128392), irregular, contact society president. CONTACT: Allen D. Jones, 5113 Greenbrook Dr., Portsmouth VA 23703.

— Virginia Philatelic Friends, (1458-173371), time varies, various locations. CONTACT: Rudolph J. Roy Jr., P.O. Box 5367, Virginia Beach, VA 23471-0367.

WARRENTON: Warrenton Stamp & Coin Club (182214), 2nd Wed., 7:30 p.m., Oak Springs of Warrenton, 614 Hastings Lane. CONTACT: Richard Herbert, Sr., 222 Elm St., Warrenton, VA 20186.

WILLIAMSBURG: * Williamsburg Stamp Society, (0610-048228), 7 p.m., 3rd Thurs., Virginia Power, 4059 Ironbound Road. CONTACT: Carl G. Finstrom, 5251-18 John Tyler Hwy.-113, Williamsburg, VA 23185.

WINCHESTER: * Shenandoah Valley Stamp Club, (0748-059428), 7:30 p.m., 3rd Fri., except Dec., Westminster-Canterbury Comm. Center, Wineberry Dr. CONTACT: Mercedes D. Lowe, 536 River Road, Woodstock, VA 22664.

WOODBRIDGE: Eastern Prince William Stamp Club, (0982-090014), 7:30 p.m., 1st & 3rd Mon., Potomac Library, Opitz Blvd. CONTACT: Joan R. Bleakley, 15906 Crest Dr., Woodbridge, VA 22191.

WASHINGTON

BELLEVUE: Greater Eastside Stamp Society, (1194-120323), 7 p.m., 1st & 3rd Thurs., Knights of Columbus Hall, 14821 S.E. 16th St. CONTACT: Donald Hoff, P.O. Box 7242, Bellevue, WA 98008-1242.

BELLINGHAM: Bellingham Stamp Club, (1454-172826), 7 p.m., Bellingham Public Library, 210 Central St. CONTACT: Rev. Al Currier, P.O. Box 6083, Bellingham, WA 98227.

EVERETT/EDMONDS: * Sno-King Stamp Club, (0642-050727), 7:30 p.m., 2nd & 3rd Wed., 2nd-8120 Hardeson Rd, Everett, 3rd-220 Railroad Ave, Edmonds. CONTACT: David W. Alexander, 14308 82nd Ave., N.E., Bothell, WA 98011.

KENT: Boeing Employees Stamp Club, (0870-072809), 6:00 p.m., 2nd Wed., Boeing Rec. Act. Center, Rm. A/B, 22649 83rd Ave., S. CONTACT: Bruce E. Landry, 12212 Marine View Dr., S.W., Seattle, WA 98146.

OAK HARBOR: Whidbey Island Stamp Club, (1262-129171), 7:30 p.m., 1st & 3rd Tues., Oak Manor Rec. Hall, 4160 400th Ave., W. CONTACT: Lee Dougherty, 6195 600th Ave., W., Oak Harbor, WA 98277.

OLYMPIA: Olympia Philatelic Society, (0895-076750), 7:30 p.m., 2nd & 4th Mon., Olympics West Retirement Inn, 929 Trosper Road, Tumwater. CONTACT: Ken Urie, P.O. Box 1554, Olympia, WA 98507.

PULLMAN: Pullman Stamp Club, (1394-155610), 7 p.m., 2nd Wed., Pullman Chamber of Commerce, N. 415 Grand Ave. CONTACT: Peter Larson, 602 S. Adams, Moscow, ID 83843.

RICHLAND: * Tri-City Stamp Club, (0715-056275), 7 p.m., 3rd Wed., Columbia Edgewater Ret. Center, 1629 George Washington Way. CONTACT: Jim Durham, 503 Buckboard Ct., Richland, WA 99352.

SEATTLE: ** Washington State Philatelic Society, (0122-013112), 7 p.m., 1st & 3rd Wed., Gethsemane Lutheran Church Library, 911 Stewart St. CONTACT: Thomas E. Ward, 12250 8th Ave., N.W., Seattle, WA 98177.

— * Collectors Club of Seattle, (0356-031488), 12 noon–3 p.m. Tues., 7 p.m., Fri., University Christian Church, 4731 15th Ave., N.E. CONTACT: Jim Hall, P.O. Box 15205, Seattle, WA 98115.

SEQUIM: Strait Stamp Society, (1453-172491), 6 p.m., 1st Thurs., Sequim Library, 800 N. Sequim Ave. CONTACT: Cathleen Osborne, P.O. Box 1781, Sequim, WA 98382.

SILVERDALE: Olympic Philatelic Society, (0985-090594), 7 p.m., 2nd & 4th Tues., Silverdale Community Center. CONTACT: Mike MacEvitt, P.O. Box 733, Silverdale, WA 98383-0733.

SPOKANE: * Inland Empire Philatelic Society, (0343-030681), 7 p.m., 2nd & 4th Tues., Riverview Terrace, 1801 Up River Dr. CONTACT: Charles Rosenstock, E. 11609 12th Ave., Spokane, WA 99206.

TACOMA: * Tacoma Stamp Club, (0511-042526), 7:30 p.m., 2nd & 4th Tues., Nov./Dec./June/July/Aug. 2nd Tues., St. Luke's Episcopal Church, 3615 N. Gove St. CONTACT: Arthur Cole, P.O. Box 1052, Tacoma, WA 98401-1052.

WALLA WALLA: Walla Walla Valley Philatelic Society, (1097-104284), 7:30 p.m., 3rd Thurs., Berney School, Pleasant & School Ave. CONTACT: Dan Gerken, 1214 Francis, Walla Walla, WA 99362.

YAKIMA: * Yakima Valley Stamp Club, (0234-023919), 7 p.m., 1st Tues., except July & Aug., 3030 W. Nob Hill-Bank. CONTACT: Glenn F. Thiesfeld, P.O. Box 952, Yakima, WA 98907-0952.

WEST VIRGINIA

CHARLESTON: * Kanawha Stamp Club, (0663-051911), 2:30 p.m., 1st Sun., Main Post Office, Lee St. CONTACT: Cathy Williams, P.O. Box 136, Sod, WV 25564.

CLARKSBURG; Harrison County Stamp Club, (1244-127078), 7:30 p.m., 3rd Mon., Harrison County Senior Center. CONTACT: Michael Ravis, P.O. Box 68, Philippi, WV 26416.

MORGANTOWN: Morgantown Area Stamp Club, (1402-157239), 7 p.m., 2nd Thurs., Mileground Medical Center, 1526 Mileground. CONTACT: Norval L. Rasmussen, 1526 Mileground. Morgantown, WV 26506.

PARKERSBURG: Blennerhassett Stamp Society, (0846-070416), 7:30 p.m., 1st Thurs. & 3rd Mon., Trinity Episcopal Church, Trinity Hall, 430 Juliana St. CONTACT: John C. Robinson, 2802 16th Ave., Vienna, WV 26105.

WISCONSIN

WISCONSIN: * Wisconsin Federation of Stamp Clubs, (0350-031025), Annually, various cities. CONTACT: Karen L. Weigt, 4184 Rose Ct., Middleton, WI 53562.

APPLETON: * Outagamie Philatelic Society, (0720-056950), 7 p.m., 3rd Thurs., except June, July, & Aug., Valley Fair Mall, Conference room, 2145 S. Memorial Dr. CONTACT: Verna Shackleton, P.O. Box 11, Appleton, WI 54912-0011.

BARABOO: Baraboo Area Stamp Club, (1361-140419), 7:30 p.m., last Thurs., University of Wisconsin, Baraboo Cafeteria, 1006 Connie Dr. CONTACT: Robert Jobe, 308 5th Ave., Baraboo, WI 53913.

ELKHORN: * Walworth County Stamp Club, (0812-

066374), 7:30 p.m., 2nd Wed., Civic Center, 109 N. Wisconsin St. CONTACT: Mike Yopp, 535 Adams St., Burlington, WI 53105.

FOND DU LAC: Fond Du Lac Stamp Club, (1331-143810), 7:30 p.m., 1st Tues. & 3rd Thurs., Fond du Lac Senior Center, 151 E. 1st. CONTACT: Fred L. Ericksen, P.O. Box 821, Fond Du Lac, WI 54936-0821.

GREEN BAY: Green Bay Philatelic Society, (1219-123324), 7:30 p.m., 3rd Thurs., Best Western-Downtowner, 321 S. Washington St. CONTACT: Gordon Lindner, 1002 Amberly Trail, Green Bay, WI 54311.

JANESVILLE: Janesville Stamp Club, (1371-150543), 7 p.m., 3rd Thurs., Trinity Episcopal Church, 411 E. Court St. CONTACT: M. Steil, 1150 Euclid Ave., Beloit, WI 53511.

KENOSHA: Kenosha Stamp & Cover Club, (1181-118223), 7:30 p.m., 3rd Wed., Swedish American Club, 7002 30th Ave. CONTACT: Dennis Mueller, 7620 10th Ave., Kenosha, WI 53143.

MANITOWOC: Manitowoc Philatelic Society, (1072-100987), 7:30 p.m., 2nd Tues., Rahr-West Museum, 8th & Park Sts. CONTACT: Mary Lou Wagner, 15 S. CTH S., Cato, WI 54206.

MIDDLETON: Badger Stamp Club, (1295-135886), 6:30 p.m.-1st Tues., 1:30 p.m.-3rd Sat., Middleton Public Library. CONTACT: Peter Smith, 9916 Dunlap Hollow Road, Mazomanie, WI 53560.

MILWAUKEE: *** Milwaukee Philatelic Society, (0024-002696),

7:30 p.m., 3rd Wed., Zablocki County Park Pavilion, 3716 W. Howard Ave. CONTACT: William Otto, P.O. Box 1980, Milwaukee, WI 53201.

— * North Shore Philatelic Society of Milwaukee, (0623-049113), 7:30 p.m., 1st Wed., Lydell School, 5205 N. Lydell Ave. CONTACT: Robert Krauss, 591 E. Fox Dale Road, Milwaukee, WI 53217-3935.

— Philatelic Society at University of Wisconsin-Madison, (0975-088234), 2nd weekend in Dec., Annual meeting at annual exhibition. CONTACT: Bruce W. Ramme, P.O. Box 407, Okauchee, WI 53069.

— Germany Philatelic Society, Chapter 18, (1252-128125), 7 p.m., 4th Sun., 8229 W. Capitol Dr. CONTACT: John R. Fagan, W140 N7470 Lilly Road, Menomonee Falls, WI 53051.

OSHKOSH: Oshkosh Philatelic Society (1238-125516), 7 p.m., 1st Tues. & 3rd, Mon., Oshkosh Post Office Building, 1025 W. 20th Ave. CONTACT: Henry J. Schmidt, P.O. Box 3153, Oshkosh, WI 54903-3153.

PORT EDWARDS: Central Wisconsin Stamp Club, (1013-094280), 7 p.m., 1st & 3rd Thurs., 1st-Stevens Point, 3rd-Port Edwards. CONTACT: Roy E. Northwood, 5520 Barberry, Wisconsin Rapids, WI 54494.

RHINELANDER: Northwoods Stamp & Coin Club, (1254-128127), 7 p.m., 2nd & 4th Tues., Oneida City Senior Citizen Center. CONTACT: Bill Julian, P.O. Box 126, Rhinelander, WI 54501.

RIPON: ** Ripon Philatelic Society, (0101-011633), 7:30 p.m., 2nd Thurs., Braun's Family Restaurant, 306 Blackburn St. CONTACT: Martha Parfitt, 625 Washington St., Ripon, WI 54971.

SHEBOYGAN: ** Sheboygan Stamp Club, (0124-013296), 7:30 p.m., 1st & 3rd Wed., Sheboygan Rehabilition Center, 1305 St. Clair Ave. CONTACT: Vern Witt, 2422 N. 9th St., Sheboygan, WI 53083.

STEVENS POINT: See Port Edwards.

WAUKESHA: * Waukesha County Philatelic Society, (0756-059700), 7:30 p.m., 2nd & 4th Thurs., except July & Aug., First Financial, 100 E. Sunset Dr. CONTACT: MaryAnn J. Bowman, P.O. Box 1451, Waukesha, WI 53187.

WAUSAU: Wisconsin Valley Philatelic Society, (0859-071592), 7 p.m., 2nd Mon., Commission on Aging Bldg., River Dr. CONTACT: William Grosnick, Sr., P.O. Box 71, Wausau, WI 54402-0071.

WAUWATOSA: Wauwatosa Philatelic Society, (1043-097006), 7:30 p.m., 3rd Tues., Wauwatosa Savings & Loan, 7500 W. State St. CONTACT: Claude Giralte, P.O. Box 13102, Wauwatosa, WI 53213.

WEST ALLIS: Polish American Stamp Club, (1191-119648), 7 p.m., 2nd Sun., except July & Aug., Cavalry United Methodist Church, 3177 S. 107th St. CONTACT: Ray Orz, P.O. Box 1920, Milwaukee, WI 53201.

WEST BEND: Kettle Moraine Coin & Stamp, (1396-155844), 7:30 p.m., 2nd Thurs., except July & Aug., Silverbrook School Library, 724 Elm St. CONTACT: Roland Essig, P.O. Box 361, West Bend, WI 53095.

WYOMING

CASPER: Central Wyoming Philatelic Association, (1353-148250), 7 p.m., 1st Thurs., Natrona County Library. CONTACT: Stephen J. Pfaff, 1045 Waterford St., Casper, WY 82609-3231.

CHEYENNE: Cheyenne Philatelic Society, (0933-082331), 7 p.m., 3rd Wed., Cheyenne Municipal Bldg., 2101 Oneil Ave. CONTACT: John Wagner, P.O. Box 1452, Cheyenne, WY 82003.

GUAM

AGANA HEIGHTS: Guam Stamp Club, (1412-161194), 1st Sun., Red Carpet Restaurant. CONTACT: Stephen F. Lander, P.O. Box 10571, Tamuning, GU 96931.

PUERTO RICO

HATO REY: * Puerto Rico Philatelic Society, (0342-030501), 9 a.m.–12 p.m., Sun., 773 Andalucia Ave., Puerto Nuevo. CONTACT: Victor R. Algarin, P.O. Box 191500, Hato Rey, PR 00919-1500.

AUSTRALIA

HOBART, TAS.: Tasmanian Philatelic Society, (1430-165212), 8 p.m., 2nd & 4th Thurs., except Jan. & Dec., 159 MacQuarie St. CONTACT: E. Genge, G.P.O. Box 594, Hobart, Tas. 7001, Australia.

CANADA

CANADA: Northwest Federation of Stamp Clubs, (1469-174562), Annual Meeting: PIPEX, various locations. CONTACT: Alex Hadden, 19-7651 Francis Road, Richmond, BC V6Y 1A3, Canada.

BATHURST, NB: Bathurst & Chaleur District Stamp Club, (1078-102415), 7 p.m., 2nd Tues., Except July & Aug., Nepisiquit Centennial Library, 360 Douglas Ave. CONTACT: C.B. Veniot, 180 York St., Bathurst, NB E2A 1G8, Canada.

CALGARY, AB: Calgary Philatelic Society, (1360-148906), 7:30 p.m., 1st Wed., except July & Aug., Kerby Centre, 1133 7th Ave., S.W., 2nd Fl. CONTACT: Dale Speirs, P.O. Box 6830, Calgary, AB T2P 2E7, Canada.

CORNWALL, ON: See New York, Massena.

EDMONTON, AB: * Edmonton Stamp Club, (0680-054000), 6:30 p.m., 1st & 3rd Mon., St. Joseph's High School, 109th St. & 108th Ave. CONTACT: Keith R. Spencer, P.O. Box 399, Edmonton, AB T5J 2J6, Canada.

ETOBICOKE, ON: West Toronto Stamp Club, (1462-174151), 7:30 p.m., every Tues., Fairfield Seniors' Centre, 80 Lothian Ave. CONTACT: Gerhard Quidzinski, 80 Lothian Ave., Etobicoke, ON M8Z 4K5, Canada.

HALIFAX, NS: Nova Scotia Stamp Club, (1340-145423), 8 p.m., 2nd Tues, except July & Aug., Nova Scotia Museum, Summer St. CONTACT: John Hall, 45 Saratoga Dr., Dartmouth, NS B2X 3P9, Canada.

HAMILTON, ON: Hamilton Philatelic Society, (1049-097889), 7:30 p.m., 2nd, 4th & 5th Mon., except July & Aug., Bishop Ryan Secondary School, Albright & Quigley Roads. CONTACT: Barry Hong, 146 Clifton Downs Road, Hamilton, ON L9C 2P6, Canada.

KELOWNA, BC: Kelowna & District Stamp Club, (1255-128389), 7 p.m., 2nd Wed., except July & Aug., Kelowna Secondary School, Harvey Ave. at Richter. CONTACT: Gary L. Geddes, P.O. Box 1185, Kelowna, BC V1Y 7P8, Canada.

OTTAWA, ON: Ottawa Philatelic Society, (1182-118224), 7:30 p.m., Thurs., except June, July & Aug., Hintonburg Community Center, 1064 Wellington Ave. CONTACT: Michel Gosselin, 51 rue du Muscatel, Aylmer, PQ J9H 5R7, Canada.

POINTE CLAIRE, PQ: * Lakeshore Stamp Club, (0769-061204), 7:30 p.m., 2nd & 4th Mon., except July & Aug., (Karnak Hall, 3350 Blvd. des Sources, Dollard des Ormeaux. CONTACT: Raymond W. Ireson, 86 Cartier, Roxboro, PQ H8Y 1G8, Canada.

QUEBEC CITY, PQ: Societe Philatelique de Quebec, (1299-136371), 7:30 p.m., 1st & 3rd Wed., except July & Aug., Montmartre Canadien, 1675 St. Louis Road. CONTACT: Andre Lafond, C.P. 2023, Quebec, PQ G1K 7M9, Canada.

REGINA, SK: Regina Philatelic Club, (1044-097437), 7:30 p.m., 1st & 3rd Wed., Library,

Sheldon Williams Collegiate, Coronation. CONTACT: Ken W. Arndt, P.O. Box 1891, Regina, SK S4P 3E1, Canada.

TORONTO, ON: Canadian Association Israel Philatelists, (1403-157892), 7:30 p.m., 2nd Mon., except July & Aug., Shaarei Shomayim Congregation, 470 Glencairn Ave. CONTACT: Joseph Berkovits, 260 Adelaide St., E., Box 33, Toronto, ON M5A 1N0, Canada.

VANCOUVER, BC: British Columbia Philatelic Society, (1379-152208), 7 p.m., Wed., Sunset Community Center, Multi-Rm. C, 404 E. 51st Ave. CONTACT: Morris Beattie, 2955 W. 38th Ave., Vancouver, BC V6N 2x2, Canada.

VICTORIA, BC: Vancouver Island Philatelic Society, (1144-112104), 8 p.m., 2nd Thurs., except July & Aug., Gordon Head Lawn Bowling Club, 1742 Lambrick Way. CONTACT: Paul Parizeau, P.O. Box 6351, Victoria, BC V8P 5M3, Canada.

WINDSOR, ON: Essex County Stamp Club, (1168-116379), 7 p.m., 2nd & 4th Wed., Teutonia Club, 55 Edinborough. CONTACT: Michael J. Barie, P.O. Box 1445, Detroit, MI 48231.

WINNIPEG, MB: * Winnipeg Philatelic Society, (0813-066375), 7:30 p.m., 1st & 3rd Thurs., except July & Aug., Union Centre, Smith St. at Broadway. CONTACT: Rich Penko, 321 Centennial St., Winnipeg, MB R3N 1P6, Canada.

COLOMBIA

BOGOTA: * Club Filatelico de Bogota, (0351-031126), 6:30 p.m., Thurs., Calle 41 #13-72. CONTACT: Brigitte Kaplan, Apartado Aereo 5258, Bogota, Colombia.

DOMINICAN REPUBLIC

SANTO DOMINGO: Sociedad Filatelica Dominicana, (1200-121277), 8 p.m., Tues.-Sun., Arz. Merino No. 358. CONTACT: Danilo A. Mueses, Apartado 1930, Santo Domingo, Dominican Republic.

ECUADOR

GUAYAQUIL: Club Filatelico Guayaquil, (0832-067630), 3–6 p.m., Local Del Club, 2ndo Pisco No. 8. CONTACT: Olaf Dobler, P.O. Box 9615, Guayaquil, Ecuador.

GERMANY

HAMBURG, FRANKFURT & MAINZ: ARGE USA/CANADA, (1057-098571), various times. CONTACT: Gernot Stephan, Moorwiese 7, W-24837 Schleswig, Germany.

GREAT BRITAIN

GREAT BRITAIN: * American Stamp Club of Great Britain, (0697-055176), various times, various locations. CONTACT: Ernest Malinow, 16 Sutherland Ave., Leeds LS8 1BZ, England.

GUATEMALA

GUATEMALA CITY: Asociacion Filatelica de Guatemala, (1327-142529), 7 p.m., Wed., Thurs., Last Sat., except Dec. 15 to Jan. 10, Old Spanish Club, 6a Av 14-68, Zona 1. CONTACT: COL Romeo J. Routhier, US MILGP (Guatemala), Unit 3301, APO, AA 34024.

MEXICO

MONTERREY, NL: Sociedad Filatelica Regiomontana, (1448-170642), 7:30 p.m., Every Mon., Imnrc Hidalgo Y.P. Diaz. CONTACT: Jose Cardenas, Apartado Postal #244, Col. Del Valle, N.L. 66250, Mexico.

NETHERLANDS

UTRECHT: USA en Canada Filatelie, (1427-164955), Bi-monthly Meetings, Throughout Netherlands. CONTACT: Arnold G. van Herk, Livingstonelaan 249, 3526 HG Utrecht, Netherlands.

NORWAY

OSLO: * Oslo Filatelist Klubb, (0685-054340), 7 p.m., Mon., except June & July, Schaftelokken, Solheimsgt 2B. CONTACT: Trygve Sommerfeldt, P.O. Box 298, Sentrum, N-0103 Oslo, Norway.

PERU

LIMA: Circulo Amigos DeLa Filatelia, (1460-174149), 1–5 p.m., Sat., Biblioteca Publica Pueblo, Libre. CONTACT: Victor M. Rojas Jr., Apartado Postal 2482, Lima 100, Peru.

SAUDI ARABIA

DHAHRAN: * Arabian Philatelic Association, (0694-055067), 7 p.m., 2nd Sat., ARAMCO facilities. CONTACT: W.A. King, c/o ARAMCO, P.O. Box 5797, Dhahran 31311, Saudi Arabia.

VENEZUELA

CARACAS: Club Filatelico De Caracas, (178564). CONTACT: Juan Diego Quintero, P.O. Box 52197, Sabana Grande, Caracas 1050 D.F., Venezuela.

IMPORTANT NOTICE: On stamps issued before 1890, prices of unused specimens are for ones without original gum. Specimens with original gum can be expected to command a premium of as much as 50 percent. Beware of regummed specimens.

Scott No.		Fine Unused Each	Ave. Unused Each	Fine Used Each	Ave. Used Each
GENERAL ISSUES					
1847. FIRST ISSUE					
☐1	5¢ Red Brown	5400.00	3500.00	515.00	365.00
☐2	10¢ Black	—	13,000.00	1400.00	800.00
1875. REPRODUCTIONS OF 1847 ISSUE					
☐3	5¢ Red Brown	800.00	650.00	—	—
☐4	10¢ Black	1000.00	850.00	—	—
1851–1856. REGULAR ISSUE—IMPERFORATE					
☐5A	1¢ Blue (1b)	—	—	3650.00	2100.00
☐6	1¢ Blue (1a)	—	—	5600.00	3300.00
☐7	1¢ Blue (II)	675.00	310.00	120.00	70.00
☐8	1¢ Blue (III)	—	—	1500.00	1000.00
☐8A	1¢ Blue (IIIa)	2750.00	1600.00	700.00	410.00
☐9	1¢ Blue (IV)	425.00	250.00	100.00	60.00
☐10	3¢ Orange Brown (I)	1500.00	1000.00	60.00	35.00
☐11	3¢ Dull Red (I)	150.00	90.00	8.00	5.50
☐12	5¢ Red Brown (I)	—	—	900.00	600.00
☐13	10¢ Green (I)	—	—	615.00	375.00
☐14	10¢ Green (II)	2000.00	1200.00	240.00	160.00
☐15	10¢ Green (III)	2000.00	1200.00	240.00	160.00
☐16	10¢ Green (IV)	—	—	1400.00	825.00
☐17	12¢ Black	—	1600.00	260.00	160.00
1857–1861. SAME DESIGNS AS 1851–1856 ISSUE—PERF. 15					
☐18	1¢ Blue (I)	850.00	500.00	375.00	225.00
☐19	1¢ Blue (Ia)	—	—	3000.00	2200.00
☐20	1¢ Blue (II)	500.00	300.00	175.00	100.00
☐21	1¢ Blue (III)	—	3650.00	1400.00	800.00
☐22	1¢ Blue (IIIa)	825.00	500.00	325.00	200.00
☐23	1¢ Blue (IV)	3200.00	1850.00	400.00	250.00

Scott No.			Fine Unused Each	Ave. Unused Each	Fine Used Each	Ave. Used Each
☐24	1¢	Blue (V)	110.00	70.00	30.00	20.00
☐25	3¢	Rose (I)	1500.00	725.00	50.00	30.00
☐26	3¢	Dull Red (II)	60.00	30.00	4.00	3.00
☐26A	3¢	Dull Red (IIa)	150.00	100.00	40.00	25.00
☐27	5¢	Brick Red (I)	—	6000.00	750.00	460.00
☐28	5¢	Red Brown (I)	1600.00	1000.00	325.00	200.00
☐28A	5¢	Indian Red (I)	—	—	1800.00	1200.00
☐29	5¢	Brown (I)	1100.00	600.00	210.00	150.00
☐30	5¢	Orange Brown (II)	715.00	390.00	900.00	525.00
☐30A	5¢	Brown (II)	800.00	500.00	200.00	120.00
☐31	10¢	Green (I)	—	5500.00	600.00	350.00
☐32	10¢	Green (II)	2500.00	1500.00	200.00	125.00
☐33	10¢	Green (III)	2500.00	1500.00	200.00	125.00
☐34	10¢	Green (IV)	—	—	1600.00	850.00
☐35	10¢	Green (IV)	200.00	100.00	60.00	40.00
☐36	12¢	Black (I)	500.00	300.00	120.00	70.00
☐36b	12¢	Black (II)	400.00	200.00	100.00	75.00
☐37	24¢	Gray Lilac	725.00	400.00	200.00	125.00
☐38	30¢	Orange	900.00	500.00	300.00	175.00
☐39	90¢	Blue	1250.00	800.00	—	—

1875. REPRINTS OF 1857–1861 ISSUE

☐40	1¢	Bright Blue	800.00	500.00	—	—
☐41	3¢	Scarlet	3400.00	2200.00	—	—
☐42	5¢	Orange Brown	1400.00	1000.00	—	—
☐43	10¢	Blue Green	2500.00	1700.00	—	—
☐44	12¢	Greenish Black	3500.00	2500.00	—	—
☐45	24¢	Blackish Violet	3400.00	2400.00	—	—
☐46	30¢	Yellow Orange	3200.00	2200.00	—	—
☐47	90¢	Deep Blue	5000.00	3600.00	—	—

1861. FIRST DESIGNS—PERF. 12

☐56	3¢	Brown Red	900.00	500.00	—	—
☐62B	10¢	Dark Green	—	—	600.00	400.00

1861–1862. SECOND DESIGNS

☐63	1¢	Blue	175.00	100.00	18.00	14.00
☐63b	1¢	Dark Blue	175.00	125.00	30.00	25.00
☐64	3¢	Pink	—	2500.00	500.00	275.00

Scott No.			Fine Unused Each	Ave. Unused Each	Fine Used Each	Ave. Used Each
☐64b	3¢	Rose Pink	400.00	220.00	110.00	60.00
☐65	3¢	Rose	100.00	50.00	2.00	1.00
☐66	3¢	Lake	—	1400.00	—	—
☐67	5¢	Buff	—	5200.00	450.00	275.00
☐68	10¢	Yellow Green	400.00	250.00	35.00	22.00
☐69	12¢	Black	600.00	350.00	75.00	40.00
☐70	24¢	Red Lilac	800.00	500.00	90.00	50.00
☐70b	24¢	Steel Blue	—	3200.00	350.00	200.00
☐70c	24¢	Violet	—	4000.00	600.00	350.00
☐71	30¢	Orange	700.00	400.00	80.00	50.00
☐72	90¢	Blue	1500.00	800.00	250.00	150.00

1861–1866. NEW VALUES OR NEW COLORS

☐73	2¢	Black	175.00	90.00	30.00	15.00
☐74	3¢	Scarlet	4000.00	3000.00	2000.00	1500.00
☐75	5¢	Red Brown	2200.00	1200.00	275.00	175.00
☐76	5¢	Brown	500.00	325.00	75.00	45.00
☐77	15¢	Black	650.00	400.00	80.00	50.00
☐78	24¢	Lilac	450.00	250.00	55.00	32.00

1867. SAME DESIGNS AS 1861–1866 ISSUE
GRILL WITH POINTS UP
A. GRILL COVERING ENTIRE STAMP

☐79	3¢	Rose	3000.00	1650.00	550.00	350.00

C. GRILL ABOUT 13 x 16 MM.

☐83	3¢	Rose	3650.00	1800.00	500.00	300.00

GRILL WITH POINTS DOWN
D. GRILL ABOUT 12 x 14 MM.

☐84	2¢	Black	8500.00	6000.00	1400.00	800.00
☐85	3¢	Rose	3000.00	1600.00	410.00	250.00

Z. GRILL ABOUT 11 x 14 MM.

☐85B	2¢	Black	3000.00	1600.00	450.00	250.00
☐85C	3¢	Rose	5000.00	3500.00	1400.00	800.00
☐85E	12¢	Black	5000.00	2500.00	650.00	400.00

E. GRILL ABOUT 11 x 13 MM.

☐86	1¢	Blue	1200.00	650.00	310.00	150.00

Scott No.			Fine Unused Each	Ave. Unused Each	Fine Used Each	Ave. Used Each
☐87	2¢	Black	550.00	350.00	70.00	40.00
☐88	3¢	Rose	400.00	210.00	15.00	7.00
☐89	10¢	Green	2000.00	1000.00	180.00	110.00
☐90	12¢	Black	2200.00	1200.00	210.00	125.00
☐91	15¢	Black	4200.00	2200.00	410.00	240.00

F. GRILL ABOUT 9 x 13 MM.

☐92	1¢	Blue	500.00	310.00	100.00	60.00
☐93	2¢	Black	200.00	120.00	28.00	16.00
☐94	3¢	Red	175.00	100.00	4.00	2.50
☐95	5¢	Brown	1500.00	800.00	350.00	210.00
☐96	10¢	Yellow Green	1200.00	650.00	120.00	75.00
☐97	12¢	Black	1400.00	800.00	140.00	80.00
☐98	15¢	Black	1500.00	800.00	175.00	100.00
☐99	24¢	Gray Lilac	2100.00	1200.00	425.00	250.00
☐100	30¢	Orange	2800.00	1600.00	400.00	250.00
☐101	90¢	Blue	4100.00	2300.00	875.00	550.00

1875. RE-ISSUE OF 1861–1866 ISSUES

☐102	1¢	Blue	600.00	400.00	1000.00	600.00
☐103	2¢	Black	3000.00	2000.00	4000.00	2700.00
☐104	3¢	Brown Red	3500.00	2400.00	4500.00	3100.00
☐105	5¢	Light Brown	1800.00	1600.00	2400.00	1800.00
☐106	10¢	Green	2200.00	1600.00	3800.00	3000.00
☐107	12¢	Black	3000.00	2100.00	4100.00	2900.00
☐108	15¢	Black	3000.00	2100.00	4800.00	3200.00
☐109	24¢	Deep Violet	4200.00	3200.00	5800.00	4500.00
☐110	30¢	Brownish Orange	4400.00	3000.00	6800.00	4400.00
☐111	90¢	Blue	6000.00	4000.00	18,000.00	11,500.00

1869. PICTORIAL ISSUES
GRILL ABOUT 9½ x 9½ MM.

☐112	1¢	Buff	275.00	150.00	70.00	45.00
☐113	2¢	Brown	225.00	150.00	30.00	16.00
☐114	3¢	Ultramarine	160.00	90.00	7.50	4.00
☐115	6¢	Ultramarine	950.00	575.00	100.00	60.00
☐116	10¢	Yellow	1000.00	600.00	90.00	60.00
☐117	12¢	Green	950.00	550.00	100.00	60.00
☐118	15¢	Brown & Blue (I)	2600.00	1600.00	350.00	200.00

Scott No.		Fine Unused Each	Ave. Unused Each	Fine Used Each	Ave. Used Each
☐ 119	15¢ Brown & Blue (II)	1100.00	600.00	170.00	90.00
☐ 120	24¢ Green & Violet	3000.00	1700.00	450.00	250.00
☐ 121	30¢ Blue & Carmine	2800.00	1600.00	280.00	160.00
☐ 122	90¢ Carmine & Black	4800.00	2600.00	1200.00	750.00

1875. RE-ISSUE OF 1869 ISSUE, HARD WHITE PAPER—WITHOUT GRILL

☐ 123	1¢ Buff	300.00	180.00	210.00	120.00
☐ 124	2¢ Brown	340.00	190.00	300.00	170.00
☐ 125	3¢ Blue	3000.00	2100.00	1200.00	1000.00
☐ 126	6¢ Blue	850.00	560.00	550.00	400.00
☐ 127	10¢ Yellow	1500.00	900.00	1400.00	900.00
☐ 128	12¢ Green	1600.00	900.00	1200.00	845.00
☐ 129	15¢ Brown & Blue (III)	1200.00	1000.00	600.00	500.00
☐ 130	24¢ Green & Violet	1200.00	700.00	600.00	360.00
☐ 131	30¢ Blue & Carmine	1500.00	1200.00	1000.00	800.00
☐ 132	90¢ Carmine & Black	4500.00	3400.00	5500.00	4000.00

1880. SAME AS ABOVE—SOFT POROUS PAPER

☐ 133	1¢ Buff	190.00	120.00	150.00	90.00

1870–1871. PRINTED BY NATIONAL BANK NOTE CO.—GRILLED

☐ 134	1¢ Ultramarine	800.00	500.00	70.00	38.00
☐ 135	2¢ Red Brown	500.00	300.00	42.00	22.00
☐ 136	3¢ Green	350.00	200.00	14.00	8.00
☐ 137	6¢ Carmine	2000.00	1100.00	300.00	175.00
☐ 138	7¢ Vermilion	1500.00	800.00	275.00	160.00
☐ 139	10¢ Brown	2000.00	1200.00	450.00	260.00
☐ 140	12¢ Light Violet	—	—	1600.00	1100.00
☐ 141	15¢ Orange	—	1600.00	700.00	400.00
☐ 142	24¢ Purple	—	—	8000.00	6200.00
☐ 143	30¢ Black	—	3200.00	1000.00	600.00
☐ 144	90¢ Carmine	—	4000.00	900.00	525.00

1870–1871. SAME AS ABOVE—WITHOUT GRILL

☐ 145	1¢ Ultramarine	200.00	120.00	9.00	5.00
☐ 146	2¢ Red Brown	150.00	80.00	5.00	3.50
☐ 147	3¢ Green	150.00	90.00	.90	.60

Scott No.		Fine Unused Each	Ave. Unused Each	Fine Used Each	Ave. Used Each
☐148 6¢	Carmine	300.00	170.00	14.00	8.00
☐149 7¢	Vermilion	350.00	200.00	60.00	35.00
☐150 10¢	Brown	350.00	200.00	14.00	8.75
☐151 12¢	Dull Violet	700.00	400.00	70.00	42.00
☐152 15¢	Bright Orange	650.00	400.00	85.00	52.00
☐153 24¢	Purple	650.00	400.00	85.00	52.00
☐154 30¢	Black	1800.00	1000.00	110.00	65.00
☐155 90¢	Carmine	1600.00	1000.00	180.00	110.00

1873. SAME DESIGNS AS 1870–1871 ISSUE— WITH SECRET MARKS PRINTED BY THE CONTINENTAL BANK NOTE CO. THIN HARD GRAYISH WHITE PAPER

☐156 1¢	Ultramarine	125.00	70.00	2.10	1.25
☐157 2¢	Brown	200.00	110.00	11.00	7.00
☐158 3¢	Green	70.00	35.00	.25	.22
☐159 6¢	Dull Pink	240.00	140.00	11.00	6.50
☐160 7¢	Orange Vermilion	480.00	300.00	60.00	30.00
☐161 10¢	Brown	350.00	200.00	14.00	8.00
☐162 12¢	Black Violet	900.00	500.00	70.00	40.00
☐163 15¢	Yellow Orange	800.00	475.00	70.00	38.00
☐165 30¢	Gray Black	1000.00	600.00	65.00	35.00
☐166 90¢	Rose Carmine	1500.00	800.00	175.00	100.00

1875. REGULAR ISSUE

☐178 2¢	Vermilion	200.00	110.00	6.00	3.50
☐179 5¢	Blue	250.00	150.00	10.00	6.00

1879. SAME DESIGNS AS 1870–1875 ISSUES PRINTED BY THE AMERICAN BANK NOTE CO. SOFT POROUS YELLOWISH WHITE PAPER

☐182 1¢	Dark Ultramarine	140.00	80.00	1.75	1.00
☐183 2¢	Vermilion	75.00	45.00	1.75	1.00
☐184 3¢	Green	58.00	35.00	.30	.20
☐185 5¢	Blue	285.00	140.00	9.00	5.25
☐186 6¢	Pink	500.00	300.00	14.00	8.00
☐187 10¢	Brown (no secret mark)	975.00	510.00	18.00	12.00

Scott No.	Fine Unused Each	Ave. Unused Each	Fine Used Each	Ave. Used Each
☐188 10¢ Brown (secret mark)	725.00	450.00	20.00	11.00
☐188b 10¢ Black Brown	700.00	370.00	70.00	27.00
☐189 15¢ Red Orange	180.00	100.00	18.00	11.00
☐190 30¢ Full Black	485.00	300.00	40.00	22.00
☐191 90¢ Carmine	1200.00	710.00	160.00	90.00

1882. REGULAR ISSUE

☐205 5¢ Yellow Brown	150.00	80.00	5.25	3.00

1881–1882. DESIGNS OF 1873 ISSUE RE-ENGRAVED (N-H ADD 95%)

☐206 1¢ Gray Blue	38.00	22.00	.75	.40
☐207 3¢ Blue Green	45.00	26.00	.30	.20
☐208 6¢ Rose	260.00	150.00	50.00	28.00
☐208a 6¢ Brown Red	240.00	130.00	58.00	32.00
☐209 10¢ Brown	90.00	52.00	2.75	1.60
☐209b 10¢ Black Brown	170.00	100.00	15.00	10.00

1883. REGULAR ISSUE

☐210 2¢ Red Brown	32.00	20.00	.30	.20
☐211 4¢ Blue Green	145.00	80.00	7.50	4.00

1887. REGULAR ISSUE

☐212 1¢ Ultramarine	60.00	35.00	.90	.60
☐213 2¢ Green	25.00	14.00	.30	.22
☐214 3¢ Vermilion	50.00	27.00	32.00	20.00

1888. SAME DESIGNS AS 1870–1883 ISSUES

☐215 4¢ Carmine	140.00	75.00	14.00	7.50
☐216 5¢ Indigo	140.00	80.00	7.00	4.00
☐217 30¢ Orange Brown	310.00	185.00	80.00	42.00
☐218 90¢ Purple	750.00	450.00	150.00	85.00

IMPORTANT NOTICE: From this point onward, values of unused stamps and blocks are for specimens with original gum. Prices given for **blocks** are for blocks of 4, **without** plate number.

Scott No.	Fine Unused Block	Ave. Unused Block	Fine Unused Each	Ave. Unused Each	Fine Used Each	Ave. Used Each
1890–1893. SMALL DESIGN (N-H ADD 70%)						
☐219 1¢ Dull Blue						
	110.00	85.00	25.00	16.00	.25	.20
☐219D 2¢ Lake						
	800.00	650.00	200.00	130.00	.50	.28
☐220 2¢ Carmine						
	94.00	72.00	20.00	14.00	.25	.16
☐220a 2¢ Carmine (Cap on left 2)						
	150.00	120.00	60.00	40.00	1.75	1.00
☐220c 2¢ Carmine (Cap both 2's)						
	170.00	135.00	175.00	120.00	10.50	5.50
☐221 3¢ Purple						
	250.00	210.00	75.00	52.00	5.00	3.50
☐222 4¢ Dark Brown						
	300.00	240.00	75.00	52.00	2.00	1.20
☐223 5¢ Chocolate						
	290.00	225.00	75.00	52.00	2.00	1.25
☐224 6¢ Brown Red						
	300.00	240.00	80.00	55.00	15.00	9.00
☐225 8¢ Lilac						
	280.00	240.00	58.00	40.00	10.00	7.00
☐226 10¢ Green						
	475.00	390.00	150.00	100.00	2.50	1.20
☐227 15¢ Indigo						
	720.00	600.00	210.00	150.00	15.00	10.00
☐228 30¢ Black						
	950.00	800.00	325.00	210.00	18.00	14.00
☐229 90¢ Orange						
	1800.00	1500.00	475.00	310.00	90.00	50.00
1893. COLUMBIAN ISSUE (N-H ADD 50%)						
☐230 1¢ Blue						
	100.00	85.00	32.00	20.00	.40	.30
☐231 2¢ Violet						
	100.00	90.00	30.00	20.00	.20	.16
☐231c 2¢ "Broken Hat"						
	260.00	210.00	85.00	52.00	.60	.30
☐232 3¢ Green						
	275.00	230.00	70.00	42.00	14.00	10.50

Scott No.			Fine Unused Block	Ave. Unused Block	Fine Unused Each	Ave. Unused Each	Fine Used Each	Ave. Used Each
☐233	4¢	Ultramarine						
			450.00	340.00	100.00	60.00	6.00	5.00
☐234	5¢	Chocolate						
			480.00	350.00	120.00	70.00	6.50	6.00
☐235	6¢	Purple						
			480.00	340.00	100.00	60.00	18.00	12.50
☐236	8¢	Magenta						
			390.00	300.00	80.00	60.00	8.00	6.00
☐237	10¢	Black Brown						
			600.00	425.00	160.00	95.00	7.00	5.25
☐238	15¢	Dark Green						
			1650.00	850.00	260.00	170.00	56.00	45.00
☐239	30¢	Orange Brown						
			2900.00	2000.00	360.00	220.00	80.00	58.00
☐240	50¢	Slate Blue						
			2900.00	2100.00	550.00	375.00	125.00	95.00
☐241	$1	Salmon						
			—	—	1700.00	1100.00	500.00	425.00
☐242	$2	Brown Red						
			—	—	1700.00	1200.00	450.00	300.00
☐243	$3	Yellow Green						
			—	—	2600.00	1800.00	900.00	700.00
☐244	$4	Crimson Lake						
			—	—	3500.00	2250.00	1200.00	875.00
☐245	$5	Black						
			—	—	4300.00	2800.00	1400.00	1050.00

1894. UNWATERMARKED (N-H ADD 60%)

Scott No.			Fine Unused Block	Ave. Unused Block	Fine Unused Each	Ave. Unused Each	Fine Used Each	Ave. Used Each
☐246	1¢	Ultramarine						
			90.00	84.00	30.00	25.00	3.10	2.30
☐247	1¢	Blue						
			210.00	175.00	70.00	48.00	2.00	1.50
☐248	2¢	Pink, Type I						
			100.00	72.00	22.00	15.00	2.50	1.25
☐249	2¢	Carmine Lake, Type I						
			550.00	430.00	130.00	100.00	2.00	1.00
☐250	2¢	Carmine, Type I						
			190.00	175.00	25.00	16.00	.40	.20

Scott No.			Fine Unused Block	Ave. Unused Block	Fine Unused Each	Ave. Unused Each	Fine Used Each	Ave. Used Each
☐251	2¢	Carmine, Type II						
			1400.00	1000.00	220.00	150.00	3.00	1.50
☐252	2¢	Carmine, Type III						
			400.00	310.00	125.00	85.00	3.10	2.00
☐253	3¢	Purple						
			400.00	300.00	95.00	60.00	7.00	4.50
☐254	4¢	Dark Brown						
			500.00	380.00	110.00	75.00	3.50	2.00
☐255	5¢	Chocolate						
			450.00	390.00	90.00	68.00	4.50	2.50
☐256	6¢	Dull Brown						
			870.00	600.00	150.00	120.00	18.00	12.00
☐257	8¢	Violet Brown						
			875.00	610.00	130.00	90.00	12.00	8.00
☐258	10¢	Dark Green						
			1400.00	910.00	210.00	150.00	8.00	6.00
☐259	15¢	Dark Blue						
			1800.00	1000.00	280.00	180.00	37.00	25.00
☐260	50¢	Orange						
			2000.00	1100.00	410.00	250.00	72.00	48.00
☐261	$1	Black (I)						
			5400.00	4000.00	830.00	560.00	225.00	150.00
☐261A	$1	Black (II)						
			—	—	2200.00	1500.00	425.00	300.00
☐262	$2	Blue						
			—	—	3000.00	1800.00	600.00	450.00
☐263	$5	Dark Green						
			—	—	4200.00	2800.00	1200.00	750.00

1895. DOUBLE LINE WATERMARKED "U.S.P.S." PERF. 12 (N-H ADD 60%)

☐264	1¢	Blue						
			46.00	38.00	8.00	5.00	.22	.18
☐265	2¢	Carmine, Type I						
			220.00	160.00	32.00	22.00	1.00	.75
☐266	2¢	Carmine, Type II						
			275.00	195.00	28.00	18.00	3.00	2.00
☐267	2¢	Carmine, Type III						
			50.00	38.00	5.00	4.00	.25	.18

Scott No.	Fine Unused Block	Ave. Unused Block	Fine Unused Each	Ave. Unused Each	Fine Used Each	Ave. Used Each
☐268 3¢ Purple						
	290.00	172.00	40.00	28.00	1.25	1.00
☐269 4¢ Dark Brown						
	300.00	250.00	40.00	26.00	1.50	1.00
☐270 5¢ Chocolate						
	300.00	260.00	40.00	28.00	2.00	1.20
☐271 6¢ Dull Brown						
	380.00	300.00	80.00	55.00	4.00	2.10
☐272 8¢ Violet Brown						
	215.00	140.00	60.00	40.00	1.50	.75
☐273 10¢ Dark Green						
	350.00	210.00	75.00	50.00	1.25	1.00
☐274 15¢ Dark Blue						
	800.00	550.00	225.00	150.00	10.00	6.00
☐275 50¢ Dull Orange						
	1200.00	900.00	300.00	200.00	20.00	14.00
☐276 $1 Black (I)						
	2400.00	1800.00	650.00	450.00	60.00	38.00
☐276A $1 Black (II)						
	—	—	1400.00	900.00	125.00	80.00
☐277 $2 Blue						
	—	—	1200.00	800.00	260.00	175.00
☐278 $5 Dark Green						
	—	—	2500.00	1600.00	375.00	275.00

1898. REGULAR ISSUE PERF. (N-H ADD 60%)

Scott No.	Fine Unused Block	Ave. Unused Block	Fine Unused Each	Ave. Unused Each	Fine Used Each	Ave. Used Each
☐279 1¢ Deep Green						
	85.00	50.00	11.00	8.00	.50	.20
☐279B 2¢ Red						
	85.00	50.00	11.00	8.00	.50	.20
☐279C 2¢ Rose Carmine						
	700.00	600.00	240.00	160.00	100.00	60.00
☐279D 2¢ Orange Red						
	80.00	55.00	12.00	10.00	.30	.20
☐280 4¢ Rose Brown						
	210.00	135.00	34.00	24.00	1.00	.75
☐281 5¢ Dark Blue						
	215.00	140.00	40.00	26.00	1.00	.75

Scott No.	Fine Unused Block	Ave. Unused Block	Fine Unused Each	Ave. Unused Each	Fine Used Each	Ave. Used Each
☐282 6¢ Lake						
	375.00	250.00	52.00	34.00	2.70	1.50
☐282a 6¢ Purplish Lake						
	500.00	380.00	70.00	48.00	3.50	1.50
☐282C 10¢ Brown (I)						
	900.00	700.00	200.00	130.00	2.40	1.50
☐283 10¢ Orange Brown (III)						
	750.00	500.00	125.00	85.00	2.25	1.50
☐284 15¢ Olive Green						
	875.00	600.00	175.00	120.00	7.50	4.00

1898. TRANS-MISSISSIPPI EXPOSITION ISSUE (N-H ADD 50%)

Scott No.	Fine Unused Block	Ave. Unused Block	Fine Unused Each	Ave. Unused Each	Fine Used Each	Ave. Used Each
☐285 1¢ Yellow Green						
	250.00	130.00	32.00	21.00	6.00	4.50
☐286 2¢ Copper Red						
	250.00	130.00	30.00	19.00	1.80	1.50
☐287 4¢ Orange						
	910.00	600.00	155.00	100.00	21.00	15.00
☐288 5¢ Dull Blue						
	900.00	650.00	150.00	100.00	20.00	14.00
☐289 8¢ Violet Brown						
	1050.00	725.00	200.00	132.00	35.00	24.00
☐290 10¢ Gray Violet						
	1100.00	1000.00	200.00	132.00	21.00	14.00
☐291 50¢ Sage Green						
	—	—	700.00	500.00	165.00	95.00
☐292 $1 Black						
	—	—	1500.00	1000.00	490.00	335.00
☐293 $2 Orange Brown						
	—	—	2450.00	1500.00	750.00	500.00

1901. PAN-AMERICAN ISSUE (N-H ADD 50%)

Scott No.	Fine Unused Block	Ave. Unused Block	Fine Unused Each	Ave. Unused Each	Fine Used Each	Ave. Used Each
☐294 1¢ Green & Black						
	250.00	200.00	22.00	14.00	3.50	3.00
☐295 2¢ Carmine & Black						
	250.00	200.00	22.00	12.00	1.50	1.00
☐296 4¢ Chocolate & Black						
	2100.00	1500.00	95.00	70.00	16.00	12.00

Scott No.	Fine Unused Block	Ave. Unused Block	Fine Unused Each	Ave. Unused Each	Fine Used Each	Ave. Used Each
☐297 5¢ Ultramarine & Black						
	2300.00	1700.00	120.00	80.00	15.00	10.00
☐298 8¢ Brown Violet Black						
	3000.00	2100.00	150.00	100.00	60.00	50.00
☐299 10¢ Yellow Brown Black						
	4900.00	3900.00	220.00	150.00	30.00	20.00

1902–1903. PERF. 12 (N-H ADD 50%)

Scott No.	Fine Unused Block	Ave. Unused Block	Fine Unused Each	Ave. Unused Each	Fine Used Each	Ave. Used Each
☐300 1¢ Blue Green						
	140.00	100.00	9.00	6.50	.25	.16
☐301 2¢ Carmine						
	140.00	100.00	14.00	9.00	.25	.16
☐302 3¢ Violet						
	480.00	325.00	60.00	36.00	3.60	2.25
☐303 4¢ Brown						
	500.00	325.00	60.00	38.00	2.50	1.00
☐304 5¢ Blue						
	600.00	500.00	60.00	40.00	1.50	1.00
☐305 6¢ Claret						
	600.00	475.00	70.00	45.00	2.75	1.50
☐306 8¢ Violet Black						
	450.00	300.00	44.00	30.00	·2.00	1.35
☐307 10¢ Red Brown						
	750.00	600.00	65.00	42.00	1.65	1.00
☐308 13¢ Purple Black						
	410.00	300.00	44.00	30.00	10.00	6.00
☐309 15¢ Olive Green						
	1100.00	750.00	160.00	110.00	7.00	5.75
☐310 50¢ Orange						
	4000.00	2800.00	425.00	300.00	25.00	15.00
☐311 $1 Black						
	5200.00	4000.00	775.00	525.00	52.00	34.00
☐312 $2 Dark Blue						
	—	—	1100.00	725.00	170.00	120.00
☐313 $5 Dark Green						
	—	—	3000.00	2000.00	550.00	400.00

1906–1908. IMPERFORATED (N-H ADD 50%)

Scott No.	Fine Unused Block	Ave. Unused Block	Fine Unused Each	Ave. Unused Each	Fine Used Each	Ave. Used Each
☐314 1¢ Blue Green						
	180.00	160.00	28.00	20.00	17.00	11.00

Scott No.	Fine Unused Block	Ave. Unused Block	Fine Unused Each	Ave. Unused Each	Fine Used Each	Ave. Used Each
☐315 5¢ Blue						
	4200.00	3500.00	500.00	400.00	300.00	240.00

1903. PERF. 12 (N-H ADD 50%)

☐319 2¢ Carmine						
	82.00	70.00	6.25	5.00	.25	.18
☐319a 2¢ Lake						
	120.00	92.00	10.00	7.00	.50	.30

1906. IMPERFORATED (N-H ADD 40%)

☐320 2¢ Carmine						
	225.00	190.00	25.00	20.00	17.00	9.50
☐320a 2¢ Lake						
	360.00	310.00	65.00	50.00	39.00	27.00

1904. LOUISIANA PURCHASE ISSUE
PERF. 12 (N-H ADD 50%)

☐323 1¢ Green						
	190.00	150.00	35.00	20.00	6.00	3.00
☐324 2¢ Carmine						
	185.00	145.00	35.00	25.00	2.00	1.50
☐325 3¢ Violet						
	825.00	575.00	100.00	60.00	32.00	22.00
☐326 5¢ Dark Blue						
	900.00	710.00	125.00	75.00	25.00	15.00
☐327 10¢ Red Brown						
	1600.00	1300.00	200.00	125.00	32.00	22.00

1907. JAMESTOWN EXPOSITION ISSUE
(N-H ADD 50%)

☐328 1¢ Green						
	250.00	200.00	30.00	22.00	4.50	3.50
☐329 2¢ Carmine						
	350.00	300.00	40.00	25.00	6.00	3.75
☐330 5¢ Blue						
	2000.00	1600.00	150.00	90.00	27.00	16.00

Scott No.	Fine Unused Block	Ave. Unused Block	Fine Unused Each	Ave. Unused Each	Fine Used Each	Ave. Used Each

1908–1909. DOUBLE LINE WATERMARKED "U.S.P.S." PERF. 12 (N-H ADD 60%)

Scott No.	Fine Unused Block	Ave. Unused Block	Fine Unused Each	Ave. Unused Each	Fine Used Each	Ave. Used Each
☐331 1¢ Green	70.00	45.00	9.00	6.00	.30	.18
☐332 2¢ Carmine	62.00	48.00	8.00	5.00	.30	.18
☐333 3¢ Violet	300.00	270.00	38.00	25.00	3.25	1.90
☐334 4¢ Orange Brown	310.00	270.00	44.00	30.00	1.50	1.00
☐335 5¢ Blue	520.00	420.00	55.00	35.00	2.30	1.50
☐336 6¢ Red Orange	425.00	330.00	65.00	45.00	5.00	3.00
☐337 8¢ Olive Green	370.00	240.00	55.00	34.00	3.15	2.00
☐338 10¢ Yellow	610.00	450.00	80.00	55.00	1.50	2.00
☐339 13¢ Blue Green	430.00	310.00	55.00	34.00	24.00	12.00
☐340 15¢ Pale Ultramarine	430.00	300.00	70.00	50.00	6.50	3.50
☐341 50¢ Violet	1700.00	1000.00	350.00	250.00	20.00	12.00
☐342 $1 Violet Black	2500.00	1800.00	550.00	370.00	80.00	46.00

IMPERFORATE (N-H ADD 30%)

Scott No.	Fine Unused Block	Ave. Unused Block	Fine Unused Each	Ave. Unused Each	Fine Used Each	Ave. Used Each
☐343 1¢ Green	62.00	43.00	8.00	6.00	4.50	3.50
☐344 2¢ Carmine	100.00	82.00	10.00	7.50	4.50	3.50
☐345 3¢ Deep Violet	200.00	160.00	25.00	18.00	14.00	11.00
☐346 4¢ Orange Brown	310.00	275.00	35.00	26.00	20.00	15.00
☐347 5¢ Blue	460.00	310.00	55.00	42.00	32.00	25.00

Scott No.	Fine Unused Line Pair	Ave. Unused Line Pair	Fine Unused Each	Ave. Unused Each	Fine Used Each	Ave. Used Each
1908–1910. COIL STAMPS						
PERF. 12 HORIZONTALLY (N-H ADD 50%)						
☐348 1¢ Green						
	175.00	120.00	32.00	22.00	12.00	7.50
☐349 2¢ Carmine						
	280.00	175.00	54.00	40.00	8.00	5.00
☐350 4¢ Orange Brown						
	700.00	425.00	130.00	85.00	68.00	45.00
☐351 5¢ Blue						
	700.00	450.00	140.00	95.00	85.00	51.00
PERF. 12 VERTICALLY (N-H ADD 40%)						
☐352 1¢ Green						
	350.00	275.00	70.00	48.00	30.00	20.00
☐353 2¢ Carmine						
	350.00	275.00	68.00	45.00	8.00	4.10
☐354 4¢ Orange Brown						
	700.00	500.00	160.00	110.00	50.00	35.00
☐355 5¢ Blue						
	780.00	610.00	175.00	120.00	75.00	45.00
☐356 10¢ Yellow						
	—	—	2100.00	1600.00	750.00	500.00

Scott No.	Fine Unused Block	Ave. Unused Block	Fine Unused Each	Ave. Unused Each	Fine Used Each	Ave. Used Each
1909. BLUISH GRAY PAPER						
PERF. 12 (N-H ADD 60%)						
☐357 1¢ Green						
	700.00	530.00	125.00	80.00	76.00	57.00
☐358 2¢ Carmine						
	690.00	500.00	120.00	75.00	70.00	45.00
☐359 3¢ Violet						
	—	—	2800.00	1600.00	—	—
☐360 4¢ Orange Brown						
	—	—	15,000.00	10,500.00	—	—
☐361 5¢ Blue						
	—	—	3000.00	2500.00	—	—

Scott No.	Fine Unused Block	Ave. Unused Block	Fine Unused Each	Ave. Unused Each	Fine Used Each	Ave. Used Each
□362 6¢ Orange						
	—	—	2000.00	1100.00	900.00	500.00
□363 8¢ Olive Green						
		—	15,000.00	10,000.00	—	—
□364 10¢ Yellow						
	—	—	2400.00	1400.00	900.00	500.00
□365 13¢ Blue Green						
	—	—	2000.00	1600.00	—	—
□366 15¢ Pale Ultramarine						
	—	—	1800.00	1000.00	800.00	450.00

1909. LINCOLN MEMORIAL ISSUE (N-H ADD 50%)

□367 2¢ Carmine						
	115.00	85.00	7.50	4.20	2.10	1.50
□368 2¢ Carmine, Impf.						
	200.00	140.00	32.00	24.00	18.00	12.00
□369 2¢ Carmine (On B.G. Paper)						
	1050.00	950.00	300.00	200.00	190.00	120.00

1909. ALASKA–YUKON ISSUE (N-H ADD 40%)

□370 2¢ Carmine						
	200.00	156.00	12.00	7.00	1.80	.60
□371 2¢ Carmine, Impf.						
	222.00	165.00	42.00	32.00	22.00	15.00

1909. HUDSON–FULTON ISSUE (N-H ADD 40%)

□372 2¢ Carmine						
	250.00	175.00	14.00	11.00	3.80	2.25
□373 2¢ Carmine, Impf.						
	300.00	200.00	50.00	40.00	22.00	18.50

1910–1911. SINGLE LINE WATERMARKED "U.S.P.S." PERF. 12 (N-H ADD 50%)

□374 1¢ Green						
	69.00	52.00	8.50	5.75	.25	.18
□375 2¢ Carmine						
	72.00	52.00	8.00	6.00	.25	.18
□376 3¢ Deep Violet						
	132.00	90.00	22.00	14.00	2.00	1.25

Scott No.	Fine Unused Block	Ave. Unused Block	Fine Unused Each	Ave. Unused Each	Fine Used Each	Ave. Used Each
☐377 4¢ Brown						
	170.00	115.00	32.00	22.00	.60	.35
☐378 5¢ Blue						
	200.00	160.00	32.00	22.00	.60	.35
☐379 6¢ Red Orange						
	310.00	165.00	40.00	28.00	.95	.65
☐380 8¢ Olive Green						
	560.00	400.00	135.00	90.00	12.00	7.50
☐381 10¢ Yellow						
	435.00	370.00	140.00	85.00	4.50	2.40
☐382 15¢ Ultramarine						
	1200.00	1000.00	310.00	210.00	13.50	9.00

IMPERFORATE (N-H ADD 50%)

☐383 1¢ Green						
	52.00	40.00	4.00	3.00	2.75	1.75
☐384 2¢ Carmine						
	130.00	95.00	6.50	5.00	2.50	1.60

Scott No.	Fine Unused Line Pair	Ave. Unused Line Pair	Fine Unused Each	Ave. Unused Each	Fine Used Each	Ave. Used Each

1910–1913. COIL STAMPS
PERF. 12 HORIZONTALLY (N-H ADD 40%)

☐385 1¢ Green						
	300.00	200.00	30.00	20.00	13.00	6.00
☐386 2¢ Carmine						
	600.00	400.00	55.00	36.00	15.00	10.00

PERF. 12 VERTICALLY (N-H ADD 50%)

☐387 1¢ Green						
	400.00	300.00	150.00	80.00	30.00	17.00
☐388 2¢ Carmine						
	4500.00	3500.00	900.00	600.00	200.00	100.00

PERF. 8½ HORIZONTALLY (N-H ADD 50%)

☐390 1¢ Green						
	30.00	20.00	6.50	4.50	4.00	3.00

Scott No.	Fine Unused Line Pair	Ave. Unused Line Pair	Fine Unused Each	Ave. Unused Each	Fine Used Each	Ave. Used Each
☐391 2¢ Carmine						
	200.00	100.00	40.00	30.00	9.00	5.00

PERF. 8½ VERTICALLY (N-H ADD 40%)

Scott No.	Fine Unused Line Pair	Ave. Unused Line Pair	Fine Unused Each	Ave. Unused Each	Fine Used Each	Ave. Used Each
☐392 1¢ Green						
	140.00	100.00	30.00	20.00	15.00	10.00
☐393 2¢ Carmine						
	200.00	150.00	55.00	36.00	8.00	5.00
☐394 3¢ Violet						
	300.00	200.00	70.00	50.00	46.00	36.00
☐395 4¢ Brown						
	300.00	200.00	70.00	50.00	46.00	36.00
☐396 5¢ Blue						
	300.00	200.00	70.00	50.00	46.00	36.00

Scott No.	Fine Unused Block	Ave. Unused Block	Fine Unused Each	Ave. Unused Each	Fine Used Each	Ave. Used Each

1913–1915. PANAMA–PACIFIC ISSUE
PERF. 12 (N-H ADD 50%)

Scott No.	Fine Unused Block	Ave. Unused Block	Fine Unused Each	Ave. Unused Each	Fine Used Each	Ave. Used Each
☐397 1¢ Green						
	125.00	92.00	20.00	15.00	2.00	1.50
☐398 2¢ Carmine						
	250.00	200.00	22.00	15.00	.85	.50
☐399 5¢ Blue						
	525.00	410.00	85.00	60.00	11.00	5.25
☐400 10¢ Orange Yellow						
	800.00	600.00	160.00	110.00	17.00	11.00
☐400A 10¢ Orange						
	1400.00	1100.00	235.00	175.00	20.00	10.50

PERF. 10 (N-H ADD 50%)

Scott No.	Fine Unused Block	Ave. Unused Block	Fine Unused Each	Ave. Unused Each	Fine Used Each	Ave. Used Each
☐401 1¢ Green						
	250.00	180.00	32.00	22.00	7.00	5.00
☐402 2¢ Carmine						
	425.00	300.00	95.00	65.00	2.10	1.60
☐403 5¢ Blue						
	1400.00	1000.00	200.00	150.00	16.00	12.00

Scott No.	Fine Unused Block	Ave. Unused Block	Fine Unused Each	Ave. Unused Each	Fine Used Each	Ave. Used Each
☐404 10¢ Orange						
	6000.00	4100.00	1200.00	800.00	66.00	40.00

1912–1914. REGULAR ISSUE
PERF. 12 (N-H ADD 50%)

Scott No.	Fine Unused Block	Ave. Unused Block	Fine Unused Each	Ave. Unused Each	Fine Used Each	Ave. Used Each
☐405 1¢ Green						
	92.00	62.00	8.00	5.00	.25	.18
☐406 2¢ Carmine						
	94.00	85.00	6.00	4.00	.25	.18
☐407 7¢ Black						
	500.00	400.00	100.00	75.00	7.60	4.50

IMPERFORATE (N-H ADD 50%)

Scott No.	Fine Unused Block	Ave. Unused Block	Fine Unused Each	Ave. Unused Each	Fine Used Each	Ave. Used Each
☐408 1¢ Green						
	20.00	15.00	1.10	.74	.75	.40
☐409 2¢ Carmine						
	36.00	26.00	1.75	1.35	.75	.40

Scott No.	Fine Unused Line Pair	Ave. Unused Line Pair	Fine Unused Each	Ave. Unused Each	Fine Used Each	Ave. Used Each

1912. COIL STAMPS
PERF. 8½ HORIZONTALLY (N-H ADD 50%)

Scott No.	Fine Unused Line Pair	Ave. Unused Line Pair	Fine Unused Each	Ave. Unused Each	Fine Used Each	Ave. Used Each
☐410 1¢ Green						
	40.00	20.00	8.00	6.00	4.50	2.50
☐411 2¢ Carmine						
	50.00	26.00	12.00	8.00	4.50	2.50

PERF. 8½ VERTICALLY (N-H ADD 50%)

Scott No.	Fine Unused Line Pair	Ave. Unused Line Pair	Fine Unused Each	Ave. Unused Each	Fine Used Each	Ave. Used Each
☐412 1¢ Green						
	100.00	60.00	30.00	20.00	5.50	3.75
☐413 2¢ Carmine						
	200.00	150.00	50.00	32.00	1.10	.75

Scott No.	Fine Unused Block	Ave. Unused Block	Fine Unused Each	Ave. Unused Each	Fine Used Each	Ave. Used Each

1912–1914. SINGLE LINE WATERMARKED "U.S.P.S." PERF. 12 (N-H ADD 50%)

Scott No.	Fine Unused Block	Ave. Unused Block	Fine Unused Each	Ave. Unused Each	Fine Used Each	Ave. Used Each
☐414 8¢ Olive Green	300.00	200.00	55.00	32.00	1.50	1.20
☐415 9¢ Salmon Red	515.00	350.00	65.00	44.00	14.00	9.00
☐416 10¢ Orange Yellow	375.00	240.00	50.00	32.00	.50	.30
☐417 12¢ Claret Brown	340.00	240.00	60.00	40.00	4.25	2.75
☐418 15¢ Gray	475.00	360.00	100.00	65.00	4.00	2.75
☐419 20¢ Ultramarine	1000.00	700.00	210.00	145.00	15.00	10.00
☐420 30¢ Orange Red	650.00	450.00	150.00	110.00	15.00	10.00
☐421 50¢ Violet	2300.00	1600.00	500.00	380.00	20.00	12.00

1912. DOUBLE LINE WATERMARKED "U.S.P.S." (N-H ADD 50%)

Scott No.	Fine Unused Block	Ave. Unused Block	Fine Unused Each	Ave. Unused Each	Fine Used Each	Ave. Used Each
☐422 50¢ Violet	1275.00	950.00	350.00	225.00	20.00	10.00
☐423 $1 Violet Black	2900.00	2100.00	600.00	400.00	62.00	40.00

1914–1915. SINGLE LINE WATERMARKED "U.S.P.S." PERF. 10 (N-H ADD 55%)

Scott No.	Fine Unused Block	Ave. Unused Block	Fine Unused Each	Ave. Unused Each	Fine Used Each	Ave. Used Each
☐424 1¢ Green	31.00	21.00	4.00	3.00	.25	.20
☐425 2¢ Carmine	24.00	17.00	6.00	4.00	.25	.20
☐426 3¢ Deep Violet	115.00	72.00	20.00	12.00	1.65	1.00
☐427 4¢ Brown	240.00	80.00	40.00	30.00	.75	.50
☐428 5¢ Blue	250.00	150.00	40.00	26.00	.60	.35

Scott No.	Fine Unused Block	Ave. Unused Block	Fine Unused Each	Ave. Unused Each	Fine Used Each	Ave. Used Each
☐429 6¢ Orange						
	285.00	175.00	62.00	45.00	2.00	1.00
☐430 7¢ Black						
	675.00	610.00	100.00	70.00	4.75	3.50
☐431 8¢ Olive Green						
	300.00	285.00	50.00	32.00	2.00	1.00
☐432 9¢ Salmon Red						
	510.00	375.00	60.00	40.00	10.00	5.50
☐433 12¢ Orange Yellow						
	510.00	390.00	60.00	40.00	.36	.20
☐434 11¢ Dark Green						
	200.00	115.00	30.00	20.00	8.00	5.50
☐435 12¢ Claret Brown						
	215.00	150.00	34.00	22.00	5.00	3.00
☐435a 12¢ Copper Red						
	260.00	160.00	40.00	25.00	6.50	4.10
☐437 15¢ Gray						
	715.00	600.00	150.00	100.00	7.25	5.10
☐438 20¢ Ultramarine						
	2000.00	1500.00	250.00	175.00	4.00	3.00
☐439 30¢ Orange Red						
	2700.00	1800.00	350.00	220.00	20.00	12.00
☐440 50¢ Violet						
	9200.00	6500.00	700.00	500.00	20.00	12.00

Scott No.	Fine Unused Line Pair	Ave. Unused Line Pair	Fine Unused Each	Ave. Unused Each	Fine Used Each	Ave. Used Each

1914. COIL STAMPS
PERF. 10 HORIZONTALLY (N-H ADD 30%)

☐441 1¢ Green						
	8.00	5.00	2.00	1.25	1.00	.80
☐442 2¢ Carmine						
	55.00	36.00	12.00	8.00	8.00	5.00

PERF. 10 VERTICALLY (N-H ADD 50%)

☐443 1¢ Green						
	150.00	100.00	30.00	20.00	7.00	5.00

Scott No.	Fine Unused Line Pair	Ave. Unused Line Pair	Fine Unused Each	Ave. Unused Each	Fine Used Each	Ave. Used Each
□444 2¢ Carmine						
	250.00	150.00	44.00	30.00	1.80	1.50
□445 3¢ Violet						
	800.00	600.00	300.00	200.00	120.00	85.00
□446 4¢ Brown						
	550.00	375.00	175.00	125.00	45.00	28.00
□447 5¢ Blue						
	300.00	200.00	65.00	44.00	30.00	18.00

1914–1916. ROTARY PRESS COIL STAMPS PERF. 10 HORIZONTALLY (N-H ADD 50%)

□448 1¢ Green						
	34.00	24.00	9.00	6.00	4.00	2.75
□449 2¢ Red (I)						
	—	—	3000.00	2000.00	310.00	220.00
□450 2¢ Carmine (III)						
	50.00	35.00	15.00	10.00	4.00	2.75

PERF. 10 VERTICALLY (N-H ADD 60%)

□452 1¢ Green						
	65.00	40.00	14.00	10.00	2.50	1.50
□453 2¢ Red (I)						
	450.00	310.00	150.00	100.00	4.00	2.75
□454 2¢ Carmine (II)						
	410.00	305.00	120.00	100.00	10.00	7.25
□455 2¢ Carmine (III)						
	51.00	41.00	14.00	9.00	1.00	.60
□456 3¢ Violet						
	510.00	405.00	350.00	220.00	100.00	70.00
□457 4¢ Brown						
	125.00	86.00	40.00	26.00	17.00	12.00
□458 5¢ Blue						
	135.00	86.00	42.00	30.00	16.00	12.50

IMPERFORATE (N-H ADD 50%)

□459 2¢ Carmine						
	1325.00	825.00	500.00	375.00	—	—

Scott No.	Fine Unused Block	Ave. Unused Block	Fine Unused Each	Ave. Unused Each	Fine Used Each	Ave. Used Each

1915. DOUBLE LINE WATERMARKED "U.S.P.S." PERF. 10 (N-H ADD 40%)

☐460 $1 Violet Black

| | 4100.00 | 3100.00 | 1000.00 | 700.00 | 100.00 | 75.00 |

1915. SINGLE LINE WATERMARKED "U.S.P.S." PERF. 11 (N-H ADD 50%)

☐461 2¢ Pale Carmine Rose

| | 310.00 | 190.00 | 165.00 | 95.00 | 120.00 | 75.00 |

1916–1917. UNWATERMARKED PERF. 10 (N-H ADD 60%)

☐462 1¢ Green

| | 112.00 | 70.00 | 8.50 | 5.75 | .60 | .30 |

☐463 2¢ Carmine

| | 100.00 | 65.00 | 5.00 | 4.00 | .30 | .25 |

☐464 3¢ Violet

| | 1100.00 | 700.00 | 90.00 | 62.00 | 14.50 | 8.50 |

☐465 4¢ Orange Brown

| | 550.00 | 410.00 | 60.00 | 40.00 | 2.50 | 1.20 |

☐466 5¢ Blue

| | 825.00 | 600.00 | 100.00 | 55.00 | 3.00 | 1.50 |

☐467 5¢ Carmine (error)

| | — | 1100.00 | 800.00 | 500.00 | — | — |

☐468 6¢ Red Orange

| | 625.00 | 460.00 | 120.00 | 75.00 | 7.00 | 4.25 |

☐469 7¢ Black

| | 525.00 | 400.00 | 140.00 | 100.00 | 12.50 | 8.00 |

☐470 58¢ Olive Green

| | 475.00 | 300.00 | 75.00 | 50.00 | 6.00 | 3.50 |

☐471 9¢ Salmon Red

| | 410.00 | 290.00 | 70.00 | 46.00 | 14.00 | 8.50 |

☐472 12¢ Orange Yellow

| | 925.00 | 650.00 | 125.00 | 84.00 | 1.25 | .75 |

☐473 11¢ Dark Green

| | 230.00 | 165.00 | 46.00 | 30.00 | 18.00 | 12.00 |

☐474 12¢ Claret Brown

| | 425.00 | 290.00 | 60.00 | 40.00 | 6.00 | 4.25 |

☐475 15¢ Gray

| | 850.00 | 700.00 | 200.00 | 160.00 | 12.00 | 7.00 |

Scott No.	Fine Unused Block	Ave. Unused Block	Fine Unused Each	Ave. Unused Each	Fine Used Each	Ave. Used Each
☐476 20¢ Ultramarine						
	2000.00	1800.00	300.00	200.00	12.00	8.00
☐477 50¢ Light Violet						
	6200.00	4500.00	1400.00	900.00	70.00	45.00
☐478 $1 Violet Black						
	4200.00	2500.00	875.00	600.00	22.00	12.00

1916–1917. DESIGN OF 1902–1903
PERF. 10 (N-H ADD 40%)

Scott No.	Fine Unused Block	Ave. Unused Block	Fine Unused Each	Ave. Unused Each	Fine Used Each	Ave. Used Each
☐479 $2 Dark Blue						
	2000.00	1500.00	440.00	285.00	45.00	30.00
☐480 $5 Light Green						
	2000.00	1500.00	330.00	230.00	46.00	30.00

IMPERFORATE (N-H ADD 40%)

Scott No.	Fine Unused Block	Ave. Unused Block	Fine Unused Each	Ave. Unused Each	Fine Used Each	Ave. Used Each
☐481 1¢ Green						
	12.00	9.00	1.20	1.00	.85	.50
☐482 2¢ Carmine						
	21.00	16.00	2.00	1.40	1.40	1.00
☐483 3¢ Violet (I)						
	110.00	80.00	18.00	14.00	8.00	5.00
☐484 3¢ Violet (II)						
	100.00	64.00	12.00	10.00	5.00	3.25

Scott No.	Fine Unused Line Pair	Ave. Unused Line Pair	Fine Unused Each	Ave. Unused Each	Fine Used Each	Ave. Used Each
1916–1922. ROTARY PRESS COIL STAMPS						
PERF. 10 HORIZONTALLY (N-H ADD 50%)						
☐486 1¢ Green						
	4.00	3.10	2.00	1.00	.30	.20
☐487 2¢ Carmine (II)						
	110.00	75.00	20.00	14.00	5.00	2.00
☐488 2¢ Carmine (III)						
	18.00	11.00	4.00	3.00	1.80	1.00
☐489 3¢ Violet						
	32.00	21.00	6.00	4.25	1.50	1.00

Scott No.	Fine Unused Line Pair	Ave. Unused Line Pair	Fine Unused Each	Ave. Unused Each	Fine Used Each	Ave. Used Each
PERF. 10 VERTICALLY (N-H ADD 50%)						
☐490 1¢ Green						
	4.50	4.00	.80	.60	.40	.22
☐491 2¢ Carmine (II)						
	—	—	2500.00	1550.00	800.00	600.00
☐492 2¢ Carmine (III)						
	51.00	38.00	12.00	8.00	.30	.20
☐493 3¢ Violet (I)						
	95.00	72.00	24.00	18.00	3.50	2.25
☐494 3¢ Violet (II)						
	60.00	49.00	14.00	10.00	1.10	.80
☐495 4¢ Orange Brown						
	85.00	48.00	14.00	10.00	5.00	3.50
☐496 5¢ Blue						
	25.00	17.50	5.00	3.25	1.10	.80
☐497 10¢ Orange Yellow						
	140.00	72.00	25.00	18.00	10.00	6.00

Scott No.	Fine Unused Block	Ave. Unused Block	Fine Unused Each	Ave. Unused Each	Fine Used Each	Ave. Used Each
1917–1919. FLAT PLATE PRINTING						
PERF. 11 (N-H ADD 50%)						
☐498 1¢ Green						
	13.50	11.00	.75	.50	.25	.20
☐499 2¢ Rose (I)						
	15.00	11.50	.60	.45	.25	.20
☐500 2¢ Deep Rose (Ia)						
	1200.00	1000.00	300.00	200.00	175.00	125.00
☐501 3¢ Violet (I)						
	150.00	87.00	15.00	10.00	.30	.22
☐502 3¢ Violet (II)						
	160.00	110.00	22.00	14.00	.45	.25
☐503 4¢ Brown						
	160.00	105.00	15.00	10.00	.30	.20
☐504 5¢ Blue						
	125.00	85.00	12.00	8.00	.30	.20
☐505 5¢ Rose (error)						
	—	—	550.00	410.00	—	—

Scott No.		Fine Unused Block	Ave. Unused Block	Fine Unused Each	Ave. Unused Each	Fine Used Each	Ave. Used Each
□506	6¢ Red Orange						
		210.00	115.00	18.00	12.00	.50	.30
□507	7¢ Black						
		325.00	210.00	36.00	25.00	1.50	1.00
□508	8¢ Olive Bistre						
		185.00	100.00	16.00	12.00	1.50	1.00
□509	9¢ Salmon Red						
		175.00	105.00	20.00	14.00	2.50	1.85
□510	10¢ Orange Yellow						
		200.00	160.00	25.00	16.00	.30	.20
□511	11¢ Light Green						
		140.00	100.00	12.00	9.00	3.50	2.75
□512	12¢ Claret Brown						
		140.00	82.00	12.00	9.00	.70	.60
□513	13¢ Apple Green						
		120.00	85.00	15.00	10.00	6.50	6.00
□514	15¢ Gray						
		550.00	340.00	50.00	34.00	1.10	.75
□515	20¢ Ultramarine						
		650.00	400.00	68.00	45.00	.50	.30
□516	30¢ Orange Red						
		510.00	340.00	50.00	35.00	1.10	.95
□517	50¢ Red Violet						
		1200.00	710.00	90.00	60.00	1.00	.75
□518	$1 Violet Brown						
		850.00	600.00	75.00	50.00	2.00	1.40
□518b	$1 Deep Brown						
		2100.00	1600.00	1600.00	1000.00	650.00	400.00

1917. DOUBLE LINE WATERMARKED "U.S.P.S." DESIGN OF 1908–1909 PERF. 11 (N-H ADD 50%)

□519	2¢ Carmine						
		1800.00	1500.00	400.00	300.00	240.00	140.00

1918. UNWATERMARKED PERF. 11 (N-H ADD 40%)

□523	$2 Orange Red & Black						
		6800.00	5200.00	900.00	600.00	210.00	150.00
□524	$5 Deep Green & Black						
		3100.00	2100.00	350.00	250.00	30.00	20.00

Scott No.	Fine Unused Block	Ave. Unused Block	Fine Unused Each	Ave. Unused Each	Fine Used Each	Ave. Used Each
1918–1920. OFFSET PRINTING PERF. 11 (N-H ADD 50%)						
☐525 1¢ Gray Green						
	15.00	13.00	3.00	2.00	.85	.60
☐526 2¢ Carmine (IV)						
	165.00	110.00	30.00	24.00	4.50	2.50
☐527 2¢ Carmine (V)						
	100.00	70.00	20.00	15.00	1.25	.75
☐528 2¢ Carmine (Va)						
	50.00	30.00	12.00	8.00	.40	.25
☐528A 2¢ Carmine (VI)						
	250.00	210.00	60.00	40.00	1.50	.85
☐528B 2¢ Carmine (VII)						
	110.00	75.00	25.00	18.00	.40	.25
☐529 3¢ Violet (III)						
	48.00	32.00	4.00	3.00	.25	.18
☐530 3¢ Purple (IV)						
	10.00	5.50	1.50	1.20	.30	.20
1918–1920. IMPERFORATE (N-H ADD 30%)						
☐531 1¢ Gray Green						
	68.00	56.00	12.00	10.00	8.50	7.00
☐532 2¢ Carmine (IV)						
	220.00	185.00	42.00	32.00	30.00	24.00
☐533 2¢ Carmine (V)						
	1000.00	800.00	220.00	180.00	60.00	50.00
☐534 2¢ Carmine (Va)						
	100.00	66.00	15.00	11.00	8.00	6.50
☐534A 2¢ Carmine (VI)						
	240.00	200.00	40.00	32.00	24.00	19.00
☐534B 2¢ Carmine (VII)						
	—	—	1800.00	1400.00	550.00	350.00
☐535 3¢ Violet						
	62.00	40.00	10.00	8.00	6.75	4.50
1918–1920. PERF. 12 ½ (N-H ADD 50%)						
☐536 1¢ Gray Green						
	130.00	88.00	20.00	12.00	16.00	8.50

IMPORTANT NOTICE: Beginning here, prices of **blocks** are for blocks of 4 with **plate number attached**. Ordinary blocks of 4 bring lower prices. Plate blocks consisting of more than 4 stamps would sell higher than these sums. Always check the **headings** of price columns to accurately value your stamps.

Scott No.	Fine Unused Plate Blk	Ave. Unused Plate Blk	Fine Unused Each	Ave. Unused Each	Fine Used Each	Ave. Used Each
1919. VICTORY ISSUE (N-H ADD 70%)						
☐537 3¢ Violet						
	92.00	75.00	12.00	8.00	4.10	2.25
1919–1921. REGULAR ISSUE ROTARY PRESS PRINTING PERF. 11 x 10 (N-H ADD 70%)						
☐538 1¢ Green						
	80.00	55.00	12.00	8.50	8.50	4.50
☐538a Same Impf. Horiz. Pair						
	—	—	70.00	50.00	—	—
☐539 2¢ Carmine Rose (II)						
			3500.00	2500.00	1000.00	600.00
☐540 2¢ Carmine Rose (III)						
	72.00	50.00	14.00	9.00	8.50	6.00
☐540a Same Impf. Horiz. Pair						
	—	—	70.00	50.00	—	—
☐541 3¢ Violet						
	310.00	210.00	50.00	30.00	28.00	22.00
PERF. 10 x 11 (N-H ADD 70%)						
☐542 1¢ Green						
	110.00	85.00	15.00	10.00	1.10	.80
PERF. 10 x 10 (N-H ADD 70%)						
☐543 1¢ Green						
	14.50	10.00	.80	.50	.25	.20
PERF. 11 x 11 (N-H ADD 70%)						
☐544 1¢ Green						
	—	—	—	—	2500.00	1800.00
☐545 1¢ Green						
	700.00	575.00	180.00	120.00	110.00	80.00

Scott No.	Fine Unused Plate Blk	Ave. Unused Plate Blk	Fine Unused Each	Ave. Unused Each	Fine Used Each	Ave. Used Each
☐546 2¢ Carmine Rose						
	500.00	410.00	130.00	90.00	80.00	60.00

FLAT PLATE PRINTING PERF. 11 (N-H ADD 50%)
☐547 $2 Carmine & Black						
	—	—	260.00	180.00	40.00	26.00

1920. PILGRIM ISSUE (N-H ADD 50%)
☐548 1¢ Green						
	40.00	38.00	5.00	3.50	3.00	1.75
☐549 2¢ Carmine Rose						
	60.00	42.00	8.00	6.00	2.50	1.75
☐550 5¢ Deep Blue						
	425.00	300.00	52.00	38.00	15.00	13.00

1922–1925. PERF. FLAT PLATE PRINTING PERF. 11 (N-H ADD 50%)
☐551 ½¢ Olive Brown						
	7.25	6.10	.35	.25	.20	.15
☐552 1¢ Deep Green						
	24.00	17.00	2.00	1.40	.30	.20
☐553 1½¢ Yellow Brown						
	32.00	24.00	3.50	2.50	.35	.24
☐554 2¢ Carmine						
	20.00	17.00	2.50	1.80	.30	.20
☐555 3¢ Violet						
	170.00	140.00	25.00	16.00	1.10	.80
☐556 4¢ Yellow Brown						
	170.00	145.00	25.00	16.00	.40	.25
☐557 5¢ Dark Blue						
	180.00	160.00	25.00	16.00	.25	.16
☐558 6¢ Red Orange						
	310.00	275.00	42.00	32.00	1.00	.75
☐559 7¢ Black						
	68.00	50.00	11.00	8.00	.75	.55
☐560 8¢ Olive Green						
	500.00	400.00	50.00	40.00	.85	.50
☐561 9¢ Rose						
	150.00	100.00	22.00	16.00	1.50	1.00

Scott No.	Fine Unused Plate Blk	Ave. Unused Plate Blk	Fine Unused Each	Ave. Unused Each	Fine Used Each	Ave. Used Each
☐562 10¢ Orange						
	220.00	180.00	30.00	20.00	.25	.18
☐563 11¢ Blue/Green						
	34.00	22.00	2.00	1.40	.50	.35
☐564 12¢ Brown Violet						
	82.00	70.00	11.00	7.75	.25	.18
☐565 14¢ Dark Blue						
	65.00	40.00	6.50	4.50	1.25	.60
☐566 15¢ Gray						
	265.00	200.00	30.00	22.00	.30	.20
☐567 20¢ Carmine Rose						
	225.00	180.00	32.00	22.00	.30	.20
☐568 25¢ Green						
	225.00	160.00	26.00	18.00	.75	.40
☐569 30¢ Olive Brown						
	320.00	240.00	44.00	32.00	.60	.35
☐570 50¢ Lilac						
	950.00	650.00	72.00	55.00	.40	.20
☐571 $1 Violet Black						
	425.00	290.00	60.00	44.00	.60	.35
☐572 $2 Deep Blue						
	1200.00	1000.00	140.00	110.00	11.00	6.50
☐573 $5 Carmine & Blue						
	7800.00	5000.00	265.00	210.00	14.00	8.00

IMPERFORATE (N-H ADD 40%)

Scott No.	Fine Unused Plate Blk	Ave. Unused Plate Blk	Fine Unused Each	Ave. Unused Each	Fine Used Each	Ave. Used Each
☐575 1¢ Green						
	75.00	60.00	9.50	7.25	4.25	2.75
☐576 1½¢ Yellow Brown						
	24.00	18.00	2.50	1.75	1.50	.86
☐577 2¢ Carmine						
	24.00	17.00	2.40	1.75	1.50	.86

1923–1926. ROTARY PRESS PRINTING
PERF. 11 x 10 (N-H ADD 50%)

Scott No.	Fine Unused Plate Blk	Ave. Unused Plate Blk	Fine Unused Each	Ave. Unused Each	Fine Used Each	Ave. Used Each
☐578 1¢ Green						
	600.00	425.00	110.00	80.00	75.00	50.00
☐579 2¢ Carmine						
	400.00	240.00	90.00	60.00	48.00	30.00

Scott No.	Fine Unused Plate Blk	Ave. Unused Plate Blk	Fine Unused Each	Ave. Unused Each	Fine Used Each	Ave. Used Each
1923–1296. PERF. 10 (N-H ADD 50%)						
☐581 1¢ Green						
	98.00	72.00	11.00	7.00	1.00	.70
☐582 1½¢ Brown						
	45.00	25.00	5.50	4.00	.80	.60
☐583 2¢ Carmine						
	28.00	21.00	3.00	2.00	.30	.20
☐584 3¢ Violet						
	210.00	160.00	30.00	20.00	2.50	1.75
☐585 4¢ Yellow Brown						
	150.00	115.00	20.00	15.00	.80	.40
☐586 5¢ Blue						
	140.00	105.00	20.00	15.00	.40	.20
☐587 6¢ Red Orange						
	70.00	55.00	10.00	7.00	.85	.50
☐588 7¢ Black						
	100.00	70.00	13.00	9.00	6.00	3.50
☐589 8¢ Olive Green						
	200.00	165.00	30.00	20.00	4.00	2.50
☐590 9¢ Rose						
	50.00	26.00	6.00	4.25	2.50	1.60
☐591 10¢ Orange						
	575.00	425.00	70.00	50.00	.35	.20

1923–1926. ROTARY PRESS COIL STAMPS PERF. 11 (N-H ADD 50%)

Scott No.	Fine Unused Plate Blk	Ave. Unused Plate Blk	Fine Unused Each	Ave. Unused Each	Fine Used Each	Ave. Used Each
☐595 2¢ Carmine						
	1300.00	1000.00	325.00	275.00	250.00	150.00

Scott No.	Fine Unused Line Pair	Ave. Unused Line Pair	Fine Unused Each	Ave. Unused Each	Fine Used Each	Ave. Used Each
1923–1929. ROTARY PRESS COIL STAMPS PERF. 10 VERTICALLY (N-H ADD 50%)						
☐597 1¢ Green						
	2.10	1.50	.50	.35	.21	.15
☐598 1½¢ Deep Brown						
	4.50	3.50	1.00	.70	.25	.18
☐599 2¢ Carmine (I)						
	2.00	1.25	.55	.40	.25	.15

Scott No.	Fine Unused Line Pair	Ave. Unused Line Pair	Fine Unused Each	Ave. Unused Each	Fine Used Each	Ave. Used Each
☐599A 2¢ Carmine (II)						
	550.00	340.00	160.00	100.00	13.00	7.50
☐600 3¢ Deep Violet						
	26.00	21.00	6.75	5.25	.30	.20
☐601 4¢ Yellow Brown						
	29.00	20.00	5.00	3.75	.60	.35
☐602 5¢ Dark Blue						
	12.00	7.00	2.00	1.40	.30	.20
☐603 10¢ Orange						
	22.00	15.00	4.50	3.00	.25	.18

PERF. 10 HORIZONTALLY (N-H ADD 40%)

Scott No.	Fine Unused Line Pair	Ave. Unused Line Pair	Fine Unused Each	Ave. Unused Each	Fine Used Each	Ave. Used Each
☐604 1¢ Green						
	3.10	1.50	.40	.25	.24	.16
☐605 1¹/₂¢ Yellow Brown						
	2.80	1.50	.40	.25	.28	.17
☐606 2¢ Carmine						
	2.80	1.10	.40	.25	.28	.16

Scott No.	Fine Unused Plate Blk	Ave. Unused Plate Blk	Fine Unused Each	Ave. Unused Each	Fine Used Each	Ave. Used Each

1923. HARDING MEMORIAL ISSUE (N-H ADD 40%)

Scott No.	Fine Unused Plate Blk	Ave. Unused Plate Blk	Fine Unused Each	Ave. Unused Each	Fine Used Each	Ave. Used Each
☐610 2¢ Black, pf. 11						
	24.00	15.00	.75	.55	.25	.20
☐611 2¢ Black, imperf.						
	110.00	80.00	9.00	7.00	4.75	3.80
☐612 2¢ Black, pf. 10 rotary						
	280.00	190.00	20.00	15.00	2.25	1.80

1924. HUGUENOT–WALLOON ISSUE (N-H ADD 40%)

Scott No.	Fine Unused Plate Blk	Ave. Unused Plate Blk	Fine Unused Each	Ave. Unused Each	Fine Used Each	Ave. Used Each
☐614 1¢ Green						
	42.00	25.00	4.00	2.80	3.00	2.40
☐615 2¢ Carmine Rose						
	75.00	58.00	7.25	5.00	3.00	2.00
☐616 5¢ Dark Blue						
	350.00	250.00	40.00	30.00	17.00	12.00

Scott No.	Fine Unused Plate Blk	Ave. Unused Plate Blk	Fine Unused Each	Ave. Unused Each	Fine Used Each	Ave. Used Each
1925. LEXINGTON–CONCORD SESQUICENTENNIAL (N-H ADD 40%)						
☐617 1¢ Green						
	41.00	31.00	4.25	3.10	2.75	1.80
☐618 2¢ Carmine Rose						
	67.00	50.00	7.00	5.00	3.75	3.10
☐619 5¢ Dark Blue						
	310.00	210.00	35.00	25.00	16.00	11.00
1925. NORSE–AMERICAN ISSUE (N-H ADD 50%)						
☐620 2¢ Carmine & Black						
	170.00	120.00	6.00	4.10	3.75	2.30
☐621 5¢ Dark Blue & Black						
	600.00	410.00	20.00	17.00	14.00	11.00
1925–1926. PERF 11. (N-H ADD 40%)						
☐622 13¢ Green						
	150.00	95.00	18.00	14.00	1.00	.80
☐623 17¢ Black						
	170.00	125.00	22.00	16.00	.75	.40
1926–1927. COMMEMORATIVES **1926. SESQUICENTENNIAL EXPOSITION (N-H ADD 40%)**						
☐627 2¢ Carmine Rose						
	42.00	32.00	4.00	3.00	.65	.45
1926. ERICSSON MEMORIAL ISSUE (N-H ADD 40%)						
☐628 5¢ Gray Lilac						
	92.00	70.00	8.50	6.00	3.75	2.60
1926. BATTLE OF WHITE PLAINS (N-H ADD 40%)						
☐629 2¢ Carmine Rose						
	—	42.00	3.00	2.00	2.10	1.15
☐630 2¢ Souvenir Sheet of 25						
	—	—	600.00	450.00	—	—

Scott No.	Fine Unused Plate Blk	Ave. Unused Plate Blk	Fine Unused Each	Ave. Unused Each	Fine Used Each	Ave. Used Each

1926 ROTARY PRESS PRINTING IMPERFORATE (N-H ADD 30%)

☐631 1½¢ Brown

| | 60.00 | 46.00 | 3.00 | 2.00 | 1.75 | 1.10 |

1926–1928 DESIGNS OF 1926–1928 PERF. 11 x 10½ (N-H ADD 30%)

☐632 1¢ Green

| | 2.65 | 1.70 | .35 | .25 | .20 | .16 |

☐633 1½¢ Yellow Brown

| | 75.00 | 61.00 | 2.50 | 1.75 | .25 | .18 |

☐634 2¢ Carmine (I)

| | 1.60 | 1.10 | .32 | .22 | .20 | .16 |

☐634A 2¢ Carmine (II)

| | — | — | 350.00 | 225.00 | 16.00 | 12.00 |

☐635 3¢ Violet

| | 7.00 | 6.10 | .60 | .50 | .25 | .20 |

☐636 4¢ Yellow Brown

| | 76.00 | 60.00 | 3.50 | 2.75 | .40 | .25 |

☐637 5¢ Dark Blue

| | 21.00 | 16.00 | 2.75 | 2.00 | .40 | .25 |

☐638 6¢ Red Orange

| | 21.00 | 16.00 | 2.75 | 2.00 | .40 | .25 |

☐639 7¢ Black

| | 21.00 | 16.00 | 2.75 | 2.00 | .40 | .25 |

☐640 8¢ Olive Green

| | 21.00 | 16.00 | 3.00 | 2.00 | .40 | .25 |

☐641 9¢ Orange Red

| | 21.00 | 16.00 | 3.00 | 2.00 | .40 | .25 |

☐642 10¢ Orange

| | 29.00 | 21.00 | 5.50 | 4.25 | .60 | .30 |

1927. VERMONT SESQUICENTENNIAL (N-H ADD 45%)

☐643 2¢ Carmine Rose

| | 42.00 | 35.00 | 2.00 | 1.50 | 1.00 | .85 |

1927. BURGOYNE CAMPAIGN ISSUE (N-H ADD 45%)

☐644 2¢ Carmine

| | 44.00 | 38.00 | 5.00 | 4.00 | 3.00 | 1.80 |

Scott No.	Fine Unused Plate Blk	Ave. Unused Plate Blk	Fine Unused Each	Ave. Unused Each	Fine Used Each	Ave. Used Each

1928. VALLEY FORGE ISSUE (N-H ADD 40%)

☐645 2¢ Carmine

| | 31.00 | 25.00 | 1.50 | 1.00 | .60 | .40 |

1928. BATTLE OF MONMOUTH (N-H ADD 40%)

☐646 2¢ Carmine

| | 40.00 | 30.00 | 1.75 | 1.25 | 1.00 | .70 |

1928. DISCOVERY OF HAWAII (N-H ADD 30%)

☐647 2¢ Carmine Rose

| | 120.00 | 70.00 | 7.00 | 5.00 | 4.25 | 2.25 |

☐648 5¢ Blue

| | 230.00 | 160.00 | 20.00 | 15.00 | 11.00 | 6.50 |

1928. AERONAUTICS CONFERENCE (N-H ADD 30%)

☐649 2¢ Carmine

| | 12.00 | 10.00 | 1.75 | 1.25 | 1.00 | .60 |

☐650 5¢ Blue

| | 65.00 | 42.00 | 7.00 | 5.00 | 3.75 | 2.60 |

1929. GEORGE ROGERS CLARK (N-H ADD 30%)

☐651 2¢ Carmine & Black

| | 10.00 | 7.00 | .85 | .70 | .65 | .40 |

1929. DESIGNS OF 1922–1925 ROTARY PRESS PRINTING—PERF. 11 x 10½ (N-H ADD 30%)

☐653 ½¢ Olive Brown

| | 1.00 | .75 | .35 | .25 | .20 | .16 |

1929. EDISON COMMEMORATIVE FLAT PLATE PRINTING—PERF. 11 (N-H ADD 30%)

☐654 2¢ Carmine Rose

| | 28.00 | 20.00 | 1.00 | .80 | .75 | .56 |

1929. EDISON COMMEMORATIVE ROTARY PRESS PRINTING—PERF. 11 x 10½ (N-H ADD 40%)

☐655 2¢ Carmine Rose

| | 45.00 | 28.00 | 1.00 | .80 | .40 | .32 |

Scott No.	Fine Unused Line Pair	Ave. Unused Line Pair	Fine Unused Each	Ave. Unused Each	Fine Used Each	Ave. Used Each

1929. EDISON COMMEMORATIVE ROTARY PRESS COIL STAMPS—PERF. 10 VERTICALLY (N-H ADD 40%)

☐656 2¢ Carmine Rose

	65.00	40.00	17.00	14.00	2.50	1.50

Scott No.	Fine Unused Plate Blk	Ave. Unused Plate Blk	Fine Unused Each	Ave. Unused Each	Fine Used Each	Ave. Used Each

1929. SULLIVAN EXPEDITION (N-H ADD 40%)

☐657 2¢ Carmine Rose

	30.00	18.00	1.00	.75	.60	.50

1929. 632–42 OVERPRINTED (KANS.) (N-H ADD 30%)

☐658 1¢ Green

	30.00	20.00	3.00	2.00	1.85	1.20

☐659 ½¢ Brown

	46.00	30.00	4.25	3.00	2.50	2.25

☐660 2¢ Carmine

	38.00	28.00	4.25	3.00	.90	.80

☐661 3¢ Violet

	140.00	100.00	22.00	15.00	11.00	5.50

☐662 4¢ Yellow Brown

	200.00	150.00	22.00	15.00	8.75	6.50

☐663 5¢ Deep Blue

	125.00	80.00	18.00	12.00	8.75	7.00

☐664 6¢ Red Orange

	350.00	225.00	35.00	25.00	15.00	12.00

☐665 7¢ Black

	325.00	210.00	35.00	25.00	18.50	15.00

☐666 8¢ Olive Green

	800.00	600.00	100.00	70.00	62.00	45.00

☐667 9¢ Light Rose

	180.00	120.00	18.00	12.00	10.00	8.25

☐668 10¢ Orange Yellow

	300.00	220.00	30.00	20.00	10.00	8.25

Scott No.	Fine Unused Plate Blk	Ave. Unused Plate Blk	Fine Unused Each	Ave. Unused Each	Fine Used Each	Ave. Used Each

1929. 632–42 OVERPRINTED (NEBR.) (N-H ADD 45%)

Scott No.	Fine Unused Plate Blk	Ave. Unused Plate Blk	Fine Unused Each	Ave. Unused Each	Fine Used Each	Ave. Used Each
☐669 1¢ Green	32.00	22.00	3.75	2.50	2.00	1.25
☐670 1½¢ Brown	45.00	34.00	3.50	2.50	2.00	1.25
☐671 2¢ Carmine	28.00	23.00	3.00	2.00	1.00	.50
☐672 3¢ Violet	150.00	100.00	15.00	10.00	8.00	5.50
☐673 4¢ Brown	160.00	110.00	25.00	15.00	10.50	7.25
☐674 5¢ Blue	165.00	120.00	20.00	14.00	12.00	8.00
☐675 6¢ Orange	420.00	325.00	56.00	35.00	17.00	12.00
☐676 7¢ Black	215.00	175.00	30.00	19.00	13.00	7.50
☐677 8¢ Olive Green	330.00	250.00	40.00	26.00	19.00	12.00
☐678 9¢ Rose	360.00	250.00	50.00	30.00	21.00	14.00
☐679 10¢ Orange Yellow	725.00	500.00	125.00	85.00	18.00	10.00

1929. BATTLE OF FALLEN TIMBERS (N-H ADD 30%)

Scott No.	Fine Unused Plate Blk	Ave. Unused Plate Blk	Fine Unused Each	Ave. Unused Each	Fine Used Each	Ave. Used Each
☐680 2¢ Carmine Rose	28.00	20.00	2.25	1.75	1.00	.75

1929. OHIO RIVER CANALIZATION (N-H ADD 30%)

Scott No.	Fine Unused Plate Blk	Ave. Unused Plate Blk	Fine Unused Each	Ave. Unused Each	Fine Used Each	Ave. Used Each
☐681 2¢ Carmine Rose	20.00	15.00	1.80	.56	.75	.55

1930–1931. COMMEMORATIVES
1930. MASSACHUSETTS BAY COLONY (N-H ADD 35%)

Scott No.	Fine Unused Plate Blk	Ave. Unused Plate Blk	Fine Unused Each	Ave. Unused Each	Fine Used Each	Ave. Used Each
☐682 2¢ Carmine Rose	29.00	21.00	.90	.80	.50	.40

Scott No.	Fine Unused Plate Blk	Ave. Unused Plate Blk	Fine Unused Each	Ave. Unused Each	Fine Used Each	Ave. Used Each

1930. CAROLINA-CHARLESTON ISSUE (N-H ADD 35%)

☐683 2¢ Carmine Rose

| | 50.00 | 41.00 | 1.70 | 1.50 | 1.25 | 1.10 |

1930. REGULAR ISSUE ROTARY PRESS PRINTING—PERF. 11 x 10½ (N-H ADD 35%)

☐684 1½¢ Brown

| | 3.10 | 2.20 | .45 | .30 | .20 | .18 |

☐685 4¢ Brown

| | 11.00 | 7.50 | 1.10 | .80 | .20 | .18 |

Scott No.	Fine Unused Line Pair	Ave. Unused Line Pair	Fine Unused Each	Ave. Unused Each	Fine Used Each	Ave. Used Each

1930. ROTARY PRESS COIL STAMPS PERF. 10 VERTICALLY (N-H ADD 40%)

☐686 1½¢ Brown

| | 8.00 | 6.00 | 3.00 | 2.00 | .20 | .15 |

☐687 4¢ Brown

| | 15.00 | 11.00 | 4.00 | 3.00 | .70 | .30 |

Scott No.	Fine Unused Plate Blk	Ave. Unused Plate Blk	Fine Unused Each	Ave. Unused Each	Fine Used Each	Ave. Used Each

1930. BATTLE OF BRADDOCK'S FIELD (N-H ADD 40%)

☐688 2¢ Carmine Rose

| | 40.00 | 32.00 | 2.10 | 1.00 | .90 | .75 |

1930. VON STEUBEN ISSUE (N-H ADD 40%)

☐689 2¢ Carmine Rose

| | 22.00 | 17.00 | 1.00 | .75 | .60 | .40 |

1931. PULASKI ISSUE (N-H ADD 40%)

☐690 2¢ Carmine Rose

| | 16.00 | 11.00 | .30 | .23 | .20 | .17 |

Scott No.	Fine Unused Plate Blk	Ave. Unused Plate Blk	Fine Unused Each	Ave. Unused Each	Fine Used Each	Ave. Used Each

1931. DESIGNS OF 1922–1926 ROTARY PRESS PRINTING—PERF. 11 x 10½ (N-H ADD 40%)

☐692 11¢ Light Blue

| | 14.00 | 10.00 | 3.40 | 2.50 | .30 | .18 |

☐693 12¢ Brown Violet

| | 26.00 | 19.00 | 8.00 | 5.75 | .30 | .18 |

☐694 13¢ Yellow Green

| | 16.00 | 11.00 | 3.00 | 2.10 | .25 | .16 |

☐695 14¢ Dark Blue

| | 16.00 | 11.00 | 5.25 | 4.00 | .60 | .30 |

☐696 15¢ Gray

| | 42.00 | 30.00 | 11.00 | 8.25 | 2.00 | .75 |

1931. DESIGNS OF 1922–1926 ROTARY PRESS PRINTING—PERF. 10½ x 11 (N-H ADD 40%)

☐697 17¢ Black

| | 24.00 | 19.00 | 7.00 | 5.50 | .75 | .30 |

☐698 20¢ Carmine Rose

| | 40.00 | 26.00 | 12.50 | 9.50 | 1.20 | .60 |

☐699 25¢ Blue Green

| | 42.00 | 25.00 | 14.00 | 10.00 | .30 | .18 |

☐700 30¢ Brown

| | 70.00 | 42.00 | 22.00 | 16.50 | .30 | .18 |

☐701 50¢ Lilac

| | 260.00 | 140.00 | 54.00 | 40.00 | .30 | .18 |

1931. RED CROSS ISSUE (N-H ADD 10%)

☐702 2¢ Black & Red

| | 3.00 | 2.00 | .40 | .25 | .20 | .18 |

1931. SURRENDER OF YORKTOWN (N-H ADD 10%)

☐703 2¢ Carmine Rose & Black

| | 4.00 | 3.25 | .75 | .60 | .50 | .38 |

1932. WASHINGTON BICENTENNIAL (N-H ADD 10%)

☐704 ½¢ Olive Brown

| | 4.50 | 3.60 | .40 | .30 | .20 | .16 |

☐705 1¢ Green

| | 5.00 | 4.10 | .40 | .30 | .20 | .16 |

Scott No.	Fine Unused Plate Blk	Ave. Unused Plate Blk	Fine Unused Each	Ave. Unused Each	Fine Used Each	Ave. Used Each
□706 1½¢ Brown						
	18.00	14.00	.75	.60	.40	.20
□707 2¢ Carmine						
	2.00	1.25	.40	.25	.25	.20
□708 3¢ Purple						
	15.00	10.00	.80	.60	.25	.20
□709 4¢ Light Brown						
	6.00	5.00	.50	.35	.25	.20
□710 5¢ Blue						
	18.00	15.00	2.50	1.75	.25	.20
□711 6¢ Orange						
	70.00	55.00	5.00	3.75	.25	.20
□712 7¢ Black						
	7.50	5.75	.45	.35	.23	.19
□713 8¢ Olive Bistre						
	67.00	50.00	4.00	3.25	1.00	.60
□714 9¢ Pale Red						
	48.00	40.00	3.50	2.75	.40	.20
□715 10¢ Orange Yellow						
	120.00	92.00	15.00	12.00	.25	.20

1932. COMMEMORATIVES
1932. OLYMPIC WINTER GAMES (N-H ADD 30%)

□716 2¢ Carmine Rose						
	14.00	11.00	.70	.40	.30	.22

1932. ARBOR DAY ISSUE (N-H ADD 30%)

□717 2¢ Carmine Rose						
	8.00	7.00	.35	.22	.18	.16

1932. OLYMPIC SUMMER GAMES (N-H ADD 30%)

□718 3¢ Purple						
	18.00	12.00	2.00	1.60	.25	.18
□719 5¢ Blue						
	26.00	19.00	3.10	2.20	.40	.25

Scott No.	Fine Unused Line Pair	Ave. Unused Line Pair	Fine Unused Each	Ave. Unused Each	Fine Used Each	Ave. Used Each

1932. WASHINGTON ROTARY PRESS (N–H ADD 30%)
☐720 3¢ Deep Violet

			.40	.30	.25	.18
—	—					

1932. COIL PERF. 10 VERTICALLY (N-H ADD 30%)
☐721 3¢ Deep Violet

7.00	4.50	3.00	2.15	.25	.18

1932. COIL PERF. 10 HORIZONTALLY (N-H ADD 30%)
☐722 3¢ Deep Violet

5.50	4.25	1.80	1.10	.75	.62

1932. COIL DESIGN OF 1922–1925—PERF. 10 VERTICALLY (N-H ADD 30%)
☐723 6¢ Deep Orange

50.00	36.00	12.00	10.00	.40	.25

Scott No.	Fine Unused Plate Blk	Ave. Unused Plate Blk	Fine Unused Each	Ave. Unused Each	Fine Used Each	Ave. Used Each

1932. WILLIAM PENN ISSUE (N-H ADD 30%)
☐724 3¢ Violet

15.00	10.50	.50	.32	.28	.20

1932. DANIEL WEBSTER ISSUE (N-H ADD 30%)
☐725 3¢ Violet

25.00	20.00	.50	.40	.35	.30

1933. COMMEMORATIVES
1933. GEORGIA BICENTENNIAL (N-H ADD 30%)
☐726 3¢ Violet

15.00	12.00	.50	.34	.30	.20

1933. PEACE SESQUICENTENNIAL (N-H ADD 30%)
☐727 3¢ Violet

7.25	5.00	.35	.25	.20	.16

Scott No.	Fine Unused Plate Blk	Ave. Unused Plate Blk	Fine Unused Each	Ave. Unused Each	Fine Used Each	Ave. Used Each

1933. CENTURY OF PROGRESS EXPOSITION (N-H ADD 30%)

☐728 1¢ Yellow Green						
	3.00	2.50	.40	.30	.20	.18
☐729 3¢ Purple						
	4.00	3.10	.40	.30	.20	.18

1933. A.P.S. CONVENTION AND EXHIBITION AT CHICAGO IMPERFORATE—UNGUMMED (N-H ADD 30%)

☐730 1¢ Yellow Green, sheet of 25						
	—	—	34.00	30.00	—	—
☐730a 1¢ Yellow Green, sgl.						
	—	—	.80	.60	.55	.35
☐731 3¢ Violet, sheet of 25						
	—	—	35.00	26.00	—	—
☐731a 3¢ Violet, single						
	—	—	.70	.60	.50	.36

1933. N.R.A. ISSUE (N-H ADD 25%)

☐732 3¢ Violet						
	2.50	1.85	.40	.30	.20	.15

1933. BYRD ANTARCTIC EXPEDITION (N-H ADD 30%)

☐733 3¢ Dark Blue						
	18.00	14.00	.80	.70	.60	.50

1933. KOSCIUSZKO ISSUE (N-H ADD 30%)

☐734 5¢ Blue						
	36.00	29.00	.80	.65	.50	.28

1934. NATIONAL PHILATELIC EXHIBITION IMPERFORATE—UNGUMMED (N-H ADD 30%)

☐735 3¢ Dark Blue, sheet of 6						
	—	—	20.00	17.00	15.00	11.00
☐735a 3¢ Dark Blue, sgl.						
	—	—	3.25	3.00	2.75	1.65

Scott No.	Fine Unused Plate Blk	Ave. Unused Plate Blk	Fine Unused Each	Ave. Unused Each	Fine Used Each	Ave. Used Each

1934. COMMEMORATIVES
1934. MARYLAND TERCENTENARY (N-H ADD 30%)

☐736 3¢ Rose						
	12.00	8.50	.40	.30	.20	.16

1934. MOTHER'S DAY ISSUE ROTARY PRESS PRINTING—PERF. 11 x 10½ (N-H ADD 30%)

☐737 3¢ Deep Violet						
	2.00	1.50	.40	.30	.20	.18

FLAT PRESS PRINTING—PERF. 11 (N-H ADD 30%)

☐738 3¢ Deep Violet						
	5.00	4.00	.40	.30	.20	.18

1934. WISCONSIN TERCENTENARY (N-H ADD 30%)

☐739 3¢ Deep Violet						
	5.00	3.60	.40	.30	.20	.18

1934. NATIONAL PARKS ISSUE (N-H ADD 25%)

Scott No.	Fine Unused Plate Blk	Ave. Unused Plate Blk	Fine Unused Each	Ave. Unused Each	Fine Used Each	Ave. Used Each
☐740 1¢ Green	1.90	1.25	.35	.25	.20	.16
☐741 2¢ Red	1.80	1.40	.35	.25	.20	.16
☐742 3¢ Purple	2.40	1.60	.35	.25	.20	.16
☐743 4¢ Brown	9.25	7.00	.60	.50	.45	.30
☐744 5¢ Blue	12.00	9.50	1.25	1.00	.75	.50
☐745 6¢ Indigo	20.00	15.00	1.60	1.30	1.00	.75
☐746 7¢ Black	15.00	8.50	1.25	.85	.70	.55
☐747 8¢ Green	25.00	16.00	3.00	2.00	1.75	1.10
☐748 9¢ Salmon	19.00	16.00	3.00	2.00	.80	.60
☐749 10¢ Gray Black	30.00	22.00	4.25	3.50	1.50	.85

Scott No.	Fine Unused Plate Blk	Ave. Unused Plate Blk	Fine Unused Each	Ave. Unused Each	Fine Used Each	Ave. Used Each

1934. A.P.S. CONVENTION AND EXHIBITION AT ATLANTIC CITY IMPERFORATE SOUVENIR SHEET (N-H ADD 25%)

Scott No.	Fine Unused Plate Blk	Ave. Unused Plate Blk	Fine Unused Each	Ave. Unused Each	Fine Used Each	Ave. Used Each
☐750 3¢ Purple, sheet of 6	—	—	45.00	—	30.00	19.00
☐750a 3¢ Purple, single	—	—	5.50	4.75	4.00	3.00

1934. TRANS-MISSISSIPPI PHILATELIC EXPOSITION AND CONVENTION AT OMAHA IMPERFORATE SOUVENIR SHEET (N-H ADD 25%)

Scott No.	Fine Unused Plate Blk	Ave. Unused Plate Blk	Fine Unused Each	Ave. Unused Each	Fine Used Each	Ave. Used Each
☐751 1¢ Green, sheet of 6	—	—	15.00	—	11.00	8.50
☐751a 1¢ Green, single	—	—	2.00	1.70	1.50	1.25

Scott No.	Plate Block	Block Plain	Mint Each	Used Each

1935. "FARLEY SPECIAL PRINTINGS" DESIGNS OF 1933–1934 PERF. 10½ x 11—UNGUMMED (N-H ADD 25%)

Scott No.	Plate Block	Block Plain	Mint Each	Used Each
☐752 3¢ Violet	18.00	4.50	.25	.18

1935. PERF. 11—GUMMED (N-H ADD 25%)

Scott No.	Plate Block	Block Plain	Mint Each	Used Each
☐753 3¢ Dark Blue	19.00	2.00	.60	.50

1935. IMPERFORATE—UNGUMMED (N-H ADD 25%)

Scott No.	Plate Block	Block Plain	Mint Each	Used Each
☐754 3¢ Deep Violet	19.00	3.50	.65	.60
☐755 3¢ Deep Violet	19.00	3.50	.65	.60

1935. NATIONAL PARKS IMPERFORATE—UNGUMMED (N-H ADD 25%)

Scott No.	Plate Block	Block Plain	Mint Each	Used Each
☐756 1¢ Green	7.00	1.60	.30	.20
☐757 2¢ Red	8.50	1.50	.30	.20

Scott No.	Plate Block	Block Plain	Mint Each	Used Each
☐758 3¢ Deep Violet	18.00	12.00	.62	.55

Scott No.			Plate Block	Block Plain	Mint Each	Used Each
☐759	4¢	Brown	25.00	12.00	1.15	1.00
☐760	5¢	Blue	30.00	17.00	2.75	2.00
☐761	6¢	Dark Blue	51.00	25.00	2.80	2.50
☐762	7¢	Black	40.00	20.00	2.00	1.80
☐763	8¢	Sage Green	50.00	21.00	2.50	2.00
☐764	9¢	Red Orange	50.00	30.00	2.50	2.20
☐765	10¢	Gray Black	60.00	40.00	4.50	3.80

1935. IMPERFORATE—UNGUMMED (N–H ADD 25%)

☐766a	1¢	Yellow Green	—	15.00	1.00	.55
☐767a	3¢	Violet	—	15.00	1.00	.55
☐768a	3¢	Dark Blue	—	20.00	3.25	2.80
☐769a	1¢	Green	—	12.00	2.00	1.50
☐770a	3¢	Deep Violet	—	26.00	4.00	3.25

1935. DESIGN OF CE 1 (N–H ADD 30%)

☐771	16¢	Dark Blue	87.00	41.00	3.10	2.60

1935–1936. COMMEMORATIVES

Scott No.			Fine Unused Plate Blk	Ave. Unused Plate Blk	Mint Each	Used Each

1935. CONNECTICUT TERCENTENARY (N-H ADD 25%)

☐772	3¢	Red Violet	2.60	2.25	.25	.18

1935. CALIFORNIA PACIFIC EXPOSITION (N-H ADD 25%)

☐773	3¢	Purple	2.75	2.25	.25	.18

1935. BOULDER DAM ISSUE (N-H ADD 25%)

☐774	3¢	Purple	2.50	2.15	.25	.18

1935. MICHIGAN CENTENARY (N-H ADD 25%)

☐775	3¢	Purple	2.75	2.25	.25	.18

1936. TEXAS CENTENNIAL (N-H ADD 25%)

☐776	3¢	Purple	2.10	1.75	.25	.18

Scott No.	Plate Block	Block Plain	Mint Each	Used Each

1936. RHODE ISLAND TERCENTENARY (N-H ADD 25%)

Scott No.	Plate Block	Block Plain	Mint Each	Used Each
☐777 3¢ Purple	2.50	2.25	.25	.18

1936. THIRD INTL. PHILATELIC EXHIBITION "TIPEX" IMPERFORATE SOUVENIR SHEET DESIGNS OF 772, 773, 775, 776 (N-H ADD 25%)

Scott No.	Plate Block	Block Plain	Mint Each	Used Each
☐778 3¢ Red Violet, sheet of 4	—	—	3.10	2.70
☐778a 3¢ Red Violet, single	—	—	.90	.70
☐778b 3¢ Red Violet, single	—	—	.90	.70
☐778c 3¢ Red Violet, single	—	—	.90	.70
☐778d 3¢ Red Violet, single	—	—	.90	.70

1936. ARKANSAS CENTENNIAL (N-H ADD 25%)

Scott No.	Plate Block	Block Plain	Mint Each	Used Each
☐782 3¢ Purple	2.40	1.80	.25	.18

Scott No.	Fine Unused Plate Blk	Ave. Unused Plate Blk	Fine Unused Each	Ave. Unused Each	Fine Used Each	Ave. Used Each

1936. OREGON TERRITORY CENTENNIAL (N-H ADD 25%)

Scott No.	Fine Unused Plate Blk	Ave. Unused Plate Blk	Fine Unused Each	Ave. Unused Each	Fine Used Each	Ave. Used Each
☐783 3¢ Purple						
	2.00	1.55	.40	.30	.25	.20

1936. SUFFRAGE FOR WOMEN ISSUE (N-H ADD 25%)

☐784 3¢ Dark Violet						
	1.75	1.00	.40	.30	.25	.20

1936–1937. ARMY AND NAVY ISSUE ARMY COMMEMORATIVES (N-H ADD 20%)

☐785 1¢ Green						
	1.75	1.20	.35	.25	.22	.20
☐786 2¢ Carmine						
	1.75	1.20	.35	.25	.22	.20
☐787 3¢ Purple						
	1.85	1.60	.35	.28	.22	.20

Scott No.	Fine Unused Plate Blk	Ave. Unused Plate Blk	Fine Unused Each	Ave. Unused Each	Fine Used Each	Ave. Used Each
☐788 4¢ Gray						
	13.00	11.00	.75	.45	.40	.22
☐789 5¢ Ultramarine						
	14.00	11.00	.90	.55	.41	.22

NAVY COMMEMORATIVES (N-H ADD 25%)

☐790 1¢ Green						
	—	1.25	.35	.25	.20	.18
☐791 2¢ Carmine						
	1.50	1.25	.35	.25	.20	.18
☐792 3¢ Purple						
	1.90	1.55	.28	.25	.20	.18
☐793 4¢ Gray						
	13.00	12.00	.55	.40	.38	.18
☐794 5¢ Ultramarine						
	16.00	12.50	.90	.60	.40	.23

1937. COMMEMORATIVES
1937. NORTHWEST ORDINANCE ISSUE (N-H ADD 25%)

☐795 3¢ Violet						
	2.00	1.40	.40	.30	.25	.18

1937. VIRGINIA DARE ISSUE (N-H ADD 20%)

☐796 5¢ Gray Blue						
	10.00	8.75	.45	.28	.25	.18

1937. S.P.A. CONVENTION ISSUE (N-H ADD 25%)
DESIGN OF 749 IMPERFORATE SOUVENIR SHEET

☐797 10¢ Blue Green						
	—	—	1.75	1.25	.85	.60

1937. CONSTITUTIONAL SESQUICENTENNIAL (N-H ADD 25%)

☐798 3¢ Red Violet						
	2.10	1.85	.40	.30	.22	.18

Scott No.	Fine Unused Plate Blk	Ave. Unused Plate Blk	Fine Unused Each	Ave. Unused Each	Fine Used Each	Ave. Used Each

1937. TERRITORIAL PUBLICITY ISSUE (N-H ADD 25%)

Scott No.	Fine Unused Plate Blk	Ave. Unused Plate Blk	Fine Unused Each	Ave. Unused Each	Fine Used Each	Ave. Used Each
□799 3¢ Violet						
	2.90	1.55	.30	.25	.20	.16
□800 3¢ Violet						
	2.90	1.55	.30	.25	.20	.16
□801 3¢ Bright Violet						
	2.90	1.55	.30	.25	.20	.16
□802 3¢ Light Violet						
	2.90	1.55	.30	.25	.20	.16

1938. PRESIDENTIAL SERIES ROTARY PRESS PRINTING—PERF. 11 x 10½ (N-H ADD 25%)

Scott No.	Fine Unused Plate Blk	Ave. Unused Plate Blk	Fine Unused Each	Ave. Unused Each	Fine Used Each	Ave. Used Each
□803 ½¢ Red Orange						
	.75	.50	.30	.28	.20	.16
□804 1¢ Green						
	.65	.40	.30	.28	.20	.16
□805 1½¢ Bistre Brown						
	.65	.40	.30	.28	.20	.16
□806 2¢ Rose Carmine						
	.75	.45	.30	.28	.20	.16
□807 3¢ Deep Violet						
	.75	.40	.30	.28	.20	.16
□808 4¢ Red Violet						
	2.90	2.60	1.40	.28	.20	.16
□809 4½¢ Dark Gray						
	2.00	1.60	.30	.22	.20	.16
□810 5¢ Bright Blue						
	1.50	1.30	.35	.28	.24	.18
□811 6¢ Red Orange						
	2.00	1.60	.35	.28	.24	.18
□812 7¢ Sepia						
	2.00	1.70	.40	.30	.24	.18
□813 8¢ Olive Green						
	2.10	1.90	.45	.30	.24	.18
□814 9¢ Rose Pink						
	2.40	2.00	.46	.30	.24	.18
□815 10¢ Brown Red						
	2.00	1.70	.45	.30	.24	.18

Scott No.	Fine Unused Plate Blk	Ave. Unused Plate Blk	Fine Unused Each	Ave. Unused Each	Fine Used Each	Ave. Used Each
☐816 11¢ Ultramarine						
	5.00	4.00	.80	.40	.22	.18
☐817 12¢ Bright Violet						
	7.00	6.00	1.40	.75	.22	.18
☐818 13¢ Blue Green						
	10.00	8.50	2.30	.75	.22	.18
☐819 14¢ Blue						
	6.00	5.00	1.10	.75	.22	.18
☐820 15¢ Blue Gray						
	3.00	2.00	.70	.60	.22	.18
☐821 16¢ Black						
	8.00	7.00	1.50	.80	.60	.46
☐822 17¢ Rose Red						
	6.50	5.50	1.50	.80	.22	.18
☐823 18¢ Brown Carmine						
	12.00	10.00	2.40	1.60	.22	.18
☐824 19¢ Bright Violet						
	10.00	8.50	2.00	1.25	.60	.50
☐825 20¢ Bright Blue Green						
	5.00	4.00	1.50	1.00	.25	.18
☐826 21¢ Dull Blue						
	11.00	8.00	2.30	1.75	.25	.18
☐827 22¢ Vermilion						
	15.00	12.00	1.60	1.00	.60	.45
☐828 24¢ Gray Black						
	20.00	17.00	4.30	2.75	.35	.22
☐829 25¢ Deep Red Lilac						
	5.00	3.50	1.25	.80	.25	.18
☐830 30¢ Deep Ultramarine						
	25.00	20.00	5.00	3.75	.25	.18
☐831 50¢ Light Red Violet						
	40.00	34.00	9.00	6.00	.25	.18

FLAT PLATE PRINTING—PERF. 11 (N-H ADD 20%)

Scott No.	Fine Unused Plate Blk	Ave. Unused Plate Blk	Fine Unused Each	Ave. Unused Each	Fine Used Each	Ave. Used Each
☐832 $1 Purple & Black						
	46.00	38.00	10.00	6.50	.40	.18
☐832b $1 Watermarked						
	—	—	300.00	240.00	67.00	50.00

Scott No.	Fine Unused Plate Blk	Ave. Unused Plate Blk	Fine Unused Each	Ave. Unused Each	Fine Used Each	Ave. Used Each
☐832c $1 Dry Printing, Thick Paper (1954)						
	40.00	36.00	10.00	6.50	.30	.20
☐833 $2 Green & Black						
	140.00	140.00	32.00	22.00	7.00	5.50
☐834 $5 Carmine & Black						
	540.00	400.00	150.00	110.00	8.00	5.00

1938–1939. COMMEMORATIVES
1938. CONSTITUTION RATIFICATION (N-H ADD 25%)

☐835 3¢ Deep Violet						
	6.00	4.00	.50	.40	.30	.18

1938. SWEDISH-FINNISH TERCENTENARY (N-H ADD 25%)

☐836 3¢ Red Violet						
	5.50	3.00	.60	.40	.30	.18

1938. NORTHWEST COLONIZATION (N-H ADD 25%)

☐837 3¢ Bright Violet						
	13.00	10.00	.60	.40	.30	.18

1938. IOWA TERRITORY CENTENNIAL (N-H ADD 25%)

☐838 3¢ Violet						
	9.00	7.00	.60	.40	.30	.18

Scott No.	Fine Unused Line Pair	Ave. Unused Line Pair	Fine Unused Each	Ave. Unused Each	Fine Used Each	Ave. Used Each

1939. ROTARY PRESS COIL STAMPS
PERF. 10 VERTICALLY (N-H ADD 25%)

☐839 1¢ Green						
	1.30	1.25	.60	.30	.22	.18
☐840 1½¢ Bistre Brown						
	1.50	1.30	.60	.30	.22	.18
☐841 2¢ Rose Carmine						
	1.90	1.75	.60	.30	.22	.18
☐842 3¢ Deep Violet						
	1.60	1.40	.75	.40	.25	.18

Scott No.	Fine Unused Line Pair	Ave. Unused Line Pair	Fine Unused Each	Ave. Unused Each	Fine Used Each	Ave. Used Each
☐843 4¢ Red Violet						
	30.00	22.00	8.50	7.00	.70	.50
☐844 4¹/₂¢ Dark Gray						
	5.50	4.00	1.75	.85	.70	.50
☐845 5¢ Bright Blue						
	26.00	20.00	7.00	5.00	.50	.36
☐846 6¢ Red Orange						
	7.25	5.50	2.50	1.40	.30	.20
☐847 10¢ Brown Red						
	40.00	30.00	12.00	9.00	.72	.50

PERF. 10 HORIZONTALLY (N-H ADD 25%)

Scott No.	Fine Unused Line Pair	Ave. Unused Line Pair	Fine Unused Each	Ave. Unused Each	Fine Used Each	Ave. Used Each
☐848 1¢ Green						
	2.90	2.40	1.00	.80	.30	.20
☐849 1¹/₂¢ Bistre Brown						
	3.50	3.00	1.75	1.25	.60	.55
☐850 2¢ Rose Carmine						
	6.00	4.50	3.40	2.40	.80	.60
☐851 3¢ Deep Violet						
	6.00	5.75	3.00	2.25	.80	.55

Scott No.	Fine Unused Plate Blk	Ave. Unused Plate Blk	Fine Unused Each	Ave. Unused Each	Fine Used Each	Ave. Used Each

1939. GOLDEN GATE INTERNATIONAL EXPOSITION (N-H ADD 25%)

Scott No.	Fine Unused Plate Blk	Ave. Unused Plate Blk	Fine Unused Each	Ave. Unused Each	Fine Used Each	Ave. Used Each
☐852 3¢ Bright Purple						
	2.10	1.75	.45	.30	.22	.18

1939. NEW YORK WORLD'S FAIR (N-H ADD 20%)

Scott No.	Fine Unused Plate Blk	Ave. Unused Plate Blk	Fine Unused Each	Ave. Unused Each	Fine Used Each	Ave. Used Each
☐853 3¢ Deep Purple						
	2.40	1.80	.45	.30	.22	.18

1939. WASHINGTON INAUGURATION SESQUICENTENNIAL (N-H ADD 20%)

Scott No.	Fine Unused Plate Blk	Ave. Unused Plate Blk	Fine Unused Each	Ave. Unused Each	Fine Used Each	Ave. Used Each
☐854 3¢ Bright Red Violet						
	6.75	3.75	.65	.40	.25	.18

Scott No.	Fine Unused Plate Blk	Ave. Unused Plate Blk	Fine Unused Each	Ave. Unused Each	Fine Used Each	Ave. Used Each

1939. BASEBALL CENTENNIAL (N-H ADD 20%)

☐855 3¢ Violet

| | 11.00 | 7.00 | 2.50 | .70 | .24 | .18 |

1939. 25TH ANNIVERSARY PANAMA CANAL (N-H ADD 20%)

☐856 3¢ Deep Red Violet

| | 5.00 | 3.25 | .45 | .28 | .20 | .18 |

1939. COLONIAL PRINTING TERCENTENARY (N-H ADD 20%)

☐857 3¢ Rose Violet

| | 2.00 | 1.75 | .40 | .30 | .20 | .18 |

1939. 50TH ANNIVERSARY OF STATEHOOD (N-H ADD 20%)

☐858 3¢ Rose Violet

| | 2.10 | 1.60 | .40 | .30 | .20 | .18 |

1940. FAMOUS AMERICANS SERIES
AMERICAN AUTHORS (N-H ADD 20%)

☐859 1¢ Bright Blue Green

| | 1.70 | 1.50 | .30 | .28 | .22 | .18 |

☐860 2¢ Rose Carmine

| | 1.70 | 1.40 | .30 | .28 | .22 | .18 |

☐861 3¢ Bright Red Violet

| | 1.80 | 1.50 | .30 | .28 | .22 | .18 |

☐862 5¢ Ultramarine

| | 16.00 | 12.00 | .45 | .40 | .36 | .35 |

☐863 10¢ Dark Brown

| | 55.00 | 40.00 | 2.60 | 2.10 | 1.80 | 1.45 |

AMERICAN POETS (N-H ADD 20%)

☐864 1¢ Bright Blue Green

| | 2.50 | 2.25 | .30 | .28 | .22 | .18 |

Scott No.	Fine Unused Plate Blk	Ave. Unused Plate Blk	Fine Unused Each	Ave. Unused Each	Fine Used Each	Ave. Used Each
☐865 2¢ Rose Carmine						
	2.60	2.35	.40	.32	.22	.18
☐866 3¢ Bright Red Violet						
	3.25	3.00	.40	.32	.22	.18
☐867 5¢ Ultramarine						
	15.00	11.00	.55	.45	.35	.30
☐868 10¢ Dark Brown						
	50.00	38.00	2.60	2.30	2.25	1.90

AMERICAN EDUCATORS (N-H ADD 20%)

Scott No.	Fine Unused Plate Blk	Ave. Unused Plate Blk	Fine Unused Each	Ave. Unused Each	Fine Used Each	Ave. Used Each
☐869 1¢ Bright Blue Green						
	3.25	2.60	.32	.28	.22	.18
☐870 2¢ Rose Carmine						
	2.00	1.75	.32	.28	.22	.18
☐871 3¢ Bright Red Violet						
	4.20	3.00	.35	.28	.22	.18
☐872 5¢ Ultramarine						
	16.00	12.00	.55	.45	.40	.26
☐873 10¢ Dark Brown						
	40.00	30.00	2.75	2.00	1.90	1.70

AMERICAN SCIENTISTS (N-H ADD 20%)

Scott No.	Fine Unused Plate Blk	Ave. Unused Plate Blk	Fine Unused Each	Ave. Unused Each	Fine Used Each	Ave. Used Each
☐874 1¢ Bright Blue Green						
	1.80	1.60	.30	.26	.22	.18
☐875 2¢ Rose Carmine						
	1.50	1.40	.30	.26	.22	.18
☐876 3¢ Bright Red Violet						
	1.75	1.50	.30	.26	.22	.18
☐877 5¢ Ultramarine						
	10.00	7.00	.40	.38	.35	.29
☐878 10¢ Dark Brown						
	33.00	26.00	1.80	1.65	1.60	1.30

AMERICAN COMPOSERS (N-H ADD 20%)

Scott No.	Fine Unused Plate Blk	Ave. Unused Plate Blk	Fine Unused Each	Ave. Unused Each	Fine Used Each	Ave. Used Each
☐879 1¢ Bright Blue Green						
	1.85	1.70	.30	.26	.22	.18
☐880 2¢ Rose Carmine						
	1.80	1.70	.30	.26	.22	.18
☐881 3¢ Bright Red Violet						
	1.85	1.70	.30	.26	.22	.18

Scott No.	Fine Unused Plate Blk	Ave. Unused Plate Blk	Fine Unused Each	Ave. Unused Each	Fine Used Each	Ave. Used Each
☐882 5¢ Ultramarine						
	13.00	11.00	.70	.50	.33	.31
☐883 10¢ Dark Brown						
	50.00	38.00	5.00	3.50	2.00	1.60

AMERICAN ARTISTS (N-H ADD 20%)

☐884 1¢ Bright Blue Green						
	1.40	1.10	.30	.22	.20	.16
☐885 2¢ Rose Carmine						
	1.35	1.10	.30	.22	.20	.16
☐886 3¢ Bright Red Violet						
	1.35	1.00	.30	.22	.20	.16
☐887 5¢ Ultramarine						
	13.00	9.00	.70	.60	.40	.35
☐888 10¢ Dark Brown						
	42.00	34.00	2.40	1.90	1.60	1.35

AMERICAN INVENTORS (N-H ADD 20%)

☐889 1¢ Bright Blue Green						
	3.00	2.50	.30	.24	.20	.18
☐890 2¢ Rose Carmine						
	1.75	1.25	.30	.24	.20	.18
☐891 3¢ Bright Red Violet						
	2.40	2.00	.42	.26	.20	.18
☐892 5¢ Ultramarine						
	20.00	16.00	1.30	.85	.52	.45
☐893 10¢ Dark Brown						
	110.00	85.00	13.00	11.00	3.20	2.75

1940. COMMEMORATIVES
1940. 80TH ANNIVERSARY OF PONY EXPRESS (N-H ADD 20%)

☐894 3¢ Henna Brown						
	5.00	3.25	.45	.30	.22	.18

1940. 50TH ANNIVERSARY OF PAN-AMERICAN UNION (N-H ADD 20%)

☐895 3¢ Light Violet						
	5.00	3.50	.40	.28	.22	.18

Scott No.	Fine Unused Plate Blk	Ave. Unused Plate Blk	Fine Unused Each	Ave. Unused Each	Fine Used Each	Ave. Used Each

1940. 50TH ANNIVERSARY OF IDAHO (N-H ADD 20%)

☐896 3¢ Bright Violet						
	3.50	2.50	.35	.25	.20	.18

1940. 50TH ANNIVERSARY OF WYOMING (N-H ADD 20%)

☐897 3¢ Brown Violet						
	2.75	2.00	.35	.25	.20	.18

1940. 400TH ANNIVERSARY OF COLORADO EXPEDITION (N-H ADD 20%)

☐898 3¢ Violet						
	2.40	2.00	.26	.25	.20	.18

1940. NATIONAL DEFENSE ISSUE (N-H ADD 20%)

☐899 1¢ Bright Blue Green						
	.75	.50	.26	.25	.20	.18
☐900 2¢ Rose Carmine						
	.75	.50	.26	.25	.20	.18
☐901 3¢ Bright Violet						
	.90	.78	.26	.25	.20	.18

1940. 75TH ANNIVERSARY EMANCIPATION AMENDMENT (N-H ADD 20%)

☐902 3¢ Deep Violet						
	4.50	3.75	.40	.30	.25	.20

IMPORTANT NOTICE: Values for mint sheets are provided for the following listings. To command the stated prices, sheets must be complete as issued with the plate number (or numbers) intact.

Scott No.	Mint Sheet	Plate Block	Fine Unused Each	Fine Used Each

1941–1943. COMMEMORATIVES
1941. VERMONT STATEHOOD

☐903 3¢ Light Violet	12.00	2.30	.30	.20

Scott No.	Mint Sheet	Plate Block	Fine Unused Each	Fine Used Each
1942. KENTUCKY SESQUICENTENNIAL ISSUE				
☐904 3¢ Violet	10.00	1.65	.30	.18
1942. WIN THE WAR ISSUE				
☐905 3¢ Violet	15.00	1.00	.30	18
1942. CHINA ISSUE				
☐906 5¢ Bright Blue	25.00	12.00	.60	.30
1943. ALLIED NATIONS ISSUE				
☐907 2¢ Rose Carmine	7.50	.75	.30	.18
1943. FOUR FREEDOMS ISSUE				
☐908 1¢ Green	7.50	.75	.30	.18
1943–1944. OVERRUN COUNTRIES SERIES				
☐909 5¢ (Poland)	18.00	8.00	.30	.19
☐910 5¢ (Czechoslovakia)	14.00	4.50	.30	.20
☐911 5¢ (Norway)	9.50	2.00	.30	.18
☐912 5¢ (Luxembourg)	9.50	1.75	.30	.20
☐913 5¢ (Netherlands)	9.50	1.50	.30	.20
☐914 5¢ (Belgium)	9.50	1.50	.30	.20
☐915 5¢ (France)	9.50	1.50	.30	.20
☐916 5¢ (Greece)	40.00	15.00	.60	.45
☐917 5¢ (Yugoslavia)	22.00	8.00	.38	.29
☐918 5¢ (Albania)	20.00	8.00	.30	.22
☐919 5¢ (Austria)	15.00	6.00	.30	.23
☐920 5¢ (Denmark)	22.00	6.50	.30	.27
☐921 5¢ (Korea)	14.00	6.00	.26	.24
1944. COMMEMORATIVES **1944. RAILROAD ISSUE**				
☐922 3¢ Violet	18.00	2.00	.35	.25
1944. STEAMSHIP ISSUE				
☐923 3¢ Violet	9.00	2.00	.26	.18

*No hinge pricing from 1941 to date is figured at (N-H ADD 10%)

Scott No.			Mint Sheet	Plate Block	Fine Unused Each	Fine Used Each

1944. TELEGRAPH ISSUE

☐924	3¢ Bright Red Violet	7.50	1.25	.30	.20

1944. CORREGIDOR ISSUE

☐925	3¢ Deep Violet	7.50	1.35	.30	.20

1944. MOTION PICTURE ISSUE

☐926	3¢ Deep Violet	8.00	1.35	.30	.20

1945. COMMEMORATIVES
1945. FLORIDA ISSUE

☐927	3¢ Bright Red Violet	6.00	1.00	.30	.20

1945. PEACE CONFERENCE ISSUE

☐928	5¢ Ultramarine	6.00	.85	.30	.20

1945. IWO JIMA ISSUE

☐929	3¢ Yellow Green	6.00	.85	.30	.20

1945–1946. ROOSEVELT MEMORIAL ISSUE

☐930	1¢ Blue Green	3.00	.50	.30	.20
☐931	2¢ Carmine Rose	5.00	.55	.30	.20
☐932	3¢ Purple	6.00	.72	.30	.20
☐933	5¢ Bright Blue	7.00	.70	.30	.20

1945. ARMY ISSUE

☐934	3¢ Olive Gray	6.00	.75	.28	.18

1945. NAVY ISSUE

☐935	3¢ Blue	6.00	.75	.28	.18

1945. COAST GUARD ISSUE

☐936	3¢ Bright Blue Green	6.00	.75	.28	.18

1945. ALFRED SMITH ISSUE

☐937	3¢ Purple	12.00	.75	.28	.18

1945. TEXAS CENTENNIAL ISSUE

☐938	3¢ Blue	6.00	.75	.28	.18

*No hinge pricing from 1941 to date is figured at (N-H ADD 10%)

Scott No.	Mint Sheet	Plate Block	Fine Unused Each	Fine Used Each

1946–1947. COMMEMORATIVES
1946. MERCHANT MARINE ISSUE
| ☐939 3¢ Blue Green | 6.00 | .85 | .26 | .18 |

1946. HONORABLE DISCHARGE EMBLEM ISSUE
| ☐940 3¢ Dark Violet | 12.00 | .85 | .26 | .18 |

1946. TENNESSEE ISSUE
| ☐941 3¢ Dark Violet | 6.00 | .85 | .26 | .18 |

1946. IOWA STATEHOOD ISSUE
| ☐942 3¢ Deep Blue | 6.00 | .85 | .26 | .18 |

1946. SMITHSONIAN INSTITUTION ISSUE
| ☐943 3¢ Violet Brown | 6.00 | .85 | .26 | .18 |

1946. NEW MEXICO ISSUE
| ☐944 3¢ Brown Violet | 6.00 | .85 | .26 | .18 |

1947. EDISON ISSUE
| ☐945 3¢ Bright Red Violet | 8.00 | .85 | .26 | .18 |

1947. PULITZER PRIZE
| ☐946 3¢ Purple | 6.00 | .85 | .26 | .18 |

1947. U.S. POSTAGE STAMP CENTENARY
| ☐947 3¢ Deep Blue | 6.00 | .85 | .26 | .18 |

1947. "CIPEX" SOUVENIR SHEET
☐948 5¢ & 10¢ Sheet of 2	—	—	1.00	.90
☐948a 5¢ Blue, sgl. stp.	—	—	.42	.30
☐948b 10¢ Brown Orange, sgl. stp.	—	—	.60	.42

1947. DOCTORS ISSUE
| ☐949 3¢ Brown Violet | 6.00 | 1.00 | .26 | 18 |

1947. UTAH ISSUE
| ☐950 3¢ Dark Violet | 6.00 | 85 | .26 | .18 |

*No hinge pricing from 1941 to date is figured at (N-H ADD 10%)

Scott No.	Mint Sheet	Plate Block	Fine Unused Each	Fine Used Each

1947. U.S.F. CONSTITUTION ISSUE
☐951 3¢ Blue Green	6.00	.90	.27	.19

1947. EVERGLADES ISSUE
☐952 3¢ Bright Green	6.00	.90	.27	.19

1948. COMMEMORATIVES
1948. CARVER ISSUE
☐953 3¢ Red Violet	8.00	.90	.27	.19

1948. GOLD RUSH ISSUE
☐954 3¢ Dark Violet	6.00	.90	.27	.19

1948. MISSISSIPPI TERRITORY ISSUE
☐955 3¢ Brown Violet	6.00	.90	.27	.19

1948. FOUR CHAPLAINS ISSUE
☐956 3¢ Gray Black	6.00	.90	.27	.21

1948. WISCONSIN CENTENNIAL ISSUE
☐957 3¢ Dark Violet	6.00	.90	.27	.21

1948. SWEDISH PIONEER ISSUE
☐958 5¢ Deep Blue	7.00	.90	.27	.21

1948. 100 YEARS PROGRESS OF WOMEN
☐959 3¢ Dark Violet	6.00	.90	.27	.21

1948. WILLIAM ALLEN WHITE ISSUE
☐960 3¢ Red Violet	8.00	1.00	.27	.21

1948. U.S.-CANADA FRIENDSHIP
☐961 3¢ Blue	6.00	.90	.27	.21

1948. FRANCIS SCOTT KEY ISSUE
☐962 3¢ Rose Pink	6.00	.90	.27	.21

*No hinge pricing from 1941 to date is figured at (N-H ADD 10%)

Scott No.	Mint Sheet	Plate Block	Fine Unused Each	Fine Used Each

1948. SALUTE TO YOUTH ISSUE
| ☐963 3¢ Deep Blue | 6.00 | .95 | .26 | .20 |

1948. OREGON TERRITORY ISSUE
| ☐964 3¢ Brown Red | 6.00 | .95 | .26 | .20 |

1948. HARLAN FISKE STONE
| ☐965 3¢ Bright Red Violet | 7.00 | .95 | .26 | .20 |

1948. MT. PALOMAR OBSERVATORY
| ☐966 3¢ Blue | 8.00 | .85 | .26 | .20 |

1948. CLARA BARTON ISSUE
| ☐967 3¢ Rose Pink | 6.00 | .85 | .26 | .20 |

1948. POULTRY ISSUE
| ☐968 3¢ Sepia | 6.00 | .95 | .26 | .20 |

1948. GOLD STAR MOTHERS
| ☐969 3¢ Orange Yellow | 6.00 | .85 | .26 | .20 |

1948. FORT KEARNY ISSUE
| ☐970 3¢ Violet | 6.00 | .85 | .26 | .20 |

1948. VOLUNTEER FIREMEN
| ☐971 3¢ Bright Rose Carmine | 6.00 | .95 | .26 | .20 |

1948. INDIAN CENTENNIAL
| ☐972 3¢ Dark Brown | 6.00 | .85 | .26 | .20 |

1948. ROUGH RIDERS
| ☐973 3¢ Violet Brown | 6.00 | .95 | .26 | .20 |

1948. JULIETTE LOW
| ☐974 3¢ Blue Green | 6.00 | 1.00 | .30 | .22 |

*No hinge pricing from 1941 to date is figured at (N-H ADD 10%)

Scott No.	Mint Sheet	Plate Block	Fine Unused Each	Fine Used Each

1948. WILL ROGERS
| ☐975 3¢ Bright Red Violet | 6.00 | .85 | .26 | .19 |

1948. FORT BLISS
| ☐976 3¢ Henna Brown | 10.00 | .95 | .26 | .19 |

1948. MOINA MICHAEL
| ☐977 3¢ Rose Pink | 7.50 | .95 | .26 | .22 |

1948. GETTYSBURG ADDRESS
| ☐978 3¢ Bright Blue | 6.00 | .85 | .26 | .19 |

1948. AMERICAN TURNERS
| ☐979 3¢ Carmine | 6.00 | .95 | .26 | .19 |

1948. JOEL CHANDLER HARRIS
| ☐980 3¢ Bright Red Violet | 8.00 | 1.00 | .30 | .22 |

1949–1950. COMMEMORATIVES
1949. MINNESOTA CENTENNIAL
| ☐981 3¢ Blue Green | 6.00 | .95 | .26 | .19 |

1949. WASHINGTON & LEE UNIVERSITY
| ☐982 3¢ Ultramarine | 6.00 | .85 | .26 | .19 |

1949. PUERTO RICO ISSUE
| ☐983 3¢ Green | 6.00 | .85 | .30 | .22 |

1949. ANNAPOLIS TERCENTENARY
| ☐984 3¢ Aquamarine | 6.00 | .85 | .26 | .22 |

1949. G.A.R. ISSUE
| ☐985 3¢ Bright Rose Carmine | 6.00 | .85 | .30 | .22 |

1950. EDGAR ALLAN POE
| ☐986 3¢ Bright Red Violet | 8.00 | .85 | .26 | .19 |

1950. BANKERS ASSOCIATION
| ☐987 3¢ Yellow Green | 6.00 | .85 | .26 | .19 |

*No hinge pricing from 1941 to date is figured at (N-H ADD 10%)

Scott No.	Mint Sheet	Plate Block	Fine Unused Each	Fine Used Each

1950. SAMUEL GOMPERS
| ☐988 3¢ Bright Red Violet | 8.00 | .70 | .26 | .19 |

1950. WASHINGTON SESQUICENTENNIAL
☐989 3¢ Bright Blue	6.00	.75	.26	.19
☐990 3¢ Deep Green	6.00	.75	.26	.19
☐991 3¢ Light Violet	6.00	.75	.26	.19
☐992 3¢ Rose Violet	6.00	.75	.26	.19

1950. RAILROAD ENGINEERS
| ☐993 3¢ Violet Brown | 6.00 | .70 | .26 | .22 |

1950. KANSAS CITY CENTENARY
| ☐994 3¢ Violet | 6.00 | .80 | .26 | .19 |

1950. BOY SCOUTS ISSUE
| ☐995 3¢ Sepia | 6.00 | .80 | .26 | .22 |

1950. INDIANA SESQUICENTENNIAL
| ☐996 3¢ Bright Blue | 6.00 | .80 | .26 | .19 |

1950. CALIFORNIA STATEHOOD
| ☐997 3¢ Yellow Orange | 6.00 | .70 | .26 | .19 |

1951–1952. COMMEMORATIVES
1951. UNITED CONFEDERATE VETERANS
| ☐998 3¢ Gray | 6.00 | 1.00 | .30 | .22 |

1951. NEVADA SETTLEMENT
| ☐999 3¢ Light Olive Green | 6.00 | .70 | .26 | .19 |

1951. LANDING OF CADILLAC
| ☐1000 3¢ Bright Blue | 6.00 | .80 | .26 | .22 |

1951. COLORADO STATEHOOD
| ☐1001 3¢ Violet Blue | 6.00 | .70 | .26 | .19 |

*No hinge pricing from 1941 to date is figured at (N-H ADD 10%)

Scott No.	Mint Sheet	Plate Block	Fine Unused Each	Fine Used Each

1951. AMERICAN CHEMICAL SOCIETY
| ☐1002 3¢ Violet Brown | 6.00 | .80 | .24 | .19 |

1951. BATTLE OF BROOKLYN ISSUE
| ☐1003 3¢ Violet | 6.00 | .70 | .24 | .19 |

1952. BETSY ROSS ISSUE
| ☐1004 3¢ Carmine Rose | 6.00 | .70 | .24 | .22 |

1952. 4-H CLUB ISSUE
| ☐1005 3¢ Blue Green | 6.00 | .80 | .24 | .22 |

1952. BALTIMORE & OHIO RAILROAD
| ☐1006 3¢ Bright Blue | 6.25 | .70 | .24 | .22 |

1952. AMERICAN AUTOMOBILE ASSOCIATION (AAA)
| ☐1007 3¢ Deep Blue | 6.00 | .70 | .24 | .22 |

1952. NORTH ATLANTIC TREATY ORGANIZATION
| ☐1008 3¢ Deep Violet | 11.25 | .80 | .24 | .19 |

1952. GRAND COULEE DAM ISSUE
| ☐1009 3¢ Blue Green | 6.00 | .70 | .24 | .19 |

1952. ARRIVAL OF LAFAYETTE
| ☐1010 3¢ Ultramarine | 6.00 | .70 | .24 | .19 |

1952. MOUNT RUSHMORE
| ☐1011 3¢ Blue Green | 6.00 | .80 | .26 | .22 |

1952. SOCIETY OF CIVIL ENGINEERS
| ☐1012 3¢ Violet Blue | 6.00 | .70 | .24 | .19 |

1952. WOMEN IN ARMED FORCES
| ☐1013 3¢ Deep Blue | 6.00 | .80 | .25 | .22 |

*No hinge pricing from 1941 to date is figured at (N-H ADD 10%)

Scott No.	Mint Sheet	Plate Block	Fine Unused Each	Fine Used Each

1952. GUTENBERG PRINTING
☐ 1014 3¢ Violet 6.00 .95 .18 .21

1952. NEWSPAPERBOYS
☐ 1015 3¢ Violet 6.00 .85 .18 .19

1952. INTERNATIONAL RED CROSS
☐ 1016 3¢ Deep Blue & Carmine
    6.00 .85 .18 .19

1953–1954. COMMEMORATIVES
1953. NATIONAL GUARD
☐ 1017 3¢ Bright Blue 7.50 .85 .18 .19

1953. OHIO STATEHOOD
☐ 1018 3¢ Chocolate 8.25 .95 .18 .21

1953. WASHINGTON TERRITORY
☐ 1019 3¢ Green 6.00 .85 .18 .19

1953. LOUISIANA PURCHASE
☐ 1020 3¢ Violet Brown 6.00 .85 .18 .19

1953. OPENING OF JAPAN
☐ 1021 3¢ Green 8.00 1.20 .18 .21

1953. AMERICAN BAR ASSOCIATION
☐ 1022 3¢ Rose Violet 6.00 1.00 .29 .21

1953. SAGAMORE HILL
☐ 1023 3¢ Yellow Green 6.00 .95 .18 .21

1953. FUTURE FARMERS
☐ 1024 3¢ Deep Blue 6.00 .85 .18 .19

1953. TRUCKING INDUSTRY
☐ 1025 3¢ Violet 6.00 .95 .18 .21

1953. GENERAL PATTON
☐ 1026 3¢ Blue Violet 7.50 .95 .29 .19

*No hinge pricing from 1941 to date is figured at (N-H ADD 10%)

Scott No.	Mint Sheet	Plate Block	Fine Unused Each	Fine Used Each
1953. NEW YORK CITY				
☐1027 3¢ Bright Red Violet	6.00	.85	.18	.19
1953. GADSDEN PURCHASE				
☐1028 3¢ Copper Brown	6.00	.85	.18	.19
1954. COLUMBIA UNIVERSITY				
☐1029 3¢ Blue	6.00	.95	.30	.22
1954–1961. LIBERTY SERIES				
☐1030 ½¢ Red Orange	7.00	.95	.30	.22
☐1031 1¢ Dark Green	6.00	.95	.30	.22
☐1031A 1¼¢ Turquoise	7.50	.85	.18	.22
☐1032 1½¢ Brown	14.00	3.50	.18	.22
☐1033 2¢ Rose Carmine	9.00	.85	.18	.22
☐1034 2½¢ Dark Blue	14.00	.85	.18	.22
☐1035 3¢ Deep Violet	14.00	.85	.18	.22
☐1036 4¢ Red Violet	20.00	.95	.18	.22
☐1037 4½¢ Green	22.00	.95	.18	.22
☐1038 5¢ Deep Blue	26.00	.85	.18	.22
☐1039 6¢ Orange Red	60.00	2.00	.36	.22
☐1040 7¢ Deep Carmine	45.00	3.00	.35	.22
☐1041 8¢ Dark Violet Blue, Carmine	42.00	3.50	.24	.22
☐1042 8¢ Violet Blue, Carmine (Re-engraved)	52.00	1.40	.28	.21
☐1042A 8¢ Brown	30.00	1.40	.30	.21
☐1043 9¢ Rose Lilac	60.00	2.00	.45	.21
☐1044 10¢ Rose Lake	52.00	1.40	.34	.21
☐1044A 11¢ Carmine, Violet Blue	52.00	1.60	.45	.21
☐1045 12¢ Red	72.00	2.00	.45	.21
☐1046 15¢ Maroon	120.00	4.50	1.10	.21
☐1047 20¢ Ultramarine	110.00	3.00	.60	.21
☐1048 25¢ Green	250.00	7.00	1.50	.21
☐1049 30¢ Black	200.00	5.50	1.35	.21
☐1050 40¢ Brown Carmine	400.00	13.00	2.40	.21

*No hinge pricing from 1941 to date is figured at (N-H ADD 10%)

Scott No.	Mint Sheet	Plate Block	Fine Unused Each	Fine Used Each
☐1051 50¢ Bright Violet	400.00	8.50	2.00	.19
☐1052 $1 Deep Violet	700.00	29.00	6.50	.30
☐1053 $5 Black	10,000.00	450.00	90.00	8.50

1954–1965. ROTARY PRESS COIL STAMPS PERF. 10 VERTICALLY OR HORIZONTALLY

Scott No.	Fine Unused Line Pair	Ave. Unused Line Pair	Fine Unused Each	Ave. Unused Each	Fine Used Each	Ave. Used Each
☐1054 1¢ Deep Green	4.00	1.00	.30	.26	.25	.22
☐1055 2¢ Rose Carmine	2.00	1.00	.30	.26	.25	.22
☐1056 2½¢ Gray Blue	4.00	3.50	.40	.26	.25	.22
☐1057 3¢ Deep Violet	3.00	.65	.28	.26	.25	.22
☐1058 4¢ Red Violet	85.00	.65	.30	.26	.25	.22
☐1059 4½¢ Green	20.00	12.00	2.50	2.00	1.75	1.40
☐1059A 25¢ Green	4.00	1.75	.80	.52	1.10	.29

Scott No.	Mint Sheet	Plate Block	Fine Unused Each	Fine Used Each

1954. NEBRASKA TERRITORY

☐1060 3¢ Violet	6.00	.85	.30	.22

1954. KANSAS TERRITORY

☐1061 3¢ Brown Orange	6.00	.85	.30	.22

1954. GEORGE EASTMAN ISSUE

☐1062 3¢ Violet Brown	8.25	.85	.30	.22

*No hinge pricing from 1941 to date is figured at (N-H ADD 10%)

Scott No.	Mint Sheet	Plate Block	Fine Unused Each	Fine Used Each

1954. LEWIS & CLARK EXPEDITION

| ☐1063 3¢ Dark Brown | 6.00 | .85 | .28 | .22 |

1955. COMMEMORATIVES
1955. PENNSYLVANIA ACADEMY OF FINE ARTS

| ☐1064 3¢ Rose Brown | 6.00 | .85 | .28 | .22 |

1955. LAND GRANT COLLEGES

| ☐1065 3¢ Green | 5.75 | .95 | .28 | .22 |

1955. ROTARY INTERNATIONAL ISSUE

| ☐1066 8¢ Deep Blue | 12.00 | 1.85 | .28 | .22 |

1955. ARMED FORCES RESERVE

| ☐1067 3¢ Red Violet | 6.00 | .85 | .28 | .22 |

1955. OLD MAN OF THE MOUNTAINS

| ☐1068 3¢ Blue Green | 6.00 | .85 | .28 | .22 |

1955. SOO LOCKS CENTENNIAL

| ☐1069 3¢ Blue | 6.00 | .95 | .28 | .22 |

1955. ATOMS FOR PEACE

| ☐1070 3¢ Blue | 6.00 | .85 | .28 | .22 |

1955. FORT TICONDEROGA BICENTENNIAL

| ☐1071 3¢ Sepia | 6.00 | .95 | .28 | .22 |

1955. ANDREW MELLON ISSUE

| ☐1072 3¢ Deep Carmine | 6.00 | .85 | .28 | .22 |

1956. COMMEMORATIVES
1956. 250TH ANNIVERSARY FRANKLIN'S BIRTH

| ☐1073 3¢ Rose Carmine | 6.50 | .95 | .22 | .18 |

1956. BOOKER T. WASHINGTON ISSUE

| ☐1074 3¢ Deep Blue | 5.75 | .85 | .22 | .18 |

*No hinge pricing from 1941 to date is figured at (N-H ADD 10%)

Scott No.	Mint Sheet	Plate Block	Fine Unused Each	Fine Used Each

1956. FIFTH INTL. PHILATELIC EXHIBITION DESIGNS OF 1035 & 1041 IN IMPERF. SOUVENIR SHEET

| ☐1075 3¢ & 8¢ Sheet of 2 | — | — | 3.75 | 2.75 |

1956. FIFTH INTL. PHILATELIC EXHIBITION

| ☐1076 3¢ Deep Violet | 6.25 | .70 | .26 | — |

1956. WILDLIFE CONSERVATION ISSUE

☐1077 3¢ Rose Lake	6.00	.85	.26	.21
☐1078 3¢ Brown	6.00	.85	.26	.21
☐1079 3¢ Green	6.00	.85	.26	.21

1956. PURE FOOD & DRUG ACT

| ☐1080 3¢ Dark Blue Green | 6.00 | .95 | .26 | .21 |

1956. HOME OF PRESIDENT BUCHANAN

| ☐1081 3¢ Black Brown | 6.00 | .85 | .26 | .21 |

1956. LABOR DAY ISSUE

| ☐1082 3¢ Deep Blue | 6.00 | .85 | .26 | .21 |

1956. NASSAU HALL—PRINCETON

| ☐1083 3¢ Black on Orange | 6.00 | .95 | .26 | .21 |

1956. DEVIL'S TOWER

| ☐1084 3¢ Purple | 6.00 | .95 | .26 | .21 |

1956. CHILDREN'S ISSUE

| ☐1085 3¢ Dark Blue | 6.00 | .85 | .26 | .21 |

1957. COMMEMORATIVES
1957. ALEXANDER HAMILTON ISSUE

| ☐1086 3¢ Rose Red | 6.00 | .85 | .26 | .21 |

1957. POLIO ISSUE

| ☐1087 3¢ Light Purple | 6.00 | .85 | .26 | .21 |

*No hinge pricing from 1941 to date is figured at (N-H ADD 10%)

Scott No.	Mint Sheet	Plate Block	Fine Unused Each	Fine Used Each

1957. COAST & GEODETIC SURVEY

| ☐1088 3¢ Dark Blue | 6.00 | .85 | .26 | .21 |

1957. ARCHITECTS ISSUE

| ☐1089 3¢ Red Lilac | 6.00 | .85 | .26 | .21 |

1957. STEEL INDUSTRY CENTENNIAL

| ☐1090 3¢ Bright Ultra | 6.00 | .85 | .26 | .21 |

1957. INTERNATIONAL NAVAL REVIEW

| ☐1091 3¢ Blue Green | 6.25 | .95 | .26 | .21 |

1957. OKLAHOMA STATEHOOD

| ☐1092 3¢ Dark Blue | 6.00 | .85 | .26 | .21 |

1957. SCHOOL TEACHERS

| ☐1093 3¢ Rose Lake | 6.00 | .85 | .26 | .21 |

1957. U.S. FLAG ISSUE

| ☐1094 4¢ Blue & Red | 7.25 | .85 | .26 | .21 |

1957. 350TH SHIPBUILDING ANNIVERSARY

| ☐1095 3¢ Purple | 9.00 | .80 | .26 | .21 |

1957. PHILIPPINES—CHAMPION OF LIBERTY

| ☐1096 8¢ Red, Blue & Gold | 12.00 | 1.50 | .30 | .21 |

1957. BIRTH OF LAFAYETTE

| ☐1097 3¢ Maroon | 6.50 | .85 | .26 | .21 |

1957. WILDLIFE CONSERVATION ISSUE

| ☐1098 3¢ Blue, Green & Yellow | 6.00 | .90 | .26 | .21 |

1957. RELIGIOUS FREEDOM

| ☐1099 3¢ Black | 6.00 | .85 | .26 | .21 |

*No hinge pricing from 1941 to date is figured at (N-H ADD 10%)

Scott No.	Mint Sheet	Plate Block	Fine Unused Each	Fine Used Each

1958. COMMEMORATIVES
1958. GARDENING & HORTICULTURE

	Mint Sheet	Plate Block	Fine Unused Each	Fine Used Each
☐ 1100 3¢ Deep Green	6.00	.95	.30	.21

1958. BRUSSELS EXHIBITION

☐ 1104 3¢ Deep Claret	6.00	.95	.30	.21

1958. JAMES MONROE BICENTENNIAL

☐ 1105 3¢ Purple	8.00	.85	.26	.19

1958. MINNESOTA STATEHOOD

☐ 1106 3¢ Green	6.00	.85	.26	.19

1958. INTERNATIONAL GEOPHYSICAL YEAR

☐ 1107 3¢ Black & Orange	6.00	.85	.26	.19

1958. GUNSTON HALL BICENTENARY

☐ 1108 3¢ Light Green	6.00	.85	.26	.19

1958. MACKINAC BRIDGE ISSUE

☐ 1109 3¢ Bluish Green	6.00	.85	.26	.19

1958. SOUTH AMERICA—CHAMPION OF LIBERTY

☐ 1110 4¢ Olive Bistre	9.00	.85	.26	.19
☐ 1111 8¢ Red, Blue & Gold	20.00	2.10	.36	.22

1958. ATLANTIC CABLE CENTENNIAL

☐ 1112 4¢ Reddish Purple	6.50	.70	.26	.19

1958–1959. LINCOLN COMMEMORATIVE ISSUE

☐ 1113 1¢ Green	2.75	.60	.26	.19
☐ 1114 3¢ Rust Brown	6.00	.85	.26	.19
☐ 1115 4¢ Sepia	8.00	.85	.28	.19
☐ 1116 4¢ Blue	7.50	2.50	.36	.22

1958. HUNGARY—CHAMPION OF LIBERTY

☐ 1117 4¢ Bluish Green	8.75	.85	.26	.19
☐ 1118 8¢ Red, Blue & Gold	18.00	1.75	.31	.19

*No hinge pricing from 1941 to date is figured at (N-H ADD 10%)

Scott No.	Mint Sheet	Plate Block	Fine Unused Each	Fine Used Each
1958. FREEDOM OF THE PRESS				
☐1119 4¢ Black	6.50	.95	.30	.21
1958. OVERLAND MAIL CENTENNIAL				
☐1120 4¢ Crimson Rose	6.50	.95	.30	.21
1958. NOAH WEBSTER				
☐1121 4¢ Dark Carmine Rose				
	8.75	.85	.26	.19
1958. FOREST CONSERVATION				
☐1122 4¢ Yellow, Brown & Green				
	6.75	.95	.30	.21
1958. FORT DUQUESNE BICENTENNIAL				
☐1123 4¢ Blue	6.75	.85	.26	.19
1959. COMMEMORATIVES				
1959. OREGON STATEHOOD				
☐1124 4¢ Blue Green	6.75	.85	.26	.19
1959. ARGENTINA & CHILE—CHAMPION OF LIBERTY				
☐1125 4¢ Blue	8.75	.85	.26	.19
☐1126 8¢ Red, Blue & Gold	18.25	1.75	.30	.21
1959. 10TH ANNIVERSARY N.A.T.O.				
☐1127 4¢ Blue	8.75	.85	.26	.19
1959. ARCTIC EXPLORATIONS				
☐1128 4¢ Blue	6.75	.85	.26	.19
1959. WORLD PEACE & TRUST				
☐1129 8¢ Maroon	12.00	1.50	.36	.21
1959. SILVER DISCOVERY CENTENNIAL				
☐1130 4¢ Black	6.75	.85	.26	.19

*No hinge pricing from 1941 to date is figured at (N-H ADD 10%)

Scott No.	Mint Sheet	Plate Block	Fine Unused Each	Fine Used Each

1959. ST. LAWRENCE SEAWAY ISSUE

☐1131 4¢ Red & Blue	6.75	.85	.26	.19

1959. 49-STAR FLAG ISSUE

☐1132 4¢ Blue, Red & Yellow				
	6.75	.85	.26	.19

1959. SOIL CONSERVATION

☐1133 4¢ Yellow, Green & Blue				
	6.75	.95	.30	.21

1959. PETROLEUM INDUSTRY CENTENNIAL

☐1134 4¢ Brown	6.50	.85	.26	.19

1959. DENTAL HEALTH ISSUE

☐1135 4¢ Green	6.75	1.50	.36	.21

1959. GERMANY—CHAMPION OF LIBERTY

☐1136 4¢ Gray	9.00	.70	.26	.19
☐1137 8¢ Red, Blue & Gold	18.00	1.75	.36	.17

1959. DR. EPHRAIM McDOWELL

☐1138 4¢ Maroon	8.50	.85	.26	.19

1960–1961. CREDO OF AMERICA SERIES

☐1139 4¢ Dark Violet, Blue & Carmine				
	6.50	.88	.30	.21
☐1140 4¢ Olive Bistre & Green				
	6.50	.88	.30	.21
☐1141 4¢ Gray & Red	7.50	.88	.30	.21
☐1142 4¢ Red & Blue	7.50	.88	.30	.21
☐1143 4¢ Violet & Green	10.00	.88	.34	.21
☐1144 4¢ Green & Brown	10.00	.88	.34	.21

1960. COMMEMORATIVES
1960. BOY SCOUTS GOLDEN JUBILEE

☐1145 4¢ Red, Khaki & Blue	12.00	1.20	.30	.21

*No hinge pricing from 1941 to date is figured at (N-H ADD 10%)

Scott No.	Mint Sheet	Plate Block	Fine Unused Each	Fine Used Each

1960. WINTER OLYMPIC GAMES

☐1146 4¢ Blue	7.75	.95	.30	.21

1960. CZECHOSLOVAKIA—CHAMPION OF LIBERTY

☐1147 4¢ Blue	8.50	.85	.26	.19
☐1148 8¢ Yellow, Blue & Red	17.50	1.80	.31	.19

1960. WORLD REFUGEE YEAR

☐1149 4¢ Gray Black	6.50	.85	.26	.19

1960. WATER CONSERVATION

☐1150 4¢ Blue, Green & Orange Brown	6.50	.85	.26	.19

1960. SOUTHEAST ASIA TREATY ORGANIZATION

☐1151 4¢ Blue	8.50	.85	.26	.19

1960. HONORING AMERICAN WOMEN

☐1152 4¢ Violet	6.75	.95	.30	.21

1960. 50-STAR FLAG ISSUE

☐1153 4¢ Red & Blue	6.50	.85	.26	.19

1960. PONY EXPRESS CENTENNIAL

☐1154 4¢ Sepia	7.00	.85	.24	.19

1960. EMPLOY THE HANDICAPPED

☐1155 4¢ Blue	6.75	.95	.30	.21

1960. WORLD FORESTRY CONGRESS

☐1156 4¢ Green	6.50	.85	.26	.19

1960. MEXICAN INDEPENDENCE SESQUICENTENNIAL

☐1157 4¢ Red & Green	6.75	.95	.30	.21

1960. UNITED STATES—JAPAN TREATY CENTENNIAL

☐1158 4¢ Blue & Pink	6.50	.85	.26	.19

*No hinge pricing from 1941 to date is figured at (N-H ADD 10%)

Scott No.	Mint Sheet	Plate Block	Fine Unused Each	Fine Used Each

1960. POLAND—CHAMPION OF LIBERTY

Scott No.	Mint Sheet	Plate Block	Fine Unused Each	Fine Used Each
☐1159 4¢ Blue	8.50	.85	.26	.19
☐1160 8¢ Red, Blue & Gold	18.00	1.80	.31	.19

1960. ROBERT A. TAFT MEMORIAL ISSUE

Scott No.	Mint Sheet	Plate Block	Fine Unused Each	Fine Used Each
☐1161 4¢ Dull Violet	8.50	.85	.26	.19

1960. WHEELS OF FREEDOM

Scott No.	Mint Sheet	Plate Block	Fine Unused Each	Fine Used Each
☐1162 4¢ Dark Blue	6.75	.95	.30	.21

1960. BOYS' CLUBS OF AMERICA

Scott No.	Mint Sheet	Plate Block	Fine Unused Each	Fine Used Each
☐1163 4¢ Indigo, Slate & Red	6.50	.85	.26	.19

1960. FIRST AUTOMATED POST OFFICE

Scott No.	Mint Sheet	Plate Block	Fine Unused Each	Fine Used Each
☐1164 4¢ Dark Blue & Carmine	6.75	.95	.30	.21

1960. FINLAND—CHAMPION OF LIBERTY

Scott No.	Mint Sheet	Plate Block	Fine Unused Each	Fine Used Each
☐1165 4¢ Blue	8.75	.85	.26	.19
☐1166 8¢ Red, Blue & Gold	18.50	1.60	.36	.22

1960. CAMP FIRE GIRLS

Scott No.	Mint Sheet	Plate Block	Fine Unused Each	Fine Used Each
☐1167 4¢ Dark Blue & Red	6.50	.85	.26	.19

1960. ITALY—CHAMPION OF LIBERTY

Scott No.	Mint Sheet	Plate Block	Fine Unused Each	Fine Used Each
☐1168 4¢ Green	8.75	.85	.26	.19
☐1169 8¢ Red, Blue & Gold	18.50	1.40	.36	.18

1960. WALTER F. GEORGE MEMORIAL ISSUE

Scott No.	Mint Sheet	Plate Block	Fine Unused Each	Fine Used Each
☐1170 4¢ Dull Violet	8.50	.85	.26	.19

1960. ANDREW CARNEGIE

Scott No.	Mint Sheet	Plate Block	Fine Unused Each	Fine Used Each
☐1171 4¢ Deep Claret	8.65	.95	.30	.21

1960. JOHN FOSTER DULLES MEMORIAL ISSUE

Scott No.	Mint Sheet	Plate Block	Fine Unused Each	Fine Used Each
☐1172 4¢ Dull Violet	8.50	.85	.26	.19

*No hinge pricing from 1941 to date is figured at (N-H ADD 10%)

Scott No.	Mint Sheet	Plate Block	Fine Unused Each	Fine Used Each

1960. "ECHO I" SATELLITE

☐ 1173 4¢ Deep Violet	12.75	1.30	.34	.21

1961. COMMEMORATIVES
1961. INDIA—CHAMPION OF LIBERTY

☐ 1174 4¢ Red Orange	8.50	.85	.26	.19
☐ 1175 8¢ Red, Blue & Gold	18.00	1.60	.36	.21

1961. RANGE CONSERVATION

☐ 1176 4¢ Blue, Slate & Brown Orange				
	7.50	.85	.26	.19

1961. HORACE GREELEY

☐ 1177 4¢ Dull Violet	8.50	.85	.26	.19

1961–1965. CIVIL WAR CENTENNIAL SERIES
1961. FORT SUMTER

☐ 1178 4¢ Light Green	14.00	1.50	.48	.24

1962. BATTLE OF SHILOH

☐ 1179 4¢ Black on Peach	8.50	1.75	.48	.21

1963. BATTLE OF GETTYSBURG

☐ 1180 5¢ Blue & Gray	12.00	1.50	.60	.21

1964. BATTLE OF THE WILDERNESS

☐ 1181 5¢ Dark Red & Black	12.00	2.00	.58	.19

1965. APPOMATTOX

☐ 1182 5¢ Black & Blue	22.00	3.00	1.25	.24

1961. KANSAS STATEHOOD

☐ 1183 4¢ Brown, Dark Red & Green on Yellow Paper				
	6.75	.85	.26	19

1961. GEORGE W. NORRIS BIRTH CENTENARY

☐ 1184 4¢ Blue Green	6.50	.85	.26	.19

*No hinge pricing from 1941 to date is figured at (N-H ADD 10%)

Scott No.	Mint Sheet	Plate Block	Fine Unused Each	Fine Used Each

1961. NAVAL AVIATION GOLDEN JUBILEE

| ☐ 1185 4¢ Blue | 7.00 | .85 | .26 | .19 |

1961. WORKMEN'S COMPENSATION LAW

| ☐ 1186 4¢ Ultramarine | 6.75 | .80 | .30 | .21 |

1961. F. REMINGTON BIRTH CENTENNIAL

☐ 1187 4¢ Blue, Red & Yellow

| | 6.75 | .80 | .30 | .21 |

1961. REPUBLIC OF CHINA ISSUE

| ☐ 1188 4¢ Blue | 7.25 | .85 | .26 | .19 |

1961. DR. J. NAISMITH—BASKETBALL FOUNDER

| ☐ 1189 4¢ Brown | 7.25 | .85 | .31 | .19 |

1961. NURSING PROFESSION

☐ 1190 4¢ Blue, Red, Black & Green

| | 7.25 | .85 | .36 | .22 |

1962. COMMEMORATIVES
1962. NEW MEXICO STATEHOOD

☐ 1191 4¢ Blue, Maroon, Bistre

| | 6.75 | .85 | .26 | .19 |

1961. ARIZONA STATEHOOD

☐ 1192 4¢ Red, Deep Blue, Green

| | 7.50 | .85 | .26 | .19 |

1962. PROJECT MERCURY

☐ 1193 4¢ Dark Blue & Yellow

| | 7.75 | .95 | .30 | .21 |

1962. MALARIA ERADICATION

| ☐ 1194 4¢ Blue & Bistre | 6.50 | .85 | .26 | .19 |

*No hinge pricing from 1941 to date is figured at (N-H ADD 10%)

Scott No.	Mint Sheet	Plate Block	Fine Unused Each	Fine Used Each

1962. CHARLES EVANS HUGHES BIRTH CENTENNIAL

☐1195 4¢ Black on Buff	6.50	.85	.26	.19

1962. SEATTLE WORLD'S FAIR

☐1196 4¢ Red & Dark Blue	6.75	.95	.30	.22

1962. LOUISIANA STATEHOOD

☐1197 4¢ Blue, Green, Red	6.50	.85	.26	.19

1962. THE HOMESTEAD ACT

☐1198 4¢ Slate	6.50	.85	.26	.19

1962. GIRL SCOUTS 50TH ANNIVERSARY

☐1199 4¢ Red	7.00	.85	.26	.19

1962. BRIEN MCMAHON MEMORIAL ISSUE

☐1200 4¢ Purple	6.75	.95	.30	.21

1962. NATIONAL APPRENTICESHIP ACT

☐1201 4¢ Black on Buff	6.50	.85	.26	.19

1962. SAM RAYBURN MEMORIAL ISSUE

☐1202 4¢ Brown & Blue	6.50	.85	.26	.19

1962. DAG HAMMARSKJOLD MEMORIAL

☐1203 4¢ Yellow, Brown & Black	6.75	.95	.30	.21
☐1204 4¢ Yellow Color Inverted	7.50	1.75	.29	.19

1962. CHRISTMAS WREATH

☐1205 4¢ Green & Red	14.00	1.25	.30	.22

1962. HIGHER EDUCATION

☐1206 4¢ Green & Black	6.50	.85	.26	.19

*No hinge pricing from 1941 to date is figured at (N-H ADD 10%)

Scott No.	Mint Sheet	Plate Block	Fine Unused Each	Fine Used Each
1962. WINSLOW HOMER				
☐1207 4¢ Brown & Blue	7.00	.85	.26	.19
1963. 50-STAR FLAG				
☐1208 5¢ Red & Blue	25.00	1.20	.30	.21
1962–1963. REGULAR ISSUE				
☐1209 1¢ Green	7.00	.85	.26	.19
☐1213 5¢ Dark Blue Gray	25.00	1.20	.30	.22

1962–1963. ROTARY PRESS COIL STAMPS PERF. 10 VERTICALLY

Scott No.	Fine Unused Plate Blk	Ave. Unused Plate Blk	Fine Unused Each	Ave. Unused Each	Fine Used Each	Ave. Used Each
☐1225 1¢ Green						
	4.00	3.00	2.50	.36	.25	.22
☐1229 5¢ Dark Blue Gray						
	5.00	3.00	1.75	1.20	.25	.22

Scott No.	Mint Sheet	Plate Block	Fine Unused Each	Fine Used Each
1963. COMMEMORATIVES				
1963. CAROLINA CHARTER TERCENTENARY				
☐1230 5¢ Dark Carmine & Brown				
	7.50	.85	.26	.19
1963. FOOD FOR PEACE—FREEDOM FROM HUNGER				
☐1231 5¢ Green, Buff & Red				
	7.50	.85	.26	.19
1963. WEST VIRGINIA STATEHOOD				
☐1232 5¢ Green, Red & Black				
	7.50	.85	.26	.19

*No hinge pricing from 1941 to date is figured at (N-H ADD 10%)

Scott No.	Mint Sheet	Plate Block	Fine Unused Each	Fine Used Each

1963. EMANCIPATION PROCLAMATION

☐ 1233 5¢ Black, Blue & Red	7.25	.85	.31	.21

1963. ALLIANCE FOR PROGRESS

☐ 1234 5¢ Bright Blue & Green	7.25	.85	.26	.21

1963. CORDELL HULL

☐ 1235 5¢ Blue Green	7.25	.85	.26	.21

1963. ELEANOR ROOSEVELT

☐ 1236 5¢ Light Purple	7.75	.85	.26	.21

1963. THE SCIENCES

☐ 1237 5¢ Blue & Black	7.25	.85	.26	.21

1963. CITY MAIL DELIVERY

☐ 1238 5¢ Red, Blue & Gray	7.25	.85	.26	.21

1963. INTERNATIONAL RED CROSS CENTENARY

☐ 1239 5¢ Slate & Carmine	6.75	.85	.26	.21

1963. CHRISTMAS ISSUE

☐ 1240 5¢ Dark Blue, Blue Black & Red	14.00	.85	.26	.21

1963. JOHN JAMES AUDUBON

☐ 1241 5¢ Blue, Brown, Bistre	7.25	1.20	.30	.21

1964. COMMEMORATIVES
1964. SAM HOUSTON

☐ 1242 5¢ Black	9.50	1.20	.30	.21

1964. CHARLES M. RUSSELL

☐ 1243 5¢ Indigo, Red Brown & Olive	9.50	1.20	.30	.21

*No hinge pricing from 1941 to date is figured at (N-H ADD 10%)

GENERAL ISSUE—SCOTT NO. 1–138 (1847–1871)

1, 39, 48A

2, 4, 948B

5, 9, 18-24, 40

10, 11, 25, 26, 41

12, 27-30A, 42

13-16, 31-35, 43

17, 36, 44

37, 45

38, 46

39, 47

56, 63, 85, 86, 92, 102

64-66, 74, 79, 88, 94, 104

57-67, 75, 76, 80, 95, 195

58-62B, 68, 85D, 89, 96, 106

59, 69, 85E, 90 97, 107

60, 70, 78, 99, 109

61, 71, 81, 100, 110

62, 72, 101, 111

73, 84, 85B, 87, 93, 103

77, 85F, 91, 98, 108

112, 123, 133

113, 124

114, 125

115, 126

116, 127

117, 128

118,119, 129

120, 130

121, 131

122, 132

134, 156, 167, 182, 206

135, 157, 168, 203

136, 158, 169, 214

137, 148, 159, 195, 208

138, 149, 160, 171, 196

139, 150, 161, 197, 209

140-151, 162, 173, 198

141, 152, 163, 189, 199

142, 153, 164, 175, 200

143, 154, 165, 190, 201, 217

144, 155, 166, 202, 218

179, 181, 185, 204

205, 205C, 216

210, 211B, 213

211, 211D, 215

212

219

219D, 220

221

222

223

224

225

226

227

228

229

230

231

232

233

234

235

236

237

238

239

240

241

242

243

244

245

246, 247,
264, 279

248-252, 265-
267, 279B

253, 268

254, 269, 280

255, 270, 281

256, 271, 282

257, 272

258, 273
282C, 283

259, 273, 284

260, 275

261-261A,
276, 276A

262, 277

263, 278

285

286

287

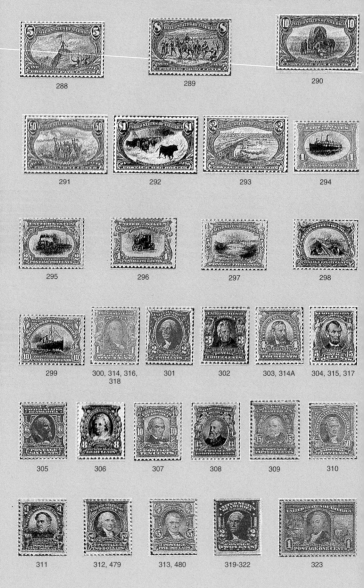

324

325

326

327

328

329

330

331, 392

332-393, 519

333-541

367, 369

370, 371

372, 373

397, 401

398, 402

399, 403

400, 400A, 404

405-545

406-546

414-518

523, 524, 547

537

548

549

550

551, 653

552, 575, 578, 604, 632

553, 576, 598, 605, 633

555, 584, 600, 635

556-585, 601, 636

557, 586, 602, 637

558, 587, 638, 723

559, 588, 639

560, 589, 640

561, 590, 641

562, 591, 603, 641

563, 692

564, 693

565, 695

566-696

567, 698

568, 699

569, 700

570, 701

571

572

573

583, 599-99A 634-34A

610-613

614

615

616

617

618

619

620

621

622, 694

623, 697

627

628

629

643

644

645

646

647

648

649

650

651

654-656

657

680

681

682

683

684, 686

685, 687

688

689

690   702   703   704   705

706   707   708   709   710   711

712   713   714   715   716   717

718   719   720-722   724   725   726

727, 752   728, 730, 766   729, 731, 767   732   733, 735, 753

734   736   737, 738, 754   739, 755

740, 751, 756, 769   741, 757   742, 750, 758, 770   743, 759

744, 760   745, 761   746, 762   747, 763

748, 764   749, 765, 797   772, 778A   773, 778B

774   775, 778C   776, 778D   777

782

783

784

785

786

787

788

789

790

791

792

793

794

795

796

798

799

800

801

802

803

804, 848

805, 849

806

807

808, 843

809, 844

810,845

811, 846

812

813

814

815, 847

816

817

818

819

820

821

822

823

824

825

826

827

828

829

830

GENERAL ISSUE—SCOTT NO. 831–867 (1938–1940)

831 832 833 834 835

836 837 838 852 853

854 855 856 857

858 859 860 861 862

863 864 865 866 867

868   869   870   871   872

873   874   875   876   877

878   879   880   881   882

883   884   885   886   887

888   889   890   891   892

893   894   895   896

897

898

899

900

901

902

903

904

905

906

907

908

909

921

922

923

924

925

926

927

GENERAL ISSUE—SCOTT NO. 928–942 (1945–1946)

928

929

930

931

932

933

934

935

936

937

938

939

940

941

942

955

956

957

958

959

960

961

962

963

964

965

966

967

968

969

970

987 988 989 990

991 992 993

994 995 996

997 998 999

1000 1001 1002

1003 1004 1005

1006

1007

1008

1009

1010

1011

1012

1013

1014

1015

1016

1017

1018

1019

1020

1021

1022

1023

1024

1025

1026

1027

1028

1029

1030

1031, 1054

1031A, 1054A

1032

1033, 1055

1034, 1056

1035-1075

1036-1058

1037, 1059

1038

1039

1040

1041, 1075B

1042A

1043

1044A

1044

1045

1046

1047

1048

1049

1050

1051

1052

1053

1060

1061

1062

1063

1064

1065

1066

1067

1068

1069

1070

1071

1072

1073

1074

1076

1075

1077

1078

1079

1080

1081

1082

1083

1084

1085

1086

1087

1088

1089

1090

1091

1092

1093

1094

1095

1096

1097

1098

1099

1100

1104

1105

1106

1107

1108

1109

1110

1111

1112

1113

1114

1115

1116

1117

1118

1119

1120

1121

1122

1123

1124

1125

1126

1127

1128

1129

1130

1131

1132

1133

1134

1135

1136

1137

1138

1139

1140

1141

1142

1143

1144

1145

1146

1147

1148

1149

1150

1151

1152

1153

1154

1155

1156

1157

1158

1159

1160

1161

1162

1163

1164

1165

1166

1167

1168

1169

1170

1171

1172

1173

1174

1175

1176

1177

1178

1179

1180

1181

1182

1183

1184

1185

1186

1187

1188

1189

1190

1191

1192

1193

1194

1195

1196

1197

1198

1199

1200

1201

1202

1203

1204

1205

1206

1207

1208

1209, 1225

1213

1230

1231

1232

1233

1234

1235

1236

1237

GENERAL ISSUE—SCOTT NO. 1274–1306 (1965–1966)

1274

1275

1276

1278

1279

1280

1281, 1297

1282, 1303

1283, 1304

1283B

1284, 1298

1285

1286

1286A

1287

1288

1289

1290

1291

1292

1293

1294, 1305C

1295

1305

1306

1307

1308

1309

1310

1311

1312

1313

1314

1315

1316

1317

1318

1319

1320

1321

GENERAL ISSUE—SCOTT NO. 1322–1343 (1966–1968)

A-36

1373

1374

1375

1376-1379

1380

1381

1382

1383

1384

1385

1386

1391

1393

1387-1390

1392

1393D

1394

1395

1396

GENERAL ISSUE—SCOTT NO. 1397–1425 (1970–1971)

1397

1398

1399

1400

1405

1406

1407

1408

1409

1410-1413

1414

1415-1418

1419

1420

1421   1422

1423   1424

1425

1426

1427-1430

1431

1432

1433

1434   1435

1436

1437   1438

1440-1443

1439   1444

1445

1446   1447

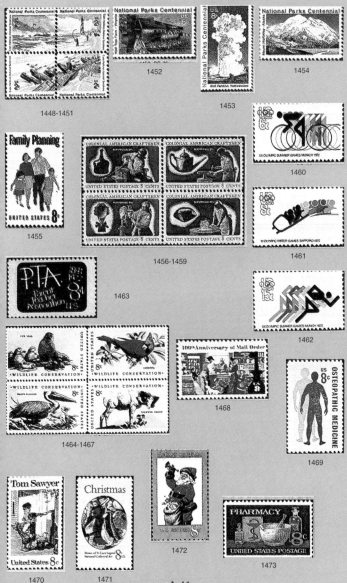

1448-1451

1452

1453

1454

1455

1456-1459

1460

1461

1463

1464-1467

1468

1469

1462

1470

1471

1472

1473

1474

1475

1476

1477

1478

1479

1480-1483

1484

1485

1486

1487

1488

1489

1490

1491

1492

1493

1494

1495

1496

1497

1498
1499
1500
1501
1502
1503
1504
1505
1506F
1507
1508
1525
1509, 1519
1510
1511
1518
1526
1527
1528
1529
1530
1531

1532

1533

1534

1535

1536

1537

1538-1539
1540-1541

1542

1543-1546

1547

1548

1549

1550

1551

1552

1553

1554

1555

GENERAL ISSUE—SCOTT NO. 1579–1623 (1975)

1579

1580

1581

1582

1584

1585

1590

1592

1593

1594

1595

1596

1597

1599

1603

1604

1605

1606

1608

1610

1611

1612

1613

1614

1615

1615C

1622

1623

1629-1630-1631

1632

1633-1682

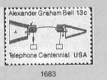

1683

1684

1685

1686

1687

1688

1689

1690

1691-1692-1693-1694

1699

1695 1696 1697 1698

1700

1701

1704

1705

1706

1702-1703

1707

1708

1709

1710

1711

1731

1732

1733

1734

1735

1737

1738-1739-1740-1741-1742

1744

1745

1746

1747

1748

1749

1750

1751

1752

1753

1754

1755

1757

1756

1758

1759

1760   1761   1762

1763

1764

1765   1766

1767   1768   1769   1770

1771   1772

1773

1774

1775

1776

1777

1778

1779

1780

1781

1782

1783

1784

1785

1786

1787

1788

1789

1790

1791

1792

1793

1794

1795

1796

1797

1798

1799

1800

1801

1802

1803

1804

1805-1806

1807-1808

1809-1810

1811

1813

1818

1821

1822

1823

1824

GENERAL ISSUE—SCOTT NO. 1825–1846 (1980–1983)

1825

1826

1827

1828

1829

1830

1831

1832

1833

1834

1835

1836

1837

1838

1839

1840

1841

1842

1843

1844

1845

1846

GENERAL ISSUE—SCOTT NO. 1885–1923 (1981–1982)

1885 1886 1887 1888 1889

1890 1891 1892 1893 1894 1903

1905 1906 1907 1908 1910

1911 1912-1919

1920 1921 1922 1923

1942-1945

1946-1948

1949

1950

1951

1952

1953-2002

2003

2004

2005

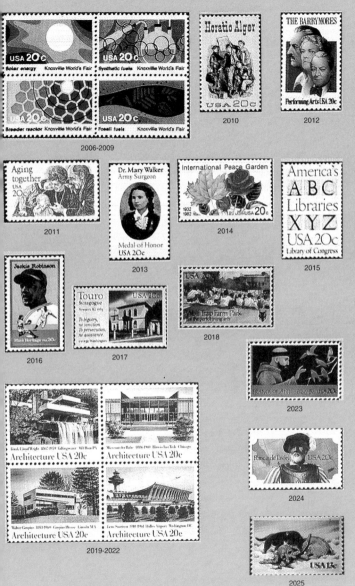

2006-2009

2010

2012

2011

2013

2014

2015

2016

2017

2018

2019-2022

2023

2024

2025

2026

2027-2030

2031

2032-2035

2036

2037

2038

2039

2040

2041

2042

2043

2044

2045

2046

2047

2048-2051

2052

2053

2054

2055

2056

2057

2058

2059

2060

2061

2062

2063

2064

2065

2066

2067-2070

2071

2072

2073

2074

2075

2076-2079

2080

2081

2086

2082-2085

2088

2089

2087

2090

2091

2092

2093

2094

2095

2096

Roberto Clemente
2097

2098

2099

2100

2101

2102

2103

2104

2105

2106

2107

2108

2109

2110

2111-2113

2114-2116

2117-2121

2122
2123
2124
2125
2126
2128
2130
2131
2132
2133
2134
2135
2136
2137
2138-2141
2142
2143
2144
2145
2146
2147
2149
2150
2152

2153

2154

2155-2158

2159

2160-2163

2164

2165

2166

2167

2168

2169

2170

2171

2172

2177

2179

2183

2191

2194

2195

2196

2198-2201

2202

2203

2204

2205-2209

2210

2211

2216

2217

2218

2219

2220-2223

2224

2235-2238

2239

2240-2243

2244

2245

2246

2247

2248

2249

2250

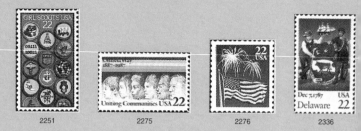

2251   2275   2276   2336

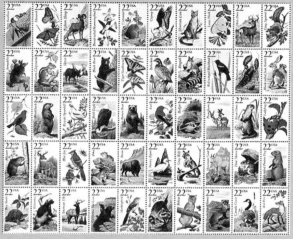

2286-2335

2337   2338   2349   2350

2351-2354

2355-2359

2360

2361

2367

2368

2369

2370

2371

2372-2375

2376

2377

2378

A-69

2379

2380

2386-2389

2381-2385

2390-2393

2394

2395

2396

2397

2398

2399

2400

2401

2402

2403

2404

2405-2409

2410

2411

2412

2413

2414

2416

2417

2418

2419

2420

2421

2422-2425

2426

2427

A-71

2428

2434-2437

2439

2440

2442

2443

2444

2445-2448

2449

2452

2496-2500

2470-2474

2501

2506-2507

2512

2508-2511

2513

2514

2515

2517

2521

2523

2524

2528

2530

2531

2532

2533

2534

2535

2537

2538

2539

2540

2541

2542

2545-2549

2550

2551

2558

2553-2557

2560

2561

2562-2566

2568-2577

2567

2578

2579

2582

2583

2584

2585

2604

2607

2608

2609

2616

2611-2615

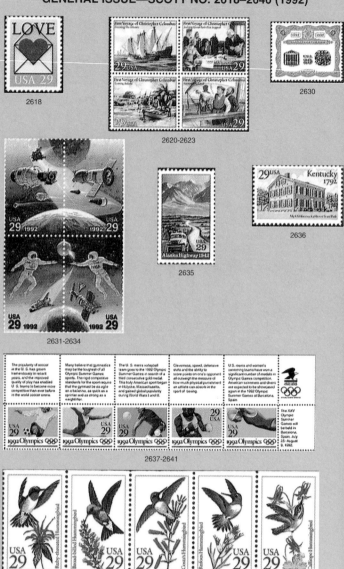

2618

2620-2623

2630

2631-2634

2635

2636

2637-2641

2642-2646

A-76

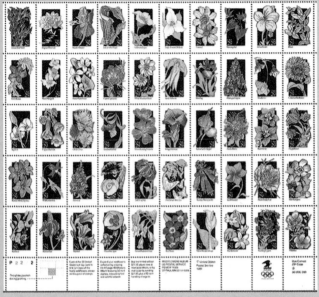

2647-2696

2697

GENERAL ISSUE—SCOTT NO. 2698–2726 (1992–1993)

2698

2699

2700-2703

2704

2705-2709

2710

2711

2712

2713

2714

2720

2721

2722

2723

2724

2725

2726

A-78

2727

2728

2729

2730

2741-2745

2746

2747

2748

2749

2754

2755

2750-2753

2756-2759

2760-2764

2765

2766

2779-2782

2767-2770

2804

2805

GENERAL ISSUE—SCOTT NO. 2806–2837(1993–1994)

2806

2812

2813

2814

2807-2811

2815

2829-2833

2818

2834-2837

A-81

2838

2840

First Moon Landing, 1969

2841

2843-2847

2848

2849

2850

2851

2852

2853

2854

2855

2856

2857

2858

2859

2860

2861

2862

2867

2863-2866

2868

2871

2872

2869

2873

2874

2876

2875

2878

2880

2882

2888

2905

A-84

2915

2933

2934

2938

2940

2943

2948

2949

2950

2951

2952

2953

2954

2955

2956

2957

2958

2960

2961

2962

2963

2964

2965

2966

2967

2968

2969

2970

2971

2972

2973

2974

2975

2976

2977

2978

2979

2980

2981

2982 LOUIS ARMSTRONG

2983 COLEMAN HAWKINS

2984 LOUIS ARMSTRONG

2985 JAMES P. JOHNSON

2986 JELLY ROLL MORTON

2987 CHARLIE PARKER

2988   2989   2990

2991   2992

2993   2994   2995   2996

2997   2998   2999

3000

3001

3002

3003

3004

3005

3006

3007

3012

3013

3019

3020

3021

3022

GENERAL ISSUE—SCOTT NO. 3023–3058 (1995–1996)

32 USA — 1901 White
3023

32 USA — Utah 1896
3024

32 USA Crocus | 32 USA Winter Aconite | 32 USA Pansy | 32 USA Snowdrop | 32 USA Anemone
3025-3029

USA 3¢ — Eastern Bluebird
3033

USA 1¢ — American Kestrel
3044

LOVE — USA 1995
3030

USA 2¢ — Red-headed Woodpecker
3032

USA 20 — Blue Jay
3048

USA 32 — Rose
3049

BLACK HERITAGE — USA 32 — Ernest E. Just — Biologist
3058

A-91

3059

3060

3061-3064

3065

3066

3067

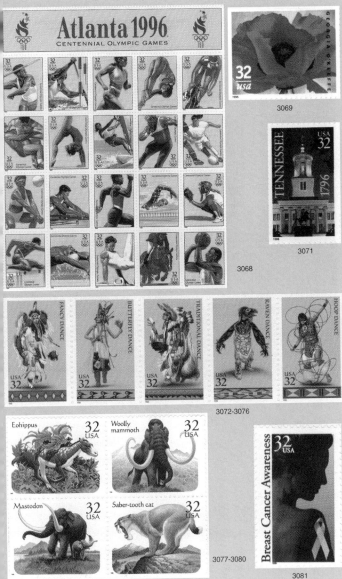

3069

3071

3068

3072-3076

3077-3080

A-93

3081

3082

3083-3086

PAUL BUNYAN

MIGHTY CASEY

PECOS BILL

JOHN HENRY

Centennial Olympic Games
1896 1996
3087

1846 IOWA
3088

RURAL FREE DELIVERY
RFD
3090

COUNT BASIE
3096

TOMMY & JIMMY DORSEY
3097

GLENN MILLER
3098

BENNY GOODMAN
3099

ROBT. E. LEE

SYLVAN DELL

FAR WEST

REBECCA EVERINGHAM

BAILEY GATZERT
3091-3095

GENERAL ISSUE—SCOTT NO. 3100–3110 (1996)

3100

3101

3102

3103

3104

3106

3105

3107 & 3112

3108

3109

3110

3111

3117

3118

3119

Scott No.	Mint Sheet	Plate Block	Fine Unused Each	Fine Used Each
1964. NEW YORK WORLD'S FAIR				
☐ 1244 5¢ Green	7.50	.95	.30	.21
1964. JOHN MUIR—CONSERVATIONIST				
☐ 1245 5¢ Brown, Green & Olive				
	7.50	.95	.30	.21
1964. JOHN F. KENNEDY MEMORIAL				
☐ 1246 5¢ Blue Gray	7.50	1.80	.48	.22
1964. NEW JERSEY TERCENTENARY				
☐ 1247 5¢ Ultramarine	7.50	.95	.31	.19
1964. NEVADA STATEHOOD				
☐ 1248 5¢ Red, Yellow & Blue				
	7.50	.95	.26	.19
1964. REGISTER AND VOTE				
☐ 1249 5¢ Dark Blue & Red	7.50	.95	.26	.19
1964. WILLIAM SHAKESPEARE				
☐ 1250 5¢ Brown on Tan	7.50	.95	.26	.19
1964. DOCTORS MAYO				
☐ 1251 5¢ Green	7.50	2.00	.36	.22
1964. AMERICAN MUSIC				
☐ 1252 5¢ Red, Black & Blue	7.00	1.10	.30	.22
1964. AMERICAN HOMEMAKERS				
☐ 1253 5¢ Multicolored	7.00	1.10	.30	.22
1964. CHRISTMAS ISSUE				
☐ 1254 5¢ Red & Green	—	—	1.60	.19
☐ 1255 5¢ Red & Green	—	—	1.60	.19
☐ 1256 5¢ Red & Green	—	—	1.20	.19
☐ 1257 5¢ Red & Green	—	—	1.20	.19

*No hinge pricing from 1941 to date is figured at (N-H ADD 10%)

Scott No.	Mint Sheet	Plate Block	Fine Unused Each	Fine Used Each

1964. VERRAZANO–NARROWS BRIDGE

| ☐1258 5¢ Green | 7.50 | .85 | .26 | .21 |

1964. STUART DAVIS—MODERN ART

| ☐1259 5¢ Ultramarine, Black & Red | | | | |
| | 7.50 | .85 | .26 | .21 |

1964. RADIO AMATEURS

| ☐1260 5¢ Red Lilac | 7.50 | 1.30 | .31 | .21 |

1965. COMMEMORATIVES
1965. BATTLE OF NEW ORLEANS

| ☐1261 5¢ Carmine, Blue & Gray | | | | |
| | 7.25 | .95 | .30 | .21 |

1965. PHYSICAL FITNESS—SOKOL CENTENNIAL

| ☐1262 5¢ Maroon & Black | 7.25 | .95 | .30 | .21 |

1965. CRUSADE AGAINST CANCER

| ☐1263 5¢ Black, Purple, Orange | | | | |
| | 7.50 | .85 | .26 | .19 |

1965. SIR WINSTON CHURCHILL MEMORIAL

| ☐1264 5¢ Black | 7.25 | .95 | .30 | .21 |

1965. MAGNA CARTA 750TH ANNIVERSARY

| ☐1265 5¢ Black, Ochre, Red Lilac | | | | |
| | 7.50 | .85 | .26 | .19 |

1965. INTERNATIONAL COOPERATION YEAR

| ☐1266 5¢ Dull Blue & Black | 7.25 | .95 | .30 | .21 |

1965. SALVATION ARMY

| ☐1267 5¢ Red, Black & Blue | 7.25 | .75 | .26 | .21 |

1965. DANTE ALIGHIERI

| ☐1268 5¢ Maroon on Tan | 7.25 | .75 | .26 | .21 |

*No hinge pricing from 1941 to date is figured at (N-H ADD 10%)

Scott No.	Mint Sheet	Plate Block	Fine Unused Each	Fine Used Each

1965. HERBERT HOOVER
☐1269 5¢ Red Rose	7.25	.85	.30	.21

1965. ROBERT FULTON BIRTH BICENTENNIAL
☐1270 5¢ Black & Blue	7.25	.85	.30	.21

1965. FLORIDA SETTLEMENT QUADRICENTENNIAL
☐1271 5¢ Red, Yellow & Black				
	7.50	.85	.26	.19

1965. TRAFFIC SAFETY
☐1272 5¢ Green, Black, Red	7.50	.85	.26	.19

1965. JOHN SINGLETON COPLEY—ARTIST
☐1273 5¢ Black, Brown, Olive				
	7.50	1.20	.30	.21

1965. INTERNATIONAL TELECOMMUNICATION UNION
☐1274 11¢ Black, Carmine, Bistre				
	30.00	9.00	.65	.40

1965. ADLAI E. STEVENSON MEMORIAL
☐1275 5¢ Light & Dark Blue, Black & Red				
	7.50	.85	.26	.19

1965. CHRISTMAS ISSUE
☐1276 5¢ Red, Green & Yellow				
	14.00	.95	.26	.19

1965–1968. PROMINENT AMERICANS SERIES
☐1278 1¢ Green	6.00	.75	.26	.21
☐1279 1¼¢ Green	28.00	15.00	.30	.21
☐1280 2¢ Slate Blue	7.00	.80	.26	.21
☐1281 3¢ Purple	9.00	.85	.26	.19
☐1282 4¢ Black	14.00	.85	.26	.19
☐1283 5¢ Blue	14.00	.85	.26	.19

*No hinge pricing from 1941 to date is figured at (N-H ADD 10%)

Scott No.	Mint Sheet	Plate Block	Fine Unused Each	Fine Used Each
☐1283B 5¢ Blue	14.00	.85	.26	.19
☐1284 6¢ Gray Brown	20.00	.80	.26	.19
☐1285 8¢ Violet	25.00	1.25	.36	.19
☐1286 10¢ Lilac	30.00	1.40	.34	.19
☐1286A 12¢ Black	36.00	1.50	.37	.19
☐1287 13¢ Brown	38.00	2.10	.60	.19
☐1288 15¢ Rose Claret	40.00	2.00	.48	.19
☐1288A 15¢ Rose Claret II	42.00	4.50	.42	.19
☐1289 20¢ Olive Green	60.00	3.00	.85	.19
☐1290 25¢ Rose Lake	75.00	4.00	1.20	.19
☐1291 30¢ Light Purple	80.00	4.00	1.10	.19
☐1292 40¢ Dark Blue	100.00	5.00	1.30	.19
☐1293 50¢ Maroon	150.00	6.00	1.60	.19
☐1294 $1 Purple	300.00	12.00	3.50	.19
☐1295 $5 Gray	1000.00	50.00	14.00	2.50

Scott No.	Fine Unused Line Pair	Ave. Unused Line Pair	Fine Unused Each	Ave. Unused Each	Fine Used Each	Ave. Used Each
1965–1968. PERF. 10 HORIZONTALLY						
☐1297 3¢ Purple						
	.75	.65	.30	.26	.25	.18
☐1298 6¢ Gray Brown						
	1.85	1.50	.30	.26	.25	.18
1965–1968. PERF. 10 VERTICALLY						
☐1299 1¢ Green						
	.60	.46	.30	.26	.25	.18
☐1303 4¢ Black						
	.90	.75	.30	.26	.25	.18
☐1304 5¢ Blue						
	.75	.60	.30	.26	.25	.18
☐1305 6¢ Gray Brown						
	.90	.80	.30	.26	.25	.18
☐1305C $1 Purple						
	6.00	4.50	3.00	2.50	2.10	1.20

*No hinge pricing from 1941 to date is figured at (N-H ADD 10%)

Scott No.	Mint Sheet	Plate Block	Fine Unused Each	Fine Used Each

1966. COMMEMORATIVES
1966. MIGRATORY BIRD TREATY

☐1306 5¢ Red, Blue, Black	7.50	.85	.24	.18

1966. HUMANE TREATMENT OF ANIMALS
☐1307 5¢ Orange Brown & Black

	7.50	.85	.24	.18

1966. INDIANA STATEHOOD
☐1308 5¢ Ochre, Brown & Violet Blue

	7.25	.80	.22	.18

1966. AMERICAN CIRCUS
☐1309 5¢ Red, Blue, Pink, Black

	7.25	1.20	.36	.22

1966. SIXTH INTL. PHILATELIC EXHIBITION "SIPEX"

☐1310 5¢ Multicolored	7.50	1.10	.26	.18

1966. IMPERFORATE SOUVENIR SHEET

☐1311 5¢ Multicolored	—	.85	.26	.18

1966. BILL OF RIGHTS
☐1312 5¢ Red, Dark & Light Blue

	8.50	1.10	.29	.18

1966. POLISH MILLENNIUM

☐1313 5¢ Red	7.50	.85	.26	.18

1966. NATIONAL PARK SERVICE
☐1314 5¢ Yellow, Black & Green

	7.50	.95	.30	.18

1966. MARINE CORPS RESERVE
☐1315 5¢ Black, Red, Blue, Olive

	7.50	.85	.26	.18

*No hinge pricing from 1941 to date is figured at (N-H ADD 10%)

Scott No.	Mint Sheet	Plate Block	Fine Unused Each	Fine Used Each

1966. GENERAL FEDERATION OF WOMEN'S CLUBS
☐ 1316 5¢ Blue, Pink, Black — 7.50 / .85 / .26 / .18

1966. AMERICAN FOLKLORE—JOHNNY APPLESEED
☐ 1317 5¢ Red, Black, Green — 7.50 / .85 / .26 / .18

1966. BEAUTIFICATION OF AMERICA
☐ 1318 5¢ Emerald, Pink, Black — 7.75 / .95 / .30 / .18

1966. GREAT RIVER ROAD
☐ 1319 5¢ Yellow, Red, Blue, Green — 7.50 / .85 / .26 / .18

1966. SERVICEMEN & SAVINGS BONDS
☐ 1320 5¢ Red, Light Blue, Dark Blue — 7.25 / .95 / .30 / .18

1966. CHRISTMAS ISSUE
☐ 1321 5¢ Multicolored — 14.00 / .95 / .30 / .18

1966. MARY CASSATT—ARTIST
☐ 1322 5¢ Multicolored — 9.50 / 1.25 / .30 / .18

1967. COMMEMORATIVES
1967. NATIONAL GRANGE CENTENARY
☐ 1323 5¢ Orange, Yellow, Black, Brown & Green — 8.50 / .95 / .26 / .18

1967. CANADA CENTENNIAL
☐ 1324 5¢ Green, Light & Dark Blue, Black — 7.50 / .85 / .26 / .18

1967. ERIE CANAL SESQUICENTENNIAL
☐ 1325 5¢ Light & Dark Blue, Red & Black — 7.50 / .85 / .26 / .18

*No hinge pricing from 1941 to date is figured at (N-H ADD 10%)

Scott No.	Mint Sheet	Plate Block	Fine Unused Each	Fine Used Each

1967. SEARCH FOR PEACE—LIONS INTL.

| ☐1326 5¢ Red, Blue & Black | 7.75 | 1.10 | .30 | .21 |

1967. HENRY DAVID THOREAU

| ☐1327 5¢ Black, Red & Green | | | | |
| | 7.00 | .95 | .26 | .18 |

1967. NEBRASKA STATEHOOD CENTENNIAL

| ☐1328 5¢ Yellow Green & Brown | | | | |
| | 7.00 | .95 | .26 | .18 |

1967. VOICE OF AMERICA

| ☐1329 5¢ Red, Blue & Black | 7.00 | .85 | .26 | .18 |

1967. AMERICAN FOLKLORE—DAVY CROCKETT

| ☐1330 5¢ Green & Black | 7.00 | .95 | .30 | .21 |

1967. SPACE ACCOMPLISHMENTS

☐1331 5¢ Light & Dark Blue, Red, Black				
	—	1.00	1.20	.36
☐1332 5¢ Light & Dark Blue, Red, Black				
	—	1.00	1.20	.36

1967. URBAN PLANNING

| ☐1333 5¢ Blue & Black | 7.75 | .90 | .24 | .18 |

1967. FINNISH INDEPENDENCE

| ☐1334 5¢ Blue | 7.00 | .98 | .26 | .18 |

1967. THOMAS EAKINS—ARTIST

| ☐1335 5¢ Gold & Multicolored | | | | |
| | 7.00 | .98 | .26 | .18 |

1967. CHRISTMAS ISSUE

| ☐1336 5¢ Multicolored | 7.50 | .90 | .26 | .18 |

1967. MISSISSIPPI STATEHOOD

| ☐1337 5¢ Multicolored | 8.50 | .95 | .29 | .18 |

*No hinge pricing from 1941 to date is figured at (N-H ADD 10%)

Scott No.	Mint Sheet	Plate Block	Fine Unused Each	Fine Used Each

1968–1971. REGULAR ISSUES
1968. FLAG ISSUE

☐ 1338 6¢ Red, Blue, Green	18.75	1.20	.26	.18

1968. COMMEMORATIVES
1968. ILLINOIS STATEHOOD

☐ 1339 6¢ Black, Gold, Pink	9.00	1.20	.26	.18

1968. HEMISFAIR '68

☐ 1340 6¢ Indigo, Carmine, White	9.00	1.20	.26	.18

1968. AIRLIFT TO SERVICEMEN

☐ 1341 $1 Multicolored	175.00	14.00	4.50	2.30

1968. SUPPORT OUR YOUTH (ELKS)

☐ 1342 6¢ Blue & Black	8.75	1.00	.30	.22

1968. LAW AND ORDER

☐ 1343 6¢ Blue & Black	8.75	1.75	.30	.21

1968. REGISTER & VOTE

☐ 1344 6¢ Black & Gold	9.00	1.20	.30	.21

1968. HISTORIC AMERICAN FLAGS

☐ 1345 6¢ Dark Blue	—	—	.60	.48
☐ 1346 6¢ Red & Dark Blue	—	—	.50	.48
☐ 1347 6¢ Dark Blue, Olive Green	—	—	.38	.30
☐ 1348 6¢ Dark Blue & Red	—	—	.38	.30
☐ 1349 6¢ Black, Yellow, Red	—	—	.38	.30
☐ 1350 6¢ Dark Blue & Red	—	—	.38	.30
☐ 1351 6¢ Blue, Olive Green, Red	—	—	.38	.30
☐ 1352 6¢ Dark Blue & Red	—	—	.38	.30
☐ 1353 6¢ Blue, Yellow, Red	—	2.25	.38	.30
☐ 1354 6¢ Blue, Red, Yellow	—	—	.38	.30

*No hinge pricing from 1941 to date is figured at (N-H ADD 10%)

Scott No.	Mint Sheet	Plate Block	Fine Unused Each	Fine Used Each
1968. WALT DISNEY				
☐ 1355 6¢ Multicolored	26.00	2.50	.75	.18
1968. FATHER MARQUETTE—EXPLORATIONS				
☐ 1356 6¢ Black, Brown, Green				
	8.50	1.30	.29	.18
1968. AMERICAN FOLKLORE—DANIEL BOONE				
☐ 1357 6¢ Brown, Yellow, Black, Red				
	8.50	.95	.26	.18
1968. ARKANSAS RIVER NAVIGATION				
☐ 1358 6¢ Black & Blue	8.50	.95	.26	.18
1968. LEIF ERIKSON				
☐ 1359 6¢ Dark Brown on Brown				
	8.50	.95	.26	.18
1968. CHEROKEE STRIP LAND RUSH				
☐ 1360 6¢ Brown	8.50	1.10	.29	.18
1968. JOHN TRUMBULL PAINTING				
☐ 1361 6¢ Yellow Red, Black	8.50	1.30	.31	.18
1968. WILDLIFE CONSERVATION—DUCKS				
☐ 1362 6¢ Multicolored	13.50	1.50	.29	.18
1968. CHRISTMAS ISSUE				
☐ 1363 6¢ Multicolored	8.50	2.00	.28	.18
1968. AMERICAN INDIAN				
☐ 1364 6¢ Multicolored	14.00	1.50	.29	.18
1969. COMMEMORATIVES				
1969. BEAUTIFICATION OF AMERICA				
☐ 1365 6¢ Multicolored	—	—	1.75	.22
☐ 1366 6¢ Multicolored	—	—	1.75	.22

*No hinge pricing from 1941 to date is figured at (N-H ADD 10%)

Scott No.	Mint Sheet	Plate Block	Fine Unused Each	Fine Used Each
☐1367 6¢ Multicolored	—	—	1.80	.22
☐1368 6¢ Multicolored	—	—	1.80	.22

1969. AMERICAN LEGION
☐1369 6¢ Red, Blue, Black	8.50	.95	.28	.18

1969. GRANDMA MOSES PAINTING
☐1370 6¢ Multicolored	8.50	1.00	.28	.18

1969. APOLLO 8 MOON ORBIT
☐1371 6¢ Black, Blue, Ochre	14.00	1.75	.36	.22

1969. W. C. HANDY—MUSICIAN
☐1372 6¢ Multicolored	10.00	1.10	.29	.19

1969. SETTLEMENT OF CALIFORNIA
☐1373 6¢ Multicolored	8.75	1.00	.36	.22

1969. MAJOR JOHN WESLEY POWELL— GEOLOGIST
☐1374 6¢ Multicolored	8.75	1.00	.30	.21

1969. ALABAMA STATEHOOD
☐1375 6¢ Red, Yellow, Brown	8.50	.95	.26	.18

1969. XI INTL. BOTANICAL CONGRESS
☐1376 6¢ Multicolored	—	—	2.00	.75
☐1377 6¢ Multicolored	—	—	2.00	.75
☐1378 6¢ Multicolored	—	—	2.00	.75
☐1379 6¢ Multicolored	—	—	2.00	.75

1969. DARTMOUTH COLLEGE CASE
☐1380 6¢ Green	9.00	1.00	.28	.18

1969. PROFESSIONAL BASEBALL CENTENARY
☐1381 6¢ Multicolored	45.00	5.00	1.75	.24

*No hinge pricing from 1941 to date is figured at (N-H ADD 10%)

Scott No.	Mint Sheet	Plate Block	Fine Unused Each	Fine Used Each

1969. INTERCOLLEGIATE FOOTBALL CENTENARY

☐1382 6¢ Red & Green	15.00	2.25	.60	.18

1969. DWIGHT D. EISENHOWER MEMORIAL

☐1383 6¢ Blue, Black & Red	6.00	.95	.28	.18

1969. CHRISTMAS ISSUE

☐1384 6¢ Multicolored	8.50	2.10	.28	.18

1969. HOPE FOR THE CRIPPLED

☐1385 6¢ Multicolored	8.50	1.00	.28	.18

1969. WILLIAM M. HARNETT PAINTING

☐1386 6¢ Multicolored	6.00	1.00	.28	.18

1970. COMMEMORATIVES
1970. NATURAL HISTORY

☐1387 6¢ Multicolored	—	—	.40	.20
☐1388 6¢ Multicolored	—	—	.40	.20
☐1389 6¢ Multicolored	—	—	.40	.20
☐1390 6¢ Multicolored	—	—	.40	.20

1970. MAINE STATEHOOD SESQUICENTENNIAL

☐1391 6¢ Multicolored	8.50	1.00	.30	.20

1970. WILDLIFE CONSERVATION—BUFFALO

☐1392 6¢ Black on Tan	8.50	1.00	.30	.20

1970–1974. REGULAR ISSUE

☐1393 6¢ Blue Gray	19.00	1.00	.24	.19
☐1393D 7¢ Light Blue	20.00	1.20	.24	.19
☐1394 8¢ Black, Blue, Red	25.00	1.50	.28	.19
☐1395 8¢ Rose Violet	—	—	.28	.19
☐1396 8¢ Multicolored	22.00	4.00	.28	.19
☐1397 14¢ Brown	38.00	2.00	.40	.19
☐1398 16¢ Orange Brown	45.00	2.10	.45	.19
☐1399 18¢ Purple	55.00	3.00	.55	.19

*No hinge pricing from 1941 to date is figured at (N-H ADD 10%)

Scott No.	Mint Sheet	Plate Block	Fine Unused Each	Fine Used Each
☐1400 21¢ Green	60.00	3.00	.85	.28

Scott No.	Fine Unused Line Pair	Ave. Unused Line Pair	Fine Unused Each	Ave. Unused Each	Fine Used Each	Ave. Used Each

1970–1971. ROTARY PRESS COIL STAMPS—PERF. 10 VERTICALLY

Scott No.	Fine Unused Line Pair	Ave. Unused Line Pair	Fine Unused Each	Ave. Unused Each	Fine Used Each	Ave. Used Each
☐1401 6¢ Blue Gray	.70	.60	.28	.25	.24	.17
☐1402 8¢ Rose Violet	.70	.60	.28	.25	.24	.17

Scott No.	Mint Sheet	Plate Block	Fine Unused Each	Fine Used Each

1970. EDGAR LEE MASTERS—POET

	Mint Sheet	Plate Block	Fine Unused Each	Fine Used Each
☐1405 6¢ Black & Olive Bistre	15.00	.75	.25	.17

1970. 50TH ANNIVERSARY WOMEN'S SUFFRAGE

	Mint Sheet	Plate Block	Fine Unused Each	Fine Used Each
☐1406 6¢ Blue	15.00	.80	.25	.17

1970. SOUTH CAROLINA TERCENTENARY

	Mint Sheet	Plate Block	Fine Unused Each	Fine Used Each
☐1407 6¢ Multicolored	15.00	.80	.24	.17

1970. STONE MOUNTAIN MEMORIAL

	Mint Sheet	Plate Block	Fine Unused Each	Fine Used Each
☐1408 6¢ Gray Black	15.00	.80	.25	.20

1970. FORT SNELLING

	Mint Sheet	Plate Block	Fine Unused Each	Fine Used Each
☐1409 6¢ Multicolored	15.00	.80	.24	.17

1970. ANTI-POLLUTION

	Mint Sheet	Plate Block	Fine Unused Each	Fine Used Each
☐1410 6¢ Multicolored	—	—	.45	.20
☐1411 6¢ Multicolored	—	—	.45	.20
☐1412 6¢ Multicolored	—	—	.45	.20
☐1413 6¢ Multicolored	—	—	.45	.20

*No hinge pricing from 1941 to date is figured at (N-H ADD 10%)

Scott No.	Mint Sheet	Plate Block	Fine Unused Each	Fine Used Each

1970. CHRISTMAS ISSUE

Scott No.	Mint Sheet	Plate Block	Fine Unused Each	Fine Used Each
☐1414 6¢ Multicolored	8.50	2.00	.28	.18
☐1415 6¢ Multicolored	—	—	.55	.18
☐1416 6¢ Multicolored	—	—	.55	.18
☐1417 6¢ Multicolored	—	—	.55	.18
☐1418 6¢ Multicolored	—	—	.55	.18

1970. PRECANCELLED CHRISTMAS ISSUE

Scott No.	Mint Sheet	Plate Block	Fine Unused Each	Fine Used Each
☐1414a 6¢ Multicolored	9.50	3.25	.45	.18
☐1415a 6¢ Multicolored	—	—	1.10	.18
☐1416a 6¢ Multicolored	—	—	1.10	.18
☐1417a 6¢ Multicolored	—	—	1.10	.18
☐1418a 6¢ Multicolored	—	—	1.10	.18

1970. UNITED NATIONS 25TH ANNIVERSARY

Scott No.	Mint Sheet	Plate Block	Fine Unused Each	Fine Used Each
☐1419 6¢ Black, Red, Blue	8.50	.90	.25	.17

1970. PILGRIM LANDING 350TH ANNIVERSARY

Scott No.	Mint Sheet	Plate Block	Fine Unused Each	Fine Used Each
☐1420 6¢ Multicolored	8.50	.90	.25	.17

1970. DISABLED AMERICAN VETERANS AND SERVICEMEN ISSUE

Scott No.	Mint Sheet	Plate Block	Fine Unused Each	Fine Used Each
☐1421 6¢ Blue, Black, Red	—	—	.55	.30
☐1422 6¢ Blue, Black, Red	—	—	.55	.30

1971. COMMEMORATIVES
1971. ADVENT OF SHEEP TO AMERICA

Scott No.	Mint Sheet	Plate Block	Fine Unused Each	Fine Used Each
☐1423 6¢ Multicolored	8.50	.90	.25	.17

1971. GENERAL DOUGLAS MacARTHUR

Scott No.	Mint Sheet	Plate Block	Fine Unused Each	Fine Used Each
☐1424 6¢ Red, Blue, Black	8.50	.90	.25	.17

1971. BLOOD DONORS PROGRAM

Scott No.	Mint Sheet	Plate Block	Fine Unused Each	Fine Used Each
☐1425 6¢ Light Blue, Scarlet, Indigo	8.50	.90	.25	.17

1971. MISSOURI STATEHOOD

Scott No.	Mint Sheet	Plate Block	Fine Unused Each	Fine Used Each
☐1426 8¢ Multicolored	12.00	3.75	.34	.22

*No hinge pricing from 1941 to date is figured at (N-H ADD 10%)

Scott No.	Mint Sheet	Plate Block	Fine Unused Each	Fine Used Each

1971. WILDLIFE CONSERVATION
☐1427 8¢ Multicolored	—	—	1.00	.60
☐1428 8¢ Multicolored	—	—	1.00	.60
☐1429 8¢ Multicolored	—	—	1.00	.60
☐1430 8¢ Multicolored	—	—	1.00	.60

1971. ANTARCTIC TREATY
☐1431 8¢ Red & Blue	12.00	1.20	.25	.18

1971. AMERICAN REVOLUTION BICENTENNIAL
☐1432 8¢ Red, Blue, Black	14.00	1.50	.28	.18

1971. JOHN SLOAN PAINTING
☐1433 8¢ Multicolored	12.00	1.20	.25	.18

1971. DECADE OF SPACE ACHIEVEMENTS
☐1434 8¢ Multicolored	—	—	.70	.28
☐1435 8¢ Multicolored	—	—	.70	.28

1971. EMILY DICKINSON—POET
☐1436 8¢ Multicolored	12.00	1.10	.28	.18

1971. SAN JUAN 450TH ANNIVERSARY
☐1437 8¢ Brown, Carmine, Blk.	12.00	1.20	.28	.18

1971. DRUG ADDICTION
☐1438 8¢ Blue & Black	12.00	1.70	.28	.18

1971. CARE ANNIVERSARY
☐1439 8¢ Multicolored	12.00	1.85	.28	.18

1971. HISTORIC PRESERVATION
☐1440 8¢ Dark Brown & Ochre	—	—	.32	.20
☐1441 8¢ Dark Brown & Ochre	—	—	.32	.20

*No hinge pricing from 1941 to date is figured at (N-H ADD 10%)

Scott No.	Mint Sheet	Plate Block	Fine Unused Each	Fine Used Each
☐1442 8¢ Dark Brown & Ochre				
	—	—	.32	.20
☐1443 8¢ Dark Brown & Ochre				
	—	—	.32	.20

1971. CHRISTMAS
☐1444 8¢ Multicolored	12.00	3.10	.30	.20
☐1445 8¢ Multicolored	12.00	3.10	.30	.20

1972. COMMEMORATIVES
1972. SIDNEY LANIER—POET
☐1446 8¢ Multicolored	12.00	1.15	.32	.20

1972. PEACE CORPS
☐1447 8¢ Red & Blue	12.00	2.00	.32	.20

1972. NATIONAL PARKS CENTENNIAL
☐1448 2¢ Multicolored	—	—	.55	.40
☐1449 2¢ Multicolored	—	—	.55	.40
☐1450 2¢ Multicolored	—	—	.55	.40
☐1451 2¢ Multicolored	—	—	.55	.40
☐1452 6¢ Multicolored	8.50	1.00	.25	.18
☐1453 8¢ Multicolored	8.00	1.25	.26	.18
☐1454 15¢ Multicolored	22.00	2.00	.45	.40

1972. FAMILY PLANNING
☐1455 8¢ Multicolored	12.00	1.40	.32	.20

1972. AMERICAN REVOLUTION BICENTENNIAL— COLONIAL CRAFTSMEN
☐1456 8¢ Deep Brown, Yellow				
	—	—	.32	.20
☐1457 8¢ Deep Brown, Yellow				
	—	—	.32	.20
☐1458 8¢ Deep Brown, Yellow				
	—	—	.32	.20
☐1459 8¢ Deep Brown, Yellow				
	—	—	.32	.20

*No hinge pricing from 1941 to date is figured at (N-H ADD 10%)

Scott No.	Mint Sheet	Plate Block	Fine Unused Each	Fine Used Each

1972. OLYMPIC GAMES

Scott No.	Mint Sheet	Plate Block	Fine Unused Each	Fine Used Each
☐ 1460 6¢ Multicolored	10.00	2.40	.25	.18
☐ 1461 8¢ Multicolored	12.00	3.50	.25	.18
☐ 1462 15¢ Multicolored	22.00	5.50	.45	.40

1972. PARENT TEACHER ASSOCIATION

Scott No.	Mint Sheet	Plate Block	Fine Unused Each	Fine Used Each
☐ 1463 8¢ Black & Yellow	12.00	1.10	.25	.18
☐ 1463a 8¢ Black & Yellow, Reversed Pl. No.	—	1.20	—	—

1972. WILDLIFE CONSERVATION

Scott No.	Mint Sheet	Plate Block	Fine Unused Each	Fine Used Each
☐ 1464 8¢ Multicolored	—	—	.36	.20
☐ 1465 8¢ Multicolored	—	—	.36	.20
☐ 1466 8¢ Multicolored	—	—	.36	.20
☐ 1467 8¢ Multicolored	—	—	.36	.20

1972. MAIL ORDER BUSINESS

Scott No.	Mint Sheet	Plate Block	Fine Unused Each	Fine Used Each
☐ 1468 8¢ Multicolored	12.00	3.25	.28	.19

1972. OSTEOPATHIC MEDICINE

Scott No.	Mint Sheet	Plate Block	Fine Unused Each	Fine Used Each
☐ 1469 8¢ Yellow Orange, Brown	12.00	1.65	.28	.19

1972. TOM SAWYER—AMERICAN FOLKLORE

Scott No.	Mint Sheet	Plate Block	Fine Unused Each	Fine Used Each
☐ 1470 8¢ Multicolored	12.00	1.30	.28	.19

1972. CHRISTMAS

Scott No.	Mint Sheet	Plate Block	Fine Unused Each	Fine Used Each
☐ 1471 8¢ Multicolored	12.00	3.25	.28	.19
☐ 1472 8¢ Multicolored	12.00	3.25	.28	.19

1972. PHARMACY

Scott No.	Mint Sheet	Plate Block	Fine Unused Each	Fine Used Each
☐ 1473 8¢ Multicolored	12.00	1.65	.28	.19

1972. STAMP COLLECTING

Scott No.	Mint Sheet	Plate Block	Fine Unused Each	Fine Used Each
☐ 1474 8¢ Multicolored	9.00	1.20	.28	.19

*No hinge pricing from 1941 to date is figured at (N-H ADD 10%)

Scott No.	Mint Sheet	Plate Block	Fine Unused Each	Fine Used Each

1973. COMMEMORATIVES
1973. LOVE—"FOR SOMEONE SPECIAL"

☐ 1475 8¢ Red, Green, Blue	12.00	1.50	.28	.17

1973. COLONIAL COMMUNICATIONS

☐ 1476 8¢ Black, Red, Blue	12.00	1.20	.28	.17
☐ 1477 8¢ Blue, Red, Brown	12.00	1.20	.28	.17
☐ 1478 8¢ Multicolored	12.00	1.20	.28	.17
☐ 1479 8¢ Multicolored	12.00	1.20	.28	.17

1973. BOSTON TEA PARTY

☐ 1480 8¢ Multicolored	—	—	.30	.18
☐ 1481 8¢ Multicolored	—	—	.30	.18
☐ 1482 8¢ Multicolored	—	—	.30	.18
☐ 1483 8¢ Multicolored	—	—	.30	.18

1973. GEORGE GERSHWIN—COMPOSER

☐ 1484 8¢ Multicolored	10.00	3.50	.28	.17

1973. ROBINSON JEFFERS—POET

☐ 1485 8¢ Multicolored	10.00	3.00	.28	.17

1973. HENRY OSSAWA TANNER—ARTIST

☐ 1486 6¢ Multicolored	10.00	3.00	.28	.17

1973. WILLA CATHER—NOVELIST

☐ 1487 8¢ Multicolored	10.00	3.00	.28	.17

1973. NICOLAUS COPERNICUS

☐ 1488 8¢ Black & Orange	12.75	2.25	.28	.17

1973. POSTAL PEOPLE

☐ 1489 8¢ Multicolored	—	—	.30	.18
☐ 1490 8¢ Multicolored	—	—	.30	.18
☐ 1491 8¢ Multicolored	—	—	.30	.18
☐ 1492 8¢ Multicolored	—	—	.30	.18
☐ 1493 8¢ Multicolored	—	—	.30	.18
☐ 1494 8¢ Multicolored	—	—	.30	.18

*No hinge pricing from 1941 to date is figured at (N-H ADD 10%)

Scott No.	Mint Sheet	Plate Block	Fine Unused Each	Fine Used Each
☐1495 8¢ Multicolored	—	—	.32	.17
☐1496 8¢ Multicolored	—	—	.32	.17
☐1497 8¢ Multicolored	—	—	.32	.17
☐1498 8¢ Multicolored	—	—	.32	.17

1973. HARRY S TRUMAN MEMORIAL

Scott No.	Mint Sheet	Plate Block	Fine Unused Each	Fine Used Each
☐1499 8¢ Black, Red, Blue	8.00	1.50	.32	.17

1973. PROGRESS IN ELECTRONICS

Scott No.	Mint Sheet	Plate Block	Fine Unused Each	Fine Used Each
☐1500 6¢ Multicolored	8.50	1.00	.32	.17
☐1501 8¢ Multicolored	12.00	1.20	.32	.17
☐1502 15¢ Multicolored	22.00	2.00	.60	.35

1973. LYNDON B. JOHNSON MEMORIAL

Scott No.	Mint Sheet	Plate Block	Fine Unused Each	Fine Used Each
☐1503 8¢ Multicolored	8.50	3.00	.28	.20

1973. ANGUS CATTLE—RURAL AMERICA

Scott No.	Mint Sheet	Plate Block	Fine Unused Each	Fine Used Each
☐1504 8¢ Multicolored	12.00	1.20	.28	.20

1974. CHAUTAUQUA—RURAL AMERICA

Scott No.	Mint Sheet	Plate Block	Fine Unused Each	Fine Used Each
☐1505 10¢ Multicolored	15.00	1.50	.28	.20

1974. WINTER WHEAT—RURAL AMERICA

Scott No.	Mint Sheet	Plate Block	Fine Unused Each	Fine Used Each
☐1506 10¢ Multicolored	15.00	1.20	.28	.20

1973. CHRISTMAS

Scott No.	Mint Sheet	Plate Block	Fine Unused Each	Fine Used Each
☐1507 8¢ Multicolored	20.00	3.50	.28	.20
☐1508 8¢ Multicolored	20.00	3.50	.28	.20

1973–1974. REGULAR ISSUES

Scott No.	Mint Sheet	Plate Block	Fine Unused Each	Fine Used Each
☐1509 10¢ Red & Blue	36.00	7.00	.28	.20
☐1510 10¢ Blue	30.00	1.35	.28	.20
☐1511 10¢ Multicolored	28.00	3.00	.28	.20

Scott No.	Fine Unused Line Pair	Ave. Unused Line Pair	Fine Unused Each	Ave. Unused Each	Fine Used Each	Ave. Used Each

1973–1974. COIL STAMPS—PERF. 10 VERTICALLY

Scott No.	Fine Unused Line Pair	Ave. Unused Line Pair	Fine Unused Each	Ave. Unused Each	Fine Used Each	Ave. Used Each
☐1518 63¢ Orange	1.10	.90	.30	.28	.25	.18

*No hinge pricing from 1941 to date is figured at (N-H ADD 10%)

Scott No.	Fine Unused Line Pair	Ave. Unused Line Pair	Fine Unused Each	Ave. Unused Each	Fine Used Each	Ave. Used Each
☐1519 10¢ Red & Blue	—	—	.35	.28	.25	.18
☐1520 10¢ Blue	1.20	.90	.30	.28	.25	.18

Scott No.	Mint Sheet	Plate Block	Fine Unused Each	Fine Used Each

1974. COMMEMORATIVES
1974. VETERANS OF FOREIGN WARS

☐1525 10¢ Carmine & Blue	14.50	1.25	.32	.17

1974. ROBERT FROST—POET

☐1526 10¢ Black	14.50	1.25	.32	.17

1975. EXPO '74—PRESERVE THE ENVIRONMENT

☐1527 10¢ Multicolored	14.50	4.00	.32	.17

1974. HORSE RACING

☐1528 10¢ Multicolored	13.50	3.40	.32	.17

1975. SKYLAB PROJECT

☐1529 10¢ Multicolored	13.50	1.25	.32	.17

1974. UNIVERSAL POSTAL UNION CENTENARY

☐1530 10¢ Multicolored	—	—	.40	.22
☐1531 10¢ Multicolored	—	—	.40	.22
☐1532 10¢ Multicolored	—	—	.40	.22
☐1533 10¢ Multicolored	—	—	.40	.22
☐1534 10¢ Multicolored	—	—	.40	.22
☐1535 10¢ Multicolored	—	—	.40	.22
☐1536 10¢ Multicolored	—	—	.40	.22
☐1537 10¢ Multicolored	—	—	.40	.22

1974. MINERALS HERITAGE ISSUE

☐1538 10¢ Multicolored	—	—	.32	.17

*No hinge pricing from 1941 to date is figured at (N-H ADD 10%)

Scott No.	Mint Sheet	Plate Block	Fine Unused Each	Fine Used Each
☐1539 10¢ Multicolored	—	—	.35	.19
☐1540 10¢ Multicolored	—	—	.35	.19
☐1541 10¢ Multicolored	—	—	.35	.19

1974. FORT HARROD BICENTENNIAL
☐1542 10¢ Multicolored	14.00	1.50	.32	.17

1974. CONTINENTAL CONGRESS
☐1543 10¢ Red, Blue, Gray	—	—	.35	.19
☐1544 10¢ Red, Blue, Gray	—	—	.35	.19
☐1545 10¢ Red, Blue, Gray	—	—	.35	.19
☐1546 10¢ Red, Blue, Gray	—	—	.35	.19

1974. ENERGY CONSERVATION
☐1547 10¢ Multicolored	14.50	1.50	.32	.17

1974. LEGEND OF SLEEPY HOLLOW
☐1548 10¢ Multicolored	14.50	1.50	.32	.17

1974. RETARDED CHILDREN
☐1549 10¢ Light & Dark Brown	14.50	1.50	.32	.17

1974. CHRISTMAS
☐1550 10¢ Multicolored	14.50	3.20	.32	.17
☐1551 10¢ Multicolored	14.50	3.20	.32	.17
☐1552 10¢ Multicolored	14.50	6.50	.32	.17
☐1552A 10¢ Multicolored, Plate Block of 12	14.50	4.00	.32	.17

1975. COMMEMORATIVES—AMERICAN ARTS
1975. BENJAMIN WEST—ARTIST
☐1553 10¢ Multicolored	14.50	3.10	.32	.17

1975. PAUL LAURENCE DUNBAR—POET
☐1554 10¢ Multicolored	14.50	3.10	.32	.17

*No hinge pricing from 1941 to date is figured at (N-H ADD 10%)

Scott No.	Mint Sheet	Plate Block	Fine Unused Each	Fine Used Each

1975. D.W. GRIFFITH—MOTION PICTURES

☐1555 10¢ Multicolored	16.00	1.50	.40	.17

1975. PIONEER 10 SPACE MISSION

☐1556 10¢ Multicolored	16.00	1.50	.40	.17

1975. MARINER 10 SPACE MISSION

☐1557 10¢ Multicolored	16.00	1.50	.40	.17

1975. COLLECTIVE BARGAINING

☐1558 10¢ Blue, Red, Purple				
	16.00	2.75	.32	.17

1975. CONTRIBUTORS TO THE CAUSE

☐1559 8¢ Multicolored	12.00	2.75	.35	.17
☐1560 10¢ Multicolored	14.00	3.00	.35	.17
☐1561 10¢ Multicolored	14.00	3.00	.35	.17
☐1562 18¢ Multicolored	25.00	6.00	.60	.17

1975. LEXINGTON AND CONCORD BATTLES BICENTENNIAL

☐1563 10¢ Multicolored	12.00	3.50	.32	.17

1975. BATTLE OF BUNKER HILL

☐1564 10¢ Multicolored	12.00	3.50	.32	.17

1975. CONTINENTAL MILITARY SERVICE UNIFORMS

☐1565 10¢ Multicolored	—	—	.32	.17
☐1566 10¢ Multicolored	—	—	.32	.17
☐1567 10¢ Multicolored	—	—	.32	.17
☐1568 10¢ Multicolored	—	—	.32	.17

1975. U.S.–SOVIET JOINT SPACE MISSION

☐1569 10¢ Multicolored	—	—	.60	.17
☐1570 10¢ Multicolored	—	—	.60	.17

1975. INTERNATIONAL WOMEN'S YEAR

☐1571 10¢ Multicolored	14.00	2.00	.32	.17

*No hinge pricing from 1941 to date is figured at (N-H ADD 10%)

Scott No.	Mint Sheet	Plate Block	Fine Unused Each	Fine Used Each
1975. U.S. POSTAL SERVICE BICENTENNIAL				
☐1572 10¢ Multicolored	—	—	.32	.17
☐1573 10¢ Multicolored	—	—	.32	.17
☐1574 10¢ Multicolored	—	—	.32	.17
☐1575 10¢ Multicolored	—	—	.32	.17
1975. WORLD PEACE THROUGH LAW				
☐1576 10¢ Blue, Green, Brown				
	17.50	1.60	.40	.17
1975. BANKING AND COMMERCE				
☐1577 10¢ Multicolored	—	—	.32	.17
☐1578 10¢ Multicolored	—	—	.32	.17
1975. CHRISTMAS				
☐1579 10¢ Multicolored	14.00	3.75	.35	.17
☐1580 10¢ Multicolored	14.00	3.75	.35	.17
1975–1980. AMERICANA SERIES				
☐1581 1¢ Blue on Green	8.50	.80	.25	.17
☐1582 2¢ Brown on Green	8.50	.80	.25	.17
☐1584 3¢ Olive on Green	9.75	.80	.25	.17
☐1585 4¢ Maroon on Green	12.00	.65	.25	.17
☐1590 9¢ Slate on Green	—	—	.45	.17
☐1591 9¢ Green on Gray	24.00	1.10	.26	.17
☐1592 10¢ Purple	30.00	1.50	.32	.17
☐1593 11¢ Orange on Gray	30.00	1.30	.32	.17
☐1594 12¢ Maroon	34.00	2.00	.32	.17
☐1595 13¢ Brown	—	—	.40	.17
☐1596 13¢ Multicolored	40.00	4.50	.40	.17
☐1597 15¢ Multicolored	44.00	9.00	.45	.17
☐1598 15¢ Multicolored	—	—	.65	.17
☐1599 16¢ Blue & Black	52.00	2.40	.60	.17
☐1603 24¢ Red on Blue	60.00	2.60	.70	.17
☐1604 28¢ Brown & Blue	80.00	3.10	.70	.17
☐1605 29¢ Blue & Blue	80.00	3.50	.90	.17
☐1606 30¢ Green on Blue	80.00	4.00	.90	.17

*No hinge pricing from 1941 to date is figured at (N-H ADD 10%)

Scott No.	Mint Sheet	Plate Block	Fine Unused Each	Fine Used Each
☐1608 50¢ Black & Orange	150.00	6.00	1.50	.17
☐1610 $1 Multicolored	300.00	11.00	2.75	.17
☐1611 $2 Multicolored	600.00	22.00	5.50	.75
☐1612 $5 Multicolored	1400.00	50.00	12.00	3.40

Scott No.	Fine Unused Line Pair	Ave. Unused Line Pair	Fine Unused Each	Ave. Unused Each	Fine Used Each	Ave. Used Each
1975–1978. COIL STAMPS						
☐1613 3.1¢ Brown on Yellow						
	1.00	.90	.40	.28	.25	.17
☐1614 7.7¢ Gold on Yellow						
	1.25	1.00	.40	.28	.25	.17
☐1615 7.9¢ Red on Yellow						
	1.00	.90	.40	.28	.25	.17
☐1615 8.4¢ Blue on White						
	2.50	2.00	.40	.28	.25	.17
☐1616 9¢ Green on Gray						
	1.15	.95	.40	.28	.25	.17
☐1617 10¢ Purple on Gray						
	1.15	.95	.40	.28	.25	.17
☐1618 13¢ Brown						
	1.00	.95	.40	.28	.25	.17

Scott No.	Mint Sheet	Plate Block	Fine Unused Each	Fine Used Each
1975–1977. REGULAR ISSUES				
☐1622 13¢ Red, Brown, Blue	38.00	8.00	.36	.18
☐1623 13¢ Blue, Red	—	9.00	.36	.18
☐1623c 13¢ Blue, Red, pf 10	—	—	2.10	.18

Scott No.	Fine Unused Each	Ave. Unused Each	Fine Used Each	Ave. Used Each
1975. COIL STAMPS				
☐1625 13¢ Red, Brown, Blue	.75	.40	.30	.18

*No hinge pricing from 1941 to date is figured at (N-H ADD 10%)

Scott No.	Mint Sheet	Plate Block	Fine Unused Each	Fine Used Each

1976. COMMEMORATIVES—AMERICAN BICENTENNIAL
1976. SPIRIT OF '76

Scott No.	Mint Sheet	Plate Block	Fine Unused Each	Fine Used Each
☐1629 13¢ Multicolored	—	—	.40	.17
☐1630 13¢ Multicolored	—	—	.40	.17
☐1631 13¢ Multicolored	—	—	.40	.17

1976. INTERPHIL '76

Scott No.	Mint Sheet	Plate Block	Fine Unused Each	Fine Used Each
☐1632 13¢ Dark Blue, Red, Ultramarine	20.00	1.75	.45	.18

1976. STATE FLAGS

Scott No.	Mint Sheet	Plate Block	Fine Unused Each	Fine Used Each
☐ 13¢ Multicolored	28.00	7.50	.60	.40

☐1633 Delaware
☐1634 Pennsylvania
☐1635 New Jersey
☐1636 Georgia
☐1637 Connecticut
☐1638 Massachusetts
☐1639 Maryland
☐1640 South Carolina
☐1641 New Hampshire
☐1642 Virginia
☐1643 New York
☐1644 North Carolina
☐1645 Rhode Island
☐1646 Vermont
☐1647 Kentucky
☐1648 Tennessee
☐1649 Ohio
☐1650 Louisiana
☐1651 Indiana
☐1652 Mississippi
☐1653 Illinois
☐1654 Alabama
☐1655 Maine
☐1656 Missouri
☐1657 Arkansas
☐1658 Michigan
☐1659 Florida
☐1660 Texas
☐1661 Iowa
☐1662 Wisconsin
☐1663 California
☐1664 Minnesota
☐1665 Oregon
☐1666 Kansas
☐1667 West Virginia
☐1668 Nevada
☐1669 Nebraska
☐1670 Colorado
☐1671 North Dakota
☐1672 South Dakota
☐1673 Montana
☐1674 Washington
☐1675 Idaho
☐1676 Wyoming

*No hinge pricing from 1941 to date is figured at (N-H ADD 10%)

☐1677 Utah   ☐1680 Arizona
☐1678 Oklahoma   ☐1681 Alaska
☐1679 New Mexico   ☐1682 Hawaii

Scott No.	Mint Sheet	Plate Block	Fine Unused Each	Fine Used Each
1976. TELEPHONE CENTENNIAL				
☐1683 13¢ Black, Purple, Red				
	22.00	1.75	.45	.17
1976. COMMERCIAL AVIATION				
☐1684 13¢ Multicolored	22.00	4.25	.45	.17
1976. CHEMISTRY				
☐1685 13¢ Multicolored	22.00	5.00	.45	.17
1976. BICENTENNIAL SOUVENIR SHEETS				
☐1686 65¢ Sheet of 5	—	—	4.50	4.50
☐1686a 13¢ Multicolored	—	—	1.00	.85
☐1686b 13¢ Multicolored	—	—	1.00	.85
☐1686c 13¢ Multicolored	—	—	1.00	.85
☐1686d 13¢ Multicolored	—	—	1.00	.85
☐1686e 13¢ Multicolored	—	—	1.00	.85
☐1687 90¢ Sheet of 5	—	—	6.50	5.50
☐1687a 18¢ Multicolored	—	—	1.50	1.25
☐1687b 18¢ Multicolored	—	—	1.50	1.25
☐1687c 18¢ Multicolored	—	—	1.50	1.25
☐1687d 18¢ Multicolored	—	—	1.50	1.25
☐1687e 18¢ Multicolored	—	—	1.75	1.45
☐1688 1.20 Sheet of 5	—	—	8.00	9.00
☐1688a 24¢ Multicolored	—	—	2.20	1.70
☐1688b 24¢ Multicolored	—	—	2.20	1.70
☐1688c 24¢ Multicolored	—	—	2.20	1.70
☐1688d 24¢ Multicolored	—	—	2.20	1.70
☐1688e 24¢ Multicolored	—	—	2.20	1.70
☐1689 1.55 Sheet of 5	—	—	10.50	9.00

*No hinge pricing from 1941 to date is figured at (N-H ADD 10%)

Scott No.	Mint Sheet	Plate Block	Fine Unused Each	Fine Used Each
☐1689a 31¢ Multicolored	—	—	2.10	1.85
☐1689b 31¢ Multicolored	—	—	2.10	1.85
☐1689c 31¢ Multicolored	—	—	2.10	1.85
☐1689d 31¢ Multicolored	—	—	2.10	1.85
☐1689e 31¢ Multicolored	—	—	2.10	1.85

1976. BENJAMIN FRANKLIN

☐1690 13¢ Blue & Multicolored	20.00	1.75	.45	.17

1976. DECLARATION OF INDEPENDENCE

☐1691 13¢ Multicolored	—	—	.65	.17
☐1692 13¢ Multicolored	—	—	.65	.17
☐1693 13¢ Multicolored	—	—	.65	.17
☐1694 13¢ Multicolored	—	—	.65	.17

1976. OLYMPIC GAMES

☐1695 13¢ Multicolored	—	—	.50	.17
☐1696 13¢ Multicolored	—	—	.50	.17
☐1697 13¢ Multicolored	—	—	.50	.17
☐1698 13¢ Multicolored	—	—	.50	.17

1976. CLARA MAASS

☐1699 13¢ Multicolored	16.50	5.25	.50	.17

1976. ADOLPH S. OCHS

☐1700 13¢ Black, Green & White	12.00	1.75	.50	.17

1976. CHRISTMAS

☐1701 13¢ Multicolored	19.50	5.25	.50	.17
☐1702 13¢ Multicolored	19.50	4.00	.50	.17
☐1703 13¢ Multicolored	19.50	7.25	.50	.17

1977. COMMEMORATIVES
1977. WASHINGTON

☐1704 13¢ Multicolored	16.00	4.25	.50	.17

*No hinge pricing from 1941 to date is figured at (N-H ADD 10%)

Scott No.	Mint Sheet	Plate Block	Fine Unused Each	Fine Used Each
1977. SOUND RECORDING CENTENARY				
☐ 1705 13¢ Multicolored	18.75	1.50	.42	.17
1977. PUEBLO ART				
☐ 1706 13¢ Multicolored	—	—	.40	.17
☐ 1707 13¢ Multicolored	—	—	.40	.17
☐ 1708 13¢ Multicolored	—	—	.40	.17
☐ 1709 13¢ Multicolored	—	—	.40	.17
1977. TRANSATLANTIC FLIGHT				
☐ 1710 13¢ Multicolored	19.50	4.60	.40	.17
1977. COLORADO				
☐ 1711 13¢ Multicolored	19.50	4.60	.40	.17
1977. BUTTERFLIES				
☐ 1712 13¢ Multicolored	—	—	.40	.17
☐ 1713 13¢ Multicolored	—	—	.40	.17
☐ 1714 13¢ Multicolored	—	—	.40	.17
☐ 1715 13¢ Multicolored	—	—	.40	.17
1977. LAFAYETTE				
☐ 1716 13¢ Multicolored	15.50	1.60	.40	.17
1977. SKILLED HANDS				
☐ 1717 13¢ Multicolored	—	—	.40	.17
☐ 1718 13¢ Multicolored	—	—	.40	.17
☐ 1719 13¢ Multicolored	—	—	.40	.17
☐ 1720 13¢ Multicolored	—	—	.40	.17
1977. PEACE BRIDGE				
☐ 1721 13¢ Blue & White	19.50	1.60	.40	.17
1977. BATTLE OF ORISKANY				
☐ 1722 13¢ Multicolored	15.50	3.75	.40	.17

*No hinge pricing from 1941 to date is figured at (N-H ADD 10%)

Scott No.	Mint Sheet	Plate Block	Fine Unused Each	Fine Used Each
1977. ENERGY CONSERVATION AND DEVELOPMENT				
☐1723 13¢ Multicolored	—	—	.40	.17
☐1724 13¢ Multicolored	—	—	.40	.17
1977. ALTA, CALIFORNIA BICENTENNIAL				
☐1725 13¢ Multicolored	19.50	1.60	.40	.17
1977. ARTICLES OF CONFEDERATION				
☐1726 13¢ Red & Brown on Tan	19.50	1.75	.40	.17
1977. TALKING PICTURES				
☐1727 13¢ Multicolored	19.50	1.75	.40	.17
1977. SURRENDER AT SARATOGA				
☐1728 13¢ Multicolored	15.50	4.00	.40	.17
1977. CHRISTMAS				
☐1729 13¢ Multicolored	40.00	8.00	.40	.17
☐1730 13¢ Multicolored	40.00	4.00	.40	.17
1978. CARL SANDBURG				
☐1731 13¢ Brown, Black, White	19.00	1.50	.40	.17
1978. CAPTAIN COOK ISSUES				
☐1732 13¢ Dark Blue	—	1.75	.40	.17
☐1733 13¢ Green	—	1.75	.40	.17
1978. INDIAN HEAD PENNY				
☐1734 13¢ Brown & Blue Green	56.00	1.80	.40	.17
1978. NONDENOMINATED "A"				
☐1735 15¢ Orange	40.00	2.00	.40	.17
1978. ROSES				
☐1737 15¢ Multicolored	—	—	.40	.17

*No hinge pricing from 1941 to date is figured at (N-H ADD 10%)

Scott No.	Mint Sheet	Plate Block	Fine Unused Each	Fine Used Each

1980. WINDMILL—VIRGINIA
| ☐1738 15¢ Black | — | — | .55 | .17 |

1980. WINDMILL—RHODE ISLAND
| ☐1739 15¢ Black | — | — | .55 | .17 |

1980. WINDMILL—MASSACHUSETTS
| ☐1740 15¢ Black | — | — | .55 | .17 |

1980. WINDMILL—ILLINOIS
| ☐1741 15¢ Black | — | — | .55 | .17 |

1980. WINDMILL—TEXAS
| ☐1742 15¢ Black | — | — | .55 | .17 |

1978. HARRIET TUBMAN
| ☐1744 13¢ Multicolored | 25.00 | 7.00 | .42 | .17 |

1978. AMERICAN FOLK ART ISSUE
☐1745 13¢ Multicolored	—	—	.42	.17
☐1746 13¢ Multicolored	—	—	.42	.17
☐1747 13¢ Multicolored	—	—	.42	.17
☐1748 13¢ Multicolored	—	—	.42	.17

1978. AMERICAN DANCE ISSUE
☐1749 13¢ Multicolored	—	—	.42	.17
☐1750 13¢ Multicolored	—	—	.42	.17
☐1751 13¢ Multicolored	—	—	.42	.17
☐1752 13¢ Multicolored	—	—	.42	.17

1978. FRENCH ALLIANCE
| ☐1753 13¢ Blue, Black & Red | 15.00 | 1.50 | .40 | .17 |

1978. EARLY CANCER DETECTION
| ☐1754 13¢ Brown | 22.00 | 1.85 | .42 | .17 |

*No hinge pricing from 1941 to date is figured at (N-H ADD 10%)

Scott No.	Mint Sheet	Plate Block	Fine Unused Each	Fine Used Each

1978. JIMMIE RODGERS
| ☐1755 13¢ Multicolored | 22.00 | 5.25 | .50 | .17 |

1978. GEORGE M. COHAN
| ☐1756 15¢ Multicolored | 24.00 | 6.00 | .50 | .17 |

1978. "CAPAX" '78 SOUVENIR SHEET
| ☐1757 13¢ Multicolored, set of 6 | | | | |
| | 18.00 | — | 3.50 | 2.80 |

1978. PHOTOGRAPHY
| ☐1758 15¢ Multicolored | 14.50 | 6.00 | .45 | .17 |

1978. VIKING MISSION TO MARS
| ☐1759 15¢ Multicolored | 22.00 | 2.00 | .50 | .17 |

1978. AMERICAN OWL ISSUE
☐1760 15¢ Multicolored	—	—	.40	.17
☐1761 15¢ Multicolored	—	—	.40	.17
☐1762 15¢ Multicolored	—	—	.40	.17
☐1763 15¢ Multicolored	—	—	.40	.17

1978. AMERICAN TREES ISSUE
☐1764 15¢ Multicolored	—	—	.45	.17
☐1765 15¢ Multicolored	—	—	.45	.17
☐1766 15¢ Multicolored	—	—	.45	.17
☐1767 15¢ Multicolored	—	—	.45	.17

1978. CHRISTMAS ISSUES
| ☐1768 15¢ Multicolored | 40.00 | 6.25 | .45 | .17 |
| ☐1769 15¢ Multicolored | 40.00 | 6.25 | .45 | .17 |

1979. ROBERT F. KENNEDY ISSUE
| ☐1770 15¢ Blue | 19.00 | 1.90 | .45 | .17 |

1979. MARTIN LUTHER KING ISSUE
| ☐1771 15¢ Multicolored | 22.00 | 6.00 | .40 | .17 |

*No hinge pricing from 1941 to date is figured at (N-H ADD 10%)

Scott No.	Mint Sheet	Plate Block	Fine Unused Each	Fine Used Each
1979. INTERNATIONAL YEAR OF THE CHILD				
☐1772 15¢ Light Brown	22.00	2.00	.40	.17
1979. JOHN STEINBECK ISSUE				
☐1773 15¢ Dark Blue	22.00	2.00	.40	.17
1979. ALBERT EINSTEIN ISSUE				
☐1774 15¢ Brown	22.00	2.00	.40	.17
1979. PENNSYLVANIA TOLEWARE ISSUE				
☐1775 15¢ Multicolored	—	—	.50	.17
☐1776 15¢ Multicolored	—	—	.50	.17
☐1777 15¢ Multicolored	—	—	.50	.17
☐1778 15¢ Multicolored	—	—	.50	.17
1979. ARCHITECTURE U.S.A. ISSUE				
☐1779 15¢ Light Blue & Brown	—	—	.55	.17
☐1780 15¢ Light Blue & Brown	—	—	.55	.17
☐1781 15¢ Light Blue & Brown	—	—	.55	.17
☐1782 15¢ Light Blue & Brown	—	—	.55	.17
1979. ENDANGERED FLORA ISSUE				
☐1783 15¢ Multicolored	—	—	.50	.17
☐1784 15¢ Multicolored	—	—	.50	.17
☐1785 15¢ Multicolored	—	—	.50	.17
☐1786 15¢ Multicolored	—	—	.50	.17
1979. SEEING FOR ME ISSUE				
☐1787 15¢ Multicolored	22.00	8.50	.40	.17
1979. SPECIAL OLYMPICS				
☐1788 15¢ Multicolored	22.00	5.00	.40	.17

*No hinge pricing from 1941 to date is figured at (N-H ADD 10%)

Scott No.	Mint Sheet	Plate Block	Fine Unused Each	Fine Used Each
1979. JOHN PAUL JONES				
☐1789 15¢ Multicolored	22.00	5.00	.40	.17
1979. OLYMPIC DECATHALON				
☐1790 10¢ Multicolored	15.00	5.00	.40	.17
1979. OLYMPIC RUNNERS				
☐1791 15¢ Multicolored	—	—	.40	.17
1979. OLYMPIC SWIMMERS				
☐1792 15¢ Multicolored	—	—	.40	.17
1979. OLYMPIC ROWERS				
☐1793 15¢ Multicolored	—	—	.40	.17
1979. OLYMPIC EQUESTRIAN				
☐1794 15¢ Multicolored	—	—	.40	.17
1979. OLYMPIC SKATER				
☐1795 15¢ Multicolored	—	—	.40	.17
1979. OLYMPIC SKIER				
☐1796 15¢ Multicolored	—	—	.40	.17
1979. OLYMPIC SKI JUMPER				
☐1797 15¢ Multicolored	—	—	.40	.17
1979. OLYMPIC GOALTENDER				
☐1798 15¢ Multicolored	—	—	.40	.17
1979. MADONNA				
☐1799 15¢ Multicolored	42.00	6.00	.45	.17
1979. CHRISTMAS				
☐1800 15¢ Multicolored	42.00	6.00	.45	.17
1979. WILL ROGERS				
☐1801 15¢ Multicolored	22.00	5.50	.45	.17

*No hinge pricing from 1941 to date is figured at (N-H ADD 10%)

Scott No.	Mint Sheet	Plate Block	Fine Unused Each	Fine Used Each
1979. VIETNAM VETERANS				
☐1802 15¢ Multicolored	22.00	6.00	.50	.15
1980. COMMMERATIVES				
1980. W. C. FIELDS				
☐1803 15¢ Multicolored	22.00	6.50	.50	.15
1980. BENJAMIN BANNEKER				
☐1804 15¢ Multicolored	22.50	6.00	.50	.15
1980. LETTERS PRESERVE MEMORIES				
☐1805 15¢ Violet & Bistre	—	—	.45	.15
1980. PRESERVE MEMORIES—P.S. WRITE SOON				
☐1806 15¢ Violet & Pink	—	—	.45	.15
1980. LETTERS LIFT SPIRITS				
☐1807 15¢ Green, Pink & Orange				
	—	—	.45	.15
1980. LIFT SPIRITS—P.S. WRITE SOON				
☐1808 15¢ Green & Yellow Green				
	—	—	.45	.15
1980. LETTERS SHAPE OPINIONS				
☐1809 15¢ Scarlet & Blue	—	—	.45	.15
1980. SHAPE OPINIONS—P.S. WRITE SOON				
☐1810 15¢ Scarlet & Blue	—	—	.45	.15
1980. AMERICANA SERIES				
☐1811 1¢ Dark Blue & Green				
	—	.75	.25	.15
☐1813 3.5¢ Purple & Yellow	—	1.40	.25	.15
☐1816 12¢ Green	—	1.80	.25	.15
1980. NONDENOMINATED "B"				
☐1818 18¢ Purple	—	2.30	.50	.15

*No hinge pricing from 1941 to date is figured at (N-H ADD 10%)

Scott No.	Mint Sheet	Plate Block	Fine Unused Each	Fine Used Each
1980. FRANCIS PERKINS				
☐1821 15¢ Blue	22.00	2.00	.45	.16
1980. DOLLY MADISON				
☐1822 15¢ Multicolored	60.00	1.85	.45	.16
1980. EMILY BISSELL				
☐1823 15¢ Scarlet & Black	21.00	1.85	.45	.16
1980. HELLEN KELLER—ANNE SULLIVAN				
☐1824 15¢ Multicolored	22.00	1.80	.45	.16
1980. VETERANS ADMINISTRATION				
☐1825 15¢ Carmine & Blue	20.00	—	.45	.16
1980. GENERAL BERNARDO de GALVEZ				
☐1826 15¢ Multicolored	20.00	—	.45	.16
1980. CORAL REEFS—VIRGIN ISLANDS				
☐1827 15¢ Multicolored	22.00		.45	.16
1980. CORAL REEFS—FLORIDA				
☐1828 15¢ Multicolored	20.00		.45	.16
1980. CORAL REEFS—AMERICAN SAMOA				
☐1829 15¢ Multicolored	20.00	—	.45	.16
1980. CORAL REEFS—HAWAII				
☐1830 15¢ Multicolored	20.00	—	.45	.16
1980. ORGANIZED LABOR				
☐1831 15¢ Multicolored	21.00	6.00	.45	.16
1980. EDITH WHARTON				
☐1832 15¢ Violet	25.00	4.00	.45	.16
1980. EDUCATION				
☐1833 15¢ Multicolored	30.00	7.00	.45	.16

*No hinge pricing from 1941 to date is figured at (N-H ADD 10%)

Scott No.	Mint Sheet	Plate Block	Fine Unused Each	Fine Used Each

1980. INDIAN ARTS

Scott No.	Mint Sheet	Plate Block	Fine Unused Each	Fine Used Each
☐1834 15¢ Multicolored	—	—	.55	.16
☐1835 15¢ Multicolored	—	—	.55	.16
☐1836 15¢ Multicolored	—	—	.55	.16
☐1837 15¢ Multicolored	—	—	.55	.16

1980. ARCHITECTURE

☐1838 15¢ Black & Red	—	—	.50	.16
☐1839 15¢ Black & Red	—	—	.50	.16
☐1840 15¢ Black & Red	—	—	.50	.16
☐1841 15¢ Black & Red	—	—	.50	.16

1980. CHRISTMAS ISSUE

☐1842 15¢ Multicolored	20.00	6.00	.40	.16
☐1843 15¢ Multicolored	22.00	10.00	.40	.16

1980–1985. GREAT AMERICANS

1982. DOROTHEA DIX

☐1844 1¢ Black	9.00	3.50	.24	.16

1983. IGOR STRAVINSKY

☐1845 2¢ Brown	8.25	.90	.24	.16

1983. HENRY CLAY

☐1846 3¢ Green	13.00	.90	.24	.16

1983. CARL SCHURZ

☐1847 4¢ Purple	14.00	.90	.24	.16

1985. PEARL BUCK

☐1848 5¢ Reddish Brown	15.00	.90	.24	.16

1985. WALTER LIPPMANN

☐1849 6¢ Orange	14.00	4.25	.24	.16

1985. ABRAHAM BALDWIN

☐1850 7¢ Red	16.00	5.00	.24	.16

1985. HENRY KNOX

☐1851 8¢ Black	25.00	1.40	.28	.16

*No hinge pricing from 1941 to date is figured at (N-H ADD 10%)

Scott No.	Mint Sheet	Plate Block	Fine Unused Each	Fine Used Each

1985. SYLVANUS THAYER

☐1852 9¢ Green	26.00	6.50	.28	.16

1984. RICHARD RUSSELL

☐1853 10¢ Blue	26.00	7.50	.30	.16

1985. ALDEN PARTRIDGE

☐1854 11¢ Blue	30.00	2.00	.30	.16

1982. CRAZY HORSE

☐1855 13¢ Brown	40.00	2.50	.42	.16

1985. SINCLAIR LEWIS

☐1856 14¢ Green	40.00	10.00	.45	.16

1981. RACHEL CARSON

☐1857 17¢ Blue Green	45.00	2.50	.45	.16

1981. GEORGE MASON

☐1958 18¢ Dark Blue	52.00	3.75	.55	.16

1980. SEQUOYAH

☐1859 19¢ Light Brown	52.00	3.25	.65	.16

1982. RALPH BUNCHE

☐1860 20¢ Carmine	60.00	4.00	.70	.16

1983. THOMAS H. GALLAUDET

☐1861 20¢ Green	60.00	5.00	.65	.16

1984. HARRY S TRUMAN

☐1862 20¢ Black & White	60.00	15.50	.70	.16

1985. JOHN J. AUDUBON

☐1863 22¢ Blue	60.00	15.00	.80	.16

1984. FRANK C. LAUBACH

☐1864 30¢ Dark Green	90.00	20.00	.95	.16

*No hinge pricing from 1941 to date is figured at (N-H ADD 10%)

Scott No.	Mint Sheet	Plate Block	Fine Unused Each	Fine Used Each
1981. CHARLES DREW				
☐1865 35¢ Gray	90.00	5.00	1.10	.16
1982. ROBERT MILLIKAN				
☐1866 37¢ Blue	90.00	5.00	1.10	.16
1985. GRENVILLE CLARK				
☐1867 39¢ Reddish Purple	100.00	25.00	1.00	.16
1984. LILLIAN M. GILBRETH				
☐1868 40¢ Green	110.00	22.00	1.00	.16
1985. CHESTER W. NIMITZ				
☐1869 50¢ Dark Brown	125.00	7.00	1.40	.16
1981. COMMEMORATIVES				
1981. EVERETT M. DIRKSEN				
☐1874 15¢ Dark Green	20.00	1.85	.45	.16
1981. WHITNEY M. YOUNG				
☐1875 15¢ Multicolored	20.00	1.85	.45	.16
1981. FLOWERS				
☐1876 18¢ Multicolored	—	—	.65	.16
☐1877 18¢ Multicolored	—	—	.65	.16
☐1878 18¢ Multicolored	—	—	.65	.16
☐1879 18¢ Multicolored	—	—	.65	.16
1981. AMERICAN WILDLIFE				
☐1880 18¢ Light Brown	—	—	1.10	.16
☐1881 18¢ Light Brown	—	—	1.10	.16
☐1882 18¢ Light Brown	—	—	1.10	.16
☐1883 18¢ Light Brown	—	—	1.10	.16
☐1884 18¢ Light Brown	—	—	1.10	.16
☐1885 18¢ Light Brown	—	—	1.10	.16
☐1886 18¢ Light Brown	—	—	1.10	.16
☐1887 18¢ Light Brown	—	—	1.10	.16
☐1888 18¢ Light Brown	—	—	1.10	.16
☐1889 18¢ Light Brown	—	—	1.10	.16

*No hinge pricing from 1941 to date is figured at (N-H ADD 10%)

Scott No.	Mint Sheet	Plate Block	Fine Unused Each	Fine Used Each

1981. FLAG—FOR AMBER WAVES OF GRAIN

| ☐1890 18¢ Multicolored | 55.00 | 12.00 | .65 | .16 |

1981. FLAG—FROM SEA TO SHINING SEA

| ☐1891 18¢ Multicolored | — | 7.00 | .65 | .16 |

1981. U.S.A.

| ☐1892 6¢ Carmine & Dark Blue | — | — | .80 | .16 |

1981. FLAG—FOR PURPLE MOUNTAIN MAJESTIES

| ☐1893 18¢ Multicolored | — | — | .55 | .16 |

1981. FLAG OVER SUPREME COURT

| ☐1894 20¢ Carmine & Dark Blue | 85.00 | 22.00 | 1.20 | .16 |

1981–1984. TRANSPORTATION
1983. OMNIBUS

| ☐1897 1¢ Violet | — | — | .28 | .16 |

1982. LOCOMOTIVE

| ☐1897a 2¢ Black | — | — | .28 | .16 |

1983. HANDCAR

| ☐1898 3¢ Dark Green | — | — | .28 | .16 |

1982. STAGECOACH

| ☐1898a 4¢ Red Brown | — | — | .28 | .16 |

1983. MOTORCYCLE

| ☐1899 5¢ Gray Green | — | — | .28 | .16 |

1983. SLEIGH

| ☐1900 5.2¢ Carmine | — | — | .32 | .16 |

1982. BICYCLE

| ☐1901 5.9¢ Blue | — | — | .32 | .16 |

*No hinge pricing from 1941 to date is figured at (N-H ADD 10%)

Scott No.	Mint Sheet	Plate Block	Fine Unused Each	Fine Used Each
1984. BABY BUGGY				
☐1902 7.4¢ Brown	—	—	.32	.16
1982. MAIL WAGON				
☐1903 9.3¢ Carmine	—	—	.32	.16
1982. HANSOM CAB				
☐1904 10.9¢ Purple	—	—	.60	.16
1984. RAILROAD CABOOSE				
☐1905 11¢ Red	—	—	.35	.16
1981. ELECTRIC CAR				
☐1906 17¢ Ultramarine	—LP.	5.50	.55	.16
1981. SURREY				
☐1907 18¢ Brown	—LP.	6.00	.55	.16
1982. FIRE PUMPER				
☐1908 20¢ Vermilion	—	—	.60	.16
1981. AMERICAN RED CROSS				
☐1910 18¢ Multicolored	—	3.00	.55	.16
1981. SAVINGS AND LOAN				
☐1911 19¢ Multicolored	—	3.00	.55	.16
1981. COMMEMORATIVES				
1981. SPACE ACHIEVEMENT				
☐1912 18¢ Multicolored	—	—	.70	.16
☐1913 18¢ Multicolored	—	—	.70	.16
☐1914 18¢ Multicolored	—	—	.70	.16
☐1915 18¢ Multicolored	—	—	.70	.16
☐1916 18¢ Multicolored	—	—	.70	.16
☐1917 18¢ Multicolored	—	—	.70	.16
☐1918 18¢ Multicolored	—	—	.70	.16
☐1919 18¢ Multicolored	—	—	.70	.16

*No hinge pricing from 1941 to date is figured at (N-H ADD 10%)

Scott No.	Mint Sheet	Plate Block	Fine Unused Each	Fine Used Each
1981. PROFESSIONAL MANAGEMENT				
☐1920 18¢ Dark Blue & Black	26.00	2.40	.60	.16
1981. PRESERVATION OF WILDLIFE HABITATS				
☐1921 18¢ Multicolored	—	—	.65	.16
☐1922 18¢ Multicolored	—	—	.65	.16
☐1923 18¢ Multicolored	—	—	.65	.16
☐1924 18¢ Multicolored	—	—	.65	.16
1981. DISABLED PERSONS				
☐1925 18¢ Multicolored	26.00	2.40	.55	.16
1981. EDNA ST. VINCENT MILLAY				
☐1926 18¢ Multicolored	26.00	2.60	.55	.16
1981. ALCOHOLISM				
☐1927 18¢ Dark Blue	70.00	48.00	.90	.16
1981. ARCHITECTURE				
☐1928 18¢ Brown & Black	—	—	.85	.16
☐1929 18¢ Brown & Black	—	—	.85	.16
☐1930 18¢ Brown & Black	—	—	.85	.16
☐1931 18¢ Brown & Black	—	—	.85	.16
1981. BABE ZAHARIAS				
☐1932 18¢ Purple	—	4.10	1.00	.16
1981. BOBBY JONES				
☐1933 18¢ Dark Green	—	8.00	1.05	.16
1981. FREDERIC REMINGTON				
☐1934 18¢ Light Brown & Green	26.00	2.50	.60	.16
1981. JAMES HOBAN				
☐1935 18¢ Multicolored	26.00	2.50	.60	.16

*No hinge pricing from 1941 to date is figured at (N-H ADD 10%)

Scott No.	Mint Sheet	Plate Block	Fine Unused Each	Fine Used Each
1981. JAMES HOBAN				
☐1936 20¢ Multicolored	28.00	2.60	.60	.16
1981. YORKTOWN MAP				
☐1937 18¢ Multicolored	—	—	.60	.16
1981. VIRGINIA CAPES MAP				
☐1938 18¢ Multicolored	—	—	.60	.16
1981. CHRISTMAS—BOTTICELLI				
☐1939 20¢ Multicolored	52.00	2.40	.60	.16
1981. SEASONS GREETINGS				
☐1940 20¢ Multicolored	28.00	2.40	.60	.16
1981. JOHN HANSON				
☐1941 20¢ Multicolored	28.00	2.60	.60	.16
1981. DESERT PLANTS				
☐1942 20¢ Multicolored	—	—	.70	.16
☐1943 20¢ Multicolored	—	—	.70	.16
☐1944 20¢ Multicolored	—	—	.70	.16
☐1945 20¢ Multicolored	—	—	.70	.16
1981. "C" EAGLE—SINGLE				
☐1946 20¢ Light Brown	55.00	2.60	.60	.16
1981. "C" EAGLE—COIL SINGLE				
☐1947 20¢ Light Brown	—	—	.80	.16
1981. "C" EAGLE—BOOKLET SINGLE				
☐1948 20¢ Light Brown	—	—	.65	.16
1981. BIGHORN SHEEP				
☐1949 20¢ Dark Blue	—	—	.65	.16
1982. COMMEMORATIVES **1982. FRANKLIN ROOSEVELT**				
☐1950 20¢ Dark Blue	30.00	6.00	.65	.16

*No hinge pricing from 1941 to date is figured at (N-H ADD 10%)

Scott No.	Mint Sheet	Plate Block	Fine Unused Each	Fine Used Each
1982. "LOVE" FLOWERS				
☐1951 20¢ Multicolored	52.00	6.00	1.00	.16
1982. GEORGE WASHINGTON				
☐1952 20¢ Multicolored	32.00	3.00	.70	.16
1982. STATE BIRDS AND FLOWERS				
☐1953– 2002 20¢ Multicolored	52.00	—	.80	.16
1982. THE NETHERLANDS				
☐2003 20¢ Dark Blue & Red	38.00	17.50	.70	.16
1982. LIBRARY OF CONGRESS				
☐2004 20¢ Rose & Dark Gray	30.00	2.60	.65	.16
1982. CONSUMER EDUCATION				
☐2005 20¢ Light Blue & Dark Blue	—	40.00	1.25	.16
1982. KNOXVILLE WORLD'S FAIR				
☐2006 20¢ Multicolored	32.00	3.50	.75	.16
☐2007 20¢ Multicolored	32.00	3.50	.75	.16
☐2008 20¢ Multicolored	32.00	3.50	.75	.16
☐2009 20¢ Multicolored	32.00	3.50	.75	.16
1982. HORATIO ALGER				
☐2010 20¢ Carmine & Black	30.00	2.60	.60	.16
1982. AGING TOGETHER				
☐2011 20¢ Light Rose	30.00	2.60	.60	.16
1982. THE BARRYMORES				
☐2012 20¢ Multicolored	32.00	2.65	.60	.16
1982. DR. MARY WALKER				
☐2013 20¢ Multicolored	30.00	2.70	.60	.16

*No hinge pricing from 1941 to date is figured at (N-H ADD 10%)

Scott No.	Mint Sheet	Plate Block	Fine Unused Each	Fine Used Each

1982. INTERNATIONAL PEACE GARDEN

| ☐2014 20¢ Multicolored | 28.00 | 2.45 | .65 | .16 |

1982. AMERICA'S LIBRARIES

| ☐2015 20¢ Orange Red & Black | 28.00 | 2.45 | .65 | .16 |

1982. JACKIE ROBINSON

| ☐2016 20¢ Multicolored | 100.00 | 9.00 | 2.00 | .16 |

1982. TOURO SYNAGOGUE

| ☐2017 20¢ Multicolored | 38.00 | 18.00 | 1.00 | .16 |

1982. WOLF TRAP FARM PARK

| ☐2018 20¢ Multicolored | 28.00 | 2.45 | .60 | .16 |

1982. ARCHITECTURE—WRIGHT

| ☐2019 20¢ Black and Brown | — | — | .85 | .16 |

1982. ARCHITECTURE—VAN DER ROHE

| ☐2020 20¢ Black and Brown | — | — | .85 | .16 |

1982. ARCHITECTURE—GROPIUS

| ☐2021 20¢ Black and Brown | — | — | .85 | .16 |

1982. ARCHITECTURE—SAARINEN

| ☐2022 20¢ Black and Brown | — | — | .85 | .16 |
| ☐Architecture, above four attached | 36.00 | — | — | — |

1982. FRANCIS OF ASSISI

| ☐2023 20¢ Multicolored | 30.00 | 2.95 | .65 | .16 |

1982. PONCE DE LEON

| ☐2024 20¢ Multicolored | 38.00 | 19.00 | .90 | .16 |

1982. CHRISTMAS ISSUE—CAT AND DOG

| ☐2025 13¢ Multicolored | 22.00 | 2.00 | .50 | .16 |

*No hinge pricing from 1941 to date is figured at (N-H ADD 10%)

Scott No.	Mint Sheet	Plate Block	Fine Unused Each	Fine Used Each

1982. CHRISTMAS ISSUE—TIEPOLO'S "MADONNA AND CHILD"

☐2026 20¢ Multicolored	31.50	16.00	.70	.16

1982. SEASON'S GREETINGS—SLEDDING

☐2027 20¢ Multicolored	—	—	.85	.16

1982. SEASON'S GREETINGS—BUILDING SNOWMAN

☐2028 20¢ Multicolored	—	—	.90	.16

1982. SEASON'S GREETINGS—ICE SKATING

☐2029 20¢ Multicolored	—	—	.90	.16

1982. SEASON'S GREETINGS—TRIMMING TREE

☐2030 20¢ Multicolored	—	—	.90	.16
☐Season's Greetings, above four attached	42.00	—	—	—

1982. SCIENCE AND INDUSTRY

☐2031 20¢ Multicolored	30.00	2.45	.70	.16

1983. BALLOONING—INTREPID

☐2032 20¢ Multicolored	—	—	.70	.16

1982. BALLOONING—RED, WHITE & BLUE

☐2033 20¢ Multicolored	—	—	.70	.16

1982. BALLOONING—YELLOW & GOLD

☐2034 20¢ Multicolored	—	—	.70	.16

1982. BALLOONING—EXPLORER II

☐2035 20¢ Multicolored	—	—	.70	.16
☐Ballooning, above four attached	28.00	—	—	—

1983. COMMEMORATIVES
1983. TREATY OF AMITY

☐2036 20¢ Blue and Black	28.00	2.45	.65	.16

*No hinge pricing from 1941 to date is figured at (N-H ADD 10%)

Scott No.	Mint Sheet	Plate Block	Fine Unused Each	Fine Used Each

1983. CIVILIAN CONSERVATION CORPS

| ☐2037 20¢ Multicolored | 28.00 | 2.60 | .70 | .16 |

1983. JOSEPH PRIESTLEY

| ☐2038 20¢ Rust Brown | 32.00 | 2.60 | .70 | .16 |

1983. VOLUNTEER—LEND A HAND

| ☐2039 20¢ Black and Red | 40.00 | 19.00 | .80 | .16 |

1983. CONCORD 1683

| ☐2040 20¢ Beige | 28.00 | 2.60 | .70 | .16 |

1983. BROOKLYN BRIDGE

| ☐2041 20¢ Blue | 30.00 | 2.60 | .70 | .16 |

1983. TENNESSEE VALLEY AUTHORITY

| ☐2042 20¢ Multicolored | 40.00 | 18.50 | .70 | .16 |

1983. PHYSICAL FITNESS

| ☐2043 20¢ Multicolored | 40.00 | 18.50 | .70 | .16 |

1982. SCOTT JOPLIN

| ☐2044 20¢ Multicolored | 32.00 | 3.00 | .80 | .16 |

1983. MEDAL OF HONOR

| ☐2045 20¢ Multicolored | 28.00 | 3.00 | .65 | .16 |

1983. BABE RUTH

| ☐2046 20¢ Blue | 110.00 | 10.50 | 2.10 | .16 |

1983. NATHANIEL HAWTHORNE

| ☐2047 20¢ Multicolored | 28.00 | 2.60 | .70 | .16 |

1983. SUMMER OLYMPICS 1984—DISCUS

| ☐2048 13¢ Multicolored | — | — | .55 | .16 |

1983. SUMMER OLYMPICS 1984—HIGH JUMP

| ☐2049 13¢ Multicolored | — | — | .55 | .16 |

*No hinge pricing from 1941 to date is figured at (N-H ADD 10%)

Scott No.	Mint Sheet	Plate Block	Fine Unused Each	Fine Used Each

1983. SUMMER OLYMPICS 1984—ARCHERY

| ☐2050 13¢ Multicolored | — | — | .43 | .16 |

1983. SUMMER OLYMPICS 1984—BOXING

| ☐2051 13¢ Multicolored | — | — | .42 | .16 |

1983. TREATY OF PARIS

| ☐2052 20¢ Multicolored | 26.00 | 2.90 | .70 | .16 |

1983. CIVIL SERVICE

| ☐2053 20¢ Multicolored | 36.00 | 18.00 (20) | .70 | .16 |

1983. METROPOLITAN OPERA

| ☐2054 20¢ Yellow & Brown | 30.00 | 3.00 | .75 | .16 |

1983. INVENTORS—CHARLES STEINMETZ

| ☐2055 20¢ Multicolored | 34.00 | 4.00 | .85 | .16 |

1983. INVENTORS—EDWIN ARMSTRONG

| ☐2056 20¢ Multicolored | 34.00 | 4.00 | .85 | .16 |

1983. INVENTORS—NIKOLA TESLA

| ☐2057 20¢ Multicolored | 34.00 | 4.00 | .85 | .16 |

1983. INVENTORS—PHILO T. FARNSWORTH

| ☐2058 20¢ Multicolored | 34.00 | 4.00 | .85 | :16 |

1983. STREETCARS—FIRST

| ☐2059 20¢ Multicolored | 32.00 | 3.75 | .75 | .16 |

1983. STREETCARS—ELECTRIC TROLLEY

| ☐2060 20¢ Multicolored | 32.00 | 2.60 | .75 | .16 |

1983. STREETCARS—BOBTAIL HORSECAR

| ☐2061 20¢ Multicolored | 32.00 | 2.60 | .75 | .16 |

1983. STREETCARS—ST. CHARLES

| ☐2061 20¢ Multicolored | 32.00 | 2.60 | .75 | .16 |

*No hinge pricing from 1941 to date is figured at (N-H ADD 10%)

Scott No.	Mint Sheet	Plate Block	Fine Unused Each	Fine Used Each
1983. CHRISTMAS—MADONNA				
☐2063 20¢ Multicolored	28.00	2.60	.65	.16
1983. CHRISTMAS—SEASON'S GREETINGS				
☐2064 20¢ Multicolored	33.00	18.50	.65	.16
1983. MARTIN LUTHER				
☐2065 20¢ Multicolored	28.00	2.60	.65	.16
1984. COMMEMORATIVES				
1984. ALASKA STATEHOOD				
☐2066 20¢ Multicolored	28.00	4.00	.65	.16
1984. WINTER OLYMPICS 1984—ICE DANCING				
☐2067 20¢ Multicolored	36.00	4.25	.80	.16
1984. WINTER OLYMPICS 1984—DOWNHILL SKIING				
☐2068 20¢ Multicolored	36.00	4.25	.80	.16
1984. WINTER OLYMPICS 1984—CROSS COUNTRY CLINIC				
☐2069 20¢ Multicolored	36.00	4.25	.80	.16
1984. WINTER OLYMPICS 1984—HOCKEY				
☐2070 20¢ Multicolored	36.00	4.25	.80	.16
1984. FEDERAL DEPOSIT INSURANCE CORPORATION				
☐2071 20¢ Red & Yellow	28.00	2.60	.65	.16
1984. LOVE				
☐2072 20¢ Multicolored	36.00	18.50 (20)	.65	.16
1984. CARTER G. WOODSON				
☐2073 20¢ Multicolored	30.00	2.60	.65	.16
1984. SOIL AND WATER CONSERVATION				
☐2074 20¢ Multicolored	28.00	2.60	.65	.16
1984. CREDIT UNION				
☐2075 20¢ Multicolored	28.00	2.60	.65	.16

*No hinge pricing from 1941 to date is figured at (N-H ADD 10%)

Scott No.	Mint Sheet	Plate Block	Fine Unused Each	Fine Used Each

1984. ORCHIDS—WILD PINK
| ☐2076 20¢ Multicolored | 36.00 | 3.60 | .75 | .16 |

1984. ORCHIDS—YELLOW LADY SLIPPER
| ☐2077 20¢ Multicolored | 36.00 | 3.60 | .75 | .16 |

1984. ORCHIDS—SPREADING POGONIA
| ☐2078 20¢ Multicolored | 36.00 | 3.60 | .75 | .16 |

1984. ORCHIDS—PACIFIC CALYPSO
| ☐2079 20¢ Multicolored | 36.00 | 3.00 | .75 | .16 |

1984. HAWAII STATEHOOD
| ☐2080 20¢ Blue & Yellow | 32.00 | 3.10 | .70 | .16 |

1984. NATIONAL ARCHIVES
| ☐2081 20¢ Brown & Black | 32.00 | 3.00 | .70 | .16 |

1984. SUMMER OLYMPICS 1984—MEN'S DIVING
| ☐2082 20¢ Multicolored | 52.00 | 5.50 | 1.20 | .16 |

1984. SUMMER OLYMPICS 1984—LONG JUMP
| ☐2083 20¢ Multicolored | 52.00 | 5.50 | 1.20 | .16 |

1984. SUMMER OLYMPICS 1984—WRESTLING
| ☐2084 20¢ Multicolored | 52.00 | 5.50 | 1.20 | .16 |

1984. SUMMER OLYMPICS 1984—WOMEN'S KAYAK
| ☐2085 20¢ Multicolored | 52.00 | 5.50 | 1.20 | .16 |

1984. LOUISIANA WORLD'S EXPOSITION
| ☐2086 20¢ Multicolored | 24.00 | 2.80 | .65 | .16 |

1984. HEALTH RESEARCH—USA
| ☐2087 20¢ Multicolored | 32.00 | 3.10 | .70 | .16 |

1984. DOUGLAS FAIRBANKS
| ☐2088 20¢ Black & White | 36.00 | 21.00 | .70 | .16 |

*No hinge pricing from 1941 to date is figured at (N-H ADD 10%)

Scott No.	Mint Sheet	Plate Block	Fine Unused Each	Fine Used Each

1984. JIM THORPE

☐2089 20¢ Black & White	34.00	3.50	.75	.16

1984. JOHN McCORMACK

☐2090 20¢ Multicolored	30.00	2.75	.70	.16

1984. ST. LAWRENCE SEAWAY

☐2091 20¢ Multicolored	30.00	3.25	.70	.16

1984. PRESERVING WETLANDS

☐2092 20¢ Multicolored	45.00	2.75	1.00	.16

1984. ROANOKE VOYAGES 1584

☐2093 20¢ Multicolored	32.00	3.00	.70	.16

1984. HERMAN MELVILLE

☐2094 20¢ Green	28.00	2.60	.70	.16

1984. HORACE MOSES

☐2095 20¢ Orange & Brown	52.00	24.00	1.10	.16

1984. SMOKEY THE BEAR

☐2096 20¢ Multicolored	30.00	3.50	.70	.16

1984. ROBERTO CLEMENTE

☐2097 20¢ Multicolored	120.00	12.00	2.50	.16

1984. DOGS: BEAGLE & BOSTON TERRIER

☐2098 20¢ Multicolored	36.00	3.50	.70	.16

1984. DOGS: RETRIEVER & COCKER SPANIEL

☐2099 20¢ Multicolored	36.00	3.50	.70	.16

1984. DOGS: MALAMUTE & COLLIE

☐2100 20¢ Multicolored	36.00	3.50	.70	.16

1984. DOGS: COONHOUND & FOXHOUND

☐2101 20¢ Multicolored	36.00	3.50	.70	.16

*No hinge pricing from 1941 to date is figured at (N-H ADD 10%)

Scott No.	Mint Sheet	Plate Block	Fine Unused Each	Fine Used Each

1984. CRIME PREVENTION
| ☐2102 20¢ Multicolored | 28.00 | 2.60 | .70 | .16 |

1984. HISPANIC AMERICANS
| ☐2103 20¢ Multicolored | 22.00 | 2.20 | .70 | .16 |

1984. FAMILY UNITY
| ☐2104 20¢ Multicolored | 38.00 | 22.00 (20) | .70 | .16 |

1984. ELEANOR ROOSEVELT
| ☐2105 20¢ Blue | 28.00 | 2.60 | .70 | .16 |

1984. NATION OF READERS
| ☐2106 20¢ Brown & Maroon | 30.00 | 2.70 | .70 | .16 |

1984. MADONNA AND CHILD
| ☐2107 20¢ Multicolored | 28.00 | 2.60 | .70 | .16 |

1984. SANTA CLAUS
| ☐2108 20¢ Multicolored | 28.00 | 2.20 | .70 | .16 |

1984. VIETNAM VETERANS MEMORIAL
| ☐2109 20¢ Multicolored | 26.00 | 4.00 | .70 | .16 |

1985 COMMEMORATIVES
1985. JEROME KERN
| ☐2110 22¢ Multicolored | 32.00 | 3.10 | .75 | .16 |

1985. REGULAR ISSUES
1985. "D" NON-DENOMINATIONAL
| ☐2111 22¢ Green | 100.00 | 36.00 (20) | 1.00 | .16 |

1985. "D" NON-DENOMINATIONAL COIL
| ☐2112 22¢ Green | — | 7.00 | .75 | .16 |

1985. "D" NON-DENOMINATIONAL BOOKLET
| ☐2113 22¢ Green | — | — | 1.00 | .16 |

1985. FLAG OVER DOME
| ☐2114 22¢ Multicolored | 50.00 | 3.00 | .30 | .16 |

*No hinge pricing from 1941 to date is figured at (N-H ADD 10%)

Scott No.	Mint Sheet	Plate Block	Fine Unused Each	Fine Used Each

1985. FLAG OVER DOME COIL
| ☐2115 22¢ Multicolored | — | — | .70 | .16 |

1985. FLAG OVER DOME BOOKLET
| ☐2116 22¢ Multicolored | — | — | 1.00 | .16 |

1985. SEASHELLS: FRILLED DOGWINKLE
| ☐2117 22¢ Brown | — | — | .80 | .16 |

1985. SEASHELLS: RETICULATED HELMET
| ☐2118 22¢ Brown | — | — | .80 | .16 |

1985. SEASHELLS: NEW ENGLAND NEPTUNE
| ☐2119 22¢ Brown | — | — | .80 | .16 |

1985. SEASHELLS: CALICO SCALLOP
| ☐2120 22¢ Pink | — | — | .80 | .16 |

1985. SEASHELLS: LIGHTNING WHELK
| ☐2121 22¢ Brown | — | — | .80 | .16 |

1985. EXPRESS MAIL U.S.A.
| ☐2122 $10.75 Multicolored | — | — | 25.00 | 12.00 |

1985. SCHOOL BUS 1920s
| ☐2123 3.4¢ Dark Brown | — | — | .24 | .16 |

1985. BUCKBOARD 1880s
| ☐2124 4.9¢ Dark Brown | — | — | .24 | .16 |

1986. STAR ROUTE TRUCK 1910s
| ☐2125 5.5¢ Carmine | — | — | .24 | .16 |

1985. TRICYCLE 1880s
| ☐2126 6¢ Red | — | — | .24 | .16 |

1985. TRACTOR 1920s
| ☐2127 71¢ Lake | — | — | .24 | .16 |

*No hinge pricing from 1941 to date is figured at (N-H ADD 10%)

Scott No.	Mint Sheet	Plate Block	Fine Unused Each	Fine Used Each
1985. AMBULANCE 1860s				
☐2128 8.3¢ Green	—	—	.25	.16
1985. TOW TRUCK 1920s				
☐2129 8.5¢ Dark Green	—	—	.25	.16
1985. OIL WAGON 1890s				
☐2130 10.1¢ Black	—	—	.35	.16
1985. STUTZ BEARCAT 1933				
☐2131 11¢ Blue	—	—	.35	.16
1985. STANLEY STEAMER 1909				
☐2132 12¢ Blue	—	—	.40	.16
1985. PUSHCART 1880s				
☐2133 12.5¢ Black	—	—	.40	.16
1985. ICEBOAT 1880s				
☐2134 14¢ Blue	—	—	.50	.16
1986. DOG SLED 1920s				
☐2135 17¢ Blue	—	—	.60	.16
1986. BREAD WAGON 1880s				
☐2136 25¢ Brown	—	—	.70	.16
1985. MARY McCLEOD BETHUNE				
☐2137 22¢ Multicolored	36.00	3.50	.75	.16
1985. DUCKS: BROADBILL				
☐2138 22¢ Multicolored	80.00	8.50	.85	.16
1985. DUCKS: MALLARD				
☐2139 22¢ Multicolored	80.00	8.50	.85	.16
1985. DUCKS: CANVASBACK				
☐2140 22¢ Multicolored	80.00	8.50	.85	.16

*No hinge pricing from 1941 to date is figured at (N-H ADD 10%)

Scott No.	Mint Sheet	Plate Block	Fine Unused Each	Fine Used Each

1985. DUCKS: REDHEAD
| ☐2141 22¢ Multicolored | 80.00 | 8.50 | .85 | .16 |

1985. WINTER SPECIAL OLYMPICS
| ☐2142 22¢ Multicolored | 24.00 | 3.25 | .70 | .16 |

1985. LOVE
| ☐2143 22¢ Multicolored | 34.00 | 3.25 | .70 | .16 |

1985. RURAL ELECTRIFICATION ADMINISTRATION
| ☐2144 22¢ Multicolored | 60.00 | 35.00 (20) | .90 | .16 |

1985. AMERIPEX SHOW
| ☐2145 22¢ Multicolored | 28.00 | 3.00 | .70 | .16 |

1985. ABIGAIL ADAMS
| ☐2146 22¢ Multicolored | 30.00 | 3.10 | .70 | .16 |

1985. BARTHOLDI—STATUE OF LIBERTY
| ☐2147 22¢ Multicolored | 30.00 | 3.10 | .70 | .16 |

1985. GEORGE WASHINGTON
| ☐2149 18¢ Multicolored | — | — | .60 | .16 |

1985. ENVELOPES
| ☐2150 2.1¢ Multicolored | — | — | .60 | .16 |

1985. KOREAN VETERANS
| ☐2152 22¢ Red & Green | 34.00 | 3.50 | .75 | .16 |

1985. SOCIAL SECURITY
| ☐2153 22¢ Blue | 30.00 | 3.40 | .70 | .16 |

1985. WORLD WAR I VETERANS
| ☐2154 22¢ Red & Green | 34.00 | 4.00 | .75 | .16 |

1985. HORSES: QUARTER HORSE
| ☐2155 22¢ Multicolored | 110.00 | 12.00 | 2.50 | .16 |

*No hinge pricing from 1941 to date is figured at (N-H ADD 10%)

Scott No.	Mint Sheet	Plate Block	Fine Unused Each	Fine Used Each
1985. HORSES: MORGAN				
☐2156 22¢ Multicolored	110.00	12.00	2.50	.16
1985. HORSES: SADDLEBRED				
☐2157 22¢ Multicolored	110.00	12.00	2.50	.16
1985. HORSES: APPALOOSA				
☐2158 22¢ Multicolored	110.00	12.00	2.50	.16
1985. PUBLIC EDUCATION				
☐2159 22¢ Multicolored	30.00	3.50	.75	.16
1985. YOUTH YEAR: Y.M.C.A.				
☐2160 22¢ Multicolored	60.00	6.00	1.25	.16
1985. YOUTH YEAR: BOY SCOUTS				
☐2161 22¢ Multicolored	60.00	6.00	1.25	.16
1985. YOUTH YEAR: BIG BROTHERS				
☐2162 22¢ Multicolored	60.00	6.00	1.25	.16
1985. YOUTH YEAR: CAMPFIRE				
☐2163 22¢ Multicolored	60.00	6.00	1.25	.16
1985. HELP END HUNGER				
☐2164 22¢ Multicolored	34.00	3.25	.75	.16
1985. MADONNA AND CHILD				
☐2165 22¢ Multicolored	30.00	3.00	.70	.16
1985. SEASON GREETINGS—POINSETTIA				
☐2166 22¢ Multicolored	30.00	3.00	.70	.16
1985. ARKANSAS—STATEHOOD				
☐2167 22¢ Multicolored	34.00	3.10	.80	.16
1986–1993 GREAT AMERICANS **1986. MARGARET MITCHELL**				
☐2168 1¢ Brown	6.00	—	.35	.16

*No hinge pricing from 1941 to date is figured at (N-H ADD 10%)

Scott No.	Mint Sheet	Plate Block	Fine Unused Each	Fine Used Each

1987. MARY LYON
| ☐2169 2¢ Blue | 6.00 | .50 | .25 | .16 |

1986. DR. PAUL DUDLEY WHITE M.D.
| ☐2170 3¢ Blue | 11.00 | .60 | .25 | .16 |

1986. FATHER FLANAGAN
| ☐2171 4¢ Blue | 12.00 | .70 | .25 | .16 |

1986. HUGO L. BLACK
| ☐2172 5¢ Olive Green | 15.00 | .80 | .25 | .16 |

1990. LUIS MUÑOZ MARIN
| ☐2173 5¢ Carmine | 15.00 | .90 | .25 | .16 |

1988. RED CLOUD
| ☐2175 10¢ Lake | 26.00 | 1.80 | .30 | .16 |

1987. JULIA WARD HOWE
| ☐2176 14¢ Red | 32.00 | 2.00 | .35 | .16 |

1988. BUFFALO BILL CODY
| ☐2177 15¢ Claret | 45.00 | 3.00 | .60 | .16 |

1986. BELVA ANN LOCKWOOD
| ☐2178 17¢ Blue Green | 36.00 | 3.00 | .60 | .16 |

1986. VIRGINIA APGAR
| ☐2179 20¢ Multicolored | 45.00 | 3.00 | .60 | .16 |

1988. CHESTER CARLSON
| ☐2180 21¢ Blue Violet | 45.00 | 3.50 | .60 | .16 |

1988. MARY CASSATT
| ☐2181 23¢ Purple | 50.00 | 4.00 | .60 | .16 |

1986. JACK LONDON
| ☐2182 25¢ Blue | 62.00 | 3.50 | .70 | .16 |

1989. SITTING BULL
| ☐2183 28¢ Myrtle Green | 65.00 | 4.25 | .70 | .16 |

*No hinge pricing from 1941 to date is figured at (N-H ADD 10%)

Scott No.	Mint Sheet	Plate Block	Fine Unused Each	Fine Used Each
1992. EARL WARREN				
☐2184 29¢ Blue	60.00	4.00	.70	.16
1993. THOMAS JEFFERSON				
☐2185 29¢ Black	62.00	3.50 (4)	.75	.16
1986. DENNIS CHAVEZ				
☐2186 35¢ Black	70.00	4.00	.80	.16
1990. CLAIRE CHENAULT				
☐2187 40¢ Dark Blue	90.00	5.75	.85	.16
1988. DR. HARVEY CUSHING				
☐2188 45¢ Blue	110.00	6.25	1.30	.16
1991. HUBERT HUMPHREY				
☐2189 52¢ Purple	110.00.	6.00	1.10	.16
1986. JOHN HARVARD				
☐2190 56¢ Brown	125.00	8.00	1.75	.16
1988. H.H. ARNOLD				
☐2191 65¢ Blue/Gray	135.00	9.00	1.60	.16
1992. WENDELL WILKIE				
☐2192 75¢ Magenta	165.00	9.00	1.85	.16
1986. BERNARD REVEL				
☐2193 $1.00 Green	250.00	16.00	4.00	.16
1989. JOHNS HOPKINS				
☐2194 $1.00 Dark Green	50.00	12.00	4.00	.16
1986. WILLIAM JENNINGS BRYAN				
☐2195 $2.00 Violet	400.00	22.00	5.00	.16
1987. BRET HARTE				
☐2196 $5.00 Brown	225.00	50.00	12.00	.16
1988. JACK LONDON				
☐2197 25¢ Black	—	—	.75	.16
1986. COMMEMORATIVES				
1986. STAMP COLLECTING: AMERICAN PHILATELIC ASSOC.				
☐2198 22¢ Multicolored	—	—	.85	.16

*No hinge pricing from 1941 to date is figured at (N-H ADD 10%)

Scott No.	Mint Sheet	Plate Block	Fine Unused Each	Fine Used Each

1986. STAMP COLLECTING: LITTLE BOY

| ☐2199 22¢ Multicolored | — | — | .85 | .16 |

1986. STAMP COLLECTING: MAGNIFIER

| ☐2200 22¢ Multicolored | — | — | .85 | .16 |

1986. STAMP COLLECTING: RUBBER STAMP

| ☐2201 22¢ Multicolored | — | — | .85 | .16 |

1986. LOVE

| ☐2202 22¢ Multicolored | 30.00 | 3.10 | .75 | .16 |

1986. SOJOURNER TRUTH

| ☐2203 22¢ Multicolored | 32.00 | 3.10 | .75 | .16 |

1986. TEXAS—SAN JACINTO 1836

| ☐2204 22¢ Multicolored | 36.00 | 3.25 | .75 | .16 |

1986. FISH: MUSKELLUNGE

| ☐2205 22¢ Multicolored | — | — | 2.50 | .16 |

1986. FISH: ATLANTIC COD

| ☐2206 22¢ Multicolored | — | — | 2.50 | .16 |

1986. FISH: LARGEMOUTH BASS

| ☐2207 22¢ Multicolored | — | — | 2.50 | .16 |

1986. FISH: BLUEFIN TUNA

| ☐2208 22¢ Multicolored | — | — | 2.50 | .16 |

1986. FISH: CATFISH

| ☐2209 22¢ Multicolored | — | — | 2.50 | .16 |

1986. PUBLIC HOSPITALS

| ☐2210 22¢ Multicolored | 32.00 | 3.25 | .65 | .16 |

1986. DUKE ELLINGTON

| ☐2211 22¢ Multicolored | 34.00 | 3.15 | .70 | .16 |

*No hinge pricing from 1941 to date is figured at (N-H ADD 10%)

Scott No.	Mint Sheet	Plate Block	Fine Unused Each	Fine Used Each

1986. AMERIPEX '86-PRESIDENTS I
| ☐2216 22¢ Brown & Black | — | 5.50 (9) | .75 | .45 |

1986. AMERIPEX '86-PRESIDENTS II
| ☐2217 22¢ Brown & Black | — | 5.50 (9) | .75 | .45 |

1986. AMERIPEX '86-PRESIDENTS III
| ☐2218 22¢ Brown & Black | — | 5.50 (9) | .75 | .45 |

1986. AMERIPEX '86-PRESIDENTS IV
| ☐2219 22¢ Brown & Black | — | 5.50 (9) | .75 | .45 |

1986. POLAR EXPLORERS: ELISHA KANE KENT
| ☐2220 22¢ Multicolored | — | — | 2.00 | .45 |

1986. POLAR EXPLORERS: ADOLPHUS W. GREELY
| ☐2221 22¢ Multicolored | — | — | 2.00 | .45 |

1986. POLAR EXPLORERS: VILHJALMUR STEFANSSON
| ☐2222 22¢ Multicolored | — | — | 2.00 | .45 |

1986. POLAR EXPLORERS: ROBERT PERRY & MATTHEW HENSON
| ☐2223 22¢ Multicolored | — | — | 2.00 | .45 |

1986. STATUE OF LIBERTY
| ☐2224 22¢ Carmine & Blue | 32.00 | 3.00 | .70 | .16 |

1986. COMMEMORATIVES
1986. NAVAJO ART
| ☐2235 22¢ Multicolored | 38.00 | 4.00 | .90 | .16 |

1986. NAVAJO ART
| ☐2236 22¢ Multicolored | 38.00 | 4.00 | .90 | .16 |

1986. NAVAJO ART
| ☐2237 22¢ Multicolored | 38.00 | 4.00 | .90 | .16 |

1986. NAVAJO ART
| ☐2238 22¢ Multicolored | 38.00 | 4.00 | .90 | .16 |

*No hinge pricing from 1941 to date is figured at (N-H ADD 10%)

Scott No.	Mint Sheet	Plate Block	Fine Unused Each	Fine Used Each

1986. T.S. ELIOT
| ☐ 2239 22¢ Brown | 30.00 | 3.00 | .70 | .16 |

1986. FOLK ART: HIGHLANDER
| ☐ 2240 22¢ Multicolored | 36.00 | 4.00 | .95 | .16 |

1986. FOLK ART: SHIP
| ☐ 2241 22¢ Multicolored | 36.00 | 4.00 | .95 | .16 |

1986. FOLK ART: NAUTICAL
| ☐ 2242 22¢ Multicolored | 36.00 | 4.00 | .95 | .16 |

1986. FOLK ART: CIGAR STORE
| ☐ 2243 22¢ Multicolored | 36.00 | 4.00 | .95 | .16 |

1986. CHRISTMAS: PEROGINO GALLERY
| ☐ 2244 22¢ Multicolored | 52.00 | 2.90 | .70 | .16 |

1986. CHRISTMAS: GREETINGS—VILLAGE
| ☐ 2245 22¢ Multicolored | 52.00 | 2.90 | .70 | .16 |

1987. MICHIGAN STATEHOOD
| ☐ 2246 22¢ Multicolored | 32.00 | 3.00 | .70 | .16 |

1987. PAN AMERICAN GAMES
| ☐ 2247 22¢ Multicolored | 30.00 | 3.00 | .70 | .16 |

1987. LOVE
| ☐ 2248 22¢ Multicolored | 54.00 | 3.00 | .70 | .16 |

1987. JEAN BAPTISTE POINTE DU SABLE
| ☐ 2249 22¢ Multicolored | 30.00 | 3.00 | .70 | .16 |

1987. ENRICO CARUSO
| ☐ 2250 22¢ Multicolored | 32.00 | 3.00 | .70 | .16 |

1987. GIRL SCOUTS
| ☐ 2251 22¢ Multicolored | 28.00 | 3.00 | .70 | .16 |

*No hinge pricing from 1941 to date is figured at (N-H ADD 10%)

Scott No.	Mint Sheet	Plate Strip	Fine Unused Each	Fine Used Each

1987–1993. TRANSPORTATION COILS
1988. CONESTOGA WAGON

Scott No.	Mint Sheet	Plate Strip	Fine Unused Each	Fine Used Each
☐2252 3¢ Claret	—	1.50	.25	.16

1988. MILK WAGON

☐2253 5¢ Black	—	1.75	.25	.18

1988. ELEVATOR

☐2254 5.3¢ Black	—	2.00	.25	.16

1988. CARRETA

☐2255 7.6¢ Brown	—	3.50	.25	.16

1988. WHEELCHAIR

☐2256 8.4¢ Claret	—	3.50	.30	.16

1988. CANAL BOAT

☐2257 10¢ Sky Blue	—	2.25	.35	.16

1988. POLICE WAGON

☐2258 13¢ Black	—	3.75	.40	.16

1988. RAILROAD COALCAR

☐2259 13.2¢ Slate Green	—	3.75	.50	.16

1988. TUG BOAT

☐2260 15¢ Violet	—	3.75	.50	.16

1988. POPCORN WAGON

☐2261 16.7¢ Rose	—	4.00	.50	.16

1988. RACING CAR

☐2262 17.5¢ Violet	—	5.00	.50	.16

1988. CABLE CAR

☐2263 20¢ Blue Violet	—	4.75	.65	.16

1988. FIRE ENGINE

☐2264 20.5¢ Rose	—	5.00	.70	.16

*No hinge pricing from 1941 to date is figured at (N-H ADD 10%)

Scott No.	Mint Sheet	Plate Strip	Fine Unused Each	Fine Used Each
1988. RAILROAD MAILCAR				
☐2265 21¢ Green	—	5.00	.70	.16
1988. TANDEM BICYCLE				
☐2266 24.1¢ Ultramarine	—	5.50	.70	.16
1987. SPECIAL OCCASIONS				
☐2267–				
2274 22¢ Multicolored	—	—	2.00	.16
1987. UNITED WAY UNITING COMMUNITIES				
☐2275 22¢ Multicolored	30.00	3.00	.70	.16
1987. AMERICAN FLAG				
☐2276 22¢ Multicolored	54.00	3.00	.70	.16
1987. "E" EARTH				
☐2277 25¢ Multicolored	65.00	3.40	.70	.16
1987. FLAG ON CLOUDS				
☐2278 25¢ Multicolored	64.00	3.10	.70	.16
1987. "E" EARTH				
☐2279 25¢ Multicolored	—	4.75	.70	.16
1987. FLAG YOSEMITE				
☐2280 25¢ Multicolored	—	4.75	.70	.16
1987. HONEY BEE				
☐2281 25¢ Multicolored	—	3.75	.70	.16
1987. "E" EARTH				
☐2282 25¢ Multicolored	—	—	.70	.16
1987. PHEASANT				
☐2283 25¢ Multicolored	—	—	.70	.16
1987. GROSBEAK				
☐2284 25¢ Multicolored	—	—	.75	.16
1987. OWL				
☐2285 25¢ Multicolored	—	—	.75	.16

*No hinge pricing from 1941 to date is figured at (N-H ADD 10%)

Scott No.	Mint Sheet	Plate Block	Fine Unused Each	Fine Used Each

1987. AMERICAN WILDLIFE

☐2286–
2335 22¢ Multicolored 70.00 — — .35

1987–1990. COMMEMORATIVES
1987. DELAWARE

☐2336 22¢ Multicolored 32.00 3.25 .70 .16

1987. PENNSYLVANIA

☐2337 22¢ Multicolored 42.00 3.75 .95 .16

1987. BICENTENNIAL SERIES

☐2338–
2348 22¢ Multicolored 32.00 3.25 .70 .16

1987. FRIENDSHIP WITH MOROCCO

☐2349 22¢ Multicolored 31.00 2.85 .70 .16

1987. WILLIAM FAULKNER

☐2350 22¢ Green 30.00 2.85 .70 .16

1987. LACEMAKING

☐2351–
2354 22¢ Blue 38.00 4.00 .95 .16

1987. CONSTITUTION (BICENTENNIAL)

☐2355 22¢ Multicolored — — .95 .16

1987. CONSTITUTION (WE THE PEOPLE)

☐2356 22¢ Multicolored — — .95 .16

1987. CONSTITUTION (ESTABLISH JUSTICE)

☐2357 22¢ Multicolored — — .95 .16

1987. CONSTITUTION (AND SECURE)

☐2358 22¢ Multicolored — — .95 .16

1987. CONSTITUTION (DO ORDAIN)

☐2359 22¢ Multicolored — — .95 .16

*No hinge pricing from 1941 to date is figured at (N-H ADD 10%)

Scott No.	Mint Sheet	Plate Block	Fine Unused Each	Fine Used Each

1987. U.S. CONSTITUTION
| ☐ 2360 22¢ Multicolored | 34.00 | 3.50 | .80 | .16 |

1987. C.P.A. CERTIFIED PUBLIC ACCOUNTANTS
| ☐ 2361 22¢ Multicolored | 180.00 | 15.00 | 4.00 | .16 |

1987. LOCOMOTIVES
| ☐ 2362– |
| 2366 22¢ Multicolored | — | — | .95 | .16 |

1987. CHRISTMAS: MARONI, NATIONAL GALLERY
| ☐ 2367 22¢ Multicolored | 50.00 | 3.00 | .70 | .16 |

1987. GREETINGS
| ☐ 2368 22¢ Multicolored | 50.00 | 3.00 | .70 | .16 |

1988. COMMEMORATIVES
1988. OLYMPICS (WINTER)
| ☐ 2369 22¢ Multicolored | 42.00 | 4.00 | .95 | .16 |

1988. AUSTRALIA BICENTENNIAL
| ☐ 2370 22¢ Multicolored | 24.00 | 3.00 | .65 | .16 |

1988. J. W. JOHNSON
| ☐ 2371 22¢ Multicolored | 30.00 | 3.00 | .65 | .16 |

1988. CATS (SHORT HAIR)
| ☐ 2372 22¢ Multicolored | 34.00 | 4.00 | 1.00 | .16 |

1988. CATS (HIMALAYAN)
| ☐ 2373 22¢ Multicolored | 34.00 | 4.00 | 1.00 | .16 |

1988. CATS (BURMESE)
| ☐ 2374 22¢ Multicolored | 34.00 | 4.00 | 1.00 | .16 |

1988. CATS (PERSIAN)
| ☐ 2375 22¢ Multicolored | 34.00 | 4.00 | 1.00 | .16 |

1988. KNUTE ROCKNE
| ☐ 2376 22¢ Multicolored | 34.00 | 4.00 | .80 | .16 |

*No hinge pricing from 1941 to date is figured at (N-H ADD 10%)

Scott No.	Mint Sheet	Plate Block	Fine Unused Each	Fine Used Each
1988. FRANCIS OUIMET				
☐2377 25¢ Multicolored	50.00	5.00	1.20	.16
1988. LOVE				
☐2378 25¢ Multicolored	65.00	3.50	.75	.16
1988. LOVE				
☐2379 45¢ Multicolored	52.00	6.00	1.20	.16
1988. OLYMPICS (SUMMER)				
☐2380 25¢ Multicolored	42.00	4.00	.95	.16
1988. CARS (LOCOMOBILE)				
☐2381 25¢ Multicolored	—	—	2.25	.16
1988. CARS (PIERCE-ARROW)				
☐2382 25¢ Multicolored	—	—	2.25	.16
1988. CARS (CORD)				
☐2383 25¢ Multicolored	—	—	2.25	.16
1988. CARS (PACKARD)				
☐2384 25¢ Multicolored	—	—	2.25	.16
1988. CARS (DUESENBERG)				
☐2385 25¢ Multicolored	—	—	2.25	.16
1988. ANTARCTIC: NATHANIEL PALMER				
☐2386 25¢ Multicolored	56.00	8.00	1.50	.16
1988. ANTARCTIC: LT. CHARLES WILKES				
☐2387 25¢ Multicolored	56.00	8.00	1.50	.16
1988. ANTARCTIC: RICHARD E. BYRD				
☐2388 25¢ Multicolored	56.00	8.00	1.50	.16
1988. ANTARCTIC: LINCOLN ELLSWORTH				
☐2389 25¢ Multicolored	56.00	8.00	1.50	.16

*No hinge pricing from 1941 to date is figured at (N-H ADD 10%)

Scott No.	Mint Sheet	Plate Block	Fine Unused Each	Fine Used Each
1988. CAROUSEL: DEER				
☐2390 25¢ Multicolored	50.00	6.25	1.50	.16
1988. CAROUSEL: HORSE				
☐2391 25¢ Multicolored	50.00	6.25	1.50	.16
1988. CAROUSEL: CAMEL				
☐2392 25¢ Multicolored	50.00	6.25	1.50	.16
1988. CAROUSEL: GOAT				
☐2393 25¢ Multicolored	50.00	6.25	1.50	.16
1988. EXPRESS MAIL				
☐2394 $8.75 Multicolored	500.00	120.00	26.00	9.50
1988. OCCASIONS: HAPPY BIRTHDAY				
☐2395 25¢ Multicolored	—	—	.85	.16
1988. OCCASIONS: BEST WISHES				
☐2396 25¢ Multicolored	—	—	.85	.16
1988. OCCASIONS: THINKING OF YOU				
☐2397 25¢ Multicolored	—	—	.85	.16
1988. OCCASIONS: LOVE YOU				
☐2398 25¢ Multicolored	—	—	.85	.16
1988. CHRISTMAS (BOTTICELLI)				
☐2399 25¢ Multicolored	32.00	3.20	.70	.16
1988. GREETINGS (CHRISTMAS)				
☐2400 25¢ Multicolored	32.00	3.20	.70	.16
1989. COMMEMORATIVES				
1989. MONTANA				
☐2401 25¢ Multicolored	32.00	3.50	.70	.16
1989. A. PHILIPP RANDOLPH				
☐2402 25¢ Multicolored	32.00	3.00	.70	.16

*No hinge pricing from 1941 to date is figured at (N-H ADD 10%)

Scott No.	Mint Sheet	Plate Block	Fine Unused Each	Fine Used Each
1989. NORTH DAKOTA				
☐2403 25¢ Multicolored	32.00	3.20	.75	.16
1989. WASHINGTON				
☐2404 25¢ Multicolored	32.00	3.20	.75	.16
1989. STEAMBOATS: EXPERIMENT				
☐2405 25¢ Multicolored	—	—	.95	.16
1989. STEAMBOATS: PHOENIX				
☐2406 25¢ Multicolored	—	—	.95	.16
1989. STEAMBOATS: NEW ORLEANS				
☐2407 25¢ Multicolored	—	—	.95	.16
1989. STEAMBOATS: WASHINGTON				
☐2408 25¢ Multicolored	—	—	.95	.16
1989. STEAMBOATS: WALK IN THE WATER				
☐2409 25¢ Multicolored	—	—	.95	.16
1989. WORLD STAMP EXPO '89				
☐2410 25¢ Black & Carmine	32.00	3.20	.75	.16
1989. ARTURO TOSCANINI				
☐2411 25¢ Multicolored	32.00	3.20	.75	.16
1989. BICENTENNIAL: HOUSE OF REPRESENTATIVES				
☐2412 25¢ Multicolored	32.00	3.20	.75	.16
1989. BICENTENNIAL: UNITED STATES SENATE				
☐2413 25¢ Multicolored	32.00	3.20	.75	.16
1989. BICENTENNIAL: EXECUTIVE BRANCH				
☐2414 25¢ Multicolored	32.00	3.20	.75	.16
1989. U.S. SUPREME COURT				
☐2415 25¢ Multicolored	32.00	3.20	.75	.16

*No hinge pricing from 1941 to date is figured at (N-H ADD 10%)

Scott No.	Mint Sheet	Plate Block	Fine Unused Each	Fine Used Each
1989. SOUTH DAKOTA 1889: STATEHOOD				
☐2416 25¢ Multicolored	32.00	3.25	.75	.16
1989. LOU GEHRIG				
☐2417 25¢ Multicolored	48.00	4.25	1.00	.16
1989. ERNEST HEMINGWAY				
☐2418 25¢ Multicolored	32.00	3.25	.75	.16
1989. MOON LANDING				
☐2419 $2.40 Multicolored	120.00	25.00	6.00	.16
1989. LETTER CARRIERS				
☐2420 25¢ Multicolored	24.00	3.20	.70	.16
1989. BILL OF RIGHTS				
☐2421 25¢ Multicolored	56.00	6.50	1.25	.16
1989. DINOSAURS: TYRANNOSAURUS				
☐2422 25¢ Multicolored	56.00	6.50	1.45	.16
1989. DINOSAURS: PTERANODON				
☐2423 25¢ Multicolored	56.00	6.50	1.45	.16
1989. DINOSAURS: STEGOSAURUS				
☐2424 25¢ Multicolored	56.00	6.50	1.45	.16
1989. DINOSAURS: BRONTOSAURUS				
☐2425 25¢ Multicolored	56.00	6.50	1.45	.16
1989. COLUMBIAN ARTIFACTS				
☐2426 25¢ Multicolored	32.00	3.25	.75	.16
1989. CHRISTMAS: MADONNA				
☐2427 25¢ Multicolored	32.00	3.25	.75	.16
1989. CHRISTMAS: SLEIGH				
☐2428 25¢ Multicolored	32.00	3.25	.75	.16

*No hinge pricing from 1941 to date is figured at (N-H ADD 10%)

Scott No.	Mint Sheet	Plate Block	Fine Unused Each	Fine Used Each

1989. MAIL DELIVERY: STAGECOACH

☐2434 25¢ Multicolored	45.00	4.50	1.20	.16

1989. MAIL DELIVERY: PADDLEWHEEL

☐2435 25¢ Multicolored	45.00	4.50	1.20	.16

1989. MAIL DELIVERY: BIPLANE

☐2436 25¢ Multicolored	45.00	4.50	1.20	.16

1989. MAIL DELIVERY: AUTOMOBILE

☐2437 25¢ Multicolored	45.00	4.50	1.20	.16

1990. COMMEMORATIVE
1990. IDAHO CENTENARY: BLUEBIRD

☐2439 25¢ Multicolored	32.00	3.75	.75	.16

1990. LOVE

☐2440 25¢ Multicolored	32.00	3.75	.75	.16

1990. BLACK HERITAGE: IDA B. WELLS

☐2442 25¢ Multicolored	32.00	3.50	.75	.16

1990. BEACH UMBRELLA

☐2443 25¢ Multicolored	—	—	.50	.16

1990. WYOMING CENTENARY—MOUNTAIN

☐2444 25¢ Multicolored	30.00	4.00	.75	.16

1990. CLASSIC FILMS: WIZARD OF OZ

☐2445 25¢ Multicolored	85.00	12.00	2.15	.16

1990. CLASSIC FILMS: GONE WITH THE WIND

☐2446 25¢ Multicolored	85.00	12.00	2.15	.16

1990. CLASSIC FILMS: BEAU GESTE

☐2447 25¢ Multicolored	85.00	12.00	2.15	.16

1990. CLASSIC FILMS: STAGECOACH

☐2448 25¢ Multicolored	85.00	12.00	2.15	.16

*No hinge pricing from 1941 to date is figured at (N-H ADD 10%)

Scott No.	Mint Sheet	Plate Block	Fine Unused Each	Fine Used Each

1990. LITERARY ARTS: MARIANNE MOORE

☐ 2449 25¢ Multicolored	32.00	3.10	.75	.16

1990. TRANSPORTATION

☐ 2451–2464 4¢, 5¢, 10¢, 23¢ Multicolored				
	—	2.75	.70	.16

1990. LIGHTHOUSES: ADMIRALTY HEAD

☐ 2470 25¢ Multicolored	—	—	1.00	.16

1990. LIGHTHOUSES: CAPE HATTERAS

☐ 2471 25¢ Multicolored	—	—	1.00	.16

1990. LIGHTHOUSES: WEST QUODDY HEAD

☐ 2472 25¢ Multicolored	—	—	1.00	.16

1990. LIGHTHOUSES: AMERICAN SHOALS

☐ 2473 25¢ Multicolored	—	—	1.00	.16

1990. LIGHTHOUSES: SANDY HOOK

☐ 2474 25¢ Multicolored	—	—	1.00	.16

1990. KESTRAL

☐ 2476 1¢ Multicolored	6.00	.80	.25	.16

1990. BLUEBIRD

☐ 2478 3¢ Multicolored	8.00	.75	.25	.16

1990. FAWN

☐ 2479 19¢ Multicolored	64.00	4.25	.50	.16

1990. CARDINAL

☐ 2480 30¢ Multicolored	64.00	3.75	.65	.16

1990. BOBCAT

☐ 2482 $2.00 Multicolored	84.00	20.00	4.50	.55

1990. WOOD DUCK

☐ 2484 29¢ Black & Multicolored	—	—	.85	.16

*No hinge pricing from 1941 to date is figured at (N-H ADD 10%)

Scott No.	Mint Sheet	Plate Block	Fine Unused Each	Fine Used Each

1990. OLYMPIANS: JESSE OWENS
| ☐2496 25¢ Multicolored | 40.00 | 12.00 | 1.10 | .25 |

1990. OLYMPIANS: RAY EWRY
| ☐2497 25¢ Multicolored | 40.00 | 12.00 | 1.10 | .25 |

1990. OLYMPIANS: HAZEL WIGHTMAN
| ☐2498 25¢ Multicolored | 40.00 | 12.00 | 1.10 | .25 |

1990. OLYMPIANS: EDDIE EAGAN
| ☐2499 25¢ Multicolored | 40.00 | 12.00 | 1.10 | .25 |

1990. OLYMPIANS: HELENE MADISON
| ☐2500 25¢ Multicolored | 40.00 | 10.00 | 1.10 | .25 |

1990. INDIAN: ASSINIBOINE
| ☐2501 25¢ Multicolored | — | — | .80 | .16 |

1990. INDIAN: CHEYENNE
| ☐2502 25¢ Multicolored | — | — | .80 | .16 |

1990. INDIAN: COMANCHE
| ☐2503 25¢ Multicolored | — | — | .80 | .16 |

1990. INDIAN: FLATHEAD
| ☐2504 25¢ Multicolored | — | — | .80 | .16 |

1990. INDIAN: SHOSHONE
| ☐2505 25¢ Multicolored | — | — | .80 | .16 |

1990. MICRONESIA
| ☐2506 25¢ Multicolored | 40.00 | 4.25 | 1.00 | .25 |

1990. MARSHALL ISLANDS
| ☐2507 25¢ Multicolored | 40.00 | 4.25 | 1.00 | .25 |

1990. SEA CREATURES: KILLER WHALE
| ☐2508 25¢ Multicolored | 36.00 | 4.25 | 1.00 | .25 |

*No hinge pricing from 1941 to date is figured at (N-H ADD 10%)

Scott No.	Mint Sheet	Plate Block	Fine Unused Each	Fine Used Each

1990. SEA CREATURES: NORTHERN SEA LION

☐2509 25¢ Multicolored	36.00	4.25	1.00	.16

1990. SEA CREATURES: SEA OTTER

☐2510 25¢ Multicolored	36.00	4.25	1.00	.16

1990. SEA CREATURES: DOLPHIN

☐2511 25¢ Multicolored	36.00	4.25	1.00	.16

1990. GRAND CANYON

☐2512 25¢ Multicolored	32.00	3.10	.75	.16

1990. DWIGHT D. EISENHOWER

☐2513 25¢ Multicolored	26.00	3.50	.75	.16

1990. CHRISTMAS: MADONNA

☐2514 25¢ Multicolored	32.00	3.00	.75	.16

1990. CHRISTMAS: CHRISTMAS TREE

☐2515 25¢ Multicolored	32.00	3.00	.75	.16

1991. "F" FLOWER: TULIP

☐2517 29¢ Multicolored	65.00	4.00	.75	.16

1991. "F" STAMP RATE: EXTRA POSTAGE

☐2521 4¢ Multicolored	19.00	.85	.50	.16

1991. FLAG: MT. RUSHMORE

☐2523 29¢ Multicolored	—	6.25	.75	.16

1991. FLOWER: TULIP

☐2524 29¢ Multicolored	70.00	4.00	.75	.16

1991. FLAG: OLYMPIC RINGS

☐2528 29¢ Multicolored	—	—	.80	.16

1991. FISHING BOAT

☐2529 19¢ Multicolored	—	5.00	.55	.16

*No hinge pricing from 1941 to date is figured at (N-H ADD 10%)

Scott No.	Mint Sheet	Plate Block	Fine Unused Each	Fine Used Each
1991. BALLOONING				
☐2530 19¢ Multicolored	—	—	.50	.16
1991. FLAGS: ON PARADE				
☐2531 29¢ Multicolored	68.00	3.50	.75	.16
1991. COMMEMORATIVES				
1991. SWITZERLAND: 700TH ANNIVERSARY				
☐2532 50¢ Multicolored	45.00	5.50	1.30	.30
1991. VERMONT: BICENTENNIAL				
☐2533 29¢ Multicolored	35.00	3.50	.80	.25
1991. SAVINGS BONDS: 50TH ANNIVERSARY				
☐2534 29¢ Multicolored	34.00	3.50	.80	.25
1991. LOVE: HEART				
☐2535 29¢ Multicolored	34.00	3.50	.80	.25
1991. LOVE				
☐2536 29¢ Multicolored	—	—	.80	.25
1991. LOVE: LOVE BIRDS				
☐2537 52¢ Multicolored	55.00	6.00	1.25	.45
1991. LITERARY ARTS: WILLIAM SAROYAN				
☐2538 29¢ Multicolored	36.00	3.50	.40	.25
1991. USPS: OLYMPIC RINGS				
☐2539 $1.00 Multicolored	50.00	11.50	2.60	.45
1991. EAGLE: OLYMPIC RINGS				
☐2540 $2.90 Multicolored	140.00	35.00	8.00	2.50
1991. DOMESTIC: EXPRESS MAIL				
☐2541 $9.95 Multicolored	375.00	95.00	22.00	8.00
1991. INTERNATIONAL: EXPRESS MAIL				
☐2542 $14.00 Multicolored	550.00	130.00	30.00	24.00
1991. SPACE VEHICLE				
☐2543 $2.90 Multicolored	240.00	26.00	7.00	2.50
1991. SPACE SHUTTLE				
☐2544 $3.00 Multicolored	125.00	30.00	7.00	3.50
1991. FISHING FLIES				
☐2545 29¢ Multicolored	—	—	1.20	.25
☐2546 29¢ Multicolored	—	—	1.20	.25

*No hinge pricing from 1941 to date is figured at (N-H ADD 10%)

Scott No.	Mint Sheet	Plate Block	Fine Unused Each	Fine Used Each
☐2547 29¢ Multicolored	—	—	1.20	.25
☐2548 29¢ Multicolored	—	—	1.20	.25
☐2549 29¢ Multicolored	—	—	1.20	.25

1991. PERFORMING ARTS: COLE PORTER
☐2550 29¢ Multicolored	38.00	3.75	.85	.25

1991. DESERT STORM: SOUTHWEST ASIA
☐2551 29¢ Multicolored	38.00	3.75	.85	.25

1991. 1992 SUMMER OLYMPICS: BARCELONA
☐2553 29¢ Multicolored	34.00	11.00	1.00	.25
☐2554 29¢ Multicolored	34.00	11.00	1.00	.25
☐2555 29¢ Multicolored	34.00	11.00	1.00	.25
☐2556 29¢ Multicolored	34.00	11.00	1.00	.25
☐2557 29¢ Multicolored	34.00	11.00	1.00	.25

1991. NUMISMATICS: COINS AND NOTES
☐2558 29¢ Multicolored	45.00	4.25	.95	.25

1991. WORLD WAR II
☐2559 29¢ Multicolored	16.00	5.00	.85	.60

1991. BASKETBALL: 100TH ANNIVERSARY
☐2560 29¢ Multicolored	50.00	4.50	1.00	.50

1991. DISTRICT OF COLUMBIA: BICENTENNIAL
☐2561 29¢ Multicolored	36.00	3.50	.80	.25

1991. COMEDIANS
☐2562 29¢ Multicolored	—	—	.85	.25
☐2563 29¢ Multicolored	—	—	.85	.25
☐2564 29¢ Multicolored	—	—	.85	.25
☐2565 29¢ Multicolored	—	—	.85	.25
☐2566 29¢ Multicolored	—	—	.85	.25

1991. BLACK HERITAGE
☐2567 29¢ Multicolored	36.00	4.00	.80	.25

*No hinge pricing from 1941 to date is figured at (N-H ADD 10%)

Scott No.	Mint Sheet	Plate Block	Fine Unused Each	Fine Used Each
1991. SPACE EXPLORATION				
☐2568 29¢ Multicolored	—	—	.85	.25
☐2569 29¢ Multicolored	—	—	.85	.25
☐2570 29¢ Multicolored	—	—	.85	.25
☐2571 29¢ Multicolored	—	—	.85	.25
☐2572 29¢ Multicolored	—	—	.85	.25
☐2573 29¢ Multicolored	—	—	.85	.25
☐2574 29¢ Multicolored	—	—	.85	.25
☐2575 29¢ Multicolored	—	—	.85	.25
☐2576 29¢ Multicolored	—	—	.85	.25
☐2577 29¢ Multicolored	—	—	.85	.25
1991. CHRISTMAS				
☐2578 29¢ Multicolored	36.00	3.75	.80	.25
☐2579 29¢ Multicolored	36.00	3.75	.80	.25
☐2582 29¢ Multicolored	36.00	3.75	.80	.25
☐2583 29¢ Multicolored	36.00	3.75	.80	.25
☐2584 29¢ Multicolored	36.00	3.75	.80	.25
☐2585 29¢ Multicolored	36.00	3.75	.80	.25
1992. BULK RATE				
☐2604 10¢ Multicolored	—	3.25	.35	.17
☐2607 23¢ Multicolored	—	6.00	.65	.17
☐2608 23¢ Multicolored	—	6.00	.65	.17
☐2609 29¢ Multicolored	—	6.00	.80	.17
1992. WINTER OLYMPICS				
☐2611 29¢ Multicolored	36.00	12.00	1.00	.17
☐2612 29¢ Multicolored	—	—	1.00	.17
☐2613 29¢ Multicolored	—	—	1.00	.17
☐2614 29¢ Multicolored	—	—	1.00	.17
☐2615 29¢ Multicolored	—	—	1.00	.17
1992. WORLD COLUMBIAN STAMP EXPO				
☐2616 29¢ Multicolored	36.00	3.50	.80	.17

*No hinge pricing from 1941 to date is figured at (N-H ADD 10%)

Scott No.	Mint Sheet	Plate Block	Fine Unused Each	Fine Used Each
1992. BLACK HERITAGE				
☐2617 29¢ Multicolored	34.00	3.50	.80	.17
1992. LOVE				
☐2618 29¢ Multicolored	34.00	3.50	.80	.17
1992. OLYMPIC BASEBALL				
☐2619 29¢ Multicolored	60.00	6.00	1.50	.17
1992. VOYAGES OF COLUMBUS				
☐2620 29¢ Multicolored	38.00	4.25	1.00	.17
☐2621 29¢ Multicolored	38.00	—	1.00	.17
☐2622 29¢ Multicolored	38.00	—	1.00	.17
☐2623 29¢ Multicolored	38.00	—	1.00	.17
1992. NEW YORK STOCK EXCHANGE BICENTENNIAL				
☐2630 29¢ Green, Red & Black				
	30.00	3.50	.85	.17
1992. SPACE ACCOMPLISHMENTS				
☐2631 29¢ Multicolored	40.00	5.00	.95	.17
☐2632 29¢ Multicolored	—	—	.95	.17
☐2633 29¢ Multicolored	—	—	.95	.17
☐2634 29¢ Multicolored	—	—	.95	.17
1992. ALASKA HIGHWAY—50TH ANNIVERSARY				
☐2635 29¢ Multicolored	36.00	3.50	.80	.17
1992. KENTUCKY STATEHOOD BICENTENNIAL				
☐2636 29¢ Multicolored	36.00	3.50	.80	.17
1992. SUMMER OLYMPICS				
☐2637 29¢ Multicolored	34.00	10.50	.95	.17
☐2638 29¢ Multicolored	34.00	10.50	.95	.17
☐2639 29¢ Multicolored	34.00	10.50	.95	.17
☐2640 29¢ Multicolored	34.00	10.50	.95	.17
☐2641 29¢ Multicolored	34.00	10.50	.95	.17

*No hinge pricing from 1941 to date is figured at (N-H ADD 10%)

Scott No.	Mint Sheet	Plate Block	Fine Unused Each	Fine Used Each

1992. HUMMINGBIRDS

Scott No.	Mint Sheet	Plate Block	Fine Unused Each	Fine Used Each
☐2642 29¢ Multicolored	—	—	.95	.17
☐2643 29¢ Multicolored	—	—	.95	.17
☐2644 29¢ Multicolored	—	—	.95	.17
☐2645 29¢ Multicolored	—	—	.95	.17
☐2646 29¢ Multicolored	—	—	.95	.17

1992. WILD FLOWERS

Scott No.	Mint Sheet	Plate Block	Fine Unused Each	Fine Used Each
☐ 29¢ Multicolored	44.00	40.00 (50)	1.25	.50

☐2647 Indian Paintbrush
☐2648 Fragrant Water Lily
☐2649 Meadow Beauty
☐2650 Jack-in-the-Pulpit
☐2651 California Poppy
☐2652 Large Flower Trillium
☐2653 Tickseed
☐2654 Shooting Star
☐2655 Stream Violet
☐2656 Bluets
☐2657 Herb Robert
☐2658 Marsh Marigold
☐2659 Sweet White Violet
☐2660 Claret Cup Cactus
☐2661 White Mountain Avens
☐2662 Sessile Bellwort
☐2663 Blue Flag
☐2664 Harlequin Lupine
☐2665 Twin Flower
☐2666 Common Sunflower
☐2667 Sego Lily
☐2668 Virginia Bluebells
☐2669 Ohi'a Lehua

☐2670 Rosebud Orchid
☐2671 Showy Evening Primrose
☐2672 Fringed Gentian
☐2673 Yellow Lady's Slipper
☐2674 Passion Flower
☐2675 Bunch Berry
☐2676 Pasque Flower
☐2677 Round-Lobed Hepatica
☐2678 Wild Columbine
☐2679 Firewood
☐2680 Indian Pond Lily
☐2681 Turk's Cap Lily
☐2682 Dutchman's Breeches
☐2683 Trumpet Honeysuckle
☐2684 Jacob's Ladder
☐2685 Plains Prickly Pear
☐2686 Mots Campion
☐2687 Bearberry
☐2688 Mexican Hat
☐2689 Harebell
☐2690 Desert Five Spot
☐2691 Smooth Solomon's Seal
☐2692 Red Maids

*No hinge pricing from 1941 to date is figured at (N-H ADD 10%)

☐2693 Yellow Skunk Cabbage   ☐2695 Standing Cypress
☐2694 Rue Anemone   ☐2696 Wild Flax

Scott No.	Mint Sheet	Plate Block	Fine Unused Each	Fine Used Each
1992. WORLD WAR II				
☐2697 29¢ Multicolored	15.00	—	.80	.50
1992. LITERARY ART SERIES				
☐2698 29¢ Multicolored	36.00	3.40	.80	.17
1992. THEODORE VON KÁRMÁN				
☐2699 29¢ Multicolored	36.00	3.40	.80	.17
1992. MINERALS				
☐2700 29¢ Multicolored	38.00	4.25	.95	.17
☐2701 29¢ Multicolored	38.00	4.25	.95	.17
☐2702 29¢ Multicolored	38.00	4.25	.95	.17
☐2703 29¢ Multicolored	38.00	4.25	.95	.17
1992. JUAN RODRÍGUEZ CABRILLO				
☐2704 29¢ Multicolored	36.00	3.75	.80	.17
1992. WILD ANIMALS				
☐2705 29¢ Multicolored	—	—	.95	.17
☐2706 29¢ Multicolored	—	—	.95	.17
☐2707 29¢ Multicolored	—	—	.95	.17
☐2708 29¢ Multicolored	—	—	.95	.17
☐2709 29¢ Multicolored	—	—	.95	.17
☐2709a 29¢ Multicolored Five Above Attached				
	—	—	5.00	.17
1992. MADONNA AND CHILD				
☐2710 29¢ Multicolored	36.00	3.40	.80	.17
1992. GREETINGS—HORSE AND RIDER				
☐2711 29¢ Multicolored	38.00	4.25	.95	.17

*No hinge pricing from 1941 to date is figured at (N-H ADD 10%)

Scott No.	Mint Sheet	Plate Block	Fine Unused Each	Fine Used Each

1992. GREETINGS—TOY LOCOMOTIVE

☐2712 29¢ Multicolored	38.00	4.25	.95	.17

1992. GREETINGS—TOY FIRE PUMPER

☐2713 29¢ Multicolored	38.00	4.25	.95	.17

1992. GREETINGS—RIVERBOAT ON WHEELS

☐2714 29¢ Multicolored	38.00	4.25	.95	.17

1992. HAPPY NEW YEAR

☐2720 29¢ Multicolored	15.00	3.40	.85	.17

1993. ELVIS

☐2721 29¢ Multicolored	28.00	3.75	.80	.17

1993. OKLAHOMA

☐2722 29¢ Multicolored	28.00	3.75	.80	.17

1993. HANK WILLIAMS

☐2723 29¢ Multicolored	28.00	3.75	.80	.17

1993. AMERICAN MUSIC—ELVIS PRESLEY

☐2724 29¢ Multicolored	25.00	9.00 (10)	.80	.17

1993. AMERICAN MUSIC—BILL HALEY

☐2725 29¢ Multicolored	25.00	9.00 (10)	.80	.17

1993. AMERICAN MUSIC—CLYDE McPHATTER

☐2726 29¢ Multicolored	25.00	9.00 (10)	.80	.17

1993. AMERICAN MUSIC—RITCHIE VALENS

☐2727 29¢ Multicolored	25.00	9.00 (10)	.80	.17

1993. AMERICAN MUSIC—OTIS REDDING

☐2728 29¢ Multicolored	25.00	9.00 (10)	.80	.17

1993. AMERICAN MUSIC—BUDDY HOLLY

☐2729 29¢ Multicolored	25.00	9.00 (10)	.80	.17

*No hinge pricing from 1941 to date is figured at (N-H ADD 10%)

Scott No.	Mint Sheet	Plate Block	Fine Unused Each	Fine Used Each

1993. AMERICAN MUSIC—DINAH WASHINGTON

☐2730 29¢ Multicolored	25.00	9.00 (10)	.80	.25

1993. SPACE FANTASY

☐2741 29¢ Multicolored	—	—	.85	.25
☐2742 29¢ Multicolored	—	—	.85	.25
☐2743 29¢ Multicolored	—	—	.85	.25
☐2744 29¢ Multicolored	—	—	.85	.25
☐2745 29¢ Multicolored	—	—	.85	.25

1993. PERCY LAVON JULIAN

☐2746 29¢ Multicolored	36.00	3.50	.80	.25

1993. OREGON TRAIL

☐2747 29¢ Multicolored	36.00	3.50	.80	.25

1993. WORLD UNIVERSITY GAMES

☐2748 29¢ Multicolored	36.00	3.50	.80	.25

1993. GRACE KELLY

☐2749 29¢ Multicolored	36.00	3.50	.80	.25

1993. CIRCUS

☐2750 29¢ Multicolored	32.00	6.50 (6)	.80	.25
☐2751 29¢ Multicolored	32.00	6.50 (6)	.80	.25
☐2752 29¢ Multicolored	32.00	6.50 (6)	.80	.25
☐2753 29¢ Multicolored	32.00	6.50 (6)	.80	.25

1993. CHEROKEE STRIP LAND RUN

☐2754 29¢ Multicolored	34.00	3.50	.80	.25

1993. DEAN ACHESON

☐2755 29¢ Multicolored	34.00	3.50	.80	.25

1993. SPORTING HORSES

☐2756 29¢ Multicolored	36.00	5.00	.95	.25
☐2757 29¢ Multicolored	36.00	5.00	.95	.25

*No hinge pricing from 1941 to date is figured at (N-H ADD 10%)

Scott No.	Mint Sheet	Plate Block	Fine Unused Each	Fine Used Each
☐2758 29¢ Multicolored	36.00	5.00	.95	.25
☐2759 29¢ Multicolored	36.00	5.00	.95	.25

1993. GARDEN FLOWERS

☐2760 29¢ Multicolored	—	—	.95	.25
☐2761 29¢ Multicolored	—	—	.95	.25
☐2762 29¢ Multicolored	—	—	.95	.25
☐2763 29¢ Multicolored	—	—	.95	.25
☐2764 29¢ Multicolored	—	—	.95	.25

1993. WORLD WAR II 1943

☐2765 29¢ Multicolored	15.00	—	.80	.50

1993. JOE LOUIS

☐2766 Multicolored	38.00	4.50	.85	.25

1993. BROADWAY MUSICALS

☐2767 29¢ Multicolored	38.00	4.00	.85	.25
☐2768 29¢ Multicolored	38.00	4.00	.85	.25
☐2769 29¢ Multicolored	38.00	4.00	.85	.25
☐2770 29¢ Multicolored	38.00	4.00	.85	.25

1993. NATIONAL POSTAL MUSEUM

☐2779 29¢ Multicolored	20.00	4.00	.85	.25
☐2780 29¢ Multicolored	20.00	4.00	.85	.25
☐2781 29¢ Multicolored	20.00	4.00	.85	.25
☐2782 29¢ Multicolored	20.00	4.00	.85	.25

1993. MARIANA ISLANDS

☐2804 29¢ Multicolored	15.00	4.00	.85	.25

1993. COLUMBUS LANDING

☐2805 29¢ Multicolored	36.00	4.00	.85	.25

1993. AIDS AWARENESS

☐2806 29¢ Multicolored	36.00	4.00	.85	.25

*No hinge pricing from 1941 to date is figured at (N-H ADD 10%)

Scott No.	Mint Sheet	Plate Block	Fine Unused Each	Fine Used Each

1994. WINTER OLYMPICS

Scott No.	Mint Sheet	Plate Block	Fine Unused Each	Fine Used Each
☐2807 29¢ Multicolored	16.00	9.00	.80	.25
☐2808 29¢ Multicolored	16.00	9.00	.80	.25
☐2809 29¢ Multicolored	16.00	9.00	.80	.25
☐2810 29¢ Multicolored	16.00	9.00	.80	.25
☐2811 29¢ Multicolored	16.00	9.00	.80	.25

1994. EDWARD R. MURROW

☐2812 29¢ Brown	34.00	3.75	.80	.25

1994. LOVE

☐2813 29¢ Multicolored	—	—	.80	.25
☐2814 29¢ Multicolored	—	—	.80	.25
☐2815 52¢ Multicolored	55.00	6.00	1.25	.25

1994. BLACK HERITAGE

☐2816 29¢ Multicolored	16.00	4.00	.80	.25

1994. CHINESE NEW YEAR

☐2817 29¢ Multicolored	15.00	3.50	.80	.25

1994. BUFFALO SOLDIERS

☐2818 29¢ Multicolored	16.00	4.00	.80	.25

1994. SILENT SCREEN STARS

☐2819 29¢ Multicolored	—	—	.85	.25
☐2820 29¢ Multicolored	—	—	.85	.25
☐2821 29¢ Multicolored	—	—	.85	.25
☐2822 29¢ Multicolored	—	—	.85	.25
☐2823 29¢ Multicolored	—	—	.85	.25
☐2824 29¢ Multicolored	—	—	.85	.25
☐2825 29¢ Multicolored	—	—	.85	.25
☐2826 29¢ Multicolored	—	—	.85	.25
☐2827 29¢ Multicolored	—	—	.85	.25
☐2828 29¢ Multicolored	—	—	.85	.25
☐2828a 29¢ Multicolored	32.00	7.00	.85	.25

1994. GARDEN FLOWERS

☐2829 29¢ Multicolored	—	—	.85	.25

*No hinge pricing from 1941 to date is figured at (N-H ADD 10%)

Scott No.	Mint Sheet	Plate Block	Fine Unused Each	Fine Used Each
☐2830 29¢ Multicolored	—	—	.85	.25
☐2831 29¢ Multicolored	—	—	.85	.25
☐2832 29¢ Multicolored	—	—	.85	.25
☐2833 29¢ Multicolored	—	—	.85	.25

1994. WORLD CUP SOCCER

☐2834 29¢ Multicolored	16.00	4.00	.85	.25
☐2835 40¢ Multicolored	20.00	5.00	.90	.25
☐2836 50¢ Multicolored	25.00	6.00	1.25	.25
☐2837 29¢ -40¢ -50¢ Souvenir Sheet				
	—	—	4.00	3.00

1994. WORLD WAR II

☐2838 29¢ Multicolored	15.00	8.00	.85	.50

1994. NORMAN ROCKWELL

☐2839 29¢ Multicolored	35.00	4.00	.85	.25
☐2840 50¢ Multicolored	—	—	5.00	4.00

1994. MOON LANDING ANNIVERSARY

☐2841 29¢ Multicolored	—	—	.95	.75
☐2842 $9.95 Multicolored	400.00	100.00	25.00	14.00

1994. LOCOMOTIVES

☐2843 29¢ Multicolored	—	—	.80	.25
☐2844 29¢ Multicolored	—	—	.80	.25
☐2845 29¢ Multicolored	—	—	.80	.25
☐2846 29¢ Multicolored	—	—	.80	.25
☐2847 29¢ Multicolored	—	—	.80	.25

1994. GEORGE MEANY

☐2848 29¢ Multicolored	34.00	4.00	.85	.25

1995. POPULAR SINGERS

☐2849–53 29¢ Multicolored	14.00	5.00 (10)	.85	.25

1995. JAZZ/BLUES SINGERS

☐2854–61 29¢ Multicolored	23.00	9.00 (10)	.85	.25

1995. JAMES THURBER

☐2862 29¢ Red, Blue, Black	34.00	4.00	.85	.25

*No hinge pricing from 1941 to date is figured at (N-H ADD 10%)

Scott No.	Mint Sheet	Plate Block	Fine Unused Each	Fine Used Each

1995. WONDERS OF THE SEA
| ☐2863–66 29¢ Multicolored | 20.00 | 4.00 | .85 | .25 |

1995. CRANES
| ☐2867–68 29¢ Multicolored | 15.00 | 3.75 | .85 | .25 |

1995. LEGENDS OF THE WEST (SHEET OF 20)
☐2869 29¢ Multicolored	15.00	—	14.00	11.00
Single Stamps			.95	.50
☐2870* 29¢ Multicolored	330.00	—	35.00	20.00

*error sheet Bill Picket recalled.

1995. CHRISTMAS
☐2871 29¢ "Elisabetta Sirani," Multicolored				
	34.00	3.50	.80	.25
☐2872 29¢ Teddy bear stocking, Multicolored				
	34.00	3.50	.80	.25
☐2873 Self-adhesive, 29¢ Santa	—	—	.80	.25
☐2874 Self-adhesive, 29¢ Cardinal	—	—	.80	.25

1995. BUREAU OF PRINTING AND ENGRAVING (SHEET OF 4)
| ☐2875 2¢ Multicolored | — | — | 18.00 | 14.00 |
| Single Stamps | — | — | 4.50 | 2.50 |

1995. YEAR OF THE BOAR
| ☐2876 29¢ Multicolored | 15.00 | 3.75 | .80 | .25 |

1995. DOVES
☐2877 4¢ Tan, Bright Blue, Red G, Make up rate				
	9.00	1.00	.25	.16
☐2878 4¢ Tan, Dark Blue, Red G, Make up rate				
	9.00	1.00	.25	.16

1995. SERIES G STAMP FLAGS
☐2879 20¢ Black G, Yellow, Multicolored				
	50.00	4.00	.60	.16
☐2880 20¢ Red G, Yellow, Multicolored				
	50.00	4.00	.60	.16

*No hinge pricing from 1941 to date is figured at (N-H ADD 10%)

Scott No.	Mint Sheet	Plate Block	Fine Unused Each	Fine Used Each
☐2881 32¢ Black G, White, Multicolored				
	70.00	4.00	.80	.25
☐2882 32¢ Red G, White, Multicolored				
	70.00	4.00	.80	.25
☐2883 Booklet 32¢ Black G, White, Multicolored				
	—	—	.80	.25
☐2884 Booklet 32¢ Blue G, White, Multicolored				
	—	—	.80	.25
☐2885 Booklet 32¢ Red G, White, Multicolored				
	—	—	.80	.25
☐2886 Booklet, Self adhesive 32¢ Black G, White, Multicolored				
	—	—	.80	.25
☐2887 Self adhesive 32¢ Black G, White, Multicolored				
	—	—	.80	.25
☐2888 Coil 25¢ Black G, First class presort, Blue, Multicolored				
	—	6.00	.75	.25
☐2889 Coil 32¢ Black G, White, Multicolored				
	—	6.25	.80	.25
☐2890 Coil 32¢ Blue G, White, Multicolored				
	—	5.25	.80	.25
☐2891 Coil 32¢ Red G, White, Multicolored				
	—	5.25	.80	.25
☐2892 Coil, Rouletted, 32¢ Red G, White, Multicolored				
	—	6.25	.80	.25
☐2893 Coil 5¢ Black G, Non-profit, Green, Multicolored				
	—	2.00	.30	.25
☐2894–96 NOT ISSUED				
☐2897 32¢ Flag over porch, Multicolored				
	65.00	4.00	.80	.25
☐2898–01 NOT ISSUED				
☐2902 Coil 5¢ Butte, Non-Profit, Multicolored				
	—	2.00	.30	.25
☐2903–04 NOT ISSUED				
☐2905 Coil 10¢ Automobile, Bulk rate, Black Orange				
	—	3.00	.30	.25
☐2906–07 NOT ISSUED				
☐2908–09 Coil 15¢ Auto Tailfin, First class presort, Multicolored				
	—	4.00	.50	.25
☐2910 NOT ISSUED				

*No hinge pricing from 1941 to date is figured at (N-H ADD 10%)

Scott No.	Mint Sheet	Plate Block	Fine Unused Each	Fine Used Each
☐2911–12 Coil 25¢ Juke Box, First class presort, Multicolored				
	—	5.00	.80	.45
☐2913–14 Coil 25¢ Flag over porch, Presort, Multicolored				
	—	5.50	.80	.45
☐2915 Self-adhesive, 25¢ Flag over porch, Presort, Multicolored				
	—	8.00	.90	.45
☐2916 Booklet, 25¢ Flag over porch, Presort, Multicolored				
	—	—	.80	.25
☐2917–18 NOT ISSUED				
☐2919 Booklet, Self-adhesive 32¢ Flag over field				
	—	—	.80	.30
☐2920 Booklet, Self-adhesive 32¢ Flag over porch				
	—	—	.80	.30
☐2921–32 NOT ISSUED				

1995. GREAT AMERICAN ISSUE—MILTON HERSHEY

Scott No.	Mint Sheet	Plate Block	Fine Unused Each	Fine Used Each
☐2933 32¢ Brown	65.00	3.50	.80	.25

1996. HUMANITARY—FARLEY

☐2934 32¢ Green	65.00	3.50	.80	.25
☐2935–37 NOT ISSUED				

1995. GREAT AMERICAN ISSUE—RUTH BENEDICT

☐2938 46¢ Red	100.00	5.25	1.10	.30
☐2939 NOT ISSUED				

1995. GREAT AMERICAN ISSUE—ALICE HAMILTON, MD

☐2940 55¢ Green	120.00	6.00	1.40	.28
☐2941–42 NOT ISSUED				

1995. GREAT AMERICAN ISSUE—ALICE PAUL

☐2943 78¢ Purple	165.00	8.50	2.00	.28
☐2944–47 NOT ISSUED				

1995. NON-DENOMINATIONAL LOVE

☐2948 32¢ Multicolored	36.00	3.00	.80	.25
☐2949 Booklet self-adhesive	—	—	.80	.25

1995. FLORIDA STATEHOOD

☐2950 32¢ Multicolored	15.00	3.50	.80	.25

*No hinge pricing from 1941 to date is figured at (N-H ADD 10%)

Scott No.	Mint Sheet	Plate Block	Fine Unused Each	Fine Used Each
1995. KID'S CARE (EARTH DAY)				
☐2951–54 32¢ Multicolored	14.00	3.50	3.00	1.25
1995. RICHARD NIXON				
☐2955 32¢ Multicolored	34.00	3.50	.80	.25
1995. BESSIE COLEMAN				
☐2956 32¢ Black, Red	34.00	3.50	.80	.25
1995. LOVE CHERUB				
☐2957 32¢ Multicolored	34.00	4.00	.80	.25
☐2958 55¢ Multicolored	60.00	—	1.25	.45
☐2959 Booklet 32¢ Multicolored	—	—	.80	.25
☐2960 Self adhesive 55¢ Multicolored				
	—	—	1.25	.45
1995. RECREATIONAL SPORTS				
☐2961–65 32¢ Multicolored	15.00	9.00 (10)	.80	.25
1995. POWs/MIAs				
☐2966 32¢ Multicolored	14.00	4.00	.80	.25
1995. MARILYN MONROE				
☐2967 32¢ Multicolored	16.00	4.00	.80	.25
1995. TEXAS STATEHOOD				
☐2968 32¢ Multicolored	15.00	4.00	.80	.25
1995. GREAT LAKES LIGHTHOUSES				
☐2969–73 Booklet 32¢ Multicolored				
	—	—	4.50	3.75
Single Stamps			.80	.25
1995. UNITED NATIONS				
☐2974 32¢ Light Blue	15.00	3.50	.80	.25
1995. CIVIL WAR (SHEET OF 20 DIFFERENT)				
☐2975 32¢ Multicolored	16.00	—	1.10	.60

*No hinge pricing from 1941 to date is figured at (N-H ADD 10%)

Scott No.	Mint Sheet	Plate Block	Fine Unused Each	Fine Used Each
1995. CAROUSEL HORSES				
☐2976–79 32¢ Multicolored	15.00	3.50	.80	.25
1995. WOMEN'S SUFFERAGE				
☐2980 32¢ Multicolored	30.00	3.50	.80	.25
1995. 1945: WW II VICTORY AT LAST (SHEET OF 10)				
☐2981 32¢ Multicolored	15.00	—	.80	.60
1995. LOUIS ARMSTRONG				
☐2982 32¢ (White 32¢) Multicolored	14.00	4.00	.80	.25
1995. JAZZ MUSICIANS				
☐2983–92 32¢ Multicolored	15.00	8.75 (10)	.80	.45
1995. FALL GARDEN FLOWERS				
☐2993–97 32¢ Multicolored	—	—	.85	.25
1995. EDDIE RICKENBACKER				
☐2998 60¢ Multicolored	68.00	7.00	1.50	.60
1995. REPUBLIC OF PALAU				
☐2999 32¢ Multicolored	34.00	3.50	.80	.25
1995. COMIC STRIP CLASSICS (SHEET OF 20)				
☐3000 32¢ Multicolored	15.00	—	14.00	11.50
Single Stamps			1.00	.60
1995. U.S. NAVAL ACADEMY				
☐3001 32¢ Multicolored	15.00	3.50	.80	.25
1995. TENNESSEE WILLIAMS				
☐3002 32¢ Multicolored	15.00	3.50	.80	.25
1995. HOLIDAY MADONNA AND CHILD				
☐3003 32¢ Multicolored	34.00	3.50	.80	.25
1995. HOLIDAY CHILDREN AND SANTA				
☐3004–07 32¢ Multicolored	35.00	3.50	.80	.25

*No hinge pricing from 1941 to date is figured at (N-H ADD 10%)

Scott No.	Mint Sheet	Plate Block	Fine Unused Each	Fine Used Each
☐3008–11 Self-adhesive	—	—	.80	.25

1995. MIDNIGHT ANGEL
☐3012 Self-adhesive, 32¢ Multicolored	—	—	.80	.25

1995. CHILDREN SLEDDING
☐3013 32¢ Multicolored	—	—	.80	.25
☐3014–18 NOT ISSUED				

1995. ANTIQUE AUTOMOBILES
☐3019–23 32¢ Multicolored	16.00	9.00 (10)	.80	.30

1996. UTAH 1896
☐3024 32¢ Multicolored	32.00	3.50	.80	.30

1996. FLOWER—CROCUS
☐3025 32¢ Multicolored	—	—	.80	.30

1996. FLOWER—WINTER ACONITE
☐3026 32¢ Multicolored	—	—	.80	.30

1996. FLOWER—PANSY
☐3027 32¢ Multicolored	—	—	.80	.30

1996. FLOWER—SNOWDROP
☐3028 32¢ Multicolored	—	—	.80	.30

1996. FLOWER—ANEMONE
☐3029 32¢ Multicolored	—	—	.80	.30

1996. LOVE ANGEL
☐3030 Self-adhesive 32¢ Multicolored	—	—	.80	.30

1996 WOODPECKER
☐3032 2¢ Multicolored	6.00	.85	.40	.30

1996. EASTER BLUEBIRD
☐3033 3¢ Multicolored	9.00	.85	.40	.30

*No hinge pricing from 1941 to date is figured at (N-H ADD 10%)

Scott No.	Mint Sheet	Plate Block	Fine Unused Each	Fine Used Each

1996. AMERICAN KESTREL
| ☐3044 1¢ Multicolored | 6.00 | 1.10 | .30 | .25 |

1996. BLUE JAY
| ☐3048 Self-adhesive 20¢ Multicolored | — | — | .60 | .25 |

1996. YELLOW ROSE
| ☐3049 Self-adhesive 32¢ Multicolored | — | — | .80 | .25 |

1996. BLACK HERITAGE—ERNEST E. JUST: BIOLOGIST
| ☐3058 32¢ Multicolored | 14.00 | 3.50 | .80 | .25 |

1996. SMITHSONIAN INSTITUTION 1846–1996
| ☐3059 32¢ Multicolored | 14.00 | 3.50 | .80 | .25 |

1996. HAPPY NEW YEAR—RAT
| ☐3060 32¢ Multicolored | 14.00 | 3.50 | .80 | .25 |

1996. COMMUNICATION—EADWEARD MUYBRIDGE
| ☐3061 32¢ Multicolored | 14.00 | 3.50 | .80 | .25 |

1996. COMMUNICATION—OTTMAR MERGENTHALER
| ☐3062 32¢ Multicolored | 14.00 | 3.50 | .80 | .25 |

1996. COMMUNICATION—FREDRICK E. IVES
| ☐3063 32¢ Multicolored | 14.00 | 3.50 | .80 | .25 |

1996. COMMUNICATION—WILLIAM DICKSON
| ☐3064 32¢ Multicolored | 14.00 | 3.50 | .80 | .25 |

1996. FULBRIGHT SCHOLARSHIPS
| ☐3065 32¢ Multicolored | 34.00 | 3.50 | .80 | .25 |

1996. PIONEER PILOT—JACQUELINE COCHRAN
| ☐3066 50¢ Multicolored | 55.00 | 5.50 | 1.25 | .30 |

*No hinge pricing from 1941 to date is figured at (N-H ADD 10%)

Scott No.	Mint Sheet	Plate Block	Fine Unused Each	Fine Used Each

1996. MARATHON
☐3067 32¢ Multicolored	14.00	3.50	.80	.25

1996. ATLANTA OLYMPIC GAMES (SHEET OF 20)
☐3068 32¢ Multicolored	16.00	—	15.00	12.00
Single Stamps	—	—	1.00	.60

1996. GEORGIA O'KEEFE
☐3069 32¢ Multicolored	14.00	—	.80	.25

1996. TENNESSEE—1796
☐3070 32¢ Multicolored	34.00	3.50	.80	.25
☐3071 Self-adhesive 32¢ Multicolored				
	—	—	.80	.25

1996. INDIAN—FANCY DANCE
☐3072 32¢ Multicolored	15.00	9.00 (10)	.80	.25

1996. INDIAN—BUTTERFLY DANCE
☐3073 32¢ Multicolored	15.00	9.00 (10)	.80	.25

1996. INDIAN—TRADITIONAL DANCE
☐3074 32¢ Multicolored	15.00	9.00 (10)	.80	.25

1996. INDIAN—RAVEN DANCE
☐3075 32¢ Multicolored	15.00	9.00 (10)	.80	.25

1996. INDIAN—HOOP DANCE
☐3076 32¢ Multicolored	15.00	9.00 (10)	.80	.25

1996. PREHISTORIC ANIMALS—EOHIPPUS
☐3077 32¢ Multicolored	16.00	3.50	.80	.25

1996. PREHISTORIC ANIMALS—WOOLY MAMMOTH
☐3078 32¢ Multicolored	16.00	3.50	.80	.25

1996. PREHISTORIC ANIMALS—MASTODON
☐3079 32¢ Multicolored	16.00	3.50	.80	.25

*No hinge pricing from 1941 to date is figured at (N-H ADD 10%)

Scott No.	Mint Sheet	Plate Block	Fine Unused Each	Fine Used Each

1996. PREHISTORIC ANIMALS—SABER-TOOTH CAT

☐3080 32¢ Multicolored	16.00	3.50	.80	.25

1996. BREAST CANCER AWARENESS

☐3082 32¢ Multicolored	15.00	3.50	.80	.25

1996. JAMES DEAN

☐3082 32¢ Multicolored	15.00	3.50	.80	.25

1996. FOLK HEROES—MIGHTY CASEY

☐3083 32¢ Multicolored	15.00	3.50	.80	.25

1996. FOLK HEROES—PAUL BUNYAN

☐3084 32¢ Multicolored	15.00	3.50	.80	.25

1996. FOLK HEROES—JOHN HENRY

☐3085 32¢ Multicolored	15.00	3.50	.80	.25

1996. FOLK HEROES—PECOS BILL

☐3086 32¢ Multicolored	15.00	3.50	.80	.25

1996. CENTENNIAL OLYMPIC GAMES—DISCUS THROWER

☐3087 32¢ Brown/Black	15.00	3.50	.80	.25

1996. IOWA—1846

☐3088 Water-adhesive 32¢ Multicolored	32.00	3.50	.80	.25
☐3089 Self-adhesive 32¢ Multicolored	—	—	.80	.25

1996. RURAL FREE DELIVERY—RFD

☐3090 32¢ Multicolored	32.00	3.50	.80	.25

1996. RIVERBOATS—ROBT. E. LEE

☐3091 Self-adhesive 32¢ Multicolored	13.75	9.00 (10)	.80	.25

1996. RIVERBOATS—SYLVAN DELL

☐3092 Self-adhesive 32¢ Multicolored	13.75	9.00 (10)	.80	.25

*No hinge pricing from 1941 to date is figured at (N-H ADD 10%)

Scott No.	Mint Sheet	Plate Block	Fine Unused Each	Fine Used Each

1996. RIVERBOATS—FAR WEST
☐3093 Self-adhesive 32¢ Multicolored

| | 13.75 | 9.00 (10) | .80 | .25 |

1996. RIVERBOATS—REBECCA EVERINGHAM
☐3094 Self-adhesive 32¢ Multicolored

| | 13.75 | — | .80 | .25 |

1996. RIVERBOATS—BAILEY GATZERT
☐3095 Self-adhesive 32¢ Multicolored

| | 13.75 | — | .80 | .25 |

1996. BIG BAND LEADERS—COUNT BASIE: PIANIST AND BANDLEADER
☐3096 32¢ Multicolored 15.00 3.50 .80 .25

1996. BIG BAND LEADERS—TOMMY & JIMMY DORSEY: BANDLEADERS
☐3097 32¢ Multicolored 15.00 3.50 .80 .25

1996. BIG BAND LEADERS—GLEN MILLER: TROMBONIST AND BANDLEADER
☐3098 32¢ Multicolored 15.00 3.50 .80 .25

1996. BIG BAND LEADERS—BENNY GOODMAN: CLARINETIST AND BANDLEADER
☐3099 32¢ Multicolored 15.00 3.50 .80 .25

1996. SONGWRITERS—HAROLD ARLEN: COMPOSER
☐3100 32¢ Multicolored 15.00 3.50 .80 .25

1996. SONGWRITERS—JOHNNY MERCER: LYRICIST
☐3101 32¢ Multicolored 15.00 3.50 .80 .25

1996. SONGWRITERS—DOROTHY FIELDS: LYRICIST
☐3102 32¢ Multicolored 15.00 3.50 .80 .25

*No hinge pricing from 1941 to date is figured at (N-H ADD 10%)

Scott No.	Mint Sheet	Plate Block	Fine Unused Each	Fine Used Each
1996. SONGWRITERS—HOAGY CHARMICHAEL: COMPOSER				
☐3103 32¢ Multicolored	15.00	3.50	.80	.25
1996. F. SCOTT FITZGERALD				
☐3104 23¢ Multicolored	32.00	3.50	.80	.25
1996. ENDANGERED SPECIES (SHEET OF 15)				
☐3105 32¢ Multicolored	12.00	—	12.00	9.00
Single Stamps	—	—	1.00	.50
1996. COMPUTER TECHNOLOGY				
☐3106 32¢ Multicolored	30.00	3.50	.80	.25
1996. MADONNA AND CHILD				
☐3107 Water-adhesive 32¢ Multicolored	32.00	3.50	.80	.25
1996. CHRISTMAS FAMILY SCENES—FIREPLACE				
☐3108 Self-adhesive 32¢ Multicolored	32.00	3.50	.80	.25
1996. CHRISTMAS FAMILY SCENES—TREE				
☐3109 Self-adhesive 32¢ Multicolored	32.00	3.50	.80	.25
1996. CHRISTMAS FAMILY SCENES—DREAMING				
☐3110 Self-adhesive 32¢ Multicolored	32.00	3.50	.80	.25
1996. CHRISTMAS FAMILY SCENES—SHOPPING				
☐3111 Self-adhesive 32¢ Multicolored	32.00	3.50	.80	.25
1996. MADONNA AND CHILD				
☐3112 Self-adhesive 32¢ Multicolored	—	—	.80	.25

☐3113–3116 NOT ISSUED

*No hinge pricing from 1941 to date is figured at (N-H ADD 10%)

Scott No.	Mint Sheet	Plate Block	Fine Unused Each	Fine Used Each

1996. SKATERS

	Mint Sheet	Plate Block	Fine Unused Each	Fine Used Each
☐3117 32¢ Multicolored	—	—	.80	.25

1996. HANUKKAH

☐3118 Self-adhesive 32¢ Multicolored	15.00	—	.80	.25

1996. CYCLING (SHEET OF 2)

☐3119 32¢ Multicolored	—	—	2.50	1.00

1997. YEAR OF THE OX

☐3120 32¢ Multicolored	15.00 (20)	3.50 (4)	.85	.25

1997. BENJAMIN O. DAVIS, SR.

☐3121 Self-adhesive 32¢ Multicolored	15.00 (20)	3.50 (4)	.85	.25

1997. STATUE OF LIBERTY

☐3122 Self-adhesive 32¢ Multicolored	—	—	.85	.25

1997. SWANS

☐3123 Self-adhesive 32¢ Multicolored	—	—	.85	.25

1997. SWANS

☐3124 Self-adhesive 55¢ Multicolored	—	—	1.50	.50

1997. HELPING CHILDREN LEARN

☐3125 Self-adhesive 32¢ Multicolored	15.00 (20)	3.50 (4)	.85	.25

1997. MERIAN BOTANICAL PRINT—CITRON (FROM PANE OF 20)

☐3126 Self-adhesive 32¢ Multicolored	—	—	.85	.25

*No hinge pricing from 1941 to date is figured at (N-H ADD 10%)

Scott No.	Mint Sheet	Plate Block	Fine Unused Each	Fine Used Each

1997. MERIAN BOTANICAL PRINT—FLOWERING PINEAPPLE (PANE OF 20)
☐3127 Self-adhesive 32¢ Multicolored

	—	—	.85	.25

1997. MERIAN BOTANICAL PRINT—CITRON (FROM BOOK OF 15)
☐3128 Self-adhesive 32¢ Multicolored

	—	—	.85	.25

1997. MERIAN BOTANICAL PRINT—FLOWERING PINEAPPLE (FROM BOOK OF 15)
☐3129 Self-adhesive 32¢ Multicolored

	—	—	.85	.25

1997. SHIP PACIFIC 1997
☐3130 32¢ Blue

	—	—	.85	.25

1997. STAGECOACH PACIFIC 1997
☐3131 32¢ Red

	—	—	.85	.25

1997. JUKEBOX (EXPERIMENTAL LINERLESS COIL)
☐3132 Self-adhesive 25¢ Multicolored

	—	—	.60	.20

1997. FLAG OVER PORCH (EXPERIMENTAL LINERLESS COIL)
☐3133 Self-adhesive 32¢ Multicolored

	—	—	.60	.20

1997. THORNTON WILDER

☐3134 32¢ Multicolored	15.00 (20)	3.50 (4)	.85	.25

1997. RAOUL WALLENBERG

☐3135 32¢ Multicolored	15.00 (20)	3.50 (4)	.85	.25

*No hinge pricing from 1941 to date is figured at (N-H ADD 10%)

Scott No.	Mint Sheet	Plate Block	Fine Unused Each	Fine Used Each

1997. DINOSAURS (15 VARIETIES)
☐3136 32¢ Multicolored   28.00 (15)   —   1.20   .80
(1)Ceratosaurus, (2)Camptosaurus, (3)Camarasaurus,
(4)Brachiosaurus, (5)Goniopholis, (6)Stegosaurus, (7)Allosaurus,
(8)Ophisthias, (9)Edmontonia, (10)Einiosaurus,
(11)Daspletosaurus, (12)Palaeosaniwa, (13)Corythosaurus,
(14)Ornithomimus, (15)Parasaurolophus

1997. BUGS BUNNY
☐3137 Self-adhesive 32¢ Multicolored
  45.00   —   .85   .25

1997. BUGS BUNNY (DIE-CUT)
☐3138 Self-adhesive 32¢ Multicolored
  8.00   —   .85   .25

1997. BENJAMIN FRANKLIN
☐3139 50¢ Multicolored   14.00 (12)   —   1.50   1.00

1997. GEORGE WASHINGTON
☐3140 60¢ Multicolored   18.00 (12)   —   1.50   1.00

1997. MARSHALL PLAN
☐3141 32¢ Multicolored   15.00 (20)   3.50 (4)   .85   .25

997. CLASSIC AMERICAN AIRCRAFT (20 VARIETIES)
☐3142 32¢ Multicolored   16.00 (20)   —   .85   .25
(1)Mustang, (2)Model B, (3)Cub, (4)Vega, (5)Alpha, (6)B-10,
(7)Corsair, (8)Stratojet, (9)GeeBee, (10)Staggerwing, (11)Flying Fortress, (12)Stearman, (13)Constellation, (14)Lightning, (15)Peashooter, (16)Tri-Motor, (17)DC-3, (18)Clipper, (19)Jenny, (20)Wildcat

1997. PAUL "BEAR" BRYANT
☐3143 32¢ Multicolored   —   —   .85   .25

1997. GLEN "POP" WARNER
☐3144 32¢ Multicolored   —   —   .85   .25
*No hinge pricing from 1941 to date is figured at (N-H ADD 10%)

Scott No.	Mint Sheet	Plate Block	Fine Unused Each	Fine Used Each

1997. VINCE LOMBARDI

☐3145 32¢ Multicolored — — .85 .25

1997. GEORGE HALAS

☐3146 32¢ Multicolored — — .85 .25

1997. VINCE LOMBARDI (RED STRIPE)

☐3147 32¢ Multicolored — — .85 .25

1997. PAUL "BEAR" BRYANT (RED STRIPE)

☐3148 32¢ Multicolored — — .85 .25

1997. GLEN "POP" WARNER

☐3149 32¢ Multicolored — — .85 .25

1997. GEORGE HALAS

☐3150 32¢ Multicolored — — .85 .25

1997. CLASSIC AMERICAN DOLLS (15 VARIETIES)

☐3151 32¢ Multicolored 16.00 (15) — .85 .25

(1)"Alabama Baby" and Martha Chase, (2)"The Columbian Doll," (3)Johnny Gruelle's "Raggedy Ann," (4)Martha Chase, (5)"American Child," (6)"Baby Coos," (7)Plains Indian, (8)Izannah Walker, (9)"Babyland Rag," (10)"Scooties," (11)Ludwig Greiner, (12)"Betsy McCall," (13)Percy Cosby's "Skippy," (14)"Maggie Mix-up," (15)Albert Schoenhut.

1997. HUMPHREY BOGART

☐3152 32¢ Multicolored 14.00 (20) 3.50 (4) .85 .25

1997. THE STARS AND STRIPES FOREVER

☐3153 32¢ Multicolored 35.00 (50) 3.50 (4) .85 .25

1997. LEGENDS OF AMERICAN MUSIC SERIES— OPERA SINGERS (4 VARIETIES)

☐32¢ Multicolored 14.00 (20) 3.50 (4) — —

*No hinge pricing from 1941 to date is figured at (N-H ADD 10%)

Scott No.	Mint Sheet	Plate Block	Fine Unused Each	Fine Used Each

1997. OPERA SINGERS—LILY PONS

Scott No.	Mint Sheet	Plate Block	Fine Unused Each	Fine Used Each
☐3154 32¢ Multicolored	—	—	.85	.25

1997. OPERA SINGERS—RICHARD TUCKER

☐3155 32¢ Multicolored	—	—	.85	.25

1997. OPERA SINGERS—LAWRENCE TIBBETT

☐3156 32¢ Multicolored	—	—	.85	.25

1997. OPERA SINGERS—ROSA PONSELLE

☐3157 32¢ Multicolored	—	—	.85	.25

1997. COMPOSERS AND CONDUCTORS (8 VARIETIES)

☐32¢ Multicolored	14.00 (20)	7.50 (8)	—	—

1997. COMPOSERS AND CONDUCTORS— LEOPOLD STOKOWSKI

☐3158 32¢ Multicolored	—	—	.80	.20

1997. COMPOSERS AND CONDUCTORS— ARTHUR FIEDLER

☐3159 32¢ Multicolored	—	—	.80	.20

1997. COMPOSERS AND CONDUCTORS— GEORGE SZELL

☐3160 32¢ Multicolored	—	—	.80	.20

1997. COMPOSERS AND CONDUCTORS— EUGENE ORMANDY

☐3161 32¢ Multicolored	—	—	.80	.20

1997. COMPOSERS AND CONDUCTORS— SAMUEL BARBER

☐3162 32¢ Multicolored	—	—	.80	.20

*No hinge pricing from 1941 to date is figured at (N-H ADD 10%)

Scott No.	Mint Sheet	Plate Block	Fine Unused Each	Fine Used Each

1997. COMPOSERS AND CONDUCTORS—FERDE GROFÉ

☐3163 32¢ Multicolored	—	—	.80	.20

1997. COMPOSERS AND CONDUCTORS—CHARLES IVES

☐3164 32¢ Multicolored	—	—	.80	.20

1997. COMPOSERS AND CONDUCTORS—LOUIS MOREAU GOTTSCHALK

☐3165 32¢ Multicolored	—	—	.80	.20

1997. PADRE FÉLIX VARELA

☐3166 32¢ Multicolored	15.00 (20)	3.50 (4)	.80	.20

1997. U. S. DEPARTMENT OF AIR FORCE (1947–1997)

☐3167 32¢ Multicolored	14.00 (20)	3.50 (4)	.70	.20

1997. CLASSIC MOVIE MONSTERS (4 VARIETIES)

☐32¢ Multicolored	15.00 (20)	3.50 (4)	—	—

1997. CLASSIC MOVIE MONSTERS—PHANTOM OF THE OPERA

☐3168 32¢ Multicolored	—	—	.70	.20

1997. CLASSIC MOVIE MONSTERS—DRACULA

☐3169 32¢ Multicolored	—	—	.70	.20

1997. CLASSIC MOVIE MONSTERS—FRANKENSTEIN

☐3170 32¢ Multicolored	—	—	.70	.20

1997. CLASSIC MOVIE MONSTERS—THE MUMMY

☐3171 32¢ Multicolored	—	—	.70	.20

1997. CLASSIC MOVIE MONSTERS—WOLF MAN

☐3172 32¢ Multicolored	—	—	.70	.20

*No hinge pricing from 1941 to date is figured at (N-H ADD 10%)

Scott No.	Mint Sheet	Plate Block	Fine Unused Each	Fine Used Each

1997. SUPERSONIC FLIGHT
☐3173 Self-adhesive 32¢ Multicolored

| | 14.00 (20) | 3.50 (4) | .70 | .20 |

1997. WOMEN IN MILITARY
☐3174 32¢ Multicolored | 14.00 (20) | 3.50 (4) | .70 | .20 |

1997. KWANZAA
☐3175 Self-adhesive 32¢ Multicolored

| | 25.00 (50) | 3.50 (4) | .70 | .20 |

1997. MADONNA AND CHILD
☐3176 Self-adhesive 32¢ Multicolored

| | 14.00 (20) | — | .70 | .20 |

1997. AMERICAN HOLLY
☐3177 Self-adhesive 32¢ Multicolored

| | 14.00 (20) | — | .70 | .20 |

*No hinge pricing from 1941 to date is figured at (N-H ADD 10%)

AIRMAIL STAMPS

THE AMERICAN AIR MAIL SOCIETY

The American Air Mail Society, organized in 1923, is one of the oldest and largest aerophilatelic societies in existence. The dues are as low as possible; privileges and services to members are many. It is not necessary that a person be an advanced collector or a wealthy specialist to attain membership—or to enjoy aerophilately to its fullest extent. Over twenty AAMS chapters and study units offer members a chance to interact either by mail or at regular meetings held throughout the United States. With two national meetings per year, the AAMS makes it possible for members and friends to meet each year in different parts of the United States. For three days or more the subject is always airmail stamps and covers, as well as the plans and progress of the AAMS itself.

The Airpost Journal (APJ) has been supported and published by the AAMS since October 1931. The *APJ* is a generously illustrated magazine covering a wide range of aerophilately. AAMS news appears regularly to keep members apprised of the organization. Feature articles, written by leading scholars in each field, are published each month covering areas of worldwide interest. Regular columns of a continuing interest include areas such as astrophilately, air postal stationery, auction results, first flight cover news, new airmail stamp issues, show news, Zeppelin posts, book reviews, and members exchange ads.

The *Jack Knight Air Log (JKAL)* became an AAMS publication after the 1995 merger of the AAMS and the Aerophilatelic Federation of the Americas. This diverse 100-page publication includes an auction of airmail material, reports and research studies by various airmail specialty groups, and member exchange ads. AAMS study units on Canadian

Air Mails, Lindbergh, 1934 Emergency Air Mail, Pan American Airlines, Rocket Mail, and Zeppelin posts publish regular sections in the *JKAL*.

The AAMS is one of the world's largest and most successful publishers of airmail literature. The *American Air Mail Catalogue (AAMC)* has been published since 1935. Other AAMS handbooks and monographs treat a variety of specialist U.S. and foreign airmail topics, from pioneer airmails worldwide to specialty topics. Members receive a discount on many of these handbooks. To receive a list of current publications for sale, write the AAMS Publications Sales Manager, 1978 Fox Burrow Court, Neenah, WI 54956.

Please join with us to bring airmail into the 21st century as a continuing, exciting hobby! For a membership application, write to: The American Air Mail Society, P.O. Box 110, Mineola, NY 11501-0110.

COLLECTING AIRMAIL STAMPS
by Ken Kobersteen

Airmail stamps can provide a fascinating, aesthetically pleasing, historically informative topic for the collector. You can build a collection of airmail stamps which is as broad as a single copy of every airmail stamp which has been issued worldwide, or as narrow as a specialized look at a single series or a single issue. Airmail postcards, stationery, and aerogrammes provide yet another area of specialization.

A collection of worldwide airmail stamps will show not only the development of aircraft and air-related events, but also will show how the airmail service developed worldwide. So too, will the collection of a single country's airmail issues tell the story of the development of airmail in that country. In the case of the United States, for instance, the development of the airmail both domestically and internationally, and the rates for this service, can be traced through a collection of U.S. airmail stamps.

You can also specialize in a single series, such as the U.S. Transport issue of the early 1940s, or a single stamp such as the Beacon airmail stamp of 1928. At first glance you might assume such specialization would limit your collecting options. Quite the contrary. After avidly collecting the Beacon airmail stamp for over fifteen years, one continually finds new material in usages on covers and in an extensive representation of the stamps.

A first step in building such a specialized collection of a single issue or series is to consult catalogues and specialized literature. *The American Air Mail Catalogue, Scott's Specialized U.S. Stamp Catalogue*, and Max. G. Johl's *The United States Postage Stamp of the Twentieth Century, Volume III,* will indicate plate positions, recuts, varieties, and errors which have been found by other specialists. Many aerophilatelists have published works based on their research; a search of the philatelic literature will reveal new information in a variety of areas. It is extremely gratifying to make a discovery that has been overlooked by earlier experts.

You might begin with the design itself, researching its origins. Essays of some stamps may be on the market, others exist only in the archives of the Bureau of Engraving and Printing in Washington, D.C.

Mint stamps can be obtained showing various plate positions, guide lines, plate numbers, and other marginal markings, as well as sideographer and plate finisher's initials—if they occur on the issue being studied.

It is also important to learn about the appropriate printing and perforating processes to analyze production varieties of the stamp or stamps in question. As you look at more copies of the stamp, you will find slight variations due to production differences. The archives of the Bureau of Engraving and Printing contain a wealth of information about the production of United States issues.

Used copies of airmail stamps offer unusual and interesting cancellations with numerous possibilities: fancy cancels, slogan cancels, socked-on-the-nose cancels, numeral cancels, paquebot and foreign cancels—the list is nearly endless. You can also search for stamps with perforated insignia or perfins and precancels. Many pleasant hours can be had pouring over dealers' stocks or large lots of relatively common stamps. And, when mounted, the display of various cancellation varieties can be impressive.

Once you feel you have exhausted the possibilities of your stamp study, keep looking, and examine other stamp exhibits for ideas of new directions to pursue. You can always find more fascinating material to add to your stamp collection, and through study and scholarship you can contribute to the overall body of knowledge of your specialty.

Scott No.	Fine Unused Plate Blk	Ave. Unused Plate Blk	Fine Unused Each	Ave. Unused Each	Fine Used Each	Ave. Used Each

AIRMAIL STAMPS
1918. FIRST ISSUE—(N-H ADD 45%)

☐C1 6¢ Orange

| | 900.00 | 600.00 | 100.00 | 75.00 | 35.00 | 22.00 |

☐C2 16¢ Green

| | 1500.00 | 1200.00 | 120.00 | 100.00 | 38.00 | 26.00 |

☐C3 24¢ Carmine & Blue

| | 1800.00 | 1400.00 | 110.00 | 85.00 | 50.00 | 28.00 |

1923. SECOND ISSUE—(N-H ADD 35%)

☐C4 8¢ Dark Green

| | 400.00 | 300.00 | 40.00 | 24.00 | 16.00 | 12.00 |

☐C5 16¢ Dark Blue

| | 2500.00 | 1800.00 | 110.00 | 75.00 | 45.00 | 32.00 |

☐C6 24¢ Carmine

| | 3000.00 | 2200.00 | 130.00 | 85.00 | 35.00 | 25.00 |

1926–1927. LONG MAP (N-H ADD 35%)

☐C7 10¢ Dark Blue

| | 60.00 | 40.00 | 3.25 | 2.50 | .45 | .30 |

☐C8 15¢ Olive Brown

| | 70.00 | 50.00 | 3.75 | 3.00 | 2.30 | 1.90 |

☐C9 20¢ Yellow Green

| | 120.00 | 80.00 | 10.00 | 7.50 | 1.90 | 1.60 |

1927. LINDBERGH TRIBUTE ISSUE (N-H ADD 25%)

☐C10 10¢ Dark Blue

| | 180.00 | 120.00 | 8.75 | 6.00 | 2.30 | 1.40 |

1928. BEACON (N-H ADD 20%)

☐C11 5¢ Carmine & Blue

| | 60.00 | 35.00 | 4.00 | 3.00 | .60 | .30 |

1930. WINGED GLOBE—FLAT PRESS (N-H ADD 35%)

☐C12 5¢ Violet

| | 200.00 | 150.00 | 10.00 | 8.00 | .45 | .30 |

1930. GRAF ZEPPELIN ISSUE (N-H ADD 20%)

☐C13 65¢ Green

| | 2300.00 | 2000.00 | 300.00 | 240.00 | 230.00 | 200.00 |

Scott No.	Fine Unused Plate Blk	Ave. Unused Plate Blk	Fine Unused Each	Ave. Unused Each	Fine Used Each	Ave. Used Each
☐C14 $1.30 Brown						
	6200.00	5000.00	800.00	600.00	550.00	450.00
☐C15 $2.60 Blue						
	10,000.00	8000.00	1200.00	850.00	700.00	600.00

1931–1932.
WINGED GLOBE—ROTARY PRESS (N-H ADD 25%)

☐C16 5¢ Violet						
	150.00	110.00	6.00	3.80	.60	.35
☐C17 8¢ Olive Bistre						
	50.00	36.00	2.40	1.80	.30	.24

1933. CENTURY OF PROGRESS ISSUE
(N-H ADD 25%)

☐C18 50¢ Green						
	900.00	750.00	100.00	80.00	81.00	55.00

1934. DESIGN OF 1930 (N-H ADD 25%)

☐C19 6¢ Orange						
	35.00	25.00	2.70	2.10	.20	.15

1935–1937. TRANS-PACIFIC ISSUE
(N-H ADD 10%)

☐C20 25¢ Blue						
	30.00	22.00	1.30	1.00	.95	.75
☐C21 20¢ Green						
	130.00	100.00	9.00	7.00	1.75	1.30
☐C22 50¢ Carmine						
	130.00	100.00	12.00	9.00	4.75	3.20

1938. EAGLE (N-H ADD 20%)

☐C23 6¢ Blue & Carmine						
	8.00	6.50	.50	.36	.21	.15

1939. TRANS-ATLANTIC (N-H ADD 20%)

☐C24 30¢ Dull Blue						
	170.00	135.00	11.00	9.00	1.50	1.00

Scott No.	Mint Sheet	Plate Block	Fine Unused Each	Fine Used Each
1941–1944. TRANSPORT PLANE*				
☐C25 6¢ Carmine				
	8.50	.80	.18	.15
☐C26 8¢ Olive Green				
	12.00	2.00	.18	.15
☐C27 10¢ Violet				
	85.00	10.00	1.20	.15
☐C28 15¢ Brown Carmine				
	160.00	12.00	3.00	.50
☐C29 20¢ Bright Green				
	120.00	11.00	2.75	.40
☐C30 30¢ Blue	150.00	13.00	3.00	.40
☐C31 50¢ Orange				
	700.00	75.00	14.00	5.00
1946–1947. DC-4 SKYMASTER*				
☐C32 5¢ Carmine	8.00	.75	.24	.15
☐C33 5¢ Carmine	15.00	.75	.24	.15
1947. REGULAR ISSUE*				
☐C34 10¢ Black	14.00	1.50	.32	.15
☐C35 15¢ Bright Blue Green	20.00	2.00	.46	.15
☐C36 25¢ Blue	55.00	5.00	1.00	.15

Scott No.	Fine Unused Line Pair	Ave. Unused Line Pair	Fine Unused Each	Ave. Unused Each	Fine Used Each	Ave. Used Each
1948. DESIGN OF 1947*						
☐C37 5¢ Carmine						
	10.00	8.50	1.00	.85	.95	.60

Scott No.	Mint Sheet	Plate Block	Fine Unused Each	Fine Used Each
1948. NEW YORK CITY JUBILEE ISSUE*				
☐C38 5¢ Red	20.00	5.00	.23	.16

*No hinge pricing from 1941 to date is figured at (N-H ADD 10%)

Scott No.	Mint Sheet	Plate Block	Fine Unused Each	Fine Used Each

1949. DESIGN OF 1947*
☐C39 6¢ Carmine   15.00   .80   .23   .16

1949. ALEXANDRIA BICENTENNIAL*
☐C40 6¢ Carmine   8.00   .70   .23   .16

Scott No.	Fine Unused Line Pair	Ave. Unused Line Pair	Fine Unused Each	Ave. Unused Each	Fine Used Each	Ave. Used Each

1949. DESIGN OF 1947*
☐C41 6¢ Carmine

    14.00   11.00   3.40   2.70   .23   .16

Scott No.	Mint Sheet	Plate Block	Fine Unused Each	Fine Used Each

1949. U.P.U.—UNIVERSAL POSTAL UNION ISSUE*
☐C42 10¢ Purple   15.00   1.75   .32   .27
☐C43 15¢ Ultramarine   20.00   1.90   .40   .35
☐C44 25¢ Carmine   40.00   7.00   .50   .40

1949. WRIGHT BROTHERS ISSUE*
☐C45 6¢ Magenta   10.00   .60   .20   .16

1952. HAWAII—DIAMOND HEAD*
☐C46 80¢ Bright Red Violet   400.00   32.00   7.00   1.40

1953. 50TH ANNIVERSARY POWERED FLIGHT*
☐C47 6¢ Carmine   8.00   .60   .20   .16

1954. EAGLE IN FLIGHT*
☐C48 4¢ Bright Blue   14.00   2.00   .23   .16
*No hinge pricing from 1941 to date is figured at (N-H ADD 10%)

Scott No.	Mint Sheet	Plate Block	Fine Unused Each	Fine Used Each

1957. 50TH ANNIVERSARY AIR FORCE*

☐ C49 6¢ Blue	8.00	.75	.23	.16

1958. DESIGN OF 1954*

☐ C50 5¢ Red	15.00	1.50	.23	.16

1958. JETLINER SILHOUETTE*

☐ C51 7¢ Blue	18.00	.80	.23	.16

Scott No.	Fine Unused Line Pair	Ave. Unused Line Pair	Fine Unused Each	Ave. Unused Each	Fine Used Each	Ave. Used Each
☐ C52 7¢ Blue	18.00	15.00	2.10	1.75	.23	.16

1959. COMMEMORATIVES*

Scott No.	Mint Sheet	Plate Block	Fine Unused Each	Fine Used Each

1959. ALASKA STATEHOOD*

☐ C53 7¢ Dark Blue	8.00	.70	.20	.16

1959. BALLOON JUPITER FLIGHT*

☐ C54 7¢ Dark Blue & Red	8.00	.70	.20	.16

1959. HAWAII STATEHOOD*

☐ C55 7¢ Rose Red	8.00	.70	.20	.16

1959. PAN AMERICAN GAMES*

☐ C56 10¢ Red & Blue	14.00	1.50	.28	.16

*No hinge pricing from 1941 to date is figured at (N-H ADD 10%)

Scott No.	Mint Sheet	Plate Block	Fine Unused Each	Fine Used Each

1959–1961. REGULAR ISSUE*

Scott No.		Mint Sheet	Plate Block	Fine Unused Each	Fine Used Each
☐C57 10¢ Black & Green		90.00	7.00	1.25	1.00
☐C58 15¢ Black & Orange		28.00	1.75	.40	.16
☐C59 25¢ Black & Maroon		32.00	2.00	.50	.16

1960. DESIGN OF 1958*

	Mint Sheet	Plate Block	Fine Unused Each	Fine Used Each
☐C60 7¢ Carmine	18.00	.70	.20	.16

Scott No.	Fine Unused Line Pair	Ave. Unused Line Pair	Fine Unused Each	Ave. Unused Each	Fine Used Each	Ave. Used Each
☐C61 7¢ Carmine	42.00	35.00	5.50	4.00	.32	.24

Scott No.	Mint Sheet	Plate Block	Fine Unused Each	Fine Used Each

1961. DESIGNS OF 1959–1960*

Scott No.	Mint Sheet	Plate Block	Fine Unused Each	Fine Used Each
☐C62 13¢ Black & Red	22.00	2.00	.40	.16
☐C63 15¢ Black & Orange	18.00	1.25	.40	.16

1962. JETLINER OVER CAPITOL*

	Mint Sheet	Plate Block	Fine Unused Each	Fine Used Each
☐C64 8¢ Carmine	24.00	1.00	.26	.16

Scott No.	Fine Unused Line Pair	Ave. Unused Line Pair	Fine Unused Each	Ave. Unused Each	Fine Used Each	Ave. Used Each
☐C65 8¢ Carmine	7.00	6.00	.51	.36	.22	.14

*No hinge pricing from 1941 to date is figured at (N-H ADD 10%)

Scott No.	Mint Sheet	Plate Block	Fine Unused Each	Fine Used Each

1963. FIRST INTERNATIONAL POSTAL CONFERENCE CENTENARY*
☐C66 15¢ Dull Red, Dark Brown & Blue

| | 36.00 | 3.50 | .60 | .50 |

1963. POSTAL CARD RATE*
☐C67 6¢ Red

| | 22.00 | 2.00 | .25 | .15 |

1963. AMELIA EARHART*
☐C68 8¢ Carmine & Maroon

| | 12.00 | 1.00 | .30 | .16 |

1964. DR. ROBERT H. GODDARD*
☐C69 8¢ Blue, Red, Bistre 24.00 2.30 .55 .19

1967.
1967. ALASKA PURCHASE CENTENARY*
☐C70 8¢ Dark Brown 15.00 2.00 .35 .20

1967. COLUMBIA JAYS*
☐C71 20¢ Blue, Brown, Bistre

| | 52.00 | 5.00 | 1.10 | .16 |

1967. 50 STARS*
☐C72 10¢ Carmine 28.00 1.25 .33 .16

Scott No.	Fine Unused Line Pair	Ave. Unused Line Pair	Fine Unused Each	Ave. Unused Each	Fine Used Each	Ave. Used Each

1968. 50 STARS*
☐C73 10¢ Carmine

| | 2.45 | 2.00 | .45 | .32 | .18 | .15 |

1968. 50TH ANNIVERSARY AIRMAIL SERVICE*
☐C74 10¢ Black, Blue, Red 20.00 3.15 .36 .16

1968. U.S.A.*
☐C75 20¢ Red, Blue, Black 30.00 3.00 .70 .18

*No hinge pricing from 1941 to date is figured at (N-H ADD 10%)

Scott No.	Fine Unused Line Pair	Ave. Unused Line Pair	Fine Unused Each	Ave. Unused Each	Fine Used Each	Ave. Used Each
1969. FIRST MAN ON THE MOON*						
☐C76 10¢ Red, Blue, Brown		10.50	2.00		.45	.18
1971–1973.						
☐C77 9¢ Red		21.00	1.25		.29	.22
☐C78 11¢ Carmine		28.00	1.40		.36	.16
☐C79 13¢ Carmine		40.00	1.70		.38	.16
☐C80 17¢ Green, Blue, Red		28.00	2.60		.55	.16
☐C81 21¢ Blue, Red, Black		26.00	2.00		.60	.16
☐C82 11¢ Carmine	1.25	1.10	.42	.32	.20	.16
☐C83 13¢ Carmine	1.30	1.15	.46	.35	.20	.16

Scott No.	Mint Sheet	Plate Block	Fine Unused Each	Fine Used Each
1972. NATIONAL PARKS CENTENNIAL*				
☐C84 11¢ Multicolored	14.00	1.00	.35	.16

Scott No.	Mint Sheet	Plate Block	Fine Unused Each	Fine Used Each
1972. OLYMPIC GAMES*				
☐C85 11¢ Multicolored	14.00	3.00	.34	.16
1973. PROGRESS IN ELECTRONICS*				
☐C86 11¢ Multicolored	14.00	1.40	.34	.16
1974. STATUE OF LIBERTY*				
☐C87 18¢ Red, Blue, Black	30.00	2.50	.65	.40
1974. MOUNT RUSHMORE*				
☐C88 26¢ Red, Blue, Black	40.00	3.00	.65	.16
1976. PLANE*				
☐C89 25¢ Red, Blue, Black	38.00	3.00	.65	.16
☐C90 31¢ Red, Blue, Black	45.00	4.10	.70	.16

*No hinge pricing from 1941 to date is figured at (N-H ADD 10%)

Scott No.	Mint Sheet	Plate Block	Fine Unused Each	Fine Used Each
1979. WRIGHT BROTHERS*				
☐C91 31¢ Blue, Brown, Red	100.00	5.00	1.00	.20
☐C92 31¢ Blue, Brown, Red	100.00	5.00	1.00	.20
1979. CHANUTE AND PLANE*				
☐C93 21¢ Blue, Brown, Red	98.00	5.00	1.00	.35
☐C94 21¢ Blue, Brown, Red	98.00	5.00	1.00	.35
1980. PLANE AND WILEY POST*				
☐C95 25¢ Multicolored	180.00	14.00	2.10	.24
☐C96 25¢ Multicolored	180.00	14.00	2.10	.24
1980. HIGH JUMPER*				
☐C97 31¢ Multicolored	40.00	13.00	.85	.34
1981. PHILIP MAZZEI*				
☐C98 40¢ Multicolored	60.00	12.50	1.00	.17
1981. BLANCHE SCOTT*				
☐C99 28¢ Multicolored	42.00	9.00	.85	.19
1981. GLENN CURTIS*				
☐C100 35¢ Multicolored	55.00	11.00	1.00	.19
1983. SUMMER OLYMPICS*				
☐C101 28¢ Multicolored	60.00	6.50	1.50	.30
☐C102 28¢ Multicolored	60.00	6.50	1.50	.30
☐C103 28¢ Multicolored	60.00	6.50	1.50	.30
☐C104 28¢ Multicolored	60.00	6.50	1.50	.30
☐C105 40¢ Multicolored	70.00	7.00	1.30	.30
☐C106 40¢ Multicolored	70.00	7.00	1.30	.30
☐C107 40¢ Multicolored	70.00	7.00	1.30	.30
☐C108 40¢ Multicolored	70.00	7.00	1.30	.30
☐C109 35¢ Multicolored	60.00	8.00	1.25	.32
☐C110 35¢ Multicolored	60.00	8.00	1.25	.32
☐C111 35¢ Multicolored	60.00	8.00	1.25	.32
☐C112 35¢ Multicolored	60.00	8.00	1.25	.32
1985. ALFRED VERVILLE*				
☐C113 33¢ Multicolored	50.00	5.00	1.00	.28
1985. LAWRENCE AND ELMER SPERRY*				
☐C114 39¢ Multicolored	50.00	6.00	1.20	.28

*No hinge pricing from 1941 to date is figured at (N-H ADD 10%)

Scott No.	Mint Sheet	Plate Block	Fine Unused Each	Fine Used Each

1985. TRANSPACIFIC*
| ☐C115 44¢ Multicolored | 65.00 | 6.00 | 1.30 | .28 |

1985. JUNIPERO SERRA*
| ☐C116 44¢ Multicolored | 70.00 | 10.00 | 1.40 | .28 |

1988. NEW SWEDEN*
| ☐C117 44¢ Multicolored | 60.00 | 9.00 | 1.15 | .28 |

1988. SAMUEL LANGLEY*
| ☐C118 45¢ Multicolored | 65.00 | 6.00 | 1.15 | .28 |

1988. IGOR SIKORSKY*
| ☐C119 36¢ Multicolored | 55.00 | 5.00 | 1.00 | .28 |

1989. FRENCH REVOLUTION*
| ☐C120 45¢ Multicolored | 40.00 | 6.50 | 1.50 | .28 |

1989. AMERICA*
| ☐C121 45¢ Multicolored | 65.00 | 6.50 | 1.50 | .28 |

1989. SPACE SHUTTLE*
| ☐C122 45¢ Multicolored | 70.00 | 7.50 | 2.00 | .28 |

1989. SPACE MAIL DELIVERY*
| ☐C123 45¢ Multicolored | 70.00 | 7.50 | 2.00 | .28 |

1989. MOON ROVER*
| ☐C124 45¢ Multicolored | 75.00 | 7.50 | 1.75 | .28 |

1989. SPACE SHUTTLE STATION*
| ☐C125 45¢ Multicolored | 75.00 | 7.50 | 1.75 | .28 |

1989. SPACE MAIL*
| ☐C126 1.80 Multicolored | — | — | 7.00 | 2.00 |

1990. AMERICA*
| ☐C127 45¢ Multicolored | 60.00 | 6.00 | 1.25 | .26 |

1991. HARRIET QUIMBY*
| ☐C128 50¢ Multicolored | 65.00 | 7.00 | 1.25 | .26 |

*No hinge pricing from 1941 to date is figured at (N-H ADD 10%)

Scott No.	Mint Sheet	Plate Block	Fine Unused Each	Fine Used Each
1991. WILLIAM PIPER*				
☐C129 40¢ Multicolored	55.00	6.00	1.00	.26
1991. ANARTIC TREATY*				
☐C130 50¢ Multicolored	66.00	7.00	1.00	.26
1991. AMERICA*				
☐C131 50¢ Multicolored	70.00	7.00	1.25	.26
1993. WILLIAM PIPER				
☐C132 40¢ Multicolored	60.00	6.00	1.15	.25

Scott No.	Fine Unused Plate Blk	Ave. Unused Plate Blk	Fine Unused Each	Ave. Unused Each	Fine Used Each	Ave. Used Each
AIRMAIL SPECIAL DELIVERY						
☐CE1 16¢ Dark Blue						
	20.00	15.00	.90	.50	.74	.50
☐CE2 16¢ Red & Blue						
	7.00	5.50	.60	.45	.42	.16
SPECIAL DELIVERY STAMPS						
1885.						
☐E1 10¢ Blue						
	—	—	220.00	150.00	34.00	20.00
1888.						
☐E2 10¢ Blue						
	—	—	225.00	130.00	9.00	6.00
1893. (N-H ADD 60%)						
☐E3 10¢ Orange						
	—	—	150.00	90.00	13.00	9.00
1894. (N-H ADD 40%)						
☐E4 10¢ Blue—	—	650.00	350.00	19.00	11.00

Scott No.	Fine Unused Plate Blk	Ave. Unused Plate Blk	Fine Unused Each	Ave. Unused Each	Fine Used Each	Ave. Used Each
1895. (N-H ADD 50%)						
☐ E5 10¢ Blue						
	—	—	120.00	80.00	2.60	1.70
1902. (N-H ADD 40%)						
☐ E6 10¢ Ultramarine						
	—	—	70.00	50.00	3.00	2.00
1908. (N-H ADD 20%)						
☐ E7 10¢ Green						
	—	—	60.00	38.00	30.00	15.00
1911. (N-H ADD 40%)						
☐ E8 10¢ Ultramarine						
	—	—	75.00	60.00	4.00	2.50
1914. (N-H ADD 40%)						
☐ E9 10¢ Ultramarine						
	—	—	135.00	95.00	6.00	3.00
1916. (N-H ADD 40%)						
☐ E10 10¢ Pale Ultramarine						
	—	—	230.00	180.00	16.00	12.00
1917. (N-H ADD 40%)						
☐ E11 10¢ Ultramarine						
	—	—	15.00	10.00	.45	.35
1922–1925. (N-H ADD 30%)						
☐ E12 10¢ Deep Ultramarine						
	260.00	210.00	20.00	14.00	.26	.20
☐ E13 10¢ Deep Orange						
	210.00	150.00	19.00	16.00	1.00	.50
☐ E14 20¢ Black						
	50.00	35.00	3.10	2.25	1.70	.65

Scott No.	Fine Unused Plate Blk	Ave. Unused Plate Blk	Fine Unused Each	Ave. Unused Each	Fine Used Each	Ave. Used Each
1927–1951. (N–H ADD 30%)						
☐E15 10¢ Gray Violet						
	9.00	7.00	.80	.62	.22	.16
☐E16 15¢ Orange						
	7.00	6.00	.95	.75	.22	.16
☐E17 13¢ Blue						
	6.00	5.00	.80	.45	.22	.16
☐E18 17¢ Yellow						
	36.00	28.00	3.70	2.50	1.50	1.40
☐E19 20¢ Black						
	12.00	9.00	2.20	1.50	.21	.14

Scott No.	Mint Sheet	Plate Block	Fine Unused Each	Fine Used Each
1954. (N–H ADD 10%)				
☐E20 20¢ Blue	30.00	2.50	.45	.15
1957. (N–H ADD 20%)				
☐E21 30¢ Maroon	36.00	2.50	.80	.15
1969. (N–H ADD 30%)				
☐E22 45¢ Red & Blue	70.00	7.00	1.25	.15
1971.				
☐E23 60¢ Blue & Red	60.00	7.00	1.25	.15

THE UNITED NATIONS PHILATELISTS, INC.

UNPI is an organization of philatelists devoted to the collection, study, and exhibition of the issues of the United Nations Postal Administration, the postal history of the U.N., the issues and postal history of its branches, specialized agencies and forerunners, as well as worldwide topical issues that call attention to the U.N., its agencies, and programs. The annual domestic dues of the UNPI are U.S. $15, of which U.S. $14 applies to the subscription to *The Journal.*

The Journal (ISSN 0164-6842) is published bimonthly by United Nations Philatelists, Inc. (UNPI), 18 Portola Drive, San Francisco, CA 94131. First-class postage is paid at the United Nations, New York.

Please make your check payable to: "UNPI." Please send payment to the UNPI Secretary: Blanton Clement, Jr., UNPI Secretary, 292 Springdale Terrace, Yardley, PA 19067-3421

Scott No.			Name Block 4	Plain Block 4	Unused Each	Used Each
UNITED NATIONS STAMPS						
1951.						
☐1	1¢	Magenta	.65	.40	.10	.16
☐2	1½¢	Blue Green	.65	.40	.10	.16
☐2a	1½¢	Precancelled	—	—	20.00	31.00
☐3	2¢	Purple	.65	.55	.10	.16
☐4	3¢	Magenta & Blue	.65	.55	.10	.16
☐5	5¢	Blue	.75	.60	.10	.16
☐6	10¢	Chocolate	1.40	1.25	.40	.21
☐7	15¢	Violet & Blue	1.50	1.35	.25	.21
☐8	20¢	Dark Brown	5.00	3.75	1.00	.50
☐9	25¢	Olive Gray & Blue	4.00	3.00	.50	.48
☐10	50¢	Indigo	32.00	20.00	5.00	2.00
☐11	$1	Red	10.00	8.00	2.00	1.20

Scott No.		Name Block 4	Plain Block 4	Unused Each	Used Each
☐1–11	First Postage Set Complete				
		42.00	25.00	6.00	4.25

1952.

☐12	5¢ War Memorial Bldg.	2.50	1.00	.25	.20
☐13–14	3¢, 5¢ Fourth H.R. Day	4.00	2.50	.50	.45

1953.

☐15–16	3¢, 5¢ Refugees	6.00	3.50	.80	.85
☐17–18	3¢, 5¢ U.P.U.	9.00	6.00	1.30	.92
☐19–20	3¢, 5¢ Technical Assist	6.00	4.00	.90	.92
☐21–22	3¢, 5¢ Human Rights	12.00	9.00	1.70	.92

1954.

☐23–24	3¢, FAO (Agriculture)	8.00	6.00	1.40	1.00
☐25–26	3¢, 8¢ OIT (Labor Org.)	15.00	10.00	2.50	1.30
☐27–28	3¢, 8¢ UN Day	20.00	16.00	3.00	2.50
☐29–30	3¢, 8¢ H.R. Day	55.00	50.00	7.75	4.00

*No hinge pricing from 1941 to date is figured at (N-H ADD 15%)

1955.

☐31–32	3¢, 8¢ I.C.A.O	20.00	14.00	3.25	2.10
☐33–34	3¢, 8¢ UNESCO	4.00	3.00	.70	.50
☐35–37	3¢, 4¢, 8¢ UN Day	14.00	12.00	2.75	1.50
☐38	3¢, 4¢, 8¢ UN Day Sheet	—	—	120.00	55.00
☐39–40	3¢, 8¢ Human Rights	5.00	3.50	.80	.80

1956.

☐41–42	3¢, 8¢ Telecommunication	5.00	3.50	.80	.40
☐43–44	3¢, 8¢ World Health	5.00	3.00	.90	.40
☐45–46	3¢, 8¢ UN Day	1.00	.75	.15	.15
☐47–48	3¢, 8¢ Human Rights	1.00	.75	.15	.15

1957.

☐49–50	3¢, 8¢ W.M.O. Meteorological				
		1.00	.75	.15	.15
☐51–52	3¢, 8¢ U.N.E.F. 1st Printing				
		1.00	.75	.15	.15
☐53–54	3¢, 8¢ U.N.E.F. 2nd Printing	1.70	1.25	.15	.15
☐55–56	3¢, 8¢ Security Council	1.00	.75	.15	.15
☐57–58	3¢, 8¢ Human Rights	1.00	.75	.15	.15

Scott No.	Name Block 4	Plain Block 4	Unused Each	Used Each
1958.				
☐59–60 3¢, 8¢ Atomic Energy	1.00	.75	.15	.15
☐61–62 3¢, 8¢ General Assembly	1.00	.75	.15	.15
☐63–64 4¢, 8¢ Regular Issues	1.00	.75	.15	.15
☐65–66 4¢, 8¢ Economic Council	1.00	.75	.15	.15
☐67–68 4¢, 8¢ Human Rights	1.00	.75	.15	.15
☐69–70 4¢, 8¢ Flushing Meadows	1.00	.75	.15	.15
☐71–72 4¢, 8¢ E.C.E.	1.50	1.25	.25	.20
☐73–74 4¢, 8¢ Trusteeship	1.00	.75	.15	.15
☐75–76 4¢, 8¢ World Refugee Year				
	1.00	.75	.15	.15
1960.				
☐77–78 4¢, 8¢ Palais de Chaillot				
	1.25	1.00	.20	.15

*No hinge pricing from 1941 to date is figured at (N-H ADD 15%)

☐79–80 4¢, 8¢ Forestry Congress				
	1.25	1.00	.20	.15
☐83–84 4¢, 8¢ 15th Anniv.	1.25	1.00	.20	.15
☐85 4¢, 8¢ 15th Anniv. Souv. Sheet				
	—	—	—	1.00	1.85
☐86–87 4¢, 8¢ International	1.25	1.00	.20	.15
1961.				
☐88–89 4¢, 8¢ Court of Justice	1.25	1.00	.20	.20
☐90–91 4¢, 7¢ Monetary Fund	1.25	1.00	.20	.20
☐92 30¢ Regular Issue	1.75	1.60	.40	.20
☐93–94 4¢, 11¢ E.C. for Latin Am.				
	2.00	1.60	.40	.20
☐95–96 4¢,11¢ E.C. for Africa	1.25	1.00	.25	.20
☐97–99 3¢,4¢,13¢ Children's Fund				
	1.50	1.20	.30	.20
1962.				
☐100–01 4¢, 7¢ Housing	1.00	.80	.20	.20
☐102–03 4¢, 11¢ Malaria	1.25	1.00	.25	.20
☐104–07 1¢, 3¢, 5¢, 11¢ Reg. Issue				
	2.00	1.75	.40	.30

Scott No.		Name Block 4	Plain Block 4	Unused Each	Used Each
☐108–09	5¢, 15¢ Hammarskjold 9.50	2.00	1.75	.40	.25
☐110–11	4¢, 11¢ UN Congo	2.00	1.75	.35	.25
☐112–13	4¢, 11¢ Peaceful Space Use				
		1.25	1.00	.25	.20

1963.

☐114–15	5¢, 11¢ Econ. Development				
		1.25	1.00	.25	.32
☐116–17	5¢, 11¢ Freedom—Hunger				
		1.25	1.00	.25	.20
☐118	25¢, UNTEA W. Irian	2.00	1.60	.40	.20
☐119–20	5¢, 11¢, 10th Hdqrs. Anniv.				
		1.25	1.00	.25	.20
☐121–22	5¢, 11¢, 15th Anniv. H. Rights				
		1.50	1.20	.30	.20

1964.

☐123–24	5¢, 11¢ Maritime	1.00	.75	.20	.20
☐125–27	2¢, 7¢, 10¢ Reg. Issue	1.50	1.40	.35	.42
☐128	50¢ New Regular	4.50	4.00	1.00	.70
☐129–30	5¢, 11¢ Trade & Develop				
		2.00	1.75	.40	.20
☐131–32	5¢, 11¢ Narcotics Control				
		2.00	1.75	.35	.20
☐133	5¢ Nuclear Tests End	1.00	.80	.15	.10
☐134–36	4¢, 5¢, 11¢ Education	1.25	1.00	.25	.20

1965.

☐137–38	5¢, 11¢ Special Fund	1.20	1.00	.25	.20
☐139–40	5¢, 11¢ UN in Cyprus	1.20	1.00	.25	.20
☐141–42	5¢, 11¢ I.T.U. (Satellite)				
		1.25	1.00	.25	.20
☐143–44	5¢, 15¢ Co-operation	1.40	1.20	.30	.30
☐145	5¢, 15¢ Min. Sheet	—	—	.40	.25
☐146–49	1¢, 15¢, 20¢, 25¢ Regular				
		5.50	4.75	1.20	1.00
☐150	$1 Regular Issue (1966)				
		7.00	5.00	1.25	.95
☐151–53	4¢, 5¢, 11¢ Population Trends				
		1.30	1.20	.30	.20

Scott No.	Name Block 4	Plain Block 4	Unused Each	Used Each
1966.				
☐154–55 5¢, 15¢ World Federation				
	1.00	.90	.25	.20
☐156–57 5¢, 11¢ W.H.O. Building				
	1.00	.90	.25	.20
☐158–59 5¢, 11¢ Coffee Agreement				
	1.00	.90	.25	.20
☐160 15¢ Peacekeeping	1.20	1.00	.25	.20
☐161–63 4¢, 5¢, 11¢ UNICEF Anniv.				
	1.75	1.60	.40	.20
1967.				
☐164–65 5¢, 11¢ Development	1.25	1.00	.25	.20
☐166–67 1½¢, 5¢ Regular Issue	1.25	1.00	.25	.20
☐168–69 5¢, 11¢ Independence	1.25	1.00	.25	.20
1967.				
☐170–74 4¢, 5¢, 8¢, 10¢, 15¢ EXPO				
	3.00	2.75	.70	.50
☐175–76 5¢, 15¢ Int'l. Tourist Year				
	1.75	1.50	.35	.20
☐177–78 6¢, 13¢ Toward Disarm	1.75	1.50	.30	.20
☐179 6¢ Chagall Sheet of Six	—	—	.45	.50
☐180 6¢ Chagall Window	.70	.60	.15	.10
1968.				
☐181–82 6¢, 13¢, Secretariat	1.35	1.20	.30	.20
☐183–84 6¢, 75¢ Starcke Statue	6.00	4.25	1.30	1.75
☐185–86 6¢, 13¢ ONUDI	1.50	1.20	.30	.20
☐187 6¢ Regular Issue	.80	.70	.15	.10
☐188–89 6¢, 20¢ Weather Watch	1.50	1.20	.30	.20
☐190–91 6¢, 13¢ Int'l. Year Human Rts.				
	1.50	1.20	.30	.20
1969.				
☐192–93 6¢, 13¢ UNITAR	1.50	1.75	.30	.20
☐194–95 6¢, 15¢ ECLA Bldg	1.50	1.25	.30	.20
☐196 13¢, Regular Issue	1.20	1.00	.25	.20
☐197–98 6¢, 13¢ Peace thru Law	1.50	1.20	.30	.20
☐199–00 6¢, 20¢ Labor & Devl	1.50	1.20	.30	.20

Scott No.		Name Block 4	Plain Block 4	Unused Each	Used Each
☐201–02	6¢, 13¢ Art Series	1.50	1.20	.30	.20
☐203–04	6¢, 25¢ Japan Peace Bell				
		2.00	1.60	.40	.20
☐205–06	6¢, 13¢ Mekong Basin	2.00	1.60	.30	.20
☐207–08	6¢, 13¢ Cancer	2.00	1.60	.30	.20
☐209–11	6¢, 13¢, 25¢ 25th UN Anniv.				
		3.00	2.40	.60	.87
☐212	Same, Souvenir Sheet				
		—	—	.50	.40
☐213–14	6¢, 13¢ Peace, Just. Prog.				
		1.30	1.20	.30	.35

1971.
Scott No.		Name Block 4	Plain Block 4	Unused Each	Used Each
☐215	6¢ Sea Bed	.50	.40	.10	.10
☐216–17	6¢, 13¢ Refugees	1.50	1.25	.25	.20
☐218	13¢ World Food Prog.	1.50	1.25	.25	.20
☐219	20¢ U.P.U. Building	1.50	1.25	.25	.20
☐220–21	3¢, 13¢ Anti-Discrim.	1.50	1.25	.25	.20
☐222–23	8¢, 60¢ Regular Issue	6.00	4.00	1.00	1.25
☐224–25	8¢, 21¢ Int'l. Schools	1.50	1.20	.40	.30

1972.
Scott No.		Name Block 4	Plain Block 4	Unused Each	Used Each
☐226	95¢ Regular Issue	7.50	6.00	1.50	.75
☐227	8¢ Non-Proliferation	.60	.50	.15	.10
☐228	15¢ World Health	1.25	1.00	.25	.20
☐229–30	8¢, 15¢ Environment	1.50	1.40	.35	.20
☐231	21¢ E.C. Europe	1.50	1.40	.35	.20
☐232–33	8¢, 15¢ UN Art Sert.	1.50	1.40	.35	.20

1973.
Scott No.		Name Block 4	Plain Block 4	Unused Each	Used Each
☐234–35	8¢, 15¢ Disarmament	1.70	—	.30	.20
☐236–37	8¢, 15¢ Drug Abuse	1.70	—	.35	.20
☐238–39	8¢, 21¢ UN Volunteers	1.70	1.50	.40	.20
☐240–41	8¢, 15¢ Namibia	1.70	1.50	.40	.20
☐242–43	8¢, 21¢ Human Rights	1.70	1.50	.30	.20

1974.
Scott No.		Name Block 4	Plain Block 4	Unused Each	Used Each
☐244–45	10¢, 21¢ ILO Hdqr.	1.75	1.60	.40	.30
☐246	10¢ UPU Centenary	1.00	.70	.15	.10
☐247–48	10¢, 18¢ Brazil Mural	2.00	1.80	.45	.40

Scott No.	Name Block 4	Plain Block 4	Unused Each	Used Each
☐249–51 2¢, 10¢, 18¢ Regular	2.00	1.75	.35	.30
☐252–53 10¢, 18¢ Population	2.00	1.75	.50	.40
☐254–55 10¢, 26¢ Law of Sea	2.25	2.00	.80	.35

1975.

☐256–57 10¢, 26¢ Space Usage	2.50	2.00	.50	.35
☐258–59 10¢, 18¢ Women's Year	2.50	2.00	.50	.30
☐260–61 10¢, 26¢ UN 30th Anniv	2.50	2.00	.50	.35
☐262 36¢ Same Souv. Sheet	—	—	.70	.30
☐263–64 10¢, 18¢ Namibia	1.75	1.60	.40	.30
☐265–66 13¢, 26¢ Peacekeeping	2.50	2.00	.50	.40

1976.

☐267–71 3¢, 4¢, 9¢, 30¢, 50¢ Regular				
	6.50	5.25	1.30	.95
☐272–73 13¢, 26¢ WFUNA	2.25	2.00	.50	.50
☐274–75 13¢, 31¢ UNCTAD	2.25	2.00	.50	.50
☐276–77 13¢, 25¢ HABITAT	2.25	2.00	.55	.50
☐278–79 13¢, 31¢ 25th Postal Anniv.				
	14.00	12.00	3.00	2.50
☐280 13¢ Food Council	1.25	1.00	.25	.15

1977.

☐281–82 13¢, 31¢ WIPO	2.25	2.00	.50	.40
☐283–84 13¢, 25¢ Water Conf.	2.25	2.00	.50	.40
☐285–86 13¢, 31¢ Security Council				
	2.25	2.00	.50	.40
☐287–88 13¢, 25¢ Combat Racism				
	2.25	2.00	.50	.40
☐289–90 13¢,18¢ Atomic Energy	2.25	2.00	.50	.40

1978.

☐291–93 1¢, 25¢, $1 Regular	7.50	6.25	1.60	1.00
☐294–95 13¢, 31¢ Small Pox	2.50	2.40	.60	.50
☐296–97 13¢, 18¢ Namibia	2.50	2.40	.60	.50
☐298–99 13¢, 25¢ ICAO-Air Safety				
	2.25	2.00	.50	.50
☐300–01 13¢, 18¢ General Assembly	2.25	2.00	.50	.40
☐302–03 13¢, 31¢ Technical Cooperation				
	3.00	2.80	.70	.50

Scott No.	Name Block 4	Plain Block 4	Unused Each	Used Each
1979.				
☐304–07 5¢, 14¢, 15¢, 20¢ Regular Issues				
	3.50	3.00	.75	.50
☐308–09 15¢, 20¢ UNDRO	3.50	3.00	.70	.50
☐310–11 15¢, 31¢ Int'l. Year of Child				
	3.50	3.00	.75	.50
☐312–13 15¢, 31¢ Namibia	2.50	2.00	.50	.50
☐314–15 15¢, 31¢ Court of Justice				
	2.78	2.50	.60	.50
1980.				
☐316–17 15¢, 31¢ Economic Order	3.25	2.80	.70	.50
☐318–19 15¢, 20¢ Women's Decade				
	2.75	2.40	.60	.50
☐320–21 15¢, 31¢ Peacekeeping	5.00	4.00	1.00	.50
☐322–23 15¢, 31¢ 35th Anniversary				
	4.00	3.20	.80	.50
☐324 15¢ Same, Souvenir Sheet				
	—	—	.60	.60
☐325–40 15¢ World Flags	12.00	—	2.25	2.00
☐341–42 15¢, 20¢ Economic and Social Council				
	5.50	4.00	.70	.60
1981.				
☐343 15¢ Palestinian People	1.50	1.20	.30	.30
☐344–45 20¢, 35¢ Disabled Persons				
	3.75	3.40	.85	.70
☐346–47 20¢, 31¢ Fresco	3.75	3.40	.80	.80
☐348–49 20¢, 40¢ Sources of Energy				
	4.50	4.00	.95	.80
☐350–65 1981 World Flags	20.00	—	3.75	4.50
☐366–67 18¢, 28¢ Volunteers Program				
	4.00	3.60	.90	.70
1982.				
☐368–70 17¢, 28¢, 40¢ Definitives				
	4.00	3.90	1.20	1.00
☐371–72 20¢, 40¢ Human Environment				
	5.00	4.80	1.20	.90
☐373 20¢ Space Exploration	2.75	2.50	.60	.45
☐374–89 World Flags	22.00	20.00	4.25	4.00

Scott No.	Name Block 4	Plain Block 4	Unused Each	Used Each
☐390–91 20¢, 28¢ Nature Conservation				
	4.50	4.00	1.00	1.05
1983.				
☐392–93 20¢, 40¢ Communication				
	4.50	4.00	1.00	1.15
☐394–95 20¢, 37¢ Safety at Sea				
	5.00	4.40	1.10	1.35
☐396 20¢ World Food	2.50	2.00	.50	.45
☐397–98 20¢, 28¢ Trade	4.50	4.00	1.00	.90
☐399–14 World Flags	22.00	20.00	5.00	5.00
☐415–16 20¢, 40¢ Human Rights	8.00	7.00	1.75	1.65
1984.				
☐417–18 20¢, 40¢ Population Conference				
	6.00	5.25	1.30	1.20
☐419–20 20¢, 40¢ World Food Day				
	7.00	6.80	1.70	1.20
☐421–22 20¢, 50¢ Heritage	10.00	9.00	2.25	1.20
☐423–24 20¢, 50¢ Refugees	8.00	7.25	1.80	1.30
☐425–40 World Flags	40.00	38.00	9.00	2.00
☐441–42 20¢, 35¢ Youth Year	9.00	8.00	2.00	1.50
1985.				
☐443 23¢ Turin Centre	3.00	2.80	.70	.45
☐444 50¢ UN University	6.00	5.20	1.30	1.25
☐445–46 22¢, $3.00 People of the World				
	18.00	16.00	4.00	2.00
☐447–48 22¢, 45¢ 40th UN Anniversary	7.50	6.50	1.60	1.35
☐449 22¢, 45¢ 40th Anniversary Souvenir Sheet				
	—	—	2.00	1.50
☐450–65 22¢ World Flags	—	40.00	10.00	1.50
☐466–67 22¢, 33¢ UNICEF	7.50	6.00	1.50	1.30
1986.				
☐468 22¢ Africa in Crisis	3.80	3.20	.80	.50
☐469–72 22¢ UN Resources	9.00	7.00	—	5.00
☐473–74 22¢, 44¢ Philately	9.00	8.00	1.80	1.15
☐475–76 22¢, 33¢ Peace Year	10.00	9.00	1.80	1.30
☐477–92 22¢ World Flags	40.00	36.00	9.00	1.75
☐493 22¢, 44¢ WFUNA Souvenir Sheet				
	—	—	5.00	4.50

Scott No.	Name Block 4	Plain Block 4	Unused Each	Used Each
1987.				
☐494 22¢ Trygve H. Lie	3.25	3.00	.75	.38
☐495–96 22¢, 44¢ Shelter Homeless				
	7.00	6.50	1.65	1.00
☐497–98 22¢, 33¢ Fight Drugs	6.00	5.20	1.30	1.00
☐499–514 22¢ World Flags	30.00	36.00	9.00	4.00
☐515–16 22¢, 39¢ United Nations Day				
	6.00	5.60	1.40	1.20
☐517–518 22¢, 44¢ Child Immunizations				
	6.00	5.50	1.40	1.20
1988.				
☐519–20 22¢, 33¢ World Hunger				
	6.00	5.50	1.40	1.00
☐521 3¢ UN A Better World				
	.60	.40	.10	.10
☐522–23 25¢, 44¢ Forest Survival				
	30.00	28.00	7.00	1.50
☐524–25 25¢, 50¢ Int. Volunteers				
	7.00	6.25	1.55	1.50
☐526–27 25¢, 38¢ Health Sports				
	8.00	7.25	1.80	1.50
☐528–43 25¢ World Flags	38.00	36.00	9.00	2.10
☐544 25¢ Human Rights	—	—	.40	—
☐545 25¢ Human Rights Souvenir Sheet				
	—	—	1.50	1.50
1989.				
☐546–47 25¢, 45¢ World Bank	5.00	4.50	1.10	1.10
☐548 25¢ Nobel Peace Prize	2.50	2.00	.50	.40
☐549 45¢ UN Building	2.50	2.25	.60	.40
☐550–51 25¢, 36¢ World Weather				
	5.50	5.00	1.20	1.00
☐552–53 25¢, 90¢ UN Vienna	9.00	8.00	2.00	1.25
☐554–69 World Flags	34.00	32.00	8.00	1.80
☐570–71 Human Rights	5.50	4.90	1.25	1.00
1990.				
☐572 25¢ Int'l Trade Center	2.50	2.00	.50	.35
☐573–74 25¢, 40¢ AIDS	6.00	5.00	1.25	.85

Scott No.	Name Block 4	Plain Block 4	Unused Each	Used Each
☐575–76 25¢, 90¢ Medicinal Plants				
	8.00	7.30	1.80	1.60
☐577–78 25¢,45¢ UN 45th Anniversary				
	6.00	5.60	1.40	1.00
☐579 25¢, 45¢ UN 45th Anniversary Souvenir Sheet				
	—	—	1.40	.90
☐580–81 25¢, 96¢ Crime Prevention				
	6.00	5.60	1.40	.90
☐582–83 25¢, 45¢ Human Rights				
	7.00	6.00	1.35	.85

1991.

Scott No.	Name Block 4	Plain Block 4	Unused Each	Used Each
☐584–87 30¢ Economic Comm. Europe				
	9.00	8.00	2.00	1.60
☐588–89 30¢, 36¢ Namibia	6.00	5.60	1.40	1.00
☐590–91 30¢, 50¢ UN Golden Rule				
	6.00	5.60	1.40	1.10
☐592 $2 UN Building	10.00	9.50	2.50	1.50
☐593–94 30¢, 70¢ Children's Rights	8.00	7.50	1.75	1.20
☐595–96 30¢, 90¢ Banning Chem. Weapons				
	8.00	7.00	1.70	1.70
☐597–98 30¢, 40¢ UNPA 40th Anniversary				
	8.00	6.50	1.20	1.10
☐599–600 30¢, 50¢ Human Rights	—	—	1.50	1.25

1992.

Scott No.	Name Block 4	Plain Block 4	Unused Each	Used Each
☐601–02 29¢, 50¢ UNESCO Heritage				
	5.50	5.00	1.20	1.10
☐603–04 29¢ Clean Oceans	6.50	5.00	1.25	.75
☐605–08 29¢ UNICEF Summit	9.00	8.00	2.00	1.75
☐609–10 29¢ Mission to Earth	10.00	8.00	2.00	2.50
☐611–12 29¢, 59¢ Science and Technology				
	5.50	5.00	1.20	1.00
☐613–15 4¢, 40¢ Definitives	3.00	2.80	.70	.70
☐616–17 29¢, 50¢ Human Rights				
	5.00	4.40	1.10	1.00

1993.

Scott No.	Name Block 4	Plain Block 4	Unused Each	Used Each
☐618–19 29¢, 52¢ Aging	—	8.00	2.00	1.00
☐620–23 29¢ Endangered Species				
	—	11.00	2.75	1.50

Scott No.	Name Block 4	Plain Block 4	Unused Each	Used Each
□624–25 29¢, 50¢ Health Environment				
	—	8.00	2.00	1.00
□626 5¢ Definitive	—	1.00	.15	.15
□627–28 29¢, 30¢ Human Rights				
	—	15.00	4.00	1.50
□629–32 29¢ Peace	—	3.50	3.00	1.50
□633–36 29¢ Environment	—	6.25	3.00	1.50

1994.

□637–38 29¢, 45¢ Year of the Family	—	8.00	2.00	1.00
□639–42 29¢ Endangered Species	—	3.50	2.50	1.40
□643 50¢ Refugees	—	5.00	1.50	.50
□644–46 10¢, $1 Definitives	—	12.00	3.00	1.25
□647–50 29¢ Natural Disaster	—	3.50	3.00	1.50
□651–52 29¢, 52¢ Population Development				
	—	8.00	2.00	1.00
□653–54 29¢, 50¢ Development Partnership				
	—	8.00	2.00	1.00

1995.

□655 32¢ 50th Anniversary of the UN				
	—	4.00	1.00	.50
□656 50¢ Social Summit	—	6.00	1.50	.50
□657–60 29¢ Endangered Species				
	—	4.00	3.00	1.50

UNITED NATIONS AIRMAILS
1951–1957.

□C1 6¢ Airmail (1951)	1.75	1.50	.35	.30
□C2 10¢ Airmail	3.00	1.50	.35	.30
□C3 15¢ Airmail	3.50	1.90	.45	.40
□C4 25¢ Airmail	4.00	2.50	.60	.50
□C1–4 First Issue Airmails				
	11.00	8.00	1.50	1.50
□C5–7 4¢, 5¢, 7¢ Airmail (1957)				
	1.75	1.25	.30	.25

1963–1964.

□C8–10 6¢, 8¢, 13¢ Airmail (1963)				
	2.00	1.60	.40	.35
□C11–12 15¢, 25¢ Airmail (1964)	5.00	4.80	1.20	.75

Scott No.	Name Block 4	Plain Block 4	Unused Each	Used Each
1968–1972.				
☐C13 20¢ Airmail (1968)	1.50	1.00	.25	.20
☐C14 10¢ Airmail (1969)	1.50	1.00	.25	.20
☐C15–18 9¢, 11¢, 17¢, 21¢ (1972)	3.80	3.00	.75	.70
1974–1977.				
☐C19–21 13¢, 18¢, 26¢ (1974)	3.50	3.00	.70	1.00
☐C22–23 25¢, 31¢ (1977)	3.50	3.00	.70	1.00

	Unused Each	Used Each

UNITED NATIONS SOUVENIR CARDS

		Unused Each	Used Each
☐1	WHO, First Printing	1.00	—
☐1a	WHO, Second Printing	5.50	—
☐2	Art at UN	.70	—
☐3	Disarmament	.50	—
☐4	Human Rights	1.50	—
☐5	Universal Postal Union	1.50	—
☐6	World Population	7.00	—
☐7	Outer Space	3.00	—
☐8	Peacekeeping	2.00	—
☐9	World Federation of UN	5.00	—
☐10	World Food Council	2.50	—
☐11	World Intellectual Property	1.50	—
☐12	Combat Racism	1.60	—
☐13	Namibia	1.00	—
☐14	ICAO-Air Safety	1.25	—
☐15	International Year of the Child	.70	—
☐16	Court of Justice	1.50	—
☐17	Women's Decade	10.00	—
☐18	Economic and Social Council	1.30	—
☐19	Disabled Persons	1.30	—
☐20	Energy Sources	1.60	—

Scott No.		Name Block 4	Plain Block 4	Unused Each	Used Each

UNITED NATIONS—GENEVA, SWITZERLAND ISSUES. DENOMINATIONS ARE GIVEN IN SWISS CURRENCY, DESIGNS ARE SIMILAR TO U.N. NEW YORK ISSUES

1969–1970.

Scott No.		Name Block 4	Plain Block 4	Unused Each	Used Each
☐1–14	5¢ to 10 franc	35.00	32.00	8.50	7.00

1971.

☐15	30¢ Sea Bed	.75	.60	.15	.15
☐16	50¢ Refugees	1.25	1.00	.25	.40
☐17	50¢ World Food Prog.	1.50	1.20	.30	.40
☐18	75¢ U.P.U. Building	4.00	3.00	.80	.80
☐19–20	30¢,50¢ Anti-Discrim.	5.00	4.00	.55	.60
☐21	1.10fr Int'l. Schools	5.00	4.50	1.00	1.10

1972.

☐22	40¢ Regular Issue	2.50	2.10	.25	.36
☐23	40¢ Non-Proliferation	3.00	2.70	.50	.70
☐24	80¢ World Health	4.00	3.50	.60	.70
☐25–26	40¢,80¢ Environment	7.00	6.00	1.00	1.00
☐27	1.10fr E.C. Europe	7.00	6.50	1.00	1.00
☐28–29	40¢,80¢ UN Art-Sert	10.00	6.00	1.10	1.10

1973.

☐30–31	60¢,1.10fr Disarm.	6.00	5.00	1.20	1.50
☐32	60¢ Drug Abuse	2.50	2.00	.50	.50
☐33	80¢ UN Volunteers	2.50	2.00	.50	.50
☐34	60¢ Namibia	2.50	2.00	.50	.50
☐35–36	40¢, 80¢ Human Rights	4.50	4.00	.90	.70

1974.

☐37–38	60¢, 80¢ ILO Hdqrs.	5.00	4.00	1.00	.95
☐39–40	30¢, 60¢ UPU Centenary	3.00	3.00	.70	.70
☐41–42	60¢, 1fr Brazil Mural	5.00	4.00	1.00	.95
☐43–44	60¢, 80¢ Population	5.00	4.00	1.00	.95
☐45	1.30fr Law of Sea	5.00	4.00	1.00	.95

1975.

☐46–47	60¢, 80¢ Space Usage	5.00	4.00	.90	.90
☐48–49	60¢, 90¢ Women's Year	5.00	4.00	1.00	1.00

Scott No.		Name Block 4	Plain Block 4	Unused Each	Used Each
☐50–51	60¢, 90¢ UN Anniv.	4.00	3.00	.90	.90
☐52	1.50fr Same, Souv. Sheet	—	—	.90	.90
☐53–54	50¢, 1.30fr Namibia	4.00	3.00	1.00	.90
☐55–56	60¢, 70¢ Peacekeeping	4.00	3.00	1.00	.90

1976.

☐57	90¢ WFUNA	4.00	3.00	.75	.75
☐58	.10fr UNCTAD	4.00	3.00	.75	.75
☐59–60	40¢ 1.50fr HABITAT	5.00	4.00	1.00	1.00
☐61–62	80¢, 1.10fr UN Postal Anniv.	20.00	16.00	4.00	4.00
☐63	70¢ World Food Council	2.50	2.00	.50	.50

1977.

☐64	80¢ WIPO	3.00	2.00	.50	.50
☐65–66	80¢, 1.10fr Water Conf.	6.00	5.00	1.25	1.20
☐67–68	80¢, 1.10fr Security Council	6.00	5.00	1.25	1.20
☐69–70	40¢, 1.10fr Combat Racism	5.00	4.00	1.00	1.20
☐71–72	80¢, 1.10fr Atomic Energy	6.00	5.00	1.20	1.20
☐73	35¢ Doves	1.50	1.00	.25	.25
☐74–75	80¢, 1.10fr Smallpox	6.00	5.00	1.25	1.15
☐76	80¢ Namibia	4.00	3.00	.75	.80
☐77–78	70¢, 80¢ ICAO-Air Safety	5.00	4.00	1.00	1.00
☐79–80	70¢, 1.10fr General Assembly	5.00	4.00	1.00	1.30
☐81	80¢ Technical Cooperation	3.00	2.00	.50	.70

1979.

☐82–83	80¢, 1.50fr UNDRO	7.00	6.00	1.50	1.50
☐84–85	80¢, 1.10fr Int'l. Year of the Child				
		4.50	4.00	1.00	.75
☐86	1.10fr Namibia	4.00	3.00	.75	.75
☐87–88	80¢, 1.10fr Court of Justice	6.00	5.00	1.25	.95

1980.

☐89	80¢ Economic Order	3.00	3.00	.65	.70
☐90–91	40¢, 70¢ Women's Decade	3.50	3.00	.75	.75
☐92	1.10fr Peacekeeping	3.50	3.00	.75	.75
☐93–94	40¢, 70¢ 35th Anniversary	3.50	3.00	.75	.75
☐95	40¢, 70¢ Sheet	—	—	.85	.75
☐96–97	40¢, 70¢ Economic and Social Council				
		3.50	3.00	.75	1.00

Scott No.	Name Block 4	Plain Block 4	Unused Each	Used Each
1981.				
☐98 80¢ Palestinian People	6.00	4.00	.60	.50
☐99–100 40¢, 1.50fr Disabled Persons	6.00	5.50	1.30	1.00
☐101 80¢ Bulgarian Mural	3.00	2.50	.60	.50
☐102 1.10fr Energy Sources	5.00	4.00	1.00	1.10
☐103–04 40¢, 70¢ Volunteers	5.00	4.00	1.00	1.00
1982.				
☐105–06 1fr Definitives	5.00	4.00	1.00	1.00
☐107–08 40¢, 1.20fr Human Environment				
	5.00	4.00	1.25	1.00
☐109–10 80¢, 1fr Space	—	7.00	1.40	1.00
☐111–12 40¢, 1. 50fr Nature Conservation				
	—	7.50	1.80	1.00
1983.				
☐113 1.20fr Communications	—	5.00	1.25	1.50
☐114–15 40¢, 80¢ Safety at Sea	—	4.00	1.00	1.50
☐116 1.50fr World Food Program	—	6.00	1.40	1.50
☐117–18 80¢, 1.10fr Trade & Development				
	—	6.50	1.60	1.50
☐119–20 40¢, 1.20fr Human Rights	—	7.00	1.70	1.50
1984.				
☐121 1.20fr Population Conference	—	8.00	1.75	1.50
☐122–23 50¢, 80¢ Food Day	—	8.00	1.75	1.50
☐124–25 50¢, 70¢ UNESCO	—	8.00	1.75	1.50
☐126–27 35¢, 1.50fr Refugees	—	8.00	1.70	2.00
☐128 1.20fr Youth Year	—	7.50	1.80	2.00
1985.				
☐129–30 80¢, 1.20fr Turin Centre	—	9.00	2.15	2.00
☐131–32 50¢, 80¢ UN University of Japan				
	—	7.00	1.60	1.50
☐133–34 20¢, 1.20fr Definitives	—	7.50	1.60	1.50
☐135–36 50¢, 70¢ 40th Anniversary	—	7.00	1.60	1.50
☐137 same, souvenir sheet			2.50	1.50
☐138–39 50¢, 4fr UNICEF	—	13.00	3.00	3.00

Scott No.	Name Block 4	Plain Block 4	Unused Each	Used Each
1986.				
☐140 1.40fr Africa	—	8.00	2.00	1.50
☐141–44 35¢ UN Development	—	9.00	6.00	4.50
☐145 5¢ Definitive	—	.75	.15	.15
☐146–47 50¢, 80¢ Philately	—	8.00	2.00	1.00
☐148–49 45¢, 1.40fr Peace	—	10.00	2.50	1.75
☐150 35¢, 70¢ WFUNA, souv. sheet \	—	—	5.00	3.00
1987.				
☐151 1.40fr Trygve Lie	—	8.00	1.75	1.50
☐152–53 90¢, 1.40fr Definitive	—	9.00	2.00	2.50
☐154–55 50¢, 90¢ Homeless Shelter	—	8.00	2.00	1.00
☐156–57 70¢, 1.20fr Anti-Drug	—	11.00	2.50	3.00
☐158–59 35¢, 50¢ United Nations	—	7.00	1.40	1.00
☐160–61 Immunization	—	14.00	3.25	2.00
1988.				
☐162–63 35¢, 1.40fr UN Better World	—	9.00	2.00	2.00
☐164 50¢ For a Better World	—	3.50	.80	.80
☐165–66 50¢, 1.10fr Forest Conservation	30.00	7.00	6.00	
☐167–68 80¢, 90¢ International Volunteers Day				
	9.00	2.00	1.50	
☐169–70 50¢, 1.40fr Health in Sports	9.00	2.00	1.50	
☐171 90¢ Human Rights 40th Anniversary	4.00	1.00	1.00	
☐172 2fr Human Rights 40th Anniversary souvenir sheet				
	—	2.25	3.00	
1989.				
☐173–74 80¢, 1.40fr World Bank				
	10.00	2.40	2.00	
☐175 90¢ Peace Nobel Prize	5.00	1.10	1.00	
☐176–77 90¢, 1.10fr Weather Watch	10.00	2.50	2.00	
☐178–79 50¢ & 2fr UN Offices in Vienna	10.00	2.50	2.00	
☐180–81 35¢, 80¢ Human rights 40th Ann.	6.50	1.50	1.50	
1990.				
☐182 1.50fr International Trade Center	8.00	1.75	1.50	
☐183 5fr Definitive	21.00	5.00	4.00	
☐184–85 35¢, 80¢ Fight Against AIDS	10.00	2.50	1.50	
☐186–87 90¢, 1.40fr Plants	10.00	2.50	2.00	

Scott No.	Plain Block 4	Unused Each	Used Each
☐188–89 90¢, 1.10fr 45th Anniversary of UN	9.00	2.00	2.00
☐190 same, souvenir sheet	—	2.00	4.00
☐191–92 50¢, 2fr Crime Prevention	11.50	2.75	4.00
☐193–94 35¢, 90¢ Declarations of Human Rights			
	17.00	4.00	2.00

1991.

☐195–98 90¢ Economy Commission	7.50	4.75	3.00
☐199–200 70¢, 90¢ Namibia	9.00	2.00	2.00
☐201–02 80¢, 1.50fr Definitives	13.00	3.00	2.00
☐203–04 80¢, 1.10fr Children's Rights	11.00	2.50	2.00
☐205–06 80¢, 1.40fr Chemical Weapons Ban	11.00	2.75	2.00
☐207–08 50¢, 1.60fr UNPA 40th Anniversary	11.00	2.75	2.00
☐209–10 50¢, 90¢ Human Rights	8.50	2.00	1.75

1992.

☐211–12 50¢, 1.10fr World Heritage			
	8.00	1.75	2.00
☐213 3fr Definitive	11.00	2.50	2.00
☐214–15 80¢ Clean Oceans	8.50	2.00	1.75
☐216–19 75¢ Earth Summit	5.50	3.00	2.00
☐220–21 1.10fr Plant Earth	11.00	3.00	2.50
☐222–23 90¢, 1.60fr Science and Technology	11.00	2.50	2.50
☐224–25 50¢, 90¢ Human Rights	28.50	7.00	1.50

1993.

☐226–27 50¢, 1.60fr Aging	26.00	6.00	2.00
☐228–31 80¢ Endangered Species	5.50	4.50	2.00
☐232–33 6¢, 1fr Healthy Environment	12.00	3.00	2.00
☐234–35 50¢, 90¢ Declaration of Human Rights			
	37.00	6.00	1.50
☐236–39 60¢ Peace	6.00	5.00	2.00
☐240–43 1.10fr Environment	24.00	6.00	4.00
☐244–45 80¢, 1fr Int'l Year of the Family	12.00	3.00	1.75
☐246–49 80¢ Endangered Species	19.00	5.00	3.00
☐250 1.20fr Refugees	10.50	2.50	1.00
☐251–254 60¢ Natural Disaster	14.00	3.50	2.50
☐255–56 60¢, 80¢ Population and Development			
	12.00	3.00	2.00
☐257–59 60¢, 1.80fr Definitives	18.00	4.50	2.00

Scott No.	Plain Block 4	Unused Each	Used Each
1995.			
☐262 80¢ UN 50th Anniversary	8.00	2.00	1.00
☐263 1fr. Social Summit	8.00	2.00	1.00
☐264–67 80¢ Endangered Species			
	5.00	4.00	3.00
☐268 80¢, 1fr Youth	12.00	3.00	2.00
☐269–70 60¢, 80fr UN 50th Anniversary	20.00	5.00	2.00
☐271 2.40fr UN 50th Anniversary souvenir sheet			
	—	4.00	2.00
☐272–73 60¢, 1fr 4th Conference on Women	12.00	3.00	2.00
☐274 25¢ UN 50th Anniversary booklet single	7.75	2.00	1.00

SOUVENIR CARDS

Scott No.		Fine
☐1	Truck w/gum	80.00
☐	Truck w/o gum	14.00
☐2	Barcelona	430.00
☐3	SIPEX Scenes	180.00
☐3a	SIPEX Miner	12.00
☐4	EFIMEX	4.00
☐5	SANDIPEX	70.00
☐	Ana '69	70.00
☐	FRESNO	510.00
☐6	ASDA '69	24.00
☐7	INTERPEX '70	56.00
☐8	COMPEX '70	15.00
☐	ANA 1970	120.00
☐9	PHILYMPIA	2.80
☐10	HAPEX	18.00
☐11	INTERPEX '71	2.50
☐12	WESTPEX	2.50
☐13	NAPEX '71	3.00
☐	ANA 1971	4.50
☐14	TEXANEX	3.00
☐15	EXFILIMA	2.10
☐16	ASDA '71	2.75
☐17	ANPHILEX	1.90
☐18	INTERPEX '72	1.90
☐19	NOPEX	1.90
☐20	BELGICA	1.90
☐	ANA 1972	4.00
☐21	Olympia Phil. Munchen	1.85
☐22	EXFILBRA	1.85
☐23	Postal Forum	2.10
☐24	SEPAD '72	2.10
☐25	ASDA '72	2.10
☐26	Stamp Expo '75	2.10
☐27	INTERPEX '73	2.10
☐28	IBRA	2.40
☐29	COMPEX '73	2.10
☐30	APEX	2.30

Scott No.		Fine
☐	ANA 1973	7.10
☐31	PLOSKA	2.30
☐32	NAPEX '73	2.30
☐33	ASDA '73	2.00
☐34	Stamps Expo '73	2.40
☐35	Hobby Show Chicago	3.10
☐36	MILCOPEX '72	3.00
☐37	INTERNABA 1974	2.60
☐	ANA 1974	12.00
☐38	STOCKHOLMIA '74	4.00
☐39	EXFILMEX '74	2.60
☐40	ESPANA '75	2.50
☐41	NAPEX '75	9.50
☐42	ARPHILA '75	2.90
☐43	Women's Year	24.00
☐	ANA 1975	12.00
☐44	ASDA '75	38.00
☐45	WERABA '76	4.10
☐46	INTERPHIL '76	8.00
☐	INTERPHIL Program with BEP Card.	12.00
☐47	Science BEP	9.00
☐48	Science U.S.P.S.	4.00
☐49	Stamp Expo '76	8.50
☐50	Colorado Statehood	3.75
☐51	HAFNIA '76	4.00
☐	ANA 1976	8.00
☐52	ITALIA '76	4.15
☐53	NORDPOSTA '76	4.10
☐54	MILCOPEX '77	3.15
☐55	ROMPEX '77	3.00
☐56	AMPHILEX '77	4.50
☐	ANA 1977	4.00
☐57	SAN MARCO	4.10
☐58	Puripex	3.15
☐59	ASDA '77	4.00

Scott No.		Fine	Scott No.		Fine
☐60	ROPEX '78	4.75	☐69	ESSEN '80	6.00
☐	Paper Money		☐70	STAMP EXPO '81	19.00
	Show	4.50	☐	Visitor Center	8.00
☐61	NAPOSTA '78	4.25	☐71	WIPA '81	5.50
☐62	CENTEX '78	5.00	☐	Paper Money	18.00
☐63	BRASILIANA '79	6.50	☐	ANA '81	18.00
☐64	JAPEX '79	6.50	☐72	STAMP COLLECTORS	
☐	ANA '80	21.00		MONTH	6.00
☐65	LONDON '80	7.50	☐73	PHILATOKYO	
☐	Money Show '80	12.00		'81	6.00
☐66	NORWEX '80	5.50	☐74	NORD POSKTA	
☐67	NAPEX '80	14.00		'81	6.00
☐	Visitor Center	9.00			
☐68	ASDA STAMP				
	FESTIVAL '80	18.00			

Scott No.		Fine Unused Each	Ave. Unused Each	Fine Used Each	Ave. Used Each

POSTAGE DUE STAMPS—1879.
PERFORATED 12 (N-H ADD 20%)

Scott No.			Fine Unused Each	Ave. Unused Each	Fine Used Each	Ave. Used Each
☐J1	1¢	Brown	33.00	21.00	6.50	4.00
☐J2	2¢	Brown	190.00	110.00	5.00	3.00
☐J3	3¢	Brown	23.00	15.00	3.00	2.00
☐J4	5¢	Brown	310.00	200.00	40.00	20.00
☐J5	10¢	Brown	350.00	200.00	16.00	10.00
☐J6	30¢	Brown	175.00	100.00	33.00	18.00
☐J7	50¢	Brown	210.00	130.00	39.00	21.00

POSTAGE DUE STAMPS—1884–1889.
SAME DESIGN—PERF. 12 (N-H ADD 20%)

Scott No.			Fine Unused Each	Ave. Unused Each	Fine Used Each	Ave. Used Each
☐J15	1¢	Red Brown	34.00	18.00	3.40	2.10
☐J16	2¢	Red Brown	40.00	21.00	3.40	2.10
☐J17	3¢	Red Brown	500.00	300.00	95.00	56.00
☐J18	5¢	Red Brown	210.00	150.00	16.00	8.00
☐J19	10¢	Red Brown	200.00	120.00	10.00	7.00
☐J20	30¢	Red Brown	100.00	60.00	30.00	17.00
☐J21	50¢	Red Brown	910.00	600.00	130.00	72.00

Scott No.	Fine Unused Each	Ave. Unused Each	Fine Used Each	Ave. Used Each
POSTAGE DUE STAMPS—1891–1893.				
SAME DESIGN—PERF. 12 (N-H ADD 20%)				
☐J22 1¢ Bright Claret	12.00	7.50	.62	.40
☐J23 2¢ Bright Claret	13.00	8.00	.63	.34
☐J24 3¢ Bright Claret	30.00	17.00	5.00	2.50
☐J25 5¢ Bright Claret	36.00	21.00	4.50	2.50
☐J26 10¢ Bright Claret	65.00	38.00	12.00	6.50
☐J27 30¢ Bright Claret	220.00	140.00	100.00	48.00
☐J28 50¢ Bright Claret	250.00	150.00	100.00	49.00
1894. POSTAGE DUE STAMPS—NEW SMALL				
DESIGN—NO WTMK.—PERF. 12 (N-H ADD 20%)				
☐J29 1¢ Vermilion	700.00	500.00	175.00	90.00
☐J30 2¢ Vermilion	300.00	200.00	70.00	38.00
☐J31 1¢ Claret	22.00	18.00	6.00	4.00
☐J32 2¢ Claret	21.00	12.00	3.00	2.00
☐J33 3¢ Claret	80.00	50.00	19.00	12.00
☐J34 5¢ Claret	100.00	75.00	30.00	20.00
☐J35 10¢ Claret	110.00	75.00	16.00	12.00
☐J36 30¢ Claret	250.00	160.00	60.00	50.00
☐J37 50¢ Claret	550.00	400.00	140.00	100.00
1895. POSTAGE DUE STAMPS—SAME NEW SMALL				
DESIGN—D.L. WTMK.—PERF. 12 (N-H ADD 70%)				
☐J38 1¢ Claret	6.00	4.00	.42	.37
☐J39 2¢ Claret	6.00	3.00	.30	.20
☐J40 3¢ Claret	34.00	21.00	1.35	1.00
☐J41 5¢ Claret	36.00	21.00	2.00	1.00
☐J42 10¢ Claret	40.00	25.00	3.00	2.00
☐J43 30¢ Claret	350.00	150.00	31.00	13.50
☐J44 50¢ Claret	300.00	210.00	30.00	20.00
1910–1912. POSTAGE DUE STAMPS—SMALL				
DESIGN—S.L. WTMK.—PERF. 12 (N-H ADD 50%)				
☐J45 1¢ Claret	18.00	12.00	2.50	2.00
☐J46 2¢ Claret	18.00	12.00	.35	.25
☐J47 3¢ Claret	350.00	275.00	20.00	12.00
☐J48 5¢ Claret	56.00	31.00	5.00	2.00

Scott No.	Fine Unused Each	Ave. Unused Each	Fine Used Each	Ave. Used Each
☐J49 10¢ Claret	72.00	42.00	9.00	4.50
☐J50 50¢ Claret	600.00	310.00	76.00	40.00

1914–1916. POSTAGE DUE STAMPS—SAME SMALL DESIGN—S.L. WTMK.—PERF. 10. (N-H ADD 50%)

	Fine Unused Each	Ave. Unused Each	Fine Used Each	Ave. Used Each
☐J52 1¢ Carmine	37.00	25.00	7.50	5.85
☐J53 2¢ Carmine	31.00	20.00	.30	.18
☐J54 3¢ Carmine	500.00	250.00	20.00	15.00
☐J55 5¢ Carmine	22.00	15.00	2.00	1.50

Scott No.	Fine Unused Each	Ave. Unused Each	Fine Used Each	Ave. Used Each
☐J56 10¢ Carmine	36.00	20.00	1.10	1.00
☐J57 30¢ Carmine	135.00	90.00	14.00	10.00
☐J58 50¢ Carmine	5800.00	3500.00	400.00	275.00
☐J59 1¢ Rose (No Wtmk.)				
	1100.00	750.00	200.00	120.00
☐J60 2¢ Rose (No Wtmk.)				
	90.00	45.00	13.00	7.50

Scott No.	Fine Unused Plate Blk	Ave. Unused Plate Blk	Fine Unused Each	Ave. Unused Each	Fine Used Each	Ave. Used Each

1917–1926. POSTAGE DUE STAMPS—SAME SMALL DESIGN—NO WTMK.—PERF. 11(N-H ADD 40%)

Scott No.	Fine Unused Plate Blk	Ave. Unused Plate Blk	Fine Unused Each	Ave. Unused Each	Fine Used Each	Ave. Used Each
☐J61 1¢ Carmine Rose						
	40.00	27.00	1.65	1.00	.22	.16
☐J62 2¢ Carmine Rose						
	34.00	27.00	1.60	1.00	.22	.16
☐J63 3¢ Carmine Rose						
	100.00	74.00	8.25	5.00	.22	.16
☐J64 5¢ Carmine Rose						
	98.00	74.00	8.25	5.00	.22	.16
☐J65 10¢ Carmine Rose						
	140.00	100.00	12.00	6.50	.22	.16

Scott No.	Fine Unused Plate Blk	Ave. Unused Plate Blk	Fine Unused Each	Ave. Unused Each	Fine Used Each	Ave. Used Each
☐J66 30¢ Carmine Rose						
	410.00	310.00	55.00	36.00	.60	.40
☐J67 50¢ Carmine Rose						
	675.00	510.00	72.00	50.00	.21	.16
☐J68 ½¢ Dull Red						
	11.00	9.00	.68	.40	.21	.16

1930–1931. POSTAGE DUE STAMPS— NEW DESIGN FLAT PRESS— PERF. 11 x 11 (N-H ADD 30%)

Scott No.	Fine Unused Plate Blk	Ave. Unused Plate Blk	Fine Unused Each	Ave. Unused Each	Fine Used Each	Ave. Used Each
☐J69 ½¢ Carmine						
	35.00	25.00	3.60	1.80	.90	.60
☐J70 1¢ Carmine						
	30.00	27.00	3.00	2.00	.22	.16
☐J71 2¢ Carmine						
	38.00	30.00	3.25	2.50	.22	.16
☐J72 3¢ Carmine						
	260.00	200.00	24.00	16.00	1.50	.80
☐J73 5¢ Carmine						
	225.00	180.00	18.00	12.00	2.00	1.50
☐J74 10¢ Carmine						
	450.00	350.00	40.00	30.00	.85	.50
☐J75 30¢ Carmine						
	1250.00	1000.00	100.00	80.00	1.50	1.00
☐J76 50¢ Carmine						
	1400.00	140.00	120.00	90.00	.50	.40
☐J77 $1 Carmine						
	250.00	200.00	23.00	18.00	.22	.16
☐J78 $5 Carmine						
	350.00	265.00	30.00	24.00	.22	.16

1931–1956. POSTAGE DUE STAMPS— SAME DESIGN—ROTARY PRESS— PERF. 10 x 10½ (N-H ADD 20%)

Scott No.	Fine Unused Plate Blk	Ave. Unused Plate Blk	Fine Unused Each	Ave. Unused Each	Fine Used Each	Ave. Used Each
☐J79 ½¢ Carmine						
	30.00	15.00	1.00	.70	.25	.18
☐J80 1¢ Carmine						
	2.10	1.50	.24	.20	.25	.18

Scott No.			Fine Unused Plate Blk	Ave. Unused Plate Blk	Fine Unused Each	Ave. Unused Each	Fine Used Each	Ave. Used Each
☐ J81	2¢	Carmine	2.15	1.50	.24	.20	.25	.18
☐ J82	3¢	Carmine	3.20	1.60	.26	.22	.25	.18
☐ J83	5¢	Carmine	4.60	2.00	.45	.26	.25	.18
☐ J84	10¢	Carmine	10.00	6.00	1.25	.72	.25	.18
☐ J85	30¢	Carmine	40.00	25.00	8.50	5.10	.25	.18
☐ J86	50¢	Carmine	60.00	35.00	8.50	5.10	.25	.18
☐ J87	$1	Red (10½ x 11)	260.00	220.00	38.00	29.00	.25	.18

Scott No.			Mint Sheet	Plate Block	Fine Unused Each	Fine Used Each

1959. POSTAGE DUE STAMPS— NEW SERIES—NEW DESIGN— ROTARY PRESS—PERF. 11 x 10½ (N-H ADD 20%)

Scott No.			Mint Sheet	Plate Block	Fine Unused Each	Fine Used Each
☐ J88	½¢	Red & Black	390.00	210.00	1.50	1.00
☐ J89	1¢	Red & Black	3.50	.40	.22	.18
☐ J90	2¢	Red & Black	5.75	.46	.22	.18
☐ J91	3¢	Red & Black	7.00	.50	.22	.18
☐ J92	4¢	Red & Black	8.50	.86	.22	.18
☐ J93	5¢	Red & Black	11.00	.78	.22	.18
☐ J94	6¢	Red & Black	16.00	1.00	.22	.18
☐ J95	7¢	Red & Black	18.00	2.10	.22	.18
☐ J96	8¢	Red & Black	20.00	1.60	.22	.18
☐ J97	10¢	Red & Black	25.00	1.65	.22	.18
☐ J98	30¢	Red & Black	60.00	5.00	.60	.18
☐ J99	50¢	Red & Black	100.00	6.00	1.00	.20
☐ J100	$1	Red & Black	200.00	10.00	2.00	.20
☐ J101	$5	Red & Black	900.00	55.00	10.00	.21

Scott No.			Mint Sheet	Plate Block	Fine Unused Each	Fine Used Each

1978. POSTAGE DUE STAMPS— SAME DESIGN, NEW VALUES

Scott No.			Mint Sheet	Plate Block	Fine Unused Each	Fine Used Each
☐J102	11¢	Red & Black	29.00	4.00	.32	.21
☐J103	13¢	Red & Black	36.00	3.00	.38	.25
☐J104	17¢	Red & Black	85.00	25.00	.40	.25

1985. POSTAGE DUE STAMPS— SAME DESIGN, NEW VALUES

☐J104	17¢	Red & Black	75.00	40.00	.85	.45

Scott No.		Fine
1927–1940. MINT SHEETS		
☐643	2¢ Vermont	200.00
☐644	2¢ Burgoyne	275.00
☐645	2¢ Valley Forge	180.00
☐646	2¢ Molly Pitcher	190.00
☐647	2¢ Hawaii	660.00
☐648	5¢ Hawaii	1800.00
☐649	2¢ Aeronautics	95.00
☐650	5¢ Aeronautics	400.00
☐651	2¢ George R. Clark	45.00
☐653	½¢ Hale	20.00
☐654	2¢ Edison-Flat	130.00
☐655	2¢ Edison-Rotary	135.00
☐657	2¢ Sullivan	140.00
☐680	2¢ Fallen Timbers	150.00
☐681	2¢ Ohio River Canal	125.00
☐682	2¢ Mass. Bay	150.00
☐683	2¢ Carolina-Charleston	200.00
☐684	1½¢ Harding	40.00
☐685	4¢ Taft	150.00
☐688	2¢ Braddock	150.00
☐689	2¢ Von Steuben	80.00
☐690	2¢ Pulaski	46.00
☐702	2¢ Red Cross	21.00
☐703	2¢ Yorktown	27.00
☐704	½¢ Wash. Bicent'l	17.00
☐705	1¢ Wash. Bicent'l	20.00
☐706	1½¢ Wash. Bicent'l	70.00
☐707	2¢ Wash. Bicent'l	15.00
☐708	3¢ Wash. Bicent'l	100.00
☐709	4¢ Wash. Bicent'l	42.00
☐710	5¢ Wash. Bicent'l	240.00
☐711	6¢ Wash. Bicent'l	600.00
☐712	7¢ Wash. Bicent'l	42.00
☐713	8¢ Wash. Bicent'l	520.00
☐714	9¢ Wash. Bicent'l	415.00
☐715	10¢ Wash. Bicent'l	1800.00
☐716	2¢ Lake Placid	68.00
☐717	2¢ Arbor Day	30.00
☐718	2¢ Olympics	200.00
☐719	5¢ Olympics	300.00
☐720	3¢ Washington	30.00
☐724	3¢ Penn	52.00
☐725	3¢ Webster	80.00
☐726	3¢ Oglethorpe	52.00
☐727	3¢ Newburgh	23.00
☐728	1¢ Chicago	20.00
☐729	3¢ Chicago	23.00
☐732	3¢ N.R.A.	20.00
☐733	3¢ Byrd	55.00
☐734	5¢ Kosciuszko	110.00
☐736	3¢ Maryland	32.00
☐737	3¢ Mother's Day Rotary	12.00
☐738	3¢ Mother's Day Flat	14.00
☐739	3¢ Wisconsin	16.00
☐740	1¢ Nat'l. Parks	10.00
☐741	2¢ Nat'l. Parks	12.00
☐742	3¢ Nat'l. Parks	14.00
☐743	4¢ Nat'l. Parks	35.00
☐744	5¢ Nat'l. Parks	60.00
☐745	6¢ Nat'l. Parks	90.00
☐746	7¢ Nat'l. Parks	60.00
☐747	8¢ Nat'l. Parks	130.00
☐748	9¢ Nat'l. Parks	120.00
☐749	10¢ Nat'l. Parks	225.00
☐752	3¢ Newburg	400.00
☐753	3¢ Byrd	550.00
☐754	3¢ Mother's Day	200.00
☐755	3¢ Wisconsin	200.00

Scott No.		Fine
☐756	1¢ Park	70.00
☐757	2¢ Park	80.00
☐758	3¢ Park	200.00
☐759	4¢ Park	300.00
☐760	5¢ Park	500.00
☐761	6¢ Park	650.00
☐762	7¢ Park	500.00
☐763	8¢ Park	600.00
☐764	9¢ Park	600.00
☐765	10¢ Park	1000.00
☐766a	1¢ Chicago	500.00
☐767a	3¢ Chicago	500.00
☐768a	3¢ Byrd	600.00
☐769	1¢ Park	300.00
☐770	3¢ Park	600.00
☐771	16¢ Air Spec. Deal	800.00
☐772	3¢ Connecticut	11.00
☐773	3¢ San Diego	7.00
☐774	3¢ Boulder Dam	10.00
☐775	3¢ Michigan	10.00
☐776	3¢ Texas	10.00
☐777	3¢ Rhode Island	10.00
☐782	3¢ Arkansas	8.00
☐783	3¢ Oregon	7.50
☐784	3¢ Susan B. Anthony	14.00
☐785	1¢ Army	10.00
☐786	2¢ Army	10.00
☐787	3¢ Army	13.00
☐788	4¢ Army	32.00
☐789	5¢ Army	46.00
☐790	1¢ Navy	10.00
☐791	2¢ Navy	10.00
☐792	3¢ Navy	9.00
☐793	4¢ Navy	32.00
☐794	5¢ Navy	55.00
☐795	3¢ N.W. Territory	7.50
☐796	5¢ Virginia Dare	16.00
☐798	3¢ Constitution	12.00
☐799	3¢ Hawaii	12.00

Scott No.		Fine
☐800	3¢ Alaska	9.50
☐801	3¢ Puerto Rico	9.50
☐802	3¢ Virgin Islands	9.50
☐835	3¢ Ratification	20.00
☐836	3¢ Swede-Finn	9.00
☐837	3¢ N.W. Territory	25.00
☐838	3¢ Iowa	15.00
☐852	3¢ Golden Gate	8.50
☐853	3¢ N.Y. Fair	9.00
☐854	3¢ Inauguration	27.00
☐855	3¢ Baseball	100.00
☐856	3¢ Canal Zone	13.00
☐857	3¢ Printing	8.00
☐858	3¢ Four States	8.00
☐859	1¢ Irving	7.00
☐860	2¢ Cooper	7.00
☐861	3¢ Emerson	8.00
☐862	5¢ Alcott	35.00
☐863	10¢ Clemens	175.00
☐864	1¢ Longfellow	8.00
☐865	2¢ Whittier	8.50
☐866	3¢ Lowell	10.00
☐867	5¢ Whitman	38.00
☐868	10¢ Riley	250.00
☐869	1¢ Mann	8.00
☐870	2¢ Hopkins	7.75
☐871	3¢ Elliot	16.00
☐872	5¢ Willard	48.00
☐873	10¢ B.T. Washington	175.00
☐874	1¢ Audubon	6.50
☐875	2¢ Long	7.00
☐876	3¢ Burbank	9.00
☐877	5¢ Reed	30.00
☐878	10¢ Addams	125.00
☐879	1¢ Fosters	6.00
☐880	2¢ Sousa	11.00
☐881	3¢ Herbert	10.00
☐882	5¢ MacDowell	41.00
☐883	10¢ Nevin	400.00
☐884	1¢ Sturat	5.00

Scott No.		Fine	Scott No.		Fine
☐885	2¢ Whistler	7.00	☐894	3¢ Pony Express	20.00
☐886	3¢ St. Gaudens	8.00	☐895	3¢ Pan American	20.00
☐887	5¢ French	46.00	☐896	3¢ Idaho	11.00
☐888	10¢ Remington	200.00	☐897	3¢ Wyoming	9.50
☐889	1¢ Whitney	9.10	☐898	3¢ Coronado	9.50
☐890	2¢ Morse	8.50	☐899	1¢ Defense	7.00
☐891	3¢ McCormick	25.00	☐900	2¢ Defense	10.00
☐892	5¢ Howe	90.00	☐901	3¢ Defense	11.00
☐893	10¢ Bell	1000.00	☐902	3¢ Emancipation	14.25

Scott No.		Fine Unused Each	Ave. Unused Each	Fine Used Each	Ave. Used Each

OFFICIAL STAMPS—
1873. CONTINENTAL PRINTING AGRICULTURAL DEPARMENT (N-H ADD 70%)

Scott No.		Fine Unused Each	Ave. Unused Each	Fine Used Each	Ave. Used Each
☐O1	1¢ Yellow	82.00	50.00	65.00	38.00
☐O2	2¢ Yellow	65.00	45.00	25.00	18.00
☐O3	3¢ Yellow	65.00	40.00	5.00	4.00
☐O4	6¢ Yellow	70.00	50.00	20.00	12.00
☐O5	10¢ Yellow	140.00	90.00	80.00	50.00
☐O6	12¢ Yellow	200.00	120.00	100.00	60.00
☐O7	15¢ Yellow	150.00	100.00	90.00	60.00
☐O8	24¢ Yellow	170.00	100.00	80.00	50.00
☐O9	30¢ Yellow	220.00	130.00	120.00	80.00

1873. OFFICIAL STAMPS—EXECUTIVE DEPARTMENT

☐O10	1¢ Carmine	350.00	220.00	200.00	140.00
☐O11	2¢ Carmine	225.00	150.00	100.00	70.00
☐O12	3¢ Carmine	300.00	180.00	100.00	60.00
☐O13	6¢ Carmine	400.00	250.00	300.00	180.00
☐O14	10¢ Carmine	400.00	250.00	250.00	150.00

1873. OFFICIAL STAMPS—INTERIOR DEPARTMENT

☐O15	1¢ Vermillion	22.00	15.00	6.50	4.10
☐O16	2¢ Vermillion	21.00	12.00	3.40	2.30
☐O17	3¢ Vermillion	30.00	20.00	4.00	2.25
☐O18	6¢ Vermillion	20.00	12.00	3.00	2.40

Scott No.		Fine Unused Each	Ave. Unused Each	Fine Used Each	Ave. Used Each
☐019	10¢ Vermillion	20.00	14.00	7.00	4.40
☐020	12¢ Vermillion	32.00	20.00	6.00	3.50
☐021	15¢ Vermillion	50.00	30.00	14.00	7.50
☐022	24¢ Vermillion	40.00	25.00	8.50	5.50
☐023	30¢ Vermillion	50.00	28.00	10.00	6.00
☐024	90¢ Vermillion	120.00	70.00	22.00	15.00

1873. OFFICIAL STAMPS—JUSTICE DEPARTMENT

☐025	1¢ Purple	65.00	40.00	38.00	30.00
☐026	2¢ Purple	100.00	70.00	40.00	28.00
☐027	3¢ Purple	100.00	65.00	10.00	6.00
☐028	6¢ Purple	90.00	65.00	15.00	10.00
☐029	10¢ Purple	110.00	65.00	40.00	25.00
☐030	12¢ Purple	80.00	50.00	20.00	12.00
☐031	15¢ Purple	175.00	100.00	60.00	45.00
☐032	24¢ Purple	450.00	300.00	160.00	100.00
☐033	30¢ Purple	400.00	250.00	100.00	65.00
☐034	90¢ Purple	600.00	400.00	220.00	150.00

1873. OFFICIAL STAMPS—NAVY DEPARTMENT

☐035	1¢ Ultra Marine	50.00	30.00	15.00	10.50
☐036	2¢ Ultra Marine	40.00	25.00	13.00	9.00
☐037	3¢ Ultra Marine	40.00	25.00	5.50	3.50
☐038	6¢ Ultra Marine	40.00	22.00	8.00	5.00
☐039	7¢ Ultra Marine	210.00	160.00	80.00	55.00
☐040	10¢ Ultra Marine	50.00	30.00	16.00	10.00
☐041	12¢ Ultra Marine	60.00	40.00	12.00	9.00
☐042	15¢ Ultra Marine	100.00	60.00	35.00	25.00
☐043	24¢ Ultra Marine	100.00	60.00	40.00	28.00
☐044	30¢ Ultra Marine	90.00	50.00	20.00	12.00
☐045	90¢ Ultra Marine	450.00	300.00	100.00	70.00

1873. OFFICIAL STAMPS—POST OFFICE DEPARTMENT

☐047	1¢ Black	9.00	5.50	4.00	2.90
☐048	2¢ Black	11.00	8.00	3.00	2.70
☐049	3¢ Black	3.50	2.15	1.95	1.00
☐050	6¢ Black	9.00	6.00	3.00	1.25
☐051	10¢ Black	45.00	28.00	21.00	15.00
☐052	12¢ Black	26.00	16.00	6.00	4.00
☐053	15¢ Black	32.00	18.00	11.00	5.00

Scott No.		Fine Unused Each	Ave. Unused Each	Fine Used Each	Ave. Used Each
☐O54	24¢ Black	40.00	25.00	15.00	9.00
☐O55	30¢ Black	40.00	25.00	12.00	8.00
☐O56	90¢ Black	60.00	30.00	16.00	9.00

1873. OFFICIAL STAMPS—STATE DEPARTMENT

☐O57	1¢ Green	60.00	40.00	18.00	10.00
☐O58	2¢ Green	125.00	75.00	35.00	21.00
☐O59	3¢ Green	50.00	35.00	12.00	8.00
☐O60	6¢ Green	45.00	30.00	12.00	8.00
☐O61	7¢ Green	95.00	60.00	25.00	15.00
☐O62	10¢ Green	80.00	50.00	20.00	12.00
☐O63	12¢ Green	105.00	65.00	45.00	28.00
☐O64	15¢ Green	115.00	80.00	30.00	19.00
☐O65	24¢ Green	230.00	150.00	75.00	40.00
☐O66	30¢ Green	210.00	150.00	65.00	40.00
☐O67	90¢ Green	475.00	300.00	150.00	100.00
☐O68	$2 Green	600.00	350.00	300.00	250.00
☐O69	$5 Green & Black	4800.00	3000.00	2000.00	1200.00
☐O70	$10 Green & Black	2800.00	1500.00	1200.00	900.00
☐O71	$20 Green & Black	2400.00	1200.00	1000.00	700.00

1873. OFFICIAL STAMPS—TREASURY DEPARTMENT

☐O72	1¢ Brown	22.00	12.00	3.00	1.40
☐O73	2¢ Brown	25.00	16.00	3.00	1.40
☐O74	3¢ Brown	15.00	10.00	2.00	1.00
☐O75	6¢ Brown	20.00	12.00	2.00	1.25
☐O76	7¢ Brown	60.00	35.00	16.00	10.00
☐O77	10¢ Brown	60.00	35.00	6.00	4.40
☐O78	12¢ Brown	65.00	35.00	4.10	3.00
☐O79	15¢ Brown	50.00	25.00	6.00	4.00
☐O80	24¢ Brown	250.00	175.00	60.00	30.00
☐O81	30¢ Brown	85.00.	50.00	6.00	3.50
☐O82	90¢ Brown	79.00	50.00	6.50	3.50

1873. OFFICIAL STAMPS—WAR DEPARTMENT

☐O83	1¢ Rose	80.00	60.00	5.00	3.00
☐O84	2¢ Rose	70.00	50.00	8.00	3.50
☐O85	3¢ Rose	70.00	40.00	2.00	1.00
☐O86	6¢ Rose	260.00	150.00	5.00	3.00

Scott No.		Fine Unused Each	Ave. Unused Each	Fine Used Each	Ave. Used Each
☐087	7¢ Rose	70.00	45.00	40.00	26.00
☐088	10¢ Rose	25.00	12.00	4.00	3.00
☐089	12¢ Rose	75.00	50.00	4.50	3.00
☐090	15¢ Rose	20.00	12.00	3.50	2.10
☐091	24¢ Rose	20.00	12.00	4.15	2.00
☐092	30¢ Rose	22.00	16.00	4.15	2.00
☐093	90¢ Rose	55.00	30.00	16.00	10.00

1879. OFFICIAL STAMPS—AMERICAN PRINTING—SOFT POROUS PAPER AGRICULTURAL DEPARTMENT (N-H ADD 80%)

☐094	1¢ Yellow	1500.00	1000.00	—	—
☐095	3¢ Yellow	200.00	125.00	40.00	25.00

1879. OFFICIAL STAMPS—INTERIOR DEPARTMENT

☐096	1¢ Vermillion	140.00	100.00	80.00	50.00
☐097	2¢ Vermillion	2.50	2.00	1.00	.75
☐098	3¢ Vermillion	3.00	1.75	1.00	.75
☐099	6¢ Vermillion	4.00	3.00	2.00	1.00
☐0100	10¢ Vermillion	38.00	28.00	25.00	20.00
☐0101	12¢ Vermillion	80.00	50.00	40.00	30.00
☐0102	15¢ Vermillion	175.00	100.00	80.00	50.00
☐0103	24¢ Vermillion	2000.00	1100.00	—	—

1879. OFFICIAL STAMPS—JUSTICE DEPARTMENT

☐0106	3¢ Purple	60.00	30.00	24.00	15.00
☐0107	6¢ Purple	125.00	80.00	75.00	50.00

1879. OFFICIAL STAMPS—POST OFFICE DEPARTMENT

☐0108	3¢ Black	10.00	6.00	2.00	1.75

1879. OFFICIAL STAMPS—TREASURY DEPARTMENT

☐0109	3¢ Brown	28.00	16.00	5.00	2.75
☐0110	6¢ Brown	60.00	36.00	18.00	12.00
☐0111	10¢ Brown	75.00	50.00	20.00	12.00
☐0112	30¢ Brown	800.00	500.00	160.00	100.00
☐0113	90¢ Brown	800.00	500.00	160.00	100.00

Scott No.	Fine Unused Each	Ave. Unused Each	Fine Used Each	Ave. Used Each

1879. OFFICIAL STAMPS—WAR DEPARTMENT

Scott No.	Fine Unused Each	Ave. Unused Each	Fine Used Each	Ave. Used Each
☐O114 1¢ Rose	2.40	1.15	1.00	.85
☐O115 2¢ Rose	4.50	1.80	1.20	.85
☐O116 3¢ Rose	3.00	1.50	1.00	.85
☐O117 6¢ Rose	4.50	2.00	1.00	.85
☐O118 10¢ Rose	24.00	16.00	14.00	10.00
☐O119 12¢ Rose	20.00	10.00	3.10	2.75
☐O120 30¢ Rose	55.00	30.00	30.00	20.00

1910–1911. POSTAL SAVINGS STAMPS (N-H ADD 50%)

Scott No.	Fine Unused Each	Ave. Unused Each	Fine Used Each	Ave. Used Each
☐O121 2¢ Black, D.L. Wmk	11.00	5.00	1.35	.90
☐O122 50¢ Dark Green, D.L. Wmk	110.00	60.00	32.00	20.00
☐O123 $1 Ultramarine, D.L. Wmk	110.00	60.00	12.00	7.00
☐O124 1¢ Dark Violet, S.L. Wmk	4.00	3.00	1.50	1.00
☐O125 2¢ Black, S.L. Wmk	45.00	20.00	5.00	3.00
☐O126 10¢ Carmine, S.L. Wmk	10.00	5.00	1.30	1.00

1983–1989. OFFICIAL STAMPS—GREAT SEAL SERIES

Scott No.		Mint Sheet	Plate Block	Fine Used Each	Fine Used Each
☐O127	1¢	10.00	.60	.25	.20
☐O128	4¢	10.00	.60	.25	.20
☐O129	13¢	25.00	1.75	1.00	.50
☐O130	17¢	35.00	2.00	.75	.50
☐O132	$1	210.00	11.00	2.50	1.75
☐O133	$5	900.00	45.00	11.00	7.00
☐O135	20¢	—	—	1.25	1.00
☐O136	22¢	—	—	1.00	.75
☐O138	14¢	300.00	—	3.75	1.75
☐O139	22¢	—	—	3.50	2.25
☐O140	25¢	—	—	1.00	.75
☐O141	25¢	—	—	1.00	.50
☐O143	1¢	10.00	—	.40	.20
☐O144	29¢	—	—	2.00	1.00
☐O145	29¢	—	—	1.00	.50
☐O146	4¢	10.00	—	.45	.25
☐O147	19¢	42.00	—	.75	.50
☐O148	23¢	52.00	—	.75	.50
☐O151	$1	200.00	—	2.50	2.00
☐O152	32¢	—	—	1.00	.50
☐O153	32¢	—	—	1.00	.50
☐O154	1¢	10.00	—	.50	.25
☐O155	20¢	45.00	—	1.00	.50
☐O156	23¢	50.00	—	1.00	.50

Scott No.	Fine Unused Block	Ave. Unused Block	Fine Unused Each	Ave. Unused Each	Fine Used Each	Ave. Used Each

1912. PARCEL POST DUE STAMPS (N-H ADD 70%)

Scott No.		Fine Unused Block	Ave. Unused Block	Fine Unused Each	Ave. Unused Each	Fine Used Each	Ave. Used Each
☐JQ1	1¢ Dark Green	275.00	200.00	8.00	6.00	4.10	2.65
☐JQ2	2¢ Dark Green	400.00	300.00	70.00	50.00	15.00	10.00
☐JQ3	5¢ Dark Green	100.00	60.00	9.25	7.25	4.15	3.50
☐JQ4	10¢ Dark Green	1100.00	900.00	150.00	100.00	38.00	24.00
☐JQ5	25¢ Dark Green	510.00	400.00	85.00	50.00	4.75	2.75

1912–1913. PARCEL POST STAMPS (N-H ADD 60%)

Scott No.		Fine Unused Block	Ave. Unused Block	Fine Unused Each	Ave. Unused Each	Fine Used Each	Ave. Used Each
☐Q1	1¢ P.O. Clerk	70.00	60.00	3.50	2.40	1.25	1.00
☐Q2	2¢ City Carrier	68.00	50.00	3.75	3.00	1.00	.72
☐Q3	3¢ Railway Clerk	120.00	90.00	6.50	5.00	4.50	3.50
☐Q4	4¢ Rural Carrier	600.00	420.00	18.00	14.00	2.60	1.80
☐Q5	5¢ Mail Train	600.00	420.00	18.00	12.00	2.00	1.25
☐Q6	10¢ Steamship	310.00	165.00	30.00	20.00	3.00	1.50
☐Q7	15¢ Mail Truck	360.00	230.00	41.00	28.00	9.00	6.10
☐Q8	20¢ Airplane	410.00	360.00	91.00	60.00	18.00	12.00
☐Q9	25¢ Manufacturing	390.00	325.00	43.00	29.00	6.50	4.50
☐Q10	50¢ Dairying	1500.00	1200.00	200.00	140.00	34.00	25.10
☐Q11	75¢ Harvesting	525.00	390.00	58.00	40.00	24.00	16.00
☐Q12	$1 Fruit Growing	1600.00	1100.00	300.00	180.00	20.00	13.00

Scott No.	Fine Unused Block	Ave. Unused Block	Fine Unused Each	Ave. Unused Each	Fine Used Each	Ave. Used Each

1925–1929 SPECIAL HANDLING STAMPS (N-H ADD 40%)

Scott No.	Fine Unused Block	Ave. Unused Block	Fine Unused Each	Ave. Unused Each	Fine Used Each	Ave. Used Each
☐QE1 10¢ Yellow Green	26.00	18.00	1.50	1.00	1.00	.72
☐QE2 15¢ Yellow Green	32.00	24.00	1.60	1.00	.95	.72
☐QE3 20¢ Yellow Green	42.00	24.00	3.00	2.00	2.10	1.50
☐QE4 25¢ Yellow Green	260.00	150.00	17.00	13.00	8.50	4.60
☐QE4A 25¢ Deep Green	320.00	200.00	23.00	16.00	5.25	3.60

1919–1922 U.S. OFFICES IN CHINA ISSUES (N-H ADD 20%) SHANGHAI 2¢ CHINA

Scott No.	Fine Unused Block	Ave. Unused Block	Fine Unused Each	Ave. Unused Each	Fine Used Each	Ave. Used Each
☐K1 2¢ on 1¢ Green	25.00	15.00	20.00	12.00	21.00	14.00
☐K2 4¢ on 2¢ Rose	25.00	15.00	20.00	12.00	21.00	14.00
☐K3 6¢ on 3¢ Violet	50.00	30.00	40.00	24.00	48.00	28.00
☐K4 8¢ on 4¢ Brown	70.00	45.00	45.00	24.00	48.00	28.00
☐K5 10¢ on 2¢ Blue	80.00	45.00	54.00	32.00	52.00	31.00
☐K6 12¢ on 6¢ Orange	90.00	50.00	60.00	40.00	68.00	42.00
☐K7 14¢ on 7¢ Black	100.00	50.00	70.00	40.00	80.00	50.00
☐K8 16¢ on 8¢ Olive Bistre	80.00	40.00	55.00	30.00	54.00	32.00
☐K8a 16¢ on 8¢ Olive Green	80.00	40.00	54.00	29.00	48.00	32.00
☐K9 18¢ on 9¢ Orange Red	80.00	40.00	50.00	30.00	60.00	36.00
☐K10 20¢ on 10¢ Yellow Orange	70.00	40.00	50.00	29.00	52.00	33.00
☐K11 24¢ on 12¢ Brown	80.00	50.00	54.00	33.00	60.00	36.00

Scott No.	Fine Unused Block	Ave. Unused Block	Fine Unused Each	Ave. Unused Each	Fine Used Each	Ave. Used Each
☐K11a 24¢ on 12¢ Brown	100.00	65.00	80.00	46.00	78.00	50.00
☐K12 30¢ on 15¢ Gray	100.00	50.00	60.00	40.00	75.00	46.00
☐K13 40¢ on 20¢ Ultramarine	140.00	90.00	100.00	60.00	110.00	70.00
☐K14 60¢ on 30¢ Orange Red	130.00	75.00	90.00	60.00	100.00	68.00
☐K15 $1 on 50¢ Violet	600.00	500.00	450.00	300.00	450.00	300.00
☐K16 $2 on $1	500.00	350.00	350.00	250.00	380.00	275.00
☐K17 2¢ on 1¢ Green	120.00	100.00	90.00	44.00	75.00	45.00
☐K18 4¢ on 2¢ Carmine	110.00	80.00	80.00	46.00	70.00	48.00

Scott No.	Imperforated (a) Fine	Ave.	Part Perforated (b) Fine	Ave.	Perforated (c) Fine	Ave.

1862–1971. U.S. REVENUE STAMPS

Scott No.	Imperforated (a) Fine	Ave.	Part Perforated (b) Fine	Ave.	Perforated (c) Fine	Ave.
☐R1 1¢ Express	51.00	28.00	34.00	18.50	1.00	.60
☐R2 1¢ Play Cards	770.00	450.00	400.00	260.00	95.00	50.00
☐R3 1¢ Proprietary	500.00	270.00	95.00	60.00	.42	.26
☐R4 1¢ Telegraph	300.00	175.00	—	—	7.60	4.00
☐R5 2¢ Bank Ck., Blue	1.00	.75	1.00	.65	.21	.16
☐R6 2¢ Bank Ck., Orange	—	—	70.00	40.00	.21	.16
☐R7 2¢ Certif., Blue	10.50	6.00	—	—	28.00	12.50
☐R8 2¢ Certif., Orange	—	—	—	—	26.00	12.50
☐R9 2¢ Express, Blue	12.00	6.00	14.00	8.00	.30	.16
☐R10 2¢ Express, Orange	—	—	—	—	6.00	3.15

Scott No.		Imperforated (a) Fine	Ave.	Part Perforated (b) Fine	Ave.	Perforated (c) Fine	Ave.
☐R11	2¢ Ply. Cds., Blue	—	—	110.00	61.00	2.90	1.50
☐R12	2¢ Ply. Cds., Orange	—	—	—	—	26.00	15.00
☐R13	2¢ Proprietary, Blue	—	—	100.00	54.00	.34	.21
☐R14	2¢ Proprietary, Orange	—	—	—	—	34.00	18.00
☐R15	2¢ U.S.I.R.	—	—	—	—	.20	.15
☐R16	3¢ Foreign Ex.	—	—	155.00	90.00	2.50	1.25
☐R17	3¢ Playing Cds.	—	—	—	—	100.00	53.00
☐R18	3¢ Proprietary	—	—	181.00	110.00	1.80	.95
☐R19	3¢ Telegraph	50.00	42.00	22.00	7.50	2.80	1.45
☐R20	4¢ Inland Exch.	—	—	—	—	1.70	.95
☐R21	4¢ Playing Cards	—	—	—	—	360.00	183.00
☐R22	4¢ Proprietary	—	—	180.00	110.00	4.00	2.50
☐R23	5¢ Agreement	—	—	—	—	.30	.16
☐R24	5¢ Certificate	3.00	3.00	8.50	5.00	.21	.16
☐R25	5¢ Express	3.70	4.00	5.00	3.00	.34	.20
☐R26	5¢ Foreign Ex.	—	—	—	—	.36	.21
☐R27	5¢ Inland Exch.	4.00	4.00	3.50	2.10	.26	.16
☐R28	5¢ Playing Cds.	—	—	—	—	14.00	9.00
☐R29	5¢ Proprietary	—	—	—	—	19.00	8.50
☐R30	6¢ Inland Exch.	—	—	—	—	1.25	.70
☐R32	10¢ Bill of Ldg.	45.00	48.00	145.00	78.00	.80	.41

Scott No.	Imperforated (a) Fine	Ave.	Part Perforated (b) Fine	Ave.	Perforated (c) Fine	Ave.
☐R33 10¢ Certificate	95.00	84.00	110.00	65.00	.37	.21
☐R34 10¢ Contract Bill	—	—	100.00	54.00	.32	.18
☐R35 10¢ For Ex. Bill	—	—	—	—	5.50	3.00
☐R36 10¢ Inland Exch.	122.00	75.00	3.00	1.90	.24	.16
☐R37 10¢ Power of Att'y.	340.00	190.00	18.00	12.00	.40	.26
☐R38 10¢ Proprietary	—	—	—	—	14.00	6.80
☐R39 15¢ Foreign Exch.	—	—	—	—	13.00	7.00
☐R40 15¢ Inland Exch.	25.00	15.00	10.00	6.10	1.00	.62
☐R41 20¢ Foreign Exch.	44.00	24.00	—	—	30.00	16.00
☐R42 20¢ Inland Exch.	13.00	7.20	17.00	10.00	.40	.25
☐R43 25¢ Bond	98.00	60.00	6.00	3.40	1.80	1.00
☐R44 25¢ Certificate	7.00	3.10	6.00	3.00	.20	.18
☐R45 25¢ Entry of Gds.	18.00	10.00	34.00	19.00	.60	.30
☐R46 25¢ Insurance	9.00	6.00	10.00	6.00	.32	.18
☐R47 25¢ Life Insur.	32.00	18.00	110.00	55.00	5.50	3.50
☐R48 25¢ Power of Atty.	5.00	3.50	18.00	9.00	.28	.16
☐R49 25¢ Protest	25.00	11.00	145.00	80.00	6.00	3.00
☐R50 25¢ Warehouse Rct.	37.00	20.00	139.00	77.00	22.00	12.00
☐R51 30¢ Foreign Exch.	55.00	25.00	500.00	250.00	34.00	18.00
☐R52 30¢ Inland Exch.	39.00	22.00	44.00	23.00	2.50	1.25
☐R53 40¢ Inland Exch.	428.00	250.00	5.00	2.35	2.60	1.60

Scott No.	Imperforated (a) Fine	Ave.	Part Perforated (b) Fine	Ave.	Perforated (c) Fine	Ave.
□R54 50¢ Convey, Blue	10.00	7.00	2.00	.75	.21	.16
□R55 50¢ Entry of Gds.	—	—	12.00	6.00	.31	.16
□R56 50¢ Foreign Exch.	38.00	22.00	32.00	19.00	4.20	2.20
□R57 50¢ Lease	22.00	12.00	57.00	30.00	4.75	2.75
□R58 50¢ Life Insur.	29.00	15.60	54.00	29.00	.80	.45
□R59 50¢ Mortgage	9.50	5.00	1.50	1.00	.40	.26
□R60 50¢ Orig. Process	2.50	1.50	—	—	.35	.21
□R61 50¢ Passage Tkt.	67.00	36.00	105.00	56.00	.54	.30
□R62 50¢ Prob. of Will	32.75	17.00	45.00	24.00	17.50	9.50
□R63 50¢ Sty. Bond, Bl.	112.00	61.00	2.60	1.40	.30	.16
□R64 60¢ Inland Exch.	78.00	45.00	45.00	25.00	4.85	2.85
□R65 70¢ Foreign Exch.	292.00	167.00	82.00	50.00	4.50	2.75
□R66 $1 Conveyance	10.00	6.00	250.00	140.00	2.40	1.15
□R67 $1 Entry of Gds.	26.00	14.00	—	—	1.60	.82
□R68 $1 Foreign Exch.	51.00	27.00	—	—	.70	.40
□R69 $1 Inland Exch.	12.00	7.00	220.00	120.00	.58	.30
□R70 $1 Lease	34.00	18.00	—	—	1.30	.80
□R71 $1 Life Insur.	140.00	80.00	—	—	4.50	2.15
□R72 $1 Manifest	50.50	29.00	—	—	20.90	12.00
□R73 $1 Mortgage	16.00	9.00	—	—	128.00	67.00

Scott No.	Imperforated (a)		Part Perforated (b)		Perforated (c)	
	Fine	Ave.	Fine	Ave.	Fine	Ave.
☐R74 $1 Passage Tkt.						
	160.00	90.00	—	—	136.00	69.00
☐R75 $1 Power of Atty.						
	59.00	32.00	—	—	1.75	.95
☐R76 $1 Prob. of Will						
	56.00	31.00	—	—	33.00	18.50
☐R77 $1.30 Foreign Exch.						
	1400.00	1100.00	—	—	45.00	26.00
☐R78 $1.50 Finland Exch.						
	22.00	11.00	—	—	3.00	1.50
☐R79 $1.60 Foreign Exch.						
	625.00	350.00	—	—	86.00	46.00
☐R80 $1.90 Foreign Exch.						
	1800.00	1400.00	—	—	59.00	30.00
☐R81 $2 Conveyance						
	88.00	48.50	870.00	500.00	2.00	1.00
☐R82 $2 Mortgage						
	80.00	42.50	—	—	2.40	1.35
☐R83 $2 Prob. of Will						
	1800.00	1400.00	—	—	41.00	21.00
☐R84 $2.50 Inland Exch.						
	964.00	540.00	—	—	3.00	1.60
☐R85 $3 Chart. Pty.						
	90.00	60.00	—	—	3.75	1.85
☐R86 $3 Manifest						
	89.00	50.00	—	—	20.00	12.00
☐R87 $3.50 Inland Exch.						
	1000.00	750.00	—	—	45.00	24.00
☐R88 $5 Chtr. Party						
	215.00	120.50	—	—	5.00	2.70
☐R89 $5 Conveyance						
	31.00	16.50	—	—	5.00	2.80
☐R90 $5 Manifest						
	90.00	46.00	—	—	84.00	47.00
☐R91 $5 Mortgage						
	80.00	43.00	—	—	16.00	9.00
☐R92 $5 Prob. of Will						
	370.00	210.00	—	—	16.00	9.00
☐R93 $10 Chrt. Party						
	415.00	225.00	—	—	20.00	12.00
☐R94 $10 Conveyance						
	80.00	50.00	—	—	51.00	30.00

Scott No.	Imperforated (a) Fine	Ave.	Part Perforated (b) Fine	Ave.	Perforated (c) Fine	Ave.
☐R95 $10 Mortgage						
	301.00	165.00	—	—	21.00	11.00
☐R96 $10 Prob. of Will						
	1000.00	600.00	—	—	21.00	11.00
☐R97 $15 Mortgage						
	850.00	475.00	—	—	90.00	49.00
☐R98 $20 Conveyance						
	75.00	36.00	—	—	32.00	18.00
☐R99 $20 Prob. of Will						
	856.00	480.00	—	—	795.00	450.00
☐R100 $25 Mortgage						
	700.00	390.00	—	—	84.00	46.00
☐R101 $50 U.S.I.R						
	151.00	92.00	—	—	76.00	43.00
☐R102 $200 U.S.I.R.						
	1000.00	540.00	—	—	520.00	300.00

Scott No.	Fine Used Each	Ave. Used Each

1871. U.S. REVENUE—SECOND ISSUE

Scott No.			Fine Used Each	Ave. Used Each
☐R103	1¢	Blue and Black	30.00	13.00
☐R104	2¢	Blue and Black	1.20	.60
☐R105	3¢	Blue and Black	12.00	6.50
☐R106	4¢	Blue and Black	41.00	24.00
☐R107	5¢	Blue and Black	1.00	.62
☐R108	6¢	Blue and Black	68.00	37.00
☐R109	10¢	Blue and Black	.82	.48
☐R110	15¢	Blue and Black	19.50	11.00
☐R111	20¢	Blue and Black	4.80	2.40
☐R112	25¢	Blue and Black	.65	.36
☐R113	30¢	Blue and Black	50.00	29.00
☐R114	40¢	Blue and Black	30.00	20.00
☐R115	50¢	Blue and Black	.60	.36
☐R116	60¢	Blue and Black	58.00	34.00
☐R117	70¢	Blue and Black	30.00	18.00

Scott No.			Fine Used Each	Ave. Used Each
☐R118	$1	Blue and Black	3.00	1.60
☐R119	$1.30	Blue and Black	220.00	122.00
☐R120	$1.50	Blue and Black	12.00	6.00
☐R121	$1.60	Blue and Black	300.00	160.00
☐R122	$1.90	Blue and Black	125.00	62.00
☐R123	$2	Blue and Black	10.00	5.50
☐R124	$2.50	Blue and Black	20.00	11.00
☐R125	$3	Blue and Black	30.00	18.00
☐R126	$3.50	Blue and Black	115.00	60.00
☐R127	$5	Blue and Black	16.00	9.00
☐R128	$10	Blue and Black	90.00	48.00
☐R129	$20	Blue and Black	267.00	150.00
☐R130	$25	Blue and Black	267.00	150.00
☐R131	$50	Blue and Black	303.00	175.00

1871-1872. U.S. REVENUE—THIRD ISSUE

☐R134	1¢	Claret and Black	24.00	13.00
☐R135	2¢	Orange and Black	.25	.18
☐R136	4¢	Brown and Black	28.00	16.00
☐R137	5¢	Orange and Black	.30	.16
☐R138	6¢	Orange and Black	27.00	15.00
☐R139	15¢	Brown and Black	10.00	6.00
☐R140	30¢	Orange and Black	11.00	7.00
☐R141	40¢	Brown and Black	22.00	15.00
☐R142	60¢	Orange and Black	47.00	28.00
☐R143	70¢	Green and Black	30.00	20.00
☐R144	$1	Green and Black	1.25	.70
☐R145	$2	Vermillion and Black	19.00	10.00
☐R146	$2.50	Claret and Black	30.00	20.00
☐R147	$3	Green and Black	32.50	22.00
☐R148	$5	Vermillion and Black	17.25	9.40
☐R149	$10	Green and Black	67.00	39.00
☐R150	$20	Orange and Black	425.00	240.00

1874. U.S. REVENUE—FOURTH ISSUE

☐R151	2¢	Orange and Black, Green Paper	.25	.18

Scott No.			Fine Used Each	Ave. Used Each

1875. U.S. REVENUE— FIFTH ISSUE

Scott No.			Fine Used Each	Ave. Used Each
☐R152a	2¢	Blue, Silk Paper	.25	.18
☐R152b	2¢	Blue, Watermarked	.25	.18
☐R152c	2¢	Blue, Rouletted	30.00	18.00

Scott No.			Fine Unused Each	Ave. Unused Each	Fine Used Each	Ave. Used Each
1898. U.S. REVENUE—POSTAGE AND NEWS-PAPER STAMPS SURCHARGED I.R.						
☐R153	1¢	Green, Small I.R.	1.50	.75	1.00	.65
☐R154	1¢	Green, Large I.R.	.30	.25	.21	.16
☐R154a	1¢	Green Inverted Surch.				
			9.00	5.00	6.00	3.00
☐R155	2¢	Carmine, Large I.R.	.25	.21	.60	.37
☐R155a	2¢	Carmine, Inverted Surch.				
			1.25	.75	1.00	.72
☐R159	$5	Blue, Surch. down	185.00	100.00	127.00	80.00
☐R160	$5	Blue, Surch. up	86.00	48.00	58.00	32.00
1898. U.S. REVENUE—DOCUMENTARY "BATTLESHIP" DESIGN						
☐R161	½¢	Orange	2.90	5.00	6.00	3.60
☐R162	½¢	Dark Gray	.29	.25	.21	.18
☐R163	1¢	Pale Blue	.30	.25	.21	.18
☐R164	2¢	Carmine	.30	.25	.21	.18
☐R165	3¢	Dark Blue	1.00	.55	.21	.18
☐R166	4¢	Pale Rose	.40	.26	.20	.18
☐R167	5¢	Lilac	.30	.25	.20	.18
☐R168	10¢	Dark Brown	.75	.30	.20	.18
☐R169	25¢	Purple Brown	1.00	.50	.20	.18
☐R170	40¢	Blue Lilac (cut .25)	60.00	30.00	1.50	.90
☐R171	50¢	Slate Violet	7.00	4.00	.20	.18
☐R172	80¢	Bistre (cut .15)	28.00	18.00	.50	.40
☐R173	$1	Dark Green	5.00	3.10	.20	.16
☐R174	$3	Dark Brown (cut .18)				
			12.00	7.00	.50	.36

Scott No.	Fine Un-Used Each	Ave. Un-Used Each	Fine Used Each	Ave. Used Each
☐R175 $5 Orange (cut .25)	12.00	8.00	1.25	.70
☐R176 $10 Black (cut .75)	33.00	25.00	2.60	1.60
☐R177 $30 Red (cut 25.00)	117.00	68.00	85.00	50.00
☐R178 $50 Gray Brown (cut 1.50)				
	55.00	32.00	4.00	3.00

1899. U.S. REVENUE—DOCUMENTARY STAMPS

Scott No.	Fine Un-Used Each	Ave. Un-Used Each	Fine Used Each	Ave. Used Each
☐R179 $100 Brown & Black (cut 15.00)				
	—	—	29.00	17.00
☐R180 $500 Lake & Black (cut 190.00)				
	—	—	442.00	279.00
☐R181 $100 Green & Black (cut 120.00)				
	—	—	334.00	270.00

1900. U.S. REVENUE—DOCUMENTARY STAMPS

Scott No.	Fine Un-Used Each	Ave. Un-Used Each	Fine Used Each	Ave. Used Each
☐R182 $1 Carmine (cut .15)	8.00	4.75	.52	.36
☐R183 $3 Lake (cut 8.00)	64.00	40.00	44.00	26.00

1900–1902. U.S. REVENUE—DOCUMENTARY STAMPS SURCHARGED

Scott No.	Fine Un-Used Each	Ave. Un-Used Each	Fine Used Each	Ave. Used Each
☐R184 $1 Gray (cut .09)	5.00	3.00	.21	.16
☐R185 $2 Gray (cut .09)	5.00	3.00	.21	.16
☐R186 $3 Gray (cut 1.15)	32.00	18.00	10.00	6.10
☐R187 $5 Gray (cut .40)	24.00	14.00	5.00	3.10
☐R188 $10 Gray (cut 3.25)	41.00	25.00	11.00	6.50
☐R189 $50 Gray (cut 80.00)	550.00	303.00	330.00	190.00
☐R190 $1 Green (cut .35)	10.00	5.00	3.00	1.75
☐R191 $2 Green (cut .30)	10.00	6.00	2.00	1.00
☐R192 $5 Green (cut 1.60)	72.00	40.00	21.00	16.00
☐R193 $10 Green (cut 27.50)	225.00	120.00	138.00	79.00
☐R194 $50 Green (cut 220.00)				
	1000.00	545.00	775.00	400.00

1914. U.S. REVENUE—STAMPS DOCUMENTARY SINGLE LINE WATERMARK

Scott No.	Fine Un-Used Each	Ave. Un-Used Each	Fine Used Each	Ave. Used Each
☐R195 ½¢ Rose	6.00	4.00	3.00	2.00

Scott No.	Fine Un-Used Each	Ave. Un-Used Each	Fine Used Each	Ave. Used Each
☐R196 1¢ Rose	1.15	.60	.21	.16
☐R197 2¢ Rose	1.50	.90	.21	.16
☐R198 3¢ Rose	29.00	17.00	22.00	12.00
☐R199 4¢ Rose	7.80	5.00	1.25	.70
☐R200 5¢ Rose	2.80	1.50	.21	.16
☐R201 10¢ Rose	2.90	1.50	.21	.16
☐R202 25¢ Rose	18.00	9.00	.55	.34
☐R203 40¢ Rose	9.50	5.00	.60	.32
☐R204 50¢ Rose	4.00	3.00	.21	.16
☐R205 80¢ Rose	50.00	28.00	7.00	4.50

1914–1915. U.S. REVENUE—DOCUMENTARY STAMPS DOUBLE LINE WATERMARK

Scott No.	Fine Un-Used Each	Ave. Un-Used Each	Fine Used Each	Ave. Used Each
☐R206 ½¢ Rose	1.10	.55	.51	.35
☐R207 1¢ Rose	.27	.23	.23	.16
☐R208 2¢ Rose	.23	.21	.21	.16
☐R209 3¢ Rose	1.25	.60	.26	.20
☐R210 4¢ Rose	2.50	1.40	.34	.21
☐R211 5¢ Rose	1.25	.60	.21	.16
☐R212 10¢ Rose	.70	.24	.21	.16
☐R213 25¢ Rose	4.00	3.00	.95	.60
☐R214 40¢ Rose (cut .60)	42.00	21.00	9.00	5.00
☐R215 50¢ Rose	7.50	4.75	.21	.16
☐R216 80¢ Rose (cut 1.10)	51.00	29.00	9.00	6.00
☐R217 $1 Green (cut .20)	18.00	10.00	.21	.16
☐R218 $2 Carmine (cut .20)	28.00	15.00	.21	.16
☐R219 $2 Carmine (cut .25)	38.00	21.00	1.00	.60
☐R220 $5 Blue (cut .65)	33.00	20.00	2.00	1.00
☐R221 $10 Orange (cut 1.10)	74.00	41.00	4.50	3.00
☐R222 $30 Vermilion (cut 2.35)	210.00	85.00	9.00	6.00
☐R223 $50 Violet (cut 210.00)	875.00	500.00	625.00	349.00
☐R224 $60 Brown (cut 47.50)	—	—	110.00	64.00
☐R225 $100 Green (cut 16.00)	—	—	43.00	24.00
☐R226 $500 Blue (cut 210.00)	—	—	500.00	300.00
☐R227 $1000 Orange (cut 225.00)	—	—	500.00	300.00

Scott No.	Fine Un- Used Each	Ave. Un- Used Each	Fine Used Each	Ave. Used Each
1917–1933. U.S. REVENUE—DOCUMENTARY STAMPS—PERF. 11				
☐R228 1¢ Rose	.30	.26	.24	.20
☐R229 2¢ Rose	.30	.26	.24	.20
☐R230 3¢ Rose	.50	.30	.26	.20
☐R231 4¢ Rose	.35	.22	.21	.20
☐R232 5¢ Rose	.30	.22	.21	.20
☐R233 8¢ Rose	1.40	.95	.21	.20
☐R234 10¢ Rose	.26	.21	.21	.20
☐R235 20¢ Rose	.55	.35	.24	.20
☐R236 25¢ Rose	.95	.55	.24	.20
☐R237 40¢ Rose	.95	.55	.24	.20
☐R238 50¢ Rose	1.15	.65	.24	.20
☐R239 80¢ Rose	3.25	1.70	.24	.20
☐R240 $1 Green	4.50	2.50	.22	.20
☐R241 $2 Rose	8.00	5.00	.22	.20
☐R242 $3 Violet (cut .15)	24.00	15.00	.60	.30
☐R243 $4 Brown (cut .20)	15.00	9.00	1.20	.64
☐R244 $5 Blue (cut .13)	10.00	5.50	.26	.16
☐R245 $10 Orange (cut .20)	24.00	14.00	1.00	.60
1917. U.S. REVENUE—DOCUMENTARY STAMPS—PERF. 12				
☐R246 $30 Vermilion (cut .80)	34.00	20.00	6.00	5.00
☐R247 $60 Brown (cut 1.00)	40.00	25.00	7.00	5.00
☐R248 $100 Green (cut .45)	24.00	14.00	1.00	.60
☐R249 $500 Blue (cut 9.50)	—	—	32.00	20.00
☐R250 $1000 Orange (cut 3.50)	92.00	60.00	15.00	7.00
1928–1929. U.S. REVENUE—DOCUMENTARY STAMPS—PERF. 10				
☐R251 1¢ Carmine Rose	1.90	1.10	.90	.65
☐R252 2¢ Carmine Rose	.52	.36	.21	.16
☐R253 4¢ Carmine Rose	6.00	3.00	3.50	2.00
☐R254 5¢ Carmine Rose	1.15	.50	.40	.30
☐R255 10¢ Carmine Rose	1.60	1.00	1.00	.60
☐R256 20¢ Carmine Rose	5.25	3.00	5.00	3.00
☐R257 $1 Green (cut 1.90)	60.00	36.00	26.00	20.00
☐R258 $2 Rose	22.00	10.00	2.00	1.00
☐R259 $10 Orange (cut 8.00)	80.00	54.00	30.00	20.00

Scott No.	Fine Un-Used Each	Ave. Un-Used Each	Fine Used Each	Ave. Used Each

1929–1930. U.S. REVENUE—DOCUMENTARY STAMPS—PERF. 11 x 10

Scott No.	Fine Un-Used Each	Ave. Un-Used Each	Fine Used Each	Ave. Used Each
☐R260 2¢ Carmine Rose	2.60	1.50	2.25	1.25
☐R261 5¢ Carmine Rose	1.80	1.25	1.50	1.00
☐R262 10¢ Carmine Rose	7.00	5.00	6.00	3.75
☐R263 20¢ Carmine Rose	15.00	9.00	8.00	5.00

Scott No.	Fine Used Each	Ave. Used Each	Fine Used Each	Ave. Used Each
	Violet Paper (a)		Green Paper (b)	

1871–1874. U.S. REVENUE—PROPRIETARY STAMPS—PERFORATED 12

Scott No.	Fine Used Each (Violet Paper a)	Ave. Used Each	Fine Used Each (Green Paper b)	Ave. Used Each
☐RB1 1¢ Green & Black	4.00	2.00	6.00	3.00
☐RB2 2¢ Green & Black	5.00	2.40	13.00	9.15
☐RB3 3¢ Green & Black	13.00	6.00	37.00	21.00
☐RB4 4¢ Green & Black	7.00	4.00	11.00	6.75
☐RB5 4¢ Green & Black	106.00	58.00	112.00	62.00
☐RB6 6¢ Green & Black	29.00	15.00	85.00	47.00
☐RB7 10¢ Green & Black	200.00	100.00	33.00	18.00
☐RB8 50¢ Green & Black	652.50	361.00	890.00	500.00

Scott No.	Silk Paper (a) Fine	Ave.	Watermarked (b) Fine	Ave.	Rouletted (c) Fine	Ave.

1875–1881. U.S. REVENUE—PROPRIETARY STAMPS—NATIONAL BANK NOTE

Scott No.	Silk Paper (a) Fine	Ave.	Watermarked (b) Fine	Ave.	Rouletted (c) Fine	Ave.
☐RB11 1¢ Green						
	2.00	1.00	.38	.21	41.00	21.00
☐RB12 2¢ Brown						
	2.00	1.25	1.25	.75	55.00	28.00
☐RB13 3¢ Orange						
	9.00	4.50	2.00	1.50	56.00	31.00
☐RB14 4¢ Red Brown						
	4.60	2.50	4.00	2.20	—	—
☐RB15 4¢ Red						
	—	—	3.95	2.20	65.00	41.00
☐RB16 5¢ Black						
	100.00	60.00	80.00	36.00	480.00	250.00

Scott No.	Silk Paper (a) Fine	Ave.	Watermarked (b) Fine	Ave.	Rouletted (c) Fine	Ave.
☐RB17 6¢ Violet Blue	19.00	12.00	13.00	7.00	160.00	95.00
☐RB18 6¢ Violet	—	—	20.00	15.00	180.00	103.00
☐RB19 10¢ Blue	—	—	210.00	120.00	—	—

Scott No.	Fine Un-Used Each	Ave. Un-Used Each	Fine Used Each	Ave. Used Each

1898. U.S. REVENUE—PROPRIETARY STAMPS—BATTLESHIP

Scott No.	Fine Un-Used Each	Ave. Un-Used Each	Fine Used Each	Ave. Used Each
☐RB20 ⅛¢ Yellow Green	.25	.22	.20	.18
☐RB21 ¼¢ Pale Green	.25	.22	.20	.18
☐RB22 ⅜¢ Deep Orange	.26	.22	.20	.18
☐RB23 ⅝¢ Deep Ultramarine	.26	.22	.20	.18
☐RB24 1¢ Dark Green	.46	.28	.26	.19
☐RB25 1¼¢ Violet	.26	.21	.21	.16
☐RB26 1⅞¢ Dull Blue	3.00	2.10	1.00	.60
☐RB27 2¢ Violet Brown	.41	.28	.26	.16
☐RB28 2½¢ Lake	1.50	70.00	.21	.16
☐RB29 3¾¢ Olive Gray	11.00	7.00	6.00	3.00
☐RB30 4¢ Purple	4.00	2.40	.90	.60
☐RB31 5¢ Brown Orange	4.00	2.60	.95	.50

1914. U.S. REVENUE—BLACK PROPRIETARY STAMPS—WATERMARKED USPS

Scott No.	Fine Un-Used Each	Ave. Un-Used Each	Fine Used Each	Ave. Used Each
☐RB32 ⅛¢ Black	.26	.21	.21	.16
☐RB33 ¼¢ Black	1.20	.70	.98	.50
☐RB34 ⅜¢ Black	.26	.21	.21	.16
☐RB35 ⅝¢ Black	2.40	1.60	1.70	1.05
☐RB36 1¼¢ Black	1.50	1.10	.75	.49
☐RB37 1⅞¢ Black	25.00	15.00	15.00	9.00
☐RB38 2¼¢ Black	4.10	2.60	2.50	1.60
☐RB39 3⅛¢ Black	67.50	39.00	47.00	28.50
☐RB40 3¾¢ Black	24.00	16.00	19.00	11.00
☐RB41 4¢ Black	42.00	25.00	26.50	15.00
☐RB42 4⅜¢ Black	750.00	600.00	—	—
☐RB43 5¢ Black	87.50	50.00	59.00	35.00

Scott No.	Fine Un-Used Each	Ave. Un-Used Each	Fine Used Each	Ave. Used Each

1914. U.S. REVENUE—PROPRIETARY STAMPS—WATERMARKED USIR

Scott No.	Fine Un-Used Each	Ave. Un-Used Each	Fine Used Each	Ave. Used Each
☐RB44 ⅛¢ Black	.26	.21	.20	.17
☐RB45 ¼¢ Black	.26	.21	.20	.17
☐RB46 ⅜¢ Black	.62	.35	.32	.21
☐RB47 ½¢ Black	3.00	1.85	2.10	1.15
☐RB48 ⅝¢ Black	.26	.22	.21	.16
☐RB49 1¢ Black	4.00	2.10	3.00	1.50
☐RB50 1¼¢ Black	.38	.22	.21	.16
☐RB51 1½¢ Black	3.00	1.90	2.10	1.15
☐RB52 1⅞¢ Black	1.00	.60	.55	.36
☐RB53 2¢ Black	5.00	3.00	3.30	2.00
☐RB54 2½¢ Black	1.20	.75	.95	.60
☐RB55 3¢ Black	3.50	1.90	2.30	1.50
☐RB56 3⅛¢ Black	4.50	2.50	2.75	1.60
☐RB57 3¾¢ Black	9.00	5.00	7.00	4.20
☐RB58 4¢ Black	.45	.26	.20	.16
☐RB59 4⅜¢ Black	12.00	7.00	7.10	4.25
☐RB60 5¢ Black	2.50	1.40	2.40	1.10
☐RB61 6¢ Black	47.00	28.00	38.00	22.00
☐RB62 8¢ Black	14.00	8.00	10.00	6.00
☐RB63 10¢ Black	9.00	6.00	7.00	4.00
☐RB64 20¢ Black	17.00	10.00	14.50	9.50

1919. U.S. REVENUE—PROPRIETARY STAMPS—OFFSET

Scott No.	Fine Un-Used Each	Ave. Un-Used Each	Fine Used Each	Ave. Used Each
☐RB65 1¢ Dark Blue	.30	.25	.17	.15
☐RB66 2¢ Dark Blue	.30	.25	.17	.15
☐RB67 3¢ Dark Blue	1.15	.60	.59	.35
☐RB68 4¢ Dark Blue	1.15	.60	.52	.32
☐RB69 5¢ Dark Blue	1.25	.70	.55	.40
☐RB70 8¢ Dark Blue	10.00	6.00	8.00	5.00
☐RB71 10¢ Dark Blue	3.00	2.00	2.10	1.40
☐RB72 20¢ Dark Blue	5.00	3.25	3.00	1.75
☐RB73 40¢ Dark Blue	25.00	14.00	10.00	5.50

1918–1934. U.S. REVENUE—FUTURE DELIVERY STAMPS—PERFORATED 11&12

Scott No.	Fine Un-Used Each	Ave. Un-Used Each	Fine Used Each	Ave. Used Each
☐RC1 2¢ Carmine Rose	1.75	1.20	.21	.16
☐RC2 3¢ Carmine Rose (cut 7.50)	29.50	19.00	20.00	13.70

Scott No.	Fine Un-Used Each	Ave. Un-Used Each	Fine Used Each	Ave. Used Each
☐ RC3 4¢ Carmine Rose	3.00	1.60	.21	.16
☐ RC3a 5¢ Carmine Rose	—	—	3.10	2.25
☐ RC4 10¢ Carmine Rose	5.00	3.00	.21	.16
☐ RC5 20¢ Carmine Rose	5.00	3.00	.22	.16
☐ RC6 25¢ Carmine Rose (cut .10)				
	13.00	9.00	.70	.46
☐ RC7 40¢ Carmine Rose (cut .10)				
	13.00	7.00	.75	.45
☐ RC8 50¢ Carmine Rose	3.80	2.40	.38	.16
☐ RC9 80¢ Carmine Rose (cut 1.00)				
	21.00	15.50	7.00	4.50
☐ RC10 $1 Green (cut .10)	—	—	.26	.16
☐ RC11 $2 Rose (cut .10)	—	—	.26	.16
☐ RC12 $3 Violet (cut .12)	—	—	2.00	1.00
☐ RC13 $5 Dark Blue (cut .12)	—	—	.45	.26
☐ RC14 $10 Orange (cut .20)	—	—	1.00	.50
☐ RC15 $20 Olive Bistre (cut .50)	—	—	4.00	2.50
☐ RC16 $30 Vermilion (cut .95)	—	—	3.40	1.85
☐ RC17 $50 Olive Green (cut .30)	—	—	1.50	.60
☐ RC18 $60 Brown (cut .55)	—	—	2.00	1.25
☐ RC19 $100 Yellow Green (cut 5.50)				
	—	26.50	24.00	17.00
☐ RC20 $500 Blue (cut 3.00)	—	—	10.00	6.25
☐ RC21 $1000 Orange (cut 1.60)	—	1.50	5.00	3.00
☐ RC22 1¢ Carmine Rose Narrow Overprint				
	1.15	.60	.19	.16
☐ RC23 80¢ Narrow Overprint (cut .30)				
	—	—	2.75	1.75
☐ RC25 $1 Serif Overprint (cut .08)				
	7.50	4.50	.70	.40
☐ RC26 $10 Serif Overprint (cut 5.00)				
	—	—	15.00	12.00

1918–1928. U.S. REVENUE—STOCK TRANSFER STAMPS—PERFORATED 11 OR 12

☐ RD1 1¢ Carmine Rose, Perf. 11				
	.70	.40	.21	.18
☐ RD2 1¢ Carmine Rose, Perf. 11				
	.25	.21	.21	.18

Scott No.	Fine Un-Used Each	Ave. Un-Used Each	Fine Used Each	Ave. Used Each
☐RD3 4¢ Carmine Rose, Perf. 11				
	.40	.25	.21	.18
☐RD4 5¢ Carmine Rose, Perf. 11				
	.40	.25	.21	.18
☐RD5 10¢ Carmine Rose, Perf. 11				
	.40	.25	.21	.18
☐RD6 20¢ Carmine Rose, Perf. 11				
	.40	.26	.21	.18
☐RD7 25¢ Carmine Rose, Perf. 12 (cut .07)				
	1.00	.60	.24	.18
☐RD8 40¢ Carmine Rose, Perf. 11				
	.90	.60	.21	.18
☐RD9 50¢ Carmine Rose, Perf. 11				
	.45	.40	.21	.18
☐RD10 80¢ Carmine Rose, Perf. 11 (cut .07)				
	1.35	.75	.26	.18
☐RD11 $1 Green, Perf. 11, Red Ovpt. (cut .40)				
	35.00	22.00	10.00	5.00
☐RD12 $1 Green, Perf. 11, Black Ovpt				
	1.50	.80	.21	.18
☐RD13 $2 Rose, Perf. 11	1.50	.80	.21	.18
☐RD14 $3 Violet, Perf. 11 (cut .17)				
	10.00	5.00	3.00	1.00
☐RD15 $4 Y. Brown, Perf. 11 (cut .07)				
	5.00	2.50	.24	.18
☐RD16 $5 Blue, Perf. 11 (cut .07)				
	4.00	2.10	.24	.18
☐RD17 $10 Orange, Perf. 11 (cut .07)				
	8.00	4.50	.24	.18
☐RD18 $20 Bistre, Perf. 11 (cut 4.25)				
	50.00	30.00	19.00	14.00
☐RD19 $30 Vermilion (cut 1.05)				
	15.00	10.00	4.00	2.65
☐RD20 $50 Olive Green (cut 9.75)				
	80.00	49.00	42.00	37.00
☐RD21 $60 Brown (cut 4.60)				
	75.00	45.00	19.00	12.00
☐RD22 $100 Green (cut 1.10)				
	20.00	12.00	5.00	4.50

Scott No.	Fine Un- Used Each	Ave. Un- Used Each	Fine Used Each	Ave. Used Each
☐RD23 $500 Blue (cut 38.00)	—	—	115.00	75.00
☐RD24 $1000 Strange (cut 10.00)	—	—	79.50	54.00
☐RD25 2¢ Carmine Rose, Perf. 10	.90	.70	.26	.16
☐RD26 4¢ Carmine Rose, Perf. 10	.70	.70	.26	.16
☐RD27 10¢ Carmine Rose, Perf. 10	.70	.70	.26	.16
☐RD28 20¢ Carmine Rose, Perf. 10	.95	1.00	.26	.16
☐RD29 50¢ Carmine Rose, Perf. 10	1.50	1.00	.26	.16
☐RD30 $1 Green, Perf. 10	14.00	10.00	.26	.16
☐RD31 $2 Carmine Rose, Perf. 10	14.00	10.00	.21	.16
☐RD32 $10 Orange, Perf. 10 (cut .07)	14.00	10.00	.21	.16
☐RD33 2¢ Carmine Rose, Perf. 11	4.00	2.10	.65	.36
☐RD34 10¢ Carmine Rose, Perf. 11	.95	.40	.21	.18
☐RD35 20¢ Carmine Rose, Perf. 11	.95	.40	.22	.18
☐RD36 50¢ Carmine Rose, Perf. 11	1.90	.70	.30	.18
☐RD37 $1 Green, Perf. 11 (cut .11)	14.00	8.50	6.50	4.00
☐RD38 $2 Rose, Perf, 11 (cut .12)	11.00	7.00	6.50	3.50
☐RD39 2¢ Rose, Perf. 11 (cut .12)	3.00	1.90	.42	.21
☐RD40 10¢ Carmine Rose, Perf. 10	1.00	.70	.30	.18
☐RD41 20¢ Carmine Rose, Perf. 10	1.15	.70	.26	.18

Scott No.		Fine Unused Block	Ave. Unused Block	Fine Unused Each	Ave. Unused Each	Fine Used Each	Ave. Used Each

1861–1862. CONFEDERATE STATES OF AMERICA STAMPS (N-H ADD 40%)

Scott No.		Fine Unused Block	Ave. Unused Block	Fine Unused Each	Ave. Unused Each	Fine Used Each	Ave. Used Each
☐1	5¢ Jefferson Davis, Green						
		—	1300.00	150.00	100.00	110.00	65.00
☐2	10¢ Thomas Jefferson, Blue						
		—	1400.00	200.00	115.00	155.00	100.00
☐3	2¢ Andrew Jackson, Green						
		—	—	430.00	265.00	460.00	350.00
☐4	5¢ Jefferson Davis, Blue						
		700.00	550.00	110.00	65.00	82.00	50.00
☐5	10¢ Thomas Jefferson, Rose						
		—	—	750.00	465.00	500.00	280.00
☐6	5¢ Jefferson Davis, London Print						
		100.00	100.00	19.00	10.00	8.00	6.00
☐7	5¢ Jefferson Davis, Local Print						
		135.00	100.00	12.00	7.00	10.00	7.00

1863.

Scott No.		Fine Unused Block	Ave. Unused Block	Fine Unused Each	Ave. Unused Each	Fine Used Each	Ave. Used Each
☐8	2¢ Andrew Jackson, Brown Red						
		400.00	320.00	50.00	26.00	260.00	165.00
☐9	10¢ Jefferson Davis (ten)						
		—	—	710.00	440.00	460.00	280.00
☐10	10¢ Jefferson Davis (with frame line)						
		—	—	2500.00	1800.00	1100.00	725.00
☐11	10¢ Jefferson Davis (no frame.)						
		78.00	64.00	9.00	7.00	8.00	7.50
☐12	10¢ Jefferson Davis (filled corner)						
		90.00	85.00	9.50	7.00	8.00	7.50
☐13	20¢ George Washington						
		380.00	300.00	360.00	240.00	36.00	24.00

1862.

Scott No.		Fine Unused Block	Ave. Unused Block	Fine Unused Each	Ave. Unused Each	Fine Used Each	Ave. Used Each
☐14	1¢ John.C. Calhoun						
		800.00	600.00	75.00	55.00	—	—

FEDERAL DUCK STAMPS

Courtesy of Sam Houston Duck Company
P. O. Box 820087, Houston TX 77282
(Specialized Duck Catalog Gratis)

JUST WHAT ARE DUCK STAMPS?

The federal duck stamp was created through a wetlands conservation program. President Herbert Hoover signed the Migratory Bird Conservation Act in 1929 to authorize the acquisition and preservation of wetlands as waterfowl habitat.

The law, however, did not provide a permanent source of money to buy and preserve the wetlands. On March 16, 1934, Congress passed, and President Franklin Roosevelt signed, the Migratory Bird Hunting Stamp Act. Popularly known as the Duck Stamp Act, the bill's whole purpose was to generate revenue designated for only one use: acquiring wetlands for what is now known as the National Refuge System.

It has been proven that sales of duck stamps increase when the public has been informed of how the revenue generated through stamp sales is used.

Jay N. "Ding" Darling, a conservationist and Pulitzer Prize-winning political cartoonist, was appointed the head of the Duck Stamp Program. Darling's pencil sketch of mallards alighting was used on the first duck stamp. The same design was reproduced on Scott 2092, a commemorative marking the 50th anniversary of the Migratory Bird Hunting Stamp Act.

In reality, a "duck stamp" is a permit to hunt, basically a receipt for payment of fees collected. Funds generated are used for the preservation and conservation of wetlands.

The term "duck stamp" is a shortened term for the message "Migratory Bird Hunting and Conservation Stamp," which appears on the federal duck stamp.

In fact, use of the word "duck" is inaccurate, since all waterfowl, *including geese, swans, brants and more,* are intended to benefit from the sale of duck stamps.

WHO ISSUES DUCK STAMPS?

Duck stamps are now issued by the United States Government and by all state governments.

Many foreign countries, including Canada, Australia, Russia, Iceland, the United Kingdom, Costa Rica, Venezuela and New Zealand also issue duck stamps.

The issuing authorities within the various governments that release duck stamps are usually conservation and wildlife departments. These programs must be created by some form of legislation for the resulting stamps to be accepted as a valid governmental issue.

Labels featuring ducks are also issued by various special interest groups, such as Ducks Unlimited, the National Fish and Wildlife Foundation, and the National Wildlife Federation. Their issues are referred to as "society stamps." These items technically are not duck stamps, because the fee structure and disposition of funds are not legislated. However, society stamps are very collectible and often appreciate in value. Funds raised by these organizations are also used for waterfowl and conservation efforts.

Valid organizations and societies of this type perform a major service to conservation by their donations and efforts, and they merit public support.

WHEN ARE DUCK STAMPS ISSUED?

Duck stamps are issued once a year. In most states, hunters are required to purchase both a federal and state stamp before hunting waterfowl.

Waterfowl hunting seasons vary, but most begin in September or October, so naturally, stamps are needed prior to opening day of the hunting season.

Currently, the federal stamp and more than half of the state stamps are issued in July. Some are issued on the first day of the new year, and a few at the last minute in September or early October.

THE COST OF DUCK STAMPS

The annual federal duck stamp had a face value of $1 in 1934, jumped to $2 in 1949, and to $3 in 1959. In 1972 the price increased to $5, then up to $7.50 in 1979, $10 in 1987, $12.50 in 1989 and to $15 beginning in 1991.

For every $15 stamp sold, the federal government retains $14.70 for wetlands acquisition and conservation, so very little gets lost in the system for overhead.

Most state conservation stamps have a face value of $5. Maine has the lowest price at $2.50 and Tennessee the highest at $14.

Funds generated from state stamps are designated for wetlands restoration and preservation, much like the federal funds, but with a more localized purpose.

Most state agencies sell their stamps at face value. However, some also charge a premium to collectors buying single stamps, to help cover overhead costs. Some states also produce special limited editions for collectors.

FORMAT OF STAMPS

The federal stamp is presently issued in panes of 30 stamps. Originally, the stamps were issued in panes of 28, but because of a change in the printing method (and to make stamps easier to count) the 30-stamp format was adopted in 1959.

Beginning in 1998, the department of the Interior will also issue a single-sheet, self-adhesive Federal stamp used in ATM machines and ease handling in sporting good stores.

Most states and foreign governments follow the federal format. Many states issue a ten-stamp pane for ease of handling and mailing to field offices.

TYPES OF STAMPS

Currently, about 20 states issue two types of stamps, one for collectors and another for hunter use.

Collector stamps are usually in panes of 10 or 30 without tabs. *Hunter-type stamps* are usually issued in panes of five or 10, many with tabs attached. Hunters use the tabs to list their name, address, age and other data. Some states use only serial numbers to designate their hunter-type stamp.

State stamps are therefore referred to as either collector stamps or hunter-type stamps. Most dealers will distinguish between these types on their price lists. Separate albums exist for both types and are available from most dealers.

Plate blocks or control number blocks are designations given to a block of stamps, usually four, with a plate or control number present on the selvage. Such a block is usually located in one or all four corners of a pane. Federal stamps prior to 1959 plus the 1964 issue are collected in blocks of six and must have selvage on two sides.

Governor's Editions have been issued by a several state agencies as a means of raising additional income. These stamps are printed in small quantities, most fewer than 1,000. They have a face value of approximately $50, and are imprinted with the name of the state governor.

Governors also hand-sign a limited number of stamps. These are usually available at a premium, generally twice the price of normal singles. Hand-signed or autographed stamps are issued in very small quantities and are scarce to rare.

Governor's Editions are valid for hunting by all issuing states thus far. Obviously none would be used for that purpose, however, as it would destroy the mint condition and lower the value of the stamp.

Artist Signed Stamps are mint examples of duck stamps autographed by the artist responsible for the artwork on the stamp. Such stamps are rapidly gaining popularity with collectors, and most can be purchased for a small premium over mint examples.

Early federal stamps are particularly valuable and difficult to acquire. Signed stamps by artists now deceased also command a substantial premium.

Printed Text Stamps are another popular collectible. Generally, these preceded the later pictorial issues. The term is applied to stamps required for duck hunting that contain only writing but no waterfowl illustration.

Certain American Indian reservations and tribes also issue waterfowl hunting stamps. The stamps of these sovereign Indian nations allow holders to hunt on that reservation when a federal stamp also is purchased. Reservation stamps are becoming increasingly popular with collectors as more people discover their existence.

ERRORS

With the printing of such a large number of stamps year after year by many different states and printing agencies, errors do occur, but are seldom found. A few federal stamps are known to exist with major errors, but only a few, namely on the 1934, 1946, 1957, 1982, 1986, 1990, 1991 and 1993 issues.

Stamps without perforations, with missing or incorrect color, missing or inverted writing on the reverse are all major errors. Smaller flaws, such as color shifts, misplaced perforations, hickeys (or donuts) and other such anomalies are termed *freaks*, rather than errors. These, too, are collectible and have value, but they do not command the same attention as major errors. Major errors are extremely rare and exist in small numbers. All errors and freaks on duck stamps are very desirable and add a great deal of interest and value to a collection.

HOW TO COLLECT DUCK STAMPS

The first basic rule is to remember that stamp collecting is very personal. *You can make your own rules.*

Most collectors prefer to collect mint condition duck stamps. Others prefer collecting stamps on licenses, autographed stamps, plate blocks, stamps signed by hunters, art prints, souvenir cards, first day covers, or a combination. The bottom line, however, is to collect what interests you.

Quality is a very important factor in a stamp collection. This applies not only to duck stamps, but all types. Preserving the mint condition of a stamp is crucial for determining value. A perfectly centered stamp will usually sell for a substantial premium over a stamp with normal centering. Fine to very fine is the norm in stamp collecting, and is the condition priced by Scott.

Care should be taken not to damage a stamp, including the gum. The mint state of a stamp includes the freshness and original gum, so stamp mounts should be utilized when placing a stamp in your album. When a stamp has never been hinged, the abbreviation "NH" is used by dealers.

COLLECTORS ORGANIZATION

The National Duck Stamp Collectors Society exists for the benefit of those who collect duck stamps. Dues are $20 a year and are tax exempt. The NDSCS issues a newsletter and provides a membership card and lapel pin. Send your $20 directly to the NDSCS, Membership Chairman, P.O. Box 43, Harleysville, PA 19438.

Bob Dumaine is a recognized expert in duck stamps, founder of the National Duck Stamp Collectors Society, writer for *Linn's Stamp News*, publisher of *The Duck Report*, a past judge in the Federal Duck Stamp Contest and serves on the expertizing committee of Professional Stamp Experts. Dumaine is the owner of Sam Houston Duck Co., a firm that specializes in duck stamps and related material.

Request your copy of our award-winning Duck Stamp Catalog. 100 illustrated pages jam-packed with information on federal and state duck stamps, artist signed stamps, prints, conservation issues and much more. Catalog $2, refundable with first order. Or send $5 and we'll send our catalog along with $35 *(catalog value)* of duck and conservation stamps!

Sam Houston Duck Company, P.O. Box 820087, Houston, TX 77282; 1-800-231-5926; Fax 1-713-496-1445.

FEDERAL DUCK STAMP DUCKLINGS

The Junior Duck Stamp Program, a recently created nonprofit organization to promote interest among young people, recently unveiled the design of its first federal junior duck stamp. The program also includes a conservation education curriculum that helps students of all ages. It focuses on wildlife conservation and management, wildlife art and philately. As an outgrowth, the Junior Duck Stamp Design Competition was developed during 1993.

The resulting stamp, unlike the federal issue, is not valid as a revenue, but emulates the federal program in terms of art selection, creation of stamps, prints and other items for sale. All proceeds from the junior duck stamp go to the United States Fish and Wildlife Foundation to further its efforts.

The winning design for the first junior duck stamp was

submitted by 16-year-old Jason Parsons of Canton, Ill. Parsons attends Canton High School. His highly realistic colored-pencil rendition of a male redhead duck was selected from 1,045 entries in Illinois, then competed nationally. He was honored by a special trip to Washington, D.C., along with one parent and his art teacher, Scott Snowman. There Parsons was guest at a special reception where the second and third place winners also were honored. The winning artwork is on display at the U.S. Department of the Interior and at festivals, art galleries and state fairs nationwide. Various products will be available bearing Parsons' winning design.

Participation in the program has grown steadily. From eight states in 1992, the young program expanded to 22 in 1993. The program in now in effect nationwide.

DUCK STAMP AGENCIES

(APPROXIMATE ISSUE MONTH FOLLOWS STATE NAME)

Alabama, (9) Accounting Section, Duck Stamp Dept. of Conservation & Natural Resources, 64 N. Union, Montgomery, AL 36130, (334)261-3151.

Alaska, (7) State of Alaska, Dept. of Fish & Game, Licensing Section, P.O. Box 25525, Juneau, AK 99802-5525, (907)465-2376.

Arizona, (7) Game & Fish Dept., 2222 W. Greenway Rd., Phoenix, AZ 85023, (602)942-3000.

Arkansas, (7) Game & Fish Commission, 2 Natural Resources Dr., Little Rock, AR 72205, (501)223-6300.

California, (9) Dept. of Fish & Game, License Section, 3211 S. St., Sacramento, CA 95816, (916)739-3380.

Colorado, (7) Division of Wildlife, 317 W. Prospect Rd., Ft. Collins, CO 80526, (970)484-2836 ext. 383.

Connecticut, (7) Wildlife Bureau, 79 Elm St., Hartford, CT 06106, (860)424-3011.

Delaware, (7) Division of Fish & Wildlife, 89 King's Highway, Box 1401, Dover, DE 19903, (302)739-5296.

Florida, (7) Game & Fish Commission, Farris Bryant Building, 620 S. Meridian, Rm. 204, Tallahassee, FL 32399-1600. (850)488-3831.

Georgia, (9) Dept. of Natural Resources, 2189 North Lake Pkwy. Bldg. 10 Ste. 108, Tucker, GA 30084, (770)414-3333.

Hawaii, (9) Division of Forestry & Wildlife, 1151 Punch Bowl St., Honolulu, HI 96813, (808)587-0166.

Idaho, (9) Collector Stamps, Idaho Dept. of Fish & Game, Box 25, Boise, ID 83707, (208)334-3717.

Illinois, (3) Illinois Dept. of Conservation, License Section, P.O. Box 19459, Springfield, IL 62794-9459, (217)785-5039.

Indiana, (12) Indiana Division of Fish & Wildlife, License Section (Stamp), 402 W. Washington Rm. W273, Indianapolis, IN 46204, (317)232-4080.

Iowa, (12) Dept. of Natural Resources, Wallace State Office Building, Des Moines, IA 50319, (515)281-5145.

Kansas, (8) Dept. of Wildlife & Parks, 512 SE 25th Ave., Pratt, KS 67124, (316)672-0735.

Kentucky, (4) Dept. of Fish & Wildlife Resources, Arnold L. Mitchell Bldg., 1 Game Farm Rd., Frankfort, KY 40601, (502)564-4436.

Louisiana, (6) Dept. of Wildlife & Fisheries, P.O. Box 98000, ATTN: Licensing Section, Baton Rouge, LA 70898-9000, (504)765-2347.

Maine, (8) Dept. of Inland Fisheries & Wildlife, 284 State St., State House Station 41, Augusta, ME 04333, (207) 287-8000.

Maryland, (8) Dept. of Natural Resources, Licensing & Consumer Services, 580 Taylor Ave., Box 1869, Annapolis, MD 21404, (410)974-3211.

Massachusetts, (12) Division of Fisheries & Game, Leverett Saltonstall Bldg., Gov't Center, 100 Cambridge St., Room 1902, Boston, MA 02202, (508)792-7270.

Michigan, (8) Dept. of Natural Resources, P.O. Box 30181, Lansing, MI 48909, (517)335-3272.

Minnesota, (3) Dept. of Natural Resources, 500 Lafayette Rd., St. Paul, MN 55155, (612)296-4508.

Mississippi, (7) Game & Fish Commission, Dept. of Wildlife Conservation, License Dept., Box 451, Jackson, MS 39205-0451. (601)362-9212

Missouri, (stopped issuing in 1996) Dept. of Conservation, Fiscal Section, Box 180, Jefferson, MO 65102, (573)751-4115.

Montana, (3) Fish & Game Commission, P.O. Box 200701, Helena, MT 59620, (406)444-2612.

Nebraska, (stopped issuing in 1995) Game & Parks Commission, P.O. Box 30370, Lincoln, NE 68503, (402)471-5478.

Nevada, (10) Dept. of Wildlife, ATTN: License Office, Box 10678, Reno, NV 89520, (702)688-1500.

New Hampshire, (8) Fish & Game Dept., 2 Hazen Dr., Concord, NH 03301, (603)271-3422.

New Jersey, (7) Division of Fish, Game & Wildlife, Waterfowl Stamp, P.O. Box 400, Trenton, NJ 08625, (609)292-9480.

New Mexico, (stopped issuing in 1994) Dept. of Game & Fish, State Capitol, Villagra Bldg., 408 Galisted St., Santa Fe, NM 87503, (505)827-7920.

New York, (1) Division of Fish & Wildlife, License & Promotional Sales Unit, 50 Wolf Rd., Room 526, Albany, NY 12233-4750, (518)457-4480.

North Carolina, (7) Wildlife Resources Commission, 512 N. Salisbury St., Raleigh, NC 27604-1188, (919)773-2881.

North Dakota, (7) Game & Fish Dept., 100 N. Bismark Expressway, Bismark, ND 58501, (701)328-6300.

Ohio, (8) Division of Wildlife, Survey & Inventory Section, 1840 Belcher Road., Columbus, OH 43224-1329, (614)265-6539.

Oklahoma, (8) Dept. of Wildlife Conservation, 1801 N. Lincoln, Box 53465, Oklahoma City, OK 73152, (405)521-3851.

Oregon, (7) Dept. of Fish & Wildlife, Box 59, Portland, OR 97207, (503)872-5270.

Pennsylvania, (3) Game Commission, 2001 Elmerton Ave., Harrisburg, PA 17110-9797, (717)787-6286.

Rhode Island, (9) Rhode Island Fish & Wildlife, Oliver Stedman Government Center, 4808 Tower Hill Rd., Wakefield, RI 02879-2207. (401)789-3094

South Carolina, (7) Wildlife & Resources Dept., P.O. Box 11710, Columbia, SC 29211, (803)734-3843.

South Dakota, (1) Game, Fish & Parks, License Division, 412 W. Missouri, Pierre, SD 57501, (605)773-5527.

Tennessee, (stopped issuing in 1996) Dept. of Wildlife Resources, Information and Education Division, Box 40747, Nashville, TN 37204, (615)781-6500.

Texas, (8) Parks & Wildlife Dept., License Office, 4200 Smith School Rd., Austin, TX 78744, (512)389-4820. Stamp Orders 1-800-895-4248.

Utah, (9) Natural Resources/Wildlife Resources, 1596 W. North Temple, Salt Lake City, UT 84116, (801)538-4841. 1996; 1997 Utah Stamps are only available through the publisher: Steiner Prints, 315 Cornwall St., San Francisco, CA 94118, 1-800-225-3971.

Vermont, (9) Agency of Natural Resources, 103 S. Main St., Waterbury, VT 05676, (802)241-3700.

Virginia, (7) Duck Stamp, Box 11104, Richmond, VA 23230, (804)367-9369.

Washington, (7) Dept. of Wildlife, 600 Capitol Way N., Olympia, WA 98501-1091, (360)902-2200.

West Virginia, (stopped issuing in 1996) Dept. of Natural Resources, Waterfowl Stamp Program, Box 67, Elkins, WV 26241, (304)637-0245.

Wisconsin, (8) Dept. of Natural Resources, Box 7924, Madison, WI 53707, (608)266-1877.

Wyoming, (1) Game & Fish Dept., 5440 Bishop Blvd., Cheyenne, WY 82006, (307)777-4541.

FEDERAL & INTERNATIONAL AGENCIES

U.S. Dept. of Wildlife, (7) 18th & "C" Streets, N.W. Room 2058, Washington, D.C. 20240, (202)208-5508.

Alberta, R. D. Miner, 83 Woodgreen Drive S.W., Calgary, Alberta, Canada T2W, 403-251-6475 (also British Columbia and Manitoba fishing stamps and sometimes Canada).

Argentina, Venezuela, Croatia, Spain, 4G6 and sometimes Canada National Wildlife Philatelics, Mr. Dave Boshart 11000-32 Metro Parkway, Ft. Meyers, FL 33912-1244, (941) 275-0500.

Australia, Jansec Fine Stamps, Mr. Jim Jude, 4/358 Pacific Highway, P.O. Box 214, Lindfield NSW 2070, Australia (02) 9416-6639.

Canadian Provinces (all except Quebec and the required Alberta), Hines/Proguide, P.O. Box 25012, Halifax, Nova Scotia, Canada B3M 4H4.

Iceland, Grishams, 2808 East Matthews, Jonesboro, AR 72401, (501) 972-6050.

Quebec, Darnell Stamps and Coins, P.O. Box 1104, Station B, Montreal, Quebec, Canada H3B 3K9 E-mail: dona@jonction.net.

Russia, Israel, Unicover (also goes by Fleetwood), I Unicover Center, Cheyenne, WY 82008-0001, (307) 771-3000. No dealer discounts from these people, they charge collectors and dealers alike the same price.

United Kingdom, New Zealand, Denmark, Sweden, Mexico, Ireland, Sport 'en Art, Mr. Dan Harshman, 1015 W. Jackson Sullivan, IL 61951, (217) 728-2361.

All the following have the same contact: Hines-

Proguide, 50 Eglinton Ave. W. Ste #1009, Mississauga, Ontario, Canada L5R 3P5.

   Saskatchewan
   Ontario (8)
   Prince Edward Island
   Manitoba (9)
   New Brunswick (9)
   Nova Scotia (1)
   Newfoundland & Labrador (10)

Scott No.	Very Fine Plate Block	Fine Plate Block	Very Fine Unused Each	Fine Unused Each	Very Fine Used Each	Fine Used Each
□RW1 (1934) $1 Mallards, Blue (J.N. "Ding" Darling)						
	9500.00	2500.00	725.00	375.00	110.00	85.00
□RW1a Osprey Pair						
	2000.00	—	—	—	—	—
□RW2 (1935) $1 Canvasbacks, Rose Lake (Frank Benson)						
	8500.00	6500.00	600.00	350.00	110.00	85.00
□RW3 (1936) $1 Canada Geese, Brown Blk (Richard E. Bishop)						
	3000.00	2000.00	200.00	115.00	65.00	40.00
□RW4 (1937) $1 Lt. Scaup, Lt. Green, (J.D. Knap)						
	2000.00	1600.00	175.00	90.00	50.00	35.00
□RW5 (1938) $1 Pintails, Light Violet (Roland Clark)						
	2500.00	1850.00	175.00	90.00	50.00	35.00
□RW6 (1939) $1 Green-Winged Teal, Chocolate (Lynn B. Hunt)						
	1500.00	1000.00	125.00	65.00	40.00	25.00
□RW7 (1940) $1 Black Ducks, Sepia (F.L. Jacques)						
	1500.00	900.00	125.00	65.00	40.00	25.00
□RW8 (1941) $1 Ruddy Ducks, Brown Carmine (E.R. Kalmbach)						
	1500.00	900.00	125.00	65.00	40.00	25.00
□RW9 (1942) $1 Widgeon, Violet Brown (A. L. Ripley)						
	1500.00	900.00	125.00	65.00	40.00	25.00
□RW10 (1943) $1 Wood Ducks, Deep Rose (Walter E. Bohl)						
	400.00	250.00	65.00	35.00	30.00	20.00
□RW11 (1944) $1 White Fronted Geese, Red Orange (Walter A. Weber)						
	350.00	240.00	55.00	30.00	20.00	15.00
□RW12 (1945) $1 Shovelers, Black (Owen J. Gramme)						
	325.00	175.00	40.00	25.00	17.00	14.00
□RW13 (1946) $1 Redheads, Red Brown (Robert W. Hines)						
	260.00	175.00	35.00	20.00	15.00	11.00
□RW13a Error						
	3500.00	—	—	—	—	—

Scott No.	Very Fine Plate Block	Fine Plate Block	Very Fine Unused Each	Fine Unused Each	Very Fine Used Each	Fine Used Each
☐RW14 (1947)$1 Snow Geese, Black (Jack Murray)						
	260.00	175.00	35.00	20.00	14.00	11.00
☐RW15 (1948)$1 Buffleheads, Bright Blue (Maynard Reece)						
	275.00	175.00	40.00	20.00	14.50	11.00
☐RW16 (1949)$2 Goldeneyes, Bright Green (Roger E. Preuss)						
	300.00	180.00	50.00	30.00	15.00	11.00
☐RW17 (1950)$1 Trumpeter Swans, Violet (Walter A. Weber)						
	400.00	250.00	55.00	32.00	11.00	8.00
☐RW18 (1951)$2 Gadwalls, Gray Black (Maynard Reese)						
	400.00	250.00	55.00	32.00	9.00	6.00
☐RW19 (1952)$2 Harlequins, Ultramarine (John H. Dick)						
	400.00	250.00	55.00	32.00	9.00	6.00
☐RW20 (1953)$2 Blue-winged Teal, Dark Rose Brown (C. B. Seagers)						
	400.00	250.00	55.00	32.00	9.00	6.00
☐RW21 (1954)$2 Ring-necked Ducks, Black (H.D. Sandstrom)						
	400.00	250.00	55.00	32.00	9.00	6.00
☐RW22 (1955)$2 Blue Geese, Dark Blue (Stanley Stearns)						
	400.00	250.00	55.00	32.00	9.00	6.00
☐RW23 (1956)$2 Mergansers, Black (E.J. Bierly)						
	400.00	250.00	55.00	32.00	9.00	6.00
☐RW24 (1957)$2 American Eider, Emerald (J.M. Abbott)						
	400.00	250.00	55.00	32.00	9.00	6.00
☐RW24a Writing Reversed						
	3500.00	—	—	—	—	—
☐RW25 (1958)$2 Canada Geese, Black (Leslie C. Kouba)						
	400.00	250.00	55.00	32.00	9.00	6.00
☐RW26 (1959)$3 Labrador, Blue/Ochre/Black (Maynard Reece)						
	375.00	220.00	65.00	40.00	9.00	6.00
☐RW27 (1960)$3 Redheads, Red Brown/Blue/Bist (John A. Ruthven)						
	375.00	220.00	65.00	40.00	9.00	8.00
☐RW28 (1961)$3 Mallards, Blue/Bist/Brown (E. A. Morris)						
	375.00	210.00	65.00	40.00	9.00	8.00
☐RW29 (1962)$3 Pintails, Blue/Brown/Black (E.A. Morris)						
	425.00	240.00	75.00	45.00	11.00	8.00
☐RW30 (1963)$3 American Brant, Black/Blue/Yellow/Green (E.J. Bierly)						
	425.00	240.00	75.00	45.00	11.00	8.00

Scott No.	Very Fine Plate Block	Fine Plate Block	Very Fine Unused Each	Fine Unused Each	Very Fine Used Each	Fine Used Each
☐RW31 (1964)$3 Nene Geese, Black/Blue//Bist. (Stanley Stearns)						
	2000.00	1600.00	75.00	45.00	11.00	8.00
☐RW32 (1965)$3 Canvasbacks, Green/Black/Brown (Ron Jenkins)						
	425.00	240.00	75.00	45.00	11.00	8.00
☐RW33 (1966)$3 Whistling Swans, Blue/Green/Black (Stanley Stearns)						
	425.00	240.00	75.00	40.00	11.00	8.00
☐RW34 (1967)$3 Oldsquaws, Multicolored (Leslie C. Kouba)						
	425.00	240.00	75.00	40.00	11.00	8.00
☐RW35 (1968)$3 Mergansers, Green/Black/Brown (C.G. Pritchard)						
	250.00	170.00	50.00	30.00	11.00	8.00
☐RW36 (1969)$3 White-winged Scoters, Multicolored (Maynard Reece)						
	250.00	130.00	50.00	30.00	11.00	7.00
☐RW37 (1970)$3 Ross' Geese, Multicolored (E.J. Bierly)						
	250.00	130.00	50.00	30.00	11.00	7.00
☐RW38 (1971)$3 Cinnamon Teal, Multicolored (Maynard Reece)						
	225.00	130.00	45.00	30.00	11.00	7.00
☐RW39 (1972)$5 Emperor Geese, Multicolored (Arthur M. Cook)						
	130.00	80.00	24.00	19.00	8.00	6.00
☐RW40 (1973)$5 Steller's Eiders, Multicolored (Lee LeBlanc)						
	110.00	80.00	23.00	18.00	8.00	6.00
☐RW41 (1974)$5 Wood Ducks, Multicolored (David A. Maass)						
	90.00	46.00	18.00	12.00	8.00	6.00
☐RW42 (1975)$5 Decoy/Canvasbacks, Multicolored (James P. Fisher)						
	65.00	46.00	14.00	11.00	7.50	6.00
☐RW43 (1976)$5 Canada Geese, Emerald & Black (Aldersen, "Sandy" Magee)						
	65.00	46.00	14.00	11.00	7.50	5.00
☐RW44 (1977)$5 Ross' Geese, Multicolored (Martin R. Murk)						
	70.00	46.00	18.00	13.00	7.50	5.00
☐RW45 (1978)$5 Mergansers, Multicolored (Albert Gilbert)						
	75.00	46.00	15.00	12.00	7.50	5.00
☐RW46 (1979)$7.50 Green-winged Teal, Multicolored (Ken Michaelsen)						
	70.00	44.00	18.00	16.00	7.50	5.00
☐RW47 (1980)$7.50 Mallards, Multicolored (Richard Plasschaert)						
	70.00	44.00	18.00	16.00	7.50	5.00

Scott No.	Very Fine Plate Block	Fine Plate Block	Very Fine Unused Each	Fine Unused Each	Very Fine Used Each	Fine Used Each
☐RW48 (1981)$7.50 Ruddy Ducks, Multicolored (John S. Wilson)						
	70.00	44.00	18.00	16.00	7.50	5.00
☐RW49 (1982)$7.50 Canvasbacks, Multicolored (David A. Maass)						
	70.00	44.00	18.00	16.00	7.50	5.00
☐RW49a Black and Orange Omitted						
	3500.00	—	—	—	—	—
☐RW50 (1983)$7.50 Pintails, Multicolored (Phil Scholer)						
	70.00	44.00	18.00	16.00	7.50	5.00
☐RW51 (1984)$7.50 Widgeons, Multicolored (W.C. Morris)						
	70.00	44.00	18.00	16.00	7.50	5.00
☐RW52 (1985)$7.50 Cinnamon Teal, Multicolored (Gerald Moblex)						
	70.00	44.00	18.00	16.00	7.50	5.00
☐RW53 (1986)$7.50 Fulvous Whistling Duck, Multicolored (Burton E. Moore)						
	70.00	44.00	18.00	16.00	7.50	5.00
☐RW53a Black Engraved Omitted						
	4000.00	—	—	—	—	—
☐RW54 (1987)$10.00 Redheads, Multicolored (Arthur Anderson)						
	95.00	60.00	21.00	16.00	10.00	8.00
☐RW55 (1988)$10.00 Snow Goose, Multicolored (Daniel Smith)						
	90.00	65.00	21.00	17.00	10.00	8.00
☐RW56 (1989)$12.50 Lesser Scaup, Multicolored (Neal Anderson)						
	90.00	65.00	23.00	17.00	11.00	9.00
☐RW57 (1990)$12.50 Black-bellied Whistling Duck, Multicolored (Jim Hautman)						
	90.00	65.00	23.00	17.00	11.00	9.00
☐RW58 (1991)$15.00 King Eider, Multicolored (Nancy Howe)						
	100.00	90.00	25.00	20.00	14.00	12.00
☐RW58a Error Black Engraved Omitted						
	$10,000.00	—	—	—	—	—
☐RW59 (1992)$15.00 Spectacled Eiders, Multicolored (Joe Hautman)						
	110.00	90.00	25.00	20.00	14.00	12.00
☐RW60 (1993)$15.00 Canvasbacks, Multicolored (Bruce Miller)						
	110.00	90.00	25.00	20.00	14.00	12.00
☐RW60a Error Black Engraved Omitted						
	$4,000.00	—	—	—	—	—

Scott No.			Fine Unused Each	Ave. Unused Each	Fine Used Each	Ave. Used Each
☐RW61 (1994)$15.00 Red-breasted Mergansers, Multicolored (Neal Anderson)						
			110.00	90.00	25.00 20.00	14.00 12.00
☐RW62 (1995)$15.00 Mallards, Multicolored (Jim Hautman)						
			110.00	90.00	25.00 20.00	14.00 12.00
☐RW63 (1996)$15.00 Sun Scoter, Multicolored (Wilhelm Goebel)						
			110.00	90.00	25.00 20.00	14.00 12.00
☐RW64 (1997)$15.00 Canada Goose, Multicolored (Robert Hautman)						
			110.00	90.00	25.00 20.00	14.00 12.00

HAWAIIAN ISSUES
1851–1952. "MISSIONARIES"

☐1	2¢	Blue	—	450,000.00	—	200,000.00
☐		On Cover				425,000.00
☐2	5¢	Blue	—	50,000.00	—	24.000.00
☐		On Cover				50,000.00
☐3	13¢	Blue	—	21,000.00	—	11,000.00
☐		On Cover				35,000.00
☐4	13¢	Blue	—	50,000.00	—	25,000.00
☐		On Cover				40,000.00

NOTE: Prices on the above classic stamps of Hawaii vary greatly depending on the individual specimen and circumstances of sale.

NOTE: Beware of fake cancels on Hawaiian stamps, when the value is higher used than unused.

1853. KING KAMEHAMEHA III

☐5	5¢	Blue	—	1500.00	—	900.00
☐6	13¢	Dark Red	—	600.00	—	450.00
☐7	5¢ on 13¢ Dark Red		—	6500.00	—	5500.00

1857.

☐8	5¢	Blue	—	400.00	—	350.00

1861.

☐9	5¢	Blue	—	120.00	—	100.00

1868. RE-ISSUE

☐10	5¢	Blue	—	18.00	—	—
☐11	13¢	Rose	—	150.00	—	—

Scott No.		Fine Unused Each	Ave. Unused Each	Fine Used Each	Ave. Used Each
1869–1862.					
☐12	1¢ Light Blue	—	3200.00	—	2750.00
☐13	2¢ Light Blue	—	3200.00	—	2750.00
☐14	2¢ Black	—	3200.00	—	2750.00
1863.					
☐15	1¢ Black	—	400.00	—	310.00
☐16	2¢ Black	—	375.00	—	340.00
☐17	2¢ Dark Blue	—	5000.00	—	2400.00
☐18	2¢ Black	—	1200.00	—	900.00
1864–1865.					
☐19	1¢ Black	—	330.00	—	—
☐20	2¢ Black	—	380.00	—	—
☐21	5¢ Blue	—	400.00	—	—
☐22	5¢ Blue	—	300.00	—	—
1864. LAID PAPER					
☐23	1¢ Black	160.00	100.00	—	—
☐24	2¢ Black	160.00	100.00	—	—
1865. WOVE PAPER					
☐25	1¢ Blue	180.00	110.00	135.00	100.00
☐26	2¢ Blue	150.00	100.00	140.00	80.00
☐27	2¢ Rose	185.00	120.00	140.00	100.00
☐28	2¢ Rose Vert	185.00	120.00	140.00	100.00
1869. ENGRAVED					
☐29	2¢ Red	65.00	38.00	40.00	20.00
1864–1871.					
☐30	1¢ Purple	8.50	5.00	6.00	3.00
☐31	2¢ Vermilion	11.00	6.00	7.00	4.00
☐32	5¢ Blue	75.00	40.00	16.00	10.00
☐33	6¢ Green	18.50	10.00	6.00	4.00
☐34	18¢ Rose	90.00	60.00	16.00	8.50
1875.					
☐35	2¢ Brown	6.00	3.50	2.50	1.70

Scott No.			Fine Unused Each	Ave. Unused Each	Fine Used Each	Ave. Used Each
☐36	12¢	Black	36.00	24.00	19.00	11.00
☐37	1¢	Blue	6.00	4.00	4.00	2.50
☐38	2¢	Lilac Rose	80.00	48.00	27.00	17.00
☐39	5¢	Ultramarine	15.00	8.00	2.10	1.50
☐40	10¢	Black	28.00	14.00	17.00	9.00
☐41	15¢	Red Brown	45.00	22.00	19.00	12.00

1883–1886.

☐42	1¢	Green	2.15	1.45	1.45	.80
☐43	2¢	Rose	4.00	3.00	.90	.50
☐44	10¢	Red Brown	17.50	11.00	7.00	4.00
☐45	10¢	Vermilion	22.00	13.00	11.00	8.00
☐46	12¢	Red Lilac	60.00	33.00	28.00	18.00
☐47	25¢	Dark Violet	82.00	50.00	42.00	25.00
☐48	50¢	Red	120.00	90.00	68.00	45.00
☐49	$1	Rose Red	200.00	120.00	100.00	48.00
☐50	2¢	Orange	125.00	95.00	—	—
☐51	2¢	Carmine	21.00	15.00	—	—

1890–1891.

☐52	2¢	Dull Violet	6.00	2.50	1.25	.80
☐52c	5¢	Dark Blue	100.00	70.00	90.00	50.00

1893. PROVISIONAL GOVT. RED OVERPRINT

☐53	1¢	Purple	4.00	2.60	3.50	2.15
☐54	1¢	Blue	4.00	2.50	3.50	2.00
☐55	1¢	Green	1.50	.80	1.00	.50
☐56	2¢	Brown	4.50	2.50	3.50	2.00
☐57	2¢	Dull Violet	1.50	.90	1.30	.85
☐58	5¢	Dark Blue	8.50	5.00	6.00	4.00
☐59	5¢	Ultramarine	5.00	2.75	3.25	2.10
☐60	6¢	Green	10.00	6.00	9.00	5.00
☐61	10¢	Black	8.00	4.00	7.00	3.25
☐62	12¢	Black	8.00	4.00	7.00	3.00
☐63	12¢	Red Lilac	140.00	62.00	110.00	50.00
☐64	25¢	Dark Violet	25.00	11.00	20.00	9.00

BLACK OVERPRINT

☐65	2¢	Vermilion	50.00	28.00	43.00	25.00

Scott No.		Fine Unused Each	Ave. Unused Each	Fine Used Each	Ave. Used Each
☐66	2¢ Rose	1.40	.95	1.00	.80
☐67	10¢ Vermilion	9.50	6.00	8.00	5.00
☐68	10¢ Red Brown	8.00	5.00	7.00	4.50
☐69	12¢ Red Lilac	210.00	115.00	200.00	100.00
☐70	15¢ Red Brown	17.00	11.00	15.00	10.00
☐71	18¢ Dull Rose	21.00	11.00	19.00	15.00
☐72	50¢ Red	50.00	28.00	40.00	25.00
☐73	$1 Rose Red	100.00	60.00	90.00	50.00
☐74	1¢ Yellow	2.10	1.75	1.50	.80
☐75	2¢ Brown	2.50	2.00	.80	.50
☐76	5¢ Rose Lake	4.00	3.00	1.75	1.10
☐77	10¢ Yellow Green	5.00	4.00	4.10	3.00
☐78	12¢ Blue	10.00	6.50	9.00	5.00
☐79	25¢ Deep Blue	10.00	6.50	9.00	5.00

1899.

☐80	1¢ Dark Green	2.00	1.20	1.25	.90
☐81	2¢ Rose	2.00	1.20	1.25	.90
☐82	5¢ Blue	5.00	3.50	3.40	2.00

1896. OFFICIAL STAMPS

☐O1	2¢ Green	32.00	18.00	17.00	11.00
☐O2	5¢ Dark Brown	32.00	18.00	17.00	11.00
☐O3	6¢ Deep Ultramarine	40.00	19.00	17.00	11.00
☐O4	10¢ Rose	30.00	16.00	17.00	11.00
☐O5	12¢ Orange	60.00	38.00	25.00	11.00
☐O6	25¢ Gray Violet	80.00	42.00	17.00	11.00

AMERICAN FIRST
DAY COVERS

THE AMERICAN FIRST DAY COVER SOCIETY

The FIRST and ONLY not-for-profit, non-commercial, International Society devoted exclusively to First Day Covers and First Day Cover collecting.

FIRST DAYS **IS THE AWARD WINNING OFFICIAL PUBLICATION OF THE AMERICAN FIRST DAY COVER SOCIETY.** FDC collecting is a hands-on hobby of personal involvement—much more than simple collecting. It encourages the individual collector to fully develop his range of interests so that his collection is a reflection of his personal tastes. FDCs will encourage your creativity to reach full expression by adapting cachets or cancellations or using combinations (related stamps). In this hobby uniqueness is the rule, not the exception.

BUT ... *FIRST DAYS* **IS AVAILABLE ONLY TO MEMBERS OF THE AFDCS.** It's just ONE of the many benefits of membership. Whether you are interested in topical areas of collecting, working on serious research or just learning more about the hobby in general, this is the organization for you.

AMERICAN FIRST DAY COVER SOCIETY
CHAPTERS

The AFDCS has over 50 active chapters. Some are groups of FDC specialists, featuring lively newsletters on their speciality. Other AFDCS Chapters are regional affilates, giving AFDCSers opportunities to meet other local FDC collectors at regular meeting times.

For further information contact the chapter of your choice. To form a chapter, contact AFDCS Chapter Coordinator Julian Pugh, P.O. Box 8789, The Woodlands, TX 77387.

#1, Queen City Stamp & Cover Club: Fred Sprague, 503 King George Rd., Basking Ridge, NJ 07920

#3, Baltimore Philatelic Society, Inc.: Alice M. L. Robinson, 1221 N. Calvert St., Baltimore, MD 21202

#5, Motor City Stamp & Cover Club: Robert Quintero, 22608 Poplar Ct., Hazel Park, MI 48030

#6, Chicagoland FDC Society: Richard W. Sandowski, 22W432 Rt. 53, Glen Ellyn, IL 60137

#7, W. Suburban Stamp Club of Plymouth: Editor, Newsletter, P.O. Box 70049, Plymouth, MI 48170

#9, Harford County Stamp Club: Arch Handy, P.O. Box 632, Bel Air, MD 21014-0632

#12, Carroll County Philatelic Assoc.: Blair H. Law, 4510 Willow View St., Hampstead, VA 21074

#17, Robert C. Graebner Chapter of AFDCS: Lorraine Bailey, P.O. Box 1483, Arlington, VA 22210

#19, Metropolitan FDC Society: Benjamin Green, 66-15 Thornton Pl., Rego Park, NY 11374

#20, FDC Collectors Club: Stephen Neulander, P.O. Box 25, Deerfield, IL 60015

#25, Coryell's Ferry Stamp Club: Mrs. Frank Davis, P.O. Box 52, Penns Park, PA 18943-0052

#26, Ft Findley Stamp Club: Tom Foust, 5578 State Rt. 186, McComb, OH 45858

#27, Hazlet Stamp Club: Oscar Strandberg, 54 Crestview Dr., Middletown, NJ 07748

#34, Columbus Philatelic Club: Paul Gault, 140 West 18th Ave., Columbus, OH 43210

#35, Rumex Stamp Club: Al Dalbec, 550 Kennebec St., Rumford, ME 04276

#36, Autograph Chapter of AFDCS: George Haggas, P.O. Box 42, Audubon, NJ 08106-0042

#39, Samuel Gompers Stamp Club: Edwin M. Schmidt, P.O. Box 1233, Springfield, VA 22151-1233

#40, Columbia Philatelic Society: Harold T. Babb, P.O. Box 627, Columbia, SC 29202

#41, FDC Unit of Clifton Stamp Society: Andrew Boyajian, P.O. Box 229, Hasbrouck Heights, NJ J07604

#42, North Georgia Chapter of AFDCS: Gene Ramsey, 3082 Argonne Dr. NW, Atlanta, GA 30305

#43, George Washington Masonic Stamp Club: Melville Rodermond, 3111 Eastern Blvd., York, PA 17402

#44, Hamilton Township Philatelic Society: John Ranto, P.O. Box 8683, Trenton, NJ 06850-0683

#45, Joplin Stamp Club: Fred Roesel, 4225 East 25th, Joplin, MO 64801

#46, Gulf Coast FDC Group: Mrs. Monte Eiserman, 14359 Chadbourne, Houston, TX 77079

#48, Claude C Ries Chapter of AFDCS: Rick Whyte, 1175 W. Base Line RD., Claremont, CA 91711

#50, The 7/1/71 Affair, Roy E. Mooney, P.O. Box 2539, Cleveland, GA 30528

#53, Central NY FDC Society: Rick Kase, P.O. Box 10833, Rochester, NY 14610-083

#54, Journalists, Authors and Poets On Stamps: Lin Collette, 78 Gooding St., Pawtucket, RI 02860

#55, Louisville FDC Society: Arthur S. Buchter, 5410 Cannonwood Ct., Louisville, KY 40229

#56, North Texas Chapter of AFDCS: Fred Sawyer, 3520 Pebble Beach Dr., Farmers Branch, TX 75234

#57, Long Island Cover Society: Charles Breyer, P.O. Box 2095, Port Washington, NY 11050

#58, American Ceremony Program Society: Michael Litvak, 1866 Loma Vista St., Pasadena, CA 91106

#59, North Eastern New York State Chapter: Daniel Goldstein, P.O. Box 533, Newtonville, NY 12128

#60, Florida Chapter of AFDCS: George Athens, 3295 Datura Rd., Venice, FL 34293

#61, Ohio Cachetmakers Assoc.: Chris & Denise Lazaroff, 2967 Aylesbury St. NW, N. Canton, OH 44720

#62, Gateway to the West Chpt. of AFDCS: Art Rosenberg, 8686 Delmar Blvd. #2W, St. Louis, MO 63124

#63, Delaware Valley Chpt. of AFDCS: George Mullen, P.O. Box 11185, Philadelphia, PA 19111

#64, Society of Philatelists & Numismatists: Joe R. Ramos, 1929 Willis St., Montebello, CA 90640

#65, Cachetmakers Association: Pam Roberts, 83 N. 22nd St., Newark, OH 43055

#66, The Magnolia FDC Society: John D. Michaelis, 104 Bradford Circle, Ocean Springs, MS 39564

#67, Maximum Card Study Unit: Gary Denis, 3284 Winterberry Ln., Virginia Beach, VA 23456

#68, Professor Earl Planty Chpt. of AFDCS: Doris Gold, 1849 Williamsburg #146, LaMesa, CA 91941

#69, Rochester Philatelic Assoc.: Brad Sterling, 3114 Elmood Ave., Apt. #8, Rochester, NY 14618

#70, Tucson Stamp Club: Alex Lutgendorf, 5260 West Arroyo Pl., Tucson, AZ 85745-9430

#71, North Carolina Chapter of AFDCS: Eric Wile, 2202 James St., Greensboro, NC 27401

#72, Gay and Lesbian History on Stamps: Ed Centeno, P.O. Box 230940, Hartford, CT 06123

#73, Hand Painted Cover Collectors Club: Dave Dube, P.O. Box 9003, Helena, MT 59604

#74. Multnomah Children's Covers: Tommy Lee, 4572 Catalpa St., Los Angeles, CA 90032

#75, American Indian Philatelic Society: Bud Keeton, P.O. Box 523, Warrenton, MO 63383

#76, Harry C. Ioor Chapter of AFDCS: Patrick Tudor, 920 N. Bolton Ave, Indianapolis, IN 46219

#77, Molly Pitcher Stamp Club: Gary Dubnik, 1489 Canterbury Rd., Lakewood, NJ 08701

#78, National Duck Stamp Collectors Society: Edmond A. Ambrogi, P.O. Box 43, Harleysville, PA 19438

#79, Art Cover Exchange (ACE): Gary Chicoine, 207 Lyons Rd., Geneva, NY 14456

#80, Waterbury Stamp Club: Laurent Corriveau, P.O. Box 581, Waterbury, CT 06720

#81, Artcraft Collectors Club: David Sofferman, 5225 Poohs Hill Rd., Bethesda, MD 20814

#82, AFDCS Chapter for Computer Users: Kerry L. Heffner, P.O. Box 460787, Papillion, NE 68046

A GLOSSARY OF FIRST DAY COVER TERMS

Compiled by *FIRST DAYS* Staff

Add-on—A cachet design added to a cover which was originally uncacheted. An add-on cachet should be identified by maker and date so that it is clear that it is not contemporary with the cover. Unfortunately, many add-ons are not so identified.

Aerogramme—Postal stationery characterized by a single sheet which may be folded into an envelope, sealed and then sent at a rate less than the air mail letter rate. Postage is usually but not always imprinted. Also known as aerogram.

AFDCS—American First Day Cover Society.

All-over cachet—A cachet design that covers most of or the entire face (front) of the envelope, as compared to one that occupies just the left side.

All-purpose cachet—A cachet with a general design that can be used for any stamp subject. It has no specific theme. Also, General Purpose.

Alternate cancel—Any First Day cancellation from the official First Day city, other than the official First Day of Issue postmarks supplied by the USPS. (These are sometimes referred to as semi-officials, or by the specific name of the cancel, such as plug, slogan, show or ship cancels, etc.)

AMF—Air Mail Field. Found in many postmarks of postal facilities located in airports.

Autographed—An autographed envelope bears one or more signatures of individuals who are usually associated with the stamp. The autograph relationships may be the stamp subject, the designer, the local postmaster, dignitaries present at the dedication ceremony, etc. Authenticity and possible mechanical application of an autograph are significant considerations.

Auxiliary markings—Postal markings which are occasionally found on First Day Covers such as "Registered," "Insured," "Return to Sender," "Postage Due ____¢," etc.

B/4—Block of four stamps. Also B4.

Back stamp—The arrival mark of the destination city which usually appears on the reverse of the cover. Most registered covers are back stamped on arrival.

Booklet pane—A sheetlet of stamps removed from a stamp booklet which may have one or more such panes. On FDC it is desirable to include the tab which is used to bind the pane into the booklet. This may not be possible with some modern issues.

Bullseye—also, bull's-eye. 1) The dial or circular portion of a postmark used by itself as a cancel. 2) Any circular postmark struck directly on the center of a stamp. (See Socked-on-the-nose.)

Cachet—Any textual or graphic design which has been applied to a cover usually, but not always, on the left side of the envelope. A cachet may be produced by any means— printed, rubberstamped, handdrawn, etc. A First Day cachet should be related specifically to the stamp on the cover.

Cachetmaker—One who designs and/or produces cacheted envelopes. Cachets may be identified by the artist's name, brand name, or manufacturing firm.

Cancel—The portion of a postmark which defaces or "kills" the stamp. Often loosely used interchangeably with "postmark."

CDS—Circular date stamp, ie. the dial or circular portion of the postmark.

Ceremony program—The printed program usually distributed by the Post Office or sponsoring organization at the First Day dedication of a new stamp. These are usually collected with the new stamp affixed and cancelled on the First Day.

Classic—The period prior to 1930 during which few First Day Covers were serviced and cachets were not common.

Coil—Stamps produced in rolls for use in vending machines. They are characterized by two opposite edges being straight or imperforate. A horizontal coil stamp is imperforate top and bottom and a vertical coil is straight-edged at the left and right sides.

Combo—One or more thematically related stamps affixed to a FDC. Also, combination cover.

Commemorative—A stamp, usually of large format, which is issued to salute or honor a person, event, state, organization, place, etc. Typically issued on an anniversary in a multiple of 10, 50, 100 years, etc. and produced in limited quantities. Contrasted with "definitive."

Commercial FDCs—FDCs sponsored by an individual, company or organization used for promoting a service, product or as a gesture of good will.

Contract station—A sub-unit of a larger post office which is contracted to a private individual. Most contract stations are located in private business establishments.

Corner card—The imprint at the upper left corner of a cover which may be the return address or other identification of the sender.

Counterfeit—A stamp, postmark, or cachet created in direct imitation of a genuine item and intended to deceive. It is a Federal offense to counterfeit any postal marking or postal issue.

Cover—An envelope that has seen postal service or has a cancelled stamp on it, usually one with philatelic interest. May exemplify some segment of postal history or simply be a souvenir of an event or a place.

Crash cover—Any cover or FDC salvaged from the crash of a plane or vehicle in which it was carried. Usually bears postal markings explaining its damaged condition.

CXL—Abbreviation for "cancel." Also, cxl.

Definitive—Stamp issued for an indefinite period in an indefinite quantity to meet an ordinary postal rate. Designs do not usually honor a specific time dated event or person; most frequently in small format. Contrasted with "commemorative." Also known as "regular issue."

Designated First Day—The date officially announced by the Post Office for the sale of a new postal issue. Many issues prior to 1922 had no designated First Day. Covers cancelled prior to the designated dates are predates.

Dial—Circular portion of a postmark, usually containing the city, date and time. See bullseye.

Dual cancel—Two related or unrelated cancellations on a cover, each cancelling a stamp. One or both cancels may be for a First Day.

Duplex cancel—A metal handstamp containing both cancel and postmark in a single unit. Often found on FDCs before the mid-1930s.

EDC—Earliest documented cover. The earliest known postmark on a postal issue which had no designated First Day. Used interchangeably with EKU.

EFO—Errors, Freaks and Oddities, ie. stamps, cachets, cancellations, etc. that contain unintended mistakes or design faults.

EKU—Earliest known use. A designation for the earliest identified postmark on a stamp for which a first day of issue was not designated.

Electric eye (EE)—An electronic device which guides the perforating equipment during stamp manufacture. This is accomplished by heavy ink dashes in the selvage, which are used for detection and alignment. FDCs of EE stamps must have the selvage with dashes attached to the stamps.

Embossing—The process of impressing a design in relief into the paper of an envelope.

Engraved—A method of printing in which the lines of the design are cut into metal, which are recessed to retain the ink. The paper is forced under pressure into these lines to pick up the ink. Hence engraved cachets appear to have the design raised above the paper surface.

Error—A consistent abnormal variety created by a mistake in the production of a stamp or postmark. For example, the name of a city may be misspelled in the First Day cancel. Used in contrast to "freak."

Esoterica—Any item, other than a cover or envelope, that has been First Day cancelled that doesn't fit any of the regular collecting categories.

Event Cover—A cacheted cover, not a FDC, prepared as a souvenir of a specific event or an anniversary of an event.

Event Program—A list of events or speakers in any program related to the stamp release, such as a stamp show, any function at which a stamp is released, or any event honoring the same event as the stamp.

Fancy Cancel—A cancellation which is or includes a design. The term is normally used for 19th century cancels which were created by local postal officials according to personal whim. Also, see pictorial.

Favor Cancel—Any postal marking supplied as a favor or accommodation for a stamp collector.

FD—First Day.

FDC—First Day Cover. (FDCs - plural)

FDOI—First Day Of Issue. The slogan found in most First Day cancellations since Sc. 795, released in 1937.

FFC—First flight cover, ie. a cover flown on the inaugural flight of a new air route.

Filler—A stiff piece of paper, cardboard or plastic found inside a First Day Cover. It provides necessary stiffness for a clearer cancellation. It also protects the cover from bending when it travels through the mail stream. Fillers, also termed stuffers, occasionally are imprinted with an advertising message or information pertaining to the stamp or cachet on the cover.

First Cachet—The initial cachet commercially produced by a cachetmaker.

First Day—The day on which a stamp for the first time is officially sold by the Post Office.

First Day Cover—Cover with a new stamp(s) or postal indicia, cancelled on the First Day.

Flag Cancel—A cancellation used during the early 20th century incorporating a flag design. The stripes of the flag are the killer bars. Also, any more recent cancel with a similar design.

Flocked—A cachet production method in which powdered cloth is adhered to the envelope in the desired design.

Forgery—A fraudulently produced or altered philatelic item intended to deceive the collector.

Frank—A stamp, mark or signature that shows payment of postage on a piece of mail. (A signature, with no stamp or paid marking, is called a Free Frank. Free as available to Congress and the President.)

Freak—An abnormal variety created by an unusual circumstance and not repeated with regularity. For example, a FDC may bear only a portion of a postmark because the cover was misfed into the cancelling machine. Used in contrast to "error."

General purpose (GP)—A cachet with a general design that is non-specific and may be used with any stamp subject. Also, All-purpose.

Hand cancel (HC)—A canceller which is applied to stamps individually and by hand. May be manufactured of plastic, rubber or steel and is similar to a rubberstamp.

Hand drawn (H/D)—A cachet applied to a cover by hand with pen, pencil, brush, chalk, or other art media. Each cachet is made individually and is an original.

Handmade (H/M)—A cachet applied to a cover by hand by adding seals, paste-ups, collage or similar materials. Each cachet is made individually and is an original.

Hand painted (H/P) or Hand colored (H/C)—A printed, handdrawn or handmade cachet to which hand painting or hand coloring has been added.

HC, H/C, H/D, H/M, H/P—See preceding definitions.

HPO—Highway Post Office. The Post Office sorted mail on special motor vehicles in transit between cities. This system was in use from the late 1930s through the mid-1970s. FDCs were occasionally cancelled with HPO markings.

IA—Ink addressed. Refers to the method of addressing a cover.

Inaugural cover—A cover cancelled on the day that a president is sworn into office. Since 1957 the words INAUGURATION DAY have been incorporated into the cancel. The site was usually Washington, D.C., although other locations, like the President's city of birth, are now being designated. (In 1957 and 1985 the inauguration date fell on a Sunday. In both cases, covers of January 20, the private swearing in ceremony, and January 21, the date of the public ceremony, both exist, and both are considered collectible.)

Indicia—An imprint on postal stationery indicating prepayment of postage. The plural is also "indicia."

Joint Issue—Two or more stamps issued by different countries to commemorate the same event, topic, place or person. Officially sanctioned joint issues are intentionally issued with the cooperation of the postal services of the countries involved.

Killer Bars—The horizontal lines of a postmark which cancel the stamp. Since 1937 the FIRST DAY OF ISSUE slogan has appeared between the bars of most First Day cancels.

LA—Label addressed. Refers to the addressing method on a cover.

LSASE—A legal-sized stamped, self-addressed envelope. See SASE.

Last Day—The final day of a postal rate, post office operation or similar occurrence. A cover cancelled on this day is referred to as a last day cover.

Lithography, or litho—A common method of printing stamps and cachets in which the design is transferred from a smooth plate by selective inks which wet only the design portion of the printing plate.

LL—Lower left. Refers to the plate number or marginal marking position on a sheet of stamps.

LR—Lower right. Refers to the marginal marking position.

Luminescent—The condition of a stamp or postal stationery which has been treated with chemicals which are sensitive to and glow under ultraviolet (UV) light. This permits automatic cancelling equipment to detect the position of the postage on the cover and to orient it for rapid mechanical cancelling.

Machine cancel (MC)—A cancellation applied by an automatic cancelling device or machine.

Maximum card—A picture (post) card with a reproduction of the stamp or related subject from which the stamp was derived. Maximum card specialists prefer that the card and the stamp be as directly related as possible, but not be reproduced. The attempt is to achieve maximum agreement or concordance between the stamp subject and post card. The stamp and cancel are usually placed on the illustrated side. This may be cancelled on the First Day of the stamp. See "Souvenir card."

Mellone catalog—A series of cachet catalogs for various time periods. They feature cachet illustrations with assigned code numbers for identification.

Mylar—Dupont's trademark for a durable plastic (polyester) film often recommended for storing stamps or covers because of its excellent chemical stability and the protection offered.

Nondenominated—Stamp or postal stationery without denomination or value in the design. These were created by the Post Office in anticipation of postal rate change when the exact rates could not be determined in advance.

Obliterator—Another term for the cancel portion of a postmark which defaces or obliterates the stamp.

OE—An abbreviation which indicates that a cover has been opened at the end or side.

Official—1) Of or related to the Federal government. USPS postmarks are official markings. 2) Stamps or stationery issued for use by government departments in the course of official business.

Official cachet—1) A cachet produced and applied by or for postal administrations. Official cachets are rare on U.S. FDCs but are common for many other countries. 2) Loosely used to refer to cachets authorized or sponsored by an organization closely associated with the issuance of a stamp, more properly called a sponsored cachet. The word "official" is abused by some cachetmakers.

Official FDC—Any First Day Cover with an official government postmark. This term is often misused for covers with sponsored cachets.

Offset—A printing method in which the design is transferred by ink from the image to another surface and then applied to the paper.

OT—An abbreviation indicating that a cover has been opened at the top.

PA—Pencil addressed. Refers to the method of cover addressing.

Patriotic or patriotic cachet—Design with patriotic or nationalistic theme, most often used to bolster public spirit during periods of war or national stress.

PB—Plate block. A group of stamps with the plate number in the selvage. May contain four or more stamps depending on the configuration of the printed numbers.

Peelable label—A self-stick label that can be easily removed from a cover without leaving adhesive or blemish. Used for addressing covers—later removed to create unaddressed covers.

Philatelic center—A post office window or station where most currently available stamps may be purchased by collectors. Created for the convenience of stamp collectors. Also postique.

Photocachet—A cachet consisting in part or entirely of a photograph.

Pictorial—A cancellation incorporating a pictorial design. Pictorial First Day cancels were used by the United States from 1958 to 1962 and are becoming more widespread on FDC issues of the 1980s and 90s. Many postiques each have a unique pictorial cancel. Many non-FD pictorial cancels are available nationwide, and are used for a limited time at special public or philatelic events.

Planty Catalogue—Catalog of U.S. cachets, for various year periods in individual volumes, assembled by Prof. Earl Planty. Planty identification designations are referred to as Planty Numbers.

Plug cancel—Colloquial name for a round, double circle marking, officially known as a validator stamp. The plug is chiefly used on postal receipts and registered envelopes. Also called a registry cancel or round-dater.

PNC—1) Plate Number Coil, ie. a coil stamp with a plate number thereon. 2) Philatelic-numismatic cover, ie. a cover with a cancelled stamp and a visible coin on the front, both thematically related. May be a FDC for the stamp.

POD—Post Office Department, the predecessor of the USPS. Also USPOD.

Polysleeve—Any of a variety of generally clear plastic sleeves, usually closed on two or three sides, to contain covers so they may be handled without soiling or damage.

Postage due—Stamps issued to indicate a penalty for insufficient postage. Postage due stamps are not used to pay postage, yet some issues are known on FDCs. These FDCs were cancelled inadvertently or by favor.

Postal card—A government produced post card with an indicia indicating prepayment of postage.

Postal stationery—Postal cards, aerogrammes, and envelopes on which postage has been imprinted. Created as a convenience for the public so postage need not be applied.

Postcancelled (post dated, back dated)—A cover which has been cancelled on a date later than that indicated on the postmark.

Post card—A privately produced card usually bearing an illustration on one side and spaces for message, address and postage on the other.

Postique—A special station or location at a post office where collectors may obtain currently available stamps. Each office usually has its own pictorial cancellation.

Postmark—A postal marking which indicates the time and point of origin of the mail to which it is applied. Often loosely used interchangeably with "Cancel."

Precancel—Stamps or stationery issued by the Post Office with words or lines printed thereon which prevent further use of the stamp. Precancelled stamps need not be cancelled again during mail handling. The standard First Day postmarks, however, are applied to FDCs of precancels.

Predate—A cover with a stamp cancelled earlier than the officially designated First Day of sale. Predates usually are created when stamps are sold prior to the official release date, contrary to postal regulations. Predates can exist only for issues with a designated First Day date.

Presentation album—Album containing a pane of a new stamp which is distributed to each dignitary at a First Day dedication ceremony. The album may have the recipient's name engraved on it. The first album is always for the President of the United States.

Presidentials—The 1938 series of definitive stamps featuring the Presidents of the United States.

Prexy—An information alternative term to designate the Presidential series of definitives.

PR—Pair of stamps.

Printed cachets—A cachet design type that is produced by printing, using any one of many methods.

Program—See Ceremony Program.

Rag content—Pertains to the use of cotton fiber rather than wood pulp in the manufacture of envelopes. High rag content or 100 percent rag envelopes resist the ravages of time much better than do wood fiber covers, which contain processing chemicals that eventually discolor the paper and make the envelope more brittle.

Regular issue—Stamp issued for an indefinite period and quantity for ordinary postal use. See definitive.

RPO—Railway post office. A system once used by the POD to process mail in railroad cars enroute between cities. A distinctive cancel was used and FDCs exist with RPO postmarks.

Registry cancel—See plug.

RSA—Rubberstamp addressed. A cover addressing method.

RSC—Rubberstamp cachet.

Rubberstamps (R/S) cachet—A cachet applied to a cover using a rubberstamp. This method or device was very popular in the 1930s.

SASE—Self-addressed stamped envelope or *SAE*—self-addressed envelope. See also "LSASE."

Scott—Philatelic Publishing Company which produces Scott catalogues. A Scott (Sc.) number refers to a Scott catalog number to identify a stamp—a widely accepted practice.

Second day cover—A cover postmarked on the day following the First Day Of Issue. These were popular in the 1940s when the stamps were available at the Philatelic Agency in Washington, DC, on the second day.

Self-Adhesive—A pre-gummed postage stamp on a peelable backing which requires no moisture for affixing to an envelope.

Selvage—The edges of a stamp pane beyond the perforations—including the portions that contain marginal markings as plate numbers, copyright notice, and other symbols/text. The plain selvage is usually removed from stamps when preparing FDCs, except for plate numbers and other collectible markings. Also spelled "selvedge."

Service—The act of affixing a stamp to and having it cancelled on a cover.

Servicer—One who performs the act of servicing. Frequently a person who does so on a commercial and large volume basis.

SGL—Single stamp. Also "sgl."

Ship cancel—A cancellation applied aboard a vessel—most frequently US Navy although there are others. Ship cancels are fairly common but such strikes on FDCs are considered unusual because they represent a special effort in order to be obtained.

Show cancel—Special Post Office cancellation designed for and applied at a philatelic show or exhibition station.

Silk cachet—A cachet type with a pictorial design printed on a piece of fabric with a silky finish.

Slogan cancel—A cancellation with a message incorporated, such as—"Mail Early Before Christmas" or "Fight Tuberculosis."

Socked-on-the-nose (SOTN)—Designation for a stamp where the circle of the postmark falls exactly on the center. Another designation for "bullseye."

Souvenir card—A commemorative card, usually with reproductions of previously issued stamps and an inscription, issued by postal authorities in conjunction with a special philatelic event. The card or stamp units cannot be used for postal purposes but are often enhanced by collectors with an actual stamp and cancel.

Souvenir program—See ceremony program.

Sponsor (cachet)—Individual or organization that has commissioned an established cachetmaker to prepare a special design in addition to the regular cachet for a particular issue. The term is sometimes used interchangeably with "cachetmaker."

Sponsored cachet—A cachet authorized or sponsored by an organization closely associated with the issuance of a stamp. See also "Official cachet," No. 2.

Station cancel—A cancellation applied at a temporary postal station established for a convention, exhibition, or other special event.

Stuffer—See filler.

Tagged—Stamp or postal stationery which has had the postage area treated with a material sensitive to ultraviolet (UV) light, so that the cover can be mechanically oriented for canceling. Also luminescent.

Thermography—A printing method for producing raised

designs by use of a special powder and heat. Often called, "poor man's embossing."

Tied—The cancellation overlaps the stamp, falling on both the postage and the cover thus affirming that the stamp was affixed prior to the postmarking. Also may be applied to non-postal labels or adhesives to show contemporaneous usage.

Toning—A deleterious condition of a cover resembling darkening or discoloration caused by excess gum at the edge of the stamp or a stain from the gum of the envelope flap. May also result from chemicals used in the production of inexpensive envelopes.

Tradename—A name or identification assigned to a cachet line by the producer. Example: Washington Press produces Artcraft Cachets.

UA—Unaddressed. A cover which does not have an address.

UL—Upper left. Refers to the position of stamp marginal markings.

Unaddressed (UA)—A cover which has no address.

Uncacheted—A cover which has no cachet design.

Unofficial cancel—A private, non-postal marking, usually resembling an official postmark, applied to a stamp or cover.

Unofficial FDC (UO)—A FDC cancelled with other than the official FIRST DAY OF ISSUE slogan cancel or official First Day pictorial cancelled supplied by the USPS for the First Day. For FDCs before the initial use of the FDOI slogan, this term refers to any city other than that which was officially designated. (There is much controversy among specialists and purists about this definition. Some dislike the use of the word "unofficial" as all postmarks are official cancellations of the USPS. Some would like to make a further distinction between stamps purchased in the official FD city, versus stamps sold in error on or before the FD in cities other than the FD city. Both of these are points well taken, but basically UOs are any FDC serviced in the city of issue or another location with any cancel other than the official FD cancel supplied by the USPS. A UO FDC must have the correct First Day date.)

UO—Unofficial First Day Cover.

UR—Upper right. Refers to the position of the marginal markings on stamp selvage.

USPS—United States Postal Service, established in 1971.

Validator—See plug.

Please Note: DC indicates Washington, D. C. as the official city and date of issue. Other cities with significantly different values are also listed. When no city is indicated, the number of cities the stamps were issued in is indicated.

Scott No.			Single	Block Of 4
FIRST DAY COVER ISSUES				
UNCACHETED				
☐551	½¢	Hale (DC & New Haven, CT, 4/4/25)	14.00	15.00
☐552	1¢	Franklin (DC, 1/17/23)	20.00	32.00
☐552	1¢	Franklin (Philadelphia, PA)	36.00	52.00
☐553	1½¢	Harding (DC, 3/19/25)	24.00	28.00
☐554	2¢	Washington (DC, 1/15/23)	36.00	48.00
☐555	3¢	Lincoln (DC, 2/12/23)	35.00	45.00
☐555	3¢	Lincoln (Hodgenville, KY)	200.00	400.00
☐556	4¢	Martha Washington (DC, 1/15/23)	65.00	95.00
☐557	5¢	Roosevelt (DC, 10/27/22)	120.00	155.00
☐557	5¢	Roosevelt (New York, NY)	200.00	400.00
☐557	5¢	Roosevelt (Oyster Bay, NY)	1200.00	—
☐558	6¢	Garfield (DC, 11/20/22)	180.00	225.00
☐559	7¢	McKinley (DC, 5/1/23)	140.00	175.00
☐559	7¢	McKinley (Niles, OH)	200.00	—
☐560	8¢	Grant (DC, 5/1/23)	150.00	190.00
☐561	9¢	Jefferson (DC, 1/15/23)	150.00	190.00
☐562	10¢	Monroe (DC, 1/15/23)	150.00	192.00
☐563	11¢	Hayes (DC, 10/4/22)	625.00	875.00
☐563	11¢	Hayes (Fremont, OH)	2000.00	—
☐564	12¢	Cleveland (DC, Boston, MA, Caldwell, NJ, 3/20/23)	200.00	300.00
☐565	14¢	Indian (DC, 5/1/23)	400.00	475.00
☐565	14¢	Indian (Muskogee, OK)	1850.00	5000.00
☐566	15¢	Statue of Liberty (DC, 11/11/22)	500.00	850.00
☐567	20¢	Golden Gate (5/1/23)	625.00	925.00
☐567	20¢	Golden Gate (San Francisco)	3000.00	—
☐568	25¢	Niagara Falls (DC, 11/11/22)	650.00	900.00
☐569	30¢	Bison (DC, 3/20/23)	750.00	1000.00
☐570	50¢	Arlington (DC, 11/11/22)	1500.00	—
☐571	$1	Lincoln Memorial (DC, Springfield, IL 2/12/23)	5000.00	—
☐572	$2	U.S. Capitol (DC, 3/20/23)	18,000.00	—
☐573	$5	America (DC, 3/20/23)	30,000.00	—

Scott No.			Single	Block Of 4
☐576	1½¢	Harding (DC, 4/4/25)	42.00	45.00
☐581	1¢	Franklin (DC, 10/17/23)	5000.00	—
☐582	1½¢	Harding (DC, 3/19/25)	38.00	40.00
☐583a	2¢	Washington (Booklet Pane, DC, 8/27/26)	1200.00	—
☐584	3¢	Lincoln (DC, 8/1/25)	50.00	70.00
☐585	4¢	Martha Washington (DC, 4/4/25)	50.00	75.00
☐586	5¢	Roosevelt (DC, 4/4/25)	50.00	70.00
☐587	6¢	Garfield (DC, 4/4/25)	50.00	70.00
☐588	7¢	McKinley (DC, 5/29/26)	60.00	75.00
☐589	8¢	Grant (DC, 5/29/26)	60.00	75.00
☐590	9¢	Jefferson (DC, 5/29/26)	60.00	75.00
☐591	10¢	Monroe (DC, 6/8/25)	90.00	110.00
☐597	1¢	Franklin (coil, DC, 7/18/23)	550.00	—
☐598	1½¢	Harding (coil, DC, 3/19/25)	40.00	—
☐599	2¢	Washington (coil, DC, 1/15/23)	2500.00	—
☐600	3¢	Lincoln (coil, DC, 5/10/24)	100.00	—
☐602	5¢	Roosevelt (coil, DC, 3/5/24)	100.00	—
☐603	10¢	Monroe (coil, DC, 2/1/24)	110.00	—
☐604	1¢	Franklin (coil, DC, 7/19/24)	80.00	—
☐605	1½¢	Harding (coil, DC, 5/9/25)	40.00	—
☐606	2¢	Washington (coil, DC, 12/31/23)	130.00	—
☐610	2¢	Harding (DC, Marion, OH 9/1/25)	25.00	40.00
☐611	2¢	Harding (imperf., DC, 11/15/23)	85.00	110.00
☐612	2¢	Harding (perf. 10, DC, 9/12/23)	110.00	130.00
☐614–16		Huguenot-Walloon, set on one cover 5/1/24 were issued in eleven cities: Albany, NY, Allentown, PA, Charleston, SC, Jacksonville, FL, Lancaster, PA, Mayport, FL, New Rochelle, NY, New York, NY, Philadelphia, PA, Reading, PA, and Washington, D.C.	150.00	—
☐614	1¢	Huguenot-Walloon (5/1/24)	32.00	42.00
☐615	2¢	Huguenot-Walloon (5/1/24)	37.00	47.00
☐616	5¢	Huguenot-Walloon (5/1/24)	60.00	90.00
☐617–19		Lexington-Concord, set on one cover 4/4/25 were issued in six cities: prices are for Boston, MA, Cambridge, MA, Concord, MA, Lexington, MA, and Washington, D.C., Concord, MA sells for 25% more.	140.00	—

Scott No.			Single	Block Of 4
☐617	1¢	Lexington-Concord (4/4/25)	35.00	40.00
☐618	2¢	Lexington-Concord (4/4/25)	36.00	45.00
☐619	5¢	Lexington-Concord (4/4/25)	80.00	110.00
☐620	2¢	Norse-American (5/18/25)	22.00	37.00
☐620–21		Norse-American, set on one cover 5/18/25 were issued in seven cities: Angola, IN, Benson, MN, Decoran, IA, Minneapolis, MN, Northfield, MN, St. Paul, MN, and Washington, D.C.	60.00	100.00
☐621	5¢	Norse-American (5/18/25)	30.00	45.00
☐622	13¢	Harrison	20.00	30.00
☐622	13¢	Harrison (Indianapolis, IN, 1/11/26)	30.00	50.00
☐622	13¢	Harrison (North Bend, OH, 1/11/26)	175.00	400.00
☐623	17¢	Wilson (New York, NY, Princeton, NJ, Staunton, VA, Washington, D.C., 12/28/25)	20.00	27.00
☐627	2¢	Sesquicentennial (Boston, MA, Philadelphia, PA, D.C., 5/10/26)	8.00	15.00
☐628	5¢	Erikson (Chicago, IL, Minneapolis, MN, New York, NY, D.C. 5/29/26)	18.00	30.00
☐629	2¢	White Plains (White Plains, NY, New York, NY, Philadelphia, PA Expo 10/18/26)	7.00	10.00
☐630	2¢	White Plains (complete sheet, 10/18/26)	2000.00	—
☐631	1½¢	Harding (DC, 8/27/26)	40.00	50.00
☐632	1¢	Franklin (DC, 6/10/27)	45.00	60.00
☐633	1½¢	Harding (DC, 5/17/27)	45.00	60.00
☐634	2¢	Washington (DC, 12/10/26)	45.00	50.00
☐635	3¢	Lincoln (DC, 2/3/27)	45.00	60.00
☐635a	3¢	Bright Violet (DC, 2/7/34)	25.00	35.00
☐636	4¢	Martha Washington (DC, 5/17/27)	50.00	60.00
☐637	5¢	Roosevelt (DC, 3/24/27)	50.00	60.00
☐638	6¢	Garfield (DC, 7/27/27)	55.00	65.00
☐639	7¢	McKinley (D.C., 3/24/27)	55.00	65.00
☐640	8¢	Grant (D.C., 6/10/27)	65.00	85.00
☐641	9¢	Jefferson (D.C., 5/17/27)	65.00	85.00
☐642	10¢	Monroe (D.C., 2/3/27)	80.00	110.00
☐643	2¢	Vermont (Burlington, VT, D.C., 8/3/27)	5.50	7.00

Scott No.			Single	Block Of 4
☐644	2¢	Burgoyne	11.00	14.00
☐		(Albany, NY, Rome, NY, Syracuse, NY, Utica, NY, and D.C., 8/3/27)		
☐645	2¢	Valley Forge	4.50	7.00
☐		(Cleveland Phil Sta., OH, Lancaster, PA, Norriston, PA, Philadelphia, PA, Valley Forge, PA, West Chester, PA, and D.C., 5/26/28)		
☐646	2¢	Molly Pitcher	15.00	14.00
☐		(Freehold, NJ, Red Bank, NJ, D.C., 10/20/18)		
☐647	2¢	Hawaii (Honolulu, HI, D.C., 8/13/28)	15.00	20.00
☐647–48		Hawaiian set on one cover (8/13/28)	35.00	75.00
☐648	5¢	Hawaii (Honolulu, HI, D.C., 8/13/28)	20.00	25.00
☐649	2¢	Aero Conf. (D.C., 12/12/28)	7.00	9.00
☐649–50		Areo Conf. set on one cover (12/12/18)	11.00	20.00
☐650	5¢	Aero Conf. (D.C., 12/12/28)	9.00	12.00
☐651	2¢	Clark (Vincennes, IN, 2/25/29)	5.00	6.00
☐653	½¢	Hale (D.C., 5/25/29)	—	30.00
☐654	2¢	Electric Light (Menlopark, NJ, 6/5/29)	8.00	12.00
☐655	2¢	Electric Light (D.C., 6/11/29)	80.00	100.00
☐656	2¢	Electric Light (coil, 6/11/29)	95.00	—
☐657	2¢	Sullivan (16 different New York cities, D.C., 6/17/29)	3.50	5.00
☐658	1¢	Kansas (D.C., 5/1/29)	30.00	40.00
☐658–68		Kansas set on one cover, D.C., 5/1/29	1000.00	—
☐659	1½¢	Kansas (D.C., 5/1/29)	35.00	45.00
☐660	2¢	Kansas (D.C., 5/1/29)	35.00	45.00
☐661	3¢	Kansas (D.C., 5/1/29)	40.00	55.00
☐662	4¢	Kansas (D.C., 5/1/29)	50.00	70.00
☐663	5¢	Kansas (D.C., 5/1/29)	50.00	70.00
☐664	6¢	Kansas (D.C., 5/1/29)	70.00	100.00
☐665	7¢	Kansas (D.C., 5/1/29)	90.00	125.00
☐666	8¢	Kansas (D.C., 5/1/29)	90.00	200.00
☐667	9¢	Kansas (D.C., 5/1/29)	95.00	140.00
☐668	10¢	Kansas (D.C., 5/1/29)	110.00	150.00
☐669	1¢	Nebraska (D.C., 5/1/29)	30.00	40.00
☐659–669		Nebraska set on one cover, D.C., 5/1/29	1000.00	—
☐670	1½¢	Nebraska (D.C., 5/1/29)	35.00	45.00

Scott No.			Single	Block Of 4
☐671	2¢	Nebraska (D.C., 5/1/29)	35.00	45.00
☐672	3¢	Nebraska (D.C., 5/1/29)	40.00	55.00
☐673	4¢	Nebraska (D.C., 5/1/29)	50.00	70.00
☐674	5¢	Nebraska (D.C., 5/1/29)	50.00	70.00
☐675	6¢	Nebraska (D.C., 5/1/29)	70.00	90.00
☐676	7¢	Nebraska (D.C., 5/1/29)	90.00	125.00
☐677	8¢	Nebraska (D.C., 5/1/29)	90.00	140.00
☐678	9¢	Nebraska (D.C., 5/1/29)	95.00	140.00
☐679	10¢	Nebraska (D.C., 5/1/29)	110.00	150.00
☐670–679		Kanas Section Cover (D.C., 5/1/29)	1000.00	—
☐680	2¢	Fallen Timbers (5 cities 9/14/29)	3.25	5.00
☐681	2¢	Ohio River (7 cities 10/19/29)	3.25	5.00
☐682	2¢	Massachusetts Bay Colony (2 cities 4/8/30)	3.25	5.00
☐683	2¢	Carolina-Charleston (4/10/30)	3.25	5.00
☐684	1½¢	Harding Marion, OH (12/1/30)	4.25	5.50
☐685	4¢	Taft Cinncinnati, OH (6/4/30)	5.50	7.50
☐686	1½¢	Harding Marion, OH (coil, 12/1/30)	4.25	6.00
☐687	4¢	Taft (coil, D.C., 9/18/30)	30.00	—
☐688	2¢	Braddock (7/9/30)	4.00	6.00
☐689	2¢	Von Steuben	4.25	6.00
☐690	2¢	Pulaski (12 cities, 1/16/31)	3.75	5.00
☐692	11¢	Hayes (D.C., 9/4/31)	110.00	125.00
☐693	12¢	Cleveland (D.C., 8/25/31)	110.00	125.00
☐694	13¢	Harrison (D.C., 9/4/31)	110.00	125.00
☐695	14¢	Indian (D.C., 9/8/31)	110.00	125.00
☐696	15¢	Liberty (D.C., 8/27/31)	135.00	175.00
☐697	17¢	Wilson (D.C., 7/27/31)	300.00	400.00
☐698	20¢	Golden Gate (D.C., 9/8/31)	300.00	400.00
☐699	25¢	Niagara Falls (D.C., 7/27/31)	350.00	450.00
☐700	30¢	Bison (D.C., 9/8/31)	350.00	450.00
☐701	50¢	Arlington (D.C., 9/4/31)	400.00	500.00
☐702	2¢	Red Cross (2 cities 5/21/31)	3.25	4.00
☐703	2¢	Yorktown (2 cities, 10/19/31)	3.25	5.00
☐704	½¢	Olive Brown (D.C., 1/1/32)	—	2.75
☐704–15		set on one cover	35.00	—
☐705	1¢	Green (D.C., 1/1/32)	2.75	3.25
☐706	1½¢	Brown (D.C., 1/1/32)	2.75	3.25
☐707	2¢	Carmine Rose (D.C., 1/1/32)	2.75	3.75
☐708	3¢	Deep Violet (D.C., 1/1/32)	2.75	3.75
☐709	4¢	Light Brown (D.C., 1/1/32)	2.75	3.75

Scott No.			Single	Block Of 4
☐710	5¢	Blue (D.C., 1/1/32)	2.75	3.75
☐711	6¢	Red Orange (D.C., 1/1/32)	2.75	3.75
☐712	7¢	Black (D.C., 1/1/32)	2.75	3.75
☐713	8¢	Olive Bistre (D.C., 1/1/32)	3.25	4.25
☐714	9¢	Pale Red (D.C., 1/1/32)	3.25	4.25
☐715	10¢	Orange Yellow (D.C., 1/1/32)	3.25	4.25
☐716	2¢	Olympic Winter Games (1/25/32)	2.75	3.75
☐717	2¢	Arbor Day (4/22/32)	2.25	3.75
☐718	3¢	Olympic Summer Games (6/15/32)	2.75	3.75
☐718–19		Olympic Summer Games set on one cover	4.50	6.25
☐719	5¢	Olympic Summer Games (6/15/32)	3.25	4.25
☐720	3¢	Washington (D.C., 6/16/32)	3.25	4.25
☐720b	3¢	Washington (booklet of 6, D.C., 7/25/32)	32.00	—
☐721	3¢	Washington (coil, D.C., 6/24/32)	4.25	—
☐722	3¢	Washington (coil, D.C., 10/12/32)	4.25	—
☐723	6¢	Garfield (coil, 8/18/32)	4.25	—
☐724	3¢	William Penn (3 cities, 10/24/32)	2.75	3.75
☐725	3¢	Daniel Webster (3 cities, 10/24/32)	2.75	3.75
☐726	3¢	Gen. Oglethorpe (2/12/32)	2.75	3.75
☐727	3¢	Peace Proclamation (4/19/32)	2.75	3.75
☐728	1¢	Century of Progress (5/25/32)	2.00	2.50
☐728–29		Century of Progress set on one cover	3.25	4.25
☐729	3¢	Century of Progress (5/25/32)	2.50	3.50
☐730	1¢	American Philatelic Society (full sheet on cover)	55.00	—
☐730a	1¢	American Philatelic Society (8/25/33)	2.75	3.25
☐731	3¢	American Philatelic Society (full sheet)	60.00	—
☐731a	3¢	American Philatelic Society (8/25/33)	2.75	3.25
☐732	3¢	National Recovery Administration (D.C., 8/15/33)	2.50	3.00
☐733	3¢	Byrd Antarctic (D.C., 10/9/33)	4.25	6.00
☐734	5¢	Kosciuszko (6 cities, 10/13/33)	4.25	6.00
☐734		Kosciuszko (Pittsburg, PA)	16.00	20.00
☐735	3¢	National Exhibition (full sheet)	32.00	—
☐735a	3¢	National Exhibition (2/10/34)	4.25	8.00
☐736	3¢	Maryland Tercentenary (3/23/34)	2.50	3.50
☐737	3¢	Mothers of America (D.C., 5/2/34)	2.50	3.50

Scott No.			Single	Block Of 4
☐738	3¢	Mothers of America (flatplate, D.C., 5/2/34)	3.00	4.00
☐739	3¢	Wisconsin (7/9/34)	2.50	3.50
☐740	1¢	Parks, Yosemite (2 cities, 7/16/34)	2.00	3.00
☐741	2¢	Parks, Grand Canyon (2 cities, 7/24/34)	2.00	3.00
☐742	3¢	Parks, Mt. Rainier (2 cities, 8/3/34)	2.00	3.00
☐743	4¢	Parks, Mesa Verde (2 cities, 9/25/34)	2.00	3.00
☐744	5¢	Parks, Yellowstone (2 cities, 7/30/34)	2.00	4.00
☐745	6¢	Parks, Crater Lake (2 cities, 9/5/34)	2.00	4.00
☐746	7¢	Parks, Acadia (2 cities, 10/2/34)	3.00	5.00
☐747	8¢	Parks, Zion (2 cities, 9/18/34)	4.00	6.00
☐748	9¢	Parks, Glacier Park (2 cities, 8/27/34)	4.00	6.00
☐749	10¢	Parks, Smoky Mountains (2 cities, 10/8/34)	4.00	6.00
☐750	3¢	American Philatelic Society (full sheet on cover)	32.00	—
☐750a	3¢	American Philatelic Society (8/28/34)	4.00	—
☐751	1¢	Trans-Mississippi Philatelic Expo, (full sheet on cover)	18.00	—
☐751a	1¢	Trans-Mississippi Philatelic Expo. (10/10/34)	3.00	—
☐752	3¢	Peace Commemoration (D.C., 3/15/35)	5.25	7.25
☐753	34¢	Byrd (D.C., 3/15/35)	5.25	7.25
☐754	3¢	Mothers of America (D.C., 3/15/35)	5.25	7.25
☐755	3¢	Wisconsin (D.C., 3/15/35)	5.25	7.25
☐756	1¢	Parks, Yosemite (D.C., 3/15/35)	5.25	7.25
☐757	2¢	Parks, Grand Canyon (D.C., 3/15/35)	5.25	7.25
☐758	3¢	Parks, Mount Ranier (D.C., 3/15/35)	5.25	7.25
☐759	4¢	Parks, Mesa Verde (D.C., 3/15/35)	5.25	7.25
☐760	5¢	Parks, Yellowstone (D.C., 3/15/35)	5.25	8.00
☐761	6¢	Parks, Crater Lake (D.C., 3/15/35)	6.00	9.00
☐762	7¢	Parks, Acadia (D.C., 3/15/35)	6.00	9.00
☐763	8¢	Parks, Zion (D.C., 3/15/35)	6.00	9.00
☐764	9¢	Parks, Glacier Park (D.C., 3/15/35)	6.00	9.00
☐765	10¢	Parks, Smoky Mountains (D.C., 3/15/35)	6.00	12.00
☐766a	1¢	Century of Progress (D.C., 3/15/35)	5.00	7.00
☐767a	3¢	Century of Progress (D.C., 3/15/35)	5.00	7.00
☐768a	3¢	Byrd (D.C., 3/15/35)	6.00	12.00

Scott No.			Single	Block Of 4
☐769a	1¢	Parks, Yosemite (D.C., 3/15/35)	5.00	7.00
☐770a	3¢	Parks, Mount Ranier (D.C., 3/15/35)	6.00	12.00
☐771	16¢	Airmail, special delivery (D.C., 3/15/35)	7.00	14.00

FIRST DAY COVER ISSUES CACHETED (FOR DATES SEE UNCACHETED STAMPS)

☐610	2¢	Harding	1000.00	—
☐617	1¢	Lexington-Concord	135.00	—
☐618	2¢	Lexington-Concord	135.00	—
☐619	5¢	Lexington-Concord	180.00	—
☐623	17¢	Wilson	295.00	—
☐627	2¢	Sesquicentennial	65.00	—
☐628	5¢	Erikson	450.00	—
☐629	2¢	White Plains	50.00	—
☐630	2¢	White Plains (sheet) single	60.00	—
☐635a	3¢	Bright Violet	32.00	—
☐643	2¢	Vermont	50.00	90.00
☐644	2¢	Burgoyne	52.00	80.00
☐645	2¢	Valley Forge	45.00	60.00
☐646	2¢	Molly Pitcher	85.00	—
☐647	2¢	Hawaii	60.00	75.00
☐647–48		Hawaii set on one cover	140.00	—
☐648	5¢	Hawaii	75.00	85.00
☐649	2¢	Aero Conf.	48.00	62.00
☐649–50		Aero Conf. set on one cover	60.00	—
☐650	5¢	Aero Conf.	50.00	65.00
☐651	2¢	Clark	30.00	42.00
☐654	2¢	Electric Light	30.00	42.00
☐655	2¢	Electric Light	165.00	—
☐656	2¢	Electric Light (coil)	250.00	—
☐657	2¢	Sullivan, Auburn N.Y.	30.00	43.00
☐680	2¢	Fallen Timbers	30.00	43.00
☐681	2¢	Ohio River	30.00	42.00
☐682	2¢	Massachusetts Bay Colony	32.00	46.00
☐683	2¢	California-Charleston	32.00	46.00
☐684	1½¢	Harding (coil)	32.00	46.00
☐685	4¢	Taft (coil)	48.00	60.00
☐686	1½¢	Harding	48.00	60.00
☐687	4¢	Taft	75.00	90.00
☐688	2¢	Braddock	30.00	42.00

Scott No.			Single	Block Of 4
☐689	2¢	Von Steuben	30.00	42.00
☐690	2¢	Pulaski	30.00	42.00
☐702	2¢	Red Cross	30.00	42.00
☐703	2¢	Yorktown	42.00	60.00
☐704	1½¢	Olive Brown	15.00	18.00
☐705	1¢	Green	15.00	18.00
☐706	1½¢	Brown	15.00	18.00
☐707	2¢	Carmine Rose	15.00	18.00
☐708	3¢	Deep Violet	15.00	18.00
☐709	4¢	Light Brown	15.00	18.00
☐710	5¢	Blue	15.00	18.00
☐711	6¢	Red Orange	15.00	18.00
☐712	7¢	Black	15.00	18.00
☐713	8¢	Olive Bistre	18.00	25.00
☐714	9¢	Pale Red	18.00	25.00
☐715	10¢	Orange Yellow	18.00	25.00
☐716	2¢	Olympic Winter Games	21.00	30.00
☐717	2¢	Arbor Day	17.00	26.00
☐718	3¢	Olympic Summer Games	21.00	30.00
☐719	5¢	Olympic Summer Games	21.00	30.00
☐720	3¢	Washington	35.00	42.00
☐720b	3¢	Booklet pane of 6	170.00	—
☐721	3¢	Washington (coil)	50.00	—
☐722	3¢	Washington (coil)	50.00	—
☐723	6¢	Garfield (coil)	48.00	—
☐724	3¢	William Penn	17.00	22.00
☐725	3¢	Daniel Webster	17.00	22.00
☐726	3¢	Gen. Oglethorpe	17.00	22.00
☐727	3¢	Peace Proclamation	17.00	22.00
☐728	1¢	Century of Progress	12.00	16.00
☐729	3¢	Century of Progress	16.00	22.00
☐730	1¢	American Philatelic Society, full sheet on cover	165.00	—
☐730a	1¢	American Philatelic Society (single)	15.00	21.00
☐731	3¢	American Philatelic Society	165.00	—
☐731a	3¢	American Philatelic Society (single)	15.00	21.00
☐732	3¢	National Recovery Administration	16.00	22.00
☐733	3¢	Byrd Antarctic	26.00	36.00
☐734	5¢	Kosciuszko	21.00	29.00
☐734b	5¢	Kosciuszko (Pittsburgh, PA)	50.00	70.00

Scott No.			Single	Block Of 4
☐735	3¢	National Exhibition (full sheet)	55.00	—
☐735a	3¢	National Exhibition (single)	16.00	—
☐736	3¢	Maryland Tercentenary	17.00	22.00
☐737	3¢	Mothers of America	11.00	16.00
☐738	3¢	Mothers of America	11.00	16.00
☐739	2¢	Wisconsin	11.00	16.00
☐740	1¢	Parks, Yosemite	11.00	16.00
☐741	2¢	Parks, Grand Canyon	11.00	16.00
☐742	3¢	Parks, Mt. Ranier	11.00	16.00
☐743	4¢	Parks, Mesa Verde	11.00	16.00
☐744	5¢	Parks, Yellowstone	11.00	16.00
☐745	6¢	Parks, Crater Lake	12.00	16.50
☐746	7¢	Parks, Acadia	12.00	16.50
☐747	8¢	Parks, Zion	12.00	16.50
☐748	9¢	Parks, Glacier Park	12.00	16.50
☐749	10¢	Parks, Smoky Mountains	12.00	16.50
☐750	3¢	American Philatelic Society, full sheet on cover	55.00	—
☐750a	3¢	American Philatelic Society (single)	14.00	17.00
☐751	1¢	Trans-Mississippi Philatelic Expo., full sheet on cover	55.00	—
☐751a	1¢	Trans-Mississippi Philatelic Expo. (single)	12.00	17.00
☐752	3¢	Peace Commemoration	35.00	42.00
☐753	3¢	Byrd	35.00	42.00
☐754	3¢	Mothers of America	36.00	42.00
☐755	3¢	Wisconsin Tercentenary	34.00	40.00
☐756	1¢	Parks, Yosemite	26.00	34.00
☐757	2¢	Parks, Grand Canyon	26.00	34.00
☐758	3¢	Parks, Mount Rainier	26.00	34.00
☐759	4¢	Parks, Mesa Verde	26.00	34.00
☐760	5¢	Parks, Yellowstone	26.00	34.00
☐761	6¢	Parks, Crater Lake	26.00	34.00
☐762	7¢	Parks, Acadia	26.00	34.00
☐763	8¢	Parks, Zion	26.00	34.00
☐764	9¢	Parks, Glacier Park	26.00	34.00
☐765	10¢	Parks, Smoky Mountains	26.00	34.00
☐766a	1¢	Century of Progress	42.00	60.00
☐767a	3¢	Century of Progress	42.00	60.00
☐768a	3¢	Byrd	42.00	60.00

Scott No.			Single	Block Of 4
☐769a	1¢	Parks, Yosemite	42.00	60.00
☐770a	3¢	Parks, Mount Rainier	42.00	60.00
☐771	16¢	Airmail, special delivery	45.00	60.00

Scott No.			Single	Block	Plate Block
☐772	3¢	Connecticut Tercentenary	7.00	8.50	15.00
☐773	3¢	California Exposition	7.00	8.50	16.00
☐774	3¢	Boulder Dam	9.00	10.00	17.00
☐775	3¢	Michigan Centenary	7.50	8.50	15.00
☐776	3¢	Texas Centennial	10.00	14.00	20.00
☐777	3¢	Rhode Island Tercentenary	7.00	8.50	16.00
☐778	3¢	TIPEX	5.25	16.00	—
☐782	3¢	Arkansas Centennial	7.00	8.50	15.00
☐783	3¢	Oregon Territory	7.00	8.50	15.00
☐784	3¢	Susan B. Anthony	7.00	8.50	15.00
☐785	1¢	Army	4.25	6.00	12.00
☐786	2¢	Army	5.25	7.00	12.00
☐787	3¢	Army	5.25	7.00	12.00
☐788	4¢	Army	5.25	7.00	12.00
☐789	5¢	Army	5.25	7.00	12.00
☐790	1¢	Navy	4.25	6.00	12.00
☐791	2¢	Navy	5.25	7.00	12.00
☐792	3¢	Navy	5.25	7.00	12.00
☐793	4¢	Navy	5.25	7.00	12.00
☐794	5¢	Navy	5.25	7.00	12.00

Note: Beginning with number 795, First Day Covers have a cancellation "First Day Issue."

Scott No.			Single	Block	Plate Block
☐795	3¢	Ordinance of 1787	6.25	7.00	14.00
☐796	5¢	Virginia Dare	6.75	7.00	14.00
☐797	10¢	Souvenir Sheet	6.75	—	—
☐798	3¢	Constitution	7.25	8.50	14.00
☐799	3¢	Hawaii	7.25	8.50	14.00
☐800	3¢	Alaska	7.25	8.50	14.00
☐801	3¢	Puerto Rico	7.25	8.50	14.00
☐802	3¢	Virgin Islands	7.25	8.50	14.00
☐803	½¢	Franklin	3.25	4.50	8.50
☐804	1¢	Washington	3.25	4.50	8.50
☐805	1½¢	Martha Washington	3.25	4.50	8.50
☐806	2¢	Adams	3.00	4.50	8.50

Scott No.			Single	Block	Plate Block
☐807	3¢	Jefferson	3.25	4.50	8.50
☐808	4¢	Madison	3.25	4.50	8.50
☐809	4½¢	White House	3.25	4.50	8.50
☐810	5¢	Monroe	3.25	4.50	8.50
☐811	6¢	Adams	3.25	4.50	8.50
☐812	7¢	Jackson	3.25	4.50	8.50
☐813	8¢	VanBuren	3.25	4.50	8.50
☐814	9¢	Harrison	3.25	4.50	8.50
☐815	10¢	Tyler	3.25	4.50	8.75
☐816	11¢	Polk	4.25	6.00	8.75
☐817	12¢	Taylor	4.25	6.00	8.75
☐818	13¢	Fillmore	4.25	6.00	8.75
☐819	14¢	Pierce	4.25	6.00	8.75
☐820	15¢	Buchanan	4.25	6.00	8.75
☐821	16¢	Lincoln	6.00	7.00	9.00
☐822	17¢	Johnson	5.00	6.50	7.50
☐823	18¢	Grant	4.50	6.50	8.00
☐824	19¢	Hayes	4.50	6.50	8.00
☐825	20¢	Garfield	5.50	6.50	8.00
☐826	21¢	Arthur	5.50	6.50	11.50
☐827	22¢	Cleveland	5.50	6.50	11.50
☐828	24¢	Harrison	5.50	6.50	11.50
☐829	25¢	McKinley	5.50	6.50	12.00
☐830	30¢	Roosevelt	7.50	9.50	14.00
☐831	50¢	Taft	14.00	18.00	25.00
☐832	$1	Wilson	60.00	75.00	125.00
☐832c	$1	Wilson	20.00	28.00	60.00
☐833	$2	Harding	125.00	190.00	275.00
☐834	$5	Coolidge	210.00	275.00	525.00
☐835	3¢	Constitution	5.75	8.50	11.50
☐836	3¢	Swedes and Finns	5.75	8.50	11.50
☐837	3¢	Northwest Sesquicentennial	5.75	8.50	11.50
☐838	3¢	Iowa	5.75	8.50	11.50
☐852	3¢	Golden Gate Expo	5.75	8.50	11.50
☐853	3¢	N.Y. World's Fair	5.75	8.50	11.50
☐854	3¢	Washington Inauguration	5.75	8.50	11.50
☐855	3¢	Baseball Centennial	25.00	37.00	55.00
☐856	3¢	Panama Canal	5.75	8.50	11.00
☐857	3¢	Printing Tercentenary	5.75	8.50	11.00
☐858	3¢	50th Statehood Anniversary	5.75	7.50	12.00
☐859	1¢	Washington Irving	3.00	4.00	5.00

Scott No.			Single	Block	Plate Block
☐860	2¢	James Fenimore Cooper	3.00	4.00	5.00
☐861	3¢	Ralph Waldo Emerson	3.00	4.00	5.00
☐862	5¢	Louisa May Alcott	3.50	7.00	12.00
☐863	10¢	Samuel L. Clemens	5.00	8.00	30.00
☐864	1¢	Henry W. Longfellow	3.00	4.00	7.50
☐865	2¢	John Greenleaf Whittier	3.00	4.00	7.50
☐866	3¢	James Russell Lowell	3.00	4.00	7.50
☐867	5¢	Walt Whitman	3.50	8.00	12.00
☐868	10¢	James Whitcomb Riley	5.00	7.50	30.00
☐869	1¢	Horace Mann	3.00	4.00	6.00
☐870	2¢	Mark Hopkins	3.00	4.00	6.00
☐871	3¢	Charles W. Eliot	3.00	4.00	6.00
☐872	5¢	Frances E. Willard	3.50	6.50	12.00
☐873	10¢	Booker T. Washington	7.50	13.00	30.00
☐874	1¢	John James Audubon	3.00	4.00	6.00
☐875	2¢	Dr. Crawford W. Long	3.00	4.00	6.00
☐876	3¢	Luther Burbank	3.00	4.00	6.00
☐877	5¢	Dr. Walter Reed	4.00	5.00	10.00
☐878	10¢	Jane Addams	5.50	8.50	30.00
☐879	1¢	Stephen Collins Foster	3.00	4.50	6.00
☐880	2¢	John Philip Sousa	3.00	4.50	6.00
☐881	3¢	Victor Herbert	3.00	4.50	6.00
☐882	5¢	Edward A. MacDowell	4.00	5.00	15.00
☐883	10¢	Ethelbert Nevin	4.50	8.00	40.00
☐884	1¢	Gilbert Charles Stuart	3.00	4.00	5.00
☐885	2¢	James A. McNeill Whistler	3.00	4.00	5.00
☐886	3¢	Augustus Saint-Gaudens	3.00	4.00	5.00
☐887	5¢	Daniel Chester French	4.00	7.50	15.00
☐888	10¢	Frederic Remington	5.00	7.50	40.00
☐889	1¢	Eli Whitney	3.25	4.50	7.00
☐890	2¢	Samuel F.B. Morse	3.25	4.50	7.00
☐891	3¢	Cyrus Hall McCormick	3.25	4.50	7.00
☐892	5¢	Elias Howe	3.50	8.00	25.00
☐893	10¢	Alexander Graham Bell	6.00	8.50	50.00
☐894	3¢	Pony Express	6.00	8.00	11.00
☐895	3¢	Pan American Union	4.25	7.50	11.00
☐896	3¢	Idaho Statehood	4.25	7.50	11.00
☐897	3¢	Wyoming Statehood	4.25	7.50	11.00
☐898	3¢	Coronado Expedition	4.25	7.50	11.00
☐899	1¢	Defense	4.00	7.50	11.00

Scott No.			Single	Block	Plate Block
☐899–901		Defense set on one cover		6.00	—
☐900	2¢	Defense	4.00	7.50	11.00
☐901	3¢	Defense	4.00	7.50	11.00
☐902	3¢	Thirteenth Amendment	7.00	8.50	12.00
☐903	3¢	Vermont Statehood	7.00	8.50	12.00
☐904	3¢	Kentucky Statehood	3.00	4.50	7.50
☐905	3¢	"Win the War"	3.00	7.00	10.00
☐906	5¢	Chinese Commemorative	7.50	10.00	15.00
☐907	2¢	United Nations	3.50	6.00	7.00
☐908	1¢	Four Freedoms	4.25	7.50	10.00
☐909	5¢	Poland	4.25	7.50	11.00
☐910	5¢	Czechoslovakia	3.50	7.00	8.50
☐911	5¢	Norway	3.50	7.00	8.50
☐912	5¢	Luxembourg	3.50	7.00	8.50
☐913	5¢	Netherlands	3.50	7.00	8.50
☐914	5¢	Belgium	3.50	7.00	8.50
☐915	5¢	France	3.50	5.25	8.50
☐916	5¢	Greece	3.50	5.25	10.00
☐917	5¢	Yugoslavia	3.50	5.25	8.50
☐918	5¢	Albany	3.50	5.25	8.50
☐919	5¢	Austria	3.50	5.25	8.50
☐920	5¢	Denmark	3.50	5.25	8.50
☐921	5¢	Korea	3.50	5.25	8.50
☐922	3¢	Railroad	5.00	7.50	9.00
☐923	3¢	Steamship	4.00	4.75	7.50
☐924	3¢	Telegraph	4.00	4.75	7.50
☐925	3¢	Philippines	4.00	4.75	7.50
☐926	3¢	Motion Picture	4.00	4.75	7.50
☐927	3¢	Florida	4.00	4.75	7.50
☐928	5¢	United Nations Conference	4.00	4.75	7.50
☐929	3¢	Iwo Jima	10.00	12.00	15.00
☐929, 934–36		Set on one cover		8.00	—
☐930	1¢	Roosevelt	3.10	4.30	6.50
☐930–33		Roosevelt set on one cover		8.00	—
☐931	2¢	Roosevelt	3.10	4.30	6.50
☐932	3¢	Roosevelt	3.10	4.30	6.50
☐933	3¢	Roosevelt	3.10	4.30	6.50
☐934	3¢	Army	4.00	5.00	6.50
☐935	3¢	Navy	4.00	5.00	6.50
☐936	3¢	Coast Guard	4.00	5.00	7.00

Scott No.			Single	Block	Plate Block
☐937	3¢	Alfred E. Smith	3.50	4.30	7.00
☐938	3¢	Texas	4.00	5.00	7.00
☐939	3¢	Merchant Marine	4.00	5.00	7.00
☐940	3¢	Honorable Discharge	4.00	5.00	7.00
☐941	3¢	Tennessee	2.90	4.30	7.00
☐942	3¢	Iowa	2.90	4.30	7.00
☐943	3¢	Smithsonian	2.90	4.30	7.00
☐944	3¢	Santa Fe	2.90	4.30	7.00
☐945	3¢	Thomas A. Edison	3.00	4.40	7.00
☐946	3¢	Joseph Pulitzer	2.90	4.30	7.00
☐947	3¢	Stamp Centenary	2.90	4.30	7.00
☐948	5¢, 10¢	Centenary Exhibition Sheet	3.50	—	—
☐949	3¢	Doctors	4.00	5.00	7.00
☐950	3¢	Utah	2.90	4.30	7.00
☐951	3¢	"Constitution"	3.50	4.30	7.00
☐952	3¢	Everglades Park	2.90	4.30	7.00
☐953	3¢	Carver	2.90	4.30	7.00
☐954	3¢	California Gold	2.15	4.00	4.50
☐955	3¢	Mississippi Territory	2.15	4.00	4.50
☐956	3¢	Four Chaplains	2.15	4.00	4.50
☐957	3¢	Wisconsin Centennial	2.15	4.00	4.50
☐958	5¢	Swedish Pioneers	2.15	4.00	4.50
☐959	3¢	Women's Progress	2.15	4.00	4.50
☐960	3¢	William Allen White	2.15	4.00	4.50
☐961	3¢	U.S.-Canada Friendship	2.15	4.00	4.50
☐962	3¢	Francis Scott Key	2.50	4.00	5.00
☐963	3¢	Salute to Youth	2.15	4.00	4.50
☐964	3¢	Oregon Territory	2.15	4.00	4.50
☐965	3¢	Harlan Fiske Stone	2.15	4.00	4.50
☐966	3¢	Palomar Observatory	2.50	4.00	4.50
☐967	3¢	Clara Barton	2.50	4.00	5.50
☐968	3¢	Poultry Industry	2.15	4.25	4.50
☐969	3¢	Gold Star Mothers	2.15	4.25	4.50
☐970	3¢	Volunteer Fireman	3.00	5.00	6.00
☐971	3¢	Ft. Kearney, Nebraska	2.15	4.25	4.50
☐972	3¢	Indian Centennial	2.15	4.25	4.50
☐973	3¢	Rough Riders	2.15	4.25	4.50
☐974	3¢	Juliette Low	3.50	4.50	7.50
☐975	3¢	Will Rogers	2.15	4.25	4.50

Scott No.			Single	Block	Plate Block
☐976	3¢	Fort Bliss	3.00	4.75	6.00
☐977	3¢	Moina Michael	2.15	3.75	6.00
☐978	3¢	Gettysburg Address	3.00	7.00	7.50
☐979	3¢	American Turners Society	2.15	3.75	6.00
☐980	3¢	Joel Chandler Harris	2.10	3.75	6.00
☐981	3¢	Minnesota Territory	1.95	4.00	6.00
☐982	3¢	Washington and Lee University	1.95	4.00	6.00
☐983	3¢	Puerto Rico Election	1.95	4.00	6.00
☐984	3¢	Annapolis, Md.	1.95	4.00	6.00
☐985	3¢	G.A.R.	1.95	4.00	6.00
☐986	3¢	Edgar Allan Poe	2.25	4.00	5.50
☐987	3¢	American Bankers Association	1.95	4.25	5.50
☐988	3¢	Samuel Gompers	1.95	4.25	5.50
☐989	3¢	Freedom Statue	1.95	4.25	5.50
☐989–992		Nat. Capital Sesquicentennial set on one cover	4.00	—	—
☐990	3¢	Nat. Capital Sesqui. (Executive)	1.95	4.25	5.50
☐991	3¢	Nat. Capital Sesqui. (Judicial)	1.95	4.25	5.50
☐992	3¢	Nat. Capital Sesqui. (Legislative)	1.95	4.25	5.50
☐993	3¢	Railroad Engineers	1.95	4.25	5.50
☐994	3¢	Kansas City Centenary	1.95	4.25	5.50
☐995	3¢	Boy Scout	3.75	7.50	8.50
☐996	3¢	Indiana Ter. Sesquicentennial	1.95	4.00	5.00
☐997	3¢	California Statehood	1.95	4.00	5.00
☐998	3¢	United Confederate Veterans	1.95	4.00	5.00
☐999	3¢	Nevada Centennial	1.95	4.00	5.00
☐1000	3¢	Landing of Cadillac	1.95	4.00	5.00
☐1001	3¢	Colorado Statehood	1.95	4.00	5.00
☐1002	3¢	American Chemical Society	1.95	4.00	5.00
☐1003	3¢	Battle of Brooklyn	1.95	4.00	5.00
☐1004	3¢	Betsy Ross	1.95	4.00	5.00
☐1005	3¢	4-H Clubs	1.95	4.00	5.00
☐1006	3¢	B & O Railroad	1.95	4.00	5.00
☐1007	3¢	American Automobile Assoc.	1.95	4.00	5.00
☐1008	3¢	NATO	1.95	4.00	5.00
☐1009	3¢	Grand Coulee Dam	1.95	4.00	5.00
☐1010	3¢	Lafayette	1.95	4.00	5.00

Scott No.		Single	Block	Plate Block
☐1011 3¢	Mt. Rushmore Memorial	1.95	4.00	5.00
☐1012 3¢	Civil Engineers	1.95	4.00	5.00
☐1013 3¢	Service Women	1.95	4.00	5.00
☐1014 3¢	Gutenberg Bible	1.95	4.00	5.00
☐1015 3¢	Newspaper Boys	1.95	4.00	5.00
☐1016 3¢	Red Cross	1.95	4.00	5.00
☐1017 3¢	National Guard	1.95	4.00	5.00
☐1018 3¢	Ohio Sesquicentennial	1.95	4.00	5.00
☐1019 3¢	Washington Territory	1.95	4.00	5.00
☐1020 3¢	Louisiana Purchase	1.95	4.00	5.00
☐1021 5¢	Opening of Japan	1.95	4.00	5.00
☐1022 3¢	American Bar Association	1.95	4.00	5.00
☐1023 3¢	Sagamore Hill	1.95	4.00	5.00
☐1024 3¢	Future Farmers	1.95	4.00	5.00
☐1025 3¢	Trucking Industry	1.95	4.00	5.00
☐1026 3¢	Gen. G.S. Patton, Jr.	1.95	4.00	5.00
☐1027 3¢	New York City	1.95	4.00	5.00
☐1028 3¢	Gadsden Purchase	1.95	4.00	5.00
☐1029 3¢	Columbia University	1.95	4.00	3.50
☐1030 ½¢	Franklin	—	2.00	3.50
☐1031 1¢	Washington	—	2.00	3.50
☐1031a 1¼¢	Palace	—	2.00	4.00
☐1032 1½¢	Mount Vernon	—	2.00	4.00
☐1033 2¢	Jefferson	—	2.00	4.00
☐1034 2½¢	Bunker Hill	—	2.00	4.00
☐1035 3¢	Statue of Liberty	1.85	4.00	5.00
☐1036 4¢	Lincoln	1.85	4.00	5.00
☐1037 4½¢	Hermitage	1.85	4.00	5.00
☐1038 5¢	Monroe	1.85	4.00	5.00
☐1039 6¢	Roosevelt	1.85	4.00	5.00
☐1040 7¢	Wilson	1.85	4.00	5.00
☐1041 8¢	Statue of Liberty	1.85	4.00	5.00
☐1042 8¢	Statue of Liberty	1.85	4.00	5.00
☐1042a 8¢	Pershing	2.50	5.00	6.00
☐1043 9¢	The Alamo	1.95	4.15	5.50
☐1044 10¢	Independence Hall	1.95	4.15	5.50
☐1045 12¢	Harrison	1.95	4.15	5.50
☐1046 15¢	John Jay	1.95	4.15	5.50
☐1047 20¢	Monticello	1.95	4.15	5.50
☐1048 25¢	Paul Revere	1.95	4.15	5.50

Scott No.	Single	Block	Plate Block
☐1049 30¢ Robert E. Lee	3.25	5.50	7.50
☐1050 40¢ John Marshall	4.50	7.00	8.50
☐1051 50¢ Susan Anthony	5.50	9.00	14.00
☐1052 $1 Patrick Henry	9.50	15.00	22.00
☐1053 $5 Alexander Hamilton	50.00	80.00	110.00
☐1054 1¢ Washington (coil)	1.85	—	—
☐1055 2¢ Jefferson (coil)	1.85	—	—
☐1056 2¹/₂¢ Bunker Hill (coil)	1.85	—	—
☐1057 3¢ Statue of Liberty (coil)	1.85	—	—
☐1058 4¢ Lincoln (coil)	1.85	—	—
☐1059 4¹/₂¢ The Hermitage (coil)	1.85	—	—
☐1059a 25¢ Paul Revere (coil)	2.25	—	—
☐1060 3¢ Nebraska Territory	1.85	4.00	5.00
☐1061 3¢ Kansas Territory	1.85	4.00	5.00
☐1062 3¢ George Eastman	1.85	4.00	5.00
☐1063 3¢ Lewis & Clark	1.85	4.00	5.00
☐1064 3¢ Pennsylvania Academy of the Fine Arts	1.85	4.00	5.00
☐1065 3¢ Land Grant Colleges	2.60	4.50	6.50
☐1066 8¢ Rotary International	2.90	4.50	6.50
☐1067 3¢ Armed Forces Reserve	2.10	4.50	6.50
☐1068 3¢ New Hampshire	1.85	4.00	5.00
☐1069 3¢ Soo Locks	1.85	4.00	5.00
☐1070 3¢ Atoms for Peace	1.85	4.00	5.00
☐1071 3¢ Fort Ticonderoga	1.85	4.00	5.00
☐1072 3¢ Andrew W. Mellon	1.85	4.00	5.00
☐1073 3¢ Benjamin Franklin	1.85	4.00	5.00
☐1074 3¢ Booker T. Washington	1.85	4.00	5.00
☐1075 3¢, 8¢ FIPEX Souvenir Sheet	5.75	—	—
☐1076 3¢ FIPEX	2.65	3.50	5.00
☐1077 3¢ Wildlife (Turkey)	2.10	3.50	5.00
☐1078 3¢ Wildlife (Antelope)	2.10	3.50	5.00
☐1079 3¢ Wildlife (Salmon)	1.85	3.50	5.00
☐1080 3¢ Pure Food and Drug Laws	1.85	3.50	5.00
☐1081 3¢ Wheatland	1.85	3.50	5.00
☐1082 3¢ Labor Day	1.85	3.50	5.00
☐1083 3¢ Nassau Hall	1.85	3.50	5.00
☐1084 3¢ Devil's Tower	1.85	3.50	5.00
☐1085 3¢ Children	1.85	3.50	5.00
☐1086 3¢ Alexander Hamilton	1.85	3.50	5.00

Scott No.		Single	Block	Plate Block
☐1087	3¢ Polio	2.10	3.50	5.00
☐1088	3¢ Coast & Geodetic Survey	1.85	3.50	5.00
☐1089	3¢ Architects	1.85	3.50	5.00
☐1090	3¢ Steel Industry	1.85	3.50	5.00
☐1091	3¢ Naval Review	1.85	3.50	5.00
☐1092	3¢ Oklahoma Statehood	1.85	3.50	5.00
☐1093	3¢ School Teachers	1.85	3.50	5.00
☐1094	4¢ Flag	1.85	3.50	5.00
☐1095	3¢ Shipbuilding	1.85	3.50	4.50
☐1096	8¢ Ramon Magsaysay	1.85	3.50	4.50
☐1097	3¢ Lafayette Bicentenary	1.85	3.50	4.50
☐1098	3¢ Wildlife (Whooping Crane)	1.85	3.50	4.50
☐1099	3¢ Religious Freedom	1.85	3.50	4.50
☐1100	3¢ Gardening Horticulture	1.85	3.50	4.50
☐1104	3¢ Brussels Exhibition	1.85	3.50	4.50
☐1105	3¢ James Monroe	1.85	3.50	4.50
☐1106	3¢ Minnesota Statehood	1.85	3.50	4.50
☐1107	3¢ International Geophysical Year	1.85	3.50	4.50
☐1108	3¢ Gunston Hall	1.85	3.50	4.50
☐1109	3¢ Mackinac Bridge	1.85	3.50	4.50
☐1110	4¢ Simon Bolivar	1.85	3.50	4.50
☐1110–1	Simon Bolivar set on one cover	2.75	—	—
☐1111	8¢ Simon Bolivar	1.85	3.50	4.50
☐1112	4¢ Atlantic Cable	1.85	3.50	4.50
☐1113	1¢ Lincoln Sesquicentennial	1.85	3.50	4.50
☐1113–16	Lincoln Sesquicentennial set on one cover	6.50	—	—
☐1114	3¢ Lincoln Sesquicentennial	1.85	3.50	4.50
☐1115	4¢ Lincoln-Douglas Debates	1.85	3.50	4.50
☐1116	4¢ Lincoln Sesquicentennial	1.85	3.50	4.50
☐1117	4¢ Lajos Kossuth	1.85	3.50	4.50
☐1117–18	Lajos Kossuth set on one cover	2.75	—	—
☐1118	8¢ Lajos Kossuth	1.85	3.50	4.50
☐1119	4¢ Freedom of Press	1.85	3.50	4.50
☐1120	4¢ Overland Mail	1.85	3.50	4.50
☐1121	4¢ Noah Webster	1.85	3.50	4.50
☐1122	4¢ Forest Conservation	1.85	3.50	4.50

Scott No.	Single	Block	Plate Block
☐1123 4¢ Fort Duquesne	1.85	3.50	4.50
☐1124 4¢ Oregon Statehood	1.85	3.50	4.50
☐1125 4¢ San Martin	1.85	3.50	4.50
☐1125–26 San Martin set on one cover	2.75	—	—
☐1126 8¢ San Martin	1.85	3.50	4.50
☐1127 4¢ NATO	1.85	3.50	4.50
☐1128 4¢ Arctic Explorations	1.85	3.50	4.50
☐1129 8¢ World Trade	1.85	3.50	4.50
☐1130 4¢ Silver Centennial	1.85	3.50	4.50
☐1131 4¢ St. Lawrence Seaway	1.85	3.50	4.50
☐1132 4¢ Flag	1.85	3.50	4.50
☐1133 4¢ Soil Conservation	1.85	3.50	4.50
☐1134 4¢ Petroleum Industry	2.50	4.00	5.00
☐1135 4¢ Dental Health	2.50	4.00	5.00
☐1136 4¢ Reuter	1.85	3.50	4.50
☐1136–37 Reuter set on one cover	2.75	—	—
☐1137 8¢ Reuter	1.85	3.50	4.50
☐1138 4¢ Dr. Ephraim McDowell	1.85	3.50	4.50
☐1139 4¢ Washington "Credo"	1.85	3.50	4.50
☐1140 4¢ Franklin "Credo"	1.85	3.50	4.50
☐1141 4¢ Jefferson "Credo"	1.85	3.50	4.50
☐1142 4¢ Francis Scott Key "Credo"	1.85	3.50	4.50
☐1143 4¢ Lincoln "Credo"	1.85	3.50	4.50
☐1144 4¢ Patrick Henry "Credo"	1.85	3.50	4.50
☐1145 4¢ Boy Scouts	3.00	4.00	5.00
☐1146 4¢ Olympic Winter Games	1.85	3.50	4.50
☐1147 4¢ Masaryk	1.85	3.50	4.50
☐1147–48 Masaryk set on one cover	2.75	—	—
☐1148 8¢ Masaryk	1.85	3.50	4.50
☐1149 4¢ World Refugee Year	1.85	3.50	4.50
☐1150 4¢ Water Conservation	1.85	3.50	4.50
☐1151 4¢ SEATO	1.85	3.50	4.50
☐1152 4¢ American Woman	1.85	3.50	4.50
☐1153 4¢ 50-Star Flag	1.85	3.50	4.50
☐1154 4¢ Pony Express Centennial	2.10	3.75	5.00
☐1155 4¢ Employ the Handicapped	1.85	3.00	4.50
☐1156 4¢ World Forestry Congress	1.85	3.00	4.50

Scott No.		Single	Block	Plate Block
☐1157 4¢	Mexican Independence	1.85	3.00	4.50
☐1158 4¢	U.S. Japan Treaty	1.85	3.00	4.50
☐1159 4¢	Paderewski	1.85	3.00	4.50
☐1159–60	Paderewski set on one cover	2.75	—	—
☐1160 8¢	Paderewski	1.85	3.00	4.50
☐1161 4¢	Robert A. Taft	1.85	3.00	4.50
☐1162 4¢	Wheels of Freedom	1.85	3.00	4.50
☐1163 4¢	Boys' Clubs	1.85	3.00	4.50
☐1164 4¢	Automated P.O.	1.85	3.00	4.50
☐1165 4¢	Mannerheim	1.85	3.00	4.50
☐1165–66	Mannerheim set on one cover	2.75	—	—
☐1166 8¢	Mannerheim	1.85	3.00	4.50
☐1167 4¢	Camp Fire Girls	1.85	3.00	4.50
☐1168 4¢	Garibaldi	1.85	3.00	4.50
☐1168–69	Garibaldi set on one cover	2.75	—	—
☐1169 8¢	Garibaldi	1.85	3.00	4.50
☐1170 4¢	Senator George	1.85	3.00	4.50
☐1171 4¢	Andrew Carnegie	1.85	3.00	4.50
☐1172 4¢	John Foster Dulles	1.85	3.00	4.50
☐1173 4¢	Echo I	1.85	3.00	4.50
☐1174 4¢	Gandhi	1.85	3.00	4.50
☐1174–75	Gandhi set on one cover	2.75	—	—
☐1175 8¢	Gandhi	1.85	3.00	4.50
☐1176 4¢	Range Conservation	1.85	3.00	4.50
☐1177 4¢	Horace Greeley	1.85	3.00	4.50
☐1178 4¢	Fort Sumter	3.10	4.00	5.00
☐1179 4¢	Battle of Shiloh	3.10	4.00	5.00
☐1179–82	Set on one cover	10.00	—	—
☐1180 5¢	Battle of Gettysburg	3.10	4.00	5.00
☐1181 5¢	Battle of Wilderness	3.10	4.00	5.00
☐1182 5¢	Appomattox	3.10	4.00	5.00
☐1183 4¢	Kansas Statehood	3.10	4.00	5.00
☐1184 4¢	Senator Norris	1.85	3.50	5.00
☐1185 4¢	Naval Aviation	1.85	3.00	4.50
☐1186 4¢	Workmen's Compensation	1.85	3.00	4.50
☐1187 4¢	Frederic Remington	2.10	3.00	5.00

Scott No.		Single	Block	Plate Block
☐1188 4¢	China Republic	4.50	5.50	7.00
☐1189 4¢	Naismith	7.00	8.00	9.00
☐1190 4¢	Nursing	11.00	12.50	14.00
☐1191 4¢	New Mexico Statehood	1.85	3.00	4.50
☐1192 4¢	Arizona Statehood	1.85	3.00	4.50
☐1193 4¢	Project Mercury	3.10	5.00	7.00
☐1194 4¢	Malaria Eradication	1.85	3.00	4.00
☐1195 4¢	Charles Evans Hughes	1.85	3.00	4.00
☐1196 4¢	Seattle World's Fair	1.85	3.00	4.00
☐1197 4¢	Louisiana Statehood	1.85	3.00	4.00
☐1198 4¢	Homestead Act	1.85	3.00	4.00
☐1199 4¢	Girl Scouts	4.00	4.75	6.00
☐1200 4¢	Brien McMahon	1.85	3.00	5.00
☐1201 4¢	Apprenticeship	1.85	3.00	5.00
☐1202 4¢	Sam Rayburn	1.85	3.00	5.00
☐1203 4¢	Dag Hammarskjold	1.85	3.00	5.00
☐1204 4¢	Hammarskjold "Error"	4.50	7.50	11.00
☐1205 4¢	Christmas	2.10	3.20	4.00
☐1206 4¢	Higher Education	2.10	3.20	4.00
☐1207 4¢	Winslow Homer	2.10	3.20	4.00
☐1208 4¢	Flag	1.85	2.80	4.00
☐1209 1¢	Jackson	1.85	3.00	4.00
☐1213 5¢	Washington	1.85	3.00	4.00
☐1225 1¢	Jackson (coil)	1.85	—	—
☐1229 5¢	Washington (coil)	1.85	—	—
☐1230 5¢	Carolina Charter	1.85	3.00	4.00
☐1231 5¢	Food for Peace	1.85	3.00	4.00
☐1232 5¢	West Virginia Statehood	1.85	3.00	4.00
☐1233 5¢	Emancipation Proclamation	1.85	3.00	4.00
☐1234 5¢	Alliance for Progress	1.85	3.00	4.00
☐1235 5¢	Cordell Hull	1.85	3.00	4.00
☐1236 5¢	Eleanor Roosevelt	1.85	3.00	4.00
☐1237 5¢	Science	1.85	3.00	4.00
☐1238 5¢	City Mail Delivery	1.85	3.00	4.00
☐1239 5¢	Red Cross	1.85	3.00	4.00
☐1240 5¢	Christmas	1.85	3.00	4.00
☐1241 5¢	Audubon	1.85	3.00	4.00
☐1242 5¢	Sam Houston	1.85	3.00	4.00
☐1243 5¢	Charles Russell	2.00	3.25	5.00
☐1244 5¢	N.Y. World's Fair	1.85	3.00	4.00

Scott No.	Single	Block	Plate Block
☐ 1245 5¢ John Muir	1.85	3.00	4.00
☐ 1246 5¢ John F. Kennedy	2.75	3.50	5.00
☐ 1247 5¢ New Jersey Tercentenary	1.85	3.00	4.00
☐ 1248 5¢ Nevada Statehood	1.85	3.00	4.00
☐ 1249 5¢ Register & Vote	1.85	3.00	4.00
☐ 1250 5¢ Shakespeare	2.10	3.50	5.00
☐ 1251 5¢ Drs. Mayo	4.00	5.00	7.00
☐ 1252 5¢ American Music	2.75	3.75	5.00
☐ 1253 5¢ Homemakers	1.85	3.00	4.00
☐ 1254–57 5¢ Christmas	1.85	5.00	10.00
☐ 1258 5¢ Verrazano-Narrows Bridge	1.85	3.00	4.50
☐ 1259 5¢ Fine Arts	1.85	3.00	4.50
☐ 1260 5¢ Amateur Radio	2.60	3.10	4.50
☐ 1261 5¢ Battle of New Orleans	1.85	3.00	4.50
☐ 1262 5¢ Physical Fitness	1.85	3.00	4.50
☐ 1263 5¢ Cancer Crusade	3.00	4.00	7.00
☐ 1264 5¢ Churchill	1.85	3.00	5.00
☐ 1265 5¢ Magna Carta	1.85	3.00	5.00
☐ 1266 5¢ Int'l. Cooperation Year	1.85	3.00	5.00
☐ 1267 5¢ Salvation Army	1.85	3.00	5.00
☐ 1268 5¢ Dante	1.85	3.00	5.00
☐ 1269 5¢ Herbert Hoover	1.85	3.00	5.00
☐ 1270 5¢ Robert Fulton	1.85	3.00	5.00
☐ 1271 5¢ Florida Settlement	1.85	3.00	5.00
☐ 1272 5¢ Traffic Safety	1.85	3.00	5.00
☐ 1273 5¢ Copley	1.85	3.00	5.00
☐ 1274 11¢ Int'l. Telecommunication Union	1.85	3.00	5.00
☐ 1275 5¢ Adlai Stevenson	1.85	3.00	5.00
☐ 1276 5¢ Christmas	1.85	3.00	5.00
☐ 1278 1¢ Jefferson	1.85	3.00	5.00
☐ 1279 1¼¢ Gallatin	1.85	3.00	5.00
☐ 1280 2¢ Wright	1.85	3.00	7.00
☐ 1281 3¢ Parkman	1.85	3.00	5.00
☐ 1282 4¢ Lincoln	1.85	3.00	5.00
☐ 1283 5¢ Washington	1.85	3.00	5.00
☐ 1283b 5¢ Washington	1.85	3.00	5.00
☐ 1284 6¢ Roosevelt	1.85	3.00	5.00
☐ 1285 8¢ Einstein	2.10	3.00	4.00
☐ 1286 10¢ Jackson	1.85	3.10	4.50

Scott No.	Single	Block	Plate Block
☐1286a 12¢ Ford	1.85	3.10	4.50
☐1287 13¢ Kennedy	2.50	5.00	7.00
☐1288 15¢ Holmes	1.90	3.50	4.50
☐1289 20¢ Marshall	2.25	4.00	7.00
☐1290 25¢ Douglas	2.25	4.00	7.00
☐1291 30¢ Dewey	2.50	5.00	7.00
☐1292 40¢ Paine	3.25	6.00	8.00
☐1293 50¢ Stone	4.00	7.00	9.00
☐1294 $1 O'Neill	6.50	8.00	12.00
☐1295 $5 Moore	47.00	90.00	115.00
☐1304 5¢ Washington (coil)	—	pr. 1.60	lp. 3.25
☐1305 6¢ Roosevelt (coil)	—	pr. 1.60	lp. 3.25
☐1305c $1 O'Neill (coil)	—	pr. 1.60	lp. 3.25
☐1306 5¢ Migratory Bird Treaty	3.00	4.00	5.00
☐1307 5¢ Humane Treatment of Animals	2.25	3.00	4.00
☐1308 5¢ Indiana Statehood	1.85	3.00	4.00
☐1309 5¢ Circus	3.00	4.00	5.00
☐1310 5¢ SIPEX	1.85	3.00	4.00
☐1311 5¢ SIPEX (sheet)	2.10	3.00	4.00
☐1312 5¢ Bill of Rights	1.85	3.00	4.00
☐1313 5¢ Polish Millennium	1.85	3.00	4.00
☐1314 5¢ National Park Service	1.85	3.00	4.00
☐1315 5¢ Marine Corps Reserve	1.90	3.25	4.50
☐1316 5¢ Gen'l. Fed. of Women's Clubs	2.10	3.50	4.50
☐1317 5¢ Johnny Appleseed	1.85	3.00	4.00
☐1318 5¢ Beautification of America	1.85	3.00	4.00
☐1319 5¢ Great River Road	1.85	3.00	4.00
☐1320 5¢ Savings Bonds	1.85	3.00	6.00
☐1321 5¢ Christmas	1.85	3.00	6.00
☐1322 5¢ Mary Cassatt	2.10	3.10	5.00
☐1323 5¢ National Grange	1.85	3.00	5.00
☐1324 5¢ Canada Centenary	1.85	3.00	5.00
☐1325 5¢ Erie Canal	1.85	3.00	5.00
☐1326 5¢ Search for Peace	1.85	3.00	5.00
☐1327 5¢ Thoreau	1.85	3.00	5.00
☐1328 5¢ Nebraska Statehood	1.85	3.00	5.00
☐1329 5¢ Voice of America	1.85	3.00	5.00
☐1330 5¢ Davy Crockett	1.85	3.00	5.50

Scott No.	Single	Block	Plate Block
☐1331–1332 5¢ Space Accomplishments			
	12.00	pr. 20.00	24.00
☐1333 5¢ Urban Planning	1.80	3.00	5.00
☐1334 5¢ Finland Independence	1.80	3.00	5.00
☐1335 5¢ Thomas Eakins	1.80	3.00	5.00
☐1336 5¢ Christmas	1.80	3.00	5.00
☐1337 5¢ Mississippi Statehood	1.80	3.00	5.00
☐1338 6¢ Flag	1.80	3.00	5.00
☐1339 6¢ Illinois Statehood	1.80	3.00	5.00
☐1340 6¢ Hemis Fair '68	1.80	3.00	5.00
☐1341 $1 Airlift	8.00	12.00	17.00
☐1342 6¢ Youth-Elks	1.80	3.00	5.00
☐1343 6¢ Law and Order	3.10	4.50	7.50
☐1344 6¢ Register and Vote	2.75	3.10	5.00
☐1345–1354 6¢ Historic Flag series of 10, all on one cover	8.00	—	15.00
☐1345–54 Set on 10 covers	30.00	—	—
☐1355 6¢ Disney	12.00	15.00	20.00
☐1356 6¢ Marquette	1.80	3.00	5.00
☐1357 6¢ Daniel Boone	1.80	3.00	5.00
☐1358 6¢ Arkansas River	1.80	3.00	5.00
☐1359 6¢ Leif Erikson	1.80	3.00	5.00
☐1360 6¢ Cherokee Strip	1.80	3.00	5.00
☐1361 6¢ John Trumbull	2.25	4.00	5.50
☐1362 6¢ Waterfowl Conservation	2.25	4.00	5.50
☐1363 6¢ Christmas	2.25	4.00	5.50
☐1364 6¢ American Indian	1.80	3.00	5.00
☐1365–1368 6¢ Beautification of America	2.00	7.00	11.00
☐1369 6¢ American Legion	1.80	3.00	5.00
☐1370 6¢ Grandma Moses	2.10	3.50	5.00
☐1371 6¢ Apollo 8	3.10	6.00	8.50

NOTE: From number 1372 to date, most First Day Covers have a value of $1.50 to $2.00 for single stamps, $2.75 to $4.00 for blocks of four and $4.00 to $5.00 for plate blocks of four.

Start your U.S. collection with

MEMBERSHIP IN THE ANA COULD BE YOUR BEST INVESTMENT THIS YEAR.

As a rare coin collector or hobbyist, you continually deal with a variety of questions. How can you know that the coin you're about to purchase is not counterfeit? How can you find the detailed, current information you need to build your collection? There is no authority to help you solve all these problems. Unless you belong to the American Numismatic Association.

Coin Certification and Grading. ANA experts examine rare coins for authenticity to help safeguard against counterfeiting and misrepresentation. ANA now offers the ANACS Grading Service—third party expert opinions as to the condition of U.S. coins submitted for examination, and will issue certificates of authenticity.

Library Service. The largest circulating numismatic library in the world is maintained by the ANA. Its sole purpose is to provide you with free access to invaluable information that can't be found anywhere else.

The Numismatist. The Association's fully illustrated magazine, considered *the* outstanding publication devoted exclusively to all phases of numismatics, is mailed free to all members.

And there are more benefits available through the ANA. Like coin insurance, special seminars, free booklets and photographic services. You can't find benefits like these anywhere else. Don't you owe it to yourself to join?

I want some recognition!
Make me an ANA Member.

Check One:

☐ Regular $26 plus $6 first-year processing fee
☐ Junior $11 (age 17 or younger)
☐ Senior $22 plus $6 first-year processing fee (age 65 or older)

☐ 5-year $120
☐ Life $750
☐ Foreign $28 plus $6 first-year processing fee

☐ Mr. ☐ Mrs. ☐ Ms.

Name _____

Please Print

Street _____

City _____ State _____ Zip _____

Birthdate _____ / _____ / _____

I agree to abide by the American Numismatic Association's bylaws and Code of Ethics which require the publication of each applicant's name and state.

_____
Signature of Applicant

_____
Signature of Parent or Guardian
(required for Junior applicant)

☐ Check here if you DO NOT want your name and address forwarded to an ANA Club Representative in your area.

☐ Check here if you want your name provided to numismatic-related companies.

☐ Check
☐ MasterCard
☐ AmExpress

☐ Money Order
☐ VISA

_____
Credit Card Account No.

Expiration Date _____

_____
Signature of Cardholder (required)

SPONSOR_____ ANA No._____
(optional)

Foreign applications must be accompanied by U.S. Funds drawn on a U.S. bank.
OR JOIN BY PHONE: Use your VISA, MasterCard or American Express Card.
Call 719-632-2646

Return application with payment to:
American Numismatic Association
818 N. Cascade Ave.
Colorado Springs, CO 80903-3279

ANA

THIS BOOK IS A GOLD MINE!

How to Make Money in Coins Right Now is *the* source for coin collectors, as well as investors. Written by coin authority Scott Travers, seen on ABC's *Good Morning America*, CNN, and CNBC, this book reveals *all* the secrets of coin pricing.

- What to sell today to your advantage
- Tax-slashing strategies
- How to distinguish between legitimate business practices and marketing gimmicks
- Special chapter on "collectible coins" produced by the U.S. Mint
- And much more!

HOUSE OF COLLECTIBLES
SERVING COLLECTORS FOR MORE THAN THIRTY-FIVE YEARS